세상이 변해도
배움의 즐거움은
변함없도록

시대는 빠르게 변해도
배움의 즐거움은
변함없어야 하기에

어제의 비상은
남다른 교재부터
결이 다른 콘텐츠
전에 없던 교육 플랫폼까지

변함없는 혁신으로
교육 문화 환경의 새로운 전형을
실현해왔습니다.

비상은 오늘, 다시 한번
새로운 교육 문화 환경을 실현하기 위한
또 하나의 혁신을 시작합니다.

오늘의 내가 어제의 나를 초월하고
오늘의 교육이 어제의 교육을 초월하여
배움의 즐거움을 지속하는 혁신,

바로, 메타인지 기반 완전 학습을.

상상을 실현하는 교육 문화 기업 비상

메타인지 기반 완전 학습

초월을 뜻하는 meta와 생각을 뜻하는 인지가 결합한 메타인지는
자신이 알고 모르는 것을 스스로 구분하고 학습계획을 세우도록 하는
궁극의 학습 능력입니다. 비상의 메타인지 기반 완전 학습 시스템은
잠들어 있는 메타인지를 깨워 공부를 100% 내 것으로 만들도록 합니다.

시·도 교육청 주관 중학영어 듣기능력평가란?

시행 목적	• 영어 의사소통능력 향상을 위한 교수·학습 및 평가 방법 개선 • 중학교에서의 영어 듣기능력평가 방향 제시
시행 방침	• 2012년부터 한국 교육과정평가원과 EBS 교육방송에 문항 출제 및 녹화, 방송 등을 위탁 • 평가 문항은 EBS에서 녹음하고 EBS 라디오(FM)를 통하여 방송 • 평가 실시 및 평가 결과의 성적 반영 여부와 방법 등은 학교 성적관리위원회에서 결정 • 듣기능력평가 점수는 전국적으로 평균 15~30% 내신 성적에 반영
시행 계획	• 실시 대상 : 중학교 전 학년 • 방송 시간 : 11:00~11:20(20분) • 실시 횟수 : 연 2회 • 방송 매체 : EBS 라디오(FM) • 문항 수 : 학년 당 20문항

시험 경향	대화 및 담화 수준	중1 대화 : 20~60 words 담화 : 20~50 words	중2 대화 : 35~75 words 담화 : 35~65 words	중3 대화 : 50~90 words 담화 : 50~80 words
	내용	• 범교과적 소재를 바탕으로 중학교 교육과정의 내용과 수준에 맞춰 출제됨. • 5~8개의 단어로 이루어진 단문 문장이 주를 이룸. • 중학교 과정 기본 단어 중에서도 어려운 어휘는 출제 가능성이 낮은 편임.		
	선택지	2013년부터 5지선다형		
	녹음 발음	2013년부터 영국식 영어 발음 문항 학년 당 2~3개 내외 출제(이전에는 모든 문항 미국식 영어 발음)		

중학영어 듣기능력평가 유형 분석(3학년)

문제 유형		2014	2015	2016	2017	2018. 4	계
그림 정보 파악	사물	4	1	2	2	1	10
	인물		1				1
목적 파악		2	2	2	2		8
그림 상황에 어울리는 대화 찾기		2	2	2	2	1	9
특정 정보 파악		1	3	2	3	1	10
언급되지 않은 것		2	2	2	4	2	12
관계 추론			1	1	2		4
직업 및 장래 희망		2	1	1			4
심정 파악		2	2	2			6
어색한 대화 찾기		2	2	2	2	1	9
부탁한 일 파악		2	2	2	2	2	10
의도 파악		2	2	2	2		8
숫자 정보 파악	금액	2	2	2	2	1	9
	날짜	1				1	2
	시각				1		1
장소 추론		2	3	4		1	10
한 일 / 할 일 파악		4	4	4	4	2	18
도표 정보 파악		2	2	2	2	1	9
주제 파악		2	2	2	2	2	10
알맞은 속담 찾기		2					2
알맞은 응답 찾기		2	4	4	6	3	19
상황에 맞는 말 찾기		2	2	2	2	1	9

01	휴식을 취하다	
02	잠시 동안	
03	채식주의자	
04	몇 개의	
05	조금	
06	놓치다	
07	자료	
08	줄을 서다	
09	낯익은	
10	소설	
11	받아들이다	
12	제안	
13	~을 제출하다	
14	~로 떠나다	
15	영원히	
16	연락하다	
17	연달아, 연이은	
18	요약문	
19	바로 지금	
20	태풍	
21	난간	
22	쌍둥이의	
23	대신에	
24	참다	
25	~외에	

	영단어	뜻
☐	serve	제공하다
☐	pay	급료, 보수
☐	liquid	액체
☐	by accident	우연히, 실수로
☐	chew	씹다, 물어뜯다
☐	fasten	매다
☐	remain	머무르다
☐	necessary	필요한
☐	due	~하기로 되어 있는
☐	switch	바꾸다, 전환하다
☐	international	국제적인
☐	credit card	신용카드
☐	cab	택시
☐	row	줄
☐	even though	비록 ~일지라도
☐	hole	구멍
☐	laptop	노트북 컴퓨터
☐	schedule	일정을 잡다
☐	impossible	불가능한
☐	fall asleep	잠들다
☐	narrow	좁은
☐	mailbox	우체통
☐	suffer from	~로 고통을 겪다
☐	serious	심각한
☐	alive	살아 있는

01	제공하다	☐ relax	휴식을 취하다
02	급료, 보수	☐ for a while	잠시 동안
03	액체	☐ vegetarian	채식주의자
04	우연히, 실수로	☐ several	몇 개의
05	씹다, 물어뜯다	☐ a few	조금
06	매다	☐ miss	놓치다
07	머무르다	☐ materials	자료
08	필요한	☐ line up	줄을 서다
09	~하기로 되어 있는	☐ familiar	낯익은
10	바꾸다, 전환하다	☐ novel	소설
11	국제적인	☐ accept	받아들이다
12	신용카드	☐ proposal	제안
13	택시	☐ turn ~ in	~을 제출하다
14	줄	☐ leave for	~로 떠나다
15	비록 ~일지라도	☐ forever	영원히
16	구멍	☐ keep in touch	연락하다
17	노트북 컴퓨터	☐ in a row	연달아, 연이은
18	일정을 잡다	☐ summary	요약문
19	불가능한	☐ at the moment	바로 지금
20	잠들다	☐ typhoon	태풍
21	좁은	☐ handrail	난간
22	우체통	☐ twin	쌍둥이의
23	~로 고통을 겪다	☐ instead	대신에
24	심각한	☐ stand	참다
25	살아 있는	☐ besides	~외에

01	~와 잘 어울리다	
02	야윈, 마른	
03	백화점	
04	둘러보다	
05	가구	
06	장소, 집	
07	인기 있는	
08	이메일 친구	
09	밖에, 밖에서	
10	함께 쓰다, 공유하다	
11	인상적인, 인상[감명] 깊은	
12	다발	
13	여분의, 추가의	
14	(손 등을) 내밀다	
15	(동물의) 발	
16	실천하다	
17	관광	
18	약속	
19	알아차리다	
20	당황스러운	
21	갑자기	
22	기사	
23	모으다	
24	~을 전공하다	
25	미리	

☐ raise	들어 올리다
☐ bring	가져오다
☐ hold	잡다
☐ stamp	우표
☐ present	선물; 현재의
☐ on time	제시간에
☐ unlucky	운이 나쁜
☐ fascinated	매료된
☐ scenery	경치
☐ be out of	~를 다 쓰다
☐ participate	참여하다
☐ weight	무게
☐ sunflower	해바라기
☐ normally	보통
☐ escape	탈출, 도피
☐ useful	유용한
☐ careful	조심하는
☐ outside	밖에서
☐ appear	나타나다, 등장하다
☐ pot	화분
☐ enough	충분하게
☐ make it	시간 맞춰 가다
☐ be into	~에 빠지다
☐ war	전쟁
☐ survive	살아남다

01	들어 올리다	☐ go well with	~와 잘 어울리다
02	가져오다	☐ thin	야윈, 마른
03	잡다	☐ department store	백화점
04	우표	☐ look around	둘러보다
05	선물; 현재의	☐ furniture	가구
06	제시간에	☐ place	장소, 집
07	운이 나쁜	☐ popular	인기 있는
08	매료된	☐ e-pal	이메일 친구
09	경치	☐ outside	밖에, 밖에서
10	~를 다 쓰다	☐ share	함께 쓰다, 공유하다
11	참여하다	☐ impressive	인상적인, 인상(감명) 깊은
12	무게	☐ bunch	다발
13	해바라기	☐ extra	여분의, 추가의
14	보통	☐ hold out	(손 등을) 내밀다
15	탈출, 도피	☐ paw	(동물의) 발
16	유용한	☐ practice	실천하다
17	조심하는	☐ sightseeing	관광
18	밖에서	☐ appointment	약속
19	나타나다, 등장하다	☐ notice	알아차리다
20	화분	☐ embarrassed	당황스러운
21	충분하게	☐ suddenly	갑자기
22	시간 맞춰 가다	☐ article	기사
23	~에 빠지다	☐ gather	모으다
24	전쟁	☐ major in	~을 전공하다
25	살아남다	☐ in advance	미리

01	음료		
02	화장실 휴지		
03	즉시, 바로		
04	정리하다		
05	머물다		
06	예매하다		
07	줄거리		
08	감동적인		
09	갈망하다		
10	모으다		
11	외우다		
12	제출일, 마감일		
13	과제		
14	어쨌든		
15	딱딱한		
16	교장		
17	기대하다		
18	나이 제한		
19	물방울		
20	추측하다		
21	끝나다, 끝내다		
22	자정, 한밤중		
23	게다가, 더욱이		
24	편리한, 간편한		
25	쓰다		

☐	rabbit	토끼
☐	common	흔한
☐	install	설치하다
☐	head	향하다, 가다
☐	present	선물
☐	be about to	막 ~하려는 참이다
☐	wonder	궁금해하다
☐	relax	긴장을 풀다
☐	space	우주; 공간
☐	do the laundry	빨래를 하다
☐	empty	비우다
☐	surprise	뜻밖의 선물(일)
☐	kid	농담하다
☐	check in	투숙 수속을 밟다
☐	to be honest	솔직하게 말하면
☐	unlike	~와 달리
☐	basically	근본적으로
☐	raw fish	생선
☐	national	국가의
☐	awesome	놀라운
☐	skip	거르다, 건너뛰다
☐	background music	배경 음악
☐	director	감독
☐	suitable	적합한
☐	far from	~에서 먼

01	토끼		☐ beverage	음료
02	흔한		☐ toilet paper	화장실 휴지
03	설치하다		☐ immediately	즉시, 바로
04	향하다, 가다		☐ arrange	정리하다
05	선물		☐ stay	머물다
06	막 ~하려는 참이다		☐ book	예매하다
07	궁금해하다		☐ storyline	줄거리
08	긴장을 풀다		☐ touching	감동적인
09	우주; 공간		☐ long for	갈망하다
10	빨래를 하다		☐ gather	모으다
11	비우다		☐ memorize	외우다
12	뜻밖의 선물(일)		☐ due date	제출일, 마감일
13	농담하다		☐ assignment	과제
14	투숙 수속을 밟다		☐ anyway	어쨌든
15	솔직하게 말하면		☐ hard	딱딱한
16	~와 달리		☐ principal	교장
17	근본적으로		☐ expect	기대하다
18	생선		☐ age limit	나이 제한
19	국가의		☐ waterdrop	물방울
20	놀라운		☐ guess	추측하다
21	거르다, 건너뛰다		☐ finish	끝나다, 끝내다
22	배경 음악		☐ midnight	자정, 한밤중
23	감독		☐ moreover	게다가, 더욱이
24	적합한		☐ convenient	편리한, 간편한
25	~에서 먼		☐ write down	쓰다

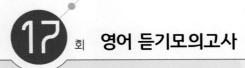

17회 영어 듣기모의고사

01	시차증	☐ cozy	아늑한
02	팔꿈치	☐ childish	어린애 같은, 유치한
03	구부리다	☐ misunderstand	잘못 이해하다
04	정확하게	☐ flight	비행
05	이용 가능한	☐ toilet	변기
06	바로 지금	☐ for sale	판매 중인
07	안전	☐ private	사적인
08	조사관	☐ a while ago	조금 전에
09	~로 전학 오다(가다)	☐ autograph	(유명인의) 사인
10	(배터리 등이) 다 닳은	☐ pretend	~인 척하다
11	매료된	☐ regret	후회하다
12	용서하다	☐ contact	연락하다
13	~을 벗다	☐ spot	자리, 장소
14	빨래, 세탁	☐ operate	작동하다
15	깨어 있는	☐ injury	부상
16	즙이 많은	☐ take a nap	낮잠을 자다
17	작성하다	☐ stomachache	복통
18	우편 요금	☐ practice	연습하다
19	초대장	☐ performance	공연; 연주회
20	아마	☐ rehearsal	리허설, 예행연습
21	훌륭한	☐ probably	아마도
22	현재로는	☐ customer	고객
23	해안	☐ fill out	작성하다
24	언젠가	☐ simple	간단한
25	제공하다	☐ survey	(설문) 조사

01	아늑한	☐ jet lag	시차증
02	어린애 같은, 유치한	☐ elbow	팔꿈치
03	잘못 이해하다	☐ bend	구부리다
04	비행	☐ exactly	정확하게
05	변기	☐ available	이용 가능한
06	판매 중인	☐ at the moment	바로 지금
07	사적인	☐ safety	안전
08	조금 전에	☐ inspector	조사관
09	(유명인의) 사인	☐ transfer to	~로 전학 오다[가다]
10	~인 척하다	☐ dead	(배터리 등이) 다 닳은
11	후회하다	☐ fascinated	매료된
12	연락하다	☐ forgive	용서하다
13	자리, 장소	☐ take off	~을 벗다
14	작동하다	☐ laundry	빨래, 세탁
15	부상	☐ awake	깨어 있는
16	낮잠을 자다	☐ juicy	즙이 많은
17	복통	☐ fill out	작성하다
18	연습하다	☐ postage	우편 요금
19	공연; 연주회	☐ invitation	초대장
20	리허설, 예행연습	☐ probably	아마
21	아마도	☐ wonderful	훌륭한
22	고객	☐ for now	현재로는
23	작성하다	☐ seashore	해안
24	간단한	☐ sometime	언젠가
25	(설문) 조사	☐ provide	제공하다

01	솔직히		☐ crosswalk	횡단보도
02	여자아이 같은		☐ pass by	(~을) 지나가다
03	이웃		☐ paint	그리다, 색칠하다
04	서로		☐ information	정보
05	~을 기억해 두다		☐ pay back	(돈 등을) 갚다
06	설치하다		☐ save	저장하다
07	승인하다		☐ totally	완전히
08	만료되다		☐ recover	복구하다, 회복하다
09	꾸준히		☐ expert	전문가, 숙련가
10	자세		☐ perfect score	만점
11	현실적인		☐ over and over	반복하여, 되풀이하여
12	굶주리다		☐ clearly	명확하게
13	콧물		☐ modern	현대의
14	신호		☐ close	친한
15	경쾌한		☐ bury	묻다
16	연습하다		☐ in case	~하면, ~하는 경우에
17	수리; 수리하다		☐ librarian	사서
18	버리다		☐ admission	입장료
19	고치다		☐ rain boots	장화
20	약속		☐ a pair of	한 쌍의
21	철자를 말하다		☐ supplies	용품, 비품
22	호의		☐ anywhere	어디에서도
23	~를 태우러 가다		☐ restroom	화장실
24	돌리다		☐ elect	선출하다
25	상세히		☐ class leader	반장

01	횡단보도	☐ honestly	솔직히
02	(~을) 지나가다	☐ girlish	여자아이 같은
03	그리다, 색칠하다	☐ neighbor	이웃
04	정보	☐ each other	서로
05	(돈 등을) 갚다	☐ keep in mind	~을 기억해 두다
06	저장하다	☐ install	설치하다
07	완전히	☐ approve	승인하다
08	복구하다, 회복하다	☐ expire	만료되다
09	전문가, 숙련가	☐ steadily	꾸준히
10	만점	☐ posture	자세
11	반복하여, 되풀이하여	☐ realistic	현실적인
12	명확하게	☐ starve	굶주리다
13	현대의	☐ runny nose	콧물
14	친한	☐ sign	신호
15	묻다	☐ rhythmical	경쾌한
16	~하면, ~하는 경우에	☐ practice	연습하다
17	사서	☐ repair	수리; 수리하다
18	입장료	☐ throw away	버리다
19	장화	☐ fix	고치다
20	한 쌍의	☐ appointment	약속
21	용품, 비품	☐ spell	철자를 말하다
22	어디에서도	☐ favor	호의
23	화장실	☐ pick up	~를 태우러 가다
24	선출하다	☐ turn	돌리다
25	반장	☐ in detail	상세히

01	더러운	
02	천재	
03	눈병	
04	앞으로	
05	땅	
06	성격	
07	~을 끄다	
08	한 병	
09	급우, 반 친구	
10	경연 대회	
11	졸업자	
12	완성하다	
13	계산서	
14	느림	
15	친밀한; 가까운	
16	상당히	
17	참석하다	
18	측정하다	
19	길이	
20	투명한	
21	명찰	
22	향, 향기	
23	점심을 먹다	
24	대출하다	
25	다림질하다; 다리미	

☐	decorate	장식하다
☐	draw	그리다
☐	make sure	반드시 ~하다
☐	delivery	배달
☐	close	아슬아슬한
☐	past	~이 지난
☐	sweat	땀을 흘리다
☐	electricity	전기
☐	seat belt	안전벨트
☐	appreciate	감사하다
☐	harm	해치다
☐	tell	알다, 판단하다
☐	owner	주인, 소유자
☐	give it a try	시도하다
☐	imported	수입된
☐	grapefruit	자몽
☐	lawyer	변호사
☐	rub	문지르다, 비비다
☐	rinse	헹구다
☐	dinosaur	공룡
☐	elementary school	초등학교
☐	relief	안도, 안심
☐	possible	가능한
☐	prescribe	처방하다
☐	find out	알게 되다

01	장식하다	☐ dirty	더러운
02	그리다	☐ genius	천재
03	반드시 ~하다	☐ eye trouble	눈병
04	배달	☐ forward	앞으로
05	아슬아슬한	☐ ground	땅
06	~이 지난	☐ personality	성격
07	땀을 흘리다	☐ turn off	~을 끄다
08	전기	☐ a bottle of	한 병
09	안전벨트	☐ classmate	급우, 반 친구
10	감사하다	☐ competition	경연 대회
11	해치다	☐ graduate	졸업자
12	알다, 판단하다	☐ complete	완성하다
13	주인, 소유자	☐ bill	계산서
14	시도하다	☐ slowness	느림
15	수입된	☐ close	친밀한; 가까운
16	자몽	☐ greatly	상당히
17	변호사	☐ attend	참석하다
18	문지르다, 비비다	☐ measure	측정하다
19	헹구다	☐ length	길이
20	공룡	☐ transparent	투명한
21	초등학교	☐ name tag	명찰
22	안도, 안심	☐ fragrance	향, 향기
23	가능한	☐ have lunch	점심을 먹다
24	처방하다	☐ check out	대출하다
25	알게 되다	☐ iron	다림질하다; 다리미

01	교과서	....	☐ explain	설명하다
02	허락	....	☐ figure	도형
03	지금 당장	....	☐ length	길이
04	공연	....	☐ traffic light	신호등
05	마감일	....	☐ gallery	미술관
06	체험학습	....	☐ stair	계단
07	오랫동안	....	☐ speech	연설
08	성적, 학점	....	☐ truth	사실, 진실
09	편안한, 안락한	....	☐ stare at	~을 응시하다
10	끄다	....	☐ try on	~을 입어 보다
11	맞는, 정확한	....	☐ imagine	상상하다
12	설명서	....	☐ kindness	친절
13	~을 전공하다	....	☐ by the way	그런데
14	쓰레기	....	☐ globe	지구본
15	유행하고 있는	....	☐ boring	지루한
16	알아보다	....	☐ purchase	구입하다
17	상담	....	☐ fit	~에게 맞다
18	전통적인	....	☐ repairman	수리 기사
19	무	....	☐ at least	적어도
20	항아리	....	☐ properly	제대로, 적절히
21	미끄러운	....	☐ price	가격
22	최근에	....	☐ accident	사고
23	소리치다	....	☐ mood	기분
24	꽉 조이는	....	☐ roommate	동거인
25	감기가 들다	....	☐ bill	청구서

01	설명하다	
02	도형	
03	길이	
04	신호등	
05	미술관	
06	계단	
07	연설	
08	사실, 진실	
09	~을 응시하다	
10	~을 입어 보다	
11	상상하다	
12	친절	
13	그런데	
14	지구본	
15	지루한	
16	구입하다	
17	~에게 맞다	
18	수리 기사	
19	적어도	
20	제대로, 적절히	
21	가격	
22	사고	
23	기분	
24	동거인	
25	청구서	

☐	textbook	교과서
☐	permission	허락
☐	right away	지금 당장
☐	performance	공연
☐	due date	마감일
☐	field trip	체험학습
☐	for a long time	오랫동안
☐	grade	성적, 학점
☐	comfortable	편안한, 안락한
☐	turn off	끄다
☐	correct	맞는, 정확한
☐	manual	설명서
☐	major in	~을 전공하다
☐	trash	쓰레기
☐	in fashion	유행하고 있는
☐	recognize	알아보다
☐	counseling	상담
☐	traditional	전통적인
☐	radish	무
☐	jar	항아리
☐	slippery	미끄러운
☐	recently	최근에
☐	shout	소리치다
☐	tight	꽉 조이는
☐	catch a cold	감기가 들다

01	꽃무늬의	
02	~을 켜다	
03	진공청소기로 청소하다	
04	참다	
05	가까운	
06	재능이 있는	
07	~을 보다	
08	잘못	
09	벌레	
10	규칙적으로	
11	마감 일자	
12	긁다	
13	일 년 내내	
14	~을 더 좋아하다	
15	자원	
16	계속되다	
17	~할 정도로 충분한	
18	다행히	
19	학원	
20	화분	
21	~을 잘하다	
22	향상되다	
23	성적, 점수	
24	라면	
25	~이내에	

☐	stripe	줄무늬
☐	shake hands	악수를 하다
☐	left-handed	왼손잡이의
☐	chopsticks	젓가락
☐	holiday	휴일
☐	possible	가능한
☐	cash	현금
☐	anywhere	어디에도
☐	cooking tool	조리 도구
☐	find out	알아내다
☐	silly	바보 같은
☐	creative	창의적인
☐	discount	할인
☐	feel sick	울렁거리다
☐	author	저자, 작가
☐	last	지속되다
☐	competition	대회
☐	deadline	마감 기한
☐	spread	펴 바르다
☐	totally	완전히
☐	volunteer work	봉사 활동
☐	wrap	싸다, 포장하다
☐	tough	힘든
☐	till	~까지
☐	wildlife	야생 동물

01	줄무늬	
02	악수를 하다	
03	왼손잡이의	
04	젓가락	
05	휴일	
06	가능한	
07	현금	
08	어디에도	
09	조리 도구	
10	알아내다	
11	바보 같은	
12	창의적인	
13	할인	
14	울렁거리다	
15	저자, 작가	
16	지속되다	
17	대회	
18	마감 기한	
19	펴 바르다	
20	완전히	
21	봉사 활동	
22	싸다, 포장하다	
23	힘든	
24	~까지	
25	야생 동물	

☐ floral	꽃무늬의
☐ turn on	~을 켜다
☐ vacuum	진공청소기로 청소하다
☐ stand	참다
☐ nearby	가까운
☐ talented	재능이 있는
☐ take a look at	~을 보다
☐ fault	잘못
☐ insect	벌레
☐ regularly	규칙적으로
☐ deadline	마감 일자
☐ scratch	긁다
☐ all year round	일 년 내내
☐ prefer	~을 더 좋아하다
☐ resource	자원
☐ continue	계속되다
☐ enough to	~할 정도로 충분한
☐ fortunately	다행히
☐ academy	학원
☐ pot	화분
☐ do well on	~을 잘하다
☐ improve	향상되다
☐ score	성적, 점수
☐ noodle	라면
☐ within	~이내에

01	고르다, 선택하다	
02	환상적인	
03	고치다, 수리하다	
04	수족관	
05	발견하다	
06	놀라움, 경이로움	
07	허용하다	
08	돌이켜 생각하다	
09	그리워하다	
10	어울리다, 놀다	
11	언제든지	
12	~을 찾아오다	
13	~을 따라잡다	
14	제품	
15	자리, 위치	
16	제출하다	
17	경력	
18	엄청난	
19	안전하게	
20	(얇게) 자르다	
21	교환하다	
22	영수증	
23	주소	
24	경쟁하다	
25	목이 마른	

☐ offer	제공하다
☐ allergic	알레르기가 있는
☐ package	소포
☐ loud	소리가 큰
☐ press	누르다
☐ huge	엄청난, 웅장한
☐ run	경영하다
☐ be sick of	~에 질리다
☐ fitting room	탈의실
☐ traveler	여행자
☐ passport	여권
☐ treat	한턱내다, 대접하다
☐ in order to	~하기 위해서
☐ cough	기침하다; 기침
☐ slight	약간의
☐ delay	지연
☐ fold	접다
☐ wipe	닦다
☐ thankful	고마워하는
☐ seasonal fruit	제철 과일
☐ satisfy	만족시키다
☐ ease	편하게 해 주다
☐ nephew	조카
☐ electronic	전자의
☐ on display	진열된, 전시된

01	제공하다	
02	알레르기가 있는	
03	소포	
04	소리가 큰	
05	누르다	
06	엄청난, 웅장한	
07	경영하다	
08	~에 질리다	
09	탈의실	
10	여행자	
11	여권	
12	한턱내다, 대접하다	
13	~하기 위해서	
14	기침하다; 기침	
15	약간의	
16	지연	
17	접다	
18	닦다	
19	고마워하는	
20	제철 과일	
21	만족시키다	
22	편하게 해 주다	
23	조카	
24	전자의	
25	진열된, 전시된	

☐	select	고르다, 선택하다
☐	fantastic	환상적인
☐	fix	고치다, 수리하다
☐	aquarium	수족관
☐	discover	발견하다
☐	wonder	놀라움, 경이로움
☐	permit	허용하다
☐	think back	돌이켜 생각하다
☐	miss	그리워하다
☐	hang out	어울리다, 놀다
☐	anytime	언제든지
☐	pick up	~을 찾아오다
☐	catch up with	~을 따라잡다
☐	product	제품
☐	position	자리, 위치
☐	hand in	제출하다
☐	experience	경력
☐	huge	엄청난
☐	safely	안전하게
☐	slice	(얇게) 자르다
☐	exchange	교환하다
☐	receipt	영수증
☐	address	주소
☐	compete	경쟁하다
☐	thirsty	목이 마른

01	정사각형	
02	곧은	
03	바닥	
04	~의 앞에	
05	건너다	
06	물러서다	
07	위험에 처한	
08	개인적인	
09	안약	
10	진단서	
11	도움을 주다	
12	실망한	
13	축하하다	
14	도망가다	
15	기운을 내다	
16	수업료	
17	~의 맞은편에 있는	
18	값비싼	
19	증가하다	
20	낙담한	
21	포기하다	
22	감명을 받은	
23	도형	
24	~에 싫증 난	
25	~로 여행가다	

☐ present	선물
☐ order	주문하다
☐ delay	미루다, 연기하다
☐ take care of	~을 돌보다
☐ allow	허락하다
☐ promise	약속하다
☐ theater	극장
☐ brief	간략한
☐ overview	개요
☐ a variety of	다양한
☐ basement	지하
☐ perform	공연하다
☐ play	연극
☐ librarian	사서
☐ announce	알리다, 공표하다
☐ break down	고장 나다
☐ facilities	설비, 시설
☐ amazing	놀라운
☐ convenient	편리한
☐ vehicle	운송 수단, 차량
☐ practical	실용적인
☐ device	기기
☐ helpful	도움이 되는
☐ join	참가하다
☐ scared	겁먹은

01	선물	
02	주문하다	
03	미루다, 연기하다	
04	~을 돌보다	
05	허락하다	
06	약속하다	
07	극장	
08	간략한	
09	개요	
10	다양한	
11	지하	
12	공연하다	
13	연극	
14	사서	
15	알리다, 공표하다	
16	고장 나다	
17	설비, 시설	
18	놀라운	
19	편리한	
20	운송 수단, 차량	
21	실용적인	
22	기기	
23	도움이 되는	
24	참가하다	
25	겁먹은	

	영어	뜻
☐	square	정사각형
☐	straight	곧은
☐	bottom	바닥
☐	in front of	~의 앞에
☐	cross	건너다
☐	step back	물러서다
☐	in danger	위험에 처한
☐	personal	개인적인
☐	eye drop	안약
☐	sick note	진단서
☐	give a hand	도움을 주다
☐	disappointed	실망한
☐	celebrate	축하하다
☐	run away	도망가다
☐	cheer up	기운을 내다
☐	fee	수업료
☐	across from	~의 맞은편에 있는
☐	expensive	값비싼
☐	increase	증가하다
☐	discouraged	낙담한
☐	give up	포기하다
☐	impressed	감명을 받은
☐	figure	도형
☐	tired of	~에 싫증 난
☐	take a trip to	~로 여행가다

01	무늬	....
02	앞쪽, 앞면	....
03	독후감	....
04	미루다, 연기하다	....
05	책장, 선반	....
06	제출하다	....
07	~을 포함하여	....
08	진정하다	....
09	이기다	....
10	속상한	....
11	~에 (잠시) 들르다	....
12	가치 있는	....
13	작가	....
14	할인	....
15	원래	....
16	반값	....
17	놀라운	....
18	제공하다	....
19	벌써	....
20	자격증	....
21	황무지	....
22	없애다, 제거하다	....
23	지저분한	....
24	공간	....
25	옷장	....

☐ balloon	풍선
☐ finish	끝마치다
☐ carry	들고 있다
☐ noisy	시끄러운
☐ stand	참다
☐ introduce	소개하다
☐ on sale	할인 중인
☐ clerk	점원
☐ miss	놓치다
☐ prefer	~을 선호하다
☐ return	반납하다
☐ borrow	~을 빌리다
☐ go out	외출하다
☐ take a class	수강하다
☐ come in	(상품 등이) 들어오다
☐ set up	준비하다
☐ experiment	실험
☐ green tea	녹차
☐ black tea	홍차
☐ bad cold	독감
☐ catch up on	만회하다
☐ be interested in	~에 관심이 있다
☐ go on a trip	여행을 가다
☐ register for	~에 등록하다
☐ take part in	~에 참가하다

01	풍선			
02	끝마치다			
03	들고 있다			
04	시끄러운			
05	참다			
06	소개하다			
07	할인 중인			
08	배달			
09	~을 들고 오다			
10	~을 선호하다			
11	반납하다			
12	~을 빌리다			
13	외출하다			
14	수강하다			
15	(상품 등이) 들어오다			
16	준비하다			
17	실험			
18	녹차			
19	홍차			
20	독감			
21	만회하다			
22	~에 관심이 있다			
23	여행을 가다			
24	~에 등록하다			
25	~에 참가하다			

☐	pattern	무늬
☐	front side	앞쪽, 앞면
☐	book report	독후감
☐	postpone	미루다, 연기하다
☐	shelf	책장, 선반
☐	submit	제출하다
☐	including	~을 포함하여
☐	calm down	진정하다
☐	beat	이기다
☐	upset	속상한
☐	drop by	~에 (잠시) 들르다
☐	valuable	가치 있는
☐	author	작가
☐	discount	할인
☐	originally	원래
☐	half price	반값
☐	amazing	놀라운
☐	offer	제공하다
☐	already	벌써
☐	license	자격증
☐	wasteland	황무지
☐	remove	없애다, 제거하다
☐	messy	지저분한
☐	space	공간
☐	closet	옷장

01	동전 지갑	....
02	경찰관	....
03	소유자, 주인	....
04	설명하다	....
05	교통 혼잡	....
06	~을 제외하고	....
07	전기의	....
08	가벼운	....
09	충전하다	....
10	훌륭한	....
11	심각한	....
12	약속하다	....
13	수다스러운	....
14	꽃병	....
15	입구	....
16	선택권	....
17	허물없는	....
18	~와 관련이 있다	....
19	예보	....
20	점토	....
21	상기시키다	....
22	다행히	....
23	보통의	....
24	추가의	....
25	쟁반	....

☐	check out	대출하다
☐	invite	초대하다
☐	beginning	처음, 시작
☐	beat	(심장이) 뛰다
☐	touched	감동 받은
☐	charity	자선 단체
☐	financial	재정의
☐	stability	안정성
☐	fold	개다
☐	mirror	거울
☐	reservation	예약
☐	unable	할 수 없는
☐	receipt	영수증
☐	pay the difference	차액을 지불하다
☐	schedule	일정
☐	stick to	~를 고수하다
☐	original	원래의
☐	check in	입실하다
☐	unhealthy	건강에 해로운
☐	nervousness	초조함
☐	puzzled	당혹스러운
☐	explain	설명하다
☐	attention	주의 (집중)
☐	principal	교장
☐	feel free to	거리낌 없이 ~하다

01	대출하다		
02	초대하다		
03	처음, 시작		
04	(심장이) 뛰다		
05	감동 받은		
06	자선 단체		
07	재정의		
08	안정성		
09	개다		
10	거울		
11	예약		
12	할 수 없는		
13	영수증		
14	차액을 지불하다		
15	일정		
16	~를 고수하다		
17	원래의		
18	입실하다		
19	건강에 해로운		
20	초조함		
21	당혹스러운		
22	설명하다		
23	주의 (집중)		
24	교장		
25	거리낌 없이 ~하다		

☐	coin purse	동전 지갑
☐	officer	경찰관
☐	owner	소유자, 주인
☐	explain	설명하다
☐	traffic jam	교통 혼잡
☐	except for	~을 제외하고
☐	electric	전기의
☐	light	가벼운
☐	charge	충전하다
☐	excellent	훌륭한
☐	serious	심각한
☐	promise	약속하다
☐	talkative	수다스러운
☐	vase	꽃병
☐	entrance	입구
☐	option	선택권
☐	informal	허물없는
☐	connect	~와 관련이 있다
☐	forecast	예보
☐	clay	점토
☐	remind	상기시키다
☐	fortunately	다행히
☐	regular	보통의
☐	extra	추가의
☐	tray	쟁반

01	한 숟갈의 양	
02	추천하다	
03	~의 옆에	
04	물론	
05	반납하다	
06	한가한; 무료의	
07	궁금하다	
08	간단히, 짧게	
09	보호하다	
10	전시	
11	요금	
12	거스름돈	
13	사실은	
14	유용한	
15	고마워하다	
16	모험	
17	~에 참가하다	
18	진공청소기	
19	무선의, 선이 없는	
20	좁은	
21	사고	
22	장갑	
23	~을 신청하다	
24	토론	
25	~할 것 같은	

☐	apologize	사과하다
☐	have ~ in mind	~을 생각하다
☐	convenient	편리한
☐	inform	알리다
☐	shortly	곧
☐	accept	받다
☐	be familiar with	익히 알다
☐	refer	참고하다
☐	list	목록을 작성하다
☐	source	자료 출처
☐	recent	최근
☐	rate	비율
☐	search	검색하다
☐	date	날짜
☐	smoothly	부드럽게
☐	various	다양한
☐	enjoyable	즐거운
☐	last long	오래 가다
☐	overdue	반납 기한이 지난
☐	exception	예외
☐	plant	나무를 심다
☐	garden	정원을 가꾸다
☐	several	몇몇의
☐	celebrate	축하하다
☐	section	구간, 구획

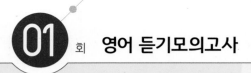
01	사과하다	_____
02	~을 생각하다	_____
03	편리한	_____
04	알리다	_____
05	곧	_____
06	받다	_____
07	익히 알다	_____
08	참고하다	_____
09	목록을 작성하다	_____
10	자료 출처	_____
11	최근	_____
12	비율	_____
13	검색하다	_____
14	날짜	_____
15	부드럽게	_____
16	다양한	_____
17	즐거운	_____
18	오래 가다	_____
19	반납 기한이 지난	_____
20	예외	_____
21	나무를 심다	_____
22	정원을 가꾸다	_____
23	몇몇의	_____
24	축하하다	_____
25	구간, 구획	_____

☐ scoop	한 숟갈의 양
☐ recommend	추천하다
☐ next to	~의 옆에
☐ certainly	물론
☐ return	반납하다
☐ free	한가한; 무료의
☐ wonder	궁금하다
☐ briefly	간단히, 짧게
☐ preserve	보호하다
☐ exhibition	전시
☐ fare	요금
☐ change	거스름돈
☐ actually	사실은
☐ useful	유용한
☐ appreciate	고마워하다
☐ adventure	모험
☐ take part in	~에 참가하다
☐ vacuum cleaner	진공청소기
☐ cordless	무선의, 선이 없는
☐ narrow	좁은
☐ accident	사고
☐ glove	장갑
☐ sign up for	~을 신청하다
☐ debate	토론
☐ likely	~할 것 같은

중학영어 **듣기모의고사**
미니 단어장

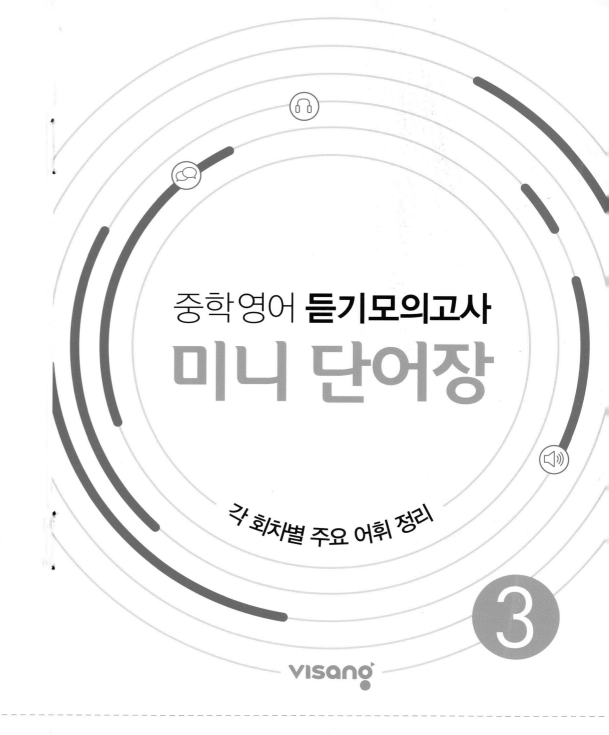

중학영어 **듣기모의고사**
미니 단어장

각 회차별 주요 어휘 정리

3

visang

중학영어
듣기모의고사 22회

3

STRUCTURE
구성 및 특징

1 영어 듣기모의고사 22회

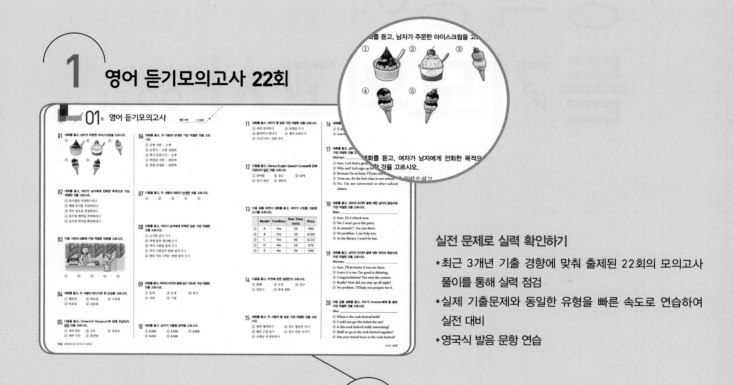

실전 문제로 실력 확인하기

- 최근 3개년 기출 경향에 맞춰 출제된 22회의 모의고사 풀이를 통해 실력 점검
- 실제 기출문제와 동일한 유형을 빠른 속도로 연습하여 실전 대비
- 영국식 발음 문항 연습

2 Dictation Test

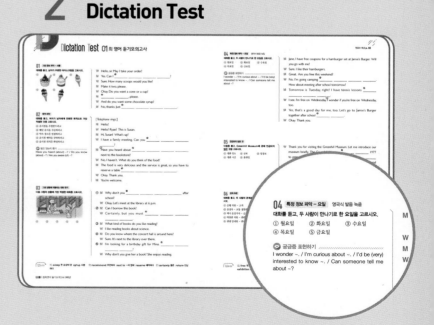

Dictation Test로 실력 다지기

- 받아쓰기 전용 MP3 파일 제공
- 받아쓰기를 통해 문제 풀이에 필요한 핵심 어휘 및 주요 표현을 완벽 이해
- 주요 의사소통 기능에 대한 설명과 발음을 tip으로 완벽 이해

3 기출문제를 활용한 FINAL TEST

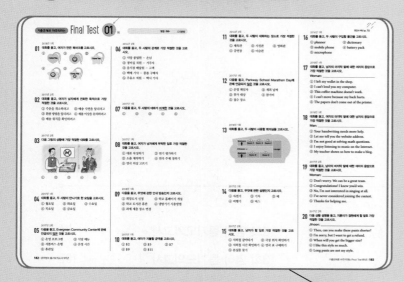

기출문제로 최종 마무리
- 최근 3개년 기출문제를 융합한 FINAL TEST 2회분을 통해 시험 전 최종 점검

4 미리 보는 수능 듣기모의고사

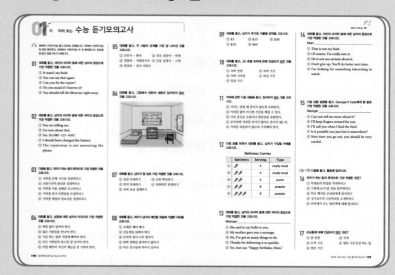

수능 듣기모의고사를 통한 수능 맛보기
- 수능 듣기모의고사 2회분을 통해 수능 유형 맛보기

미니 단어장
- 각 회차별 핵심 어휘를 단어장을 통해 완벽 학습할 수 있도록 별책 부록으로 제공

CONTENTS
차례

영어 듣기모의고사

중학영어
듣기모의고사

I have learned that success is to be measured not so much by the position that one has reached in life as by the obstacles which he has overcome while trying to succeed.

성공이란 그가 인생에서 도달해 온 지위가 아니라, 그가 성공하기 위해 애쓰는 과정에서 극복해 온 장애물에 의해 측정되는 것이라고 나는 배웠노라.

연설가 Booker Washington(1856~1915)

영어 듣기모의고사 01~22회

기출문제로 마무리하는 Final Test 01~02회

미리 보는 수능 듣기모의고사 01~02회

01 대화를 듣고, 남자가 주문한 아이스크림을 고르시오.

02 대화를 듣고, 여자가 남자에게 전화한 목적으로 가장 적절한 것을 고르시오.

① 음식점을 추천받으려고
② 배달 음식을 주문하려고
③ 약속 장소를 변경하려고
④ 음식점 예약을 부탁하려고
⑤ 음식점 위치를 확인하려고

03 다음 그림의 상황에 가장 적절한 대화를 고르시오.

① ② ③ ④ ⑤

04 대화를 듣고, 두 사람이 만나기로 한 요일을 고르시오.

① 월요일　　② 화요일　　③ 수요일
④ 목요일　　⑤ 금요일

05 다음을 듣고, Greenhill Museum에 관해 언급되지 않은 것을 고르시오.

① 개관 연도　② 규모　　③ 입장료
④ 개관 시간　⑤ 휴관일

06 대화를 듣고, 두 사람의 관계로 가장 적절한 것을 고르시오.

① 은행 직원 – 고객
② 운전자 – 교통 경찰관
③ 택시 운전기사 – 승객
④ 박물관 직원 – 관람객
⑤ 관광 안내원 – 관광객

07 다음을 듣고, 두 사람의 대화가 어색한 것을 고르시오.

① ② ③ ④ ⑤

08 대화를 듣고, 여자가 남자에게 부탁한 일로 가장 적절한 것을 고르시오.

① 도서관 같이 가기
② 과제 발표 대신해 주기
③ 역사 시험일 알려 주기
④ 역사 시험공부 방법 알려 주기
⑤ 발표 자료 구하는 방법 알려 주기

09 대화를 듣고, 여자의 마지막 말에 담긴 의도로 가장 적절한 것을 고르시오.

① 동의　　② 동정　　③ 충고
④ 사과　　⑤ 거절

10 대화를 듣고, 남자가 지불할 금액을 고르시오.

① $200　　② $300　　③ $400
④ $450　　⑤ $500

11 대화를 듣고, 여자가 할 일로 가장 적절한 것을 고르시오.

① 파티 준비하기 ② 초대장 쓰기

③ 할아버지 만나기 ④ 세차 도와주기

⑤ 크리스마스 선물 사기

12 다음을 듣고, Genius English Speech Contest에 관해 언급되지 <u>않은</u> 것을 고르시오.

① 준비물 ② 장소 ③ 날짜

④ 참가 대상 ⑤ 연락처

13 다음 표를 보면서 대화를 듣고, 여자가 구입할 진공청소기를 고르시오.

	Model	Cordless	Run Time (min)	Price
①	A	Yes	20	$90
②	B	Yes	30	$100
③	C	Yes	40	$110
④	D	No	20	$70
⑤	E	No	30	$90

14 다음을 듣고, 무엇에 관한 설명인지 고르시오.

① 볼펜 ② 모자 ③ 전구

④ 냉장고 ⑤ 휴대 전화

15 대화를 듣고, 두 사람이 할 일로 가장 적절한 것을 고르시오.

① 병원 예약하기 ② 친구 병문안 가기

③ 체육 수업 듣기 ④ 친구 마중 나가기

⑤ 선생님 댁 방문하기

16 대화를 듣고, 두 사람이 구입할 물건을 고르시오.

① T-shirts ② gloves ③ hats

④ scarves ⑤ socks

17 대화를 듣고, 남자의 마지막 말에 대한 여자의 응답으로 가장 적절한 것을 고르시오.

Woman: _____

① Sure. Let's find a good one together.

② Why not? Let's sign up for the class.

③ Because I'm so busy. I'll join you later.

④ Trust me. It's the best class in our school.

⑤ No. I'm not interested in after-school classes.

18 대화를 듣고, 여자의 마지막 말에 대한 남자의 응답으로 가장 적절한 것을 고르시오.

Man: _____

① Sure. It's 4 o'clock now.

② No. I won't go to the party.

③ At around 7. See you there.

④ No problem. I can help you.

⑤ At the library. I won't be late.

19 대화를 듣고, 남자의 마지막 말에 대한 여자의 응답으로 가장 적절한 것을 고르시오.

Woman: _____

① Sure. I'll do better if you are there.

② Leave it to me. I'm good at debating.

③ Congratulations! You won the contest.

④ Really? How did you stay up all night?

⑤ No problem. I'll help you prepare for it.

20 다음 상황 설명을 듣고, 지수가 Andrew에게 할 말로 가장 적절한 것을 고르시오.

Jisu: _____

① When is the rock festival held?

② Could you get the tickets for me?

③ Is this rock festival really interesting?

④ Shall we go to the rock festival together?

⑤ Has your friend been to the rock festival?

Dictation Test 01회 영어 듣기모의고사

01 그림 정보 파악 – 사물

대화를 듣고, 남자가 주문한 아이스크림을 고르시오.

① ② ③
④ ⑤

W Hello, sir. May I take your order?
M Yes. Can I ❶_____ _____ _____ _____?
W Sure. How many scoops would you like?
M Make it two, please.
W Okay. Do you want a cone or a cup?
M ❷_____ _____, please.
W And do you want some chocolate syrup?
M No, thanks. Just ❸_____ _____ _____ _____.

02 목적 파악

대화를 듣고, 여자가 남자에게 전화한 목적으로 가장 적절한 것을 고르시오.

① 음식점을 추천받으려고
② 배달 음식을 주문하려고
③ 약속 장소를 변경하려고
④ 음식점 예약을 부탁하려고
⑤ 음식점 위치를 확인하려고

🗣 알고 있는지 묻기 ////////////////////////
Have you heard (about) ~? / Do you know (about) ~? / Are you aware (of) ~?

[*Telephone rings.*]
M Hello?
W Hello? Ryan? This is Susan.
M Hi, Susan! What's up?
W I have a family meeting. Can you ❶_____ _____ _____ _____?
M Have you heard about ❷_____ _____ _____ _____ next to the bookstore?
W No, I haven't. What do you think of the food?
M The food is very delicious and the service is great, so you have to reserve a table ❸_____ _____ _____ _____.
W Okay. Thank you.
M You're welcome.

03 그림 상황에 어울리는 대화 찾기

다음 그림의 상황에 가장 적절한 대화를 고르시오.

① ② ③ ④ ⑤

① M Why don't you ❶_____ _____ _____ _____ after school?
　 W Okay. Let's meet at the library at 6 p.m.
② M Can I borrow this book?
　 W Certainly, but you must ❷_____ _____ _____ _____ _____.
③ M What kind of books do you like reading?
　 W I like reading books about science.
④ M Do you know where the concert hall is around here?
　 W Sure. It's next to the library over there.
⑤ M I'm looking for a birthday gift for Mina. ❸_____ _____ _____ _____?
　 W Why don't you give her a book? She enjoys reading.

Words **01 scoop** 한 숟갈의 양 **syrup** 시럽 **02 recommend** 추천하다 **next to** ~의 옆에 **reserve** 예약하다 **03 certainly** 물론 **return** 반납하다

04 특정 정보 파악 – 요일 영국식 발음 녹음

대화를 듣고, 두 사람이 만나기로 한 요일을 고르시오.

① 월요일   ② 화요일   ③ 수요일
④ 목요일   ⑤ 금요일

😀 궁금증 표현하기 ///////////////////////////////

I wonder ~. / I'm curious about ~. / I'd be (very) interested to know ~. / Can someone tell me about ~?

M Jane, I have free coupons for a hamburger set at Jamie's Burger. Will you go with me?

W Sure. I like their hamburgers.

M Great. Are you free this weekend?

W No. I'm going camping ❶ _____ _____ _____ _____. How about meeting after school tomorrow?

M Tomorrow is Tuesday, right? I have tennis lessons ❷ _____ _____ _____ _____.

W I see. I'm free on Wednesday. I wonder if you're free on Wednesday, too.

M Yes, that's a good day for me, too. Let's go to Jamie's Burger together after school ❸ _____ _____.

W Okay. Thank you.

05 언급되지 않은 것

다음을 듣고, Greenhill Museum에 관해 언급되지 않은 것을 고르시오.

① 개관 연도   ② 규모   ③ 입장료
④ 개관 시간   ⑤ 휴관일

W Thank you for visiting the Greenhill Museum. Let me introduce our museum briefly. The Greenhill Museum ❶ _____ _____ 1977 to preserve historic and artistic works. It is a ❷ _____ _____ and has 7 exhibition halls. It has more than 10,000 paintings and sculptures by Renaissance masters. It is open from 9 a.m. to 6 p.m. daily but closed ❸ _____ _____.

06 관계 추론

대화를 듣고, 두 사람의 관계로 가장 적절한 것을 고르시오.

① 은행 직원 – 고객
② 운전자 – 교통 경찰관
③ 택시 운전기사 – 승객
④ 박물관 직원 – 관람객
⑤ 관광 안내원 – 관광객

M Good afternoon, ❶ _____ _____?

W The Royal Hotel please.

M Where are you from? Japan?

W No, I'm from Korea.

M Oh, Korea! If you have enough time, ❷ _____ _____ _____ _____ and shows.

W Thank you. I will keep that in mind.

M I hope you have a nice stay here in London. Enjoy your trip.

W Thank you. How much is the fare?

M It's 26 pounds.

W Here's 30 pounds. ❸ _____ _____ _____.

M Thank you very much. Welcome to London, the city of rain.

Words **04** **free** 한가한; 무료의 **wonder** 궁금하다 **after school** 방과 후에   **05** **briefly** 간단히, 짧게 **preserve** 보호하다 **two-story** 2층인 **exhibition** 전시 **sculpture** 조각품   **06** **miss** 놓치다 **enjoy** 즐기다 **fare** 요금 **change** 거스름돈

Dictation Test

07 어색한 대화 찾기

다음을 듣고, 두 사람의 대화가 <u>어색한</u> 것을 고르시오.

① ② ③ ④ ⑤

💬 의도 묻기

Are you planning to ~? / Are you going to ~? / Will you ~? / Are you thinking of ~?

① M You passed the test. Congratulations!
   W Thanks. _____ _____ _____ _____.
② M Do you know when the concert starts?
   W Yes, it starts at 7.
③ M You ❷ _____ _____ _____. What's up?
   W I didn't sleep at all last night because of lots of homework.
④ M What great weather! How about going on a picnic?
   W Good! Let's go to Grand Park.
⑤ M Are you planning to take a swimming lesson after school?
   W I watched a ❸ _____ _____ _____ _____.

08 부탁한 일 파악 영국식 발음 녹음

대화를 듣고, 여자가 남자에게 부탁한 일로 가장 적절한 것을 고르시오.

① 도서관 같이 가기
② 과제 발표 대신해 주기
③ 역사 시험일 알려 주기
④ 역사 시험공부 방법 알려 주기
⑤ 발표 자료 구하는 방법 알려 주기

🅟 it about의 발음

What's it about?에서 it의 [t]는 모음 [i]와 [ə] 사이에서 [d] 또는 [r]로 발음된다.

M Hi, Cindy! You look busy today.
W Actually, I have to _____ _____ _____ next week, but I don't know what to do.
M What's it about? 🅟
W It's about American history and culture. You did it last week, right? Can you show me ❷ _____ _____ _____ _____ _____?
M Sure. I read some books on American history and culture. I borrowed them in the school library. You ❸ _____ _____ _____ _____ from there.
W Oh, I appreciate your help.
M You're welcome.

09 의도 파악

대화를 듣고, 여자의 마지막 말에 담긴 의도로 가장 적절한 것을 고르시오.

① 동의   ② 동정   ③ 충고
④ 사과   ⑤ 거절

M Mom, could you give me more pocket money? I have to buy some books, but I'm short of money.
W Already? Tommy, it's been ❶ _____ _____ _____ since you got the money.
M I know, but this week, I had lots of things to spend money on.
W Son, tell me ❷ _____ _____ _____ with your money.
M Actually, I spent all my money buying new game CDs.
W Oh, boy! You ❸ _____ _____ _____ _____ _____. Planned spending is very important, okay?
M Yes, Mom.

📖 Words **07 not ~ at all** 전혀 ~하지 않다 **take a lesson** 수업을 받다 **08 actually** 사실은 **give a presentation** 발표하다 **useful** 유용한 **appreciate** 고마워하다 **09 pocket money** 용돈 **be short of** ~이 부족하다 **planned** 계획된 **spending** 지출, 소비

10 숫자 정보 파악 – 금액

대화를 듣고, 남자가 지불할 금액을 고르시오.

① $200　　② $300　　③ $400
④ $450　　⑤ $500

W　Hello, this is Happy Adventure Park. Can I help you?
M　I want ❶_____ _____ _____. How much are they?
W　$20 for an adult and $10 for a child.
M　Okay. I want tickets for ❷_____ _____ _____ _____ _____.
W　In that case, one adult is free.
M　Great. Here you are.

11 한 일 / 할 일 파악

대화를 듣고, 여자가 할 일로 가장 적절한 것을 고르시오.

① 파티 준비하기　　② 초대장 쓰기
③ 할아버지 만나기　　④ 세차 도와주기
⑤ 크리스마스 선물 사기

M　Amanda! You looked busy a few minutes ago. What were you doing?
W　I ❶_____ _____ _____ _____ to friends for the Christmas party.
M　Did you finish writing them?
W　Yes, Dad. By the way, didn't you say that you would ❷_____ _____ _____ _____ this evening?
M　Yeah, but my car is so dirty. So, I'll ❸_____ _____ _____ _____. Will you help me wash my car?
W　Sure!

12 언급되지 않은 것

다음을 듣고, Genius English Speech Contest에 관해 언급되지 <u>않은</u> 것을 고르시오.

① 준비물　　② 장소　　③ 날짜
④ 참가 대상　　⑤ 연락처

😀 **확실성 정도 표현하기** ///////////////////////////
I'm sure[certain] ~. / I have no doubt. / Are you sure[certain] about ~? / How sure are you that ~?

W　We will have a Genius English Speech Contest for our students this spring. This contest ❶_____ _____ _____ _____ the Hana Culture Center on April 30. The contest is a 3-minute English speech competition. 😀 I'm sure it will be a great chance to show off your abilities. ❷_____ _____ _____ _____ can take part in this contest. For more information, please ❸_____ _____ at 800-212-6212.

13 도표 정보 파악　영국식 발음 녹음

다음 표를 보면서 대화를 듣고, 여자가 구입할 진공청소기를 고르시오.

	Model	Cordless	Run Time (min)	Price
①	A	Yes	20	$90
②	B	Yes	30	$100
③	C	Yes	40	$110
④	D	No	20	$70
⑤	E	No	30	$90

M　How may I help you?
W　I'm looking for a vacuum cleaner.
M　Okay. Look at these five models. Do you want ❶_____ _____?
W　Yes. Vacuums with a cord are a bit inconvenient to use.
M　Right. How about ❷_____ _____ _____?
W　The run time should be at least thirty minutes.
M　All right. You have two options now.
W　Hmm... for me, ❸_____ _____ _____ _____.
M　Okay. Let me go and get this one for you.

Words　**10 adventure** 모험　**11 invitation card** 초대장　**12 competition** 대회(= contest)　**take part in** ~에 참가하다　**contact** 연락하다
13 vacuum cleaner 진공청소기　**cordless** 무선의, 선이 없는　**inconvenient** 불편한　**run time** 작동 시간

Dictation Test

14 주제 파악

다음을 듣고, 무엇에 관한 설명인지 고르시오.

① 볼펜　　② 모자　　③ 전구
④ 냉장고　　⑤ 휴대 전화

M It is very important in everyday life. There are usually a few ❶ _____ _____ _____. It is also used outside. It comes in many sizes and shapes, but it is usually small. Its body is ❷ _____ _____ _____ _____, and it has a narrow neck. It is made of glass and metal. It is used to ❸ _____ _____ _____ when it's dark.

15 한 일 / 할 일 파악

대화를 듣고, 두 사람이 할 일로 가장 적절한 것을 고르시오.

① 병원 예약하기　　② 친구 병문안 가기
③ 체육 수업 듣기　　④ 친구 마중 나가기
⑤ 선생님 댁 방문하기

M Susan! Do you know where Michael is? I can't find him.
W Didn't you hear about his accident? ❶ _____ _____ _____ _____ in P. E. class.
M Really? That's too bad. Then, is he now ❷ _____ _____ _____?
W Yeah. My teacher drove him to the hospital.
M I hope he will get better soon.
W I hope so, too. Why don't we ❸ _____ _____ _____ _____ _____?
M Good idea. When shall we meet?
W After school today.

16 특정 정보 파악　영국식 발음 녹음

대화를 듣고, 두 사람이 구입할 물건을 고르시오.

① T-shirts　　② gloves　　③ hats
④ scarves　　⑤ socks

👄 의견 묻기 ////////////////////////////////////
What do you think about(of) ~? / How do you feel about ~? / What is your view(opinion) on ~?

W Peter, Mom and Dad's wedding anniversary is next week.
M Yeah. Why don't we buy T-shirts for them?
W We ❶ _____ _____ _____ last year. Let's buy another present.
M Then what do you think about gloves?
W As far as I know, Mom and Dad ❷ _____ _____ _____ last week.
M Hmm... how about ❸ _____ _____ _____?
W That's a good idea. Let's go buy them now.

📒 Words　**14 shape** 모양 **narrow** 좁은 **glass** 유리 **metal** 금속　**15 accident** 사고 **in the hospital** 입원 중인　**16 wedding anniversary** 결혼기념일 **as far as I know** 내가 아는 한 **glove** 장갑 **scarf** 스카프

17 알맞은 응답 찾기

대화를 듣고, 남자의 마지막 말에 대한 여자의 응답으로 가장 적절한 것을 고르시오.

Woman: _____

① Sure. Let's find a good one together.
② Why not? Let's sign up for the class.
③ Because I'm so busy. I'll join you later.
④ Trust me. It's the best class in our school.
⑤ No. I'm not interested in after-school classes.

💬 의도 표현하기 //////////////////
I'm thinking of ~. / I'm going to ~. / I'm planning to ~.

M Susan, are you going to take an after-school class?
W Yes, I am. How about you?
M Me, too. This time there are lots of **❶**_____ _____ like a baking class and a drum class.
W Sounds interesting.
M Then let's choose a class and **❷**_____ _____ _____.
W Good idea.
M 💬 I'm thinking of taking **❸**_____ _____ _____. Why don't we take it together?

---

18 알맞은 응답 찾기

대화를 듣고, 여자의 마지막 말에 대한 남자의 응답으로 가장 적절한 것을 고르시오.

Man: _____

① Sure. It's 4 o'clock now.
② No. I won't go to the party.
③ At around 7. See you there.
④ No problem. I can help you.
⑤ At the library. I won't be late.

W David, are you going out now?
M Yes. I'm going to **❶**_____ _____ _____ _____ with Tom. Why?
W We are invited to Uncle Kevin's housewarming party this evening.
M What time will you go to the party?
W At around 6. Will you come home by then?
M **❷**_____ _____ _____ _____.
W You know where your uncle's is, right?
M Yes. I can go there by myself.
W What time **❸**_____ _____ _____?

---

19 알맞은 응답 찾기

대화를 듣고, 남자의 마지막 말에 대한 여자의 응답으로 가장 적절한 것을 고르시오.

Woman: _____

① Sure. I'll do better if you are there.
② Leave it to me. I'm good at debating.
③ Congratulations! You won the contest.
④ Really? How did you stay up all night?
⑤ No problem. I'll help you prepare for it.

W Hi, Mark.
M Hi, Susan. You look very tired today. Did you go to sleep late last night?
W Yes. I **❶**_____ _____ _____ _____.
M Really? Why?
W I had to **❷**_____ _____ the debate contest. I'm so nervous.
M Don't worry. I'm sure you will do really well. By the way, when is the contest?
W Next Monday.
M May I go to **❸**_____ _____ _____?

---

20 상황에 맞는 말 찾기

다음 상황 설명을 듣고, 지수가 Andrew에게 할 말로 가장 적절한 것을 고르시오.

Jisu: _____

① When is the rock festival held?
② Could you get the tickets for me?
③ Is this rock festival really interesting?
④ Shall we go to the rock festival together?
⑤ Has your friend been to the rock festival?

W Jisu is fascinated by rock music. A rock festival will be held in Seoul next Saturday. So, she gets **❶**_____ _____, and she is looking for a person **❷**_____ _____ _____ _____. At that time, she hears from her friend that Andrew **❸**_____ _____ _____ _____ the rock festival. In this situation, what would Jisu most likely say to Andrew?

Ⓦords **17** think of ~할 생각이다 **sign up for** ~을 신청하다 **18** **housewarming party** 집들이 **by oneself** 혼자서 **19** **stay up all night** 밤을 새다 **prepare for** ~을 준비하다 **debate** 토론 **20** **be fascinated by** ~에 매료되다 **likely** ~할 것 같은

01 대화를 듣고, 남자가 구입할 동전 지갑을 고르시오.

① ② ③
④ ⑤

02 대화를 듣고, 여자가 방문한 목적으로 가장 적절한 것을 고르시오.

① 환불을 요청하려고
② 예약을 문의하려고
③ 선물을 구입하려고
④ 습득물을 신고하려고
⑤ 신분증을 재발급 받으려고

03 다음 그림의 상황에 가장 적절한 대화를 고르시오.

① ② ③ ④ ⑤

04 대화를 듣고, 남자가 배드민턴을 가르쳐 줄 수 <u>없는</u> 요일을 고르시오.

① 월요일 ② 화요일 ③ 수요일
④ 목요일 ⑤ 금요일

05 다음을 듣고, Joy에 관해 언급되지 <u>않은</u> 것을 고르시오.
① 제품명 ② 최대 속도 ③ 무게
④ 충전 시간 ⑤ 가격

06 대화를 듣고, 두 사람의 관계로 가장 적절한 것을 고르시오.

① 면접관 – 수험생
② 사진작가 – 모델
③ 신문 기자 – 화가
④ 신문 판매원 – 고객
⑤ 미술관 안내원 – 관람객

07 다음을 듣고, 두 사람의 대화가 <u>어색한</u> 것을 고르시오.
① ② ③ ④ ⑤

08 대화를 듣고, 남자가 여자에게 부탁한 일로 가장 적절한 것을 고르시오.

① 일찍 퇴근하기
② 피자 만들어 주기
③ 저녁 식사 준비 돕기
④ 친구 집에 데려다주기
⑤ 모르는 문제 가르쳐 주기

09 대화를 듣고, 여자의 마지막 말에 담긴 의도로 가장 적절한 것을 고르시오.
① 감사 ② 동의 ③ 후회
④ 거절 ⑤ 부탁

10 대화를 듣고, 남자가 지불할 금액을 고르시오.
① $10 ② $12 ③ $15
④ $17 ⑤ $18

11 대화를 듣고, 남자가 할 일로 가장 적절한 것을 고르시오.
① 꽃 사 오기 　　② 설거지하기
③ 생일 카드 쓰기 　④ 케이크 만들기
⑤ 부모님 마중 나가기

12 다음을 듣고, 동아리에 관해 언급되지 <u>않은</u> 것을 고르시오.
① 만들어진 시기 　② 주요 활동
③ 동아리 방 위치 　④ 가입 혜택
⑤ 가입 조건

13 다음 표를 보면서 대화를 듣고, 여자가 구입할 스케이트보드를 고르시오.

	Model	Weight(kg)	Color	Price
①	A	1.7	purple	$90
②	B	2.0	blue	$100
③	C	2.7	green	$110
④	D	2.4	blue	$70
⑤	E	3.4	green	$90

14 다음을 듣고, 무엇에 관한 설명인지 고르시오.
① 배우　② 성격　③ 별명
④ 이름　⑤ 취미

15 대화를 듣고, 여자가 할 일로 가장 적절한 것을 고르시오.
① 에어컨 켜기 　　② 방 정리하기
③ 선풍기 청소하기 　④ 일기예보 확인하기
⑤ 수리공에게 전화하기

16 대화를 듣고, 남자가 구입할 물건을 고르시오.
① glue　　② clay
③ paints　④ flowers
⑤ colored paper

17 대화를 듣고, 여자의 마지막 말에 대한 남자의 응답으로 가장 적절한 것을 고르시오.
Man: _____
① Maybe next time.
② I'm going to work.
③ How much is the fare?
④ I'll have to take the bus for a while.
⑤ It's been nice knowing you. Take care.

18 대화를 듣고, 남자의 마지막 말에 대한 여자의 응답으로 가장 적절한 것을 고르시오.
Woman: _____
① Can you help with my English?
② Make sure you arrive there in time.
③ Hey, cheer up! I'm sure you can do it well.
④ Thank you. I'm satisfied with living in Korea.
⑤ I'm supposed to go back to the United States.

19 대화를 듣고, 여자의 마지막 말에 대한 남자의 응답으로 가장 적절한 것을 고르시오.
Man: _____
① Sorry, I don't think so.
② It really doesn't matter.
③ You will like my dentist.
④ I think I should pay now.
⑤ I want a tube of toothpaste, too.

20 다음 상황 설명을 듣고, Gary가 종업원에게 할 말로 가장 적절한 것을 고르시오.
Gary: _____
① I'll have Coke instead of milk.
② I'll have a cheeseburger and fries.
③ You've given me the wrong change.
④ Could you please hurry up as I'm late?
⑤ Could you put that in a bag to take out?

01 그림 정보 파악 - 물건

대화를 듣고, 남자가 구입할 동전 지갑을 고르시오.

① ② ③

④ ⑤

M My sister's birthday is next week. I don't know what to buy for her.
W How about buying _____ _____ _____ _____ _____?
M Good idea. Can you help me choose one?
W Sure. How about this frog-shaped one?
M Well, I don't like its design. This one that ❷_____ _____ _____ _____ looks nice. What do you think about it?
W It looks cute, but its ears are too long. I think this cat-shaped one is better.
M You mean ❸_____ _____ _____ _____?
W That's right.
M It looks good to me, too. I'll get it.

02 목적 파악

대화를 듣고, 여자가 방문한 목적으로 가장 적절한 것을 고르시오.
① 환불을 요청하려고
② 예약을 문의하려고
③ 선물을 구입하려고
④ 습득물을 신고하려고
⑤ 신분증을 재발급 받으려고

🔊 Could you의 발음 ////////////////////////
Could you의 [d]는 바로 뒤에 y로 시작하는 단어가 오면, y의 영향을 받아 [ʤ]로 발음된다.

M Good morning, young lady. How can I help you?
W Good morning, officer. I ❶_____ _____ _____ on my way home. I don't know what to do with it.
M ❷Could you tell me ❷_____ _____ _____ _____?
W It was right in front of Happy Supermarket.
M Okay. Maybe we can find its owner. There's an ID card in it.
W Good. I hope you can ❸_____ _____ _____ soon.

03 그림 상황에 어울리는 대화 찾기

다음 그림의 상황에 가장 적절한 대화를 고르시오.

① ② ③ ④ ⑤

💬 설명 요청하기 //////////////////////////
Could you explain ~? / What is ~ (exactly)? / What do you mean by ~?

① M Could you explain why you're late again?
   W Sorry, I got in ❶_____ _____ _____ _____.
② M Look at those people at the bus stop.
   W Wow, there are so many people waiting for the bus.
③ M We ❷_____ _____ _____ _____ at the next stop.
   W Okay. I'll push the stop button.
④ M Does the number seven bus go to the National Museum?
   W No. Take the number five bus across the street.
⑤ M How long will it take to get to the nearest subway station?
   W It'll take at least ❸_____ _____ _____ _____.

Words **01 coin purse** 동전 지갑 **-shaped** ~의 모양의 **02 officer** 경찰관 **on one's way home** 집에 오는 길에 **owner** 소유자, 주인 **ID** 신분증(= identification) **03 explain** 설명하다 **traffic jam** 교통 혼잡 **at least** 적어도

04 특정 정보 파악 – 요일 영국식 발음 녹음

대화를 듣고, 남자가 배드민턴을 가르쳐 줄 수 없는 요일을 고르시오.

① 월요일   ② 화요일   ③ 수요일
④ 목요일   ⑤ 금요일

😊 **생각할 시간 요청하기** //////////////////////
Let me see[think]. / Just a moment (while I think).

M Jane, did you take the test in the P. E. class?
W Not yet. In fact, I'm already worried about it. You know I'm not good at ❶ _____ _____.
M I can help you. I already took the test and got an A.
W I envy you. We're going to take the test next Tuesday. Can you teach me everyday this week?
M 😊Let me see. I can help you every day ❷ _____ _____ _____.
W Why not Wednesday?
M I have to meet my friends ❸ _____ _____ _____ _____.
W Oh, I see. Thank you.
M Then see you after school today.

05 언급되지 않은 것

다음을 듣고, Joy에 관해 언급되지 않은 것을 고르시오.
① 제품명   ② 최대 속도   ③ 무게
④ 충전 시간   ⑤ 가격

W Hello, everyone. Thank you for visiting us. Today, I'm going to tell you about our new electric kickboard, "Joy". It's very fast. It can ❶ _____ _____ _____ up to 25 km/h. Also, it's ❷ _____ _____ _____ _____ _____ around, as it weighs just 7 kg. It takes about ❸ _____ _____ _____ _____ _____ to fully charge. It is very fast compared to other products. Now please line up here if you would like to take "Joy" for a short ride.

06 관계 추론

대화를 듣고, 두 사람의 관계로 가장 적절한 것을 고르시오.
① 면접관 – 수험생
② 사진작가 – 모델
③ 신문 기자 – 화가
④ 신문 판매원 – 고객
⑤ 미술관 안내원 – 관람객

😊 **만족에 대해 묻기** //////////////////////
Are you satisfied[happy] (with ~)? / How do you like[find] ~? / Is this what you want(ed)[need, meant, had] in mind?

M Good morning, Ms. Peterson. Nice to meet you.
W Nice to meet you too, Mr. Smith.
M I ❶ _____ _____ _____. They are excellent.
W Thank you.
M 😊Are you satisfied with your exhibition this time?
W Of course, I am. This is ❷ _____ _____ _____ I've ever had.
M Good for you.
W Is this interview going to be in your newspaper this Friday?
M Yes. Now, are you ❸ _____ _____ _____ _____?
W Oh, yes. Go ahead.

Words **04 worry about** ~에 대해 걱정하다 **except for** ~을 제외하고   **05 electric** 전기의 **travel** 이동하다 **up to** 최대 **light** 가벼운 **weigh** 무게가 ~이다 **charge** 충전하다   **06 excellent** 훌륭한 **be satisfied with** ~에 만족하다 **exhibition** 전시회

Dictation Test ✏️

07 어색한 대화 찾기
다음을 듣고, 두 사람의 대화가 <u>어색한</u> 것을 고르시오.

① ② ③ ④ ⑤

😊 **의무 여부 묻기** //////////////////////////

Do I need(have) to ~? / Is it necessary to ~? /
Must I ~?

① M How do you like this shirt?
  W Well, I ❶_____ _____ its color.
② M What do you hope to do in this city?
  W This is my second visit.
③ M 😊 Do I need to bring ❷_____ _____ _____ tomorrow?
  W Well, you just need to bring some drinking water.
④ M How did you like your steak?
  W It was delicious, but it was ❸_____ _____ _____.
⑤ M Can you explain what happened to you yesterday?
  W I had a car accident. It wasn't that serious.

08 부탁한 일 파악 영국식 발음 녹음
대화를 듣고, 남자가 여자에게 부탁한 일로 가장 적절한
것을 고르시오.
① 일찍 퇴근하기
② 피자 만들어 주기
③ 저녁 식사 준비 돕기
④ 친구 집에 데려다주기
⑤ 모르는 문제 가르쳐 주기

[Cellphone rings.]
W Hello, Chris. Are you coming home now?
M Yes. ❶_____ _____ _____ _____ home to study together. Is it okay?
W Yeah. How many friends are coming?
M Three. Mom, may I ask you a favor?
W Sure. What is it?
M ❷_____ _____ _____ _____ _____ for us? They'll love your pizza.
W Okay. I'll start making it so that you guys ❸_____ _____ _____ _____ _____.
M Thank you. See you soon.

09 의도 파악
대화를 듣고, 여자의 마지막 말에 담긴 의도로 가장 적절한
것을 고르시오.
① 감사   ② 동의   ③ 후회
④ 거절   ⑤ 부탁

🅟 **told her의 발음** //////////////////////////
[h]나 [ð]로 시작하는 대명사나 중요하지 않은 단어의 경우 주
로 생략되어 발음된다. 따라서 told her는 [h]가 생략되어
[toldə(r)]로 들린다.

M Cathy, have you told anyone about the surprise party for Amy?
W No. ❶_____ _____ _____ _____.
M Just tell me the truth.
W Actually, I didn't tell anyone except Sue.
M Oh, no! That's ❷_____ _____ _____ about the party.
W What? Sue promised me she would keep it a secret.
M Cathy, you didn't know how talkative she is.
W Oh, my! ❸_____ _____ _____ 🅟 told her about the party.

📖 Words   **07 salty** 짠 **accident** 사고 **serious** 심각한   **08 ask ~ a favor** ~에게 부탁하다   **09 promise** 약속하다 **keep a secret** 비밀을 지키다 **talkative** 수다스러운

10 숫자 정보 파악 – 금액

대화를 듣고, 남자가 지불할 금액을 고르시오.

① $10 ② $12 ③ $15
④ $17 ⑤ $18

W Can I help you?
M I'd like to buy a present for my mom. Can you recommend one?
W How about this hairpin?   M Good. How much is it?
W It's $10. You can get two ❶ _____ _____ _____.
M $15? Okay. I'll take two. And I need a birthday card.
W How about this one? It's ❷ _____ _____.
M Good. I'll ❸ _____ _____.

11 한 일 / 할 일 파악

대화를 듣고, 남자가 할 일로 가장 적절한 것을 고르시오.

① 꽃 사 오기 ② 설거지하기
③ 생일 카드 쓰기 ④ 케이크 만들기
⑤ 부모님 마중 나가기

M Wow! It smells delicious, Kate.
W The birthday cake will be done in a few minutes.
M Good. Mom and Dad are coming ❶ _____ _____ _____.
   We have to hurry.
W Did you put the flowers in the vase?
M Sure. I put the vase ❷ _____ _____ _____.
W Good job. Then, I will make a birthday card.
M Then, is there anything I have to do?
W Yes. Please ❸ _____ _____ _____. We have to clean up
   the kitchen before they come.   M Okay. I'll do that.

12 언급되지 않은 것

다음을 듣고, 동아리에 관해 언급되지 <u>않은</u> 것을 고르시오.

① 만들어진 시기 ② 주요 활동
③ 동아리 방 위치 ④ 가입 혜택
⑤ 가입 조건

ⓟ **flower club과 main entrance의 발음** ///////////
「명사+명사」로 된 복합명사는 대개 첫 번째 명사에 강세가
오지만, 「형용사+명사」로 된 명사구의 경우에는 뒤의 명사에
강세가 온다. 그래서 flower club은 flower에, main
entrance는 entrance에 강세가 온다.

M Thank you for your interest in our ⓟ flower club. Our club was made
   just ❶ _____ _____ _____, but we've been doing so many
   interesting things. Have you seen the flowers near the ⓟ main
   entrance? They ❷ _____ _____ _____ _____ by our
   club members. And sometimes we go outdoors to take pictures of
   plants and flowers. If you want to join us, come to Room 211. We
   give a beautiful dried-flower bookmark ❸ _____ _____
   _____.

13 도표 정보 파악 영국식 발음 녹음

다음 표를 보면서 대화를 듣고, 여자가 구입할 스케이트보드를 고르시오.

	Model	Weight(kg)	Color	Price
①	A	1.7	purple	$90
②	B	2.0	blue	$100
③	C	2.7	green	$110
④	D	2.4	blue	$70
⑤	E	3.4	green	$90

M Judy, what are you looking at on the Internet?
W I'm ❶ _____ _____ _____ _____, but I don't know
   which to choose.
M Let me help you. First, this one over 3 kg is too heavy.
W Okay, I won't buy that one.
M What color do you like among these?
W I like ❷ _____ _____ _____ more than blue.
M Now there are two options left.
W Well, I don't want to ❸ _____ _____ _____ $100 on a
   skateboard.
M Then this one seems to be perfect for you.   W Right. I'll buy it.

ⓦ **Words** **10 recommend** 추천하다 **11 be done** 끝마치다, 끝내다 **hurry** 서두르다 **vase** 꽃병 **12 interest** 관심 **entrance** 입구
bookmark 책갈피 **13 among** ~ 사이에 **purple** 보라색 **option** 선택권 **spend** 쓰다 **perfect** 완벽한

Dictation Test

14 주제 파악

다음을 듣고, 무엇에 관한 설명인지 고르시오.

① 배우　　② 성격　　③ 별명
④ 이름　　⑤ 취미

W This is an informal, often _____ _____ for a person. The name is connected with his real name, talent, personality, or appearance. For example, I call my classmate Jinsu "Michael Jackson" because _____ _____ _____ _____ just like Michael Jackson. You give this to a lot of your friends. Through this, you can _____ _____ _____ and have some fun. However, sometimes this can hurt your friends' feelings.

15 한 일 / 할 일 파악

대화를 듣고, 여자가 할 일로 가장 적절한 것을 고르시오.

① 에어컨 켜기　　　② 방 정리하기
③ 선풍기 청소하기　④ 일기예보 확인하기
⑤ 수리공에게 전화하기

😮 **희망, 기대 표현하기** ////////////////
I hope ~. / I'm looking forward to ~. / I can't wait for ~.

W Hey, brother! Isn't it _____ _____ today?
M Yeah. The weather forecast said the temperature would go up to thirty degrees today.
W Really? I hope it won't get too hot this summer.
M I hope so.
W Do you mind if I turn on the air conditioner?
M Of course not, but I'm afraid it's _____ _____.
W Oh, my! Then, how about turning on the electric fan?
M It's very dirty, so we _____ _____ _____ _____ before using it.
W Okay. I'll do that right away. I can't stand this hot weather.

16 특정 정보 파악　영국식 발음 녹음

대화를 듣고, 남자가 구입할 물건을 고르시오.

① glue　　　　② clay
③ paints　　　④ flowers
⑤ colored paper

W Peter, we have an art class tomorrow, don't we?
M Yes. What are you going to make?
W Paper flowers. _____ _____ _____ _____ _____ some colored paper and glue.
M Sounds great! You can make a bouquet with your paper flowers.
W Right. What are you going to make?
M I'm thinking of _____ _____ _____ _____.
W I'm looking forward to seeing your clay animals. Hey, don't forget to bring clay and paints.
M Oh, I ran out of clay, so I'll _____ _____ _____ _____. Thank you for reminding me.
W You're welcome.

Words 　**14 informal** 허물없는　**connect** ~와 관련이 있다　**personality** 성격　**appearance** 외모　**15 forecast** 예보　**temperature** 기온　**electric fan** 선풍기　**16 colored paper** 색종이　**clay** 점토　**look forward to** ~을 기대하다　**remind** 상기시키다

17 알맞은 응답 찾기

대화를 듣고, 여자의 마지막 말에 대한 남자의 응답으로 가장 적절한 것을 고르시오.

Man: _____

① Maybe next time.
② I'm going to work.
③ How much is the fare?
④ I'll have to take the bus for a while.
⑤ It's been nice knowing you. Take care.

😔 유감이나 동정 표현하기 ///////////////////////

That's too bad. / I'm sorry to hear that. / That's a pity(shame).

M Hi, Suji. I'm sorry I am late.　W What happened to you?
M On my way here, ❶ _____ _____ _____ right.　W Oh, that's too bad. Are you okay?
M Yes, I'm okay. Fortunately, I ❷ _____ _____ _____ _____ _____.
W What did you do with your car?
M I left my car at the garage to get it repaired.
W So, what are you going to ❸ _____ _____ _____?

18 알맞은 응답 찾기

대화를 듣고, 남자의 마지막 말에 대한 여자의 응답으로 가장 적절한 것을 고르시오.

Woman: _____

① Can you help with my English?
② Make sure you arrive there in time.
③ Hey, cheer up! I'm sure you can do it well.
④ Thank you. I'm satisfied with living in Korea.
⑤ I'm supposed to go back to the United States.

W Jinsu, I've heard your family ❶ _____ _____ _____ the United States soon.
M Yeah. I wonder if I can do well there.
W You may have some difficulty at first. But you'll ❷ _____ _____ _____ there.
M Oh, you moved into Korea two years ago! What was the most difficult thing for you?
W As for me, it is difficult to understand Korean. You know I didn't speak Korean at all then. So I studied Korean hard every day.
M Well, I've studied English for 7 years. But I'm ❸ _____ _____ _____ _____ _____.

19 알맞은 응답 찾기

대화를 듣고, 여자의 마지막 말에 대한 남자의 응답으로 가장 적절한 것을 고르시오.

Man: _____

① Sorry, I don't think so.
② It really doesn't matter.
③ You will like my dentist.
④ I think I should pay now.
⑤ I want a tube of toothpaste, too.

W Good morning. Can I help you?
M Good morning. I'm ❶ _____ _____ _____ _____, please.
W Do you want an ❷ _____ _____?
M No, just a regular one.　W Hard, soft or medium?
M Soft. My dentist says soft ones are best for my weak teeth.
W I see. ❸ _____ _____ _____ _____ _____?

20 상황에 맞는 말 찾기

다음 상황 설명을 듣고, Gary가 종업원에게 할 말로 가장 적절한 것을 고르시오.

Gary: _____

① I'll have Coke instead of milk.
② I'll have a cheeseburger and fries.
③ You've given me the wrong change.
④ Could you please hurry up as I'm late?
⑤ Could you put that in a bag to take out?

M Gary works for a computer business. Today he is ❶ _____ _____. His boss has given him extra work. So, he decided to ❷ _____ _____ _____ in his office while he is working. He goes to a fast-food restaurant and orders his lunch. A waitress begins putting his food on a tray. Maybe she thinks that he'll eat it ❸ _____ _____ _____. In this situation, what would Gary most likely say to the waitress?

Words　17 fortunately 다행히　garage 차량 정비소; 차고　transportation 이동　18 difficulty 어려움　19 regular 보통의　dentist 치과 의사　weak 약한　20 boss 상사　extra 추가의　order 주문하다　waitress 여종업원　tray 쟁반

01 대화를 듣고, 여자가 찾고 있는 가방을 고르시오.

① 　② 　③

④ 　⑤

02 대화를 듣고, 남자가 여자에게 전화한 목적으로 가장 적절한 것을 고르시오.

① 병원 예약을 하려고
② 독후감 작성을 도와주려고
③ 선생님 병문안을 제안하려고
④ 독후감 제출일을 물어보려고
⑤ 독후감 제출일 변경을 알려 주려고

03 다음 그림의 상황에 가장 적절한 대화를 고르시오.

① ② ③ ④ ⑤

04 대화를 듣고, 두 사람이 만나기로 한 요일을 고르시오.

① 월요일　② 화요일　③ 수요일
④ 목요일　⑤ 금요일

05 다음을 듣고, Bluebird Toy Museum에 관해 언급되지 않은 것을 고르시오.

① 규모　② 위치　③ 장난감 종류
④ 개관 시간　⑤ 입장료

06 대화를 듣고, 두 사람의 관계로 가장 적절한 것을 고르시오.

① 코치 – 운동선수
② 물리치료사 – 환자
③ 체육교사 – 학부모
④ 스포츠 해설가 – 아나운서
⑤ 스포츠 용품점 직원 – 고객

07 다음을 듣고, 두 사람의 대화가 <u>어색한</u> 것을 고르시오.

① ② ③ ④ ⑤

08 대화를 듣고, 여자가 남자에게 부탁한 일로 가장 적절한 것을 고르시오.

① 물건 사 오기　② 소포 보내기
③ 집에 같이 가기　④ 보고서 작성 도와주기
⑤ 휴대 전화 수리 맡기기

09 대화를 듣고, 여자의 마지막 말에 담긴 의도로 가장 적절한 것을 고르시오.

① 칭찬　② 조언　③ 거절
④ 감사　⑤ 허락

10 대화를 듣고, 남자가 지불한 금액을 고르시오.

① ₩30,000　② ₩35,000
③ ₩50,000　④ ₩55,000
⑤ ₩60,000

11 대화를 듣고, 두 사람이 대화하고 있는 장소로 가장 적절한 곳을 고르시오.

① restaurant　　② beauty shop
③ clothes shop　　④ movie theater
⑤ amusement park

12 다음을 듣고, Grand Hotel에서 방영되는 방송 프로그램으로 언급되지 <u>않은</u> 것을 고르시오.

① 호텔 정보 안내　　② 영화
③ 요리　　④ CNN뉴스
⑤ 스포츠

13 대화를 듣고, 남자가 생일 파티할 곳을 고르시오.

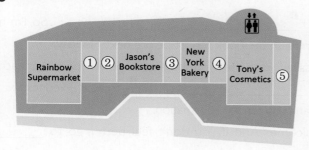

14 다음을 듣고, 무엇에 관한 설명인지 고르시오.

① 종이 제작 과정
② 자연 보호의 중요성
③ 종이를 절약하는 방법
④ 물건을 잘 고르는 방법
⑤ 재활용해야 하는 물건들

15 대화를 듣고, 여자가 대화 직후에 할 일로 가장 적절한 것을 고르시오.

① 장보기　　② 서점 가기
③ 집에 가기　　④ 저녁 식사하기
⑤ 생일 파티 참석하기

16 대화를 듣고, 여자가 구입할 물건을 고르시오.

① flower　　② book　　③ magazine
④ toy car　　⑤ pencil

17 대화를 듣고, 남자의 마지막 말에 대한 여자의 응답으로 가장 적절한 것을 고르시오.

Woman: _____

① Do you mind if I taste it?
② I wish I would pass the test.
③ Tests on Sunday are very annoying.
④ I'll keep my fingers crossed for you.
⑤ Do you know how to make *bulgogi*?

18 대화를 듣고, 여자의 마지막 말에 대한 남자의 응답으로 가장 적절한 것을 고르시오.

Man: _____

① Once or twice a week.
② Because I like gardening.
③ I have two more gardens.
④ More than five hours a day.
⑤ The garden isn't far from here.

19 대화를 듣고, 남자의 마지막 말에 대한 여자의 응답으로 가장 적절한 것을 고르시오.

Woman: _____

① I'll help you move the closet.
② I don't think so. My room is clean.
③ Sure. I don't like a messy room either.
④ No thanks. I don't need more clothes.
⑤ Thanks. I like my new room very much.

20 다음 상황 설명을 듣고, Stewart가 Judy에게 할 말로 가장 적절한 것을 고르시오.

Stewart: _____

① It's on me.
② How was the food?
③ How did you learn French?
④ What does "Thank you" mean?
⑤ How can I say "Thank you" in French?

Dictation Test 03회 영어 듣기모의고사

01 그림 정보 파악 – 사물

대화를 듣고, 여자가 찾고 있는 가방을 고르시오.

① ② ③
④ ⑤

🔵 **사물의 모양 표현** ////////////////////////
square 정사각형의 / rectangular 직사각형의 / round
둥근, 원형의 / triangular 삼각형의

W Excuse me. Is this the Lost and Found?
M Yes. What are you looking for?
W I'm looking for my bag. I left it on the seat when I was ❶ _____ _____ _____ _____. It is a square backpack.
M Does it have a special pattern?
W Yes, it has ❷ _____ _____ _____ on it. Also, there're ❸ _____ _____ _____ on the front side.
M Okay. I'll look for it. Please wait for a second.

02 목적 파악

대화를 듣고, 남자가 여자에게 전화한 목적으로 가장 적절한 것을 고르시오.
① 병원 예약을 하려고
② 독후감 작성을 도와주려고
③ 선생님 병문안을 제안하려고
④ 독후감 제출일을 물어보려고
⑤ 독후감 제출일 변경을 알려 주려고

[*Telephone rings.*]
W Hello?
M Hi, Jane. This is Daniel. You didn't come to school today. Are you sick?
W Hi, Daniel. I ❶ _____ _____ _____ _____. So, I'm not sure if I can finish the book report before next Monday.
M Actually, I called you to tell you some good news. Today, the teacher ❷ _____ _____ _____ _____ to next Wednesday.
W Really? Thank you for the information.
M You're welcome. And if you don't feel better, go to ❸ _____ _____ _____.
W Okay. I will.

03 그림 상황에 어울리는 대화 찾기

다음 그림의 상황에 가장 적절한 대화를 고르시오.

① ② ③ ④ ⑤

🔵 **좋아하는 것 표현하기** ////////////////////
I love(like) (to) ~. / I enjoy ~ (very much). / ~ is
(very) good(nice, pleasant).

① W Do you think I should wrap this box?
　 M If I were you, I would do that.
② W Happy birthday! This is ❶ _____ _____ _____ _____ for you.
　 M I love it! Thank you very much.
③ W ❷ _____ _____ _____ looks so lovely. Thank you. Here is 20,000 won.
　 M I hope your mother will like this.
④ W Did you carry all the boxes to your room?
　 M Yes, I did. They are on the top shelf.
⑤ W Jim, can you ❸ _____ _____ _____ for me?
　 M Sure. Is there anything more to throw out?

📘 **Words**　**01 the Lost and Found** 분실물 센터　**seat** 좌석　**pattern** 무늬　**front side** 앞쪽, 앞면　**02 book report** 독후감　**postpone** 미루다, 연기하다　**information** 정보　**see a doctor** 병원에 가다　**03 wrap** 포장하다　**shelf** 책장, 선반　**throw out** ~을 버리다

04 특정 정보 파악 – 요일 영국식 발음 녹음

대화를 듣고, 두 사람이 만나기로 한 요일을 고르시오.

① 월요일   ② 화요일   ③ 수요일
④ 목요일   ⑤ 금요일

M Cindy, I think we have to start our group project.
W Yeah. We ❶ _____ _____ _____ by next Monday, right?
M Right. We have about one week left.
W How about meeting ❷ _____ _____ _____ ?
M I'm sorry, I can't. I have a drum lesson every Tuesday. Why don't we meet on Wednesday?
W Well, I have to go to the dentist on Wednesday. But I'm free on Thursday and Friday.
M The sooner the better. Let's meet ❸ _____ _____ .
W Okay. See you then.

05 언급되지 않은 것

다음을 듣고, Bluebird Toy Museum에 관해 언급되지 않은 것을 고르시오.

① 규모   ② 위치   ③ 장난감 종류
④ 개관 시간   ⑤ 입장료

😀 **주제 소개하기**

I'd like to tell you ~. / I'd like to say something about ~. / (Now) let's talk about ~:

W Hello, everyone! I'd like to tell you a few things about our Bluebird Toy Museum. The Bluebird Toy Museum is ❶ _____ _____ _____ _____ in the nation. We have ❷ _____ _____ _____ _____ including hundreds of dolls, cars, boats, planes, steam engines, and so on. ❸ _____ _____ _____ _____ 9 a.m. to 7 p.m. every day. Tickets are $25 for adults and $15 for children. Visit the Bluebird Toy Museum and have a good time.

06 관계 추론

대화를 듣고, 두 사람의 관계로 가장 적절한 것을 고르시오.

① 코치 – 운동선수
② 물리치료사 – 환자
③ 체육교사 – 학부모
④ 스포츠 해설가 – 아나운서
⑤ 스포츠 용품점 직원 – 고객

M Kate, are you ready?
W Mr. Wilson, I'm so nervous now.
M Calm down, Kate. ❶ _____ _____ _____ _____ , you will beat Lisa. I'm sure of it.
W Thank you, Mr. Wilson.
M Kate, you practiced really hard. Just trust yourself.
W Thanks to you, I finally made it to ❷ _____ _____ _____ . I'll do my best.
M Good. Be sure to ❸ _____ _____ _____ _____ the ball all the time.
W Yes, I will.   M Okay. Good luck.

07 어색한 대화 찾기

다음을 듣고, 두 사람의 대화가 어색한 것을 고르시오.

①   ②   ③   ④   ⑤

😀 **허가 여부 묻기**

Do you mind if ~? / Is it all right[okay] if ~? / I wonder if I could ~. / May[Can] I ~?

① W Do you mind if I borrow this book?   M No, not at all.
② W Why are you so upset?
   M It's because I ❶ _____ _____ _____ _____ again.
③ W Do you know how to open this bottle? M Let me try it.
④ W What does an "app" mean?   M It means an "application."
⑤ W I'd like to talk about ❷ _____ _____ , ice cream.
   M Thank you for listening.

📖 **Words** **04 submit** 제출하다 **dentist** 치과의사   **05 including** ~을 포함하여 **hundreds of** 수백 개의, 수많은 **steam engine** 증기기관   **06 calm down** 진정하다 **beat** 이기다 **keep one's eye on** ~에서 눈을 떼지 않다   **07 upset** 속상한 **application** 응용 프로그램, 앱

Dictation Test

대화를 듣고, 여자가 남자에게 부탁한 일로 가장 적절한 것을 고르시오.
① 물건 사 오기   ② 소포 보내기
③ 집에 같이 가기   ④ 보고서 작성 도와주기
⑤ 휴대 전화 수리 맡기기

🔊 요청하기 /////////////////////////////////
Would(Could) you mind ~? / Could I ask you to
~? / Can you ~?

W Daddy, where are you going now?
M I'm going to _____ _____ _____.
W Well, do you have anything more to do after that?
M No, not really. Why? Do you want me to buy you something on the way home?
W No. My cellphone doesn't work. So, would you mind dropping by ❷ _____ _____ _____ instead of me? I have to ❸ _____ _____ _____ in an hour, so I don't have enough time for that.
M No problem. I'll do it for you.
W Thank you, Dad.

09 의도 파악
대화를 듣고, 여자의 마지막 말에 담긴 의도로 가장 적절한 것을 고르시오.
① 칭찬   ② 조언   ③ 거절
④ 감사   ⑤ 허락

W Dr. Smith, I really ❶ _____ _____ _____.
M Thank you.
W Well, I really like your books, and I learned some valuable lessons from them.
M Oh, what's your name?
W My name is Jisun Kim. When I grow up, I want to be ❷ _____ _____ _____ like you.
M Jisun Kim. I think I should remember your name. I believe you can be a wonderful author in the future.
W ❸ _____ _____ _____ _____ _____.

10 숫자 정보 파악 – 금액
대화를 듣고, 남자가 지불한 금액을 고르시오.
① ₩30,000   ② ₩35,000
③ ₩50,000   ④ ₩55,000
⑤ ₩60,000

W Wow, where did you buy these shoes? These look really nice.
M Thanks. I bought them at Namdaemun Market.
W Can I buy shoes ❶ _____ _____ _____ _____ there?
M Yes. If you get a discount, you can buy them cheaply. I paid just 30,000 won.
W I thought they cost around 60,000 won.
M Yes. These were originally 60,000 won, but I ❷ _____ _____ _____ _____.

📖 Words   08 on the way home 집에 오는 길에 drop by ~에 (잠시) 들르다 instead of ~ 대신에   09 valuable 가치 있는 lesson 가르침, 교훈 grow up 자라다 author 작가   10 discount 할인 cost (가격이) ~되다 originally 원래 half price 반값

11 장소 추론

대화를 듣고, 두 사람이 대화하고 있는 장소로 가장
적절한 곳을 고르시오.

① restaurant   ② beauty shop
③ clothes shop   ④ movie theater
⑤ amusement park

W   Wow, this roller coaster is amazing. So, what are we going to do next?
M   Why don't we eat something? I'm hungry.
W   No, there is no time. We should ❶ _____ _____ _____ _____.
M   I'm sorry, but I want to have something to eat.
W   Okay. Then, let's ❷ _____ _____ _____.
M   Good! Thanks.

12 언급되지 않은 것

다음을 듣고, Grand Hotel에서 방영되는 방송 프로그램
으로 언급되지 않은 것을 고르시오.

① 호텔 정보 안내   ② 영화
③ 요리   ④ CNN뉴스
⑤ 스포츠

ⓟ Channel의 발음
한 단어 안에서 동일한 자음이 연속되면 그중 마지막 자음만
발음하므로 channel은 [tʃænəl]이라고 말한다.

M   Welcome to Grand Hotel. Here's a TV guide. On Channel 1, you can get information about the ❶ _____ _____ _____ _____. Channel 2 is movies. They are playing 24 hours a day. And Channel 3 ❷ _____ _____. Channel 4 is CNN news, then 5 is ❸ _____ _____ _____. Then, Channel 6 is the fashion channel.

13 도표 정보 파악   영국식 발음 녹음

대화를 듣고, 남자가 생일 파티할 곳을 고르시오.

M   Emily, are you busy this Saturday?
W   No. Why?
M   I'd like to invite you ❶ _____ _____ _____ _____. Can you come and enjoy the party?
W   Sure. Thank you for inviting me to your party. Where are you going to have the party?
M   At Happy Pizza in the ABC mall. Do you know ❷ _____ _____ _____ _____?
W   Well, is it next to the Rainbow Supermarket?
M   No. ❸ _____ _____ Jason's Bookstore and New York Bakery.
W   Okay, I can find it. What time is the party?
M   At 12. See you on Saturday.

14 주제 파악

다음을 듣고, 무엇에 관한 설명인지 고르시오.

① 종이 제작 과정
② 자연 보호의 중요성
③ 종이를 절약하는 방법
④ 물건을 잘 고르는 방법
⑤ 재활용해야 하는 물건들

M   Take your own bag to markets. Then you won't need the paper bags that stores offer. If you buy something small and ❶ _____ _____ _____ _____ _____, say, "No, thanks" and carry it in your hands. There is another way to ❷ _____ _____ _____. You can use your handkerchief instead of tissue. These are some good ways of ❸ _____ _____.

Words   **11 amazing** 놀라운 **ride** 놀이기구   **12 guide** 안내, 가이드   **13 invite** 초대하다 **mall** 쇼핑몰 **bakery** 빵집   **14 market** 시장 **offer** 제공하다 **handkerchief** 손수건 **tissue** 화장지

Dictation Test

15 한 일 / 할 일 파악

대화를 듣고, 여자가 대화 직후에 할 일로 가장 적절한 것을 고르시오.

① 장보기   ② 서점 가기
③ 집에 가기   ④ 저녁 식사하기
⑤ 생일 파티 참석하기

M Where are you going, Yuna?
W I'm going to buy Jieun's birthday present.
M Oh! me, too. ❶ _____ _____ _____ _____ a book for her. How about you?
W Actually, I don't have a good idea. I'll follow you and see if there's a good item ❷ _____ _____ _____.
M Good. By the way, it's already 5. Why don't we have dinner together after buying her present?
W Okay. Then, let's finish ❸ _____ _____ quickly. My mother told me to come back by 6 p.m.

16 특정 정보 파악   영국식 발음 녹음

대화를 듣고, 여자가 구입할 물건을 고르시오.

① flower   ② book   ③ magazine
④ toy car   ⑤ pencil

M Ann, where are you going?
W I'm going to see my friend ❶ _____ _____ _____. He had a car accident.
M Oh, I'm sorry to hear that. I hope he's okay.
W Yes, it's not too serious. I want to buy something for him, but I don't know what to buy.
M How about buying ❷ _____ _____ _____ _____?
W Well, I've heard that many hospitals don't allow flowers.
M Hmm... then what about a book?
W Unfortunately, he doesn't like reading books.
M But he might like ❸ _____ _____ _____.
W You may be right. He likes cars, so I'll buy a car magazine. Thanks.

17 알맞은 응답 찾기

대화를 듣고, 남자의 마지막 말에 대한 여자의 응답으로 가장 적절한 것을 고르시오.

Woman: _____

① Do you mind if I taste it?
② I wish I would pass the test.
③ Tests on Sunday are very annoying.
④ I'll keep my fingers crossed for you.
⑤ Do you know how to make *bulgogi*?

😊 관심에 대해 묻기 ////////////////////
Are you interested in ~? / What are you interested in? / Do you find ~ interesting?

W Michael, what are you doing?
M I'm studying for a cooking license.
W 😊 Wow. Are you interested in cooking? I didn't know that.
M Yes, I am. My dream is to be ❶ _____ _____ _____ of Korean dishes.
W When is the test?
M It's this Sunday. Please ❷ _____ _____ _____ _____.

📖 Words   **15 already** 벌써   **16 accident** 사고 **allow** 허락하다 **magazine** 잡지   **17 license** 자격증 **dish** 요리

028 | 중학영어 듣기모의고사 **3**학년

18 알맞은 응답 찾기

대화를 듣고, 여자의 마지막 말에 대한 남자의 응답으로 가장 적절한 것을 고르시오.

Man: _____

① Once or twice a week.
② Because I like gardening.
③ I have two more gardens.
④ More than five hours a day.
⑤ The garden isn't far from here.

W Grandpa, your garden looks so much better! I love it!
M Thank you, Amy. Do you remember how it was last year?
W Of course, I do. It was a wasteland full of small rocks.
M Right. I ❶ _____ _____ _____.
W Then you planted these vegetables and trees in the garden.
M Yes, I did.
W Wow, you worked really hard ❷ _____ _____ _____.
M Yeah. I'm still working very hard on it.
W Really? ❸ _____ _____ do you work on it these days?

19 알맞은 응답 찾기

대화를 듣고, 남자의 마지막 말에 대한 여자의 응답으로 가장 적절한 것을 고르시오.

Woman: _____

① I'll help you move the closet.
② I don't think so. My room is clean.
③ Sure. I don't like a messy room either.
④ No thanks. I don't need more clothes.
⑤ Thanks. I like my new room very much.

M Lisa, your room is too messy. Why are your clothes lying on the bed and on the floor?
W I know my room is messy, but there's a reason for that.
M What is it?
W I ❶ _____ _____ _____ _____ for my clothes.
M You mean you want a bigger room?
W Well, no. I just need ❷ _____ _____ _____.
M I see. I'll buy a closet for you. But promise you will ❸ _____ _____ _____ _____ away.

20 상황에 맞는 말 찾기

다음 상황 설명을 듣고, Stewart가 Judy에게 할 말로 가장 적절한 것을 고르시오.

Stewart: _____

① It's on me.
② How was the food?
③ How did you learn French?
④ What does "Thank you" mean?
⑤ How can I say "Thank you" in French?

W Stewart is traveling to France with Judy. Judy can speak French well, so he has ❶ _____ _____ _____ from her. After having a nice lunch, he wanted to say "Thank you" to the chef. However, he did not know ❷ _____ _____ _____ "Thank you" ❸ _____ _____. In this situation, what would Stewart most likely say to Judy?

Words **18** wasteland 황무지 full of ~로 가득 찬 remove 없애다, 제거하다 **19** messy 지저분한 space 공간 clothes 옷 extra 추가의 closet 옷장 put ~ away ~을 (보관 장소에) 넣다[치우다] **20** chef 요리사

01 다음을 듣고, 지시에 따라 바르게 그린 그림을 고르시오.

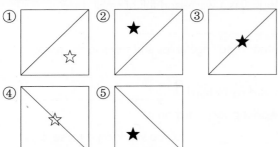

02 대화를 듣고, 남자가 여자에게 전화한 목적으로 가장 적절한 것을 고르시오.
① 여름 캠프 참가 신청을 하려고
② 어린이 도서관의 위치를 문의하려고
③ 만나기로 약속한 시간을 변경하려고
④ 버스에서 잃어버린 물건을 찾으려고
⑤ 여름 캠프 버스 타는 곳을 물어보려고

03 다음 그림의 상황에 가장 적절한 대화를 고르시오.

①   ②   ③   ④   ⑤

04 대화를 듣고, 남자가 보고서를 제출할 요일을 고르시오.
① 월요일   ② 화요일   ③ 수요일
④ 목요일   ⑤ 금요일

05 대화를 듣고, 학급 신문에 실릴 내용으로 언급되지 않은 것을 고르시오.
① 급훈   ② 단체 사진
③ 인터뷰   ④ 고등학교 정보
⑤ 학급 소식

06 대화를 듣고, 두 사람의 관계로 가장 적절한 것을 고르시오.
① 의사 – 환자
② 선생님 – 학생
③ 수의사 – 간호사
④ 식당 종업원 – 고객
⑤ 비행기 승무원 – 승객

07 다음을 듣고, 두 사람의 대화가 어색한 것을 고르시오.
①   ②   ③   ④   ⑤

08 대화를 듣고, 여자가 남자에게 부탁한 일로 가장 적절한 것을 고르시오.
① 상 차리는 것 돕기
② 스파게티 요리하기
③ 창문 열어 환기하기
④ 샐러드 재료 사 오기
⑤ 음식물 쓰레기 버리기

09 대화를 듣고, 남자의 마지막 말에 담긴 의도로 가장 적절한 것을 고르시오.
① 실망   ② 거절   ③ 제안
④ 축하   ⑤ 위로

10 대화를 듣고, 남자가 지불할 금액을 고르시오.
① $2   ② $4.50   ③ $6.50
④ $7   ⑤ $10

11 대화를 듣고, 여자가 할 일로 가장 적절한 것을 고르시오.

① 동네 청소하기
② 포스터 만들기
③ 고양이 사진 찍기
④ 애완동물 산책시키기
⑤ 애완동물 사진 편집하기

12 다음을 듣고, Summer Soccer Camp에 관해 언급되지 **않은** 것을 고르시오.

① 기간 　② 참가 대상 　③ 수업료
④ 준비물 　⑤ 인원 제한

13 대화를 듣고, 두 사람이 선택한 구역을 고르시오.

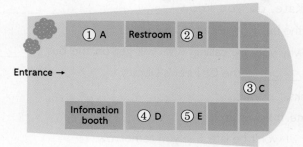

14 다음을 듣고, 무엇에 관한 설명인지 고르시오.

① 스마트폰 　　　　② 헤드폰
③ 디지털카메라 　　④ 문자 메시지
⑤ 홈쇼핑

15 대화를 듣고, 남자가 대화 직후에 할 일로 가장 적절한 것을 고르시오.

① 집에 가기 　　　② 점심 식사하기
③ 옷 갈아입기 　　④ 체육 수업 참가하기
⑤ 선생님과 상담하기

16 대화를 듣고, 두 사람이 만날 시각을 고르시오.

① 6:00 　　② 7:00 　　③ 7:30
④ 8:30 　　⑤ 9:00

17 대화를 듣고, 남자의 마지막 말에 대한 여자의 응답으로 가장 적절한 것을 고르시오.

Woman: _____

① Why not?
② Cheer up!
③ No problem.
④ You can say that again.
⑤ Next time, I won't miss it.

18 대화를 듣고, 여자의 마지막 말에 대한 남자의 응답으로 가장 적절한 것을 고르시오.

Man: _____

① Let me solve the problem.
② Well, I'm not good at history.
③ I guess you like math, right?
④ I don't know what subject I like.
⑤ I'll help you study for your exam.

19 대화를 듣고, 남자의 마지막 말에 대한 여자의 응답으로 가장 적절한 것을 고르시오.

Woman: _____

① I'd rather see a movie.
② Let's play soccer instead.
③ Do you have time next week?
④ Let's check out the movie schedule.
⑤ The running time is about 2 hours.

20 다음 상황 설명을 듣고, Cindy의 아버지가 Cindy에게 할 말로 가장 적절한 것을 고르시오.

Cindy's father: _____

① This is my first trip to Jeju-do, too.
② I'm very excited about going to Jeju-do.
③ The weather will be very cold tomorrow.
④ We can't go to Jeju-do because of heavy snow.
⑤ It's snowing a lot, so you'd better stay at home.

Dictation Test 04회 영어 듣기모의고사

01 그림 정보 파악 – 그림

다음을 듣고, 지시에 따라 바르게 그린 그림을 고르시오.

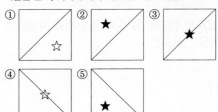

W First, _____ _____ _____ _____. Then draw a straight line from the top right corner to the bottom left. Now, you have ❷ _____ _____ in one big square. Draw one little star in one of the triangles. But the star must not touch with any other lines. Lastly, ❸ _____ _____ _____ _____ so that it becomes all black.

02 목적 파악

대화를 듣고, 남자가 여자에게 전화한 목적으로 가장 적절한 것을 고르시오.

① 여름 캠프 참가 신청을 하려고
② 어린이 도서관의 위치를 문의하려고
③ 만나기로 약속한 시간을 변경하려고
④ 버스에서 잃어버린 물건을 찾으려고
⑤ 여름 캠프 버스 타는 곳을 물어보려고

[*Telephone rings.*]

W Hello?

M Hello, Kate. It's me, Chris.

W Hi, Chris. What's up?

M ❶ _____ _____ _____ _____ for the summer camp tomorrow?

W Almost done. I'm looking forward to the camp.

M Me, too. Kate, do you know ❷ _____ _____ _____ _____ the bus for the camp? I forgot.

W Oh, that's why you are calling? We will get on the bus ❸ _____ _____ _____ the Children's Library.

M Okay. Thanks.

W Don't be late. It leaves at 9.

M Don't worry. I won't be late. See you tomorrow.

03 그림 상황에 어울리는 대화 찾기

다음 그림의 상황에 가장 적절한 대화를 고르시오.

① ② ③ ④ ⑤

① **W** Are we going to take that bus, Dad?
   M Yes, we are. Let's ❶ _____ _____ _____ when the light turns green.

② **W** I can't see the number over there. Can you see it, Dad?
   M Of course I can. Your eyesight has gotten worse.

③ **W** Stop, Dad. We must not cross the road here.
   M Oh, I didn't see the "No Crossing" sign. Thanks.

④ **W** I wonder why there isn't ❷ _____ _____ _____ here.
   M There should be one because so many people cross the street here.

⑤ **W** Dad, I'm going to cross the road. Stay there!
   M Step back! The light will ❸ _____ _____ in a few seconds.

---

04 특정 정보 파악 – 요일 영국식 발음 녹음

대화를 듣고, 남자가 보고서를 제출할 요일을 고르시오.

① 월요일　　② 화요일　　③ 수요일
④ 목요일　　⑤ 금요일

M　Mina, did you ❶ _____ _____ _____ _____ ?

W　Yes. I submitted it on Monday.

M　Good. What did you write about?

W　I wrote about animals in danger. Did you submit yours?

M　Not yet. I'm going to ❷ _____ _____ _____ _____ .

W　What are you writing about?

M　I'm writing about the ❸ _____ _____ _____ .

W　Sounds interesting. Good luck to you.

M　Thanks.

05 언급되지 않은 것

대화를 듣고, 학급 신문에 실릴 내용으로 언급되지 않은 것을 고르시오.

① 급훈　　　　　② 단체 사진
③ 인터뷰　　　　④ 고등학교 정보
⑤ 학급 소식

ⓟ **interview의 발음** ////////////////////////////
interview처럼 [n] 다음에 [t]가 나오면 [t]가 생략되어 [inərvju:]처럼 발음되는 경향이 있다.

M　Emma, did the class meeting go well? How are you going to make ❶ _____ _____ _____ ?

W　We are thinking of including our class motto, two big group pictures, and an interview with you, Mr. Brown. ⓟ

M　So far so good. Keep going.

W　And useful information about ❷ _____ _____ _____ and our cellphone numbers.

M　Wait a second. You must not ❸ _____ _____ _____ _____ . It is not safe to give out personal information.

W　Ah, that's good advice, thanks.

06 관계 추론

대화를 듣고, 두 사람의 관계로 가장 적절한 것을 고르시오.

① 의사 – 환자
② 선생님 – 학생
③ 수의사 – 간호사
④ 식당 종업원 – 고객
⑤ 비행기 승무원 – 승객

ⓟ **It seems like의 발음** ///////////////////
문장의 주어 It은 실제로 잘 안 들릴 정도로 빨리 말하는 경향이 있다. It seems like ~.의 경우 Seems like ~.로 들릴 정도로 It을 작게 말하는 경우가 흔하다.

M　Your eyes are all red. Can you open your eyes wide? (*pause*) ⓟ It seems like you have ❶ _____ _____ .

W　Oh, no. What am I supposed to do?

M　Put eye drops into your eyes three times a day. It'll be okay soon.

W　Anything else?

M　It's very important to ❷ _____ _____ _____ with soap as often as possible.

W　Thank you, Dr. Lee. Can I have ❸ _____ _____ _____ from you? I need to give it to my homeroom teacher.

M　Sure. I will write one for you.

📖 **Words**　**04 submit** 제출하다　**in danger** 위험에 처한　**05 include** 포함하다　**motto** 모토, 좌우명　**publish** 발표(공표)하다, 널리 알리다　**personal** 개인적인　**06 eye drop** 안약　**soap** 비누　**sick note** 진단서　**homeroom teacher** 담임 선생님

Dictation Test

07 어색한 대화 찾기

다음을 듣고, 두 사람의 대화가 <u>어색한</u> 것을 고르시오.

① ② ③ ④ ⑤

💬 **낙담 위로하기** ////////////////////

Don't be disappointed(discouraged). / Don't worry. / Cheer up! / Things will be better (soon).

① M ❶ _____ _____ _____ if I use your cellphone?

W No. Go ahead.

② M How do you like your new apartment?

W Actually, it's ❷ _____ _____ _____ my old one.

③ M What are you going to order?

W I'm thinking of pizza.

④ M It ❸ _____ _____ _____. Can I give you a hand?

W Of course. I'll help you.

⑤ M I got a terrible score on the midterm exam.

W 💬 Don't be disappointed. You can do better next time.

08 부탁한 일 파악   영국식 발음 녹음

대화를 듣고, 여자가 남자에게 부탁한 일로 가장 적절한 것을 고르시오.

① 상 차리는 것 돕기
② 스파게티 요리하기
③ 창문 열어 환기하기
④ 샐러드 재료 사 오기
⑤ 음식물 쓰레기 버리기

M Mom, this spaghetti looks delicious.

W Thank you. Try some if you want.

M Okay. (pause) Wow, it's so good. May I ❶ _____ _____ _____ now?

W Thank you, but not yet, Peter. I'm making salad now. I'll set the table.

M Well, is there anything ❷ _____ _____ _____ _____ with?

W Hmm... can you ❸ _____ _____ _____ to let some fresh air in?

M No problem.

W Thanks, Peter.

09 의도 파악

대화를 듣고, 남자의 마지막 말에 담긴 의도로 가장 적절한 것을 고르시오.

① 실망   ② 거절   ③ 제안
④ 축하   ⑤ 위로

💬 **축하, 칭찬하기** ////////////////////

Congratulations (on ~)! / (Very) good! / Good (for you)! / Great!(Excellent!) / (You did a) good (job)!

W Hi, David. I ❶ _____ _____ _____ in the jump rope contest.

M Oh, Amy. Congratulations!

W Thank you. I think I was lucky.

M No, I don't think so. You practiced really hard, didn't you?

W Well, that's true. I ❷ _____ _____ _____ every day.

M Then you deserve the prize.

W Thank you for saying so.

M Let's go and have ice cream to celebrate.

Words   **07 give a hand** 도움을 주다 **midterm exam** 중간고사 **disappointed** 실망한   **08 set the table** 상을 차리다 **let ~ in** ~을 (안으로) 들이다 **09 jump rope** 줄넘기; 줄넘기 줄 **Congratulations!** 축하해! **celebrate** 축하하다

10 숫자 정보 파악 – 금액

대화를 듣고, 남자가 지불할 금액을 고르시오.
① $2 ② $4.50 ③ $6.50
④ $7 ⑤ $10

W Welcome to Burger World. What would you like to have?
M Hi, I'd like to have a *bulgogi* burger and a small Coke, please.
W Do you need anything else? M No, thanks.
W Well, a *bulgogi* burger is $4.50, and a small Coke is $2. So, that will be
❶ _____ _____ _____ _____ . But if you pay
❷ _____ _____ _____ , you can order the *bulgogi*
combo meal, which is a *bulgogi* burger, a medium Coke, and fries.
M Really? Then, I'll take the combo meal.
W Okay. For here or to go? M ❸ _____ _____, please.

11 한 일 / 할 일 파악 영국식 발음 녹음

대화를 듣고, 여자가 할 일로 가장 적절한 것을 고르시오.
① 동네 청소하기
② 포스터 만들기
③ 고양이 사진 찍기
④ 애완동물 산책시키기
⑤ 애완동물 사진 편집하기

슬픔, 불만족, 실망의 원인에 대해 묻기
Why are you sad[disappointed]? / What's
wrong? / What's the matter?

M Jenny, why are you sad? W My cat ran away this morning.
M Oh no! I'm sorry to hear that.
W Where is he now? ❶ _____ _____ _____ so much.
M Cheer up, Jenny. I'm sure you'll find him soon.
W Thanks, but I don't know what to do to find him.
M How about ❷ _____ _____ _____ in the neighborhood?
W That's a good idea. I'll make posters right away.
M Don't forget to ❸ _____ _____ _____ _____ on your
poster. W Sure. Thanks.

12 언급되지 않은 것

다음을 듣고, Summer Soccer Camp에 관해 언급
되지 **않은** 것을 고르시오.
① 기간 ② 참가 대상 ③ 수업료
④ 준비물 ⑤ 인원 제한

M Hello, students! Do you want to take your soccer skills to the next
level this summer? Then join our Summer Soccer Camp. ❶ _____
_____ _____ from August 2 to August 4. Boys and girls
aged 10 and over can join the camp. ❷ _____ _____ is just
$100 including lunch. The camp ❸ _____ _____ _____ 50
participants. So, don't regret and register now!

13 도표 정보 파악

대화를 듣고, 두 사람이 선택한 구역을 고르시오.

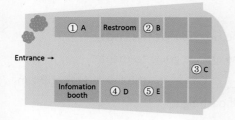

W Peter, there are ❶ _____ _____ _____ to rent at the flea
market next week. Which one would be best for us?
M Last year we took a booth next to the restroom. Remember? It
wasn't good.
W Right. This time let's not rent a booth next to the restroom.
M Okay. How about taking one of these booths that are ❷ _____
_____ _____ _____?
W Good idea. I think this one next to the information booth is better
than the other one. What do you think?
M I don't agree with you. The section next to the information booth
will be too crowded. People might skip our booth because of that.
W You may be right. Then let's ❸ _____ _____ _____ _____.

Words **10 combo meal** (햄버거, 감자튀김, 음료수가 포함된) 세트 메뉴 **11 run away** 도망가다 **cheer up** 기운을 내다 **neighborhood** 동네, 이웃
12 fee 수업료 **participant** 참가자 **register** 등록하다 **13 flea market** 벼룩시장 **next to** ~의 옆에 있는 **across from** ~의 맞은편에 있는

Dictation Test

14 주제 파악

다음을 듣고, 무엇에 관한 설명인지 고르시오.

① 스마트폰　　　　② 헤드폰
③ 디지털카메라　　④ 문자 메시지
⑤ 홈쇼핑

M This is usually a little expensive. But these days, the number of people using this is increasing. People like to ❶_____ _____ _____ and take pictures with this. They also like to ❷_____ _____ _____ and play games through this. However, people should not ❸_____ _____ _____ _____ using this.

15 한 일 / 할 일 파악

대화를 듣고, 남자가 대화 직후에 할 일로 가장 적절한 것을 고르시오.

① 집에 가기　　　　② 점심 식사하기
③ 옷 갈아입기　　　④ 체육 수업 참가하기
⑤ 선생님과 상담하기

😊 **의무 표현하기**
I have (got) to ~. / I should[ought to] ~. / It is required to ~.

M Ms. Parker, can you give me a minute of your time?
W Okay. I have time now.
M Not right now. I have ❶_____ _____ _____ the next P.E. class. Do you have a minute at lunchtime?
W Sure. By the way, what's going on?
M Actually, I need to talk to you ❷_____ _____ _____. I really want to enter a good high school, but my score doesn't seem to be going up.
W Don't be discouraged. I think I can help you out.
M Thanks. Oh, I've got to go to ❸_____ _____ _____ for the next P.E. class.
W Okay, then see you at lunchtime.

16 숫자 정보 파악 – 시각　영국식 발음 녹음

대화를 듣고, 두 사람이 만날 시각을 고르시오.

① 6:00　　② 7:00　　③ 7:30
④ 8:30　　⑤ 9:00

M Finally, we are going to see the *Gag Concert* this Friday.
W Yes, I'm so excited. What time are we going to meet?
M Hmm, they ❶_____ _____ _____ the free tickets at 9 a.m. So, why don't we meet at half past eight?
W Well, some people begin to wait from 6 a.m. to get front seat tickets. I also want to ❷_____ _____ _____ _____.
M You mean you want to go there at 6 in the morning?
W No, I know that's too early. What about ❸_____ _____ _____?
M Okay. That will be okay.

Ⓦords 　14 expensive 값비싼　increase 증가하다　15 prepare for ~을 준비하다　grade 성적　score 점수　discouraged 낙담한　16 front 앞쪽(의)

17 알맞은 응답 찾기

대화를 듣고, 남자의 마지막 말에 대한 여자의 응답으로 가장 적절한 것을 고르시오.

Woman: _____

① Why not?
② Cheer up!
③ No problem.
④ You can say that again.
⑤ Next time, I won't miss it.

😮 **놀람 표현하기** /////////////////////////////

That's surprising! / What a surprise! / I can't believe this. / I'm surprised that ~.

M We're _____ _____ _____ with the best figure skater, Yuna Kim. When did you start skating?

W I started skating when I was seven. When I was fourteen, I was selected as a member of the national team.

M Wow, that's surprising! Have you considered giving up?

W Sometimes I feel exhausted. But I've ❷ _____ _____ _____ _____ _____.

M I'm so impressed. Would you like to say something to your fans?

W Practice makes perfect, everyone. Please never give up.

M ❸ _____ _____ _____ _____ for the interview today.

18 알맞은 응답 찾기

대화를 듣고, 여자의 마지막 말에 대한 남자의 응답으로 가장 적절한 것을 고르시오.

Man: _____

① Let me solve the problem.
② Well, I'm not good at history.
③ I guess you like math, right?
④ I don't know what subject I like.
⑤ I'll help you study for your exam.

W Tony, what is your favorite subject?

M ❶ _____ _____ _____ is history.

W Oh, I didn't know that. Why do you like history?

M I like to learn what happened in the past and how people in the past lived.

W History is ❷ _____ _____ _____.

M What is your favorite subject, Bora?

W Guess what it is. It deals with numbers, figures, and graphs. I ❸ _____ _____ _____ _____.

19 알맞은 응답 찾기

대화를 듣고, 남자의 마지막 말에 대한 여자의 응답으로 가장 적절한 것을 고르시오.

Woman: _____

① I'd rather see a movie.
② Let's play soccer instead.
③ Do you have time next week?
④ Let's check out the movie schedule.
⑤ The running time is about 2 hours.

W I'm tired of TV every night. Let's go out and ❶ _____ _____ _____.

M That's a good idea. What should we go to see?

W Well, we usually see dramas. ❷ _____ _____ _____ go to see an animation film for a change?

M That's great. How about *Madagascar*?

W Good. It's playing at TTC Cinema.

M It's near here. ❸ _____ _____ does it start?

20 상황에 맞는 말 찾기

다음 상황 설명을 듣고, Cindy의 아버지가 Cindy에게 할 말로 가장 적절한 것을 고르시오.

Cindy's father: _____

① This is my first trip to Jeju-do, too.
② I'm very excited about going to Jeju-do.
③ The weather will be very cold tomorrow.
④ We can't go to Jeju-do because of heavy snow.
⑤ It's snowing a lot, so you'd better stay at home.

W Cindy is going to ❶ _____ _____ _____ to Jeju-do with her father. She is very excited about going to Jeju-do for the first time. They will leave Seoul for Jeju-do tomorrow morning, but today's news says that there is ❷ _____ _____ in Jeju-do. Cindy's father gets a phone call from the travel agency and learns that all flights to Jeju-do ❸ _____ _____ because of the heavy snow. He wants to let Cindy know about this. In this situation, what would Cindy's father most likely say to her?

📖 Words ♦ **17 national team** 국가대표 팀 **exhausted** 지친 **give up** 포기하다 **impressed** 감명을 받은 **18 happen** 발생하다 **figure** 도형 **solve** (문제 등을) 풀다 **19 tired of** ~에 싫증난 **for a change** 기분 전환으로 **20 take a trip to** ~로 여행가다 **travel agency** 여행사

01 대화를 듣고, 여자가 구입할 꽃병을 고르시오.

 ① ② ③

 ④ ⑤

02 대화를 듣고, 여자가 남자에게 전화한 목적으로 가장 적절한 것을 고르시오.

① 유기견을 입양하려고
② 애완견 사료를 주문하려고
③ 애완견 분실 신고를 하려고
④ 유기견 습득 신고를 하려고
⑤ 애완견 훈련법을 문의하려고

03 다음 그림의 상황에 가장 적절한 대화를 고르시오.

① ② ③ ④ ⑤

04 대화를 듣고, 두 사람이 만나기로 한 요일을 고르시오.

① 월요일 ② 화요일 ③ 수요일
④ 목요일 ⑤ 금요일

05 다음을 듣고, Dolphin Aquarium에 관해 언급되지 않은 것을 고르시오.

① 개장 시간 ② 입장료 ③ 편의 시설
④ 단체 할인 ⑤ 음식물 반입 여부

06 대화를 듣고, 남자의 심정으로 가장 적절한 것을 고르시오.

① pleased ② bored
③ relieved ④ embarrassed
⑤ disappointed

07 다음을 듣고, 두 사람의 대화가 <u>어색한</u> 것을 고르시오.

① ② ③ ④ ⑤

08 대화를 듣고, 여자가 남자에게 부탁한 일로 가장 적절한 것을 고르시오.

① 사진 전송하기
② 사진 찍어 주기
③ 여행 일정 짜기
④ 집에 데려다주기
⑤ 시험공부 도와주기

09 대화를 듣고, 여자의 마지막 말에 담긴 의도로 가장 적절한 것을 고르시오.

① 부탁 ② 허락 ③ 거절
④ 축하 ⑤ 위로

10 대화를 듣고, 여자가 지불할 금액을 고르시오.

① $5 ② $9 ③ $10.50
④ $12.50 ⑤ $16

11 대화를 듣고, 여자가 오늘 할 일로 가장 적절한 것을 고르시오.

① 병원 가기 　② 수업 듣기
③ 공원 산책하기 　④ 집에서 휴식 취하기
⑤ 야구 경기 보러 가기

12 다음을 듣고, Genie Smart Speaker에 관해 언급되지 않은 것을 고르시오.

① 기능 　② 무게 　③ 색깔
④ 제어 방식 　⑤ 충전 시간

13 대화를 듣고, 남자가 서류에서 수정할 항목을 고르시오.

Name	① Park Dohoon	
Gender	② ☑ Male	☐ Female
Cellphone No.	③ 100-9123-4567	
Experience	④ ☐ Yes	☑ No
Subject	⑤ ☑ English	☐ Chinese

14 다음을 듣고, 무엇에 관한 설명인지 고르시오.

① 곤충 채집 방법 　② 곤충을 기르는 방법
③ 여름철 피부 보호법 　④ 산행 시 벌레 예방법
⑤ 벌레에 물린 상처 치료법

15 대화를 듣고, 남자가 할 일로 가장 적절한 것을 고르시오.

① 운전하기 　② 화장실 청소하기
③ 물 끓이기 　④ 파스타 만들기
⑤ 식료품 쇼핑하기

16 대화를 듣고, 두 사람이 구입할 물건이 <u>아닌</u> 것을 고르시오.

① water 　② ramen 　③ snacks
④ chopsticks ⑤ instant rice

17 대화를 듣고, 남자의 마지막 말에 대한 여자의 응답으로 가장 적절한 것을 고르시오.

Woman: _____

① It's not in the top drawer.
② I need to go to the nail shop.
③ Please slice the other onions for me.
④ The drugstore is just across the street.
⑤ Me, neither. I should have been more careful.

18 대화를 듣고, 여자의 마지막 말에 대한 남자의 응답으로 가장 적절한 것을 고르시오.

Man: _____

① Do you want to try it on?
② Will this be cash or credit?
③ All right. We'll give you a new watch.
④ I think you should change the battery.
⑤ Sorry, but we don't give a discount on it.

19 대화를 듣고, 남자의 마지막 말에 대한 여자의 응답으로 가장 적절한 것을 고르시오.

Woman: _____

① Well, it doesn't matter.
② I'm sorry to bother you.
③ Shall we go there for dinner?
④ I have another appointment.
⑤ I don't want to take up your time.

20 다음 상황 설명을 듣고, Lisa가 어머니에게 할 말로 가장 적절한 것을 고르시오.

Lisa: _____

① Can you believe I won?
② Do you have any water?
③ Can we share the stage?
④ Can you teach me to dance?
⑤ Shall I go get water for you?

Dictation Test 05회 영어 듣기모의고사

01 그림 정보 파악 – 사물

대화를 듣고, 여자가 구입할 꽃병을 고르시오.

① ② ③

④ ⑤

😀 제안·권유하기 ///////////////

How[What] about ~? / Let's ~. / Why don't
we[you] ~? / Would you like to ~?

M Diana, how about selecting your birthday present here? I'll buy it for
you.

W Oh, thanks. I want to have ❶ _____ _____ _____ _____.

M The vases are over there. This one with a flower pattern looks nice.

W It does, but I want something modern.

M Then, how about this one with a checked pattern?

W I already have one. Wow, that white vase with black dots looks
fantastic.

M Oh, yeah. There is ❷ _____ _____ of the same design, but it
has a different color.

W That's much prettier! I'll take that ❸ _____ _____ _____
_____ _____.

02 목적 파악

대화를 듣고, 여자가 남자에게 전화한 목적으로 가장
적절한 것을 고르시오.

① 유기견을 입양하려고
② 애완견 사료를 주문하려고
③ 애완견 분실 신고를 하려고
④ 유기견 습득 신고를 하려고
⑤ 애완견 훈련법을 문의하려고

[*Telephone rings.*]

M Guro Police Station, how can I help you?

W Hello, ❶ _____ _____ _____ _____.

M When and where did you lose it?

W An hour ago, at my house. It ❷ _____ _____ through an open
door.

M I see. What does it look like?

W It is white and small. It is wearing a jean suit.

M I got it. I'll call you ❸ _____ _____ _____ _____.

03 그림 상황에 어울리는 대화 찾기

다음 그림의 상황에 가장 적절한 대화를 고르시오.

① ② ③ ④ ⑤

① **M** Mom, I need ❶ _____ _____ _____. Mine is too old.

   W I don't think so, honey. It's not that old.

② **M** Do you know ❷ _____ _____ _____ _____
   _____?

   W I remember seeing it on the shelf in the living room.

③ **M** My robot is broken. What should I do?

   W Don't worry. I can fix it for you.

④ **M** I can't ❸ _____ _____ _____ _____ on the shelf.
   Can you get it?

   W Sure. I'll get it for you.

⑤ **M** Mom, I'd like to have that teddy bear.

   W It's too expensive. Let's find a cheaper one.

Words **01 select** 고르다, 선택하다 **checked pattern** 체크무늬 **fantastic** 환상적인 **02 police station** 경찰서 **suit** (옷의) 한 벌 **03 teddy bear** 곰 인형 **shelf** 선반 **fix** 고치다, 수리하다 **expensive** 비싼

04 특정 정보 파악 – 요일 영국식 발음 녹음
대화를 듣고, 두 사람이 만나기로 한 요일을 고르시오.
① 월요일 ② 화요일 ③ 수요일
④ 목요일 ⑤ 금요일

[*Cellphone rings.*]
M Hi, Stella. What's up?
W I'm going to buy _____ _____ _____. But I don't know much about phones.
M Do you want me to help you buy your smartphone?
W That would be great! Are you free ❷ _____ _____ _____?
M No. I will play baseball with my friends tomorrow. We meet every Wednesday. How about meeting on Thursday?
W I have a violin lesson on Thursday.
M Then ❸ _____ _____ _____ _____?
W Sure! See you at ABC mall at 6.
M Okay. See you soon.

05 언급되지 않은 것
다음을 듣고, Dolphin Aquarium에 관해 언급되지 않은 것을 고르시오.
① 개장 시간 ② 입장료 ③ 편의 시설
④ 단체 할인 ⑤ 음식물 반입 여부

W Welcome to Dolphin Aquarium. Discover the wonders of life in the water with us. ❶ _____ _____ _____ from 9 a.m. to 8 p.m. from Monday to Saturday and closed on Sundays. ❷ _____ _____ $25 for adults and $20 for children under fifteen. Groups of 10 or more can get $2 off per person. ❸ _____ _____ _____ or drink is permitted. Please don't take pictures of the dolphins while they are taking a rest because it can disturb them. Thank you for your cooperation.

06 심정 파악
대화를 듣고, 남자의 심정으로 가장 적절한 것을 고르시오.
① pleased ② bored
③ relieved ④ embarrassed
⑤ disappointed

😊 **기억이나 망각 여부 묻기**
Don't you remember ~? / I wonder if you remember ~. / You haven't forgotten about ~, have you?

W What's the matter?
M I ❶ _____ _____ _____ _____.
W You mean you've lost them? George, it's two thirty. The train will leave in half an hour! Don't you remember ❷ _____ _____ _____ _____ after getting them from me?
M Of course, I remember.
W Now think back.
M I put them in the pocket of my jacket. But now ❸ _____ _____.

Words **04** free 한가한 mall 쇼핑몰 **05** aquarium 수족관 discover 발견하다 wonder 놀라움, 경이로움 admission 입장료 permit 허용하다 disturb 방해하다 cooperation 협조 **06** matter 문제, 일 lose 잃어버리다 think back 돌이켜 생각하다 pocket 주머니, 포켓

Dictation Test

07 어색한 대화 찾기

다음을 듣고, 두 사람의 대화가 어색한 것을 고르시오.

① ② ③ ④ ⑤

😊 격려하기 //////////////////////////////////

Don't give up! / You can do it! / That's all right. /
You'll do better next time.

① W Can I _____ _____ _____?
  M Okay. Make sure you give it back to me this week.
② W I failed the English speaking test.
  M Don't give up. You'll _____ _____ _____.
③ W I have a bad headache.
  M Why don't you go see a doctor?
④ W The blackboard is too dirty.
  M Let's clean it together.
⑤ W I think Greg will ❸ _____ _____ _____ _____.
  M It's all my fault.

08 부탁한 일 파악   영국식 발음 녹음

대화를 듣고, 여자가 남자에게 부탁한 일로 가장 적절한
것을 고르시오.
① 사진 전송하기
② 사진 찍어 주기
③ 여행 일정 짜기
④ 집에 데려다주기
⑤ 시험공부 도와주기

M Alice, today is the last day of ❶ _____ _____ _____. I
  can't believe it.
W Me, neither. We'll return to school tomorrow and midterm exams
  are next week.
M Oh, I wish we could stay here longer.
W Me, too. By the way, Chris, did you ❷ _____ _____ _____
  _____ here?
M Yes. You're in some of my pictures.
W Really? Can you ❸ _____ _____ _____ _____ now?
M Sure. I'll send them after we get on the bus.
W Thank you.
M Oh, it's time to get on the bus now. Let's go.

09 의도 파악

대화를 듣고, 여자의 마지막 말에 담긴 의도로 가장 적절한
것을 고르시오.
① 부탁   ② 허락   ③ 거절
④ 축하   ⑤ 위로

W Chris, it's been a month since we moved here. How's your new
  school life?
M So far so good. I've made many friends.
W Good to hear that. Don't you ❶ _____ _____ _____
  _____?
M Of course I do. ❷ _____ _____ _____ _____ almost
  every day.
W I remember. Would you like to invite them here?
M Really? I'd love to see them again.
W ❸ _____ _____ _____ _____ anytime you want.

📖 Words   **07 give back** 돌려주다 **fault** 잘못   **08 field trip** 수학여행, 현장학습 **midterm exam** 중간고사   **09 miss** 그리워하다 **hang out** 어울리다, 놀다 **invite** 초대하다 **anytime** 언제든지

10 숫자 정보 파악 – 금액

대화를 듣고, 여자가 지불할 금액을 고르시오.

① $5　　② $9　　③ $10.50
④ $12.50　　⑤ $16

가능성 정도 묻기

Is it possible(probable, likely) that I ~? /
Can(May) I ~?

M　Good morning. May I help you?
W　I'd like to have these clothes dry-cleaned.
M　When would you like to _____ _____ _____?
W　Is it possible that I pick them up tomorrow evening?
M　Okay, I'll try. Now, what do you have?
W　I have _____ _____ _____ _____. How much will that be?
M　Blouses are $2.50 each and _____ _____ _____ _____ each.
W　I see, here you are.

11 한 일 / 할 일 파악　영국식 발음 녹음

대화를 듣고, 여자가 오늘 할 일로 가장 적절한 것을 고르시오.

① 병원 가기　　② 수업 듣기
③ 공원 산책하기　　④ 집에서 휴식 취하기
⑤ 야구 경기 보러 가기

M　Hey, Mary, are you okay? You seem a little quiet.
W　Well, I guess I'm _____ _____ _____ _____.
M　I'm sorry to hear that. Why don't you take the day off tomorrow?
W　I have a class in the morning.
M　Skip class. I'll help you catch up with it.
W　Thanks, Eric. Anyway, I'll just _____ _____ and _____ _____ _____ today.

12 언급되지 않은 것

다음을 듣고, Genie Smart Speaker에 관해 언급되지 않은 것을 고르시오.

① 기능　　② 무게　　③ 색깔
④ 제어 방식　　⑤ 충전 시간

M　Hello, everyone. Today I'm going to tell you about _____ _____ _____, Genie Smart Speaker. With Genie Smart Speaker, you can find information and listen to music, too. It's _____ _____ _____ _____ an apple. It weighs only 2 kg. It can be controlled by either remote controller or your voice. It doesn't take long to charge the battery. It _____ _____ _____ _____ to be fully charged.

13 도표 정보 파악

대화를 듣고, 남자가 서류에서 수정할 항목을 고르시오.

Name	① Park Dohoon	
Gender	② ☑ Male	□ Female
Cellphone No.	③ 100-9123-4567	
Experience	④ □ Yes	☑ No
Subject	⑤ ☑ English	□ Chinese

M　Rebecca, I applied for an academy teacher position. _____ _____ _____ my English résumé? I'm going to hand it in tomorrow.
W　Sure. Your name, Park Dohoon is spelled correctly, and you're a male. Your phone number is 100−9123−4567.
M　Yeah, and I have _____ _____ _____ _____.
W　I see. By the way, aren't you good at Chinese as well?
M　I am, but I thought I was supposed to check only one box.
W　It doesn't say so. If you _____ _____ _____, they would want to pick you more.
M　Okay. Thank you for your help.

hand it의 발음

자음과 모음이 연달아 오면 둘은 자연스럽게 연결되어 발음된다. 따라서 hand it은 [hændit]으로 발음한다.

Words　**10** **pick up** ~을 찾아오다　**11** **take off** ~을 쉬다　**catch up with** ~을 따라잡다　**anyway** 어쨌든, 어차피　**12** **product** 제품　**weigh** 무게가 ~이다　**charge** 충전하다　**13** **position** 자리, 위치　**hand in** 제출하다　**correctly** 정확하게　**experience** 경력

Dictation Test ✐

14 주제 파악

다음을 듣고, 무엇에 관한 설명인지 고르시오.
① 곤충 채집 방법　　② 곤충을 기르는 방법
③ 여름철 피부 보호법　④ 산행 시 벌레 예방법
⑤ 벌레에 물린 상처 치료법

W There was another huge loss by dangerous insects today. Let me tell you _____ _____ _____ yourself while ❷ _____ _____. First, wear long sleeves and pants. Second, avoid sitting on the grass without a mat. Third, prepare creams or sprays to keep the insects away. Lastly, ❸ _____ _____ _____ right after you come home.

15 한 일 / 할 일 파악

대화를 듣고, 남자가 할 일로 가장 적절한 것을 고르시오.
① 운전하기　　　② 화장실 청소하기
③ 물 끓이기　　　④ 파스타 만들기
⑤ 식료품 쇼핑하기

W I'm going grocery shopping. What would you like to have for dinner?
M Well, I ❶ _____ _____ _____ cream pasta today.
W Okay. I'll make it for you.
M I can go with you if you want.
W Would you ❷ _____ _____ _____ _____?
M No problem. Do you want me to boil some water, too?
W No. I can do it ❸ _____ _____ _____ _____.
M Okay. Drive safely.

16 특정 정보 파악　영국식 발음 녹음

대화를 듣고, 두 사람이 구입할 물건이 <u>아닌</u> 것을 고르시오.
① water　　② ramen　　③ snacks
④ chopsticks　⑤ instant rice

🗣 **동의나 이의 여부 묻기** ////////////////////////////
Don't you agree? / Do(Would) you agree with me? / What do you think?

W So, did we put everything in the cart for our camping?
M I believe so. Let's check the list again.
W Okay. We bought ❶ _____, _____, paper cups and ❷ _____ _____.
M Don't we need instant rice?
W No, I can cook rice there.
M 🗣 But don't you agree that it'll make too much work?
W Well, I agree. Let's get some instant rice as well. What about chopsticks?
M Minwoo said ❸ _____ _____ _____ _____. He'll bring them.
W Great.

📖 **Words** **14 huge** 엄청난 **loss** 피해, 손실 **protect** 보호하다 **sleeve** 소매 **15 grocery shopping** 장보기 **feel like -ing** ~하고 싶다 **boil** 끓이다 **safely** 안전하게 **16 cart** 카트, 수레 **instant** 즉석의, 인스턴트의 **chopstick** 젓가락 한 쪽

17 알맞은 응답 찾기

대화를 듣고, 남자의 마지막 말에 대한 여자의 응답으로 가장 적절한 것을 고르시오.

Woman: _____

① It's not in the top drawer.
② I need to go to the nail shop.
③ Please slice the other onions for me.
④ The drugstore is just across the street.
⑤ Me, neither. I should have been more careful.

W Ouch!　　M What's up?
W I cut my finger.　M How did that happen?
W I was slicing an onion and I ❶ _____ _____ _____ _____.
M It must be painful. Is there something I can do for you?
W Yes, please. Will you get a bandage for me? It's in the top drawer.
M I will. ❷ _____ _____ _____ your cutting yourself. You're an expert in cutting.

18 알맞은 응답 찾기

대화를 듣고, 여자의 마지막 말에 대한 남자의 응답으로 가장 적절한 것을 고르시오.

Man: _____

① Do you want to try it on?
② Will this be cash or credit?
③ All right. We'll give you a new watch.
④ I think you should change the battery.
⑤ Sorry, but we don't give a discount on it.

😊 허락 요청하기 //////////////////////
Let me ~. / May[Can] I ~ (, please)? / Do you mind if ~? / Would it be possible ~? / I was wondering if I could ~.

W Hello. I just bought this watch here a week ago, and it's already stopped working. I'd like to ❶ _____ _____ for a new one.
M Really? ❷ _____ _____ _____ when you bought it?
W Yes, although it was a few minutes slow.
M Did you check the battery?
W Yes, I put in a new one, just to be sure.
M Okay. Let me see ❸ _____ _____.
W Here you are.

19 알맞은 응답 찾기

대화를 듣고, 남자의 마지막 말에 대한 여자의 응답으로 가장 적절한 것을 고르시오.

Woman: _____

① Well, it doesn't matter.
② I'm sorry to bother you.
③ Shall we go there for dinner?
④ I have another appointment.
⑤ I don't want to take up your time.

[*Telephone rings.*]
M Hello?
W Hello, Michael! Can you come to a party tomorrow? It's at my house.
M What's the address?
W As you know, 13 East Street.
M Well, ❶ _____ _____ _____ _____ who lives at that address.
W Oh, isn't this Michael Williams?
M No, this is Michael Adams. I'm afraid you've ❷ _____ _____ _____ _____.

20 상황에 맞는 말 찾기

다음 상황 설명을 듣고, Lisa가 어머니에게 할 말로 가장 적절한 것을 고르시오.

Lisa: _____

① Can you believe I won?
② Do you have any water?
③ Can we share the stage?
④ Can you teach me to dance?
⑤ Shall I go get water for you?

W Lisa is competing in ❶ _____ _____ _____. This is the first time for her to take part in a dance contest. She watches other students dancing very well. She will go on the stage soon, so she's nervous. She suddenly ❷ _____ _____ _____. She looks for water but she can't find any. She wants to ask her mom if ❸ _____ _____ _____. In this situation, what would Lisa most likely say to her mother?

Words **17** slice (얇게) 자르다 bandage 붕대 drawer 서랍 expert 전문가 **18** exchange 교환하다 although (비록) ~이기는 하지만 receipt 영수증 **19** address 주소 **20** compete 경쟁하다 take part in ~에 참가하다 stage 무대 nervous 긴장한 thirsty 목이 마른

01 대화를 듣고, 남자가 구입할 시계를 고르시오.

① ② ③

④ ⑤

02 대화를 듣고, 남자가 도서관에 전화한 목적으로 가장 적절한 것을 고르시오.

① 신간 구입을 요청하려고
② 분실된 책을 보상하려고
③ 자원봉사자에 지원하려고
④ 회원 카드 분실 신고를 하려고
⑤ 회원 카드 신청 방법을 문의하려고

03 다음 그림의 상황에 가장 적절한 대화를 고르시오.

① ② ③ ④ ⑤

04 대화를 듣고, 두 사람이 만나기로 한 장소를 고르시오.

① 학교　　② 병원　　③ 약국
④ 경찰서　　⑤ 소방서

05 다음을 듣고, Summer Reading Program에 관해 언급되지 않은 것을 고르시오.

① 개최 장소　② 참가 대상　③ 운영 기간
④ 참가비　　⑤ 참가 인원수

06 대화를 듣고, 여자의 직업으로 가장 적절한 것을 고르시오.

① editor　　　② painter
③ teacher　　④ photographer
⑤ programmer

07 다음을 듣고, 두 사람의 대화가 <u>어색한</u> 것을 고르시오.

①　　②　　③　　④　　⑤

08 대화를 듣고, 여자가 남자에게 부탁한 일로 가장 적절한 것을 고르시오.

① 라켓 빌려주기
② 함께 운동하기
③ 병원에 같이 가기
④ 학교 공부 도와주기
⑤ 배드민턴 경기 응원하기

09 대화를 듣고, 남자의 마지막 말에 담긴 의도로 가장 적절한 것을 고르시오.

① 칭찬　　② 허락　　③ 질문
④ 이해　　⑤ 제안

10 대화를 듣고, 여자가 지불할 금액을 고르시오.

① ₩1,200　② ₩4,800　③ ₩5,000
④ ₩5,800　⑤ ₩6,000

11 대화를 듣고, 여자가 내일 할 일로 가장 적절한 것을 고르시오.

① 운동하기   ② 소풍 가기   ③ 방 청소하기
④ 옷 사러 가기   ⑤ 아빠 도와 드리기

12 다음을 듣고, 고양이에 관해 언급되지 <u>않은</u> 것을 고르시오.

① 고양이의 성격
② 고양이의 평균 수명
③ 먹으면 안 되는 음식
④ 고양이의 버릇
⑤ 털이 빠지는 시기

13 대화를 듣고, 두 사람이 볼 연극을 고르시오.

	Title	Time	Ticket Price (₩)
①	The Heroes	10:30~12:30	12,000
②	The Water Babies	9:30~11:30	10,000
③	At Last	9:00~11:00	8,000
④	After the Fall	14:00~16:00	8,000
⑤	Death of a Salesman	9:30~11:30	14,000

14 다음을 듣고, 무엇에 관한 설명인지 고르시오.

① 환경오염   ② 자원 절약
③ 자연재해   ④ 사회 규범 준수
⑤ 멸종 위기 동물 보호

15 대화를 듣고, 남자가 대화 직후에 할 일로 가장 적절한 것을 고르시오.

① 세차하기   ② 휴대 전화 빌리기
③ 길가에 눈 치우기   ④ 고장 난 차 수리하기
⑤ 고객에게 전화 걸기

16 대화를 듣고, 여자가 치과에 갈 시각을 고르시오.

① 5:00   ② 5:50   ③ 6:00
④ 6:30   ⑤ 6:40

17 대화를 듣고, 남자의 마지막 말에 대한 여자의 응답으로 가장 적절한 것을 고르시오.

Woman: _____

① I think it's all my fault.
② That makes me so sad.
③ I'm sure that you are right.
④ Well, I'm sorry but I don't agree with you.
⑤ Yes. You should have watered it every two days.

18 대화를 듣고, 여자의 마지막 말에 대한 남자의 응답으로 가장 적절한 것을 고르시오.

Man: _____

① I'm so proud of you.
② I'm not good at math.
③ Don't be discouraged.
④ You didn't do your best.
⑤ Let's study math together.

19 대화를 듣고, 남자의 마지막 말에 대한 여자의 응답으로 가장 적절한 것을 고르시오.

Woman: _____

① I'm sorry, but you can't.
② I heard it from the news.
③ I think that is good news.
④ I'm planning to have it again.
⑤ I'm fascinated by instant food.

20 다음 상황 설명을 듣고, Judy가 어머니에게 할 말로 가장 적절한 것을 고르시오.

Judy: _____

① It was the best concert I've ever seen.
② I promise I'll come home at around 8.
③ I'm sorry, but I've already seen the concert.
④ I prefer watching a movie to listening to music.
⑤ We have to go out in a minute, or we'll be late.

Dictation Test 06회 영어 듣기모의고사

01 그림 정보 파악 – 사물

대화를 듣고, 남자가 구입할 시계를 고르시오.

① ② ③

④ ⑤

😊 **선호 표현하기** ///////////////////////

I prefer A to B. / I('d) prefer (to) ~ (if possible). / I think A is better than(preferable) to B.

M Hi, I want to buy a clock. Can you show me clocks?

W Of course. Which one do you prefer, ❶_____ _____ _____?

M Um, I prefer round ones to rectangular ones.

W Okay. Then, how about this clock with a floral print?

M I don't like flowers. I'd ❷_____ _____ _____ on it.

W Okay, then what about this one?

M Great! That's exactly ❸_____ _____ _____. I'll take it.

02 목적 파악

대화를 듣고, 남자가 도서관에 전화한 목적으로 가장 적절한 것을 고르시오.

① 신간 구입을 요청하려고
② 분실된 책을 보상하려고
③ 자원봉사자에 지원하려고
④ 회원 카드 분실 신고를 하려고
⑤ 회원 카드 신청 방법을 문의하려고

[*Telephone rings.*]

W Hello. This is Christine Williams at Viva Library. How may I help you?

M Hello. I'd like to sign up for ❶_____ _____ _____.

W Okay. Are you a student?

M Yes, I'm a middle school student. I want to sign up for the membership card. What do I ❷_____ _____ _____?

W You just need to visit either our library or our website. You have to ❸_____ _____ _____ _____ on the website. Bring your card with you if you sign up here.

M Thanks. I'll try on the website first.

03 그림 상황에 어울리는 대화 찾기

다음 그림의 상황에 가장 적절한 대화를 고르시오.

① ② ③ ④ ⑤

① **M** It's very hot in here. Did you turn on the air conditioner?
   W No, I didn't. I'll turn it on.

② **M** My room is too messy. I'll vacuum it now.
   W Before you vacuum it, how about ❶_____ _____ _____ first?

③ **M** I'll do the dishes for you.
   W It's okay. Would you ❷_____ _____ _____ instead?

④ **M** I'll go to the library to return these books.
   W Okay. Don't be late for dinner.

⑤ **M** I can't stand this noise. Where is it coming from?
   W ❸_____ _____ _____ outside. Some children are playing.

 01 rectangular 직사각형의 **floral** 꽃무늬의　**02 membership card** 회원 카드 **sign up for** ~을 신청하다　**03 air conditioner** 에어컨 **turn on** ~을 켜다 **messy** 지저분한 **vacuum** 진공청소기로 청소하다 **remove** 치우다 **stand** 참다

04 장소 추론 · 영국식 발음 녹음

대화를 듣고, 두 사람이 만나기로 한 장소를 고르시오.

① 학교 ② 병원 ③ 약국
④ 경찰서 ⑤ 소방서

W Peter, let's talk about our English homework.
M Okay. _____ _____ _____ write about our future jobs, right?
W Yeah. We need to include an interview with someone who has the job we want to have in the future.
M All right. Let's talk about ❷ _____ _____ _____ first. What do you want to be in the future?
W I want to be a doctor. What about you?
M Well, I wanted to be a police officer or a fire fighter when I was very young. But now I want to be a nurse.
W Good! Then let's go to ❸ _____ _____ _____ and interview a doctor and a nurse there.
M Good idea! Let's meet at the Peterson General Hospital tomorrow.

05 언급되지 않은 것

다음을 듣고, Summer Reading Program에 관해 언급되지 <u>않은</u> 것을 고르시오.

① 개최 장소 ② 참가 대상 ③ 운영 기간
④ 참가비 ⑤ 참가 인원수

W Attention, please. ❶ _____ _____ _____ _____ about our Summer Reading Program. It will be held at the National Children's Library. The program is for children and teens to ❷ _____ _____ _____ _____. It begins on March 10 and runs through May 10. ❸ _____ _____ _____. Registration begins on February 20 and it's first come, first served. So don't wait too late to register!

06 직업 및 장래 희망

대화를 듣고, 여자의 직업으로 가장 적절한 것을 고르시오.

① editor ② painter
③ teacher ④ photographer
⑤ programmer

😊 **궁금증 표현하기** ////////////////////////
I wonder ~. / I'm curious about ~. / I'd be (very) interested to know ~.

M Hello, Mrs. Ross. I really enjoyed your exhibition.
W Thank you for coming. Happy to hear that.
M I'm a student who wants to be ❶ _____ _____ _____ just like you. But I don't think I'm talented. What should I do?
W Just practice hard for your dream, and ❷ _____ _____ you see.
M Okay. Then, can you take a ❸ _____ _____ _____ later? I wonder whether my paintings are good or not.
W Sure. Here's my name card. Call me at this number.
M I will. Thank you very much.

Ⓦords **04** include 포함하다 nearby 가까운 **05** participation 참가 registration 등록 first come. first served 선착순 **06** exhibition 전시회 talented 재능이 있는 take a look at ~을 보다 whether ~ or not ~인지 아닌지

Dictation Test

07 어색한 대화 찾기

다음을 듣고, 두 사람의 대화가 <u>어색한</u> 것을 고르시오.

①   ②   ③   ④   ⑤

😊 비난을 수용하기 ///////////////
It's (all) my fault. / I am to blame. / It's (all)
because of me.

① W Which do you think ❶ _____ _____, Canada or China?

   M I want to visit Canada this time.

② W You know that girl over there, don't you?

   M Yes, she is my neighbor.

③ W I'm sorry that you ❷ _____ _____ _____.

   M It's all my fault. I should have locked my locker.

④ W What do you think about the new science teacher?

   M I think he's very smart.

⑤ W This plant ❸ _____ _____ _____ _____.

   M Wow! That interests me a lot.

---

08 부탁한 일 파악   영국식 발음 녹음

대화를 듣고, 여자가 남자에게 부탁한 일로 가장 적절한
것을 고르시오.

① 라켓 빌려주기
② 함께 운동하기
③ 병원에 같이 가기
④ 학교 공부 도와주기
⑤ 배드민턴 경기 응원하기

M Bora, you don't look well these days.

W I am very tired these days, but I don't know why.

M Did you ❶ _____ _____ _____?

W Yes, I did. But the doctor said my health seems to be fine.

M Then why don't you exercise regularly?

W I'm not sure I can exercise regularly by myself. Can you ❷ _____ _____ _____?

M Sure. ❸ _____ _____ _____ every day after school.

W Thank you.

---

09 의도 파악

대화를 듣고, 남자의 마지막 말에 담긴 의도로 가장 적절한
것을 고르시오.

① 칭찬   ② 허락   ③ 질문
④ 이해   ⑤ 제안

M Mary, what are you looking at?

W I'm looking at the movie club poster. I ❶ _____ _____ _____ this club.

M What do you mean?   W I forgot to apply, so I gave it up.

M Well, there is still one day left before the deadline. ❷ _____ _____ _____ _____ for this club now?

W But I think I'm too late. This poster says first come, first served.

M Who knows? ❸ _____ _____ the number on the poster.

---

10 숫자 정보 파악 – 금액

대화를 듣고, 여자가 지불할 금액을 고르시오.

① ₩1,200   ② ₩4,800   ③ ₩5,000
④ ₩5,800   ⑤ ₩6,000

😊 허가 여부 묻기 ///////////////
Can(May) I ~? / Is it all right(okay) if ~? / Do
you mind if ~? / I wonder if I could ~.

W How much are they?

M Two pens and one pencil case. They are 4,800 won.

W Here is 5,000 won. Oh, wait. Can I ❶ _____ _____ _____ now? How much is this?

M Of course you can. It's 1,200 won. If you give me 1,000 won more, I don't need to ❷ _____ _____ _____.

W That's good. Here is 1,000 won.   M Thanks.

📖Words   **07 fault** 잘못 **lock** 잠그다 **locker** 개인 물품 보관함 **insect** 벌레   **08 regularly** 규칙적으로 **by oneself** 혼자서   **09 apply** 지원하다,
신청하다 **deadline** 마감 일자   **10 add** 더하다 **change** 거스름돈

11 한 일 / 할 일 파악 영국식 발음 녹음

대화를 듣고, 여자가 내일 할 일로 가장 적절한 것을 고르시오.

① 운동하기   ② 소풍 가기   ③ 방 청소하기
④ 옷 사러 가기 ⑤ 아빠 도와 드리기

M Look at the mess! What are you doing, Minji?
W Daddy, I don't have anything to wear ❶ _____ _____ _____. I need to buy new clothes.
M No way. You have so many clothes. But do you still need more?
W You can't understand. Ah, what should I ❷ _____ _____ _____?
M This shirt and those pants look good. Wear them and clean up this room now.
W Oh, I don't want to wear ❸ _____ _____ _____. But I'll clean the room.

12 언급되지 않은 것

다음을 듣고, 고양이에 관해 언급되지 <u>않은</u> 것을 고르시오.

① 고양이의 성격
② 고양이의 평균 수명
③ 먹으면 안 되는 음식
④ 고양이의 버릇
⑤ 털이 빠지는 시기

M Do you like cats? If you have decided to get ❶ _____ _____ _____ _____ _____, there are some things you should think about first. Most people think cats are quiet, but actually many cats can be quite loud. You should not give cats ❷ _____ _____ like ice cream or candy. It can cause serious health problems. You also need to understand that most cats have a habit of scratching things. Lastly, many cats ❸ _____ _____ _____ _____ _____ all year round. Please think about these things carefully before you bring a cat into your family.

13 도표 정보 파악

대화를 듣고, 두 사람이 볼 연극을 고르시오.

	Title	Time	Ticket Price (₩)
①	The Heroes	10:30~12:30	12,000
②	The Water Babies	9:30~11:30	10,000
③	At Last	9:00~11:00	8,000
④	After the Fall	14:00~16:00	8,000
⑤	Death of a Salesman	9:30~11:30	14,000

W What are you planning to do this Sunday?
M I'm planning to ❶ _____ _____ _____.
W That's a great idea. Can I go with you?
M Fine. This is the list of plays I'm thinking about. Which one do you prefer?
W Well, I prefer ❷ _____ _____. 8,000 won looks fine.
M Okay. Then, of the two plays, I prefer the one that ❸ _____ _____. I have to do homework in the afternoon.
W No problem. Then let's meet at 8 a.m. this Sunday.
M Okay. I'm already excited.

😊 의도 표현하기 ////////////////////////
I'm planning to ~. / I'm going to ~. / I'm thinking of ~.

Words **11 mess** 엉망인 상태 **clean up** 청소하다 **12 decide** 결심하다, 결정하다 **treat** 음식 대접 **habit** 습관 **scratch** 긁다 **lose hair** 털이 빠지다 **all year round** 일 년 내내 **13 prefer** ~을 더 좋아하다

Dictation Test

14 주제 파악

다음을 듣고, 무엇에 관한 설명인지 고르시오.

① 환경오염   ② 자원 절약
③ 자연재해   ④ 사회 규범 준수
⑤ 멸종 위기 동물 보호

M There are many people on earth. The number of people is getting bigger and bigger. They are using _____ _____ _____ _____ on Earth. If we continue, we _____ _____ _____ to our sons and daughters. Now, it's time that we should do something to _____ _____.

15 한 일 / 할 일 파악

대화를 듣고, 남자가 대화 직후에 할 일로 가장 적절한 것을 고르시오.

① 세차하기   ② 휴대 전화 빌리기
③ 길가에 눈 치우기   ④ 고장 난 차 수리하기
⑤ 고객에게 전화 걸기

W It's ❶_____ _____ _____.
M We should have left before it began to snow. The roads are icy, and I can't run fast enough to make it on time.
W We will be late for an important ❷_____ _____ _____. What should we do?
M Fortunately, I brought my cellphone with me. I'll ❸_____ _____ _____ _____ her that we are on our way.
W That's a good idea.

16 숫자 정보 파악 – 시각   영국식 발음 녹음

대화를 듣고, 여자가 치과에 갈 시각을 고르시오.

① 5:00   ② 5:50   ③ 6:00
④ 6:30   ⑤ 6:40

ⓟ close의 발음 ////////////////////////////////
close가 동사로 쓰여 '(문 등을) 닫다'라는 의미일 때는 [klouz]로 발음되고, 형용사로 쓰여 '가까운'의 뜻일 때는 [klous]로 발음된다.

W Do you know when Dr. Kim's ❶_____ _____ _____?
M Well, I'm not sure. Why?
W I want to see the dentist after going to the academy, but I'm not sure ❷_____ _____ _____ _____ then.
M What time do you finish at the academy?
W Today, I have one more class, so my class finishes at 5:50. I think I can get there ❸_____ _____.
M Well, I'm not sure when it closes, but it is open at half past six. I have visited there at 6:40 before, and it was still open.
W That's great. I have enough time, then.

Words   **14 resource** 자원 **continue** 계속되다 **save** 구하다   **15 icy** 얼음에 뒤덮인 **enough to** ~할 정도로 충분한 **fortunately** 다행히   **16 dental clinic** 치과 **dentist** 치과 의사 **academy** 학원

17 알맞은 응답 찾기

대화를 듣고, 남자의 마지막 말에 대한 여자의 응답으로 가장 적절한 것을 고르시오.

Woman: _____

① I think it's all my fault.
② That makes me so sad.
③ I'm sure that you are right.
④ Well, I'm sorry but I don't agree with you.
⑤ Yes. You should have watered it every two days.

👁 충고하기 ///////////////////////////////////

(I think) you should[ought to] ~. / Why don't you ~? / You'd better ~. / If I were you, I'd ~.

W Why are you looking at the pot?
M My rose ❶ _____ _____. I don't know what I did wrong.
W Where did you put it?
M Right here, at the corner of my bedroom window. It ❷ _____ _____ _____.
W How often did you water it?
M Every morning.
W Well, I think you should have ❸ _____ _____ _____.
M Are you sure about that?

18 알맞은 응답 찾기

대화를 듣고, 여자의 마지막 말에 대한 남자의 응답으로 가장 적절한 것을 고르시오.

Man: _____

① I'm so proud of you.
② I'm not good at math.
③ Don't be discouraged.
④ You didn't do your best.
⑤ Let's study math together.

W Dad, I'm home.
M Emma, you look so happy. Did something good happen at school today?
W Yes. I did really well ❶ _____ _____ _____ _____.
M Wow, I'm so happy to hear that.
W You ❷ _____ _____ _____. I got 95 points.
M That's really great. Congratulations! You've improved a lot.
W Thank you. It's ❸ _____ _____ _____ in the class.

19 알맞은 응답 찾기

대화를 듣고, 남자의 마지막 말에 대한 여자의 응답으로 가장 적절한 것을 고르시오.

Woman: _____

① I'm sorry, but you can't.
② I heard it from the news.
③ I think that is good news.
④ I'm planning to have it again.
⑤ I'm fascinated by instant food.

W David, come to have dinner.
M Mom, I don't need to. I've just had cup noodles.
W Again? You ❶ _____ _____ _____ as well. I wonder why you like it so much.
M It's because instant noodles ❷ _____ _____ _____. I think I can have them every day.
W They're delicious, but they're not good for your health.
M Oh, is it okay ❸ _____ _____ _____ once a week, please?

20 상황에 맞는 말 찾기

다음 상황 설명을 듣고, Judy가 어머니에게 할 말로 가장 적절한 것을 고르시오.

Judy: _____

① It was the best concert I've ever seen.
② I promise I'll come home at around 8.
③ I'm sorry, but I've already seen the concert.
④ I prefer watching a movie to listening to music.
⑤ We have to go out in a minute, or we'll be late.

W Judy will go to her favorite singer's concert with her mother. The concert will start at 8 and it is already 7 now. But her mother ❶ _____ _____ _____ _____ and doesn't seem to be in a hurry. ❷ _____ _____ _____ within 10 minutes, they might be ❸ _____ _____ _____ _____. Judy wants to tell her mother about it. In this situation, what would Judy most likely say to her mother?

Ⓦords ❷ **17 pot** 화분 **die** 시들다, 죽다 **18 do well on** ~을 잘하다 **point** 점수 **Congratulations!** 축하해! **improve** 향상되다 **score** 성적, 점수
19 instant 인스턴트의, 즉석의 **noodle** 라면 **20 within** ~이내에

01 대화를 듣고, 남자가 먹을 음식을 고르시오.

02 대화를 듣고, 여자가 남자에게 전화한 목적으로 가장 적절한 것을 고르시오.

① 교과서를 빌리려고
② 남자에게 사과하려고
③ 방과 후 일정을 물어보려고
④ 친구의 전화번호를 물어보려고
⑤ 자신의 전화번호가 바뀐 것을 알려 주려고

03 다음 그림의 상황에 가장 적절한 대화를 고르시오.

① ② ③ ④ ⑤

04 대화를 듣고, 남자의 보고서 제출일로 알맞은 요일을 고르시오.

① 이번 주 목요일 ② 이번 주 금요일
③ 이번 주 토요일 ④ 다음 주 월요일
⑤ 다음 주 목요일

05 다음을 듣고, 체험학습 준비물로 언급되지 <u>않은</u> 것을 고르시오.

① 공책 ② 카메라
③ 야생화 관련 책 ④ 야생화 사진
⑤ 모자

06 대화를 듣고, 여자의 심정으로 가장 적절한 것을 고르시오.

① worried ② relaxed
③ surprised ④ pleased
⑤ disappointed

07 다음을 듣고, 두 사람의 대화가 <u>어색한</u> 것을 고르시오.

① ② ③ ④ ⑤

08 대화를 듣고, 남자가 여자에게 부탁한 일로 가장 적절한 것을 고르시오.

① 시계 환불받기
② 시계 시간 설정하기
③ 현재 시간 알려 주기
④ 고장 난 시계 수리하기
⑤ 일본어 설명서 읽어 주기

09 대화를 듣고, 여자의 마지막 말에 담긴 의도로 가장 적절한 것을 고르시오.

① 칭찬 ② 당부 ③ 감사
④ 위로 ⑤ 불평

10 대화를 듣고, 남자가 추가로 지불할 금액을 고르시오.

① $10 ② $15 ③ $30
④ $45 ⑤ $60

11 대화를 듣고, 두 사람이 대화하는 장소를 고르시오.
① 식당　　　② 공항　　　③ 사진관
④ 지하철　　⑤ 비행기

12 다음을 듣고, 상담 프로그램에 관해 언급되지 않은 것을 고르시오.
① 참가 학교 수　　　② 참가비
③ 시작 시간　　　　④ 열리는 장소
⑤ 얻을 수 있는 정보

13 다음 표를 보면서 대화를 듣고, 여자가 선택할 수업을 고르시오.

After-school Class	Day	Time	Place
① Easy Coding	Monday	16:40~17:50	Computer Room
② Advanced Math	Monday	16:40~17:50	A302
③ Singing Together	Wednesday	16:40~17:50	Music Room
④ Chinese Letters	Friday	15:40~16:50	A303
⑤ Let's Play Soccer	Friday	15:40~18:30	Playground

14 다음을 듣고, 무엇에 관한 설명인지 고르시오.
① 김　　　② 된장　　　③ 김치
④ 단무지　　⑤ 불고기

15 대화를 듣고, 남자가 할 일로 가장 적절한 것을 고르시오.
① 집에서 책 읽기
② 혼자서 숙제하기
③ 비옷 입고 자전거 타기
④ 체육관에서 혼자 운동하기
⑤ 여자와 함께 배드민턴 치기

16 대화를 듣고, 남자가 구입할 물건을 고르시오.
① backpack　　② hat　　　③ watch
④ sneakers　　⑤ sunglasses

17 대화를 듣고, 남자의 마지막 말에 이어질 여자의 응답으로 가장 적절한 것을 고르시오.
Woman: _____
① I had a lot of fun.
② They didn't like it.
③ I like skirts better than pants.
④ Traveling gives a good lesson.
⑤ I've never experienced Halloween.

18 대화를 듣고, 여자의 마지막 말에 대한 남자의 응답으로 가장 적절한 것을 고르시오.
Man: _____
① It's my pleasure.
② I'm sorry to hear that.
③ I don't need your help.
④ Thank you for saying that.
⑤ I'd like to learn *taekwondo*.

19 대화를 듣고, 남자의 마지막 말에 대한 여자의 응답으로 가장 적절한 것을 고르시오.
Woman: _____
① It's a good deal.
② What a sad story!
③ I hate baggy jeans.
④ That's too expensive.
⑤ Jeans are my favorite.

20 다음 상황 설명을 듣고, Mark가 Jane에게 할 말로 가장 적절한 것을 고르시오.
Mark: _____
① Enjoy your drink.
② Let me take you home.
③ I feel a little under the weather.
④ What kind of drinks do you want?
⑤ How many cups of coffee do you drink a day?

01 그림 정보 파악 – 사물

대화를 듣고, 남자가 먹을 음식을 고르시오.

① ② ③
④ ⑤

ⓟ butter의 발음 ////////////////////
강세가 있는 모음과 강세가 없는 모음 사이에 [d], [t], [rd], [rt] 소리가 오면 이들은 모두 [r]처럼 발음된다. 따라서 butter은 [bʌ́rər]라고 발음하면 된다.

W Honey, I'm going to have some toast with **ⓟ** butter and apple jam. What are you going to have? Do you want to have the same?
M No, I'm going to _____ _____ _____ _____ with ketchup on it.
W Any drinks?
M Well, I'd like to **❷** _____ _____ _____ _____. How about you?
W I'm going to have coffee. All right, honey. Just stay here. I'm going to **❸** _____ _____ _____ you want.
M Oh, thank you very much.

02 목적 파악

대화를 듣고, 여자가 남자에게 전화한 목적으로 가장 적절한 것을 고르시오.

① 교과서를 빌리려고
② 남자에게 사과하려고
③ 방과 후 일정을 물어보려고
④ 친구의 전화번호를 물어보려고
⑤ 자신의 전화번호가 바뀐 것을 알려 주려고

[*Telephone rings.*]
M Hi, Sujeong. What's up?
W Hi, Michael. I was just **❶** _____ _____ _____ _____ Sarah's cellphone number.
M Yes, it's 110-2134-5678. Can I ask why?
W I used her textbooks without permission today, and I **❷** _____ _____ _____ _____.
M You didn't say sorry?
W I was going to do that, but she just left right after school.
M Oh, she **❸** _____ _____ _____ _____. Call her and say sorry.
W Yes. I'll call her right away.

03 그림 상황에 어울리는 대화 찾기

다음 그림의 상황에 가장 적절한 대화를 고르시오.

① ② ③ ④ ⑤

① W Excuse me. Is this seat taken?
  M No, you **❶** _____ _____ _____.
② W What kind of sport do you like most?
  M I like baseball most.
③ W Why don't you stand up and go home?
  M Maybe I should.
④ W **❷** _____ _____ _____ _____ go to school by bus?
  M I never go to school by bus.
⑤ W Do I have to buy a ticket?
  M No, you don't have to. It's **❸** _____ _____ _____.

04 특정 정보 파악 – 요일   영국식 발음 녹음

대화를 듣고, 남자의 보고서 제출일로 알맞은 요일을 고르시오.

① 이번 주 목요일   ② 이번 주 금요일
③ 이번 주 토요일   ④ 다음 주 월요일
⑤ 다음 주 목요일

W Let's work on the history report together after school today.

M I'm sorry, but I can't. I have to ❶ _____ _____ _____ by this Friday. I'll write the report this Saturday.

W That will be too late. ❷ _____ _____ _____ of the report is this Thursday.

M What? Isn't it next Monday?

W Wait, you were absent yesterday, right? Mrs. Brown moved the due date ❸ _____ _____ _____.

M I see. Thank you so much for letting me know.

W No problem.

05 언급되지 않은 것

다음을 듣고, 체험학습 준비물로 언급되지 <u>않은</u> 것을 고르시오.

① 공책   ② 카메라
③ 야생화 관련 책   ④ 야생화 사진
⑤ 모자

M Guys, as you know, we are going on our field trip tomorrow. We'll look for as many wildflowers as possible. You'll need ❶ _____ _____ and a pen, and a camera for each group as well. Don't forget to bring the book about wildflowers which we read together in class. We'll use the book to check the names of flowers we find. We'll ❷ _____ _____ _____ _____, and you have to write a report with those pictures after the field trip. Because we'll be outside for a long time, it would be a good idea ❸ _____ _____ _____ _____. See you tomorrow.

06 심정 파악

대화를 듣고, 여자의 심정으로 가장 적절한 것을 고르시오.

① worried   ② relaxed
③ surprised   ④ pleased
⑤ disappointed

M Are you ready for tomorrow's presentation, Jiwoo?

W ❶ _____ _____. And it's not so good.

M How come?

W I ❷ _____ _____ _____ _____ for a surprise party with my brother because tomorrow is my mom's birthday.

M Oh, you must have been busy.

W Yes. So, I'm not ready for the presentation.

M But tomorrow's presentation is also very important for your grade.

W I know. I wish ❸ _____ _____ _____ _____. What should I do?

Words **04 work on** 착수하다 **homework assignment** 숙제 **due date** 마감일   **05 field trip** 체험학습 **wildflowers** 야생화 **take pictures of** ~의 사진을 찍다 **for a long time** 오랫동안   **06 be ready for** ~할 준비가 되다 **prepare** 준비하다 **grade** 성적, 학점

Dictation Test

07 어색한 대화 찾기

다음을 듣고, 두 사람의 대화가 <u>어색한</u> 것을 고르시오.

①   ②   ③   ④   ⑤

😮 설명 요청하기 /////////////////////////////////

What do you mean by ~? / Could you explain ~? / What is ~ (exactly)?

① **M** How do you feel about your new sofa?

   W Well, I feel it's very comfortable.

② **M** ❶ _____ _____ _____ _____? What do you mean by that?

   W It means that's very easy work.

③ **M** Why don't we go to a movie after school?

   W Sorry, I'm supposed to get home early today.

④ **M** I tried my best to win the race, but I ❷ _____ _____ _____.

   W Congratulations! You ❸ _____ _____ _____ _____.

⑤ **M** Make sure you turn off the lights when you go out.

   W Okay, I will keep it in mind.

---

08 부탁한 일 파악   영국식 발음 녹음

대화를 듣고, 남자가 여자에게 부탁한 일로 가장 적절한 것을 고르시오.

① 시계 환불받기
② 시계 시간 설정하기
③ 현재 시간 알려 주기
④ 고장 난 시계 수리하기
⑤ 일본어 설명서 읽어 주기

M Are you busy right now? Please help me a bit. I have a ❶ _____ _____ _____ _____.

W Okay. This watch looks really nice. Is it new?

M Yes, I got it yesterday, but I can't wear it yet. The time ❷ _____ _____ _____.

W Is it broken? Ask for a refund.

M No, I simply ❸ _____ _____ _____ _____. It is in Japanese. I heard that you majored in Japanese. Can you read this for me?

W Of course I can. Give it to me. I'll help you set the correct time.

---

09 의도 파악

대화를 듣고, 여자의 마지막 말에 담긴 의도로 가장 적절한 것을 고르시오.

① 칭찬   ② 당부   ③ 감사
④ 위로   ⑤ 불평

😮 경고하기 /////////////////////////////////

Be careful. / Watch(Look) out (for ~)! / Make sure you don't ~. / Don't ~.

W Did you finish packing all you need for camping?

M Yes, I did. I'm ready to go, Mom.

W I just ❶ _____ _____ _____ _____, and you don't have to worry about it. The weather will be perfect.

M Oh, really?

W Are you guys ❷ _____ _____ _____ at night?

M Yes. We are going to have a barbecue party.

W Be careful when you make a fire and ❸ _____ _____ _____ _____ _____ any trash behind.

📖 **Words**   **07 comfortable** 편안한, 안락한   **try one's best** 최선을 다하다   **turn off** 끄다   **keep ~ in mind** ~을 명심하다   **08 correct** 맞는, 정확한 **refund** 환불; 환불하다   **manual** 설명서   **major in** ~을 전공하다   **09 pack** (짐을) 싸다   **make a fire** 불을 피우다   **trash** 쓰레기

10 숫자 정보 파악 – 금액

대화를 듣고, 남자가 추가로 지불할 금액을 고르시오.

① $10   ② $15   ③ $30
④ $45   ⑤ $60

ⓟ '15'와 '50'의 발음 //////////////////////////
숫자 '15'는 [fiftíːn]으로 발음하고 숫자 '50'은 [fífti]로 발음하므로 둘을 잘 구분해서 들어야 한다.

M Excuse me, can I exchange this?
W Do you have a receipt?   **M** Yes. Here it is.
W Um, you bought a $30 T-shirt. You can get anything **❶** _____

_____ _____ _____ .

M How much are these jeans?   **W** They are $45.
M Oh, then **❷** _____ _____ _____ _____ ?
W Yes, you can get them if you pay $15 **ⓟ** extra.
M Really? Then I'll take them.

11 장소 추론

대화를 듣고, 두 사람이 대화하는 장소를 고르시오.

① 식당   ② 공항   ③ 사진관
④ 지하철   ⑤ 비행기

M Excuse me, but are you Carrie?   **W** Yes, you must be Uncle Dave.
M Wow, you grew up so much. I couldn't have recognized you without a picture. Fortunately, your mom sent me a picture of you yesterday. Is your family all okay?   **W** Yes, they are all fine. Mom said hello to you.
M I miss all of your family. **❶** _____ _____ _____ _____ , by the way? Didn't it take too long?
W Yes, it did. But, I'm okay. I'm so happy **❷** _____ _____ for the first time in my life.

12 언급되지 않은 것

다음을 듣고, 상담 프로그램에 관해 언급되지 <u>않은</u> 것을 고르시오.

① 참가 학교 수   ② 참가비
③ 시작 시간   ④ 열리는 장소
⑤ 얻을 수 있는 정보

😎 주의 끌기 ///////////////////////////
May I have your attention(, please)? / Look! /
Listen! / Hey!

W May I have your attention, please? I just want to remind you of today's counseling program. The teachers **❶** _____ _____ _____ _____ _____ are coming today. They are going to give you useful information you would like to know about. It will start at 2 o'clock right after lunch and end at 6. The program will take place in the main hall. **❷** _____ _____ _____ _____ about the high school you want to enter.

13 도표 정보 파악   영국식 발음 녹음

다음 표를 보면서 대화를 듣고, 여자가 선택할 수업을 고르시오.

After-School Class	Day	Time	Place
① Easy Coding	Monday	16:40~17:50	Computer Room
② Advanced Math	Monday	16:40~17:50	A302
③ Singing Together	Wednesday	16:40~17:50	Music Room
④ Chinese Letters	Friday	15:40~16:50	A303
⑤ Let's Play Soccer	Friday	15:40~18:30	Playground

😎 의도 표현하기 ////////////////////////
I'm planning to ~. / I'm thinking of ~. / I'm going to ~.

M Which after-school class are you going to take?
W I am planning to take one that finishes at 5:50 p.m.
M Then you should choose one of the classes **❶** _____ _____ _____ .
W Right. I think I should take the one in Room A302.
M That's a good idea. It's right just **❷** _____ _____ _____ _____ .
W That's the point. I won't have to be in a hurry. What are you going to take?
M I'm thinking of taking **❸** _____ _____ _____ .
W Then our classes finish at the same time. Let's go home together after class.   **M** That's a great idea.

Words **10 exchange** 교환하다 **receipt** 영수증 **jeans** 청바지   **11 recognize** 알아보다 **say hello (to)** (~에게) 안부를 전하다   **12 remind** 상기시키다 **counseling** 상담 **take place** 열리다   **13 coding** (컴퓨터) 코딩

Dictation Test

14 주제 파악

다음을 듣고, 무엇에 관한 설명인지 고르시오.
① 김   ② 된장   ③ 김치
④ 단무지   ⑤ 불고기

M This is a traditional Korean ❶ _____ _____ _____ _____ _____ with a variety of seasonings. This is usually made of Korean cabbage or radish. People use this to make *jjigae*, *buchimgae* or fried rice. A long time ago, people put this in jars and ❷ _____ _____ _____ for months. However, these days, people use a special refrigerator instead.

15 한 일 / 할 일 파악

대화를 듣고, 남자가 할 일로 가장 적절한 것을 고르시오.
① 집에서 책 읽기
② 혼자서 숙제하기
③ 비옷 입고 자전거 타기
④ 체육관에서 혼자 운동하기
⑤ 여자와 함께 배드민턴 치기

M Oh no, it's raining again. I can't go for a bike ride today either.
W It's been a while since you were able to ride your bike.
M I can't wait anymore. I'll ❶ _____ _____ _____ and ride my bike.
W That's too dangerous. The roads will be very slippery, and you can't see clearly.
M You are right. Maybe I should just work out ❷ _____ _____ _____, but I don't like exercising alone.
W How about ❸ _____ _____ at the gym with me?
M That sounds good. Let's go now.

16 특정 정보 파악 영국식 발음 녹음

대화를 듣고, 남자가 구입할 물건을 고르시오.
① backpack   ② hat   ③ watch
④ sneakers   ⑤ sunglasses

W How may I help you, sir?
M My son is graduating from middle school, so I'm ❶ _____ _____ _____ _____.
W Teenagers would like a new watch or a new pair of sneakers.
M Actually, he bought both of them recently. Are these caps or sunglasses popular?
W No, they are not popular with teenagers. How about buying him ❷ _____ _____ _____? This is a new product, and it's cheap.
M The backpack looks nice. I'll ❸ _____ _____.

Words **14 traditional** 전통적인 **seasoning** 양념 **Korean cabbage** 배추 **radish** 무 **jar** 항아리 **refrigerator** 냉장고   **15 slippery** 미끄러운 **clearly** 또렷하게 **gym** 체육관   **16 sneakers** 운동화 **recently** 최근에 **cheap** 값싼

17 알맞은 응답 찾기

대화를 듣고, 남자의 마지막 말에 이어질 여자의 응답으로 가장 적절한 것을 고르시오.

Woman: _____

① I had a lot of fun.
② They didn't like it.
③ I like skirts better than pants.
④ Traveling gives a good lesson.
⑤ I've never experienced Halloween.

😊 만족이나 불만족에 대해 묻기 //////////////
How do you like(find) ~? / Are you satisfied (happy) (with ~)? / Is this what you want(ed) (need, meant, had) in mind?

W How was your Halloween, Daniel?
M It was okay. I walked around town with my friends, shouting "Trick or treat."
W Sounds interesting. Did you ❶ _____ _____?
M Yes, I dressed up like Dracula.
W I ❷ _____ _____ _____ _____ _____.
M What about you? How did your Halloween go, Misun?
W We don't have Halloween in Korea, but ❸ _____ _____ _____ _____ my foreign friends. It was my first time.
M Was it? So how did you like it?

18 알맞은 응답 찾기

대화를 듣고, 여자의 마지막 말에 대한 남자의 응답으로 가장 적절한 것을 고르시오.

Man: _____

① It's my pleasure.
② I'm sorry to hear that.
③ I don't need your help.
④ Thank you for saying that.
⑤ I'd like to learn taekwondo.

😊 유감이나 동정 표현하기 //////////////
I'm (so) sorry to hear ~. / That's too bad. / That's a pity(shame).

W Hey, Jim! You don't look good today.
M I failed to get a black belt on the taekwondo test.
W I'm sorry to hear that. Was it your first time?
M No, actually, ❶ _____ _____ _____ three times before. What should I do?
W You might not have practiced enough because of a lot of stuff.
M That's true, but I don't think I'm that talented in taekwondo.
W Don't give up! ❷ _____ _____ _____ _____.

19 알맞은 응답 찾기

대화를 듣고, 남자의 마지막 말에 대한 여자의 응답으로 가장 적절한 것을 고르시오.

Woman: _____

① It's a good deal.
② What a sad story!
③ I hate baggy jeans.
④ That's too expensive.
⑤ Jeans are my favorite.

M Hi, are you looking for anything?
W Yes, I'm looking for jeans.
M It seems like people love skinny jeans a lot these days. Why don't you try on ❶ _____ _____ _____ _____ here?
W Well, I don't like skinny jeans. They are too tight.
M Then, I recommend these baggy jeans.   W Oh, I like them.
M Plus, if you buy one, you can ❷ _____ _____ _____ _____ _____.

20 상황에 맞는 말 찾기

다음 상황 설명을 듣고, Mark가 Jane에게 할 말로 가장 적절한 것을 고르시오.

Mark: _____

① Enjoy your drink.
② Let me take you home.
③ I feel a little under the weather.
④ What kind of drinks do you want?
⑤ How many cups of coffee do you drink a day?

M Mark met Jane to see a movie. However, she coughed again and again. He asked Jane if she had ❶ _____ _____ _____, and he said that she could go home to take a rest. Jane said she didn't catch a cold. She just needed ❷ _____ _____ _____. Mark wanted to buy her a drink, but he was not sure ❸ _____ _____ _____ _____. In this situation, what would Mark most likely say to Jane?

Words **17 shout** 소리치다 **trick** 장난 **treat** 대접 **foreign** 외국의 **18 stuff** 일 **be talented in** ~에 재능이 있다 **19 skinny** 몸에 딱 붙는 **tight** 꽉 조이는 **baggy** 헐렁한 **20 see a movie** 영화를 보다 **cough** 기침하다 **catch a cold** 감기가 들다

01 대화를 듣고, 남자가 만든 컵을 고르시오.

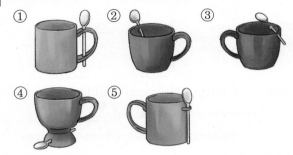

①   ②   ③   ④   ⑤

02 대화를 듣고, 남자가 여자에게 전화한 목적으로 가장 적절한 것을 고르시오.

① 약속을 취소하려고
② 약속 시간을 변경하려고
③ 진료 시간을 문의하려고
④ 병원 위치를 문의하려고
⑤ 약속 장소를 확인하려고

03 다음 그림의 상황에 가장 적절한 대화를 고르시오.

①   ②   ③   ④   ⑤

04 대화를 듣고, 남자와 여자가 만나기로 한 요일을 고르시오.

① Tuesday   ② Wednesday   ③ Thursday
④ Friday   ⑤ Saturday

05 다음을 듣고, 영어가 제2언어인 나라로 언급되지 <u>않은</u> 곳을 고르시오.

① 인도   ② 싱가포르   ③ 러시아
④ 케냐   ⑤ 필리핀

06 대화를 듣고, 남자의 심정으로 가장 적절한 것을 고르시오.

① afraid   ② anxious   ③ worried
④ relieved   ⑤ disappointed

07 다음을 듣고, 두 사람의 대화가 <u>어색한</u> 것을 고르시오.

①   ②   ③   ④   ⑤

08 대화를 듣고, 남자가 여자에게 부탁한 일로 가장 적절한 것을 고르시오.

① 축가 선정하기   ② 결혼식 사회 보기
③ 연주회 관람하기   ④ 바이올린 연주하기
⑤ 경연 대회 참가하기

09 대화를 듣고, 남자가 한 마지막 말에 담긴 의도로 가장 적절한 것을 고르시오.

① 충고   ② 위로   ③ 감사
④ 칭찬   ⑤ 질책

10 대화를 듣고, 남자가 팁으로 주려고 하는 금액을 고르시오.

① $5   ② $7   ③ $10
④ $12   ⑤ $20

11 대화를 듣고, 여자가 토요일 저녁에 할 일로 가장 적절한 것을 고르시오.
① 숙제하기
② 산책하기
③ 친구들과 테니스 치기
④ 친구의 생일 파티 가기
⑤ 가족들과 연극 보러 가기

12 다음을 듣고, Winter English Camp에 관해 언급되지 않은 것을 고르시오.
① 수업료 ② 강사명 ③ 수업 내용
④ 수업 기간 ⑤ 수업 장소

13 대화를 듣고, 내용과 일치하지 않는 것을 고르시오.

Graduation Party Schedule	
Date	① October 25th
Place	② Party House
Transportation	③ Subway Line 2
Time	④ 16:00
Fee	⑤ 10,000 won

14 다음을 듣고, 무엇에 관한 설명인지 고르시오.
① 달력 ② 자 ③ 공책
④ 연필 ⑤ 크레파스

15 대화를 듣고, 남자가 대화 직후에 할 일로 가장 적절한 것을 고르시오.
① 친구와 집에 가기
② 이름표 확인하기
③ 휴대 전화 빌려주기
④ 운동장에서 축구하기
⑤ 이름표의 전화번호로 전화하기

16 대화를 듣고, 여자가 구입할 물건을 고르시오.
① body lotion ② body cream
③ body oil ④ lip-balm
⑤ shampoo

17 대화를 듣고, 여자의 마지막 말에 대한 남자의 응답으로 가장 적절한 것을 고르시오.
Man: _____
① You'd better call the police.
② You didn't do anything wrong.
③ She won't listen to me anyway.
④ You should ask him why he's angry.
⑤ Try to talk to your sister, not your Dad.

18 대화를 듣고, 남자의 마지막 말에 대한 여자의 응답으로 가장 적절한 것을 고르시오.
Woman: _____
① I don't believe so.
② How have you been?
③ Long time no see, Jane.
④ I'm pleased to meet you, Jane.
⑤ I wonder if I have enough time.

19 대화를 듣고, 여자의 마지막 말에 대한 남자의 응답으로 가장 적절한 것을 고르시오.
Man: _____
① The book is sold out.
② I'm sorry but you can't get a refund.
③ You should have returned it last week.
④ Can I return it instead of you tomorrow?
⑤ Can you show me how to go to the library?

20 다음 상황 설명을 듣고, Coby가 어머니께 할 말로 가장 적절한 것을 고르시오.
Coby: _____
① The iron is out of order.
② Where did you put the iron?
③ Why do I have to wash my uniform?
④ Can you tell me how to use the iron?
⑤ It's not easy to use a washing machine.

Dictation Test 08회 영어 듣기모의고사

01 그림 정보 파악 – 사물

대화를 듣고, 남자가 만든 컵을 고르시오.

① ② ③
④ ⑤

M I recently ❶ _____ _____ _____.

W Oh, really? What does it look like?

M It has ❷ _____ _____ _____ _____ _____ — one at the top and the other at the bottom.

W Why did you make the holes on the handle?

M I made them ❸ _____ _____ _____. If you use this cup, you don't have to put the teaspoon on the dirty table.

W Wow! You're a genius.

02 목적 파악

대화를 듣고, 남자가 여자에게 전화한 목적으로 가장 적절한 것을 고르시오.

① 약속을 취소하려고
② 약속 시간을 변경하려고
③ 진료 시간을 문의하려고
④ 병원 위치를 문의하려고
⑤ 약속 장소를 확인하려고

[*Telephone rings.*]

W Hello.

M Hi, Sarah. This is Simon. I am sorry I ❶ _____ _____ _____ today.

W Why not?

M I'm ❷ _____ _____ _____.

W Sorry to hear that. How did you get that?

M I went to a pool yesterday. I guess I got the problem there.

W Have you gone to see the doctor?

M Not yet. I'm going to ❸ _____ _____ _____ _____ after lunch.

03 그림 상황에 어울리는 대화 찾기

다음 그림의 상황에 가장 적절한 대화를 고르시오.

① ② ③ ④ ⑤

😊 **수정하기** ///////////////////////////////

That's[It's] not right. / No, it isn't. / (I think) you've made a mistake.

① **W** My car will not move forward ❶ _____ _____ _____ _____.

M Let me move the stone.

② **W** Is this statue made of stone? It's really beautiful.

M That's not right. It's made of metal.

③ **W** Look out. There's a stone on the ground.

M Oh! I ❷ _____ _____ _____.

④ **W** There are many beautiful stones in the beach.

M Take one of them if you want.

⑤ **W** ❸ _____ _____ _____. The paint is still wet.

M Thanks for telling me.

 Words **01 recently** 최근에 **dirty** 더러운 **genius** 천재 **02 make it** (모임 등에) 가다[참석하다] **eye trouble** 눈병 **03 forward** 앞으로 **statue** 조각상 **metal** 금속 **ground** 땅 **wet** 마르지 않은, 젖은

04 특정 정보 파악 – 요일 영국식 발음 녹음

대화를 듣고, 남자와 여자가 만나기로 한 요일을 고르시오.

① Tuesday ② Wednesday ③ Thursday
④ Friday ⑤ Saturday

💬 **허가 여부 묻기** ////////////////////////

Is it okay(all right) if ~? / Do you mind if ~? / I wonder if I could ~. / May(Can) I ~?

W I like your watch. Where did you get it?
M I bought it in Namdaemoon Market.
W I'd like to visit there. Can you ❶ _____ _____ _____?
M Sure. Is it okay if I go there this Wednesday?
W I have a piano lesson ❷ _____ _____ _____. How about Saturday?
M Well, I have an appointment on Saturday. But it'll ❸ _____ _____ _____ _____ _____.
W That's great. Then, let's meet at 7 p.m.

05 언급되지 않은 것

다음을 듣고, 영어가 제2언어인 나라로 언급되지 **않은** 곳을 고르시오.

① 인도 ② 싱가포르 ③ 러시아
④ 케냐 ⑤ 필리핀

W In the world, there are many countries that use English. The United States, Canada, the United Kingdom and Australia are some countries where people use English as a first language. And English is used ❶ _____ _____ _____ _____ in India, Singapore, Kenya, the Philippines and many other countries. In other countries like Korea and Russia, people learn English ❷ _____ _____ _____ _____ _____.

06 심정 파악

대화를 듣고, 남자의 심정으로 가장 적절한 것을 고르시오.

① afraid ② anxious ③ worried
④ relieved ⑤ disappointed

M Rebecca, don't you think that girl over there is pretty?
W Who? The one with the white blouse and red pants?
M Yeah. She ❶ _____ _____ _____ _____. I'm sure she has a nice personality, too.
W Hmm.... I don't think she's as beautiful as an angel. Besides, she's ❷ _____ _____.
M Do you know her?
W I do. She's my brother's girlfriend.
M Oh, no. Does she ❸ _____ _____ _____ _____?
W I'm afraid she does.

Ⓦords **04 appointment** (만날) 약속, 예약 **05 first language** 제1언어, 모국어 **foreign language** 외국어 **06 personality** 성격 **cold-hearted** 냉정한

Dictation Test

07 어색한 대화 찾기

다음을 듣고, 두 사람의 대화가 <u>어색한</u> 것을 고르시오.

①　　②　　③　　④　　⑤

🗨 충고 구하기 ////////////////

Do you think I should ~? / Can I get your advice on ~? / What would you do if I ~?

① W ❶ _____ _____ the air conditioner, won't you?

M Isn't it too hot?

② W Aren't you late for school?

M I don't go to school today.

③ W Could you buy ❷ _____ _____ _____ _____ on your way home?

M All right. Anything else?

④ W Where is my cellphone?

M How am I supposed to know?

⑤ W Do you think I should have my hair cut?

M ❸ _____ _____ this afternoon.

08 부탁한 일 파악 　영국식 발음 녹음

대화를 듣고, 남자가 여자에게 부탁한 일로 가장 적절한 것을 고르시오.

① 축가 선정하기　　② 결혼식 사회 보기
③ 연주회 관람하기　　④ 바이올린 연주하기
⑤ 경연 대회 참가하기

🗨 바람, 소원, 요망 표현하기 ////////////////

I wish I could ~. / I'd like ~. / I want (to) ~. / I look[am looking] forward to ~.

M Sojin, can I ask you a favor?

W What is it?

M My homeroom teacher ❶ _____ _____ _____ soon. My classmates are preparing a song for the wedding. So, could you ❷ _____ _____ _____ while we sing?

W I wish I could, but I can't. I don't have much time until my violin competition.

M When is the competition?

W It's next week.

M Then, it won't be a problem. My teacher's wedding is ❸ _____ _____.

W Oh, that's great.

09 의도 파악

대화를 듣고, 남자가 한 마지막 말에 담긴 의도로 가장 적절한 것을 고르시오.

① 충고　　② 위로　　③ 감사
④ 칭찬　　⑤ 질책

M Yesterday I went to a graduate exhibition and ❶ _____ _____ _____.

W Really? Did you like it?

M It was ❷ _____ _____. Did you really draw the painting yourself?

W Yes. It took a very long time to complete the work.

M I think you will be ❸ _____ _____ _____.

W Thanks, Mr. Kim. That's very kind of you to say so.

10 숫자 정보 파악 – 금액

대화를 듣고, 남자가 팁으로 주려고 하는 금액을 고르시오.

① $5   ② $7   ③ $10
④ $12   ⑤ $20

🗨 이의 제기하기 ////////////////////

I don't agree(disagree) (with you). / I don't think(believe) so. / I'm against ~.

M   How much should I ❶_____ _____ _____?
W $10, I guess.
M   That's too much. That's 20% of our fifty-dollar bill. 20% is too high for the service we received. ❷_____ _____ _____ _____ the food because of her slowness.
W   Well, I know, but I think she was trying to offer good service.
M   🗨I don't agree with you. ❸_____ _____ 10%.

11 한 일 / 할 일 파악   영국식 발음 녹음

대화를 듣고, 여자가 토요일 저녁에 할 일로 가장 적절한 것을 고르시오.

① 숙제하기
② 산책하기
③ 친구들과 테니스 치기
④ 친구의 생일 파티 가기
⑤ 가족들과 연극 보러 가기

W   What are you planning to do this weekend?
M   I'm planning to play tennis ❶_____ _____ _____ _____ and go to my friend's birthday party this Saturday.
W   And on Sunday?
M   I'm going to ride my bicycle in the park. How about you?
W   I'm going to ❷_____ _____ _____ Hamlet ❸_____ _____ _____ Saturday night. On Sunday, I have to work on my homework.
M   Those are good plans.

12 언급되지 않은 것

다음을 듣고, Winter English Camp에 관해 언급되지 않은 것을 고르시오.

① 수업료   ② 강사명   ③ 수업 내용
④ 수업 기간   ⑤ 수업 장소

M   Do you want to improve your English during the vacation? Join Winter English Camp! It is a ❶_____ _____ _____ where you can enjoy learning English. The teacher is ❷_____ _____ _____ _____ of our school, Anna Thomson. You are going to sing songs, play games, and ❸_____ _____ with Anna. Your English will be greatly improved with this three-week camp.

13 도표 정보 파악

대화를 듣고, 내용과 일치하지 않는 것을 고르시오.

Graduation Party Schedule	
Date	① October 25th
Place	② Party House
Transportation	③ Subway Line 2
Time	④ 16:00
Fee	⑤ 10,000 won

W   Are you going to attend ❶_____ _____ _____?
M   When is the party? I have an appointment on October 25th.
W   It's at 4 p.m. on the 26th.
M   Cool. Where is the party?
W   It'll be at Party House. ❷_____ _____ _____ _____ Line Number 2. And the fee is 10,000 won.
M   I got it. See you then.

Words   **10 bill** 계산서   **receive** 받다   **slowness** 느림   **offer** 제공하다   **11 close** 친밀한; 가까운   **12 improve** 향상시키다   **during** ~동안   **greatly** 상당히   **13 attend** 참석하다   **fee** 회비

Dictation Test

14 주제 파악

다음을 듣고, 무엇에 관한 설명인지 고르시오.

① 달력 ② 자 ③ 공책
④ 연필 ⑤ 크레파스

M This is something you need when you want to ❶ _____ _____ _____ _____. You can measure the length of things with this. This varies in its size, and it can have many different colors. However, this is usually a thin, flat and wide stick ❷ _____ _____ written on it. The part where the numbers are written is mostly transparent, so you can see through it. Many students carry this ❸ _____ _____ _____ _____, so you might have one, too.

15 한 일 / 할 일 파악

대화를 듣고, 남자가 대화 직후에 할 일로 가장 적절한 것을 고르시오.

① 친구와 집에 가기
② 이름표 확인하기
③ 휴대 전화 빌려주기
④ 운동장에서 축구하기
⑤ 이름표의 전화번호로 전화하기

W Hey, Nick! Are you going home? Come along with me.
M Okay. Oh, wait! This is ❶ _____ _____ _____.
W Really? How did that happen?
M Maybe I took someone else's bag by mistake.
W Whose bag is it? Is there ❷ _____ _____ _____ or something?
M Oh, yeah. There is a name tag on it with ❸ _____ _____ _____. Can I use your phone?
W Go ahead.

16 특정 정보 파악 영국식 발음 녹음

대화를 듣고, 여자가 구입할 물건을 고르시오.

① body lotion ② body cream
③ body oil ④ lip-balm
⑤ shampoo

M How may I help you?
W I need something ❶ _____ _____ _____ after I shower.
M How about this body lotion? This is very popular nowadays.
W My skin is very dry, so I would prefer a cream.
M Then I recommend ❷ _____ _____ _____.
W Do you mind if I try this?
M Of course not. Go ahead. It smells very good.
W Yeah, it does. I'll ❸ _____ _____.
M We also have a lip-balm and shampoo with the same fragrance. Would you like to see them too?
W No, thanks. I'll try them next time.

Words **14 straight** 직선의 **measure** 측정하다 **length** 길이 **vary** 가지각색이다, 다르다 **transparent** 투명한 **15 come along** 함께 가다(오다) **name tag** 명찰 **16 nowadays** 요즘에는 **recommend** 추천하다 **fragrance** 향, 향기

17 알맞은 응답 찾기

대화를 듣고, 여자의 마지막 말에 대한 남자의 응답으로
가장 적절한 것을 고르시오.
Man: _____

① You'd better call the police.
② You didn't do anything wrong.
③ She won't listen to me anyway.
④ You should ask him why he's angry.
⑤ Try to talk to your sister, not your Dad.

😠 화냄 표현하기 //////////////////////////
I'm (very) annoyed(upset) (about ~). / I can't
stand ~. / ~ is (very) annoying (irritating).

M Why are you so upset?
W I'm having trouble with my older sister. She ❶_____ _____
_____ without asking me, so I'm annoyed about that.
M ❷_____ _____ _____ _____ how you feel about it?
W Actually, I've been telling my dad, not my sister.
M And she must be ❸_____ _____ _____ for telling him
about it.
W Exactly. What do you think I can do?

18 알맞은 응답 찾기

대화를 듣고, 남자의 마지막 말에 대한 여자의 응답으로
가장 적절한 것을 고르시오.
Woman: _____

① I don't believe so.
② How have you been?
③ Long time no see, Jane.
④ I'm pleased to meet you, Jane.
⑤ I wonder if I have enough time.

W Hi, Tom. Are you going ❶_____ _____ _____?
M Yes, I am. Do you know any good restaurants around here?
W There's a good one around that corner.
M Did you have lunch? ❷_____ _____ _____ together.
W All right. I haven't been there for a long time. Is this your friend?
M Oh, ❸_____ _____ _____ _____. This is my sister,
Jane.

19 알맞은 응답 찾기

대화를 듣고, 여자의 마지막 말에 대한 남자의 응답으로
가장 적절한 것을 고르시오.
Man: _____

① The book is sold out.
② I'm sorry but you can't get a refund.
③ You should have returned it last week.
④ Can I return it instead of you tomorrow?
⑤ Can you show me how to go to the library?

W Did you read a science book and ❶_____ _____ _____
on it?
M No, not yet. I went to the library to ❷_____ _____ _____
_____ *The Human Body*, but it was already checked out. I think
I'll have to buy a copy today.
W You mean this book?
M Yes, that's right. Did you write your report about this book?
W Yes. I checked this book out last week, and I was going to ❸_____
_____ _____ because I've finished the homework already.

20 상황에 맞는 말 찾기

다음 상황 설명을 듣고, Coby가 어머니께 할 말로 가장
적절한 것을 고르시오.
Coby: _____

① The iron is out of order.
② Where did you put the iron?
③ Why do I have to wash my uniform?
④ Can you tell me how to use the iron?
⑤ It's not easy to use a washing machine.

🔊 iron의 발음 //////////////////////////
iron은 [áirən]이 아닌 [áiərn]으로 발음된다.

W Coby decides to wash his school uniform today. So he puts it into
❶_____ _____ _____. After it's washed, he finds out
that he needs to 🔊iron the uniform. However, this is ❷_____
_____ _____ he tries ironing. So, he thinks that he needs
❸_____ _____ _____. In this situation, what would Coby
most likely say to his mom?

📖 Words **17** annoyed 짜증이 난 **18** have lunch 점심을 먹다 **19** check out 대출하다 copy 한 부, 한 권 return 반납하다, 돌려주다 **20** school
uniform 교복 iron 다림질하다; 다리미

01 대화를 듣고, 여자가 좋아하는 가수의 사진을 고르시오.

① 　② 　③

④ 　⑤

02 대화를 듣고, 여자가 남자를 방문한 목적으로 가장 적절한 것을 고르시오.

① 물건을 빌리려고
② 물건을 판매하려고
③ 음식을 배달하려고
④ 소음에 대해 항의하려고
⑤ 옆집 이웃에게 인사하려고

03 다음 그림의 상황에 가장 적절한 대화를 고르시오.

①　　②　　③　　④　　⑤

04 대화를 듣고, 두 사람이 만나기로 한 장소를 고르시오.

① 영화관　　　　② 지하철역
③ 빵 가게　　　　④ 신발 가게
⑤ 구두 수리점

05 다음을 듣고, School Notice에 관해 언급되지 않은 것을 고르시오.

① 설치 대상　　　② 주요 기능
③ 사용 조건　　　④ 회원권 만료일
⑤ 서비스 종료일

06 대화를 듣고, 두 사람의 관계로 가장 적절한 것을 고르시오.

① 의사 – 환자
② 사장 – 직원
③ 사진작가 – 모델
④ 감독 – 운동선수
⑤ 개인 운동 지도사 – 회원

07 다음을 듣고, 두 사람의 대화가 어색한 것을 고르시오.

①　　　②　　　③　　　④　　　⑤

08 대화를 듣고, 여자가 남자에게 부탁한 일로 가장 적절한 것을 고르시오.

① 고양이 밥 주기
② 휴대 전화 빌려주기
③ 공중전화 위치 알려 주기
④ 엄마에게 전화 걸어 주기
⑤ 점심시간에 집에 다녀오기

09 대화를 듣고, 여자의 마지막 말에 담긴 의도로 가장 적절한 것을 고르시오.

① 감사　　　② 거절　　　③ 불평
④ 충고　　　⑤ 후회

10 대화를 듣고, 남자가 지불할 금액을 고르시오.

① $7　　　② $10　　　③ $14
④ $17　　　⑤ $20

11 대화를 듣고, 두 사람이 대화하고 있는 장소를 고르시오.
① 식당　　　　　　② 영화관
③ 음반 가게　　　　④ 학교 운동장
⑤ 학교 음악실

12 다음을 듣고, 라디오 방송에서 언급되지 <u>않은</u> 것을 고르시오.
① 진행자 이름　　　② 프로그램 이름
③ 출연자 이름　　　④ 깜짝 손님 이름
⑤ 출연자가 부를 노래 제목

13 대화를 듣고, 전화 내용을 메모한 것 중 <u>잘못된</u> 것을 고르시오.

While You Were Out

To:　　　　① Mr. Adams
From:　　　② Max from Max Auto Repair
Message:　③ Your car is ready.
　　　　　④ The repair bill is $15.
　　　　　⑤ Call Max back.

14 다음을 듣고, 무엇에 관한 설명인지 고르시오.
① 동전　　　② 통장　　　③ 영수증
④ 신용카드　⑤ 바코드

15 대화를 듣고, 여자가 할 일로 가장 적절한 것을 고르시오.
① 새 물건으로 교환하기
② 구입한 물건을 환불받기
③ 구입한 물건 수리 맡기기
④ 구입한 물건 계속 사용하기
⑤ 다른 모델의 새 상품 구입하기

16 대화를 듣고, 두 사람이 인터뷰를 하러 갈 날짜를 고르시오.
① June 8th　② June 9th　③ June 10th
④ June 21st　⑤ June 22nd

17 대화를 듣고, 여자의 마지막 말에 대한 남자의 응답으로 가장 적절한 것을 고르시오.
Man: _____
① How can I say that?
② I'll make an order in advance.
③ Could you spell your name, please?
④ I am afraid that we are fully booked that day.
⑤ Please follow me and I'll show you to your table.

18 대화를 듣고, 남자의 마지막 말에 대한 여자의 응답으로 가장 적절한 것을 고르시오.
Woman: _____
① She's coming at around 5 p.m.
② I really look forward to seeing her.
③ Sorry, but I'm too busy to pick her up.
④ She's leaving at 10 p.m. from the airport.
⑤ She has a short hair and is wearing glasses.

19 대화를 듣고, 여자의 마지막 말에 대한 남자의 응답으로 가장 적절한 것을 고르시오.
Man: _____
① Good for you.
② Is everything clear?
③ You can say that again.
④ Do you know what I mean?
⑤ Could you explain more in detail?

20 다음 상황 설명을 듣고, 한 선생님이 정수에게 할 말로 가장 적절한 것을 고르시오.
Ms. Han: _____
① Don't mention it.
② Let me explain it again.
③ I really appreciate your help.
④ Would you like to help me again, please?
⑤ I'm worried that I will get a poor grade in math again.

Dictation Test 09회 영어 듣기모의고사

01 그림 정보 파악 – 인물

대화를 듣고, 여자가 좋아하는 가수의 사진을 고르시오.

① ② ③ ④ ⑤

😊 **이의 제기하기** //////////////////////////
I don't think[believe] so. / I don't agree
[disagree] (with you). / I'm against ~.

M What are you looking at?

W This is a picture of my favorite singer.

M Wow, he has ❶ _____ _____ _____.

W Yes. Don't you think he is a fashion leader?

M Honestly, I'm not happy with his style. He is wearing ❷ _____ _____ _____ _____. I don't think they look good on him.

W Come on. Look at ❸ _____ _____. It's so cool.

M I think that's too girlish. Why are girls crazy about singers like him? I don't get it.

02 목적 파악

대화를 듣고, 여자가 남자를 방문한 목적으로 가장 적절한 것을 고르시오.

① 물건을 빌리려고
② 물건을 판매하려고
③ 음식을 배달하려고
④ 소음에 대해 항의하려고
⑤ 옆집 이웃에게 인사하려고

W Excuse me. Is anybody here?

M Yes. Who is it?

W Hi, my name is Jessica. I ❶ _____ _____ _____ _____ yesterday.

M Oh, hi. Nice to meet you. I'm Minsu.

W Nice to meet you, too. Here, I brought ❷ _____ _____ _____ _____ _____. Please have some.

M Wow, I appreciate it. This looks very delicious.

W I hope we will ❸ _____ _____ _____ _____ each other.

M Me, too.

03 그림 상황에 어울리는 대화 찾기

다음 그림의 상황에 가장 적절한 대화를 고르시오.

① ② ③ ④ ⑤

① W When you have a good idea, it's important to take notes about it.
   M I see. I will ❶ _____ _____ _____ _____.

② W Is there anything you'd like for dinner?
   M No, how about you?

③ W What are ❷ _____ _____ _____ _____ at this restaurant?
   M *Bulgogi* is the most popular.

④ W I'm very surprised there are so many people in this restaurant.
   M Yeah. I'm curious about the taste of the dishes.

⑤ W Tommy, dinner is ready.
   M I don't ❸ _____ _____ _____ _____, Mom.

📖 Words **01 honestly** 솔직히 **necklace** 목걸이 **girlish** 여자아이 같은 **be crazy about** ~에 열광하다 **02 pumpkin** 호박 **neighbor** 이웃
each other 서로 **03 take notes** 메모하다, 필기하다 **keep in mind** ~을 기억해 두다

072 | 중학영어 듣기모의고사 **3**학년

04 [장소 추론] 영국식 발음 녹음

대화를 듣고, 두 사람이 만나기로 한 장소를 고르시오.

① 영화관 　　② 지하철역
③ 빵 가게 　　④ 신발 가게
⑤ 구두 수리점

[*cellphone rings.*]

M Hello?

W Dave. Are you at _____ _____ _____ already? ❶

M Not yet. I'm at the subway station. Why?

W On the way, my shoe heel broke. I'm _____ _____ ❷ _____ _____ _____ now.

M Is it going to take a long time?

W No, I'll _____ _____ _____ ❸ in about twenty minutes. Do you know where the repair shop is?

M Yes, I do. I'll go there now.

05 [언급되지 않은 것]

다음을 듣고, School Notice에 관해 언급되지 않은 것을 고르시오.

① 설치 대상 　　② 주요 기능
③ 사용 조건 　　④ 회원권 만료일
⑤ 서비스 종료일

W JW Middle School strongly recommends all parents to install the "School Notice" application on their cellphones. This free application _____ _____ _____ ❶ to your cellphone, so you won't need to worry about missing an important notice again. To use this application, you have to _____ _____ _____. ❷ The school will approve the membership after checking your child's grade and class. Your membership _____ _____ ❸ at the end of the school year. The service will start from next month, so please get a membership before the end of this month.

06 [관계 추론]

대화를 듣고, 두 사람의 관계로 가장 적절한 것을 고르시오.

① 의사 – 환자
② 사장 – 직원
③ 사진작가 – 모델
④ 감독 – 운동선수
⑤ 개인 운동 지도사 – 회원

💬 **의견 표현하기** ////////////////////
In my opinion(view), ~. / It seems to me ~. / I think(feel, believe) ~.

W I have a backache. I think my posture is not good.

M I'm afraid but you are right. You have _____ _____. ❶

W Is there anything I can do about it?

M It can help if you work out steadily. I'll help you _____ ❷ _____ _____.

W How often do you think I should come to exercise?

M In my opinion, you should come at least three times a week.

W Then I'll try my best. I'll exercise really hard.

M Good. Then I'll make _____ _____ _____ ❸ suitable for you. Now, let's start with stretching.

Words **04 on the way** ~ 하는 중에 　**05 install** 설치하다 **application** 응용 프로그램, 앱 **membership** 회원 (자격·신분) **approve** 승인하다 **expire** 만료되다 　**06 rounded shoulder** 굽은 어깨 **steadily** 꾸준히 **posture** 자세

Dictation Test

07 어색한 대화 찾기

다음을 듣고, 두 사람의 대화가 <u>어색한</u> 것을 고르시오.
① ② ③ ④ ⑤

😊 도움 제안하기 /////////////////////////////
Do you need any help? / Can I help you? / Can I give you a hand? / Let me help you.

① W What would you like to wear for the party tomorrow?
　 M I think it _____ _____ _____ _____ you.
② W I was surprised that the action scene was so realistic.
　 M Yeah, movies do look real these days.
③ W What should we do to keep our teeth healthy?
　 M It's very important ❷ _____ _____ _____ _____ three times a day.
④ W I made so many mistakes that I wasn't able to win the contest.
　 M Don't be disappointed. You will ❸ _____ _____ _____ _____.
⑤ W You look lost. 😊 Do you need any help?
　 M Yes. Would you please show me how to get to Seoul Station?

---

08 부탁한 일 파악　영국식 발음 녹음

대화를 듣고, 여자가 남자에게 부탁한 일로 가장 적절한 것을 고르시오.
① 고양이 밥 주기
② 휴대 전화 빌려주기
③ 공중전화 위치 알려 주기
④ 엄마에게 전화 걸어 주기
⑤ 점심시간에 집에 다녀오기

😊 걱정, 두려움 표현하기 ////////////////////
I'm (rather) worried(anxious) (about ~). / I'm scared(frightened, terrified) (to ~).

M You look worried. What's the matter?
W Well, 😊 I am worried about my cat. I forgot to ❶ _____ _____ _____ this morning. She might be starving. Maybe I should go home during lunchtime.
M Your mom may have fed her. Why don't you call her and check?
W That's a good idea, but my cellphone battery ❷ _____ _____.
M Then do you want to ❸ _____ _____?
W Can I? I won't talk for long.
M It's okay. Go ahead.

---

09 의도 파악

대화를 듣고, 여자의 마지막 말에 담긴 의도로 가장 적절한 것을 고르시오.
① 감사　② 거절　③ 불평
④ 충고　⑤ 후회

M Good morning, Dr. Kim.
W Good morning. ❶ _____ _____ _____ _____?
M Well, I have a very big headache.
W Do you have a cough or a runny nose?
M Not really. My temperature ❷ _____ _____ _____, _____. I don't think I have a cold.
W How many hours do you sleep a day?
M About four hours, but I don't feel tired or sleepy.
W That's not a good sign. In my opinion, you ❸ _____ _____ _____ _____.

📖 Words　**07 look good on** ~에게 잘 어울리다　**scene** 장면　**realistic** 현실적인　**these days** 요즈음, 최근에　**08 feed** 먹이를 주다(-fed)　**starve** 굶주리다　**dead** (배터리 등이) 다 된, 끊어진　**borrow** 빌리다　**09 runny nose** 콧물　**temperature** 체온　**sign** 신호

10 숫자 정보 파악 – 금액

대화를 듣고, 남자가 지불할 금액을 고르시오.

① $7   ② $10   ③ $14
④ $17   ⑤ $20

W May I help you?

M Hi. I'd like to buy two tickets for the dolphin show.

W Are they for two adults?

M No, ❶ _____ _____ and ❷ _____ _____ .

W The ticket for an adult is $10. The ticket for children aged 7 and under 7 is free, and above 7 is $7.   M My son is 6.

W Then, you don't need to pay for him. You just ❸ _____ _____ _____ _____ _____ .

M Okay, here's the money.

11 장소 추론   영국식 발음 녹음

대화를 듣고, 두 사람이 대화하고 있는 장소를 고르시오.

① 식당   ② 영화관
③ 음반 가게   ④ 학교 운동장
⑤ 학교 음악실

😊 **의견 묻기** ////////////////

What do you think of[about] ~? / How do you feel about ~? / What is your view[opinion] on ~?

W Jinsu, what do you think of this music?

M Um, it is very rhythmical. I like it. Why?

W I'm thinking we ❶ _____ _____ _____ _____ for the school festival.

M That's a good idea. This song will be perfect for it.

W Why don't we buy this music CD and practice playing together?

M Okay. ❷ _____ _____ _____ _____ and go out. There's a music store near this restaurant.   W Sounds great.

12 언급되지 않은 것

다음을 듣고, 라디오 방송에서 언급되지 <u>않은</u> 것을 고르시오.

① 진행자 이름   ② 프로그램 이름
③ 출연자 이름   ④ 깜짝 손님 이름
⑤ 출연자가 부를 노래 제목

M Good evening, everyone. I'm Michael, the host of *Music Camp*. Today, we are going to meet Kimberley Clark and ❶ _____ _____ _____ _____ _____ . She will sing *The Song of Wind*, the one of her hit songs. Also, she will talk on the phone with a surprise guest in the studio. The guest is her closest friend and a singer as well. I'm very curious ❷ _____ _____ _____ _____ _____ . Stay tuned with us.

13 도표 정보 파악

대화를 듣고, 전화 내용을 메모한 것 중 잘못된 것을 고르시오.

While You Were Out

To: ① Mr. Adams
From: ② Max from Max Auto Repair
Message: ③ Your car is ready.
           ④ The repair bill is $15.
           ⑤ Call Max back.

[*Telephone rings.*]

W Hello?

M Hello. May I speak to Mr. Adams?

W I'm afraid he isn't here right now. Can I take a message?

M Yes. This is Max from Max Auto Repair. I'm calling to tell him ❶ _____ _____ _____ _____ .

W Okay. Anything else?

M Could you tell him ❷ _____ _____ _____ _____ _____ is $50? And tell him to call me back.

W Okay. I'll give him the message.   M Thanks.

Words   **10 dolphin** 돌고래   **aged** ~세(살)의   **11 rhythmical** 경쾌한   **practice** 연습하다   **music store** 음반 가게   **12 host** 사회자   **closest** 가장 가까운   **as well** ~도, 역시   **stay tuned** (채널을) 고정하다   **13 repair** 수리; 수리하다   **cost** 비용

Dictation Test

14 주제 파악

다음을 듣고, 무엇에 관한 설명인지 고르시오.

① 동전　　② 통장　　③ 영수증
④ 신용카드　　⑤ 바코드

W When you ❶ _____ _____ _____ _____ _____, you will get this. Lots of people just throw this away, but actually it is very important to keep this. When you need to ❷ _____ _____ _____ or exchange something, this will ❸ _____ _____ _____ _____ _____ from the store.

15 한 일 / 할 일 파악

대화를 듣고, 여자가 할 일로 가장 적절한 것을 고르시오.

① 새 물건으로 교환하기
② 구입한 물건을 환불받기
③ 구입한 물건 수리 맡기기
④ 구입한 물건 계속 사용하기
⑤ 다른 모델의 새 상품 구입하기

😊 **만족 표현하기** //////////////////////
That will do. / I'm (very) satisfied. / Good![fine!, Excellent!]

M Hello. How may I help you, ma'am?
W Hello. I bought this electric fan last month. I just used it for a month, and it's ❶ _____ _____.
M Can we take a look at it? We can fix it for you.
W No, I want to get a refund.
M Sorry, but you've already used it for a month. It's not easy to get a refund for it.
W Then, can I exchange this ❷ _____ _____ _____ _____?
M Yes. That's possible, but only for the same model. Do you ❸ _____ _____ _____ _____ it?
W Yes. That will do.

16 숫자 정보 파악 – 날짜　영국식 발음 녹음

대화를 듣고, 두 사람이 인터뷰를 하러 갈 날짜를 고르시오.

① June 8th　　② June 9th　　③ June 10th
④ June 21st　　⑤ June 22nd

W Brian, did you finish your interview homework?
M No. I've ❶ _____ _____ _____ _____ my aunt. She is a designer.
W Really? Can I go with you? I wanted to interview a designer.
M Of course. When are we going to see her? She said she would be busy from June 10th to 21st.
W Then, how about June 9th?
M Well, I'm sorry, but I have an appointment on that day. How about ❷ _____ _____ _____ _____?
W Okay. That's fine with me.

📖 **Words**　**14 throw away** 버리다　**get a refund** 환불 받다　**exchange** 교환하다　**15 electric fan** 선풍기　**fix** 고치다　**16 aunt** 이모, 고모　**designer** 디자이너　**appointment** 약속

17 알맞은 응답 찾기

대화를 듣고, 여자의 마지막 말에 대한 남자의 응답으로 가장 적절한 것을 고르시오.

Man: _____

① How can I say that?
② I'll make an order in advance.
③ Could you spell your name, please?
④ I am afraid that we are fully booked that day.
⑤ Please follow me and I'll show you to your table.

[*Telephone rings.*]

M This is Sky Lounge. How can I help you?
W I'd like to _____ _____ _____ for four people for this Saturday.
M ❷ _____ _____ will you visit, ma'am?
W We'll be there ❸ _____ _____ _____.
M Please leave your name and phone number.
W My name is Jisoo Kim. My phone number is 010-1101-5678.

18 알맞은 응답 찾기

대화를 듣고, 남자의 마지막 말에 대한 여자의 응답으로 가장 적절한 것을 고르시오.

Woman: _____

① She's coming at around 5 p.m.
② I really look forward to seeing her.
③ Sorry, but I'm too busy to pick her up.
④ She's leaving at 10 p.m. from the airport.
⑤ She has a short hair and is wearing glasses.

[*Telephone rings.*]

M Hello?
W Hello, Kenny. This is Julie. Are you busy this afternoon?
M Not really. Why?
W Then can you do me a favor?
M Sure. ❶ _____ _____ _____ _____. What is it?
W My sister is coming home from Canada this afternoon, but I have to work late tonight. Can you pick her up for me?
M Sure. ❷ _____ _____ _____ _____ _____ the airport?

19 알맞은 응답 찾기

대화를 듣고, 여자의 마지막 말에 대한 남자의 응답으로 가장 적절한 것을 고르시오.

Man: _____

① Good for you.
② Is everything clear?
③ You can say that again.
④ Do you know what I mean?
⑤ Could you explain more in detail?

W May I help you, sir?
M Yes, please. ❶ _____ _____ _____ _____ an oven.
W Are you going to use it at home?
M Yes. I don't want it to be too big.
W This is ❷ _____ _____ _____ _____.
M I like its design. Is it easy to use?
W Yes, it is. You ❸ _____ _____ _____ by simply turning this dial.

20 상황에 맞는 말 찾기

다음 상황 설명을 듣고, 한 선생님이 정수에게 할 말로 가장 적절한 것을 고르시오.

Ms. Han: _____

① Don't mention it.
② Let me explain it again.
③ I really appreciate your help.
④ Would you like to help me again, please?
⑤ I'm worried that I will get a poor grade in math again.

M Ms. Han is ❶ _____ _____ _____. One day, Jeongsu, one of her students, asked her how to solve a math question. She showed him how to solve it, but he ❷ _____ _____ _____ _____. She thinks she has to tell him the way ❸ _____ _____ _____ again to make him understand. In this situation, what would Ms. Han most likely say to Jeongsu?

Words 17 **make a reservation** 예약하다 **in advance** 미리 **spell** 철자를 말하다 18 **favor** 호의 **pick up** ~를 태우러 가다 19 **oven** 오븐 **turn** 돌리다 **dial** 문자반, 다이얼 **in detail** 상세히 20 **solve** 풀다

01 대화를 듣고, 여자가 설명하는 동작을 고르시오.

02 대화를 듣고, 남자가 여자에게 전화한 목적으로 가장 적절한 것을 고르시오.

① 피자를 주문하려고
② 식당 예약을 부탁하려고
③ 식당 위치를 문의하려고
④ Jamie의 연락처를 문의하려고
⑤ 여자의 아파트 위치를 문의하려고

03 다음 그림의 상황에 가장 적절한 대화를 고르시오.

①   ②   ③   ④   ⑤

04 대화를 듣고, 여자가 테니스 코트를 이용할 수 있는 요일을 고르시오.

① Monday   ② Tuesday
③ Wednesday   ④ Thursday
⑤ Friday

05 다음을 듣고, 새로 전학 온 친구에 관해 언급되지 <u>않은</u> 것을 고르시오.

① 이름   ② 취미   ③ 나이
④ 출신 국가   ⑤ 사용 언어

06 대화를 듣고, 여자의 심정으로 가장 적절한 것을 고르시오.

① upset   ② bored
③ joyful   ④ nervous
⑤ regretful

07 다음을 듣고, 두 사람의 대화가 <u>어색한</u> 것을 고르시오.

①   ②   ③   ④   ⑤

08 대화를 듣고, 여자가 남자에게 부탁한 일로 가장 적절한 것을 고르시오.

① 빨래 제때 하기
② 집안일 도와주기
③ 자기 방 청소하기
④ 벗은 양말 빨래 통에 넣기
⑤ 외출 후 손발 깨끗하게 씻기

09 대화를 듣고, 여자의 마지막 말에 담긴 의도로 가장 적절한 것을 고르시오.

① 초대   ② 칭찬   ③ 동의
④ 허락   ⑤ 거절

10 대화를 듣고, 여자가 지불할 금액을 고르시오.

① $4   ② $5   ③ $9
④ $13   ⑤ $15

11 대화를 듣고, 두 사람이 대화하는 장소로 가장 적절한 곳을 고르시오.

① 공원　　　　　② 우체국
③ 분실물 센터　　④ 서비스 센터
⑤ 호텔 안내 데스크

12 다음을 듣고, 소포 발송에 관해 언급되지 <u>않은</u> 것을 고르시오.

① 접수 시간
② 요금 부과 방법
③ 요금 납부자
④ 소포의 제한 중량
⑤ 상자 위 기재 내용

13 대화를 듣고, 남자가 받은 초대 문자의 내용으로 알맞지 <u>않은</u> 것을 고르시오.

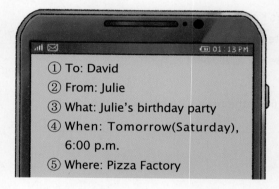

```
⊡                    01:13 PM
① To: David
② From: Julie
③ What: Julie's birthday party
④ When: Tomorrow(Saturday),
         6:00 p.m.
⑤ Where: Pizza Factory
```

14 다음을 듣고, 무엇에 관한 설명인지 고르시오.

① 정크푸드의 역사
② 트랜스 지방의 역할
③ 청소년 건강의 중요성
④ 음식물 쓰레기의 심각성
⑤ 정크푸드의 안 좋은 점

15 대화를 듣고, 남자가 할 일로 가장 적절한 것을 고르시오.

① 저녁 먹기　　　　② 치킨 배달하기
③ 설거지하기　　　　④ 학교 숙제하기
⑤ 음식물 쓰레기 버리기

16 대화를 듣고, 여자가 여행에서 돌아오는 날짜를 고르시오.

① August 6th　　　② August 7th
③ August 8th　　　④ August 9th
⑤ August 10th

17 대화를 듣고, 남자의 마지막 말에 대한 여자의 응답으로 가장 적절한 것을 고르시오.

Woman: _____

① You can do it, Dad.
② Please buy me a bike, Dad.
③ I rode a bike last week, Dad.
④ Okay. I'll try tomorrow, Dad.
⑤ Where were you just a minute ago, Dad?

18 대화를 듣고, 여자의 마지막 말에 대한 남자의 응답으로 가장 적절한 것을 고르시오.

Man: _____

① I had a lot of fun, too.
② I think that would be great.
③ My grandparents live in the city.
④ I have never been to another country.
⑤ I like the mountains better than the ocean.

19 대화를 듣고, 남자의 마지막 말에 대한 여자의 응답으로 가장 적절한 것을 고르시오.

Woman: _____

① I'll keep my fingers crossed.
② I don't need a new backpack.
③ Where do you think the shop is?
④ I don't know where N Seoul Tower is.
⑤ I would like to go, but I already have plans.

20 다음 상황 설명을 듣고, 유진이가 친구에게 할 말로 가장 적절한 것을 고르시오.

Yujin: _____

① Why don't you come back to Japan?
② When does your piano concert begin?
③ Have you ever traveled to Japan by yourself?
④ How much was the ticket you bought for me the other day?
⑤ Can you help me make a reservation on the Japanese website?

Dictation Test 10회 영어 듣기모의고사

01 그림 정보 파악 – 인물
대화를 듣고, 여자가 설명하는 동작을 고르시오.

① ② ③ ④ ⑤

W Many people feel tired when they travel by plane. Here is ❶ _____ _____ _____ _____ in your seat on a long plane flight that will reduce jet lag. First, sit up straight. Put your fingers together and ❷ _____ _____ _____ to chest level, keeping your elbows straight and your palms facing outward. Bend forward at the waist and then relax.

02 목적 파악
대화를 듣고, 남자가 여자에게 전화한 목적으로 가장 적절한 것을 고르시오.
① 피자를 주문하려고
② 식당 예약을 부탁하려고
③ 식당 위치를 문의하려고
④ Jamie의 연락처를 문의하려고
⑤ 여자의 아파트 위치를 문의하려고

😮 요청하기
Can you ~(. please)? / Could I ask you to ~? / Do(Would) you mind ~?

[cellphone rings.]
W Hi, Alex. What's up?
M Hi, Patti. You have told me there is ❶ _____ _____ _____ _____ near your apartment. A very famous chef runs the place.
W Yes, that's Jamie's Kitchen.
M Right. Can you tell me exactly ❷ _____ _____ _____?
W You know where my apartment is, right?
M Yes.
W It's right across from the main gate of my apartment.
M Oh, I think ❸ _____ _____ _____ _____. Thanks.

03 그림 상황에 어울리는 대화 찾기
다음 그림의 상황에 가장 적절한 대화를 고르시오.

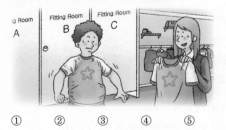

① ② ③ ④ ⑤

😮 모르고 있음 표현하기
I have no idea. / I don't know. / I haven't got a clue.

① **M** What do you want to be in the future?
W I want to be ❶ _____ _____ _____.
② **M** Are there any rooms available?
W Sorry, none at the moment.
③ **M** How can I get to the department store?
W Go straight this way. It's ❷ _____ _____ _____ _____.
④ **M** Have you heard about the new clothing store near here?
W No, I have no idea.
⑤ **M** This is too small for me. Do you have a bigger one?
W Sure. ❸ _____ _____ _____.

Words **01 jet lag** 시차증 **elbow** 팔꿈치 **palm** 손바닥 **bend** 구부리다 **relax** 휴식을 취하다 **02 chef** 요리사 **run** 경영하다 **exactly** 정확하게 **03 available** 이용 가능한 **at the moment** 바로 지금 **department store** 백화점

| 중학영어 듣기모의고사 **3학년**

04 특정 정보 파악 – 요일 영국식 발음 녹음

대화를 듣고, 여자가 테니스 코트를 이용할 수 있는 요일을
고르시오.

① Monday   ② Tuesday
③ Wednesday   ④ Thursday
⑤ Friday

W Excuse me. Is the tennis court still being repaired?
M Yes. You ❶ _____ _____ _____ today.
W Why is it taking so long? The work started last Wednesday, and it's
   already Tuesday today.
M It's almost done. I think ❷ _____ _____ _____ _____
   again from Friday.
W If the repair's almost done, can't I play on the court tomorrow?
M Safety inspectors will come on Thursday. Please come back
   ❸ _____ _____.

05 언급되지 않은 것

다음을 듣고, 새로 전학 온 친구에 관해 언급되지 <u>않은</u>
것을 고르시오.

① 이름   ② 취미   ③ 나이
④ 출신 국가 ⑤ 사용 언어

M Let me introduce a new friend who transferred to our school today.
   ❶ _____ _____ is Celine, and she is ❷ _____ _____
   _____. As you can see, she isn't Korean. She is from France and
   ❸ _____ _____. She just moved to Korea, so she is not good
   at Korean. Everything in Korea is new to her, so please understand
   her situation and be nice to her. I hope everyone can be good
   friends.

06 심정 파악

대화를 듣고, 여자의 심정으로 가장 적절한 것을 고르
시오.

① upset   ② bored
③ joyful   ④ nervous
⑤ regretful

W Tom, do you know what time it is?
M I'm so sorry, Mom. I won't be late again.
W ❶ _____ _____ _____ more than ten times. Where were
   you?
M I was playing basketball with some of my classmates. My phone's
   battery was dead, so I couldn't call you.
W You could have used one of your friends' cellphones.
M Right. I ❷ _____ _____ _____ it. I'm so sorry.
W This is not the first time. What's wrong with you?
M ❸ _____ _____ _____ _____, Mom. I promise. I
   won't be late again.

Words **04 safety** 안전 **inspector** 조사관 **05 transfer to** ~로 전학 오다(가다) **be good at** ~을 잘하다 **06 battery** 배터리, 건전지 **dead** (배터리 등이) 다 닳은

10회 | **081**

Dictation Test

07 어색한 대화 찾기

다음을 듣고, 두 사람의 대화가 <u>어색한</u> 것을 고르시오.

① ② ③ ④ ⑤

① M How was the movie?

W _____ _____ _____. I'm fascinated by the actors.

② M I lost my umbrella this morning.

W That's too bad.

③ M ❷_____ _____ _____! You'll make it next time.

W I'm sorry to hear that.

④ M Do you agree with me?

W Actually, I don't.

⑤ M It's all my fault. Please forgive me.

W Oh, it's okay. ❸_____ _____.

08 부탁한 일 파악 영국식 발음 녹음

대화를 듣고, 여자가 남자에게 부탁한 일로 가장 적절한 것을 고르시오.

① 빨래 제때 하기
② 집안일 도와주기
③ 자기 방 청소하기
④ 벗은 양말 빨래 통에 넣기
⑤ 외출 후 손발 깨끗하게 씻기

W Where are you, Ronald?

M ❶_____ _____ _____ my room, Mom.

W Come out here right now.

M Okay. What's going on?

W Look at your socks on the floor! I told you many times. You must put them ❷_____ _____ _____ _____ when you take them off.

M I'm so sorry. I'll put my ❸_____ _____ _____ _____ next time.

W Okay.

09 의도 파악

대화를 듣고, 여자의 마지막 말에 담긴 의도로 가장 적절한 것을 고르시오.

① 초대 ② 칭찬 ③ 동의
④ 허락 ⑤ 거절

W Good morning.

M Hi, are you ready for the exam?

W I ❶_____ _____ _____ _____.

M You mean you didn't sleep at all?

W Yes, I don't think I can stay awake during the exam.

M Studying without sleeping makes you ❷_____ _____ _____ _____ the exam well. I've said it before.

W Right, I didn't realize it before, but now I ❸_____ _____ _____ _____ _____.

Words 07 fascinated 매료된 fault 잘못 forgive 용서하다 08 take off ~을 벗다 laundry 빨래, 세탁 09 not ~ at all 전혀 ~하지 않다 awake 깨어 있는 realize 깨닫다

10 숫자 정보 파악 – 금액

대화를 듣고, 여자가 지불할 금액을 고르시오.

① $4 ② $5 ③ $9
④ $13 ⑤ $15

확실성 정도 표현하기
I'm sure(certain) ~. / I have no doubt. / Are you sure(certain) about ~? / How sure are you that ~?

M Hello.
W Hi, I need some fruit for my grandmother.
M Take these pears. They are sweet and juicy.
W How much are they?
M $1 each, but ❶ _____ _____ _____ _____ .
W How about these oranges?
M $2 each, but ❷ _____ _____ _____ .
W Okay. I'll take ❸ _____ _____ _____ _____ _____ .
M Thanks. I'm sure your grandmother will like them.

11 장소 추론 영국식 발음 녹음

대화를 듣고, 두 사람이 대화하는 장소로 가장 적절한 곳을 고르시오.

① 공원 ② 우체국
③ 분실물 센터 ④ 서비스 센터
⑤ 호텔 안내 데스크

W How can I help you?
M Hi, I need to ❶ _____ _____ _____ .
W What's the problem?
M The screen is broken. I can't read text messages.
W Why is that?
M I ❷ _____ _____ on the stairs by mistake.
W All right. Can you fill out this form?
M Sure. How much will it cost?
W Well, the repairman ❸ _____ _____ _____ _____ first.

12 언급되지 않은 것

다음을 듣고, 소포 발송에 관해 언급되지 않은 것을 고르시오.

① 접수 시간
② 요금 부과 방법
③ 요금 납부자
④ 소포의 제한 중량
⑤ 상자 위 기재 내용

W When you want to ❶ _____ _____ _____ at the post office, you have to take it there between 9 a.m. and 6 p.m. on weekdays. The postage rate is ❷ _____ _____ the weight of your package: the heavier the package is, the higher the rate is. You can either pay the postage when you send it, or have the receiver pay for it. For all packages, ❸ _____ _____ _____ write the name, address, and phone number of both you and the receiver on the box.

13 도표 정보 파악

대화를 듣고, 남자가 받은 초대 문자의 내용으로 알맞지 않은 것을 고르시오.

① To: David
② From: Julie
③ What: Julie's birthday party
④ When: Tomorrow(Saturday), 6:00 p.m.
⑤ Where: Pizza Factory

W Wow, it's Friday. How are you feeling today, David?
M Good. You got ❶ _____ _____ _____ _____ from Julie, right?
W What? (pause) Oh, I just checked it.
M Well, just let me know if you're going to go to ❷ _____ _____ _____ _____ .
W Yes, I would love to go. So, 6 o'clock ❸ _____ _____ _____ , right?
M You got that right.

Words **10 juicy** 즙이 많은 **11 broken** 깨진 **by mistake** 실수로 **fill out** 작성하다 **form** 서식 **12 package** 소포, 짐, 꾸러미 **on weekdays** 평일에 **postage** 우편 요금 **based on** ~에 근거하여 **either A or B** A이거나 B인 **13 invitation** 초대장

Dictation Test

14 주제 파악

다음을 듣고, 무엇에 관한 설명인지 고르시오.

① 정크푸드의 역사
② 트랜스 지방의 역할
③ 청소년 건강의 중요성
④ 음식물 쓰레기의 심각성
⑤ 정크푸드의 안 좋은 점

M Have you heard of junk food? Many people like it. That's probably because it's simple and tastes very good. However, you need to know it is _____ _____ _____ _____ _____. They are very high-calorie and sugar-rich foods. Eating too much junk food can ❷ _____ _____ _____ _____. Try not to eat those foods, and eat more vegetables.

15 한 일 / 할 일 파악

대화를 듣고, 남자가 할 일로 가장 적절한 것을 고르시오.

① 저녁 먹기   ② 치킨 배달하기
③ 설거지하기   ④ 학교 숙제하기
⑤ 음식물 쓰레기 버리기

😋 음식 권하기 //////////////////////

Do you want some more ~? / Would you like some ~? / Please try some ~. / Please go ahead. / (Please) help yourself.

M It was a wonderful dinner, Mom. I'm sure you are the best cook in the world.
W Thank you. Do you want ❶ _____ _____ _____, Eric?
M No, thanks. I've had enough.
W Okay, then now I'm going to ❷ _____ _____ _____.
M Is there anything I can help you with, Mom?
W No, it's okay. You just go to your room and do your homework.
M Mom, then I can ❸ _____ _____ _____ _____.
W Oh, really? Okay, that will be great.

16 숫자 정보 파악 – 날짜   영국식 발음 녹음

대화를 듣고, 여자가 여행에서 돌아오는 날짜를 고르시오.

① August 6th   ② August 7th
③ August 8th   ④ August 9th
⑤ August 10th

😋 허가 여부 묻기 //////////////////////

I wonder if I could ~. / Do you mind if I could ~? / Is it okay(all right) if I could ~?

M Star Travel Agency.
W Hi, I wonder if I could ❶ _____ _____ _____ of my flight.
M Let me check. Your name, please?
W Judy Park.
M Okay. You're leaving for Sydney on August 6 and coming back on August 10.
W Yes, I was going to, but ❷ _____ _____ _____ _____ _____ on August 9.
M Hold on, please. (*pause*) Yes, you can change your flight.
W Thank you.

---

 14 **junk food** 정크푸드(인스턴트 음식이나 패스트푸드) **probably** 아마 **high-calorie** 고열량의 **sugar-rich** 당분이 많은   15 **wonderful** 훌륭한 **waste** 쓰레기   16 **travel agency** 여행사

17 알맞은 응답 찾기

대화를 듣고, 남자의 마지막 말에 대한 여자의 응답으로 가장 적절한 것을 고르시오.

Woman: _____

① You can do it, Dad.
② Please buy me a bike, Dad.
③ I rode a bike last week, Dad.
④ Okay. I'll try tomorrow, Dad.
⑤ Where were you just a minute ago, Dad?

🗨 격려하기 ////////////////////////////
Don't give up! / You'll do better next time. /
That's all right. / You can do it!

W Dad, I don't think I can ride a bike any more.
M Just _____ _____ _____ _____, Dorothy. You can do it.
W Oh, no, Dad. I'm so scared.
M ❷ _____ _____ _____, honey.
W I think I should stop it for now.
M All right. Maybe ❸ _____ _____ _____ _____.
W It's very hard to ride a bike. I thought it would be easy.
M Don't give up, honey. You'll do better next time.

18 알맞은 응답 찾기

대화를 듣고, 여자의 마지막 말에 대한 남자의 응답으로 가장 적절한 것을 고르시오.

Man: _____

① I had a lot of fun, too.
② I think that would be great.
③ My grandparents live in the city.
④ I have never been to another country.
⑤ I like the mountains better than the ocean.

M How was your vacation?
W I had ❶ _____ _____ _____ _____. I stayed at my grandparents' all vacation.
M Where do they live?
W In Busan. They live ❷ _____ _____ _____. I played by the sea every day.
M It sounds like you had a lot of fun. I envy you. My vacation was boring.
W Maybe you ❸ _____ _____ _____ _____ next summer.

19 알맞은 응답 찾기

대화를 듣고, 남자의 마지막 말에 대한 여자의 응답으로 가장 적절한 것을 고르시오.

Woman: _____

① I'll keep my fingers crossed.
② I don't need a new backpack.
③ Where do you think the shop is?
④ I don't know where N Seoul Tower is.
⑤ I would like to go, but I already have plans.

W What do you think of my new backpack?
M It looks good on you. ❶ _____ _____ _____ buy it?
W I bought it at the souvenir shop at N Seoul Tower.
M I didn't know they sell backpacks, too.
W Why don't we ❷ _____ _____ _____ sometime? It's a nice place to look around and there are good restaurants, too.
M Sounds great. How about ❸ _____ _____?

20 상황에 맞는 말 찾기

다음 상황 설명을 듣고, 유진이가 친구에게 할 말로 가장 적절한 것을 고르시오.

Yujin: _____

① Why don't you come back to Japan?
② When does your piano concert begin?
③ Have you ever traveled to Japan by yourself?
④ How much was the ticket you bought for me the other day?
⑤ Can you help me make a reservation on the Japanese website?

W Yujin is planning to ❶ _____ _____ _____. During her trip, a piano concert by Yuhki Kuramoto is going to be held in Tokyo. She really wants to ❷ _____ _____ _____. However, the website provides information in Japanese only, so she ❸ _____ _____ _____ _____. She calls her friend who is good at Japanese. In this situation, what would Yujin most likely say to her friend?

Ⓦords **17 scared** 무서운 **for now** 현재로는 **18 vacation** 방학 **nearby** 인근에, 가까운 곳에 **seashore** 해안 **19 souvenir shop** 기념품 가게
sometime 언젠가 **20 provide** 제공하다 **make a reservation** 예약하다

11회 영어 듣기모의고사

맞은 개수 /20문항

01 다음을 듣고, 어떤 운동 경기에 대한 중계방송인지 고르시오.

①  ②   ③

④  ⑤

02 대화를 듣고, 여자가 남자에게 전화한 목적으로 가장 적절한 것을 고르시오.

① 책을 정리해 주려고
② 음료 구입을 부탁하려고
③ 늦은 귀가를 경고하려고
④ 화장실 휴지를 사다 달라고
⑤ 휴식 시간을 갖게 해 주려고

03 대화를 듣고, 여자가 가고자 하는 곳을 고르시오.

04 대화를 듣고, 두 사람이 내일 오후 2시에 있을 장소를 고르시오.

① 학교   ② 영화관   ③ 공원
④ 동물원   ⑤ 식당

05 대화를 듣고, 여자의 직업을 고르시오.

① artist   ② author   ③ doctor
④ actress   ⑤ musician

06 대화를 듣고, 두 사람의 관계로 가장 적절한 것을 고르시오.

① banker – client
② doctor – patient
③ teacher – student
④ cashier – customer
⑤ mailman – housekeeper

07 다음을 듣고, 두 사람의 대화가 <u>어색한</u> 것을 고르시오.

①   ②   ③   ④   ⑤

08 대화를 듣고, 여자가 남자에게 부탁한 일로 가장 적절한 것을 고르시오.

① 박물관까지 데려다주기
② 박물관으로 데리러 오기
③ 여자가 써 놓은 메모 찾기
④ 박물관 직원에게 문자 보내기
⑤ 박물관으로 가는 버스 정보 알려 주기

09 대화를 듣고, 남자의 마지막 말에 담긴 의도로 가장 적절한 것을 고르시오.

① 감사   ② 격려   ③ 동의
④ 설득   ⑤ 위로

10 대화를 듣고, 남자가 지불할 금액을 고르시오.

① $35   ② $40   ③ $45
④ $50   ⑤ $55

11 대화를 듣고, 두 사람이 대화하는 장소로 가장 적절한 것을 고르시오.

① bank ② library ③ restaurant
④ bookstore ⑤ grocery store

12 다음을 듣고, 학교를 방문하는 손님들에 관해 언급되지 않은 것을 고르시오.

① 방문 기간 ② 출신 고등학교
③ 총 방문 인원 ④ 도착 시간
⑤ 방문 기간 동안 할 일

13 대화를 듣고, 음악회에 대한 설명으로 옳지 않은 것을 고르시오.

Summer Concert
① Performer: Seoul Orchestra
② When: July 28th, 29th
③ Where: White Art Center
④ Fee: R – $20 / S – $15 / A – $10
⑤ Age limit:
Children under 5 not admitted

14 다음을 듣고, 무엇에 관한 설명인지 고르시오.

① 해 ② 별 ③ 구름
④ 달 ⑤ 무지개

15 대화를 듣고, 두 사람이 오늘 오후에 할 일로 가장 적절한 것을 고르시오.

① 책 읽기 ② 낚시하기
③ 휴식 취하기 ④ 소풍 가기
⑤ 쇼핑하러 가기

16 대화를 듣고, 두 사람이 만날 시각을 고르시오.

① 5:30 ② 5:40 ③ 6:00 ④ 6:30 ⑤ 7:00

17 다음 상황 설명을 듣고, Judy가 아버지께 할 말로 가장 적절한 것을 고르시오.

Judy: _____

① That would be really nice.
② I do not like flowers that much.
③ I'm afraid that I don't need to go.
④ Is it okay for me to go to the market?
⑤ Can you go to the flower market with me?

18 대화를 듣고, 남자가 할 일로 가장 적절한 것을 고르시오.

① 최신 모델 검색하기
② 잃어버린 이어폰 찾기
③ 여자에게 이어폰 빌리기
④ 블루투스 이어폰 구매하기
⑤ 여자에게 이어폰 빌려주기

19 대화를 듣고, 남자의 마지막 말에 대한 여자의 응답으로 가장 적절한 것을 고르시오.

Woman: _____

① I hope you can get a new one.
② Oh, great! It couldn't be better.
③ That's okay. These things happen.
④ It's kind of you to do that for me.
⑤ No problem. I can do better next time.

20 대화를 듣고, 여자의 마지막 말에 대한 남자의 응답으로 가장 적절한 것을 고르시오.

Man: _____

① I think that's a great idea.
② I wish I could get a discount.
③ Sure. How much of a discount do you give?
④ Yes. Make sure you show your card to our clerk.
⑤ No, you are supposed to bring your own shopping basket.

Dictation Test 11회 영어 듣기모의고사

01 그림 정보 파악 – 운동 경기

다음을 듣고, 어떤 운동 경기에 대한 중계방송인지 고르시오.

① ② ③

④ ⑤

M Here we are in the Olympic Stadium. The ❶_____ _____ Ted Johnson from England ❷_____ _____ _____ _____. The height of the bar is at 2.30 meters. Now he begins his last try. And he jumps! Oh! He crashes into the bar. ❸_____ _____ _____ _____. Is he hurt? No, he's all right. He's getting up and walking away, but he looks very disappointed.

02 목적 파악

대화를 듣고, 여자가 남자에게 전화한 목적으로 가장 적절한 것을 고르시오.

① 책을 정리해 주려고
② 음료 구입을 부탁하려고
③ 늦은 귀가를 경고하려고
④ 화장실 휴지를 사다 달라고
⑤ 휴식 시간을 갖게 해 주려고

[Telephone rings.]

M Hello?

W Brian, are you still at the store?

M Yes. I've picked up the beverages. Why? Do you need something else?

W Yes. I've just found we're almost ❶_____ _____ _____ _____. Can you buy some?

M No problem. What are you doing now? ❷_____ _____ _____ me to go home immediately?

W No. it's okay. I'm arranging my books on the shelf. This is ❸_____ _____ _____ _____.

M Before I go home, I'll look around the sportswear section for a while. Don't work too hard.

W Okay. I'll see you when you get home.

03 그림 정보 파악 – 길 찾기

대화를 듣고, 여자가 가고자 하는 곳을 고르시오.

☺ 감사에 답하기
No problem. / You're welcome. / (It was) my pleasure. / Don't mention it.

W Excuse me, do you know how to get to Renaissance Hotel?

M Oh, I'm staying at the hotel. I can show you the way. ❶_____ _____ _____ _____ and turn left. Oh, no, turn right.

W Go straight one block and turn right. Then?

M Go straight one more block and ❷_____ _____. It'll ❸_____ _____ _____ _____.

W I see. Thank you so much for your help.

M No problem.

Words 01 crash into ~와 충돌하다 bar 막대, 바 02 beverage 음료 be out of ~이 떨어지다 toilet paper 화장실 휴지 immediately 즉시, 바로 arrange 정리하다 section 부분, 부문 03 stay 머물다

04 　장소 추론　영국식 발음 녹음

대화를 듣고, 두 사람이 내일 오후 2시에 있을 장소를 고르시오.

① 학교　　② 영화관　　③ 공원
④ 동물원　　⑤ 식당

😊 **의도 묻기** ////////////////////////////

What are you planning to ~? / What are you going to ~? / What are you thinking of ~? / What will you ~?

W What are you planning to do after the school drawing contest tomorrow?

M ❶ _____ _____.

W Let's go to see a movie.

M Cool. Shall we book a ticket now?

W Let's do it. How about *Star Trek Into Darkness* at 2 o'clock?

M Are you kidding? We'll be at the park by that time.

W Really? Aren't we ❷ _____ _____ _____ drawing pictures around noon?

M No, we'll draw pictures in the morning, and have lunch at noon. And then we'll spend time ❸ _____ _____ _____ _____ _____ _____.

W I see. Let's see a movie at 4.

05 　직업 및 장래 희망

대화를 듣고, 여자의 직업을 고르시오.

① artist　　② author　　③ doctor
④ actress　　⑤ musician

😊 **소개에 답하기** ////////////////////////////

(It's) nice(good) to meet you. / (I'm) pleased to meet you. / It's a pleasure to meet you. / I've been looking forward to meeting you.

M Nice to meet you, Ms. Choi.

W Hello, and thanks for inviting me.

M We're happy to have you on this show. I read ❶ _____ _____ _____. The storyline was touching and creative.

W I'm glad you liked it.

M Could you tell us how you ❷ _____ _____ _____?

W People usually think fairy tales are only for children, but they're not. We all long for fairy tales from the heart.

M That's why you ❸ _____ _____ _____ _____ for adults.

W That's right.

06 　관계 추론

대화를 듣고, 두 사람의 관계로 가장 적절한 것을 고르시오.

① banker – client
② doctor – patient
③ teacher – student
④ cashier – customer
⑤ mailman – housekeeper

M May I help you?

W I'd like to ❶ _____ _____ _____ _____ _____.

M Wow, you've gathered lots of coins. Let me put these coins into the machine and see ❷ _____ _____ _____ _____ _____.

W How long will it take?

M It'll take less than two minutes. *(beep)* It's done. They're worth $45.

W Wow, it's more ❸ _____ _____ _____. Thanks.

M You're welcome.

📖 **Words**　**04 drawing contest** 사생 대회　**book** 예매하다　**05 storyline** 줄거리　**touching** 감동적인　**creative** 창의적인　**long for** 갈망하다　**from the heart** 진심으로　**06 bill** 지폐　**gather** 모으다　**machine** 기계　**worth** (몇 원) 어치

Dictation Test

07 어색한 대화 찾기

다음을 듣고, 두 사람의 대화가 <u>어색한</u> 것을 고르시오.

①   ②   ③   ④   ⑤

① **W** Could you be quiet? You're being too loud.

   M Am I? I'm sorry.

② **W** Aren't you hungry?

   M I'm starving. I want to eat something.

③ **W** Is it ❶ _____ _____ _____ _____ the theater now?

   M The theater is next to the fire station.

④ **W** Did you ❷ _____ _____ _____ at the restaurant?

   M No, I was so busy. Could you do it for me?

⑤ **W** Please tell me your ❸ _____ _____ _____.

   M Wait. I'll have to check. I haven't memorized it.

08 부탁한 일 파악   영국식 발음 녹음

대화를 듣고, 여자가 남자에게 부탁한 일로 가장 적절한 것을 고르시오.

① 박물관까지 데려다주기
② 박물관으로 데리러 오기
③ 여자가 써 놓은 메모 찾기
④ 박물관 직원에게 문자 보내기
⑤ 박물관으로 가는 버스 정보 알려 주기

[*Telephone rings.*]

M Hello?

W Dad, it's me.

M Sarah? You just stepped out. What's up?

W Well, I'm on my way to the national museum but I forgot which bus I ❶ _____ _____. Could you let me know?

M Wait a second. I'll ❷ _____ _____ _____ on my smartphone.

W I wrote it down somewhere, but I can't remember where.

M That happens. Do you want me to drive you there if you are in a hurry?

W No, it's okay. I have plenty of time.

M Okay. I'll send you a text message ❸ _____ _____ _____ _____.   **W** Okay. Thank you.

09 의도 파악

대화를 듣고, 남자의 마지막 말에 담긴 의도로 가장 적절한 것을 고르시오.

① 감사   ② 격려   ③ 동의
④ 설득   ⑤ 위로

M Let's go to an Internet cafe.

W Maybe next time. I'm going home.

M ❶ _____ _____ _____ _____ home so early? Do you have something to do?

W I should finish my history report today.

M But there's still a week before the due date.

W I tend to try to finish assignments ❷ _____ _____ _____ _____. I feel more relaxed when I can take a rest after getting important things done.

M I think ❸ _____ _____ _____ _____. Maybe I should do the same.

Words   **07 starve** 굶주리다   **bank account number** 은행 계좌번호   **memorize** 외우다   **08 step out** 나가다   **look up** 찾아보다   **09 due date** 제출일, 마감일   **assignment** 과제   **as ~ as possible** 가능한 한 ~하게

10 숫자 정보 파악 – 금액

대화를 듣고, 남자가 지불할 금액을 고르시오.

① $35 　　② $40 　　③ $45

④ $50 　　⑤ $55

🔊 선호에 대해 묻기 ////////////////////////

Which one do you prefer, A or B? / Which do you like better, A or B? / Do you like A better than B? / Do you prefer A to B?

M Hi, I want to buy a toy for my 3-year-old cousin.

W Kids that age love blocks or dolls. Which one do you prefer?

M ❶ _____ _____ _____ _____. How much are they?

W They're $50, but you can get a 10% discount if you have a coupon.

M Is this the coupon I can use?

W Let me see. Oh, ❷ _____ _____ _____ this coupon ❸ _____ _____. See? It was until last month.

M I see. I'll take the blocks anyway.

---

11 장소 추론 　영국식 발음 녹음

대화를 듣고, 두 사람이 대화하는 장소로 가장 적절한 것을 고르시오.

① bank 　　② library 　　③ restaurant

④ bookstore 　　⑤ grocery store

M What are you reading?

W It's a ❶ _____ _____ _____.

M Is there something interesting about them?

W Yes. Did you know that some bananas have hard seeds inside?

M Really? That's interesting.

W Yeah, I like this book. I'd ❷ _____ _____ _____ _____.

M If I were you, I would go to the library and borrow the book.

W Well, I like buying books. I'll be right back after ❸ _____ _____ _____.

---

12 언급되지 않은 것

다음을 듣고, 학교를 방문하는 손님들에 관해 언급되지 않은 것을 고르시오.

① 방문 기간 　　② 출신 고등학교

③ 총 방문 인원 　　④ 도착 시간

⑤ 방문 기간 동안 할 일

W Good morning. This is the principal speaking. Do you remember when your class visited a school in Hong Kong last year? ❶ _____ _____ _____ _____, we are going to have some special guests visiting our school. ❷ _____ _____ _____ _____ _____ Saint Mark's School in Hong Kong. We expect them to arrive at 9 this morning. They will ❸ _____ _____ _____ _____, and have lunch with you. Please make them feel welcome, and help them enjoy their week at our school.

Words　**10 discount** 할인 **coupon** 쿠폰, 할인권 **anyway** 어쨌든　**11 hard** 딱딱한 **seed** 씨, 씨앗 **inside** 안쪽에　**12 principal** 교장 **expect** 기대하다

Dictation Test

13 도표 정보 파악

대화를 듣고, 음악회에 대한 설명으로 옳지 <u>않은</u> 것을 고르시오.

Summer Concert
① Performer: Seoul Orchestra
② When: July 28th, 29th
③ Where: White Art Center
④ Fee: R – $20 / S – $15 / A – $10
⑤ Age limit:
　Children under 5 not admitted

😊 (도움) 제안, 권유, 요청에 답하기 ////////////
(That) sounds good. / No problem. / All right! /
Sure! / Yes!

M Did you finish the music homework?
W Not yet. I haven't decided _____ _____ _____ _____ to.
M How about going to the concert by Seoul Orchestra together?
W 😊 Sounds good. When and where is the concert?
M It's held on July 28th and 29th at White Art Center.
W The 29th ❷_____ _____ _____ with me. How much is the fee?
M Tickets are $20 for R seats, $15 for S seats and $12 for A seats.
W An A seat is good for me. By the way, I want to take my little sister with me. Is there an age limit?
M Yes. Children ❸_____ _____ _____ _____ _____ cannot enter the hall.

14 주제 파악

다음을 듣고, 무엇에 관한 설명인지 고르시오.
① 해　　　② 별　　　③ 구름
④ 달　　　⑤ 무지개

M You can see this in the sky. It's the gathering of small waterdrops in the air. Its color changes ❶_____ _____ _____ _____. For example, its color becomes red at sunset, and it becomes dark blue at night. Also, when it ❷_____ _____, you can guess that you'll ❸_____ _____ _____.

15 한 일 / 할 일 파악

대화를 듣고, 두 사람이 오늘 오후에 할 일로 가장 적절한 것을 고르시오.
① 책 읽기　　　② 낚시하기
③ 휴식 취하기　　　④ 소풍 가기
⑤ 쇼핑하러 가기

M Hi, Monica. Tell me what you are going to do this afternoon.
W I'm not sure. I'll ❶_____ _____ _____ and read a book. How about you?
M Well, I'm planning to go fishing. Would you like to join me?
W Sure. I'd be happy to. ❷_____ _____ sounds a lot more exciting than reading a book at home.
M Good! I'll ❸_____ _____ _____ at around 1 o'clock.
W See you then.

16 숫자 정보 파악 – 시각　영국식 발음 녹음

대화를 듣고, 두 사람이 만날 시각을 고르시오.
① 5:30　② 5:40　③ 6:00　④ 6:30　⑤ 7:00

🅿 make it at의 발음 ////////////////////////////
make it at은 자음 [k]와 모음 [i]가 연결되어 발음되고, it의 [t]는 모음 사이에서 부드러운 [r]소리로 발음된다.

M What time shall we meet for the basketball game tomorrow?
W What time does ❶_____ _____ _____?
M It starts at 7 p.m. How about meeting at 6:30 at the bus stop?
W There will be a traffic jam then. Why don't we 🅿 make it at 5:30?
M Well, my piano lesson finishes at 5:30. It'll ❷_____ _____ _____ _____ to get to the bus stop.
W Alright. See you at 5:40. I'll buy hamburgers and then go to the bus stop.　M Cool.

📖 Words　**13 fee** 요금　**age limit** 나이 제한　**14 waterdrop** 물방울　**sunset** 해 질 녘　**guess** 추측하다　**15 pick up** ~을 태우러 가다　**16 lesson** 수업　**finish** 끝나다, 끝내다

17 상황에 맞는 말 찾기

다음 상황 설명을 듣고, Judy가 아버지께 할 말로 가장 적절한 것을 고르시오.

Judy: _____

① That would be really nice.
② I do not like flowers that much.
③ I'm afraid that I don't need to go.
④ Is it okay for me to go to the market?
⑤ Can you go to the flower market with me?

W One of Judy's friends told her about a flower market that opens ❶ _____ _____. Judy wants to go have a look at the market, but she is worried about going there alone so late at night. Moreover, there's ❷ _____ _____ _____ at midnight, so Judy doesn't know how she can get there and come home. Judy hopes her father ❸ _____ _____ _____ there. In this situation, what would Judy most likely say to her father?

18 한 일 / 할 일 파악

대화를 듣고, 남자가 할 일로 가장 적절한 것을 고르시오.
① 최신 모델 검색하기
② 잃어버린 이어폰 찾기
③ 여자에게 이어폰 빌리기
④ 블루투스 이어폰 구매하기
⑤ 여자에게 이어폰 빌려주기

W What are you searching for?
M I'm searching for ❶ _____ _____. They look very cool and convenient.
W They need to be charged often. They are also quite easy to lose.
M But take a look at this pair. This is the latest model, and they look so cool.
W Okay, ❷ _____ _____ _____ first for a few days. Then you can decide whether to buy them or not.
M That's a great idea. Don't you use them often?
W Not really. I like my old ones better. I'll bring them tomorrow.
M Thank you so much.

19 알맞은 응답 찾기

대화를 듣고, 남자의 마지막 말에 대한 여자의 응답으로 가장 적절한 것을 고르시오.

Woman: _____

① I hope you can get a new one.
② Oh, great! It couldn't be better.
③ That's okay. These things happen.
④ It's kind of you to do that for me.
⑤ No problem. I can do better next time.

😊 유감이나 동정 표현하기 ////////////////////////
That's too bad. / I'm (so) sorry to hear that. /
That's a pity(shame).

M Hi, Helen. I'm sorry I'm late.
W What happened to you?
M I lost my bag. I left it ❶ _____ _____ _____.
W 😊 That's too bad. So, what did you do about it?
M I went to the Lost and Found in the subway station and reported it.
W Good idea! I hope you find it.
M I hope so. Anyway, I'm really sorry ❷ _____ _____ _____ _____ so long.

20 알맞은 응답 찾기

대화를 듣고, 여자의 마지막 말에 대한 남자의 응답으로 가장 적절한 것을 고르시오.

Man: _____

① I think that's a great idea.
② I wish I could get a discount.
③ Sure. How much of a discount do you give?
④ Yes. Make sure you show your card to our clerk.
⑤ No, you are supposed to bring your own shopping basket.

M How do you like the teas in our shop?
W Well, I'm ❶ _____ _____ with them.
M Thank you. Would you visit us again?
W Of course. Can I get ❷ _____ _____ _____?
M Yes. Write down your name here and sign next to it.
W Okay. Can I ❸ _____ _____ _____ with this?

ⓦords 　**17 midnight** 자정, 한밤중 **moreover** 게다가, 더욱이 **public transportation** 대중 교통 　**18 Bluetooth** 블루투스(전자 기기의 무선 연결 기법) **convenient** 편리한, 간편한 **charge** 충전하다 **latest** 최신의 　**19 Lost and Found** 분실물 취급소 　**20 write down** 쓰다

01 대화를 듣고, 남자가 온라인으로 주문한 물건이 <u>아닌</u> 것을 고르시오.

①   ②   ③

④   ⑤

02 대화를 듣고, 여자가 뉴욕에 간 목적으로 가장 적절한 것을 고르시오.

① 관광을 하려고
② 영어를 배우려고
③ 회의에 참석하려고
④ 병을 치료받으려고
⑤ 여동생을 방문하려고

03 다음 그림의 상황에 가장 적절한 대화를 고르시오.

① ② ③ ④ ⑤

04 대화를 듣고, 두 사람이 만나기로 한 장소를 고르시오.

① 식당
② 학교 앞
③ 가구 코너
④ 지하철역
⑤ 백화점 정문

05 대화를 듣고, 남자의 직업으로 가장 적절한 것을 고르시오.

① painter
② art teacher
③ designer
④ photographer
⑤ tour guide

06 대화를 듣고, 여자의 심정으로 가장 적절한 것을 고르시오.

① excited
② relaxed
③ annoyed
④ tired
⑤ disappointed

07 다음을 듣고, 두 사람의 대화가 <u>어색한</u> 것을 고르시오.

① ② ③ ④ ⑤

08 대화를 듣고, 여자가 남자에게 부탁한 일로 가장 적절한 것을 고르시오.

① 우산 사 주기
② 우산 빌려주기
③ 날씨 알려 주기
④ 집에 데려다주기
⑤ 상점에 데려다주기

09 대화를 듣고, 여자의 마지막 말에 담긴 의도로 가장 적절한 것을 고르시오.

① 비난
② 사과
③ 제안
④ 충고
⑤ 후회

10 대화를 듣고, 남자가 지불할 금액을 고르시오.

① $10
② $15
③ $25
④ $32
⑤ $37

11 대화를 듣고, 두 사람이 대화하는 장소로 가장 적절한 곳을 고르시오.

① 집   ② 식당
③ 영화관   ④ 야구 경기장
⑤ 버스 정류장

12 다음을 듣고, Bingo에 관해 언급되지 <u>않은</u> 것을 고르시오.

① 이름   ② 나이
③ 크기   ④ 좋아하는 음식
⑤ 특기

13 대화를 듣고, 내용과 일치하지 <u>않는</u> 것을 고르시오.

Subject	① Chinese
Day of the week	② Monday and Wednesday
Where	③ Room 205
When	④ 3:40 p.m.
Preparation	⑤ Two textbooks

14 다음을 듣고, 무엇에 관한 설명인지 고르시오.

① 수자원의 종류   ② 에너지의 종류
③ 자원 재생 비용   ④ 청결 유지 방법
⑤ 수자원 절약 실천

15 대화를 듣고, 여자가 캄보디아에서 할 일로 가장 적절한 것을 고르시오.

① 빵 만들기   ② 친지 방문하기
③ 한국어 가르치기   ④ 앙코르와트 방문하기
⑤ 캄보디아어 공부하기

16 대화를 듣고, 남자가 병원을 예약한 시각을 고르시오.

① 2:30   ② 3:30
③ 2:30   ④ 3:00
⑤ 4:00

17 다음 상황 설명을 듣고, 진수가 여자에게 할 말로 가장 적절한 것을 고르시오.

Jinsu: _____

① Can I give you a hand?
② Could you help me carry the bag?
③ I'd like to get a refund for this bag.
④ I wish your baby didn't cry so much.
⑤ Please give it to me. It's my turn to pay.

18 대화를 듣고, 여자가 대화 직후에 할 일로 가장 적절한 것을 고르시오.

① 경찰서에 전화하기
② 차를 직접 수리하기
③ 보험 회사에 전화하기
④ 가까운 정비소에 가기
⑤ 가까운 주유소까지 걸어가기

19 대화를 듣고, 여자의 마지막 말에 대한 남자의 응답으로 가장 적절한 것을 고르시오.

Man: _____

① Well, I don't think so.
② You'll do better next time.
③ I also respect her very much.
④ I already read the article last week.
⑤ I think she should comeback soon.

20 대화를 듣고, 남자의 마지막 말에 대한 여자의 응답으로 가장 적절한 것을 고르시오.

Woman: _____

① I've never been to France.
② Thank you for your advice.
③ Why don't you become a musician?
④ I'm not interested in French lessons.
⑤ Of course. Let me listen to the song.

01 그림 정보 파악 – 사물

대화를 듣고, 남자가 온라인으로 주문한 물건이 <u>아닌</u> 것을 고르시오.

① ② ③ ④ ⑤

W Sam, you look great today.
M Thank you. I did some ❶_____ _____.
W I like your shoes. Which site did you buy them on?
M I bought them from GD shopping mall. I also got ❷_____ _____ _____ _____.
W How about the others? Did you also order ❸_____ _____ _____ _____ _____?
M Yes, but this watch is a birthday present from my father.
W That goes very well with your shirt.

02 목적 파악

대화를 듣고, 여자가 뉴욕에 간 목적으로 가장 적절한 것을 고르시오.

① 관광을 하려고
② 영어를 배우려고
③ 회의에 참석하려고
④ 병을 치료받으려고
⑤ 여동생을 방문하려고

😮 모르고 있음 표현하기 ///////////////////////
I have no idea. / I haven't got a clue. / I don't know.

[Telephone rings.]
M Hello?
W Hi, Kevin. It's Linda. I'm calling from New York.
M Really? When did you go there?
W I came here yesterday ❶_____ _____ _____ _____. She came here alone to study.
M Oh, I had no idea. How is she doing there?
W She's fine, but ❷_____ _____ _____ _____.
M I hope you'll ❸_____ _____ _____ _____ with your sister there.
W I will. Bye-bye!

03 그림 상황에 어울리는 대화 찾기

다음 그림의 상황에 가장 적절한 대화를 고르시오.

① ② ③ ④ ⑤

① M Are you going to the library?
   W Yes. I am going to ❶_____ _____ _____.
② M How did you like this book?
   W I haven't finished it yet.
③ M Did you say ❷_____ _____ _____ _____ you borrowed last week?
   W I'm sorry. It's all my fault.
④ M Whose book is this?
   W Oh, that's mine. I've been looking everywhere for it.
⑤ M Do you have any good e-books?
   W Yes, I do. ❸_____ _____ _____ _____ this one.

Words 01 go well with ~와 잘 어울리다 02 alone 혼자서, 홀로 thin 야윈, 마른 03 look everywhere 곳곳을 살피다

04 장소 추론 영국식 발음 녹음

대화를 듣고, 두 사람이 만나기로 한 장소를 고르시오.

① 식당   ② 학교 앞
③ 가구 코너   ④ 지하철역
⑤ 백화점 정문

W Brian, do you remember that we are going shopping for your new bed today, right?

M Of course. Will we meet in front of the school?

W No. Your school is close to the department store. See you there at 4.

M ❶ _____ _____ _____ to wait for you at the subway station?

W You don't need to. Let's meet at the entrance of the department store.

M I think it would be better if you look around the furniture first. Let's meet ❷ _____ _____ _____ _____ on the 8th floor.

W That's a great idea. If it doesn't take too long to find a bed, ❸ _____ _____ _____ your favorite sushi bar after.

M Sounds perfect.

05 직업 및 장래 희망

대화를 듣고, 남자의 직업으로 가장 적절한 것을 고르시오.

① painter   ② art teacher
③ designer   ④ photographer
⑤ tour guide

😮 궁금증 표현하기

I'm curious about ~. / I wonder ~. / I'd be interested to know ~. / Can someone tell me about ~?

W Wow! Did you take all these pictures?

M Sure. They are the ones that ❶ _____ _____ _____ this time.

W They are really fantastic pictures.

M Thank you. ❷ _____ _____ _____ _____ _____, I make every effort to get the best scene.

W Great. I'm curious about ❸ _____ _____ _____ _____ _____.

M I took them at various places in Paris.

W They're wonderful! I want to go to Paris sometime.

06 심정 파악

대화를 듣고, 여자의 심정으로 가장 적절한 것을 고르시오.

① excited   ② relaxed
③ annoyed   ④ tired
⑤ disappointed

W What are you going to do after school?

M ❶ _____ _____ _____ _____ ice cream with Minsu. There is a famous ice cream shop around his place.

W Wow, I really like ice cream. Can I go with you?

M Sure. The shop is very popular, so we can't have any if we're late.

W ❷ _____ _____ _____. When shall we meet?

M Let's meet right after school.

W Then, I'll go to your classroom ❸ _____ _____ _____.

M Fine. See you then.

Words **04** in front of ~의 앞에 department store 백화점 look around 둘러보다 furniture 가구 **05** make every effort 온갖 노력을 다하다 scene 장면, 현장 **06** place 장소, 집 popular 인기 있는

Dictation Test

07 어색한 대화 찾기

다음을 듣고, 두 사람의 대화가 <u>어색한</u> 것을 고르시오.

①   ②   ③   ④   ⑤

① **W** How do you like his new album?
   M I like it a lot.
② **W** I think you ❶_____ _____ _____ again.
   M Okay. I'll come early.
③ **W** When is the bus supposed to come?
   M The bus stop is ❷_____ _____ _____.
④ **W** What would you like to have?
   M I'll have coffee.
⑤ **W** What do you hope to do this vacation?
   M I ❸_____ _____ _____ my e-pal in Japan.

08 부탁한 일 파악   영국식 발음 녹음

대화를 듣고, 여자가 남자에게 부탁한 일로 가장 적절한 것을 고르시오.

① 우산 사 주기   ② 우산 빌려주기
③ 날씨 알려 주기   ④ 집에 데려다주기
⑤ 상점에 데려다주기

W Oh, it's raining outside. Do you have an umbrella?
M Yes, I do. Don't you?
W No, ❶_____ _____ _____ _____.
M Then I'll walk home with you today. We can share mine.
W Would you take me to ❷_____ _____ _____ _____?
M Sure. Are you going to buy a new one?
W Yes, ❸_____ _____ _____ _____ one. Thank you.

09 의도 파악

대화를 듣고, 여자의 마지막 말에 담긴 의도로 가장 적절한 것을 고르시오.

① 비난   ② 사과   ③ 제안
④ 충고   ⑤ 후회

😊 **주제 바꾸기**

By the way, ~. / Let's move on to ~. / I'd like to say something else ~.

M Your presentation was great. It was so impressive.
W Thank you for ❶_____ _____ _____ _____. I couldn't have done it without you.
M Yes, you could have. I know how hard you worked on it.
W Thanks. 😊 By the way, aren't you hungry?
M Yeah, I'm hungry. It's time for dinner.
W ❷_____ _____ _____ the new restaurant in front of this building.
M That's a great idea. I really want to try the food there.
W Please ❸_____ _____ _____ _____ today. I need to thank you.

Words   **07 e-pal** 이메일 친구   **08 outside** 밖에, 밖에서   **share** 함께 쓰다, 공유하다   **09 presentation** 발표, 프레젠테이션   **impressive** 인상적인, 인상[감명] 깊은

10 숫자 정보 파악 – 금액

대화를 듣고, 남자가 지불할 금액을 고르시오.

① $10　　② $15　　③ $25
④ $32　　⑤ $37

W Good morning. How may I help you, sir?

M Well, _____ _____ _____ _____ some flowers for my daughter.

W How about these red roses?　　M I like them. How much are they?

W $15 for a bunch. How about some purple pansies to go with them? These are only $10.

M Oh, that's a good idea. I'll take them both. Can you ❷_____ _____ _____ with the flowers?

W Yes, we can. But it will cost an extra $7 ❸_____ _____ _____ _____.

M That's fine. Please make a pretty bouquet.　　W No problem.

11 장소 추론

대화를 듣고, 두 사람이 대화하는 장소로 가장 적절한 곳을 고르시오.

① 서점　　　　② 식당
③ 영화관　　　④ 야구 경기장
⑤ 버스 정류장

M Minji, I'm very sorry to be late.

W Oh, James. That's all right. I was reading a book. Are we going to ❶_____ _____ _____ now?

M Well, don't you think there are too many people here? People are waiting in a long line ❷_____ _____ _____.

W Yeah. Tickets for popular movies are already sold out.

M Why don't we ❸_____ _____ _____ _____ first? We'd better see a movie after dinner.

W That's a great idea. Let's have a delicious dinner together.

M Sounds good.

12 언급되지 않은 것

다음을 듣고, Bingo에 관해 언급되지 않은 것을 고르시오.

① 이름　　　　② 나이
③ 크기　　　　④ 좋아하는 음식
⑤ 특기

M Let me introduce ❶_____ _____ _____, Bingo. Bingo is a 2-year-old poodle with brown hair. He likes to walk a lot, so I go walking with Bingo every night if it doesn't rain. ❷_____ _____ _____, but I take care not to give him too many. He can ❸_____ _____ _____ _____. When I hold out my hand, Bingo puts his paw on it. He's really cute and smart. You can play with Bingo if you come to my place.

13 도표 정보 파악　영국식 발음 녹음

대화를 듣고, 내용과 일치하지 않는 것을 고르시오.

Subject	① Chinese
Day of the week	② Monday and Wednesday
Where	③ Room 205
When	④ 3:40 p.m.
Preparation	⑤ Two textbooks

M Mary, I want to take an after-school Chinese class. Do you know on what days of the week the classes are?

W They're ❶_____ _____ _____ _____.

M I see. Oh, I don't know where and what time I should go.

W ❷_____ _____ _____ _____ room 205 at 3:40 p.m.

M Do we have to buy textbooks?

W No, ❸_____ _____ _____ for this class, so you don't need to buy anything.

M Sounds good. Thank you for the information.

Words **10 bunch** 다발 **go with** 어울리다 **bouquet** 꽃다발 **extra** 여분의, 추가의 **11 all right** 괜찮은 **sold out** 표가 매진된 **12 trick** 재주, 요술; 묘기 **hold out** (손 등을) 내밀다 **paw** (동물의) 발 **13 after-school** 방과 후의 **textbook** 교재

Dictation Test

14 주제 파악

다음을 듣고, 무엇에 관한 설명인지 고르시오.

① 수자원의 종류
② 에너지의 종류
③ 자원 재생 비용
④ 청결 유지 방법
⑤ 수자원 절약 실천

W Everyone knows we are supposed ❶ _____ _____ _____. However, do you really practice it? Lots of people don't think that we have to save water. They say we have plenty of water to use. Yes, there is lots of water around us, but ❷ _____ _____ _____ _____ is drinking water. It ❸ _____ _____ _____ to make water we can drink. To save water is to save energy.

15 한 일 / 할 일 파악

대화를 듣고, 여자가 캄보디아에서 할 일로 가장 적절한 것을 고르시오.

① 빵 만들기
② 친지 방문하기
③ 한국어 가르치기
④ 앙코르와트 방문하기
⑤ 캄보디아어 공부하기

😊 **설명 요청하기** //////////////////////////
What do you mean by ~? / Could you explain ~? / What is ~ (exactly)?

M What are you going to ❶ _____ _____ _____?
W I'm going to Cambodia this summer.
M Wow! I heard there are many places to see, like Angkor Wat.
W Yeah, I wish I could visit there, too.
M 😊 What do you mean by that?
W Actually, I will go there to ❷ _____ _____ _____. I don't think I will have time for sightseeing.
M You're really great. What are you going to do there?
W I'm going to ❸ _____ _____ _____ _____ _____.

16 숫자 정보 파악 – 시각   영국식 발음 녹음

대화를 듣고, 남자가 병원을 예약한 시각을 고르시오.

① 2:30
② 3:30
③ 2:30
④ 3:00
⑤ 4:00

W Dr. Han's office. May I help you?
M I need to have a physical check-up, so I'd like to ❶ _____ _____ _____ to see the doctor.
W When did you have your last check-up?
M I had a check-up about a year ago.
W I see. Can you come in on Monday at 2:30?
M Sorry, I ❷ _____ _____ _____ _____ _____.
W How about Tuesday at 2:30?
M Well, can I come ❸ _____ _____ _____ _____?
W Okay. See you then.

📒 Words   **14 practice** 실천하다 **plenty of** 많은 **drinking water** 식수   **15 mean** 의미하다 **sightseeing** 관광   **16 physical check-up** 건강 검진 **appointment** 약속

17 상황에 맞는 말 찾기

다음 상황 설명을 듣고, 진수가 여자에게 할 말로 가장 적절한 것을 고르시오.

Jinsu: _____

① Can I give you a hand?
② Could you help me carry the bag?
③ I'd like to get a refund for this bag.
④ I wish your baby didn't cry so much.
⑤ Please give it to me. It's my turn to pay.

W Jinsu was going to visit his grandmother in Busan. He got on the train and waited for the train to leave. Jinsu noticed a young lady who was trying to sit near him. She was ❶_____ _____ _____ and ❷_____ _____. At that moment, the baby began to cry and she looked so embarrassed. In this situation, what would Jinsu most likely say to her ❸_____ _____ _____?

18 한 일 / 할 일 파악

대화를 듣고, 여자가 대화 직후에 할 일로 가장 적절한 것을 고르시오.

① 경찰서에 전화하기
② 차를 직접 수리하기
③ 보험 회사에 전화하기
④ 가까운 정비소에 가기
⑤ 가까운 주유소까지 걸어가기

😮 능력 여부 묻기 /////////////////////
Don't(Do) you know how to ~? / Are you good at ~? / Can you ~?

W Why are we stopping? We're right in the middle of the street.
M ❶_____ _____ _____. The car stopped suddenly.
W Don't you know how to repair it?
M I don't know what the problem is. Oh, we ran out of gas.
W Oh, my! There is a ❷_____ _____ around here. I'll ❸_____ _____ _____ _____ _____.
M Okay. Then, I'll be here.

19 알맞은 응답 찾기

대화를 듣고, 여자의 마지막 말에 대한 남자의 응답으로 가장 적절한 것을 고르시오.

Man: _____

① Well, I don't think so.
② You'll do better next time.
③ I also respect her very much.
④ I already read the article last week.
⑤ I think she should comeback soon.

😮 의견 묻기 /////////////////////
What do you think of(about) ~? / How do you feel about ~? / What is your view(opinion) on ~?

M What are you reading?
W I'm reading a news article ❶_____ _____ _____ _____.
M Can you tell me more about it?
W She made money by gathering used cans and bottles. She was poor, but with the money ❷_____ _____ _____ _____ than her.
M Tell me more in detail.
W She ❸_____ _____ _____ _____ to poor people every year. Isn't she great? What do you think of her?

20 알맞은 응답 찾기

대화를 듣고, 남자의 마지막 말에 대한 여자의 응답으로 가장 적절한 것을 고르시오.

Woman: _____

① I've never been to France.
② Thank you for your advice.
③ Why don't you become a musician?
④ I'm not interested in French lessons.
⑤ Of course. Let me listen to the song.

M I'm going to ❶_____ _____ _____ in college.
W Do you really mean it? I can't believe it.
M What's so surprising?
W You always said that you were going to be a musician.
M You know, ❷_____ _____ _____. Anyway, I'm going to take French lessons in advance.
W What made you become a French lover?
M I was fascinated by the French language while listening to French songs. Would you like to listen to ❸_____ _____ _____?

Ⓦords **17 notice** 알아차리다 **begin** 시작하다 **embarrassed** 당황스러운 **18 suddenly** 갑자기 **repair** 수리하다 **run out of** ~을 다 써버리다 **19 article** 기사 **gather** 모으다 **in detail** 상세히, 자세히 **20 major in** ~을 전공하다 **in advance** 미리 **lover** 애호가

01 대화를 듣고, 두 사람이 체육 시간에 배운 동작을 고르시오.

①   ②   ③

④   ⑤

02 대화를 듣고, 여자가 남자에게 전화한 목적으로 가장 적절한 것을 고르시오.

① 식당을 예약하려고
② 물건을 반품하려고
③ 음식을 배달시키려고
④ 호텔 예약을 취소하려고
⑤ 영수증 발급을 요청하려고

03 대화를 듣고, 여자가 가고자 하는 곳을 고르시오.

04 대화를 듣고, 남자가 조별 모임을 할 수 없는 요일을 고르시오.

① 월요일   ② 화요일   ③ 수요일
④ 목요일   ⑤ 금요일

05 대화를 듣고, 여자의 직업으로 가장 적절한 것을 고르시오.

① chef   ② student
③ teacher   ④ tour guide
⑤ office worker

06 대화를 듣고, 여자의 심정으로 가장 적절한 것을 고르시오.

① annoyed   ② worried
③ relieved   ④ nervous
⑤ disappointed

07 다음을 듣고, 두 사람의 대화가 <u>어색한</u> 것을 고르시오.

①   ②   ③   ④   ⑤

08 대화를 듣고, 여자가 남자에게 부탁한 일로 가장 적절한 것을 고르시오.

① 함께 식사하기
② 먹을 것 사 오기
③ 숙제 가져다주기
④ 다이어트 도와주기
⑤ 과학 보고서 도와주기

09 대화를 듣고, 남자의 마지막 말에 담긴 의도로 가장 적절한 것을 고르시오.

① 충고   ② 칭찬   ③ 허락
④ 거절   ⑤ 기원

10 대화를 듣고, 여자가 거스름돈으로 받을 금액을 고르시오.

① $ 20   ② $ 40   ③ $ 60
④ $ 80   ⑤ $ 100

11 대화를 듣고, 두 사람이 대화하는 장소로 가장 적절한 곳을 고르시오.

① 호텔   ② 공연장   ③ 기차역
④ 가구점   ⑤ 관광 안내소

12 다음을 듣고, 좋은 독후감을 쓰는 방법으로 언급되지 않은 것을 고르시오.

① 책의 기본 정보 쓰기
② 세 문단 이상 쓰기
③ 책 내용 요약하기
④ 책 읽고 느낀 점 쓰기
⑤ 독서 후 하고 싶은 것 쓰기

13 대화를 듣고, 메시지 내용이 잘못된 것을 고르시오.

Telephone Message

To: ① Lisa
From: ② Michelle
Message: ③ The tea time has been ④ changed to this afternoon because of ⑤ the typhoon.

14 다음을 듣고, 무엇에 관한 설명인지 고르시오.

① 다리   ② 계단
③ 저울   ④ 엘리베이터
⑤ 에스컬레이터

15 대화를 듣고, 남자가 대화 직후에 할 일로 가장 적절한 것을 고르시오.

① 교무실 가기
② 친구에게 전화하기
③ 휴대 전화 사러 가기
④ 영어 숙제 하러 가기
⑤ 휴대 전화 수리하러 가기

16 대화를 듣고, 남자가 태어난 연도를 고르시오.

① 1998년   ② 1999년   ③ 2000년
④ 2001년   ⑤ 2002년

17 다음 상황 설명을 듣고, 민수가 점원에게 할 말로 가장 적절한 것을 고르시오.

Minsu: _____

① Would you say that again, please?
② What do you think of these strawberries?
③ Can I get a discount on the strawberries?
④ Which do you like better, strawberries or apples?
⑤ Can I buy apples instead of strawberries, please?

18 대화를 듣고, 남자가 오늘 방과 후에 할 일이 아닌 것을 고르시오.

① 숙제하기   ② 피자 만들기
③ 교실 청소하기   ④ 도서관에서 책 빌리기
⑤ 사촌 동생 데리러 가기

19 대화를 듣고, 여자의 마지막 말에 대한 남자의 응답으로 가장 적절한 것을 고르시오.

Man: _____

① You should apologize to them.
② You should not make a lot of noise.
③ You shouldn't play the piano at night.
④ I should spend more time with my kids.
⑤ I think you should go upstairs and tell them about that.

20 대화를 듣고, 남자의 마지막 말에 대한 여자의 응답으로 가장 적절한 것을 고르시오.

Woman: _____

① I already had dinner.
② That sounds interesting.
③ How about eating *bibimbap*?
④ Thanks for saying so, my son.
⑤ It isn't clear to me what you means.

01 그림 정보 파악 – 인물

대화를 듣고, 두 사람이 체육 시간에 배운 동작을 고르시오.

① ② ③
④ ⑤

💬 **기억이나 망각 여부 묻기** ///////////////
Do(Don't) you remember ~? / You haven't forgotten about ~, have you? / I wonder if you remember ~.

W We have been studying for five hours.

M Oh, really?

W I think we should get some rest and relax for a while.

M Or why don't we ❶_____ _____ _____ _____ _____ in P.E. class the other day?

W That's a great idea. Do you remember how?

M Sure. It's very simple. First, we need to ❷_____ _____. And try to ❸_____ _____ _____ with both hands without bending our knees.

02 목적 파악

대화를 듣고, 여자가 남자에게 전화한 목적으로 가장 적절한 것을 고르시오.

① 식당을 예약하려고
② 물건을 반품하려고
③ 음식을 배달시키려고
④ 호텔 예약을 취소하려고
⑤ 영수증 발급을 요청하려고

[Telephone rings.]

M Hello. This is Judy Palace restaurant.

W I'd like to ❶_____ _____ _____ for tonight.

M All right. What time?

W 8 o'clock.

M 8 o'clock. How many people do you have?

W ❷_____ _____ _____ _____ _____. And do you serve vegetarian dishes? Three of us are vegetarians.

M Of course. We have several vegetarian dishes. ❸_____ _____ _____ and phone number?

W Olivia Ross. 081–2254–3312.

03 그림 정보 파악 – 길 찾기

대화를 듣고, 여자가 가고자 하는 곳을 고르시오.

W Excuse me. Do you know where the nearest bus stop is?

M Yes. Just ❶_____ _____ _____ _____ and turn right at the corner.

W Two blocks and ❷_____ _____?

M Yes. Then, if you walk down a few steps, you'll see ❸_____ _____ _____ and an animal hospital. The bus stop is between them. You can't miss it.

W I got it. Thank you very much.

M No problem.

〔Words〕 **01 relax** 휴식을 취하다 **for a while** 잠시 동안 **stretching** 스트레칭 체조 **the other day** 일전에 **bend** 구부리다 **knee** 무릎
02 vegetarian 채식주의자 **dish** 요리 **several** 몇 개의 **03 a few** 조금 **miss** 놓치다

04 특정 정보 파악 – 요일 영국식 발음 녹음

대화를 듣고, 남자가 조별 모임을 할 수 <u>없는</u> 요일을 고르시오.

① 월요일　② 화요일　③ 수요일
④ 목요일　⑤ 금요일

M I think we have to start ❶ _____ _____ _____ _____.
W Good idea. Let's meet and talk after school this week.
M I have to go to the dentist ❷ _____ _____. The other days are fine with me.
W I have afternoon school classes on Tuesday and Thursday. How about on Monday?
M Okay. Then let's ❸ _____ _____ _____ on Monday, and prepare the materials on Wednesday.
W That sounds perfect.

05 직업 및 장래 희망

대화를 듣고, 여자의 직업으로 가장 적절한 것을 고르시오.

① chef　　　② student
③ teacher　④ tour guide
⑤ office worker

W Excuse me, sir. Do I need to line up here to enter the school cafeteria?
M Yes, you do. You don't look familiar.
W I'm Jina, a third year student. I ❶ _____ _____ _____ _____ today.
M Where are you from?
W I'm from Daegu.
M Can I ask ❷ _____ _____ _____ _____ Seoul?
W My dad started working in Seoul.
M I see. I hope you like ❸ _____ _____ _____ _____ here.
W Thank you.

06 심정 파악

대화를 듣고, 여자의 심정으로 가장 적절한 것을 고르시오.

① annoyed　　② worried
③ relieved　　④ nervous
⑤ disappointed

😊 사과하기 /////////////////////////////
(I'm so) sorry (about that). / Please forgive me. / I apologize.

W David, ❶ _____ _____ _____ _____ I talk to you for a minute?
M Not at all, Jimin. What's up?
W Do you remember I borrowed an English novel from you a month ago?
M Yes, I do.
W I think ❷ _____ _____ _____. I'm so sorry.
M But Jimin, I found the book on my desk yesterday. I thought you put it there.
W No, I didn't. Oh, ❸ _____ _____ _____ _____ and saw your name on it.

Ｗords **04 prepare** 준비하다 **materials** 자료　**05 line up** 줄을 서다 **familiar** 낯익은　**06 borrow** 빌리다 **novel** 소설

Dictation Test

07 어색한 대화 찾기

다음을 듣고, 두 사람의 대화가 <u>어색한</u> 것을 고르시오.

①   ②   ③   ④   ⑤

😠 화냄 표현하기

I'm annoyed (that ~). / I feel angry. / I'm quite upset. / I can't stand ~. / ~ is (very) annoying (irritating).

① M   Do you think I should accept the proposal?
   W   Of course.
② M   Why are you so upset?
   W   😠 I'm annoyed that somebody stole my sandwich.
③ M   ❶ _____ _____ _____ taking a picture of me?
   W   Of course not. I'm busy.
④ M   I wonder when the bookstore closes.
   W   It closes at 10 p.m.
⑤ M   Thank you. I really ❷ _____ _____ _____.
   W   You're very welcome.

08 부탁한 일 파악   영국식 발음 녹음

대화를 듣고, 여자가 남자에게 부탁한 일로 가장 적절한 것을 고르시오.

① 함께 식사하기
② 먹을 것 사 오기
③ 숙제 가져다주기
④ 다이어트 도와주기
⑤ 과학 보고서 도와주기

M   Sunmi, let's go for lunch.
W   ❶ _____ _____ _____ _____ with you guys today. Go with Steve and Jane.
M   Why? Are you on a diet?
W   No. I forgot to bring my science report and I have to turn it in today.
M   So are you going to write it again during lunchtime?
W   No, I'm going home ❷ _____ _____ _____.
M   You'll have to hurry. You won't have time to have lunch.
W   So, can you ❸ _____ _____ _____ _____ for me? I'll give you the money later.
M   I can do that. See you when you get back.

09 의도 파악

대화를 듣고, 남자의 마지막 말에 담긴 의도로 가장 적절한 것을 고르시오.

① 충고   ② 칭찬   ③ 허락
④ 거절   ⑤ 기원

😊 기원하기

I'll keep my fingers crossed (for you)! / Good luck! / Have a good(nice) ~! / I hope(wish) ~.

M   Seoyoung, you're leaving for Canada in only a week, right?
W   Yes, I'm so sad.
M   Cheer up! You won't leave us forever. You can ❶ _____ _____ _____ _____ us.
W   You're right.
M   By the way, how long are you going to study in Canada?
W   I'm planning to study in Canada for three years.
M   It ❷ _____ _____ _____, _____ I'll keep my fingers crossed for you!

📖 **Words**   **07 accept** 받아들이다   **proposal** 제안   **steal** 훔치다(-stole)   **08 turn ~ in** ~을 제출하다   **09 leave for** ~로 떠나다   **forever** 영원히 **keep in touch** 연락하다

10 숫자 정보 파악 – 금액

대화를 듣고, 여자가 거스름돈으로 받을 금액을 고르시오.

① $20   ② $40   ③ $60

④ $80   ⑤ $100

M Do you need any help?   **W** Yes. How much is this T-shirt?

M It's $40. If you buy this one, you can get ❶ _____ _____ _____ another one.

W That's very nice. Then, I'd like to buy this one and that one.

M Good choice. ❷ _____ _____ _____ _____.

W Okay. Here is a hundred-dollar bill.

M Thank you. Here is your change.

11 장소 추론   영국식 발음 녹음

대화를 듣고, 두 사람이 대화하는 장소로 가장 적절한 곳을 고르시오.

① 호텔   ② 공연장   ③ 기차역

④ 가구점   ⑤ 관광 안내소

M ❶ _____ _____ _____ _____ _____ on the first floor for the next performance?

W Yes, we have some good ones on the left side.

M That's good. May I see the seating chart?

W Yes, it's right here. How many will that be?   **M** Just two.

W I'm afraid ❷ _____ _____ _____ _____ in a row.

M Oh, we'd like to sit together.

W Okay, then how about the seats ❸ _____ _____ _____ _____?   **M** Okay, good.

12 언급되지 않은 것

다음을 듣고, 좋은 독후감을 쓰는 방법으로 언급되지 않은 것을 고르시오.

① 책의 기본 정보 쓰기

② 세 문단 이상 쓰기

③ 책 내용 요약하기

④ 책 읽고 느낀 점 쓰기

⑤ 독서 후 하고 싶은 것 쓰기

W If you want to write a good book report, try the following. A good book report should include ❶ _____ _____ about the book such as the title and the author. You should also write a summary of the impressive parts and tell ❷ _____ _____ _____ _____. The most important thing is to write ❸ _____ _____ _____ _____ after reading the book. It's okay if the book report is short. Just do your best to relate the reading experience to your own life.

13 도표 정보 파악

대화를 듣고, 메시지 내용이 잘못된 것을 고르시오.

Telephone Message

To: ① Lisa
From: ② Michelle
Message: ③ The tea time has been ④ changed to this afternoon because of ⑤ the typhoon.

[*Telephone rings.*]

M Hello?

W Hi, ❶ _____ _____ _____ _____ Lisa?

M Sorry, she's not in at the moment. Can I take a message?

W Yes, please.

M Okay, hold on. (*pause*) I'm ready.

W This is Michelle. Please tell Lisa our tea time ❷ _____ _____ _____ because the typhoon will hit ❸ _____ _____.

M All right. Anything else?

W No, that's all. Thanks.

Words   **10 change** 거스름돈   **11 seating chart** 좌석 배치도   **in a row** 연달아, 연이은   **12 book report** 독후감   **the following** 다음에 말하는 것   **include** 포함하다   **summary** 요약문   **13 at the moment** 바로 지금   **hold on** (명령문 형태로 쓰여) 기다려라   **typhoon** 태풍

Dictation Test

14 주제 파악

다음을 듣고, 무엇에 관한 설명인지 고르시오.

① 다리   ② 계단
③ 저울   ④ 엘리베이터
⑤ 에스컬레이터

W People use this to move upstairs or downstairs. You can find this in big buildings. You must be careful when you use this. You'd better hold the handrail and **❶** _____ _____ _____ _____. Actually, you can move between floors much faster if you use an elevator. But I prefer using this. That's because I **❷** _____ _____ _____ _____ the elevator after pushing the button.

15 한 일 / 할 일 파악

대화를 듣고, 남자가 대화 직후에 할 일로 가장 적절한 것을 고르시오.

① 교무실 가기
② 친구에게 전화하기
③ 휴대 전화 사러 가기
④ 영어 숙제 하러 가기
⑤ 휴대 전화 수리하러 가기

M Good morning, Judy! I'm getting **❶** _____ _____ _____ _____ today.
W What do you mean?
M I bought a new cellphone a week ago, but the English teacher took it that day because **❷** _____ _____ _____ _____ _____.
W Did you use your cellphone in class?
M Yes, I know I shouldn't have done it.
W So, it's been kept **❸** _____ _____ _____ _____ for a week.
M Yes. Oh, I should go to get my cellphone back. See you.

16 숫자 정보 파악 – 연도   영국식 발음 녹음

대화를 듣고, 남자가 태어난 연도를 고르시오.

① 1998년   ② 1999년   ③ 2000년
④ 2001년   ⑤ 2002년

🗣 알고 있음 표현하기 ////////////////////////////
I heard(have heard) (about) ~. / I'm aware (of) ~. /
I've been told (about) ~. / I know (about) ~.

M Hi, Laura.
W Hi, Minho. What are you doing here?
M I'm looking for a gift for my parents because **❶** _____ _____ _____ _____ _____.
W When did they get married?
M I heard they got married in 1997. **❷** _____ _____ _____, I was born.
W What about your twin sisters? When were they born?
M They were born in 2002 when the World Cup was held in Seoul.

Ⓦⓞⓡⓓⓢ   **14 upstairs** 위층으로   **downstairs** 아래층으로   **handrail** 난간   **15 get ~ back** (잃었던 것을) 되찾다   **16 anniversary** 기념일   **get married** 결혼하다   **twin** 쌍둥이의

17 상황에 맞는 말 찾기

다음 상황 설명을 듣고, 민수가 점원에게 할 말로 가장 적절한 것을 고르시오.

Minsu: _____

① Would you say that again, please?
② What do you think of these strawberries?
③ Can I get a discount on the strawberries?
④ Which do you like better, strawberries or apples?
⑤ Can I buy apples instead of strawberries, please?

M Minsu went to the market _____ _____ _____ _____. Because he likes strawberries a lot, he asked the man at the fruit market to pack some strawberries. However, when he looked closely, he found the strawberries were not fresh. Moreover, they were ❷ _____ _____ _____. Now he doesn't want to buy strawberries and he wants to ❸ _____ _____ _____ _____. In this situation, what would Minsu most likely say to the clerk?

18 한 일 / 할 일 파악

대화를 듣고, 남자가 오늘 방과 후에 할 일이 아닌 것을 고르시오.

① 숙제하기   ② 피자 만들기
③ 교실 청소하기   ④ 도서관에서 책 빌리기
⑤ 사촌 동생 데리러 가기

W What are you going to do after school today?
M I have to ❶ _____ _____ _____ today. And I'm planning to ❷ _____ _____ _____ at the library.
W And are you going home after that?
M Yes. After ❸ _____ _____ _____, I'm going to make a pizza.
W Make a pizza?
M Yes. My cousin is coming today. I'll make it for her.
W Wow! I didn't know you're good at cooking!

19 알맞은 응답 찾기

대화를 듣고, 여자의 마지막 말에 대한 남자의 응답으로 가장 적절한 것을 고르시오.

Man: _____

① You should apologize to them.
② You should not make a lot of noise.
③ You shouldn't play the piano at night.
④ I should spend more time with my kids.
⑤ I think you should go upstairs and tell them about that.

M You look upset. What's wrong?
W I can't stand the people upstairs any more. They ❶ _____ _____ _____ _____ _____.
M What kind of noise are you talking about?
W They seem to have kids, and they ❷ _____ _____ _____ _____ _____. Besides that, somebody plays the piano even at night.
M That's too bad.
W ❸ _____ _____ _____ _____?

20 알맞은 응답 찾기

대화를 듣고, 남자의 마지막 말에 대한 여자의 응답으로 가장 적절한 것을 고르시오.

Woman: _____

① I already had dinner.
② That sounds interesting.
③ How about eating *bibimbap*?
④ Thanks for saying so, my son.
⑤ It isn't clear to me what you means.

🔊 낙담 위로하기 ////////////////////
Cheer up! / Don't worry. / Things will be better (soon). / Don't be disappointed.

W Subin, what do you want to have for dinner?
M Mom, you asked me ❶ _____ _____ _____ five minutes ago.
W Oh, did I? I remember nothing about it.
M Really? I answered that I didn't care.
W Phew, I guess ❷ _____ _____ _____. I often forget things these days.
M Don't say that. ❸ _____ _____ _____ to everyone sometimes, Mom. Cheer up!

Words   **17 instead** 대신에   **18 cousin** 사촌   **19 stand** 참다 **besides** ~외에 **even** 심지어   **20 care** 상관하다

01 대화를 듣고, 여자가 주문할 음식을 고르시오.

02 대화를 듣고, 여자가 남자와 면담한 목적으로 가장 적절한 것을 고르시오.

① 휴가를 얻으려고
② 감사 표시를 하려고
③ 직장을 소개해 달라고
④ 급여 인상을 요구하려고
⑤ 사적인 고민을 의논하려고

03 다음 그림의 상황에 가장 적절한 대화를 고르시오.

① ② ③ ④ ⑤

04 대화를 듣고, 여자가 지난 주말에 갔던 장소를 고르시오.

① park   ② pet shop
③ repair shop   ④ amusement park
⑤ department store

05 다음을 듣고, 여자의 직업으로 가장 적절한 것을 고르시오.

① 비행 승무원   ② 관광 가이드   ③ 기상 캐스터
④ 방송 진행자   ⑤ 교통 경찰관

06 대화를 듣고, 두 사람의 관계로 가장 적절한 것을 고르시오.

① boss – secretary
② clerk – customer
③ reporter – writer
④ waiter – customer
⑤ police officer – citizen

07 다음을 듣고, 두 사람의 대화가 어색한 것을 고르시오.

① ② ③ ④ ⑤

08 대화를 듣고, 남자가 여자에게 부탁한 일로 가장 적절한 것을 고르시오.

① Jake에게 사과할 것
② 도서부 일을 대신 해 줄 것
③ Jake에게 문자를 보내 줄 것
④ 수업 자료를 대신 받아 줄 것
⑤ Jake의 전화번호를 알려 줄 것

09 대화를 듣고, 여자의 마지막 말에 담긴 의도로 가장 적절한 것을 고르시오.

① 사과   ② 걱정   ③ 격려
④ 동의   ⑤ 감사

10 다음을 듣고, 여자가 지불할 금액을 고르시오.

① $19   ② $21   ③ $22
④ $23   ⑤ $24

11 대화를 듣고, 두 사람이 대화하는 장소로 가장 적절한 곳을 고르시오.

① bus stop   ② taxi stand

③ restaurant   ④ coffee shop

⑤ supermarket

12 다음을 듣고, 벨리 댄스 수업에 대해 언급되지 <u>않은</u> 것을 고르시오.

① 시작 시기   ② 지도 선생님

③ 수업 시간   ④ 등록 할인

⑤ 수업 장소

13 대화를 듣고, 여자가 앉을 자리를 고르시오.

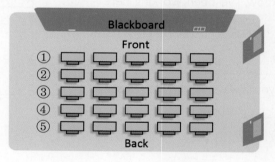

14 다음을 듣고, 무엇에 관한 설명인지 고르시오.

① 바지   ② 장갑   ③ 안경

④ 양말   ⑤ 운동화

15 대화를 듣고, 남자가 대화 직후에 할 일로 가장 적절한 것을 고르시오.

① 도서 대출하기   ② 도서관에 가기

③ 항의 전화하기   ④ 보고서 발표하기

⑤ 컴퓨터 구입하기

16 대화를 듣고, 남자가 병원 진료를 예약한 날짜와 시각을 고르시오.

① 7일, 오전 10시   ② 7일, 오후 4시

③ 17일, 오전 10시   ④ 17일, 오후 2시

⑤ 17일, 오후 4시

17 다음 상황 설명을 듣고, 민우가 Jane에게 할 말로 가장 적절한 것을 고르시오.

Minwoo: _____

① I'm glad you like it.

② I think I need one more day.

③ Thank you for understanding.

④ Why do you want me to call you?

⑤ When do we have the presentation?

18 대화를 듣고, 여자가 겨울 방학에 할 일로 가장 적절한 것을 고르시오.

① 식당에서 일하기

② 겨울 학교에 가기

③ 학원에서 공부하기

④ 미국에서 공부하기

⑤ 집에서 가정교사와 공부하기

19 대화를 듣고, 남자의 마지막 말에 대한 여자의 응답으로 가장 적절한 것을 고르시오.

Woman: _____

① Take care!

② You're right.

③ No problem.

④ How good you are!

⑤ You can go there again.

20 대화를 듣고, 여자의 마지막 말에 대한 남자의 응답으로 가장 적절한 것을 고르시오.

Man: _____

① I am happy as a singer, too.

② I'm not a singer, but a doctor.

③ I will never forget your dream.

④ You used to sing and dance very well.

⑤ My parents always wanted me to be a doctor.

Dictation Test 14회 영어 듣기모의고사

01 | 그림 정보 파악 – 사물

대화를 듣고, 여자가 주문할 음식을 고르시오.

M Let's order something quickly. I'll have Japanese ramen.

W Okay. Let me see. Wow, they serve many kinds of foods.

M You said you also wanted to eat ramen, right?

W No, I _____ _____ _____. I'd like to have sushi.

M If you are not going to have ramen, there's no reason to come here. This place is famous for ramen.

W I'll try it next time. I ❷_____ _____ _____ _____ now.

M Hmm... okay. As you wish.

02 | 목적 파악

대화를 듣고, 여자가 남자와 면담한 목적으로 가장 적절한 것을 고르시오.

① 휴가를 얻으려고
② 감사 표시를 하려고
③ 직장을 소개해 달라고
④ 급여 인상을 요구하려고
⑤ 사적인 고민을 의논하려고

W Mr. Johnson, may I talk to you for a moment?

M Sure. Come on in. What can I do for you?

W Well, as you know, I've been working here ❶_____ _____ _____ _____.

M Yes. Go on.

W But, I haven't ❷_____ _____ _____ yet in pay.

M Okay, I know you always work hard. I'll see ❸_____ _____ _____ _____ about it.

W Thank you very much.

03 | 그림 상황에 어울리는 대화 찾기

다음 그림의 상황에 가장 적절한 대화를 고르시오.

① M I didn't ❶_____ _____ _____.

   W Neither did I.

② M What's this liquid on the stairs?

   W I spilt water by accident.

③ M It's beginning to rain. What should I do?

   W ❷_____ _____ my umbrella.

④ M Do you like snowy days?

   W No, I prefer rainy days.

⑤ M Oops, my umbrella ❸_____ _____.

   W Don't worry. It's not raining any more.

 Words **01 serve** 제공하다 **sushi** 초밥, 스시 **there is no reason to** ~할 이유가 없다 **be famous for** ~로 유명하다 **02 pay** 급료, 보수
03 neither ~도 역시 아닌 **liquid** 액체 **spill** 흘리다(-spilt) **by accident** 우연히, 실수로

04 장소 추론 영국식 발음 녹음

대화를 듣고, 여자가 지난 주말에 갔던 장소를 고르시오.
① park   ② pet shop
③ repair shop   ④ amusement park
⑤ department store

😊 **유감이나 동정 표현하기** ////////////////////
That's too bad. / I'm (so) sorry to hear that. /
That's a pity(shame).

M Hey, you bought new sunglasses. You look great in them.
W Thanks. I ❶ _____ _____ _____ at the department store.
M What about your old ones?
W I was playing with my dog ❷ _____ _____ _____ _____ _____, and he chewed up my sunglasses.
M That's too bad.
W I even ❸ _____ _____ _____ _____ the next day, but it was no use.
M Forget about them. You got nicer sunglasses, any way.
W That's true.

05 직업 및 장래 희망

다음을 듣고, 여자의 직업으로 가장 적절한 것을 고르시오.
① 비행 승무원 ② 관광 가이드 ③ 기상 캐스터
④ 방송 진행자 ⑤ 교통 경찰관

😊 **주의 끌기** ////////////////////
May I have your attention(. please)? / (Oh,)
look(listen). / Hey!

W Ladies and gentlemen, may I have your attention, please? ❶ _____ _____ _____ _____ Kennedy Airport in ten minutes. Please ❷ _____ _____ _____ _____ and turn off your cellphones. Please remain in your seats until ❸ _____ _____ _____ completely. Thank you.

06 관계 추론

대화를 듣고, 두 사람의 관계로 가장 적절한 것을 고르시오.
① boss – secretary
② clerk – customer
③ reporter – writer
④ waiter – customer
⑤ police officer – citizen

M Would you please ❶ _____ _____ _____ ?
W Certainly. When do you need it by?
M I need it by 2 o'clock.
W Is that all?
M And then could you ❷ _____ _____ _____, please?
W Sure. Three copies.
M Yes. ❸ _____ _____ _____ _____ _____, one to marketing, and keep one on file, please. Thanks.
W Don't mention it. It's my work that I have to do.

07 어색한 대화 찾기

다음을 듣고, 두 사람의 대화가 <u>어색한</u> 것을 고르시오.
①   ②   ③   ④   ⑤

😊 **의견 묻기** ////////////////////
What do you think of(about) ~? / How do you
feel about ~? / What is your view(opinion) on ~?

① W What do you think of using cellphones at school?
   M In my opinion, it is necessary.
② W When does ❶ _____ _____ _____ _____ ?
   M It's due on Monday.
③ W Why don't you try some cake?
   M I'm full. I had a sandwich on my way here.
④ W ❷ _____ _____ _____ _____ for this weekend?
   M I'm going to visit my grandparents in Gwangju.
⑤ W What time do you usually go to bed?
   M At 10, but I stayed up until 12 yesterday.

Words **04 chew** 씹다, 물어뜯다 **no use** 쓸모없는 **05 fasten** 매다 **seat belt** 안전벨트 **remain** 머무르다 **completely** 완전하게 **06 copy** 복사
[복제](본) **07 necessary** 필요한 **due** ~하기로 되어 있는 **stay up** (자지 않고) 깨어 있다

Dictation Test

08 부탁한 일 파악　영국식 발음 녹음

대화를 듣고, 남자가 여자에게 부탁한 일로 가장 적절한 것을 고르시오.

① Jake에게 사과할 것
② 도서부 일을 대신 해 줄 것
③ Jake에게 문자를 보내 줄 것
④ 수업 자료를 대신 받아 줄 것
⑤ Jake의 전화번호를 알려 줄 것

[Telephone rings.]

M Hello?

W Mathew. It's Jimin. Are you feeling better?

M Yes. I'm better than yesterday, but I don't think I can go to school today. I'm worried that I'm ❶ _____ _____.

W Don't worry. I'm gathering class materials for you.

M Thank you so much. By the way, ❷ _____ _____ _____ _____ _____ Jake's phone number?

W I will text it. Why?

M He and I are on duty in the book club toady, but he will have to work alone. I think I have to ❸ _____ _____ _____ _____.

W Then switch schedules with me. I'll work with him today, and you can work on Friday.

09 의도 파악

대화를 듣고, 여자의 마지막 말에 담긴 의도로 가장 적절한 것을 고르시오.

① 사과　　② 걱정　　③ 격려
④ 동의　　⑤ 감사

😊 슬픔, 불만족, 실망의 원인에 대해 묻기 //////////
What's wrong? / What's the matter? / Why are you sad(disappointed)?

W Hey, Jinho. You look down. What's wrong?

M Well, I'm worried about my future.

W Your future? What would you like to be?

M I'd like to be an international lawyer, but I ❶ _____ _____ _____.

W What is it?

M My English isn't good enough.

W Cheer up! I'm sure ❷ _____ _____ _____ _____ _____ if you practice more.

10 숫자 정보 파악 – 금액

다음을 듣고, 여자가 지불할 금액을 고르시오.

① $19　　② $21　　③ $22
④ $23　　⑤ $24

M May I take your order?

W Yes, please. I'd like to ❶ _____ _____ _____ _____ and cream cheese toast.

M Anything else?

W No, that's all.

M Okay. That makes $21 ❷ _____ _____.

W I see. Here's my credit card.

M Um, we have been running an event. Since you bought more than $20, you can get a cup for just $2.

W All right. ❸ _____ _____ _____ _____, too.

Words **08 miss** 놓치다 **gather** 모으다 **material** 소재, 재료 **on duty** 당번인 **switch** 바꾸다, 전환하다　**09 international** 국제적인 **lawyer** 변호사 **practice** 연습하다　**10 credit card** 신용카드 **run an event** 행사를 진행하다

11 장소 추론

대화를 듣고, 두 사람이 대화하는 장소로 가장 적절한 곳을 고르시오.

① bus stop
② taxi stand
③ restaurant
④ coffee shop
⑤ supermarket

W Oh, _____ _____ _____ _____.
M Yeah. We have to wait, I guess.
W There are five of us. We won't _____ _____ _____ _____.
M Yes, you're right. We'll need two cabs.
W Ken, you take the first cab with your children.
M Okay. Wait! Is the name of the restaurant Pizza Hat?
W Yes, it is.

12 언급되지 않은 것

다음을 듣고, 벨리 댄스 수업에 대해 언급되지 않은 것을 고르시오.

① 시작 시기
② 지도 선생님
③ 수업 시간
④ 등록 할인
⑤ 수업 장소

ⓟ lose의 발음 //////////////////////////
'잃어버리다'라는 뜻의 lose는 [luːz]로 발음되고, '분실'이라는 뜻의 loss는 [lɔːs]로 발음된다는 점에 유의한다.

M Hello. We're offering a belly dancing class _____ _____ _____. If you plan to lose weight for the summer, come and take the class. The teacher is Grace Kim, _____ _____ _____ _____. The class is at 5:30 p.m. _____ _____. We have a special event as well. For those who sign up by this week, we give a 10% discount.

13 도표 정보 파악   영국식 발음 녹음

대화를 듣고, 여자가 앉을 자리를 고르시오.

W Good morning, Tom.
M Hi, Suyeong. Come and sit here.
W I don't want to sit _____ _____ _____ _____. That's too close to the blackboard.
M Are you going to _____ _____ _____ _____?
W No, I still want a good seat for the presentation. I'll sit in the second or third row.
M Then have a seat _____ _____.
W Okay, I will.

14 주제 파악

다음을 듣고, 무엇에 관한 설명인지 고르시오.

① 바지
② 장갑
③ 안경
④ 양말
⑤ 운동화

M These are something you wear very often all year round. You wear them mostly _____ _____ _____ _____. These come in different designs and sizes. These days many have cute characters on them. People might not see whether you are wearing them or not if you _____ _____ _____ _____. Even though others might not see them, you should check whether _____ _____ _____ _____ or not before you put them on.

Words   11 **cab** 택시   12 **offer** 제공하다   **lose weight** 체중을 줄이다   **sign up** 등록하다   13 **row** 줄   **presentation** 발표   14 **all year round** 일년 내내   **protect** 보호하다   **whether** ~인지 (아닌지)   **even though** 비록 ~일지라도   **hole** 구멍

Dictation Test

15 한 일 / 할 일 파악

대화를 듣고, 남자가 대화 직후에 할 일로 가장 적절한 것을 고르시오.

① 도서 대출하기 ② 도서관에 가기
③ 항의 전화하기 ④ 보고서 발표하기
⑤ 컴퓨터 구입하기

😊 **안도감 표현하기** //////////////////////////
I'm glad(relieved) to hear that. / That's a relief. /
What a relief! / Thank goodness!

M Honey, what's that sound? It's been noisy all day.
W I heard that it's the sports day of the elementary school across the street.
M I ❶ _____ _____ _____ _____ with this noise.
W Why don't you go to the library then?
M But I have to use the computer.
W There's a reading room where you can use your laptop.
M Oh, I'm glad to hear that. I ❷ _____ _____ _____ _____ _____ right now.

16 숫자 정보 파악 – 날짜와 시각 영국식 발음 녹음

대화를 듣고, 남자가 병원 진료를 예약한 날짜와 시각을 고르시오.

① 7일, 오전 10시 ② 7일, 오후 4시
③ 17일, 오전 10시 ④ 17일, 오후 2시
⑤ 17일, 오후 4시

W Dr. Smith's office. May I help you?
M This is Mickey Arnold. Can I ❶ _____ _____ _____ for Friday the 17th?
W Okay, Mr. Arnold. In the morning or afternoon?
M ❷ _____ _____ _____.
W Can you come at 4 p.m.?
M That's fine.
W So ❸ _____ _____ _____ come at 4 p.m. on Friday the 17th.
M Thank you.

17 상황에 맞는 말 찾기

다음 상황 설명을 듣고, 민우가 Jane에게 할 말로 가장 적절한 것을 고르시오.

Minwoo: _____

① I'm glad you like it.
② I think I need one more day.
③ Thank you for understanding.
④ Why do you want me to call you?
⑤ When do we have the presentation?

W Minwoo and Jane are in the same group. They have ❶ _____ _____ _____, and they decided Minwoo would make the presentation materials and Jane would give the presentation. He promised to ❷ _____ _____ _____ _____ by Monday. He worked hard during the weekend, but he couldn't finish making the materials. He thinks he can finish it if he has ❸ _____ _____ _____. In this situation, what would Minwoo most likely say to Jane?

📖 Words **15 sports day** 운동회 **reading room** 열람실 **laptop** 노트북 컴퓨터 **16 schedule** 일정을 잡다 **17 materials** 자료

18 한 일 / 할 일 파악

대화를 듣고, 여자가 겨울 방학에 할 일로 가장 적절한 것을 고르시오.

① 식당에서 일하기
② 겨울 학교에 가기
③ 학원에서 공부하기
④ 미국에서 공부하기
⑤ 집에서 가정교사와 공부하기

ⓟ fall asleep 발음 //////////////////////////
자음과 모음이 나란히 있을 때 이 둘은 자연스럽게 연음이 되므로, fall asleep은 [fɔːləslíːp]으로 연결하여 발음한다.

M What are your plans for winter vacation, Becky?
W ❶ _____ _____ _____ _____ _____ and study in America.
M That sounds exciting!
W I said, "I'd like to." It's just too expensive, so it's impossible.
M That's too bad. I'm going to take three academy classes. Why don't you take them with me?
W Well, you know I ❷ _____ _____ _____ _____ _____ in the library.
M But you always ⓟ fall asleep.
W Yes. That is why my mom has found ❸ _____ _____ _____ _____ _____ during the winter vacation.
M Oh, I see.

19 알맞은 응답 찾기

대화를 듣고, 남자의 마지막 말에 대한 여자의 응답으로 가장 적절한 것을 고르시오.
Woman: _____

① Take care!
② You're right.
③ No problem.
④ How good you are!
⑤ You can go there again.

😊 반복 요청하기 //////////////////////////
Could you say that again(, please)? / What (did you say)? / (I beg your) Pardon? / I don't know what you mean(meant).

M Excuse me. Do you know ❶ _____ _____ _____ _____ _____ is?
W Sure. Can you see the tall red building?
M Sure. I see it.
W Okay, just go straight there. You can find a very narrow street before you get to the building. If you turn right there and walk for about one minute, you'll see a big mailbox and...
M I'm sorry but, I can't get it. Could you say that again?
W Well, I'll just ❷ _____ _____ _____. Let's go.
M Oh, really? I really ❸ _____ _____.

20 알맞은 응답 찾기

대화를 듣고, 여자의 마지막 말에 대한 남자의 응답으로 가장 적절한 것을 고르시오.
Man: _____

① I am happy as a singer, too.
② I'm not a singer, but a doctor.
③ I will never forget your dream.
④ You used to sing and dance very well.
⑤ My parents always wanted me to be a doctor.

M Why did you become a doctor?
W My grandma suffered from a serious disease when she was alive, so I decided to become a doctor.
M Ah, you wanted to ❶ _____ _____ _____ like your grandma.
W Exactly.
M Good for you. You look so happy as a doctor.
W Yeah. By the way, I heard that your dream was to be a singer. ❷ _____ _____ _____ become a doctor?

Words **18** impossible 불가능한 academy class 학원 수업 fall asleep 잠들다 **19** narrow 좁은 mailbox 우체통 **20** suffer from ~로 고통을 겪다 serious 심각한 alive 살아 있는 Exactly. (맞장구치는 말로) 맞아.

01 대화를 듣고, 여자가 남자를 위해 준비한 선물을 고르시오.

02 대화를 듣고, 여자가 남자에게 전화한 목적으로 가장 적절한 것을 고르시오.

① 약속을 취소하려고　② 콘서트를 홍보하려고
③ 콘서트에 함께 가려고　④ 도서관에 함께 가려고
⑤ 도서관 위치를 물어보려고

03 다음 그림의 상황에 가장 적절한 대화를 고르시오.

①　　②　　③　　④　　⑤

04 대화를 듣고, 두 사람이 만나기로 한 장소를 고르시오.

① 제과점　　　② 음반 가게
③ 학교 정문　　④ 민지네 집
⑤ Martin의 집

05 대화를 듣고, 남자의 직업으로 가장 적절한 것을 고르시오.

① actor　　　② dentist
③ farmer　　　④ repairman
⑤ delivery man

06 대화를 듣고, 남자의 심정으로 가장 적절한 것을 고르시오.

① excited　　　② hopeful
③ annoyed　　　④ thankful
⑤ disappointed

07 다음을 듣고, 두 사람의 대화가 어색한 것을 고르시오.

①　　　②　　　③　　　④　　　⑤

08 대화를 듣고, 여자가 남자에게 부탁한 일로 가장 적절한 것을 고르시오.

① 책 빌려오기　　　② 양파 사 오기
③ 빌린 책 반납하기　④ 집에서 저녁 먹기
⑤ 5시까지 집에 오기

09 대화를 듣고, 남자의 마지막 말에 담긴 의도로 가장 적절한 것을 고르시오.

① 동의　　② 요청　　③ 격려
④ 감사　　⑤ 충고

10 대화를 듣고, 남자가 지불할 금액을 고르시오.

① ₩6,000　② ₩7,000　③ ₩8,000
④ ₩9,000　⑤ ₩10,000

11 대화를 듣고, 두 사람이 대화하는 장소로 가장 적절한 곳을 고르시오.

① 병원　　② 서점　　③ 식당
④ 은행　　⑤ 미용실

12 다음을 듣고, 해바라기에 관해 언급되지 <u>않은</u> 것을 고르시오.

① 수명　　　　　② 원산지
③ 꽃 색깔　　　　④ 심는 시기
⑤ 물을 주는 횟수

13 다음 표를 보면서 대화를 듣고, 두 사람이 선택할 게임을 고르시오.

	Game	Difficulty	Number of People	Time (min.)
①	A	★★★☆☆	2-4	60
②	B	★★★☆☆	2-6	60
③	C	★★★★☆	2-4	70
④	D	★★★★☆	2-6	70
⑤	E	★★★★★	2-6	80

14 다음을 듣고, 무엇에 관한 설명인지 고르시오.

① 스피커　　　　② 이어폰
③ 마이크　　　　④ 휴대 전화
⑤ MP3 플레이어

15 대화를 듣고, 남자가 대화 직후에 할 일로 가장 적절한 것을 고르시오.

① 축구하기　　　② 샤워하기
③ 요리 돕기　　　④ 저녁 먹기
⑤ 옷 갈아입기

16 대화를 듣고, 여자의 체육대회 날짜를 고르시오.

① October 6th　　② October 8th
③ October 10th　　④ October 11th
⑤ October 12th

17 다음 상황 설명을 듣고, Maggie가 남동생에게 할 말로 가장 적절한 것을 고르시오.

Maggie: _____

① What happened?
② It's my fault. I apologize.
③ Don't you agree with me?
④ What makes you think so?
⑤ Do you find the story interesting?

18 대화를 듣고, 여자가 대화 직후에 할 일로 가장 적절한 것을 고르시오.

① 화분에 물 주기
② 화분에 씨앗 심기
③ 화분 계속 관찰하기
④ 화분의 흙을 갈아 주기
⑤ 화분을 햇볕이 드는 곳으로 옮기기

19 대화를 듣고, 여자의 마지막 말에 대한 남자의 응답으로 가장 적절한 것을 고르시오.

Man: _____

① That's a great relief.
② I'm sorry to hear that.
③ Don't be disappointed.
④ Never drive a car again.
⑤ I hope you get well soon.

20 대화를 듣고, 남자의 마지막 말에 대한 여자의 응답으로 가장 적절한 것을 고르시오.

Woman: _____

① That interests me a lot.
② No, it wasn't your fault.
③ Yes, I'm certain about that.
④ I should have practiced more.
⑤ Don't give up. You'll finish the book.

01 그림 정보 파악 – 사물

대화를 듣고, 여자가 남자를 위해 준비한 선물을 고르시오.

① ② ③
④ ⑤

M Jean, how was your trip to Japan?
W It was very nice. Here, I ❶_____ _____ _____ for you.
M Wow, this cat looks so cute.
W See, it is ❷_____ _____ _____ _____ next to its head. I heard this doll brings us good luck.
M That's good. I like the red ribbon around its neck.
W I also liked ❸_____ _____ _____. I'm glad you like it.
M Thank you very much.

02 목적 파악

대화를 듣고, 여자가 남자에게 전화한 목적으로 가장 적절한 것을 고르시오.

① 약속을 취소하려고   ② 콘서트를 홍보하려고
③ 콘서트에 함께 가려고 ④ 도서관에 함께 가려고
⑤ 도서관 위치를 물어보려고

🔊 관심에 대해 묻기 //////////////
Are you interested in ~? / Do you find ~ interesting? / What are you interested in?

[Telephone rings.]
M Hello?
W Hi, Jim. This is Mina. Are you interested in pop music?
M Yes, I am. Why are you asking me that?
W I've just ❶_____ _____ _____ for a pop concert tonight. Can you ❷_____ _____ _____?
M Well, I was going to the library, but I don't want to ❸_____ _____ _____. What time and where is it?
W It's at 7 at Yedang Hall.
M Okay. Let's meet at 6:30 there.
W Good. See you then.

03 그림 상황에 어울리는 대화 찾기

다음 그림의 상황에 가장 적절한 대화를 고르시오.

① ② ③ ④ ⑤

🔊 의견 묻기 //////////////
What do you think of(about) ~? / How do you feel about ~? / What is your view(opinion) on ~?

① W Do I look all right in this?
   M You ❶_____ _____ _____.
② W Can you please hold it for me?
   M Sure, go ahead.
③ W Can I mail these letters?
   M Yes. Do you need some stamps?
④ W Could you ❷_____ _____ _____ _____ to the hotel?
   M Sure. Get in, please.
⑤ W What do you think of these shoes?
   M I think ❸_____ _____ _____ _____.

Words **01** raise 들어 올리다 bring 가져오다   **02** miss 놓치다   **03** hold 잡다 mail (우편으로) 보내다 stamp 우표 give ~ a ride ~을 태워주다

04 장소 추론 영국식 발음 녹음

대화를 듣고, 두 사람이 만나기로 한 장소를 고르시오.

① 제과점 ② 음반 가게
③ 학교 정문 ④ 민지네 집
⑤ Martin의 집

M ❶ _____ _____ _____ _____ buy Minji's birthday present today?

W We don't need to. I went to the music store and bought the CD she wanted yesterday.

M How about the cake then? Do you want me to go to the bakery and buy a cake?

W I think ❷ _____ _____ _____ _____ one tomorrow. Come to Martin's place after school today. Do you know where he lives?

M Yes, I do. What are we going to do there?

W We are going to prepare party accessories for her birthday party. How about meeting in front of school and going together?

M No, you finish earlier than I do today.

W Okay. Let's meet ❸ _____ _____ _____ then.

05 직업 및 장래 희망

대화를 듣고, 남자의 직업으로 가장 적절한 것을 고르시오.

① actor ② dentist
③ farmer ④ repairman
⑤ delivery man

[*Telephone rings.*]

M Hello?

W Hello. I called you to ask about ❶ _____ _____.

M Sorry, but can you tell me more about it?

W Okay. Here is 141 at Elm Street. I ordered a fried chicken over the telephone an hour ago, but it hasn't arrived yet.

M Let me check. Well, I have it here. I'll ❷ _____ _____ _____ _____.

W Sounds good. We're so hungry.

M Okay. ❸ _____ _____ _____ to you as soon as possible.

06 심정 파악

대화를 듣고, 남자의 심정으로 가장 적절한 것을 고르시오.

① excited ② hopeful
③ annoyed ④ thankful
⑤ disappointed

😊 **사과 수용하기** /////////////////////////
That's okay. / It doesn't matter. / Not at all. /
Forget it. / No problem. / Never mind.

M Ma'am, I'm sorry ❶ _____ _____.

W That's okay, but what made you late? You are usually on time.

M While I was waiting for a bus, I found I ❷ _____ _____ _____ _____.

W Did you go back home?

M Yes, I had to. When I got back to the bus stop, the bus had just left.

W You were unlucky.

M Yeah, so I took a taxi, and ❸ _____ _____ _____ _____ _____.

W That's why you are late.

M Yes. This morning was a mess.

Words 04 **present** 선물; 현재의 **party accessories** 파티용 소품 05 **as soon as possible** 되도록 빨리 06 **on time** 제시간에 **wallet** 지갑 **unlucky** 운이 나쁜 **mess** 엉망인 상황

Dictation Test

07 어색한 대화 찾기

다음을 듣고, 두 사람의 대화가 <u>어색한</u> 것을 고르시오.

①   ②   ③   ④   ⑤

😊 격려하기 ///////////////////////////

Don't give up. / You can do it! / That's all right. /
You'll do better next time.

① M   I think Mike Ashley will score a goal.

    W   Are you sure? I don't think he will.

② M   How was your trip to India?

    W   ❶ _____ _____ _____ _____ the beautiful scenery.

③ M   Oh, did you say you lost my book?

    W   I'm sorry. ❷ _____ _____ _____ _____.

④ M   I think I'm not good at singing. Maybe I can't become a singer.

    W   Don't give up. If you keep practicing, you can do it.

⑤ M   Recycling can ❸ _____ _____ _____ _____ _____. Don't you agree with me?

    W   Yes, I'm saving money for two years.

08 부탁한 일 파악   영국식 발음 녹음

대화를 듣고, 여자가 남자에게 부탁한 일로 가장 적절한
것을 고르시오.

① 책 빌려오기   ② 양파 사 오기
③ 빌린 책 반납하기   ④ 집에서 저녁 먹기
⑤ 5시까지 집에 오기

M   Mom, are you still watching that drama?

W   Yeah, this is so interesting. Let's watch it together.

M   No, I'm going out to borrow some books. I'll be back by 5.

W   Okay. So, you are going to ❶ _____ _____ _____ _____, right?

M   Yes, I am.

W   Then, could you buy ❷ _____ _____ _____ on the way home? I'm out of onions.

M   I will. Make a delicious dish for me.

W   Sure.

09 의도 파악

대화를 듣고, 남자의 마지막 말에 담긴 의도로 가장 적절한
것을 고르시오.

① 동의   ② 요청   ③ 격려
④ 감사   ⑤ 충고

😊 설명 요청하기 ///////////////////////////

What do you mean (by) ~? / Could you explain
~? / What is ~ (exactly)?

W   Did you turn off the lights at 8 last night?

M   What do you mean?

W   Didn't you know ❶ _____ _____ _____ _____ _____?

M   It was April 22nd and Monday. What's the matter with that?

W   April 22nd is "Earth Day." On this day, people turn off the lights for ten minutes from 8 o'clock to save energy.

M   That's a great idea. I want to participate in that next year.

W   ❷ _____ _____ _____ _____ _____ for next year. You can just turn off the lights when they are not in use.

M   ❸ _____ _____ _____.

Words   **07** score 득점하다 fascinated 매료된 scenery 경치   **08** on the way home 집에 오는 길에 be out of ~를 다 쓰다   **09** turn off (전기 등을) 끄다 earth 지구 participate 참여하다 be not in use 사용되지 않다

10 숫자 정보 파악 – 금액

대화를 듣고, 남자가 지불할 금액을 고르시오.

① ₩6,000　② ₩7,000　③ ₩8,000
④ ₩9,000　⑤ ₩10,000

M Excuse me. I'd like to send this package to Busan.

W Okay. I'll check the weight of it. *(pause)* It is 1kg, and that's 6,000 won. What's inside?

M There are plates.

W They're easy to break, so you should ❶ _____ _____ _____ _____ _____.

M Oh, how much is that?

W It's 3,000 won more.

M Okay, then ❷ _____ _____ _____.

11 장소 추론

대화를 듣고, 두 사람이 대화하는 장소로 가장 적절한 곳을 고르시오.

① 병원　② 서점　③ 식당
④ 은행　⑤ 미용실

💬 바람, 소원, 요망에 대해 묻기 ////////////
Would you like ~? / Do you want (to) ~? / Do you wish (you could) ~? / Are you looking forward to ~?

M Excuse me. I have been waiting for 30 minutes. How much longer do I ❶ _____ _____ _____?

W I'm sorry, but today is a busy day. However, I'm sure you can ❷ _____ _____ _____ in 10 minutes.

M I see. I've just read all the books here.

W Then, would you like some snacks there?

M Are those snacks ❸ _____ _____ _____?

W Sure.

12 언급되지 않은 것

다음을 듣고, 해바라기에 관해 언급되지 <u>않은</u> 것을 고르시오.

① 수명　② 원산지
③ 꽃 색깔　④ 심는 시기
⑤ 물을 주는 횟수

W A sunflower lives only for a year. This flower originally ❶ _____ _____ North America. It's normally 2 to 3 meters tall, and is ❷ _____ _____. If you want to grow this, you must water it ❸ _____ _____ _____ _____ a week. And you know what? Actually, this flower doesn't always face the sun.

13 도표 정보 파악　영국식 발음 녹음

다음 표를 보면서 대화를 듣고, 두 사람이 선택할 게임을 고르시오.

	Game	Difficulty	Number of People	Time (min.)
①	A	★★★☆☆	2–4	60
②	B	★★★☆☆	2–6	60
③	C	★★★★☆	2–4	70
④	D	★★★★☆	2–6	70
⑤	E	★★★★★	2–6	80

M What about going to an escape game with Jisu and Sam?

W Okay. I have always wanted to try an escape game. Why don't we invite Mary, too?

M That sounds good. Should we start with the easiest one?

W No, let's try one of the harder ones.

M So, we have ❶ _____ _____. Let's try ❷ _____ _____ _____ _____. Then we have only one option.

W You're right. What does the time mean?

M That is how long we have to solve all of the problems. ❸ _____ _____ _____ _____ is 70 minutes.

W Oh, I'm already excited. Let's make a reservation.

M Okay.

Words　10 **package** 소포　**weight** 무게　**plate** 접시　11 **patient** 환자　12 **sunflower** 해바라기　**come from** ~에서 생산되다　**normally** 보통　**face** ~을 향하다　13 **escape** 탈출, 도피　**option** 선택할 수 있는 것　**limit** 제한　**make a reservation** 예약하다

Dictation Test

14 주제 파악

다음을 듣고, 무엇에 관한 설명인지 고르시오.

① 스피커
② 이어폰
③ 마이크
④ 휴대 전화
⑤ MP3 플레이어

M When you want to ❶ _____ _____ _____ _____, these are very useful. To listen to music, you should plug these into a music player and also put them ❷ _____ _____ _____. They are not heavy or big, so you ❸ _____ _____ _____ _____. But when you carry them, the lines might get seriously twisted. So, be careful with them.

15 한 일 / 할 일 파악

대화를 듣고, 남자가 대화 직후에 할 일로 가장 적절한 것을 고르시오.

① 축구하기
② 샤워하기
③ 요리 돕기
④ 저녁 먹기
⑤ 옷 갈아입기

ⓟ friends의 발음 /////////////////////////////
세 자음이 연속하여 발음될 때는 가운데 자음 소리가 탈락한다. 따라서 friends는 가운데 자음 소리 d가 탈락되어 [frenz]로 발음한다.

M Mom, I'm home.
W Bob, did you play outside? ❶ _____ _____ _____.
M Yes, I played soccer with my ⓟfriends. I'll go to change my clothes.
W But I think you should also take a shower.
M Okay. By the way, what are you making? Smells so good.
W This is meatball spaghetti. It's almost done. Come back ❷ _____ _____ _____ _____. Let's have dinner together.
M All right.

16 숫자 정보 파악 – 날짜   영국식 발음 녹음

대화를 듣고, 여자의 체육대회 날짜를 고르시오.

① October 6th
② October 8th
③ October 10th
④ October 11th
⑤ October 12th

[*Telephone rings.*]
M Hello. This is T-zone. How may I help you?
W Hello. ❶ _____ _____ _____ _____ 30 large pink T-shirts for the school sports day. Can I get them by October 10 if I order them today?
M I'm very sorry, but that'll be hard. Today's already October 8.
W Then ❷ _____ _____ _____ _____ them?
M You should get them on the 11.
W ❸ _____ _____ _____ _____ is October 12, so that we will be okay.
M Thanks. I will send you them as soon as possible.

Words **14 useful** 유용한 **plug into** ~에 연결하다 **seriously** 심각하게 **twist** 꼬다 **careful** 조심하는   **15 outside** 밖에서 **take a shower** 샤워하다   **16 sports day** 체육대회, 운동회

17 상황에 맞는 말 찾기

다음 상황 설명을 듣고, Maggie가 남동생에게 할 말로 가장 적절한 것을 고르시오.

Maggie: _____

① What happened?
② It's my fault. I apologize.
③ Don't you agree with me?
④ What makes you think so?
⑤ Do you find the story interesting?

M Maggie was watching a music program with her younger brother, and her favorite singer appeared. She told her brother that the singer was very _____ _____ _____ and dancing. However, her brother didn't say anything. She ❷ _____ _____ _____ _____ _____. In this situation, what is Maggie most likely to say to her brother?

18 한 일 / 할 일 파악

대화를 듣고, 여자가 대화 직후에 할 일로 가장 적절한 것을 고르시오.

① 화분에 물 주기
② 화분에 씨앗 심기
③ 화분 계속 관찰하기
④ 화분의 흙을 갈아 주기
⑤ 화분을 햇볕이 드는 곳으로 옮기기

ⓟ try의 발음 //////////////////////////////
try의 [t]는 주로 [tʃ]로 발음되는데, 이는 [t]가 [r]의 영향을 받아 소리가 부드럽게 변하기 때문이다. 따라서 try는 [tʃurai] 로 발음한다.

M What are you looking at?
W I'm watching my plant.
M Your plant? There's nothing in the pot.
W I know. It's been a week since I ❶ _____ _____ _____. But nothing's happening. What is the problem?
M Well, did you water it enough?   W Of course.
M I think this room is ❷ _____ _____ _____. You might need to put it ❸ _____ _____ _____ _____.
W Oh, I should try that. ⓟ

19 알맞은 응답 찾기

대화를 듣고, 여자의 마지막 말에 대한 남자의 응답으로 가장 적절한 것을 고르시오.

Man: _____

① That's a great relief.
② I'm sorry to hear that.
③ Don't be disappointed.
④ Never drive a car again.
⑤ I hope you get well soon.

[Telephone rings.]
M Hi, Alice. What's up?
W Hey, I don't think I can make it by 3.
M What's the matter?
W I just ❶ _____ _____ _____ _____.
M What? Are you all right?
W Yeah. It ❷ _____ _____ _____ _____ one. The bus I was taking crashed with a car.
M Are you sure that you're okay?
W I ❸ _____ _____ _____ _____ _____.

20 알맞은 응답 찾기

대화를 듣고, 남자의 마지막 말에 대한 여자의 응답으로 가장 적절한 것을 고르시오.

Woman: _____

① That interests me a lot.
② No, it wasn't your fault.
③ Yes, I'm certain about that.
④ I should have practiced more.
⑤ Don't give up. You'll finish the book.

W Tom, what are you doing?
M Oh, Mom. I'm reading a book. This book is really interesting.
W You were pretty much into it. What's the story about?
M This is a story about a girl, Anne Frank. She ❶ _____ _____ _____ during World War II.
W Oh, I know that book.
M Did she survive the war? ❷ _____ _____ _____.
W As far as I know, she died before the war ends.
M That's so sad. ❸ _____ _____ _____?

Ⓦords **17 appear** 나타나다, 등장하다   **18 pot** 화분   **enough** 충분하게   **19 make it** 시간 맞춰 가다   **crash** 충돌하다   **20 be into** ~에 빠지다
war 전쟁   **survive** 살아남다

01 대화를 듣고, 여자가 구입할 휴대 전화 케이스를 고르시오.

①   ②   ③

④   ⑤

02 대화를 듣고, 여자가 남자에게 전화한 목적으로 가장 적절한 것을 고르시오.

① 주택을 구입하려고   ② 상품을 주문하려고
③ 기차표를 예매하려고   ④ 건강 검진을 받으려고
⑤ 전화 설치를 신청하려고

03 다음 그림의 상황에 가장 적절한 대화를 고르시오.

① ② ③ ④ ⑤

04 대화를 듣고, 남자가 구입할 물건을 고르시오.

①   ②   ③

④   ⑤

05 대화를 듣고, 여자의 직업으로 가장 적절한 것을 고르시오.

① vet   ② chef   ③ detective
④ astronaut   ⑤ programmer

06 대화를 듣고, 남자의 심정으로 가장 적절한 것을 고르시오.

① angry   ② excited
③ nervous   ④ pleased
⑤ satisfied

07 다음을 듣고, 두 사람의 대화가 어색한 것을 고르시오.

① ② ③ ④ ⑤

08 대화를 듣고, 여자가 남자에게 부탁한 일로 가장 적절한 것을 고르시오.

① 청소하기   ② 빨래하기
③ 설거지하기   ④ 케이크 사기
⑤ 쓰레기통 비우기

09 대화를 듣고, 여자의 마지막 말에 담긴 의도로 가장 적절한 것을 고르시오.

① 격려   ② 후회   ③ 계획
④ 승낙   ⑤ 감사

10 대화를 듣고, 남자가 지불할 금액을 고르시오.

Menu	
· Cheeseburger	$4.00
· Chicken burger	$4.50
· French fries	$2.00
· Coke(small/large)	$1.00 / $1.50

① $20.00   ② $20.50   ③ $21.00
④ $21.50   ⑤ $22.00

11 대화를 듣고, 두 사람이 대화하고 있는 장소로 가장 적절한 곳을 고르시오.
① 은행　　　② 호텔　　　③ 상점
④ 극장　　　⑤ 공항

12 다음을 듣고, Blue Planet 수족관에 관해 언급되지 않은 것을 고르시오.
① 체험 활동　　② 편의 시설　　③ 입장료
④ 운영 시간　　⑤ 가는 방법

13 다음을 듣고, 내용과 일치하지 않는 것을 고르시오.

	WORLD LEAGUE BASEBALL	
	World League Baseball	
①	Date	May 29th
②	Place	Dodger Stadium
③	Teams	Dodgers vs. Angels
④	Score	4:1
⑤	MVP	Hyunjin Ryu

14 다음을 듣고, 무엇에 관한 설명인지 고르시오.
① 치아　　　② 수염　　　③ 손톱
④ 발톱　　　⑤ 머리카락

15 대화를 듣고, 두 사람이 대화 직후에 할 일로 가장 적절한 것을 고르시오.
① 초밥 만들기　　　② 김밥 만들기
③ 장보러 가기　　　④ 김밥 사러 가기
⑤ 한국 음식 수업 듣기

16 대화를 듣고, 두 사람이 박물관 투어를 시작할 시각을 고르시오.
① 9:00　　　② 9:30　　　③ 10:00
④ 10:30　　　⑤ 11:00

17 다음 상황 설명을 듣고, 지호가 Lisa에게 할 말로 가장 적절한 것을 고르시오.
Jiho: _____
① You need to skip dinner as well.
② I think you should say sorry first.
③ Why don't you work out at the gym?
④ I'm worried that I'm gaining a lot of weight.
⑤ How about having lunch together when you're free?

18 대화를 듣고, 남자가 오늘 할 일이 아닌 것을 고르시오.
① 숙제하기　　　　　② 소포 받기
③ 자기 방 청소하기　④ Jenny 집에 놀러 가기
⑤ 컴퓨터 수리하러 가기

19 대화를 듣고, 남자의 마지막 말에 대한 여자의 응답으로 가장 적절한 것을 고르시오.
Woman: _____
① I'm surprised to hear that.
② It means, "Thank you my friend."
③ Do you know how to sing the song?
④ It is important to understand the meaning.
⑤ I think this song will be really good for the play.

20 대화를 듣고, 여자의 마지막 말에 대한 남자의 응답으로 가장 적절한 것을 고르시오.
Man: _____
① Twice a week.
② Let's take a taxi.
③ About 15 minutes.
④ Can I give you a ride?
⑤ You can say that again.

Dictation Test 16회 영어 듣기모의고사

01 그림 정보 파악 – 사물

대화를 듣고, 여자가 구입할 휴대 전화 케이스를 고르시오.

① ② ③ ④ ⑤ **Karen**

😊 **의도 표현하기** ////////////////////

I'm thinking of ~. / I'm planning to ~. / I'm going to ~.

W Hi, I'm thinking of buying _____ _____ _____ for my little sister. Can you recommend one?

M Absolutely. Look at this bear, and this rabbit is also cute.

W Well, these are too common. ❷_____ _____ _____ _____ I can get for her?

M This hand-knitted case is also good.

W But I think it gets dirty easily.

M Then, how about this one? We can ❸_____ _____ _____ of your sister's name on this one.

W Great. I'll take it.

02 목적 파악

대화를 듣고, 여자가 남자에게 전화한 목적으로 가장 적절한 것을 고르시오.

① 주택을 구입하려고　② 상품을 주문하려고
③ 기차표를 예매하려고　④ 건강 검진을 받으려고
⑤ 전화 설치를 신청하려고

[Telephone rings.]

M Hello. May I help you?

W Yes, I'd like to ❶_____ _____ _____ _____, please.

M May I have your name and address, please?

W Sure. My name is Janet Miller. My address is 20 Train Avenue.

M Thank you. ❷_____ _____ _____ we can install the phone is this Friday. Is that okay?

W That's fine. Thanks.

03 그림 상황에 어울리는 대화 찾기

다음 그림의 상황에 가장 적절한 대화를 고르시오.

① ② ③ ④ ⑤

① W For here or to go?
　M To go, please.
② W How can I get to the supermarket?
　M Oh, it's right there.
③ W Do you need ❶_____ _____ _____ for them?
　M Yes. One plastic bag, please.
④ W Where are you heading?
　M I'm ❷_____ _____ _____.
⑤ W Can I get a 3 p.m. train ticket?
　M Sorry. The seats are all sold out.

📖 **Words**　**01** recommend 추천하다　rabbit 토끼　common 흔한　hand-knitted 손으로 뜨개질한　**02** install 설치하다　avenue 거리, ~가
03 head 향하다, 가다　sold out 표가 매진된

04 그림 정보 파악 – 사물 영국식 발음 녹음
대화를 듣고, 남자가 구입할 물건을 고르시오.

① ② ③ ④ ⑤

W May I help you, sir?

M Yes, I'm looking for a present for my wife.

W I see. _____ _____ a handbag?

M No, she has many handbags already.

W Then, maybe she ❷_____ _____ _____ _____. How about this one?

M Oh, it's beautiful! How much is it?

W It's $55.75.

M I'll ❸_____ _____.

05 직업 및 장래 희망
대화를 듣고, 여자의 직업으로 가장 적절한 것을 고르시오.

① vet   ② chef   ③ detective
④ astronaut   ⑤ programmer

😊 허락 요청하기 ////////////////////////////
Do you mind if ~? / I was wondering if I could ~. /
Would it be possible ~? / Let me ~.

W Excuse me, Mr. Turner. ❶_____ _____ _____ _____ at around 7 p.m. yesterday?

M I was cooking spaghetti for dinner.

W Are you sure about that?

M Yes, ask my family. And even my neighbors, Kevin and Linda ❷_____ _____ that I was with them.

W Hmm... what time was it when you heard somebody shout?

M Maybe, around 8 o'clock. We were about to finish dinner at that time.

W Do you mind if I ❸_____ _____ _____?

M No, go ahead.

06 심정 파악
대화를 듣고, 남자의 심정으로 가장 적절한 것을 고르시오.

① angry   ② excited
③ nervous   ④ pleased
⑤ satisfied

😊 궁금증 표현하기 ////////////////////////////
I wonder ~. / I'd be (very) interested to know ~. /
I'm curious about ~. / Can someone tell me about ~?

W You ❶_____ _____.

M It's because of today's speaking test.

W What kind of test is it?

M My English teacher is going to ask me a few questions, and ❷_____ _____ _____ _____ them.

W Don't worry too much. I'm sure your English is good enough to pass the test.

M But I wonder what kind of questions he is going to ask me. I might ❸_____ _____ _____ _____ _____ the questions. What am I going to do?

W Relax. You'll be fine.

📖 Words **04 present** 선물   **05 neighbor** 이웃 **shout** 소리치다 **be about to** 막 ~하려는 참이다 **go ahead** (하던 일을) 계속 하다   **06 wonder** 궁금해하다 **relax** 긴장을 풀다

Dictation Test

다음을 듣고, 두 사람의 대화가 <u>어색한</u> 것을 고르시오.

① ② ③ ④ ⑤

😊 가능성 정도 묻기 ////////////////////////
Is it possible(probable, likely, impossible) to ~?

① **M** Which do you like better, meat or fish?

　 W I like fish better.

② **M** ❶ _____ _____ _____ _____ the read-a-thon?

　 W No, I haven't. What is it?

③ **M** What are you going to buy as a present for her?

　 W I'm thinking of buying a doll.

④ **M** We're late for school.

　 W Yes. We should ❷ _____ _____ _____ _____.

⑤ **M** Is it possible to drink water in space?

　 W No, we don't have ❸ _____ _____ _____ _____

　　 _____.

---

08 부탁한 일 파악　영국식 발음 녹음

대화를 듣고, 여자가 남자에게 부탁한 일로 가장 적절한 것을 고르시오.

① 청소하기　　　　② 빨래하기
③ 설거지하기　　　④ 케이크 사기
⑤ 쓰레기통 비우기

W Today's Mom's birthday. Let's do something special for her.

M Why don't we ❶ _____ _____ _____ _____ for her? I will do the cleaning, and you do the laundry.

W She will be pleased. What about the dishes?

M If you do the dishes, I'll empty the wastebaskets.

W Okay. Can you ❷ _____ _____ _____ for her after emptying the wastebaskets? I'll prepare ❸ _____ _____ _____.

M No problem. I hope Mom likes our surprise.

---

09 의도 파악

대화를 듣고, 여자의 마지막 말에 담긴 의도로 가장 적절한 것을 고르시오.

① 격려　　② 후회　　③ 계획
④ 승낙　　⑤ 감사

😊 알고 있는지 묻기 ////////////////////////
Did(Do) you know (about) ~? / Have you heard (about) ~? / Are you aware (of) ~?

M Where were you last night?

W What do you mean?

M We were invited to Amy's birthday party, but you weren't there.

W Ah, I ❶ _____ _____ _____ all day, but now I'm okay.

M That's the reason. Did you know that Amy's uncle is Justin Bieber's manager?

W Really? ❷ _____ _____ _____ _____.

M He brought Justin Bieber to the party to surprise her.

W You must be kidding. Justin is my favorite singer.

M I know. He even sang a song for us.

W Oh, no! I ❸ _____ _____ _____ there.

📖 **Words** **07 read-a-thon** 독서 마라톤　**space** 우주; 공간　**08 household chores** 집안일　**do the laundry** 빨래를 하다　**pleased** 기쁜, 기뻐하는 **empty** 비우다　**wastebasket** 휴지통　**surprise** 뜻밖의 선물[일]　**09 invite** 초대하다　**kid** 농담하다

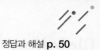

10 숫자 정보 파악 – 금액

대화를 듣고, 남자가 지불할 금액을 고르시오.

Menu	
• Cheeseburger	$4.00
• Chicken burger	$4.50
• French fries	$2.00
• Coke(small/large)	$1.00 / $1.50

① $20.00   ② $20.50   ③ $21.00
④ $21.50   ⑤ $21.00

W Welcome to King Burgers.
M Hi, what kind of burgers do you have?
W We have a variety of burgers, but cheeseburgers and chicken burgers are ❶ _____ _____ _____ _____.
M All right. Can I have one cheeseburger and two chicken burgers, please?   W Okay. Any drinks?
M ❷ _____ _____ _____ with ice, please.
W Anything else?
M Oh, ❸ _____ _____ _____ _____ _____ orders of French fries.
W Okay. For here or to go?   M To go, please.

11 장소 추론   영국식 발음 녹음

대화를 듣고, 두 사람이 대화하고 있는 장소로 가장 적절한 곳을 고르시오.

① 은행   ② 호텔   ③ 상점
④ 극장   ⑤ 공항

M Good evening, I'd like to ❶ _____ _____.
W May I have your name, please?   M Yes, my name is Larry Kim.
W Just one moment, please. Is that just ❷ _____ _____ _____?   M Right.
W How will you be paying?   M By credit card.
W May I have your credit card, please?
M Sure, here it is.   W ❸ _____ _____ _____.

12 언급되지 않은 것

다음을 듣고, Blue Planet 수족관에 관해 언급되지 않은 것을 고르시오.

① 체험 활동   ② 편의 시설   ③ 입장료
④ 운영 시간   ⑤ 가는 방법

W Have you heard about the Blue Planet Aquarium? If you plan to visit London, don't miss this wonderful place. You can watch ❶ _____ _____ _____ _____ _____ and even feed them. We also have a restaurant and a gift shop, so come and enjoy all these things. We open from 10 a.m. to 6 p.m. every day. You ❷ _____ _____ _____ _____ from Big Ben to get here. Thank you.

13 도표 정보 파악

다음을 듣고, 내용과 일치하지 않는 것을 고르시오.

World League Baseball		
①	Date	May 29th
②	Place	Dodger Stadium
③	Teams	Dodgers vs. Angels
④	Score	4:1
⑤	MVP	Hyunjin Ryu

M On May 29th, I went to Dodger Stadium to watch a baseball game. The Dodgers ❶ _____ _____ the Angels. To be honest, I prefer the Dodgers because a Korean player, Hyunjin Ryu plays for them. On that day, the final score was ❷ _____ _____ _____. Even better news was the MVP of the game was Hyunjin Ryu.

Words   **10 a variety of** 다양한   **11 check in** 투숙 수속을 밟다   **12 miss** 놓치다 **feed** 먹이를 주다 **gift shop** 선물가게   **13 stadium** 경기장, 스타디움 **to be honest** 솔직하게 말하면

Dictation Test

14 주제 파악

다음을 듣고, 무엇에 관한 설명인지 고르시오.

① 치아 ② 수염 ③ 손톱
④ 발톱 ⑤ 머리카락

W These are a part of your body. Unlike most parts of your body, these are ❶ _____ _____ _____ _____. Because they're very hard, some might think they are part of the bone. However, they are really part of your skin. ❷ _____ _____ _____ little by little, so people cut them from time to time. They basically protect ❸ _____ _____ _____ _____ _____. Many people decorate them with nail polish to make their hands look pretty.

15 한 일 / 할 일 파악

대화를 듣고, 두 사람이 대화 직후에 할 일로 가장 적절한 것을 고르시오.

① 초밥 만들기 ② 김밥 만들기
③ 장보러 가기 ④ 김밥 사러 가기
⑤ 한국 음식 수업 듣기

M I'm so hungry.
W Me, too. I ❶ _____ _____ _____ gimbap.
M Gimbap? What is it?
W It's a popular Korean food.
M What does it look like?
W It looks like sushi, but there is no raw fish in gimbap.
M ❷ _____ _____ _____ _____ at home?
W Sure, but we need a few things to make it.
M Then, let's ❸ _____ _____ _____ _____ first.
W Okay, let's go.

16 숫자 정보 파악 – 시각   영국식 발음 녹음

대화를 듣고, 두 사람이 박물관 투어를 시작할 시각을 고르시오.

① 9:00 ② 9:30 ③ 10:00
④ 10:30 ⑤ 11:00

M Wow! This national museum is one of the biggest museums in the world.
W Awesome!
M They ❶ _____ _____ _____ _____ twice a day. Are you interested?
W Sure. Let's check the time.
M Let's see. Now ❷ _____ _____ _____. The first one has already started.
W Right, the second one will ❸ _____ _____ _____ _____ _____. Are we going to wait?
M Yes, let's wait. Why don't we read this map while waiting?
W That's a great idea.

Words **14** unlike ~와 달리 from time to time 가끔(이따금) basically 근본적으로 protect 보호하다 polish 광택제 **15** raw fish 생선 **16** national 국가의 awesome 놀라운 while ~하는 동안

17 상황에 맞는 말 찾기

다음 상황 설명을 듣고, 지호가 Lisa에게 할 말로 가장 적절한 것을 고르시오.

Jiho: _____

① You need to skip dinner as well.
② I think you should say sorry first.
③ Why don't you work out at the gym?
④ I'm worried that I'm gaining a lot of weight.
⑤ How about having lunch together when you're free?

W Jiho and Lisa are best friends. Lisa thinks she is gaining weight these days, so she begins to skip lunch every day. As one of her best friends, Jiho is really ❶ _____ _____ _____ because she doesn't look healthy. Jiho wants to tell her to do something ❷ _____ _____ _____ _____ . In this situation, what would Jiho most likely say to Lisa?

18 한 일 / 할 일 파악

대화를 듣고, 남자가 오늘 할 일이 <u>아닌</u> 것을 고르시오.

① 숙제하기   ② 소포 받기
③ 자기 방 청소하기   ④ Jenny 집에 놀러 가기
⑤ 컴퓨터 수리하러 가기

😊 헤어질 때 인사하기 ////////////////////////
See you. / (Have a) nice day. / Take care. /
Goodbye. / Bye(-bye).

[*Cellphone rings.*]
M Hi, Jenny. What's up?
W Joon, ❶ _____ _____ _____ your homework?
M Yes.
W Then, would you like to come to my house? Jack and Gyuri are here, too.
M I'm afraid I can't. I need to ❷ _____ _____ _____ and clean my room now. After that, I have to go to a repair shop to fix my computer, too.
W We'll be here until 8 p.m.
M Really? Then, I can ❸ _____ _____ _____ at 5 p.m.
W Okay, see you then.

19 알맞은 응답 찾기

대화를 듣고, 남자의 마지막 말에 대한 여자의 응답으로 가장 적절한 것을 고르시오.

Woman: _____

① I'm surprised to hear that.
② It means, "Thank you my friend."
③ Do you know how to sing the song?
④ It is important to understand the meaning.
⑤ I think this song will be really good for the play.

M What are you doing?
W I'm listening to music. I'm choosing ❶ _____ _____ for the play.
M Are you the music director of the play for the school festival?
W Yes, and this is harder than I thought.
M Have you ❷ _____ _____ _____ _____ ?
W Yes, but I haven't decided which one I'll use. Would you like to listen to this?   **M** This one is good. What's the title?
W It's "Gracias Mi Amigo."
M "Gracias Mi Amigo"? ❸ _____ _____ _____ _____ ?

20 알맞은 응답 찾기

대화를 듣고, 여자의 마지막 말에 대한 남자의 응답으로 가장 적절한 것을 고르시오.

Man: _____

① Twice a week.
② Let's take a taxi.
③ About 15 minutes.
④ Can I give you a ride?
⑤ You can say that again.

W Excuse me. Can I ask you something?   **M** Sure. What is it?
W Can you tell me ❶ _____ _____ _____ _____ the Toronto Zoo?
M Oh, it isn't far from here. You can either walk or take a bus.
W ❷ _____ _____ _____ _____ if I walk?
M It'll take about half an hour.
W Then, what about ❸ _____ _____ _____ ?

Words **17** gain weight 체중이 늘다 skip 거르다, 건너뛰다   **18** repair 수리; 수리하다 fix 고치다, 수리하다   **19** background music 배경 음악 director 감독 suitable 적합한   **20** far from ~에서 먼

01 대화를 듣고, 여자가 구입할 커튼을 고르시오.

02 대화를 듣고, 여자가 남자에게 전화한 목적으로 가장 적절한 것을 고르시오.

① 모임을 초대하려고
② 비행기 표를 예매하려고
③ 모임 장소를 확인하려고
④ 비행기 시간을 확인하려고
⑤ 기차표 구매 가능 여부를 확인하려고

03 다음 그림의 상황에 가장 적절한 대화를 고르시오.

①   ②   ③   ④   ⑤

04 대화를 듣고, 두 사람이 샌드위치를 사러 가기로 한 요일을 고르시오.

① 수요일   ② 목요일   ③ 금요일
④ 토요일   ⑤ 일요일

05 대화를 듣고, 남자의 직업으로 가장 적절한 것을 고르시오.

① designer   ② mechanic
③ police officer   ④ cellphone seller
⑤ service center staff

06 대화를 듣고, 남자의 심정으로 가장 적절한 것을 고르시오.

① jealous   ② annoyed
③ satisfied   ④ expected
⑤ disappointed

07 다음을 듣고, 두 사람의 대화가 <u>어색한</u> 것을 고르시오.

①   ②   ③   ④   ⑤

08 대화를 듣고, 남자가 여자에게 부탁한 일로 가장 적절한 것을 고르시오.

① 짐 싸 주기
② 전화로 택시 부르기
③ 서울역에 데려다주기
④ 시계 배터리를 교환하기
⑤ 대신해서 사촌 마중 가기

09 대화를 듣고, 남자의 마지막 말에 담긴 의도로 가장 적절한 것을 고르시오.

① 동의   ② 감사   ③ 충고
④ 거절   ⑤ 제안

10 대화를 듣고, 남자가 거스름돈으로 받을 금액을 고르시오.

① $25   ② $30   ③ $45
④ $55   ⑤ $60

11 대화를 듣고, 두 사람이 대화하고 있는 장소로 가장 적절한 곳을 고르시오.

① 산 　　② 해변 　　③ 병원
④ 야영지 　　⑤ 백화점

12 다음을 듣고, 파티에 관해 언급되지 <u>않은</u> 것을 고르시오.

① 요일 　　② 장소 　　③ 시간
④ 교통편 　　⑤ 참석 인원

13 대화를 듣고, 여자가 화분을 놓을 곳의 위치를 고르시오.

14 다음을 듣고, 무엇에 관한 설명인지 고르시오.

① 세탁기 　　② 컴퓨터
③ 선풍기 　　④ 냉장고
⑤ 에어컨

15 대화를 듣고, 여자가 대화 직후에 할 일로 가장 적절한 것을 고르시오.

① 지하철 환승하기
② 노인의 가방 들어주기
③ 다음 정거장에서 내리기
④ 노인에게 자리 양보하기
⑤ 남자에게 자리 양보 부탁하기

16 대화를 듣고, 여자가 과제를 제출할 날짜를 고르시오.

① May 6 　　② May 12
③ May 16 　　④ May 17
⑤ May 20

17 다음 상황 설명을 듣고, Peter가 Judy에게 할 말로 가장 적절한 것을 고르시오.

Peter: _____

① Don't be late again, please.
② Are you on your way home?
③ I'm going to take the subway.
④ I'm sorry but I'll be a little late.
⑤ We need to change the meeting place.

18 대화를 듣고, 여자가 대화 직후에 할 일로 가장 적절한 것을 고르시오.

① 민주에게 전화 걸기
② 민주네 집 방문하기
③ 민주에게 약 사다 주기
④ 놀이공원으로 출발하기
⑤ 민주에게 문자 메시지 보내기

19 대화를 듣고, 여자의 마지막 말에 대한 남자의 응답으로 가장 적절한 것을 고르시오.

Man: _____

① It's probably possible.
② You've made a mistake.
③ Of course not. Come if you want.
④ Can someone tell me the time and place?
⑤ I'm sorry but I can't go to your performance.

20 대화를 듣고, 남자의 마지막 말에 대한 여자의 응답으로 가장 적절한 것을 고르시오.

Woman: _____

① Please come again tomorrow.
② This is the address of our website.
③ Thank you for carrying out the survey.
④ You can use it by the end of September.
⑤ You can have any kind of drink with this coupon.

01 그림 정보 파악 – 사물

대화를 듣고, 여자가 구입할 커튼을 고르시오.

① ② ③
④ ⑤

M How do you like your new house?
W I like it, but I want to make it a more cozy place. Help me ❶ _____ _____ _____ _____.
M Okay. What about these with the teddy bear print?
W They're not my style. They ❷ _____ _____ _____.
M You don't like flower prints either, right?
W I hate flower prints. Aren't these checked curtains nice?
M I don't know, they're not my type. Aren't these striped ones better?
W Well, I ❸ _____ _____ _____ _____.

02 목적 파악

대화를 듣고, 여자가 남자에게 전화한 목적으로 가장 적절한 것을 고르시오.

① 모임을 초대하려고
② 비행기 표를 예매하려고
③ 모임 장소를 확인하려고
④ 비행기 시간을 확인하려고
⑤ 기차표 구매 가능 여부를 확인하려고

😊 바람, 소원, 요망 표현하기 ///////////////////////
I wish I could ~. / I'd like ~. / I want (to) ~. / I look(am looking) forward to ~.

[Telephone rings.]
M Hello?
W Hi, Laurence. It's me.
M Susie, aren't you supposed to be on the plane by now? How are you calling me?
W I ❶ _____ _____ _____, so I'm at the airport now.
M How come?
W I misunderstood the flight schedule.
M Oh, dear. You ❷ _____ _____ _____ _____ in Mokpo. I wish I could help you.
W Actually, I need your help. Could you check if ❸ _____ _____ _____ _____ Mokpo is available?
M Okay. Let me check it on the Internet and call you back.

03 그림 상황에 어울리는 대화 찾기

다음 그림의 상황에 가장 적절한 대화를 고르시오.

① ② ③ ④ ⑤

① W Let's play soccer together. M No, I want to play basketball.
② W You seem to be into ❶ _____ _____.
   M Yeah. I can't stop reading it.
③ W Hey, you've been playing ❷ _____ _____ _____ _____ _____.
   M Just five more minutes. This is the last stage.
④ W For how long have you been studying?
   M I just started.
⑤ W Oh, I think my computer ❸ _____ _____ _____ _____.
   M Let me see. I'll try to fix it.

Words 01 cozy 아늑한 childish 어린애 같은, 유치한 checked 체크무늬의 striped 줄무늬가 있는 02 miss ~을 놓치다 misunderstand 잘못 이해하다(-misunderstood) flight 비행 available 구할 수 있는 03 be into ~에 빠져 있다 stage 단계 fix 고치다

04 | 특정 정보 파악 – 요일 | 영국식 발음 녹음

대화를 듣고, 두 사람이 샌드위치를 사러 가기로 한 요일을
고르시오.

① 수요일　　② 목요일　　③ 금요일

④ 토요일　　⑤ 일요일

W　This sandwich is really delicious. Where did you buy it?

M　I bought it at the bakery near my house.

W　Please take me there some day. I want to see ❶ _____ _____
_____ _____.

M　Okay. Then let's go to buy sandwiches together. How about this
Friday?

W　I'm afraid I can't. Can we go this Thursday?

M　No, I ❷ _____ _____ _____ _____. Then how about
this weekend?

W　That's fine with me. Which day is better for you?

M　Can you come over ❸ _____ _____? I'm not sure about
Sunday.

W　Saturday sounds good.

05 | 직업 및 장래 희망

대화를 듣고, 남자의 직업으로 가장 적절한 것을 고르
시오.

① designer　　② mechanic

③ police officer　　④ cellphone seller

⑤ service center staff

😊 **감사에 답하기** ////////////////////

No problem. / You're welcome. / (It was) my
pleasure. / Don't mention it.

M　How can I help you?

W　Hello, I dropped my cellphone in the toilet ❶ _____ _____,
and it isn't working.

M　We ❷ _____ _____ _____ _____, and you need to
visit the service center to fix your phone.

W　I see. Can you tell me where the nearest service center is?

M　It is located in Yongsan Station.

W　Thanks for your help.

M😊No problem, but I'm afraid it will cost a lot of money to fix it. In that
case, you'd better ❸ _____ _____ _____ _____, so
please visit here again.

W　I will, thanks.

06 | 심정 파악

대화를 듣고, 남자의 심정으로 가장 적절한 것을 고르
시오.

① jealous　　② annoyed

③ satisfied　　④ expected

⑤ disappointed

W　Hi, Ted. ❶ _____ _____ _____ _____ my house
tomorrow? We're going to have a pajama party.

M　What about your parents?

W　They're on a trip, so they're coming back in a week.

M　Cool. Have you ❷ _____ _____ _____?

W　Sure. Julie, Monica, Luke, and Tony are coming.

M　Did you say Luke? I haven't seen him since elementary school.
❸ _____ _____ _____ _____ him. Okay. I
will go to your house tomorrow.

Ⓦords　**04 bakery** 빵집, 제과점　**05 toilet** 변기　**service center** 서비스 센터　**be located in** ~에 위치하다　**06 pajama party** 파자마 파티(친구
집에서 밤새워 노는 모임)

Dictation Test

07 어색한 대화 찾기

다음을 듣고, 두 사람의 대화가 <u>어색한</u> 것을 고르시오.
①   ②   ③   ④   ⑤

ⓟ cleaned your의 발음 ////////////////////

자음과 you의 반모음 y가 만나면 자연스럽게 연결되어 발음되므로, cleaned your는 [kliːnjuər]처럼 발음된다.

① W   Could you boil some water?
   M   Okay. Let's _____ _____ _____ _____.❶
② W   Are these dolls for sale?
   M   No, they're not. They're part of the exhibits.
③ W   Where did you ❷ _____ _____ _____?
   M   I just stayed at home watching TV.
④ W   Haven't you ⓟ cleaned your room yet?
   M   No, I was busy doing my homework.
⑤ W   You cannot ❸ _____ _____ _____ here.
   M   I didn't know it was a private parking area.

08 부탁한 일 파악   영국식 발음 녹음

대화를 듣고, 남자가 여자에게 부탁한 일로 가장 적절한 것을 고르시오.
① 짐 싸 주기
② 전화로 택시 부르기
③ 서울역에 데려다주기
④ 시계 배터리를 교환하기
⑤ 대신해서 사촌 마중 가기

M   Is it still 3 o'clock?
W   That's strange. It was 3 when I saw the clock a while ago.
M   ❶ _____ _____ _____ my cellphone clock. Oh, my gosh. It's 4:30.
W   The clock's battery must have run out.
M   What'll I do? I ❷ _____ _____ _____ _____ _____ Seoul Station by 5 to meet my cousin.
W   It's impossible to get to Seoul Station in 30 minutes by subway. Why don't you take a taxi?
M   Okay. Can you ❸ _____ _____ _____ _____ while I pack my bag?
W   Sure.

09 의도 파악

대화를 듣고, 남자의 마지막 말에 담긴 의도로 가장 적절한 것을 고르시오.
① 동의   ② 감사   ③ 충고
④ 거절   ⑤ 제안

😊 사과하기 ////////////////////////////

I apologize. / I'm so (very) sorry (about that). / Please forgive me.

W   Excuse me, aren't you Josh Austin? Can I get your autograph?
M   Umm, I'm not.   W   Oops, I apologize.
M   No, no. But ❶ _____ _____ _____ I look like the singer a lot.
W   Can I ❷ _____ _____ _____ _____?
M   What is it?
W   Could you take a picture with me? My friends will believe that I met Josh.
M   ❸ _____ _____ _____. Josh Austin would not be happy if he knew I was pretending to be him.
W   Oh, you're right.

Words   **07 boil** 끓이다   **for sale** 판매 중인   **exhibit** 전시품   **private** 사적인   **parking area** 주차장   **08 a while ago** 조금 전에   **run out** 다 쓰다   **impossible** 불가능한   **pack** (짐을) 싸다   **09 autograph** (유명인의) 사인   **pretend** ~인 척하다

10 숫자 정보 파악 – 금액

대화를 듣고, 남자가 거스름돈으로 받을 금액을 고르시오.

① $25 ② $30 ③ $45
④ $55 ⑤ $60

ⓟ clothes의 발음
clothes는 [klouðz]로 발음되기보다 주로 발음의 편의상 [klouz]로 발음된다. 이는 close의 발음과 매우 유사하므로 앞뒤의 내용을 통해 단어를 파악해야 한다.

M Hello, I came to get my clothes. Are they all dry-cleaned?
W Yes. ⓟ _____ _____ _____ and a coat are yours, right?
M They are. How much are they?
W They're ❷ _____ _____ _____.
M Wow, is it that expensive?
W It's $15 to dry-clean a sweater, and $25 for a coat.
M I see. Here's a 100 dollar bill.

11 장소 추론

대화를 듣고, 두 사람이 대화하고 있는 장소로 가장 적절한 곳을 고르시오.

① 산 ② 해변 ③ 병원
④ 야영지 ⑤ 백화점

W Aren't we there yet? I want to take a rest for a while.
M Okay. Let's ❶ _____ _____ _____ here.
W If I had known ❷ _____ _____ _____ _____, I would have gone to the beach instead.
M You would have regretted it if you had gone to the beach. It's too crowded there.
W Maybe or maybe not. Anyway, my legs are killing me.
M Give me your bag. It will only take 15 minutes ❸ _____ _____ _____ _____ _____.

12 언급되지 않은 것

다음을 듣고, 파티에 관해 언급되지 않은 것을 고르시오.

① 요일 ② 장소 ③ 시간
④ 교통편 ⑤ 참석 인원

ⓒ 의도 표현하기
I'm planning to ~. / I'm thinking of ~. / I'm going to ~.

W Please leave a message. (beep)
M Hi, Natalie. I recently moved to a new house, and I'm planning to throw a party. If you are ❶ _____ _____ _____, come to my house by 12 o'clock. You can take the number 3 bus and ❷ _____ _____ _____ Jisan Station. Since Jenny has been to my house, you can contact her and come together. Hope to see you on Saturday.

13 그림 정보 파악 영국식 발음 녹음

대화를 듣고, 여자가 화분을 놓을 곳의 위치를 고르시오.

ⓒ 걱정, 두려움 표현하기
I'm worried (about ~). / I'm anxious (about ~). / I'm scared(frightened, terrified) (to ~).

W I don't know where to put this little flowerpot.
M There are many ❶ _____ _____ _____ _____. Between the door and the bookshelf is empty.
W I don't want to put it on the floor.
M How about on the head of the bed?
W I'm worried I might hit it by mistake when I'm in bed.
M Then, how about ❷ _____ _____ _____? I don't think you would hit it by mistake there.
W You are right. But the space doesn't seem to be big enough.
M Oh, I think ❸ _____ _____ will be the best. There's a big window in front of the desk.
W That's a good idea. Flowers need a lot of sun. I'll put it there.

Words 10 dry-clean 드라이클리닝하다 11 take a rest 휴식을 취하다 instead 대신에 regret 후회하다 crowd 붐비다 12 throw a party 파티를 열다 contact 연락하다 13 flowerpot 화분 spot 자리, 장소 by mistake 실수로 space 공간

Dictation Test

14 주제 파악

다음을 듣고, 무엇에 관한 설명인지 고르시오.

① 세탁기　　　　② 컴퓨터
③ 선풍기　　　　④ 냉장고
⑤ 에어컨

M It keeps ❶ _____ _____ _____ _____. Before, it was usually a wooden box with ❷ _____ _____ _____ _____ _____ in it. These days, it is made of metal. And it's a pretty big, rectangular box. And it has one or two doors. It can be operated ❸ _____ _____.

15 한 일 / 할 일 파악

대화를 듣고, 여자가 대화 직후에 할 일로 가장 적절한 것을 고르시오.

① 지하철 환승하기
② 노인의 가방 들어주기
③ 다음 정거장에서 내리기
④ 노인에게 자리 양보하기
⑤ 남자에게 자리 양보 부탁하기

W Look at that young woman in the seat for the elderly. She's not ❶ _____ _____ _____ _____ the old man in front of her.
M She might have her own reasons.
W Such as?
M Maybe she's suffering from a leg injury or ❷ _____ _____ _____ _____ a baby. Don't you think so?
W You might be right. I'd better give the old man ❸ _____ _____.
M How kind of you!

16 숫자 정보 파악 – 날짜　영국식 발음 녹음

대화를 듣고, 여자가 과제를 제출할 날짜를 고르시오.

① May 6　　　　② May 12
③ May 16　　　　④ May 17
⑤ May 20

😊 **반복 요청하기** ////////////////////////////////
(I'm) sorry? / What (did you say)? / (I beg your) pardon? / Would you say that again(, please)?

M Miran, can I talk to you for a moment?
W Sure, Mr. Kim.
M You haven't handed in the report yet.
W 😊 Sorry? Isn't ❶ _____ _____ _____ _____ May 20th?
M No, it was due on the 12th, and it's already the 16th today.
W I'll ❷ _____ _____ _____ _____ _____.
M Okay.

17 상황에 맞는 말 찾기

다음 상황 설명을 듣고, Peter가 Judy에게 할 말로 가장 적절한 것을 고르시오.

Peter: _____

① Don't be late again, please.
② Are you on your way home?
③ I'm going to take the subway.
④ I'm sorry but I'll be a little late.
⑤ We need to change the meeting place.

W Peter got on the subway to meet Judy. He was very tired, so he took a nap for a while. When Peter opened his eyes, however, he found out that he had ❶ _____ _____ _____. It was certain that he ❷ _____ _____ _____ _____ _____. Judy might be at the meeting place. In this situation, what would Peter most likely say to Judy?

📖 **Words** ● **14 metal** 금속　**rectangular** 직사각형의　**operate** 작동하다　**15 elderly** 어른들　**suffer from** ～로 고통 받다　**injury** 부상　**16 hand in** (과제물 등을) 제출하다　**due** ～하기로 예정된　**17 take a nap** 낮잠을 자다

18 한일/할일파악

대화를 듣고, 여자가 대화 직후에 할 일로 가장 적절한 것을 고르시오.

① 민주에게 전화 걸기
② 민주네 집 방문하기
③ 민주에게 약 사다 주기
④ 놀이공원으로 출발하기
⑤ 민주에게 문자 메시지 보내기

M Has everybody come? Let's leave for the amusement park.

W Wait, Minju hasn't come yet.

M Oh, didn't she say she had a stomachache yesterday?

W She did. Maybe she's still sick, so I ❶ _____ _____ _____ _____ _____ five minutes ago.

M She might not be able to check her cellphone. Would you ❷ _____ _____?

W All right.

19 알맞은 응답 찾기

대화를 듣고, 여자의 마지막 말에 대한 남자의 응답으로 가장 적절한 것을 고르시오.

Man: _____

① It's probably possible.
② You've made a mistake.
③ Of course not. Come if you want.
④ Can someone tell me the time and place?
⑤ I'm sorry but I can't go to your performance.

W Are you going to your club now?

M Yes, we have to ❶ _____ _____ _____ _____ next week.

W I'm sorry that I can't go to the show.

M I understand. You have an important family gathering.

W But I really want to ❷ _____ _____ _____.

M Well, actually, we have a rehearsal tomorrow.

W Really? Do you mind if ❸ _____ _____ _____ _____ it?

20 알맞은 응답 찾기

대화를 듣고, 남자의 마지막 말에 대한 여자의 응답으로 가장 적절한 것을 고르시오.

Woman: _____

① Please come again tomorrow.
② This is the address of our website.
③ Thank you for carrying out the survey.
④ You can use it by the end of September.
⑤ You can have any kind of drink with this coupon.

W Congratulations! You are the 100th customer of our store today.

M Am I? It's a surprise.

W As a gift, we are giving you ❶ _____ _____ _____ _____.

M That's great. Thank you.

W Here is the coupon. Please visit our homepage, enter these numbers and fill out a simple survey.

M Huh, that's ❷ _____ _____.

W It will take less than five minutes.

M Okay, I'll try. By ❸ _____ _____ _____ _____ _____?

 18 leave for ~로 떠나다 **stomachache** 복통 **19 practice** 연습하다 **family gathering** 가족 모임 **performance** 공연; 연주회 **rehearsal** 리허설, 예행연습 **probably** 아마도 **20 customer** 고객 **fill out** 작성하다 **simple** 간단한 **survey** (설문) 조사

01 대화를 듣고, 내용 중 언급되지 <u>않은</u> 표지판을 고르시오.

①
②
③
④
⑤

02 대화를 듣고, 남자가 여자에게 전화한 목적으로 가장 적절한 것을 고르시오.

① 빌렸던 것을 돌려주려고
② 여자와 학교에 같이 가려고
③ 여자와 함께 게임을 하려고
④ 여자와 함께 영화를 보려고
⑤ 내일 여자와 학교에서 만날 약속을 잡으려고

03 다음 그림의 상황에 가장 적절한 대화를 고르시오.

① ② ③ ④ ⑤

04 대화를 듣고, 두 사람이 만나기로 한 장소를 고르시오.

① 학교 정문   ② 극장
③ 여자의 집   ④ 남자의 교실
⑤ 여자의 교실

05 대화를 듣고, 여자의 심정으로 가장 적절한 것을 고르시오.

① happy   ② bored
③ lonely   ④ excited
⑤ embarrassed

06 대화를 듣고, 두 사람의 관계로 가장 적절한 것을 고르시오.

① teacher − parent
② student − student
③ teacher − student
④ father − daughter
⑤ teacher − teacher

07 다음을 듣고, 두 사람의 대화가 <u>어색한</u> 것을 고르시오.

①   ②   ③   ④   ⑤

08 대화를 듣고, 남자가 여자에게 부탁한 일로 가장 적절한 것을 고르시오.

① 아침에 깨워 주기
② 학교에 함께 오기
③ Ann의 의견 물어보기
④ Ann을 소개시켜 주기
⑤ 자신과 가까이 사는 친구 찾아보기

09 대화를 듣고, 남자의 마지막 말에 담긴 의도로 가장 적절한 것을 고르시오.

① 동의   ② 사과   ③ 격려
④ 감사   ⑤ 충고

10 대화를 듣고, 남자가 지불할 금액을 고르시오.

① $15   ② $20   ③ $25
④ $30   ⑤ $35

11 다음을 듣고, 비가 올 경우 오후 2시에 방문할 장소를 고르시오.

① Central Park
② Brooklyn Bridge
③ the Statue of Liberty
④ Radio City Music Hall
⑤ the Museum of Modern Art

12 다음을 듣고, 도서 대출에 관해 언급되지 <u>않은</u> 것을 고르시오.

① 대출 시 필요한 물품
② 대출 가능 권 수
③ 대출 기간
④ 원하는 책 찾는 법
⑤ 반납 연체 시 처리

13 대화를 듣고, 아이스 쇼에 대한 설명으로 <u>잘못된</u> 것을 고르시오.

① Title: Winter Dream
② Date: June 21st
③ Time: 7 p.m. ~ 9 p.m.
④ Admission: R–$100/S–$60/A–$20
⑤ Don't take pictures inside.

14 다음을 듣고, 무엇에 관한 설명인지 고르시오.

① 우산　　② 모자　　③ 헬멧
④ 머리띠　　⑤ 마스크

15 대화를 듣고, 남자가 대화 직후에 할 일로 가장 적절한 것을 고르시오.

① 전화 끊기　　② 남동생 바꿔 주기
③ 메시지 전달하기　　④ 전화번호 알려 주기
⑤ 남동생에게 전화 걸기

16 대화를 듣고, 두 사람이 만날 시각을 고르시오.

① 12:00　　② 1:00　　③ 3:00
④ 4:00　　⑤ 5:00

17 다음 상황 설명을 듣고, Andy가 영미에게 할 말로 가장 적절한 것을 고르시오.

Andy: _____

① Sure. Go ahead.
② Can you lend me a paintbrush?
③ What are you going to paint today?
④ Do we have to move to the art room now?
⑤ Remind me to bring more paintbrush next time.

18 대화를 듣고, 두 사람이 이번 주말에 할 일로 가장 적절한 것을 고르시오.

① bowling only
② going dancing
③ going out to dinner only
④ going out to dinner and bowling
⑤ going out to dinner and seeing a movie

19 대화를 듣고, 남자의 마지막 말에 대한 여자의 응답으로 가장 적절한 것을 고르시오.

Woman: _____

① Let me go get some medicine.
② I hope she becomes the class leader.
③ She has been waiting for you to come.
④ If I were you, I would have selected her.
⑤ Time is the best medicine. Let's just wait here.

20 대화를 듣고, 여자의 마지막 말에 대한 남자의 응답으로 가장 적절한 것을 고르시오.

Man: _____

① He's not my type.
② Jackie Chan's movie.
③ I learn judo, instead.
④ I don't know about the movie.
⑤ Michael Jackson, the king of pop.

Dictation Test 18회 영어 듣기모의고사

01 [그림 정보 파악 – 사물]

대화를 듣고, 내용 중 언급되지 않은 표지판을 고르시오.

① ② ③ ④ ⑤

W What's that sign? It has a picture of a mother and her child.
M That's ❶ _____ _____ _____.
W I see. And what does the one with the bicycle mean?
M It means you ❷ _____ _____ _____ _____ there.
W Okay. And that sign? What does it mean?
M When you see that sign, you ❸ _____ _____ _____.
W Oh, I see. How about that sign?
M It means you ❹ _____ _____ _____.

02 [목적 파악]

대화를 듣고, 남자가 여자에게 전화한 목적으로 가장 적절한 것을 고르시오.

① 빌렸던 것을 돌려주려고
② 여자와 학교에 같이 가려고
③ 여자와 함께 게임을 하려고
④ 여자와 함께 영화를 보려고
⑤ 내일 여자와 학교에서 만날 약속을 잡으려고

[Telephone rings.]
W Hello?
M Mary, this is Mike. Where are you now?
W I'm home. I am watching a movie with my brother. What's up?
M Can I ❶ _____ _____ _____ _____ now and return the game I borrowed?
W You don't have to come to my house. You can ❷ _____ _____ _____ tomorrow at school.
M I just happened to be ❸ _____ _____ _____ _____. I'll just drop this off and leave. I'll be there in 5 minutes.
W All right then. See you soon.

03 [그림 상황에 어울리는 대화 찾기]

다음 그림의 상황에 가장 적절한 대화를 고르시오.

① ② ③ ④ ⑤

😊 **동의하기** ///////////////////////////////
(Yes,) I agree. / Me, too. / Same here. / Okay! / Good! / That's a good idea.

① M Ma'am, what are we going to do today?
  W ❶ _____ _____ _____ _____ read this short story and draw the most impressive scene of it.
② M I am going to ❷ _____ _____ _____. Which color do you think is better, blue or yellow?
  W How about blue? I think blue will go better with this room.
③ M You know what? The painter of this picture is blind.
  W Really? Then how did she paint this picture?
④ M Let me take a picture of you. Go stand ❸ _____ _____ _____.
  W Okay. Do I look all right?
⑤ M This book doesn't have enough information about pictures. Don't you think so?
  W 😊 I agree. The writer should have written more about them.

Words ● **01 crosswalk** 횡단보도 **02 drop by** (~에) 들르다 **happen** 마침 ~하다 **pass by** (~을) 지나가다 **drop ~ off** ~을 배달해 주다
03 impressive 인상적인 **scene** 장면 **paint** 그리다, 색칠하다 **statue** 동상 **information** 정보

04 [장소 추론] 영국식 발음 녹음

대화를 듣고, 두 사람이 만나기로 한 장소를 고르시오.

① 학교 정문   ② 극장
③ 여자의 집   ④ 남자의 교실
⑤ 여자의 교실

M We are going to meet at the front gate of the school after class, right?

W Well, I'm sorry, but we have to ❶ _____ _____ _____. Can we meet at the movie theater?

M Sure, but what's the matter?

W I forgot to ❷ _____ _____ _____. I'll go home and get it.

M I can lend you money if you want.

W Really? I'll pay you back tomorrow. Oh, there's the bell. I have to go back to my classroom.

M Then we are going to meet ❸ _____ _____ _____ _____ as we promised?

W Sure. See you later.

05 [심정 파악]

대화를 듣고, 여자의 심정으로 가장 적절한 것을 고르시오.

① happy   ② bored
③ lonely   ④ excited
⑤ embarrassed

W Oh, my gosh!

M What's happening?

W ❶ _____ _____ _____ _____ suddenly. I was working on my computer.

M Did you save it?

W No, I totally forgot. I ❷ _____ _____ _____ _____.

M Hey, I have an idea. I'll bring Peter to help you. He will be able to recover that file. He's an expert in computers.

W But, if he can't recover it, what ❸ _____ _____ _____ _____ _____?

06 [관계 추론]

대화를 듣고, 두 사람의 관계로 가장 적절한 것을 고르시오.

① teacher – parent
② student – student
③ teacher – student
④ father – daughter
⑤ teacher – teacher

M Mina, I heard you got a perfect score on the English listening test.

W Yeah, it was the first time I got a perfect score.

M ❶ _____ _____ I were good at English, too. Please ❷ _____ _____ _____ _____ _____ your score.

W Well, there's nothing special. I bought a workbook and listened to the MP3 file over and over.

M Is that all?

W Yeah, that's true.

M Right. Maybe ❸ _____ _____ _____ _____ as well.

ⓌWords **04 front gate** 정문 **pay back** (돈 등을) 갚다 **as** ~한 대로   **05 save** 저장하다 **totally** 완전히 **recover** 복구하다, 회복하다 **expert** 전문가, 숙련가   **06 perfect score** 만점 **workbook** (연습) 문제집

Dictation Test

07 어색한 대화 찾기

다음을 듣고, 두 사람의 대화가 <u>어색한</u> 것을 고르시오.

① ② ③ ④ ⑤

ⓟ Which one is ~?의 발음 //////////////////////
Which ~, *A* or *B*?와 같은 선택의문문의 경우에는 A는 올려 말하고 B는 내려 말한다.

① W **❶** _____ _____ _____ _____?
   M Yes, but not clearly.
② W What can I call you?
   M You can call me Jake.
③ W This coffee shop is too crowded.
   M Shall we go somewhere else?
④ W **❷** _____ _____ _____ _____ the modern art museum?
   M I'm not good at painting.
⑤ W **ⓟ** Which one is better, the red one or the white one?
   M I like **❸** _____ _____ _____.

08 부탁한 일 파악   영국식 발음 녹음

대화를 듣고, 남자가 여자에게 부탁한 일로 가장 적절한 것을 고르시오.

① 아침에 깨워 주기
② 학교에 함께 오기
③ Ann의 의견 물어보기
④ Ann을 소개시켜 주기
⑤ 자신과 가까이 사는 친구 찾아보기

☺ 능력 표현하기 ////////////////////////////
I can ~. / I am able to ~. / I know how to ~. / I'm (pretty) good at ~.

M Ma'am, I'm sorry I'm late.
W What made you late? You are usually on time.
M Well, my mom started working, so I'm alone at home in the morning now. Because there's nobody to wake me up, Sometimes I have **❶** _____ _____ _____ _____ _____.
W Did you set an alarm?
M I tried, but I **❷** _____ _____ _____ today.
W Ann lives near your place. You can come with her.
M That's a good idea, but I'm not that close to her. Can you ask her if that would be okay? Then **❸** _____ _____ _____ to ring my doorbell on her way to school.
W Okay. I can do that for you.

09 의도 파악

대화를 듣고, 남자의 마지막 말에 담긴 의도로 가장 적절한 것을 고르시오.

① 동의   ② 사과   ③ 격려
④ 감사   ⑤ 충고

☺ 슬픔, 불만족, 실망의 원인에 대해 묻기 //////////
What's the matter? / What's wrong? / Why are you sad(disappointed)?

M Sarah, did you throw away this paper in the garbage can?
W Yes, I did. What's the matter?
M You have to put paper **❶** _____ _____ _____ _____. If you put it in the garbage can, it'll be buried in the ground.
W But I think it's okay to be buried.
M It takes **❷** _____ _____ _____ _____ to make paper and we can use this paper again.
W It is too much bother to care about garbage.
M I understand how you feel, but if you don't care about it now, **❸** _____ _____ _____ by it a lot more in the future.

Words • **07 clearly** 명확하게 **somewhere** 어딘가에 **modern** 현대의   **08 on time** 정각에 **set an alarm** 자명종 시계를 맞추다 **close** 친한
09 garbage can 쓰레기통 **recycling bin** 재활용 통 **bury** 묻다 **bother** 귀찮음; 귀찮게 하다 **a lot more** 더 많이

10 숫자 정보 파악 – 금액

대화를 듣고, 남자가 지불할 금액을 고르시오.

① $15   ② $20   ③ $25
④ $30   ⑤ $35

W There are many different kinds of bread in this bakery.
M Cool. I'd like to have a blueberry cookie and a chocolate muffin.
W Great choice. I'll have ❶ _____ _____ _____.
M How much are they?
W The cookie and muffin are ❷ _____ _____ _____, and the sandwich is $20.
M Let's pay ❸ _____ _____ _____. We can share the food.
W Great.

11 장소 추론

다음을 듣고, 비가 올 경우 오후 2시에 방문할 장소를 고르시오.

① Central Park
② Brooklyn Bridge
③ the Statue of Liberty
④ Radio City Music Hall
⑤ the Museum of Modern Art

W Let me tell you ❶ _____ _____ _____ _____. We're going to take the bus at 9 and move to the Statue of Liberty. After ❷ _____ _____ _____ _____ there, we're going to Brooklyn Bridge and stay there until lunchtime. At two, we're going to visit Central Park, but ❸ _____ _____ _____ _____, we are going to the Museum of the Modern Art instead. After that, we are going to go to Radio City Music Hall at 5.

12 언급되지 않은 것

다음을 듣고, 도서 대출에 관해 언급되지 <u>않은</u> 것을 고르시오.

① 대출 시 필요한 물품
② 대출 가능 권 수
③ 대출 기간
④ 원하는 책 찾는 법
⑤ 반납 연체 시 처리

M Now, let me tell you how you check out a book. Take the books you want to borrow to the librarian. You will have to ❶ _____ _____ _____ your student ID card too. The librarian will check your student number and name and let you check out the books. You can check out ❷ _____ _____ _____, and you have to return the books ❸ _____ _____ _____. You won't be able to check out more books if you don't return them within two weeks.

13 도표 정보 파악   영국식 발음 녹음

대화를 듣고, 아이스 쇼에 대한 설명으로 <u>잘못된</u> 것을 고르시오.

① Title: Winter Dream
② Date: June 21st
③ Time: 7 p.m. ~ 9 p.m.
④ Admission: R-$100 / S-$60 / A-$20
⑤ Don't take pictures inside.

😊 **허가 여부 묻기** ////////////////////////////////
Is it okay(all right) to ~? / I wonder if I could ~. /
Do you mind if ~? / May(Can) I ~?

M Why don't we go to see Yuna Kim's ice show, *Winter Dream* on June 21? It's her last ice show.
W Wow, I don't want to miss it. ❶ _____ _____ _____ _____ _____?
M It's from 7 p.m. to 9 p.m.   W And what's the admission?
M It's from $30 to $100. But, my uncle gave me two free tickets.
W Fantastic! I'll buy you dinner.
M Thanks. And don't forget to ❷ _____ _____ _____.
W 😊 Is it okay to take pictures during the show?
M No, ❸ _____ _____ _____, but we might take pictures of her after the show.

Words   **10 each** 각각   **11 stay** 머물다   **until** ~까지   **in case** ~하면, ~하는 경우에   **12 librarian** 사서   **ID card** 신분증   **in total** 다 합해서, 총
within ~이내에   **13 admission** 입장료

18회 | **147**

Dictation Test

14 주제 파악

다음을 듣고, 무엇에 관한 설명인지 고르시오.

① 우산　　② 모자　　③ 헬멧
④ 머리띠　　⑤ 마스크

M This is something _____ _____ _____ _____ _____, and it is a round shape. This is made of a special material that does not easily break, and this is not for fashion. It is ❷_____ _____ _____. In other words, people wear this to ❸_____ _____ _____. For example, people wear it when they ride bicycles or inline skates.

15 한 일 / 할 일 파악

대화를 듣고, 남자가 대화 직후에 할 일로 가장 적절한 것을 고르시오.

① 전화 끊기　　② 남동생 바꿔 주기
③ 메시지 전달하기　　④ 전화번호 알려 주기
⑤ 남동생에게 전화 걸기

[Telephone rings.]
M Hello?
W Hey, David. Let's do the homework together at my house.
M Um, who's this? David is ❶_____ _____ _____.
W This is Bella. Are you David's brother, Jack?
M Yeah. David went to the grocery store and he's coming back in 5 minutes. Do you want to ❷_____ _____ _____?
W Let me just call him later.
M Oh, ❸_____ _____ _____. Wait a second.

16 숫자 정보 파악 - 시각　영국식 발음 녹음

대화를 듣고, 두 사람이 만날 시각을 고르시오.

① 12:00　　② 1:00　　③ 3:00
④ 4:00　　⑤ 5:00

😊 희망, 기대 표현하기 ////////////////
I can't wait to ~. / I'm looking forward to ~. / I hope ~.

M Did you hear the JJ shoe store is having a 70% off sale just for today?
W Really? This is ❶_____ _____ _____ _____ rain boots.
M I'm going to buy a pair of slippers.
W Then, let's go there together.
M Cool. ❷_____ _____ _____ _____ from 3 to 5 o'clock. Except that, I'm free the whole afternoon.
W It must be crowded there after 5. Let's go there right after lunch.
M Good. ❸_____ _____ _____ at 1?
W Okay. I can't wait to go there.

Words 　**14 material** 물질 **in other words** 다시 말해　**15 grocery store** 식료품점 **leave a message** 메시지를 남기다　**16 rain boots** 장화 **a pair of** 한 쌍의 **except** ~을 제외하고는 **crowded** 붐비는, 복잡한

17 상황에 맞는 말 찾기

다음 상황 설명을 듣고, Andy가 영미에게 할 말로 가장 적절한 것을 고르시오.

Andy: _____

① Sure. Go ahead.
② Can you lend me a paintbrush?
③ What are you going to paint today?
④ Do we have to move to the art room now?
⑤ Remind me to bring more paintbrush next time.

W Andy has an art class today. He ❶ _____ _____ _____ his painting supplies, and he finds something important missing. He ❷ _____ _____ _____ his paintbrushes! He can't do anything without a paintbrush during today's art class. But then he sees that his close friend, Youngmi, has many paintbrushes and he wants her ❸ _____ _____ _____ _____. In this situation, what would Andy most likely say to Youngmi?

18 한 일 / 할 일 파악

대화를 듣고, 두 사람이 이번 주말에 할 일로 가장 적절한 것을 고르시오.

① bowling only
② going dancing
③ going out to dinner only
④ going out to dinner and bowling
⑤ going out to dinner and seeing a movie

😎 의도 묻기 ////////////////////////////////
What are you planning to ~? / What will you ~? / What are you going to ~?

M Sally, what are you planning to do this weekend?
W Let's ❶ _____ _____ _____ _____. I was thinking that we could see the new Brad Pitt movie after that.
M Dinner sounds great, but I've already seen the movie.
W Well, how about ❷ _____ _____ then?
M Sorry, but you know I don't like dancing.
W What about bowling ?
M I'm ❸ _____ _____ _____ _____, but maybe it'll be fun.
W Okay, then, let's meet at 5 o'clock on Saturday.

19 알맞은 응답 찾기

대화를 듣고, 남자의 마지막 말에 대한 여자의 응답으로 가장 적절한 것을 고르시오.

Woman: _____

① Let me go get some medicine.
② I hope she becomes the class leader.
③ She has been waiting for you to come.
④ If I were you, I would have selected her.
⑤ Time is the best medicine. Let's just wait here.

M Where's Claire? I can't find her anywhere.
W She's in the restroom.
M It's been an hour now. What is she doing in the restroom?
W ❶ _____ _____ _____.   M Why?
W She was very sure that she would be elected as the class leader, but ❷ _____ _____.
M Oh, don't you think we ❸ _____ _____ _____ _____?

20 알맞은 응답 찾기

대화를 듣고, 여자의 마지막 말에 대한 남자의 응답으로 가장 적절한 것을 고르시오.

Man: _____

① He's not my type.
② Jackie Chan's movie.
③ I learn judo, instead.
④ I don't know about the movie.
⑤ Michael Jackson, the king of pop.

M What are you watching?
W I'm watching *Rush Hour*.
M You're watching Jackie Chan's movie again?
W Yes, ❶ _____ _____ _____ _____ more than ten times.
M Why do you watch the same movie over and over again?
W That's because Jackie Chan is my hero. Someday, I will be ❷ _____ _____ _____ _____ like him.
M Oh, that's why you're learning *Taekwondo* and Kung Fu.
W Yes. By the way, ❸ _____ _____ _____ _____?

ⓦords **17 supplies** 용품, 비품 **paintbrush** 그림붓 **18 go dancing** 춤추러 가다 **19 anywhere** 어디에서도 **restroom** 화장실 **elect** 선출하다 **class leader** 반장 **20 over and over again** 반복해서

01
다음을 듣고, 지시에 따라 알맞게 꾸민 케이크를 고르시오.

①   ②   ③

④  ⑤

02
대화를 듣고, 여자가 남자에게 전화한 목적으로 가장 적절한 것을 고르시오.

① 택배 배달을 부탁하려고
② 배달 음식을 주문하려고
③ 반품 접수 문의를 하려고
④ 컴퓨터 수리를 부탁하려고
⑤ 택배 수령 여부를 확인하려고

03
다음 그림의 상황에 가장 적절한 대화를 고르시오.

① ② ③ ④ ⑤

04
대화를 듣고, 두 사람이 만나기로 한 장소를 고르시오.

① 식당　　　　　② 공원
③ 마트　　　　　④ 여자의 집
⑤ 자전거 대여소

05
대화를 듣고, 여자의 심정 변화로 가장 적절한 것을 고르시오.

① bored → joyful　　② upset → envious
③ annoyed → pleased　④ excited → nervous
⑤ relaxed → disappointed

06
대화를 듣고, 두 사람의 관계로 가장 적절한 것을 고르시오.

① 동창 – 동창　　　　② 교사 – 학생
③ 점원 – 고객　　　　④ 교사 – 학부모
⑤ 운동선수 – 감독

07
다음을 듣고, 두 사람의 대화가 어색한 것을 고르시오.

① ② ③ ④ ⑤

08
대화를 듣고, 여자가 남자에게 부탁한 일로 가장 적절한 것을 고르시오.

① 악수하기　　　　② 사인해 주기
③ 함께 TV 보기　　④ 함께 축구하기
⑤ 축구공 사 주기

09
대화를 듣고, 남자의 마지막 말에 담긴 의도로 가장 적절한 것을 고르시오.

① 기원　　② 불평　　③ 축하
④ 경고　　⑤ 허락

10
대화를 듣고, 여자가 지불한 금액을 고르시오.

① $20.65　　② $21.65　　③ $22.00
④ $23.00　　⑤ $25.00

11 대화를 듣고, 두 사람이 대화하는 장소로 가장 적절한 곳을 고르시오.

① 교실
② 화장실
③ 교내 식당
④ 농구 코트
⑤ 학교 체육관

12 다음을 듣고, Time Sale에 관해 언급되지 <u>않은</u> 것을 고르시오.

① 할인 품목
② 할인율
③ 품목별 가격
④ 종료 시각
⑤ 진행 장소

13 대화를 듣고, 명함의 내용과 일치하지 <u>않는</u> 것을 고르시오.

① **Kim & Johnson**
② First Avenue, New York
③ Elly Brown, Lawyer
④ Address: East 23rd Street
⑤ Phone: 001-0908

14 다음을 듣고, 무엇에 관한 설명인지 고르시오.

① 손 씻는 방법
② 물 절약 방법
③ 옷 세탁 방법
④ 스트레칭 방법
⑤ 머리 감는 방법

15 대화를 듣고, 두 사람이 이번 주말에 할 일로 가장 적절한 것을 고르시오.

① 음악회 가기
② 공원에 가기
③ 박물관에 가기
④ 영화 관람하기
⑤ 파티에 참석하기

16 대화를 듣고, 남자가 구입할 물건이 <u>아닌</u> 것을 고르시오.

① pencil
② eraser
③ crayon
④ sketchbook
⑤ backpack

17 다음 상황 설명을 듣고, George가 민지에게 할 말로 가장 적절한 것을 고르시오.

George: _____

① That's a relief.
② Can you tell Mr. Kim that I will be late?
③ Is it possible for you to open the classroom today?
④ Do you know how to get to the teacher's office?
⑤ You're supposed to open the classroom door instead of me.

18 대화를 듣고, 여자가 대화 직후에 할 일로 가장 적절한 것을 고르시오.

① 점심 식사를 주문한다.
② 집에 가서 휴식을 취한다.
③ 병원에 가서 진찰을 받는다.
④ 처방전을 가지고 약국에 간다.
⑤ 뜨거운 레몬차를 만들어 준다.

19 대화를 듣고, 여자의 마지막 말에 대한 남자의 응답으로 가장 적절한 것을 고르시오.

Man: _____

① Right. Let's eat some more ice cream.
② Yes, I've lost too much weight recently.
③ Not really. I think I need to gain weight.
④ She didn't tell me I should avoid ice cream.
⑤ She said I have a lot of body fat and need a diet.

20 대화를 듣고, 남자의 마지막 말에 대한 여자의 응답으로 가장 적절한 것을 고르시오.

Woman: _____

① You don't have to try harder.
② Why don't you join the contest?
③ I told you. You'd better get some sleep.
④ That's okay. I hope you understand me.
⑤ Don't be discouraged. You'll do better next time.

Dictation Test 19회 영어 듣기모의고사

01 그림 정보 파악 – 사물

다음을 듣고, 지시에 따라 알맞게 꾸민 케이크를 고르시오.

① ② ③ ④ ⑤

M I'd like to tell you the way to decorate a birthday cake with chocolate cream. First, draw ❶ _____ _____ _____ _____ _____ _____ of the cake. Then, write the ❷ _____ _____ _____ _____ _____ _____. Now, draw lines to ❸ _____ _____ _____ the heart. Make sure you don't draw lines inside the heart.

02 목적 파악

대화를 듣고, 여자가 남자에게 전화한 목적으로 가장 적절한 것을 고르시오.

① 택배 배달을 부탁하려고
② 배달 음식을 주문하려고
③ 반품 접수 문의를 하려고
④ 컴퓨터 수리를 부탁하려고
⑤ 택배 수령 여부를 확인하려고

😎 안부 묻기 //////////////////////////////
What's up? / How are you doing? / How's it going? / How are you (today)?

[Cellphone rings.]
M Hi, Michelle. What's up?
W Hi, Scott. My computer is down again. Can you come and ❶ _____ _____ _____ _____ _____ now?
M I can't leave home right now. Mom asked me to take a package. The delivery man is arriving in an hour.
W So, you can ❷ _____ _____ _____ in the afternoon, right?
M Yes. After getting the package, I'll go there ❸ _____ _____ _____ _____.
W That's fine with me. Thanks.

03 그림 상황에 어울리는 대화 찾기

다음 그림의 상황에 가장 적절한 대화를 고르시오.

① ② ③ ④ ⑤

① **M** How many times do you check the time a day?
  W I don't know. I think it's my habit.
② **M** Where did you ❶ _____ _____ _____ last time?
  W I don't have a clue.
③ **M** Watch out! A car is coming.
  W That was close. Thank you.
④ **M** Look! It's already ❷ _____ _____ _____.
  W That's not possible.
⑤ **M** You have been watching TV for 2 hours.
  W Okay. I'll go ❸ _____ _____ _____ now.

04 장소 추론 영국식 발음 녹음

대화를 듣고, 두 사람이 만나기로 한 장소를 고르시오.

① 식당 ② 공원
③ 마트 ④ 여자의 집
⑤ 자전거 대여소

M Do you remember that we will hang out together this Saturday?

W Yes. I do. Let's go on a picnic. Where do you want to meet?

M ❶ _____ _____ _____ _____ at a restaurant and buy some *gimbap* for lunch?

W I'll pack some fruit and *gimbap* at home. You just need to ❷ _____ _____ _____ .

M ❸ _____ _____ _____ _____ the Korea Mart and buy snacks together.

W Okay. We can go to the park together from there.

M How about going to a bicycle rental shop and renting bikes?

W That's a great idea. I'm already excited.

M Me, too.

05 심정 파악

대화를 듣고, 여자의 심정 변화로 가장 적절한 것을 고르시오.

① bored → joyful ② upset → envious
③ annoyed → pleased ④ excited → nervous
⑤ relaxed → disappointed

M Jenny, it was too hot, right?

W Yes, Mr. Kim. We're all sweating a lot, but the air conditioner ❶ _____ _____ _____ . Turning on the fan is not good enough.

M I understand you, but that's because we have to save electricity.

W I know, but I want to use the air conditioner ❷ _____ _____ _____ _____ , just like today.

M Instead, I'll ❸ _____ _____ _____ _____ for all of you. So, tell the class leader to come to the teacher's room right away.

W Wow! Thank you very much, Mr. Kim.

06 관계 추론

대화를 듣고, 두 사람의 관계로 가장 적절한 것을 고르시오.

① 동창 – 동창 ② 교사 – 학생
③ 점원 – 고객 ④ 교사 – 학부모
⑤ 운동선수 – 감독

😎 **기억이나 망각 여부 묻기** ////////////////
Can't[Don't] you remember ~? / I wonder if you remember ~. / You haven't forgotten about ~, have you?

M Excuse me. Are you Susan ❶ _____ _____ _____ ?

W Yes, I am. Do I know you?

M Yes, we went to ❷ _____ _____ _____ _____ — Lincoln Elementary. Can't you remember me?

W No. I'm still wondering whom I'm talking to.

M I am Jason. You used to ❸ _____ _____ _____ _____ because I was very short.

W Ah! Jason. The little kid! You grew a lot taller.

M I hear that a lot. Anyway, let's go somewhere and have a talk.

Words **04 hang out together** 함께 시간을 보내다 **pack** 싸다, 챙기다 **rental shop** 대여소 **05 sweat** 땀을 흘리다 **turn on** 켜다 **fan** 선풍기 **enough** 충분히 **electricity** 전기 **teacher's room** 교무실 **06 by any chance** 혹시(라도) **have a talk** 이야기를 나누다

Dictation Test

07 어색한 대화 찾기

다음을 듣고, 두 사람의 대화가 어색한 것을 고르시오.
① ② ③ ④ ⑤

😮 **Do you mind ~?에 대한 허가하기**
I don't mind (at all). / Of course not. / Not at all.

① M ❶ _____ _____ _____ _____ your trip to Japan?
  W I wish I could have enjoyed the trip.
② M He won first prize in the piano contest.
  W What? You're kidding.
③ M It's very important to ❷ _____ _____ _____ _____.
  W You can say that again.
④ M Do you mind if I open the windows?
  W No, I don't mind.
⑤ M What would you like to have for dinner?
  W ❸ _____ _____ _____ eating pizza.

08 부탁한 일 파악 영국식 발음 녹음

대화를 듣고, 여자가 남자에게 부탁한 일로 가장 적절한 것을 고르시오.
① 악수하기   ② 사인해 주기
③ 함께 TV 보기   ④ 함께 축구하기
⑤ 축구공 사 주기

😮 **기쁨 표현하기**
That's great! / I'm(I feel) (very) happy. / I'm (very) glad(delighted) to ~.

W Excuse me. Are you Jisung Park?
M Yes, I am.
W Oh, my gosh! I'm a ❶ _____ _____ _____.
M Thank you very much.
W I can't believe I'm looking at someone I've always watched on TV. Do you live near this park?   M No, I'm here to meet my friend.
W I see. ❷ _____ _____ _____ _____ _____ on this soccer ball?
M Sure. What's your name?
W Lisa. Oh, that's great. I really ❸ _____ _____.

09 의도 파악

대화를 듣고, 남자의 마지막 말에 담긴 의도로 가장 적절한 것을 고르시오.
① 기원   ② 불평   ③ 축하
④ 경고   ⑤ 허락

W Look at the dog! It looks so cute. I want to go pat it.
M I don't think that's a good idea. Do you know the dog?
W No, but most dogs are friendly.
M They are, but you should know that you can be ❶ _____ _____ _____ _____.
W What do you mean?
M If the dog doesn't know you, it might think you are going to harm it. If it is frightened, ❷ _____ _____ _____ _____.
W I think dogs can tell that I am friendly.
M Then you can be a huge friendly stranger to them. That's dangerous to you, too.
W Okay. Now I understand. I shouldn't ❸ _____ _____ _____ _____ I don't know.
M Right. You should ask their owners first.

〔Words〕 **07 seat belt** 안전벨트 **08 appreciate** 감사하다 **09 pat** 쓰다듬다 **friendly** 우호적인 **threat** 위협 **harm** 해치다 **frightened** 겁먹은, 무서워하는 **tell** 알다, 판단하다 **owner** 주인, 소유자

10 숫자 정보 파악 – 금액

대화를 듣고, 여자가 지불한 금액을 고르시오.

① $20.65 ② $21.65 ③ $22.00
④ $23.00 ⑤ $25.00

W I'm going to the Twin Tower Hotel.
M No problem.
W Do you know ❶ _____ _____ _____ _____ will be?
M It should be somewhere between 22 and 23 dollars.
W Okay.
M (*pause*) ❷ _____ _____ _____, the Twin Tower Hotel. That's 21 dollars 65 cents.
W Here's 25 dollars. You can ❸ _____ _____ _____.
M Thank you.

11 장소 추론

대화를 듣고, 두 사람이 대화하는 장소로 가장 적절한 곳을 고르시오.

① 교실   ② 화장실
③ 교내 식당   ④ 농구 코트
⑤ 학교 체육관

W You're really ❶ _____ _____ _____, Sanghyeok.
M Thanks, but I ❷ _____ _____ _____ _____. It's so hot today.
W Yes, and I'm hungry. What time is it?
M It's 12:30. Ten minutes left before lunchtime.
W Let's ask the P.E. teacher to ❸ _____ _____ _____ _____. Then, we don't have to wait in a long line at the cafeteria.
M Good idea, but do you think he will say yes?
W I don't know, but we can give it a try.
M Okay, let's do it. Oh, he's coming to this court.

12 언급되지 않은 것

다음을 듣고, Time Sale에 관해 언급되지 <u>않은</u> 것을 고르시오.

① 할인 품목   ② 할인율
③ 품목별 가격   ④ 종료 시각
⑤ 진행 장소

M Attention, shoppers. Our time sale on imported fruits is going to start soon. You can get 40% off ❶ _____ _____ and 20% off pineapples and grapefruits. Also, if you buy more than $10, we will give you a 10% discount coupon that you can use on your next visit. This time sale is from 2 p.m. and ❷ _____ _____ _____ 4 p.m. or earlier if we sell all of our stock. Hurry to ❸ _____ _____ _____ for these good deals.

13 도표 정보 파악 _영국식 발음 녹음_

대화를 듣고, 명함의 내용과 일치하지 <u>않는</u> 것을 고르시오.

① **Kim & Johnson**
② First Avenue, New York

③ Elly Brown, Lawyer
④ Address: East 23rd Street
⑤ Phone: 001-0908

M Hey, Cindy. Is Elly Brown ❶ _____ _____ _____?
W Yes, she is.   M Is she still working at KM Law?
W Not any more. ❷ _____ _____ _____ Kim & Johnson now. The office is on 5th Avenue in New York.
M Is she still living on East 23rd Street?   W Yes, she is.
M Does she still ❸ _____ _____ _____ _____? Is it 001-0908?   W Yes, that's right.

Ⓦords **10 between *A* and *B*** A와 B 사이의 **11 wait in line** 줄을 서서 기다리다 **cafeteria** 구내식당 **give it a try** 시도하다 **12 imported** 수입된 **grapefruit** 자몽 **stock** (상점의) 재고품 **13 lawyer** 변호사

Dictation Test

14 주제 파악

다음을 듣고, 무엇에 관한 설명인지 고르시오.

① 손 씻는 방법
② 물 절약 방법
③ 옷 세탁 방법
④ 스트레칭 방법
⑤ 머리 감는 방법

W When you return home, you have to do this. First, _____ _____ _____ in warm water. _____ _____ _____ both sides of your hands and fingers with soap. You need to do this for about 15 to 20 seconds. Lastly, rinse your hands and ❸_____ _____ with a clean towel.

15 한 일 / 할 일 파악

대화를 듣고, 두 사람이 이번 주말에 할 일로 가장 적절한 것을 고르시오.

① 음악회 가기
② 공원에 가기
③ 박물관에 가기
④ 영화 관람하기
⑤ 파티에 참석하기

W Jason, why don't we ❶_____ _____ _____ this weekend?
M There's an exhibition of dinosaurs at the museum.
W I don't like dinosaurs.
M How about concerts?
W Well, it's ❷_____ _____ _____ _____.
M Then, let's go to the movies.
W No, I'd rather be outside.
M The River Park?
W Yes. I want to relax and enjoy the fresh air ❸_____ _____ _____.
M Okay. I'll call you on Saturday.

16 특정 정보 파악   영국식 발음 녹음

대화를 듣고, 남자가 구입할 물건이 <u>아닌</u> 것을 고르시오.

① pencil
② eraser
③ crayon
④ sketchbook
⑤ backpack

😊 충고 구하기 ////////////////

Do you think I should ~? / What would you do if ~? / Can I get your advice on ~?

W Hi, Jack. What are you going to buy here?
M Hi, Hyorin. My cousin is entering an elementary school soon, so I'd like to give her small gifts. But, I can't decide what to buy.
W Why don't you ❶_____ _____ _____ _____?
M I was going to buy them, but what else?
W Well, girls like drawing. Buy these crayons and sketchbooks as well.
M That's a great idea. 😊 Do you think I should buy a backpack for her, too?
W Probably not. I'm sure her parents ❷_____ _____ _____ _____ already.
M Maybe, you're right. Thanks.

Ⓦords   **14 wet** 적시다; 젖은   **rub** 문지르다, 비비다   **rinse** 헹구다   **clean** 깨끗한   **towel** 수건   **15 exhibition** 전시회   **dinosaur** 공룡   **relax** 휴식을 취하다   **16 elementary school** 초등학교

17 상황에 맞는 말 찾기

다음 상황 설명을 듣고, George가 민지에게 할 말로 가장 적절한 것을 고르시오.

George: _____

① That's a relief.
② Can you tell Mr. Kim that I will be late?
③ Is it possible for you to open the classroom today?
④ Do you know how to get to the teacher's office?
⑤ You're supposed to open the classroom door instead of me.

M George usually gets to school first in his class. Every morning, he gets ____ ____ ____ from the teacher's office and opens his classroom. However, he got up very late today and won't get to school by his usual time. Therefore, George called Minji, his classmate. Fortunately ❷ ____ ____ ____ school. He wants to ask her to ❸ ____ ____ ____ today. In this situation, what would George most likely say to Minji?

18 한 일 / 할 일 파악

대화를 듣고, 여자가 대화 직후에 할 일로 가장 적절한 것을 고르시오.

① 점심 식사를 주문한다.
② 집에 가서 휴식을 취한다.
③ 병원에 가서 진찰을 받는다.
④ 처방전을 가지고 약국에 간다.
⑤ 뜨거운 레몬차를 만들어 준다.

W Max, what did the doctor say?
M He prescribed some ❶ ____ ____ and told me to rest.
W Rest? But I really need your help with this project we're working on.
M I know. Don't worry. I'm not going home until it's done.
W Thanks for helping me when ❷ ____ ____ ____ ____. Let's have lunch first.
M No, thanks. But I'd like to drink something hot for this sore throat.
W I will make ❸ ____ ____ ____ ____ for your throat.
M Thanks.

19 알맞은 응답 찾기

대화를 듣고, 여자의 마지막 말에 대한 남자의 응답으로 가장 적절한 것을 고르시오.

Man: _____

① Right. Let's eat some more ice cream.
② Yes, I've lost too much weight recently.
③ Not really. I think I need to gain weight.
④ She didn't tell me I should avoid ice cream.
⑤ She said I have a lot of body fat and need a diet.

음식 권하기
Would you like some ~? / Do you want some more ~? / Please try some ~.

M This ice cream is really delicious.
W Would you like some more?
M No, ❶ ____ ____ ____.
W Are you sure? What happened to the ice cream lover?
M Not any more. ❷ ____ ____ ____ that I lose weight.
W ❸ ____ ____ ____ ____ suggest that?

20 알맞은 응답 찾기

대화를 듣고, 남자의 마지막 말에 대한 여자의 응답으로 가장 적절한 것을 고르시오.

Woman: _____

① You don't have to try harder.
② Why don't you join the contest?
③ I told you. You'd better get some sleep.
④ That's okay. I hope you understand me.
⑤ Don't be discouraged. You'll do better next time.

M Mom, I'm home.
W Hi, sweetie. How was your day?   M It was okay.
W But ❶ ____ ____ ____. Is something wrong?
M Today, I found out the result of the drawing contest I joined last week.   W Oh, really? Tell me about it.
M ❷ ____ ____ ____, Mom. Sorry.
W That's okay. You did your best. That's the most important thing.
M But I practiced so hard. Maybe I have ❸ ____ ____ ____ ____ pictures.

Words 17 **fortunately** 다행스럽게도, 운 좋게도 **relief** 안도, 안심 **possible** 가능한 18 **prescribe** 처방하다 **project** 과제 **sore** 아픈, 따가운 **throat** 목구멍 19 **lover** 애호가 20 **find out** 알게 되다 **result** 결과 **talent** 재능

01 다음을 듣고, 설명하는 도형을 고르시오.

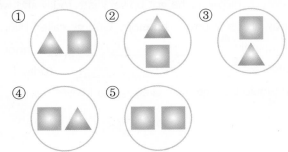

① ② ③
④ ⑤

02 대화를 듣고, 남자가 여자에게 전화한 목적으로 가장 적절한 것을 고르시오.

① 책 구입을 부탁하려고
② 수학 공부를 함께하려고
③ 빌려준 돈을 돌려 달라고
④ 어떤 책을 사야 하는지 물어보려고
⑤ 내일 학교에서 만날 약속을 정하려고

03 대화를 듣고, 남자가 가고자 하는 곳을 고르시오.

04 대화를 듣고, 두 사람이 미술관에 가기로 한 요일을 고르시오.

① 월요일   ② 화요일   ③ 수요일
④ 목요일   ⑤ 금요일

05 대화를 듣고, 남자의 직업으로 가장 적절한 것을 고르시오.

① judge   ② doctor
③ athlete   ④ police officer
⑤ ambulance driver

06 대화를 듣고, 여자의 심정으로 가장 적절한 것을 고르시오.

① excited   ② happy
③ jealous   ④ relieved
⑤ embarrassed

07 다음을 듣고, 두 사람의 대화가 어색한 것을 고르시오.

①   ②   ③   ④   ⑤

08 대화를 듣고, 여자가 이번 겨울 방학에 한 일이 아닌 것을 고르시오.

① 호주 방문하기   ② 박물관 가기
③ 동물원 가기   ④ 수영하기
⑤ 스키 타기

09 대화를 듣고, 여자의 마지막 말에 담긴 의도로 가장 적절한 것을 고르시오.

① 걱정   ② 감사   ③ 동의
④ 칭찬   ⑤ 불평

10 대화를 듣고, 여자가 거스름돈으로 받을 금액을 고르시오.

① $5   ② $10   ③ $15
④ $20   ⑤ $25

11 대화를 듣고, 두 사람이 대화하는 장소로 가장 적절한 곳을 고르시오.

① 공원
② 고급 식당
③ 대학 기숙사
④ 테니스 코트
⑤ 아파트 단지

12 다음을 듣고, Sam이 받은 생일 선물로 언급되지 <u>않은</u> 것을 고르시오.

① 우산
② 공
③ 지구본
④ 스마트폰
⑤ 책

13 대화를 듣고, 두 사람이 보려는 TV 채널을 고르시오.

	Program	Channel
①	Loving You	1
②	World Baseball Game	2
③	National Geographic	3
④	ABD News	4
⑤	Comedy House	5

14 다음을 듣고, 무엇에 관한 광고인지 고르시오.

① 치약
② 음료수
③ 영양제
④ 조미료
⑤ 식사 대용품

15 대화를 듣고, 남자가 대화 직후에 할 일로 가장 적절한 것을 고르시오.

① 바지 환불하기
② 영수증 가져오기
③ 티셔츠 추가 구매하기
④ 바지를 티셔츠로 교환하기
⑤ 바지를 더 큰 사이즈로 교환하기

16 대화를 듣고, 현재의 시각을 고르시오.

① 6:30
② 7:00
③ 7:15
④ 7:30
⑤ 8:00

17 다음 상황 설명을 듣고, Kate가 휴대 전화 수리 기사에게 할 말로 가장 적절한 것을 고르시오.

Kate: _____

① Can I have it delivered then?
② Please tell me how much it costs.
③ How long does it take to get home?
④ Then please leave your home address here.
⑤ I want to change the screen into a new one.

18 대화를 듣고, 여자가 대화 직후에 할 일로 가장 적절한 것을 고르시오.

① 해산물로 요리하기
② 집에 가서 치약 살펴보기
③ 미세 플라스틱이 든 제품 치우기
④ 미세 플라스틱에 관한 뉴스 듣기
⑤ 미세 플라스틱이 사용된 제품 찾아보기

19 대화를 듣고, 남자의 마지막 말에 대한 여자의 응답으로 가장 적절한 것을 고르시오.

Woman: _____

① I can't drive at all.
② Next weekend will be good.
③ Then, could I test-drive it?
④ Do you have a driver's license?
⑤ How long will it take to repair it?

20 대화를 듣고, 여자의 마지막 말에 대한 남자의 응답으로 가장 적절한 것을 고르시오.

Man: _____

① It's my pleasure.
② That's a great idea.
③ Glad to see you here.
④ When do I have to leave?
⑤ No, I've never lived in here.

01 그림 정보 파악 – 도형

다음을 듣고, 설명하는 도형을 고르시오.

W I'm going to explain the figures you're supposed to draw. First, there's a large circle. Inside, there're two small figures. The one on the left ❶ _____ _____ _____ and three points. The other on the right has ❷ _____ _____ _____ _____ _____. In each figure, all the lengths are the same. These two figures ❸ _____ _____ _____ _____.

02 목적 파악

대화를 듣고, 남자가 여자에게 전화한 목적으로 가장 적절한 것을 고르시오.

① 책 구입을 부탁하려고
② 수학 공부를 함께하려고
③ 빌려준 돈을 돌려 달라고
④ 어떤 책을 사야 하는지 물어보려고
⑤ 내일 학교에서 만날 약속을 정하려고

[*Telephone rings.*]
W Hello?
M Maria. This is Ken. I am at K Bookstore. ❶ _____ _____ _____ _____ buy you *Gentle Math*.
W Yes please. I need to practice problem solving more.
M But there are three different books. I don't know ❷ _____ _____ _____ _____. There is a green, yellow and red one.
W I forgot to let you know. What I need is ❸ _____ _____ _____. How much is it?
M It's 13,000 won.
W I'll give you 13,000 won later. Please bring it to school tomorrow. Thank you very much.
M No problem. See you tomorrow.

03 그림 정보 파악 – 길 찾기

대화를 듣고, 남자가 가고자 하는 곳을 고르시오.

🕐 **생각할 시간 요청하기** ///////////////////////////
Let me see. / Just a moment (while I think). /
May I think about that for a moment?

M Excuse me. Can you help me?
W Sure.
M I'm taking a tour around here, but ❶ _____ _____ _____ _____ JK hotel is.
W Um, let me see. Turn left at the third traffic light and ❷ _____ _____ _____ _____ _____. The hotel is ❸ _____ _____ _____.
M How long will it take from here?
W Maybe about 10 minutes.
M Thank you.

 Words **01 explain** 설명하다 **figure** 도형 **length** 길이 **02 ask** 부탁하다 **problem solving** 문제 풀이 **let ~ know** ~에게 알리다(말하다)
03 traffic light 신호등 **for a while** 잠시 동안

04 특정 정보 파악 – 요일 | 영국식 발음 녹음

대화를 듣고, 두 사람이 미술관에 가기로 한 요일을 고르시오.

① 월요일   ② 화요일   ③ 수요일
④ 목요일   ⑤ 금요일

M Do you like looking at paintings?

W Yes. I am really interested in paintings a lot.

M Then _____ _____ _____ _____ the gallery that just opened together?

W I'd love to. When shall we go?

M The gallery is closed on Wednesdays. How about this Thursday?

W I can't go on Thursday. I have a yoga class every Tuesday and Thursday.

M Well, I have a violin lesson ❷ _____ _____. Then shall we go on Monday? Is it too soon?

W Not at all. ❸ _____ _____. Let's go then.

05 직업 및 장래 희망

대화를 듣고, 남자의 직업으로 가장 적절한 것을 고르시오.

① judge   ② doctor
③ athlete   ④ police officer
⑤ ambulance driver

M Excuse me, I heard you scream. Can I help you?

W Yes, please. I slipped on the stairs.

M ❶ _____ _____ _____ _____ _____?

W I don't think so. It really hurts.

M Let me have a look. I ❷ _____ _____ _____ _____.

W Terrific! I'm really lucky you're here! What's wrong with my leg?

M Oh, you've broken ❸ _____ _____ _____. I'll call an ambulance first.   W Thanks a lot.

06 심정 파악

대화를 듣고, 여자의 심정으로 가장 적절한 것을 고르시오.

① excited   ② happy
③ jealous   ④ relieved
⑤ embarrassed

😀 **관심 표현하기** ////////////////////////
I'm fascinated by ~. / I'm interested in ~. / ~ interests me (a lot).

W How was my speech? Tell me the truth.

M I was fascinated by your speech, but your T-shirt was a little....

W What? Oh, my! I've been ❶ _____ _____ _____! Why didn't you tell me?

M I realized it after you started your speech.

W Oh, that was why everyone was staring at my T-shirt and ❷ _____ _____ _____.   M Don't be ❸ _____ _____.

07 어색한 대화 찾기

다음을 듣고, 두 사람의 대화가 어색한 것을 고르시오.

①   ②   ③   ④   ⑤

😀 **음식 권하기** ////////////////////////
(Please) help yourself. / Please go ahead. / Please try some ~. / Would you like some ~? / Do you want some more ~?

① W ❶ _____ _____ _____ _____ on the exam?
  M Don't even ask me about it.

② W Let me open the door for you.   M That's so kind of you.

③ W Can I ❷ _____ _____ _____ _____?
  M Help yourself. They're delicious.

④ W Here's your coffee and sandwich, sir.
  M Well, they're not what I ordered.

⑤ W Wait! Is this your cellphone? I think ❸ _____ _____ _____ in the classroom.   M Oh, it's mine. Thank you.

Words **04 gallery** 미술관   **05 scream** 비명   **stair** 계단   **terrific** 아주 좋은   **ambulance** 구급차   **06 speech** 연설   **truth** 사실, 진실
fascinated 매혹된   **realize** 알아차리다   **stare at** ~을 응시하다   **07 try on** ~을 입어 보다

Dictation Test

08 한 일 / 할 일 파악 영국식 발음 녹음

대화를 듣고, 여자가 이번 겨울 방학에 한 일이 <u>아닌</u> 것을 고르시오.

① 호주 방문하기 ② 박물관 가기
③ 동물원 가기 ④ 수영하기
⑤ 스키 타기

M Hi, Sandra. How was your winter vacation?
W To me, it was _____ _____ _____ _____ ❶ .
M What do you mean?
W I spent the winter in Australia. It's summer there.
M I can't imagine hot weather in winter. What did you do there?
W I ❷ _____ _____ _____, and the zoo, and I ❸ _____ _____ _____ _____. How about you?
M I went to a ski resort with my family. It was also fun.

09 의도 파악

대화를 듣고, 여자의 마지막 말에 담긴 의도로 가장 적절한 것을 고르시오.

① 걱정 ② 감사 ③ 동의
④ 칭찬 ⑤ 불평

W Sorry, I'm late. Oops, I left my pencil case and ❶ _____ _____ _____ at home!
M What? Are you sure?
W Yeah, I must be in math class in 30 minutes. Do you have a pencil and some paper I can use?
M Sure.
W And if you have a math textbook, ❷ _____ _____ _____ _____?
M Yeah, here you go. My first class is English, so it's okay.
W I ❸ _____ _____ _____ _____!

10 숫자 정보 파악 – 금액

대화를 듣고, 여자가 거스름돈으로 받을 금액을 고르시오.

① $5 ② $10 ③ $15
④ $20 ⑤ $25

W Hello, I'd like to buy a shoulder bag.
M How about this red one? It's $25 ❶ _____ _____ _____.
W Good. Do you have other colors besides this?
M We have blue and white ones as well, but they are $40.
W Oh, really? I'll take ❷ _____ _____ _____.
M I see. Then, why don't you ❸ _____ _____ _____ _____ the bag? They're a good match.
W It's cute. How much is it?
M It's $10.
W I'll take it as well. Here's $50.
M Here's your change.

Words 08 imagine 상상하다 resort 휴양지, 리조트 09 textbook 교과서 kindness 친절 10 shoulder bag 어깨에 메는 가방 besides ~ 외에 match 아주 잘 어울리는 것 change 거스름돈

11 [장소 추론] 영국식 발음 녹음

대화를 듣고, 두 사람이 대화하는 장소로 가장 적절한 곳을 고르시오.

① 공원
② 고급 식당
③ 대학 기숙사
④ 테니스 코트
⑤ 아파트 단지

M That's it for today, and if you want to practice, _____ _____ _____ _____ _____ until 11.

W Thank you, Mr. Kim. Your tennis lesson is always very fun.

M I'm so glad to hear that. Are you going to practice more?

W Of course. There are no tennis court in my apartment complex. By the way, I saw you having brunch last Saturday.

M Were you at the same restaurant?

W No, I just ❷_____ _____ the restaurant. I was on my way to the park to walk my dog.

M Oh, I see. I teach a tennis lesson near that restaurant.

W I heard the tennis court near that restaurant is very nice. ❸_____ _____ _____ tennis on that court sometime?

M Yeah. I'll invite you to that tennis court one day.

12 [언급되지 않은 것]

다음을 듣고, Sam이 받은 생일 선물로 언급되지 **않은** 것을 고르시오.

① 우산
② 공
③ 지구본
④ 스마트폰
⑤ 책

M Yesterday was Sam's birthday. He got a lot of presents. One square package was blue: it ❶_____ _____ _____ in it. Sam's sister gave him a big and round package. He thought it was a ball, but it was ❷_____ _____ _____ _____ _____.
His brother gave him what he wanted — a smartphone. And his father gave him some ❸_____ _____ _____.

13 [도표 정보 파악]

대화를 듣고, 두 사람이 보려는 TV 채널을 고르시오.

	Program	Channel
①	Loving You	1
②	World Baseball Game	2
③	National Geographic	3
④	ABD News	4
⑤	Comedy House	5

😊 관심에 대해 묻기 ////////////////////////////
Do you find ~ interesting? / Are you interested in ~?

M Sandy, ❶_____ _____ _____ _____. What's the title of it?

W Its title is *Loving You*.

M Do you find it interesting?

W Not really. You may turn the channel if you want.

M Thanks. Oh, the baseball game just finished. Is there anything interesting on TV?

W Let's check the TV program schedule. ❷_____ _____ _____ _____ _____ *National Geographic* or the news channel.

M They're boring. How about *Comedy House* on Channel 5?

W It is not interesting these days.

M Then, let's just watch *Loving You* that ❸_____ _____ _____.

Words ✎ **11 court** 코트 **complex** (건물) 단지 **by the way** 그런데 **on one's way to** ~로 가는 길 **12 package** 상자, 포장물 **globe** 지구본
13 title 제목 **turn the channel** 채널을 돌리다 **boring** 지루한

Dictation Test

14 주제 파악

다음을 듣고, 무엇에 관한 광고인지 고르시오.

① 치약　　　　　② 음료수
③ 영양제　　　　④ 조미료
⑤ 식사 대용품

M Do you usually skip breakfast so you won't be late for school? It is _____ _____ _____ _____, but do you not have enough time in the morning? Here is ❷ _____ _____ _____ for you. It is not only healthy but also delicious. Besides, you don't need to worry about gaining weight because it's low in calories. ❸ _____ _____ _____ _____, start your day with this cereal bar.

15 한 일 / 할 일 파악

대화를 듣고, 남자가 대화 직후에 할 일로 가장 적절한 것을 고르시오.

① 바지 환불하기
② 영수증 가져오기
③ 티셔츠 추가 구매하기
④ 바지를 티셔츠로 교환하기
⑤ 바지를 더 큰 사이즈로 교환하기

W May I help you?
M I purchased these pants last month, but they don't fit me well.
W Do you want to exchange them for another size?
M No, I want to ❶ _____ _____ _____.
W When did you purchase them? Do you have the receipt?
M Here it is. I bought them on May 25.
W Because you bought them on sale, you can ❷ _____ _____. Would you like to try on a bigger size?
M Not really. Could I exchange them for a T-shirt?
W Yes, sir. As long as the T-shirt is ❸ _____ _____ _____ _____ the pants.

16 숫자 정보 파악 – 시각　영국식 발음 녹음

대화를 듣고, 현재의 시각을 고르시오.

① 6:30　　　② 7:00　　　③ 7:15
④ 7:30　　　⑤ 8:00

😊 **이해 상태 나타내기** ////////////////////////
I don't understand. / It (still) isn't clear to me what this means.

W Hurry up! We're late.
M What do you mean? We've ❶ _____ _____ _____ _____ the movie starts.
W But it'll take 30 minutes to get there. That's the problem.
M 😊 I don't understand. Why is that a problem?
W Well, I reserved ❷ _____ _____ _____ the 8 o'clock show through the Internet, and we must pick them up 30 minutes before the show starts.　**M** Oh, I didn't know that. Let's get moving.

17 상황에 적절한 말 찾기

다음 상황 설명을 듣고, Kate가 휴대 전화 수리 기사에게 할 말로 가장 적절한 것을 고르시오.

Kate: _____

① Can I have it delivered then?
② Please tell me how much it costs.
③ How long does it take to get home?
④ Then please leave your home address here.
⑤ I want to change the screen into a new one.

M Kate's cellphone screen is broken, so ❶ _____ _____ _____ _____ to get it fixed. The repairman there said he could change the screen but it would take at least two hours. There were already many people ❷ _____ _____ _____ _____. Kate didn't have much time so she said she would visit next time again. Then he said he could send the repaired cellphone by home-delivery service. Kate wants to ❸ _____ _____ _____ _____ and send home. In this situation, what would Kate most likely say to the repairman?

📖 **Words**　**14** not only A but also B A뿐만 아니라 B도　gain weight 살이 찌다　**15** purchase 구입하다　fit ~에게 맞다　**16** through ~을 통해서　pick up 찾아오다　get moving 빨리 움직이다　**17** repairman 수리 기사　at least 적어도　home-delivery 택배

18 한 일 / 할 일 파악

대화를 듣고, 여자가 대화 직후에 할 일로 가장 적절한 것을 고르시오.

① 해산물로 요리하기
② 집에 가서 치약 살펴보기
③ 미세 플라스틱이 든 제품 치우기
④ 미세 플라스틱에 관한 뉴스 듣기
⑤ 미세 플라스틱이 사용된 제품 찾아보기

알고 있는지 묻기
Have you heard (about) ~? / Do you know (about) ~? / You know ~ (, don't you)? / Are you aware (of) ~?

M Have you heard the news about microplastics?
W No. What are microplastics?
M They are very _____ _____ _____ _____. There are a lot them in things people use every day, such as toothpaste. Unfortunately, microplastics end up in the sea.
W Does it make a problem?
M Yes, If animals eat them, _____ _____ _____ _____. And because we eat ocean animals, we can also eat the microplastics.
W Wow. I might not be able to eat seafood for a while. I'll go home right away and see if my toothpaste has microplastics.
M Look for ❸_____ _____ _____ _____ microplastics.

19 알맞은 응답 찾기

대화를 듣고, 남자의 마지막 말에 대한 여자의 응답으로 가장 적절한 것을 고르시오.
Woman: _____

① I can't drive at all.
② Next weekend will be good.
③ Then, could I test-drive it?
④ Do you have a driver's license?
⑤ How long will it take to repair it?

M May I help you?
W Hi, I'd like to get some information ❶_____ _____ _____ _____. M Do you have anything special in mind?
W I'm ❷_____ _____ _____ _____ _____.
M How about this one? It's only $9,000, a very low price.
W What year was it made? M In 2016. It's almost new.
W It's nice. Has it ever been in an accident?
M Not at all. It is in almost ❸_____ _____.

20 알맞은 응답 찾기

대화를 듣고, 여자의 마지막 말에 대한 남자의 응답으로 가장 적절한 것을 고르시오.
Man: _____

① It's my pleasure.
② That's a great idea.
③ Glad to see you here.
④ When do I have to leave?
⑤ No, I've never lived in here.

제안·권유하기
How[What] about ~? / Why don't you[we] ~? / Let's ~. / I suggest (that) we ~.

W John, do you have any plans tonight?
M Nothing special.
W How about ❶_____ _____ _____ _____ with me tonight?
M I'm afraid I can't. I'm not in a good mood.
W Come on, what's bothering you?
M I may not live in my apartment any more. The house owner told me ❷_____ _____ _____ _____ if I want to stay here longer.
W ❸_____ _____ _____ _____ a roommate and share the bill?

Words 18 **microplastic** 미세 플라스틱 **properly** 제대로, 적절히 **ocean animal** 해양 동물 19 **price** 가격 **accident** 사고 20 **mood** 기분 **owner** 주인, 소유자 **roommate** 동거인 **bill** 청구서

01
대화를 듣고, 여자가 구입할 가방을 고르시오.

02
대화를 듣고, 남자가 여자에게 전화한 목적으로 가장 적절한 것을 고르시오.
① 과제 발표를 부탁하려고
② 과제 제출을 요청하려고
③ 함께 하교하자고 제안하려고
④ 파일을 이메일로 보내 줄 것을 요청하려고
⑤ USB에 파일 저장하는 방법을 문의하려고

03
다음 그림의 상황에 가장 적절한 대화를 고르시오.

①   ②   ③   ④   ⑤

04
대화를 듣고, 여자가 티셔츠를 받을 요일을 고르시오.
① Monday   ② Tuesday
③ Wednesday   ④ Thursday
⑤ Friday

05
대화를 듣고, 남자의 직업으로 가장 적절한 것을 고르시오.
① actor   ② writer   ③ painter
④ soldier   ⑤ photographer

06
대화를 듣고, 여자의 심정으로 가장 적절한 것을 고르시오.
① bored   ② jealous   ③ thankful
④ annoyed   ⑤ embarrassed

07
다음을 듣고, 두 사람의 대화가 <u>어색한</u> 것을 고르시오.
①   ②   ③   ④   ⑤

08
대화를 듣고, 복사기가 작동되지 <u>않는</u> 이유를 고르시오.
① 용지가 없어서
② 전원이 꺼져 있어서
③ 용지가 걸려 있어서
④ 부품이 빠져 있어서
⑤ 플러그가 빠져 있어서

09
대화를 듣고, 남자의 마지막 말에 담긴 의도로 가장 적절한 것을 고르시오.
① 감사   ② 거절   ③ 격려
④ 사과   ④ 축하

10
대화를 듣고, 여자가 지불할 금액을 고르시오.
① $25   ② $30   ③ $35
④ $45   ⑤ $50

11 대화를 듣고, 두 사람이 대화하는 장소로 가장 적절한 곳을 고르시오.

① supermarket　　② concert hall
③ subway station　④ amusement park
⑤ department store

12 다음을 듣고, 저자 사인회에 관해 언급되지 <u>않은</u> 것을 고르시오.

① 저자 이름　　② 장소　　③ 시간
④ 책 내용　　⑤ 보너스 행사

13 대화를 듣고, 내용과 일치하지 <u>않는</u> 것을 고르시오.

	Design Competition	
①	Theme	The world in 50 years
②	Deadline	August 1st
③	1st Place Prize	iPad
④	How to Submit	email
⑤	More Information	www.designcompetition.com

14 다음을 듣고, 무엇에 관한 설명인지 고르시오.

① 버터　　② 우유　　③ 치즈
④ 식용유　　⑤ 생크림

15 대화를 듣고, 남자가 대화 직후에 할 일로 가장 적절한 것을 고르시오.

① 양념 맛보기　　② 양념 교환하기
③ 양념 새로 사 오기　④ 양념통 설거지하기
⑤ 음식에 양념 뿌리기

16 대화를 듣고, 남자가 Nicole과 통화 가능한 시각을 고르시오.

① 11:30 a.m.　② 12:30 p.m.　③ 1:30 p.m.
④ 2:30 p.m.　　⑤ 3:30 p.m.

17 다음 상황 설명을 듣고, Tom이 Ann에게 할 말로 가장 적절한 것을 고르시오.

Tom: _____

① That's very disappointing.
② Don't you agree with me?
③ What makes you think so?
④ I think this book is better than that book.
⑤ Which book do you find the most interesting?

18 대화를 듣고, 두 사람이 할 일로 가장 적절한 것을 고르시오.

① 남은 음식 싸 가기　　② 상한 음식 버리기
③ 결식 아동 후원하기　④ 음식 더 주문하기
⑤ 남은 음식 마저 먹기

19 대화를 듣고, 여자의 마지막 말에 대한 남자의 응답으로 가장 적절한 것을 고르시오.

Man: _____

① Thanks. I like it a lot.
② No, I haven't. What's that?
③ Maybe he'll like orange juice better.
④ I think Coke is better than orange juice.
⑤ I'm going to watch a movie after the exams.

20 대화를 듣고, 남자의 마지막 말에 대한 여자의 응답으로 가장 적절한 것을 고르시오.

Woman: _____

① Be careful of the animals.
② I keep a puppy and a cat in my house.
③ I never let my child watch TV in the evening.
④ Very interesting. I like those wildlife programs.
⑤ Good idea! I think you have to see the programs.

01 그림 정보 파악 – 사물

대화를 듣고, 여자가 구입할 가방을 고르시오.

① ② ③
④ ⑤

W Clark, how do you like this backpack with two stripes in the middle? ❶ _____ _____ _____ _____ it.

M Don't you have one in the same style? I suggest that you try a new style.

W Hmm... let me try. ❷ _____ _____ _____ one for me?

M How about this one with a ribbon?

W I don't like that.

M Then, how about this black one ❸ _____ _____ _____ ?

W That's cool. I'll take it.

02 목적 파악

대화를 듣고, 남자가 여자에게 전화한 목적으로 가장 적절한 것을 고르시오.

① 과제 발표를 부탁하려고
② 과제 제출을 요청하려고
③ 함께 하교하자고 제안하려고
④ 파일을 이메일로 보내 줄 것을 요청하려고
⑤ USB에 파일 저장하는 방법을 문의하려고

😀 **기억이나 망각 표현하기** //////////////
I forgot ~. / I (don't) remember ~. / I'll never forget ~.

W Son, what's up at this time?

M Mom, are you at home now?

W Yes. Why?

M ❶ _____ _____ _____ _____ _____ to my email? The title of the file is *Science Project*.

W Okay. You didn't take it, right?

M No. I forgot to store it on my USB and take it. ❷ _____ _____ _____ _____ on the project with my group members now.

W I got it. I'll call you ❸ _____ _____ _____ .

03 그림 상황에 어울리는 대화 찾기

다음 그림의 상황에 가장 적절한 대화를 고르시오.

① ② ③ ④ ⑤

① M Can you give me a hand?
   W Of course, what can I do for you?

② M ❶ _____ _____ _____ our left hand when shaking hands.
   W Oh, I didn't know that. Sorry.

③ M How can you write so well with your left hand?
   W Well, I'm left-handed.

④ M We only use the right hand when eating things.
   W Is there ❷ _____ _____ _____ ?

⑤ M Why don't you use a fork?
   W It is easier for me to use the chopsticks.

 01 stripe 줄무늬 **recommend** 추천하다 **02 email** 이메일; 이메일을 보내다 **project** 프로젝트, 과제 **03 shake hands** 악수를 하다 **left-handed** 왼손잡이의 **chopsticks** 젓가락

04 특정 정보 파악 – 요일 영국식 발음 녹음

대화를 듣고, 여자가 티셔츠를 받을 요일을 고르시오.

① Monday　　② Tuesday
③ Wednesday　④ Thursday
⑤ Friday

[*Telephone rings.*]
M Hello. This is T-market. May I help you?
W Hello. I'd like to order 25 teddy bear T-shirts. ❶ _____ _____ _____ _____ _____ by this Thursday.
M I'm very sorry but Wednesday is a holiday, so that's not possible. If you order today, I can send them by this Friday.
W But our sports day is Friday. We need them by this Thursday.
M If you can come to get them, you ❷ _____ _____ _____ _____ _____. But only if you send your payment today. Our shop address is on the website.
W I can go. Thank you so much. What time can I go?
M Come at around 6. I'll ❸ _____ _____ _____ for you.

05 직업 및 장래 희망

대화를 듣고, 남자의 직업으로 가장 적절한 것을 고르시오.

① actor　　② writer　　③ painter
④ soldier　⑤ photographer

😊 슬픔, 불만족, 실망의 원인에 대해 묻기 //////////
What's wrong? / What's the matter? / Why are you sad(disappointed)?

M Cut. ❶ _____ _____ _____ _____ one more time.
W Well, did I do something wrong again?
M It was not you, this time. Actually, your ❷ _____ _____ _____.
W Then, what's wrong?
M A fly has been flying around you.
W I see. I hope this is the last time.
M I hope so, too. Let's take a break ❸ _____ _____ _____ _____.

06 심정 파악

대화를 듣고, 여자의 심정으로 가장 적절한 것을 고르시오.

① bored　　② jealous　　③ thankful
④ annoyed　⑤ embarrassed

W How much is it?
M It's $15 total. Would you like to pay by cash or credit?
W I'd like to pay by credit card. ❶ _____, _____ _____ _____?
M Umm, is there something wrong?
W I ❷ _____ _____ _____ _____ anywhere. Could you wait for me for a second?
M Okay. But, could you give way to the next person? A lot of people have been ❸ _____ _____ _____ _____ _____.
W Oh, I didn't know that. I'm sorry.
M It's okay.

Words　**04 holiday** 휴일 **possible** 가능한 **payment** 지불　**05 fly** 파리 **take a break** 잠시 휴식을 취하다　**06 cash** 현금 **anywhere** 어디에도 **for a second** 잠시 **give way to** ~에게 양보하다

Dictation Test

07 어색한 대화 찾기

다음을 듣고, 두 사람의 대화가 <u>어색한</u> 것을 고르시오.

①   ②   ③   ④   ⑤

💬 의무 여부 묻기 ////////////////////////

Do I need(have) to ~? / Is it necessary to ~? / Must I ~?

① W   May I hold your bag? It looks heavy.

   M   Thanks, but I'm okay.

② W   What are you going to buy as Tim's birthday present?

   M   He ❶ _____ _____ _____.

③ W   Have you been to the new restaurant?

   M   ❷ _____, _____ _____. What is it famous for?

④ W   Is it possible that you finish the report in an hour?

   M   Of course, I can type really fast.

⑤ W 💬 Do I need to bring my own cooking tools?

   M   You ❸ _____ _____ _____. We have all the tools.

08 이유 파악   영국식 발음 녹음

대화를 듣고, 복사기가 작동되지 <u>않는</u> 이유를 고르시오.

① 용지가 없어서
② 전원이 꺼져 있어서
③ 용지가 걸려 있어서
④ 부품이 빠져 있어서
⑤ 플러그가 빠져 있어서

M   Hi, Jenny. Are you having problems with the copy machine?

W   Yes. It _____ _____. I couldn't find out what's wrong with it.

M   Did you check the paper tray?

W   Sure. It is okay. Phew, I don't know much about machines.

M   Let's see what's wrong. Why don't we start by ❷ _____ _____ _____ _____?

W   It's plugged in.

M   Oh! But the ❸ _____ _____ _____ _____ yet.

W   What a silly mistake!

09 의도 파악

대화를 듣고, 남자의 마지막 말에 담긴 의도로 가장 적절한 것을 고르시오.

① 감사   ② 거절   ③ 격려
④ 사과   ⑤ 축하

M   What are you making?

W   I'm ❶ _____ _____. Would you have a look?

M   These look so comfortable. How did you make these?

W   Let me show you.

M   You are very creative. Why don't we ❷ _____ _____ _____ and upload it on the internet?

W   That sounds interesting, but I don't think anybody would be interested.

M   Trust me. ❸ _____ _____ _____ _____ _____ by what people think of these.

📖 Words   **07 hold** 잡다, 붙들다   **be famous for** ~으로 유명하다   **type** 타자 치다   **cooking tool** 조리 도구   **08 copy machine** 복사기   **find out** 알아내다   **paper tray** 용지함   **plug in** 플러그를 꽂다   **silly** 바보 같은   **09 comfortable** 편안한   **creative** 창의적인   **upload** 업로드하다

10 숫자 정보 파악 – 금액

대화를 듣고, 여자가 지불할 금액을 고르시오.

① $25   ② $30   ③ $35
④ $45   ⑤ $50

💬 **반복 요청하기** //////////////////

(I'm) sorry? / What (did you say)? / (I beg your) pardon? / I don't know what you mean(meant).

W I like my new hair style. How much should I pay?
M I'm glad you like it. You ❶ _____ _____ _____ _____ _____.   W Sorry? Did you say $50?
M Yes. It's $20 for the haircut, $30 for coloring your hair.
W I see. I have a membership card and a discount coupon as well.
M Sorry, but you ❷ _____ _____ _____ _____ _____. You can get either a 10% discount with the membership card or 30% discount with the coupon.
W Okay. I'll ❸ _____ _____ _____.

11 장소 추론

대화를 듣고, 두 사람이 대화하는 장소로 가장 적절한 곳을 고르시오.

① supermarket   ② concert hall
③ subway station   ④ amusement park
⑤ department store

W Jack, I rode that roller coaster, and it was so fun. Can I ❶ _____ _____ one more time?
M Again? Aren't you scared?
W No, ❷ _____ _____ _____. Do you want to ride it with me?
M No way. Even looking at the rail makes me feel sick.
W Okay, let me ride it by myself.
M Have fun. Amy, I want to have some orange juice. Come to the snack bar ❸ _____ _____ _____ _____.
W I will.

12 언급되지 않은 것

다음을 듣고, 저자 사인회에 관해 언급되지 **않은** 것을 고르시오.

① 저자 이름   ② 장소   ③ 시간
④ 책 내용   ⑤ 보너스 행사

W Best-selling author, Barbara Jones, has ❶ _____ _____ _____ _____, *Jenny's Secret*. She is having an autograph event in the Jungle bookstore on May 31st. The event starts at 3 p.m. and will last for two hours. ❷ _____ _____ _____ _____. If you buy two books, we will give you a third one free.

13 도표 정보 파악 영국식 발음 녹음

대화를 듣고, 내용과 일치하지 **않는** 것을 고르시오.

Design Competition	
① Theme	The world in 50 years
② Deadline	August 1st
③ 1st Place Prize	iPad
④ How to Submit	email
⑤ More Information	www.designcompetition.com

M Amy, are you interested in this design competition?
W Oh, yes. I'd love to take part in the competition.
M Then, you need to make your own work about ❶ _____ _____ _____ _____.
W The theme sounds interesting. Do you know the deadline?
M By ❷ _____ _____ _____ _____. You know what? First prize is an iPad.
W Really? Is it possible to ❸ _____ _____ _____ _____?
M Yes. You can visit their website www.designcompetition.com for more information.

📖 **Words** **10 haircut** 이발 **color** 염색하다 **discount** 할인 **11 rail** 선로 **feel sick** 울렁거리다 **by oneself** 혼자 **12 author** 저자, 작가 **autograph event** 사인회 **last** 지속되다 **13 competition** 대회 **theme** 주제 **deadline** 마감 기한

Dictation Test

14 주제 파악

다음을 듣고, 무엇에 관한 설명인지 고르시오.

① 버터   ② 우유   ③ 치즈
④ 식용유   ⑤ 생크림

W This is ❶＿＿＿＿ ＿＿＿＿ ＿＿＿＿. It is hard in the refrigerator, but it ❷＿＿＿＿ ＿＿＿＿ ＿＿＿＿ ＿＿＿＿ if it is heated. You spread it on bread and eat it, or you can use it to fry vegetables or meat. You also need it to bake cookies or cake. It is ❸＿＿＿＿ ＿＿＿＿ ＿＿＿＿, and it's not good to eat it too much.

15 한 일 / 할 일 파악

대화를 듣고, 남자가 대화 직후에 할 일로 가장 적절한 것을 고르시오.

① 양념 맛보기   ② 양념 교환하기
③ 양념 새로 사 오기   ④ 양념통 설거지하기
⑤ 음식에 양념 뿌리기

M Mom, here's the sauce you asked me to buy.
W Thanks. Wait, this is a green bottle.
M Yeah. You said the green bottle, didn't you?
W No, I told you to buy a red one, ❶＿＿＿＿ ＿＿＿＿ ＿＿＿＿ ＿＿＿＿.
M Oops. Can we just use it?
W No, they're totally different sauces.
M Well, do you want me to ❷＿＿＿＿ ＿＿＿＿ ＿＿＿＿ ＿＿＿＿?
W Hmm, we might need this one anyway. Leave it here and ❸＿＿＿＿ ＿＿＿＿ ＿＿＿＿ ＿＿＿＿, will you?
M Okay.

16 숫자 정보 파악 – 시각   영국식 발음 녹음

대화를 듣고, 남자가 Nicole과 통화 가능한 시각을 고르시오.

① 11:30 a.m.   ② 12:30 p.m.   ③ 1:30 p.m.
④ 2:30 p.m.   ⑤ 3:30 p.m.

😀 허락 요청하기 //////////////////////////

Can I ~? / Let me ~. / Do you mind if ~? / Would it be possible ~? / I was wondering if I could ~?

[Telephone rings.]
M Hello. Can I speak to Nicole, please?
W I'm afraid she's out now.
M I see. What time ❶＿＿＿＿ ＿＿＿＿ ＿＿＿＿ ＿＿＿＿ in the office?
W I'm not sure.
M All right. What about lunchtime?
W Just one moment. I'll check. (pause) No, she's having lunch with a designer.
M Ah! So when is a good time to call her?
W ❷＿＿＿＿ ＿＿＿＿ ＿＿＿＿ 3. She will be in her office for ❸＿＿＿＿ ＿＿＿＿ ＿＿＿＿ ＿＿＿＿ ＿＿＿＿.
M Okay. I'll call back then. Thank you.

Words   **14 refrigerator** 냉장고   **spread** 펴 바르다   **fry** 볶다. 튀기다   **15 sauce** 양념   **totally** 완전히   **leave** 그대로 두다   **16 office** 사무실

17 상황에 맞는 말 찾기

다음 상황 설명을 듣고, Tom이 Ann에게 할 말로 가장 적절한 것을 고르시오.

Tom: _____

① That's very disappointing.
② Don't you agree with me?
③ What makes you think so?
④ I think this book is better than that book.
⑤ Which book do you find the most interesting?

W Tom is preparing to do _____ _____ _____ for elementary school students. He is supposed to read a book to them, so last week he chose some books. However, he isn't sure ❷ _____ _____ the kids would like the most. Fortunately, his younger sister, Ann is an elementary school student. He wants to ask Ann to ❸ _____ _____ _____ _____ among the ones he has. In this situation, what would Tom most likely say to Ann?

18 한 일 / 할 일 파악

대화를 듣고, 두 사람이 할 일로 가장 적절한 것을 고르시오.

① 남은 음식 싸 가기   ② 상한 음식 버리기
③ 결식 아동 후원하기   ④ 음식 더 주문하기
⑤ 남은 음식 마저 먹기

W Did you finish your dinner?
M Yes, I've had enough, I'm full.
W Then, why did you order this much? You ❶ _____ _____ _____ sundae at the end.
M I wanted to taste it as well, but I can't eat anymore.
W Okay. Then, let's ❷ _____ _____ _____ and ❸ _____ _____.
M That's a good idea.

19 알맞은 응답 찾기

대화를 듣고, 여자의 마지막 말에 대한 남자의 응답으로 가장 적절한 것을 고르시오.

Man: _____

① Thanks. I like it a lot.
② No, I haven't. What's that?
③ Maybe he'll like orange juice better.
④ I think Coke is better than orange juice.
⑤ I'm going to watch a movie after the exams.

👄 선호에 대해 묻기 ////////////////////////
Which one do you prefer, A or B? / Do you like A better(more) than B? / Do you prefer A to B?

W What are you doing, John?
M Oh, Mom. I'm studying for final exams.
W Aren't you sleepy? It's too late.
M I can't help it. I haven't finish this book yet, but there are more books to read. I think I have to ❶ _____ _____ _____.
W You will have a tough night. Is there anything I can do for you?
M Yes. I'm already sleepy. Would you get me ❷ _____ _____ to wake me up?
W No problem. Which one do you prefer, Coke or orange juice?

20 알맞은 응답 찾기

대화를 듣고, 남자의 마지막 말에 대한 여자의 응답으로 가장 적절한 것을 고르시오.

Woman: _____

① Be careful of the animals.
② I keep a puppy and a cat in my house.
③ I never let my child watch TV in the evening.
④ Very interesting. I like those wildlife programs.
⑤ Good idea! I think you have to see the programs.

M Excuse me. I'm from Channel 7 TV. We're ❶ _____ _____. Could I ask you a few questions? W Okay.
M First, did you watch TV last night?
W Yes, after dinner. From about 8 o'clock.
M Did you watch ❷ _____ _____ _____ _____?
W Yes, most of the evening. Till 11 o'clock.
M So, you saw *A Day of Wildlife*. ❸ _____ _____ _____ of it?

Words **17 volunteer work** 봉사 활동 **elementary school students** 초등학생   **18 wrap** 싸다, 포장하다   **19 final exam** 기말시험 **tough** 힘든 **20 till** ~까지 **wildlife** 야생 동물

01 대화를 듣고, 여자가 메인 요리로 주문한 음식을 고르시오.

02 대화를 듣고, 남자가 여자에게 전화한 목적으로 가장 적절한 것을 고르시오.

① 소포를 보내려고
② 직장을 구하려고
③ 주소 변경을 알리려고
④ 여행 경비를 빌리려고
⑤ 출장 가는 것을 알리려고

03 다음 그림의 상황에 가장 적절한 대화를 고르시오.

① ② ③ ④ ⑤

04 대화를 듣고, 두 사람이 박물관을 관람할 요일을 고르시오.

① Wednesday ② Thursday   ③ Friday
④ Saturday   ⑤ Sunday

05 대화를 듣고, 여자의 장래 희망으로 가장 적절한 것을 고르시오.

① 대학 교수   ② 의사   ③ 교사
④ 운동 선수   ⑤ 호텔 지배인

06 대화를 듣고, 여자의 심정으로 가장 적절한 것을 고르시오.

① bored   ② satisfied   ③ worried
④ ashamed   ⑤ surprised

07 다음을 듣고, 두 사람의 대화가 <u>어색한</u> 것을 고르시오.

①   ②   ③   ④   ⑤

08 대화를 듣고, 남자가 여행자 수표로 지불할 수 <u>없는</u> 이유를 고르시오.

① 수표를 잃어버려서
② 현금만 갖고 있어서
③ 신분증을 안 가져와서
④ 수표를 호텔에 두고 와서
⑤ 여행사에서 수표를 받지 않아서

09 대화를 듣고, 여자의 마지막 말에 담긴 의도로 가장 적절한 것을 고르시오.

① 감사   ② 격려   ③ 동의
④ 요청   ⑤ 위로

10 대화를 듣고, 여자가 지불할 금액을 고르시오.

① $15   ② $25   ③ $45
④ $60   ⑤ $90

11 대화를 듣고, 두 사람이 대화하는 장소로 가장 적절한 곳을 고르시오.

① hospital   ② theater   ③ library
④ drugstore   ⑤ airport

12 다음을 듣고, 안내 방송 내용 중 언급되지 않은 것을 고르시오.

① 목적지   ② 탑승구 변경
③ 기장 소개   ④ 출발 지연 사유
⑤ 탑승 시간

13 대화를 듣고, 내용과 일치하지 않는 것을 고르시오.

TELEPHONE MESSAGE	
To:	① Ms. Lopez
From:	② Mr. Smith
Message:	③ The meeting is on Friday at 11.
	④ Please call him this afternoon.
	⑤ His phone number 0356–4031

14 다음을 듣고, 무엇에 관한 설명인지 고르시오.

① 휴지   ② 수건
③ 귀마개   ④ 목도리
⑤ 손수건

15 대화를 듣고, 두 사람이 토요일에 할 일로 가장 적절한 것을 고르시오.

① TV 시청하기   ② 영화 관람하기
③ 시내 관광하기   ④ 집 청소하기
⑤ 광고 제작하기

16 대화를 듣고, 남자가 구입할 물건을 고르시오.

① grape   ② tomato
③ watermelon   ④ strawberry
⑤ blueberry

17 다음 상황 설명을 듣고, Susan이 점원에게 할 말로 가장 적절한 것을 고르시오.

Susan: _____

① I'll take it.
② I will pay in cash.
③ Can I get a discount?
④ How much are they?
⑤ No, thanks. I'm just looking around.

18 대화를 듣고, 두 사람이 오늘 저녁에 할 일로 가장 적절한 것을 고르시오.

① 쇼핑하기   ② 과제 제출하기
③ 회의 참석하기   ④ 축제 준비하기
⑤ 강의 준비하기

19 대화를 듣고, 남자의 마지막 말에 대한 여자의 응답으로 가장 적절한 것을 고르시오.

Woman: _____

① I'd like it well-done.
② Of course not. I'll eat this up.
③ I'd like to order some dessert.
④ Yes, please. That would be really nice.
⑤ I'm surprised that the dishes are so delicious.

20 대화를 듣고, 여자의 마지막 말에 대한 남자의 응답으로 가장 적절한 것을 고르시오.

Man: _____

① No, it doesn't, ma'am.
② Sorry, but I have to go now.
③ I'm sorry, but we only accept cash.
④ Thank you for giving me a great present.
⑤ No problem. Wait for a few minutes, please.

01 그림 정보 파악 – 사물

대화를 듣고, 여자가 메인 요리로 주문한 음식을 고르시오.

① ② ③ ④ ⑤

😊 **선호 표현하기** //////////////
I('d) prefer A to B. / I think A is better than B. /
I('d) prefer (to) ~ (if possible).

M May I take your order?

W I'm still trying to decide what to have. Are the burgers good here?

M Yes, they are, but we only offer mini-burgers ❶ _____ _____ _____ _____ .

W I see.

M For your main dish, we have a special seafood spaghetti.

W No, thanks. I'm ❷ _____ _____ _____ . I'd prefer meat to seafood.

M Then shall I ❸ _____ _____ _____ _____ _____ ?

W Yes, I think I'll go with that.

M Okay, ma'am.

02 목적 파악

대화를 듣고, 남자가 여자에게 전화한 목적으로 가장 적절한 것을 고르시오.

① 소포를 보내려고
② 직장을 구하려고
③ 주소 변경을 알리려고
④ 여행 경비를 빌리려고
⑤ 출장 가는 것을 알리려고

😊 **감사하기** /////////////////////
I appreciate your help[what you've done]. /
Thanks for ~. / Thank you (very much). / Thanks (a lot).

[Telephone rings.]

W Hello, this is Anna Johns of ABC company. May I help you?

M Hello. This is Fred. Can I speak to Mr. White?

W I'm sorry. He is on a business trip ❶ _____ _____ _____ . Can I take a message?

M Well, I'd like to ❷ _____ _____ _____ _____ . Could you tell me the company's address, please?

W Of course. The address is 65 Shine Road, Greehill. Anything else?

M If you ❸ _____ _____ _____ , call me back, please.

W All right.

M 😊 I appreciate your help.

03 그림 상황에 어울리는 대화 찾기

다음 그림의 상황에 가장 적절한 대화를 고르시오.

① ② ③ ④ ⑤

① W What's your favorite song?

M I love this one. And you?

② W Hey, could you please ❶ _____ _____ _____ _____ ?

M What? Speak louder. I can't hear you.

③ W I want to sing No. 342.

M ❷ _____ _____ . I'll press the number for you.

④ W Can I have two tickets for the concert, please?

M Where would you like to sit?

⑤ W ❸ _____ _____ _____ _____ with you.

M That's great. I've wanted to ask you for a long time.

📖 Words **01 offer** 제공하다 **main** 주된 **seafood** 해산물 **allergic** 알레르기가 있는 **pork cutlet** 돈가스 **02 business trip** 출장 **address** 주소 **package** 소포 **03 loud** 소리가 큰 **press** 누르다

04 특정 정보 파악 – 요일 영국식 발음 녹음

대화를 듣고, 두 사람이 박물관을 관람할 요일을 고르시오.

① Wednesday ② Thursday ③ Friday
④ Saturday ⑤ Sunday

M Wow! This National Gallery is very big, isn't it?

W Yes, it's huge. *(pause)* Oh, no! I don't think it's open today.

M What do you mean?

W Look. It says "❶_____ _____."

M Well, we'll just have to come back tomorrow.

W But, wait. We're supposed to go on ❷_____ _____ _____ _____ _____.

M That's right. Then, how about ❸_____ _____ _____ _____?

W It's okay with me.

M All right.

05 직업 및 장래 희망

대화를 듣고, 여자의 장래 희망으로 가장 적절한 것을 고르시오.

① 대학 교수 ② 의사 ③ 교사
④ 운동 선수 ⑤ 호텔 지배인

W Now we have only a few months before we finish college.

M What are you going to do when you graduate?

W Well, I'd like to get a ❶_____ _____ _____ _____.

M That sounds interesting. What are your next plans on that job?

W I want to ❷_____ _____ _____ _____ and run one someday.

M Work hard, and you'll be rich enough to buy the hotel.

06 심정 파악

대화를 듣고, 여자의 심정으로 가장 적절한 것을 고르시오.

① bored ② satisfied ③ worried
④ ashamed ⑤ surprised

M Guess where grandma and grandpa are going on vacation.

W Miami? Hawaii?

M No! Think about other places!

W I give up. Where?

M They'll go camping in Colorado! You ❶_____ _____ _____, right?

W What? Camping? ❷_____ _____ _____?

M No. They were serious. They're sick of hotels.

W That's great. I ❸_____ _____ _____ _____ in my 60's.

Words **04 huge** 엄청난, 웅장한 **say** ~라고 쓰여 있다 **05 finish college** 대학을 졸업하다 **next** 다음의 **manager** 관리인, 지배인 **run** 경영하다
06 on vacation 휴가로 **be sick of** ~에 질리다

Dictation Test

07 어색한 대화 찾기

다음을 듣고, 두 사람의 대화가 <u>어색한</u> 것을 고르시오.

①   ②   ③   ④   ⑤

① M   Can I try this shirt on?

    W   Certainly. The fitting room is over there.

② M   Do you know ❶ _____ _____ _____ _____ _____?

    W   No, I disagree.

③ M   How would you like your steak?

    W   Well done, please.

④ M   You look down. What's wrong?

    W   I ❷ _____ _____ _____ my math test.

⑤ M   I'd like to send this package.

    W   Okay. Where do you want to send it?

08 이유 파악   영국식 발음 녹음

대화를 듣고, 남자가 여행자 수표로 지불할 수 <u>없는</u> 이유를 고르시오.

① 수표를 잃어버려서

② 현금만 갖고 있어서

③ 신분증을 안 가져와서

④ 수표를 호텔에 두고 와서

⑤ 여행사에서 수표를 받지 않아서

M   I'll buy this suitcase.

W   How would you like to pay? ❶ _____ _____ _____?

M   Do you take travelers' checks?

W   Yes, sir. Do you have a passport or other ID cards?

M   No, I ❷ _____ _____ _____ my hotel room.

W   I'm sorry, sir. In that case, we ❸ _____ _____ _____ _____. I'm afraid you'll have to pay in cash.

M   Well, then, here's a 100-dollar bill.

09 의도 파악

대화를 듣고, 여자의 마지막 말에 담긴 의도로 가장 적절한 것을 고르시오.

① 감사   ② 격려   ③ 동의

④ 요청   ⑤ 위로

W   June's posters are sold out at the music store.

M   Are you coming back from the music store?

W   I am. I'm so sad. ❶ _____ _____ _____ _____ buy one of June's posters. He is my favorite singer.

M   Guess what I have.

W   What is it? June's poster? ❷ _____ _____ _____ get it?

M   I went to the music store right after school and bought two. This one is for you.

W   Oh, you ❸ _____ _____ _____! I'll treat you to lunch tomorrow.

Words   **07 fitting room** 탈의실   **08 suitcase** 서류 가방   **traveler** 여행자   **passport** 여권   **ID card** 신분증   **09 sold out** 다 팔린   **treat** 한턱 내다, 대접하다

10 숫자 정보 파악 – 금액

대화를 듣고, 여자가 지불할 금액을 고르시오.

① $15 ② $25 ③ $45
④ $60 ⑤ $90

W How much are the tickets for the best seats in the concert hall?

M They cost $60. They're just in front of the stage.

W Oh, that's much more expensive ❶ _____ _____ _____ _____.

M The cheapest ones are $15.

W Where are they located? **M** On the third floor.

W That's ❷ _____ _____ _____. I won't be able to see anything.

M The seats on the second floor cost $25 and the first floor cost $45.

W Well, I'd better get a ticket ❸ _____ _____ _____ _____ in order to enjoy the concert.

11 장소 추론 영국식 발음 녹음

대화를 듣고, 두 사람이 대화하는 장소로 가장 적절한 곳을 고르시오.

① hospital ② theater ③ library
④ drugstore ⑤ airport

😊 **도움 제안하기** ////////////////////////
Can I help you? / Let me help you. / Can I give you a hand?

M Can I help you?

W Yes, please. My daughter ❶ _____ _____ _____.

M Okay. Can you tell me more about it?

W She has been coughing quite a lot since last night. Could you ❷ _____ _____ _____?

M How old is your daughter? **W** She's four.

M These pills are good for children's coughs. Give her two pills ❸ _____ _____ _____ _____.

W Thanks, I will.

12 언급되지 않은 것

다음을 듣고, 안내 방송 내용 중 언급되지 않은 것을 고르시오.

① 목적지 ② 탑승구 변경
③ 기장 소개 ④ 출발 지연 사유
⑤ 탑승 시간

W Hello, passengers of flight CX417 to Toronto. ❶ _____ _____ _____ has been changed to 37A. Also, there will be a slight delay due to the ❷ _____ _____. We ❸ _____ _____ _____ _____ _____ 4 o'clock. We are really sorry and thank you for your understanding.

13 도표 정보 파악

대화를 듣고, 내용과 일치하지 않는 것을 고르시오.

TELEPHONE MESSAGE	
To:	① Ms. Lopez
From:	② Mr. Smith
Message:	③ The meeting is on Friday at 11.
	④ Please call him this afternoon.
	⑤ His phone number 0356–4031

[Telephone rings.]

W Hello, Belle Company.

M ❶ _____ _____ _____ _____ Ms. Lopez?

W I'm sorry. She's not in. Can I take a message?

M Yes. This is Mr. Smith. Please tell her our meeting time ❷ _____ _____ _____ from 11 to 1:30 on Friday. **W** Okay.

M And would you ask her to ❸ _____ _____ _____? My number is 0356–4031. **W** Okay. I will.

Words **10 in order to** ~하기 위해서 **11 cough** 기침하다; 기침 **medicine** 약 **pill** 알약 **12 passenger** 승객 **slight** 약간의 **delay** 지연
due to ~ 때문에 **be about to** ~할 예정이다 **13 take a message** 메시지를 받다

Dictation Test

14 주제 파악

다음을 듣고, 무엇에 관한 설명인지 고르시오.

① 휴지　　　　　　② 수건
③ 귀마개　　　　　④ 목도리
⑤ 손수건

M This is _____ _____ _____ _____ **❶** people carry, and it usually has a nice design on it. When people carry it, they fold it in a square shape and put it in their pockets or bags. They can **❷** _____ _____ _____ their faces, or dry their hands with it. When it gets dirty, they can **❸** _____ _____ _____ after washing and drying it. Some people tie this around their necks, and others put it in the front pockets of their jackets to look fashionable.

15 한 일 / 할 일 파악

대화를 듣고, 두 사람이 토요일에 할 일로 가장 적절한 것을 고르시오.

① TV 시청하기　　　② 영화 관람하기
③ 시내 관광하기　　　④ 집 청소하기
⑤ 광고 제작하기

😊 **허가 여부 묻기** ////////////////////////////////
Is it okay(all right) to ~? / I wonder if I could ~. / Do you mind if ~? / May(Can) I ~?

M I want to see *The Great Gatsby*. Are you free this Saturday?
W Is it okay to see the movie on Sunday? I'm supposed to **❶** _____ _____ _____ _____ _____.
M Fine with me. And I think I can help you clean your house.
W I would be thankful **❷** _____ _____ _____ _____ _____. Can you come to my house at 10 in the morning?
M No problem.
W By the way, the movie sounds boring.
M No, I heard it's fantastic. Believe me.

16 특정 정보 파악　영국식 발음 녹음

대화를 듣고, 남자가 구입할 물건을 고르시오.

① grape　　　　② tomato
③ watermelon　　④ strawberry
⑤ blueberry

😊 **허락 요청에 답하기** ////////////////////////////
Of course. / Yes.(Okay, All right.) / Sure. / (Yes,) you can.

W May I help you, sir?
M I'd like to **❶** _____ _____ _____. Are they good today?
W We are at the end of the strawberry season now. Why don't you try seasonal fruits?
M What do you recommend?
W Watermelons are good, and grapes and tomatoes are very fresh.
M I bought a watermelon yesterday. Can I try the grapes and tomatoes?
W Of course. **❷** _____ _____ _____ too. They are very cheap today.
M Oh, these **❸** _____ _____ _____ _____. I'll buy these.

17 상황에 맞는 말 찾기

다음 상황 설명을 듣고, Susan이 점원에게 할 말로 가장 적절한 것을 고르시오.

Susan: _____

① I'll take it.
② I will pay in cash.
③ Can I get a discount?
④ How much are they?
⑤ No, thanks. I'm just looking around.

M Susan **❶** _____ _____ _____ whenever she has free time. To her, it's just good entertainment. It gives her a chance to see what new products are on the market. When she enjoys window shopping, a **❷** _____ _____ _____ _____ _____ if she needs any help. In this situation, what would Susan most likely say to the clerk?

📖 **Words** **14 design** 무늬 **fold** 접다 **wipe** 닦다 **sweat** 땀 **tie** 묶다　**15 thankful** 고마워하는 **fantastic** 환상적인　**16 season** (농작물 등의) 제철 **seasonal fruit** 제철 과일 **cheap** (값이) 싼　**17 entertainment** 오락, 재미 **on the market** 시장에 나와 있는

18 한 일 / 할 일 파악

대화를 듣고, 두 사람이 오늘 저녁에 할 일로 가장 적절한 것을 고르시오.

① 쇼핑하기 ② 과제 제출하기
③ 회의 참석하기 ④ 축제 준비하기
⑤ 강의 준비하기

😊 **바람, 소원, 요망 표현하기** //////////////////

I wish I could ~. / I look forward to ~. / I'd like to ~.

W Brian, what are you doing?

M Oh, Cindy, I've just finished my term paper. What's up?

W Well, I'm _____ _____ _____ _____. How about going together?

M I wish I could, but I have an appointment this evening.

W Oh, what is it? ❷ _____ _____ _____ _____?

M I'll meet Susan to plan our school festival.

W Come on! Shopping will be ❸ _____ _____ _____ _____. And, I'll buy you dinner.

M Hmm... all right. I'll call up Susan.

19 알맞은 응답 찾기

대화를 듣고, 남자의 마지막 말에 대한 여자의 응답으로 가장 적절한 것을 고르시오.

Woman: _____

① I'd like it well-done.
② Of course not. I'll eat this up.
③ I'd like to order some dessert.
④ Yes, please. That would be really nice.
⑤ I'm surprised that the dishes are so delicious.

M Ma'am, is there anything I can do for you?

W No, I'm fine.

M ❶ _____ _____ _____ your meal?

W Yes, I liked it. Why are you asking?

M Because you left a lot of food, so I wondered if you were not satisfied with it.

W I liked it very much, but I guess I have ❷ _____ _____ _____. I just can't eat it.

M I see. Do you want me to bring you ❸ _____ _____ _____ _____? That might ease your stomach.

20 알맞은 응답 찾기

대화를 듣고, 여자의 마지막 말에 대한 남자의 응답으로 가장 적절한 것을 고르시오.

Man: _____

① No, it doesn't, ma'am.
② Sorry, but I have to go now.
③ I'm sorry, but we only accept cash.
④ Thank you for giving me a great present.
⑤ No problem. Wait for a few minutes, please.

M What can I show you, ma'am?

W I want to buy my nephew ❶ _____ _____ _____.

M May I recommend one?

W Of course. What is it?

M How about an electronic dictionary?

W Oh, good. ❷ _____ _____ _____ the newest model?

M Sure. The red one on display is a hot item.

W Looks nice. How much is it?

M Let me check the price. It's $120. It is on sale.

W Okay. I'll take it. ❸ _____ _____ _____ _____ _____ for me?

Ⓦords **18 term paper** 학기말 과제 **call ~ up** ~에게 전화를 걸다 **19 satisfy** 만족시키다 **have an upset stomach** 체하다 **ease** 편하게 해 주다
20 nephew 조카 **electronic** 전자의 **on display** 진열된, 전시된

01 2018년 1회
대화를 듣고, 여자가 만든 북마크를 고르시오.

①  ② ③

④ ⑤

02 2017년 2회
대화를 듣고, 여자가 남자에게 전화한 목적으로 가장 적절한 것을 고르시오.

① 주문을 취소하려고   ② 배송 지연을 알리려고
③ 환불 방법을 알리려고   ④ 제품 이상을 문의하려고
⑤ 배송 위치를 확인하려고

03 2017년 2회
다음 그림의 상황에 가장 적절한 대화를 고르시오.

①   ②   ③   ④   ⑤

04 2017년 1회
대화를 듣고, 두 사람이 만나기로 한 요일을 고르시오.

① 월요일   ② 화요일   ③ 수요일
④ 목요일   ⑤ 금요일

05 2017년 2회
다음을 듣고, Evergreen Community Center에 관해 언급되지 <u>않은</u> 것을 고르시오.

① 운영 프로그램   ② 식당 메뉴
③ 셔틀버스 운행   ④ 운영 시간
⑤ 휴관일

06 2016년 2회
대화를 듣고, 두 사람의 관계로 가장 적절한 것을 고르시오.

① 식당 종업원 – 손님
② 경비실 직원 – 거주자
③ 음식점 배달원 – 고객
④ 택배 기사 – 물품 구매자
⑤ 주유소 직원 – 택시 기사

07 2017년 1회
다음을 듣고, 두 사람의 대화가 <u>어색한</u> 것을 고르시오.

①   ②   ③   ④   ⑤

08 2017년 1회
대화를 듣고, 여자가 남자에게 부탁한 일로 가장 적절한 것을 고르시오.

① 대본 작성하기   ② 연기 평가하기
③ 소품 제작하기   ④ 연극 주제 정하기
⑤ 연극 의상 고르기

09 2018년 1회
다음을 듣고, 무엇에 관한 안내 방송인지 고르시오.

① 희망도서 신청   ② 학교 홈페이지 개설
③ 학교 도서관 휴관   ④ 냉방기기 사용방법
⑤ 과제 제출 장소 변경

10 2017년 1회
대화를 듣고, 여자가 지불할 금액을 고르시오.

① $2   ② $5   ③ $7
④ $9   ⑤ $11

11 2016년 2회
대화를 듣고, 두 사람이 대화하는 장소로 가장 적절한 것을 고르시오.

① 체육관 ② 사진관 ③ 영화관
④ 공연장 ⑤ 미술관

12 2017년 1회
다음을 듣고, Parkway School Marathon Day에 관해 언급되지 <u>않은</u> 것을 고르시오.

① 운영 책임자 ② 개최 날짜
③ 참가 대상 ④ 참가비
⑤ 접수 장소

13 2018년 1회
대화를 듣고, 두 사람이 사용할 회의실을 고르시오.

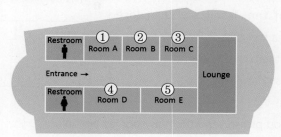

14 2017년 1회
다음을 듣고, 무엇에 관한 설명인지 고르시오.

① 자전거 ② 기차 ③ 배
④ 비행기 ⑤ 버스

15 2017년 2회
대화를 듣고, 남자가 할 일로 가장 적절한 것을 고르시오.

① 지하철 갈아타기 ② 극장 위치 확인하기
③ 지하철 시간 확인하기 ④ 연극 표 구매하기
⑤ 분실물 찾기

16 2016년 1회
대화를 듣고, 두 사람이 구입할 물건을 고르시오.

① planner ② dictionary
③ mobile phone ④ battery pack
⑤ microphone

17 2018년 1회
대화를 듣고, 남자의 마지막 말에 대한 여자의 응답으로 가장 적절한 것을 고르시오.

Woman: _____

① I left my wallet in the shop.
② I can't lend you my computer.
③ This coffee machine doesn't work.
④ I can't move because my back hurts.
⑤ The papers don't come out of the printer.

18 2018년 1회
대화를 듣고, 여자의 마지막 말에 대한 남자의 응답으로 가장 적절한 것을 고르시오.

Man: _____

① Your handwriting needs more help.
② Let me tell you the website address.
③ I'm not good at solving math questions.
④ I enjoy listening to music on the Internet.
⑤ My teacher shows us how to make a blog.

19 2017년 2회
대화를 듣고, 남자의 마지막 말에 대한 여자의 응답으로 가장 적절한 것을 고르시오.

Woman: _____

① Don't worry. We can be a great team.
② Congratulations! I knew you'd win.
③ No, I'm not interested in singing at all.
④ I've never considered joining the contest.
⑤ Thanks for helping me.

20 2017년 2회
다음 상황 설명을 듣고, 지훈이가 점원에게 할 말로 가장 적절한 것을 고르시오.

Jihoon: _____

① Then, can you make these pants shorter?
② I'm sorry, but I want to get a refund.
③ When will you get the bigger size?
④ I like this style so much.
⑤ Long pants are not my style.

Dictation Test 기출문제로 마무리하는 Final Test **01** 회

01 그림 정보 파악 – 사물

대화를 듣고, 여자가 만든 북마크를 고르시오.

①   ②   ③

④   ⑤

M Emily, there's a bookmark on your desk. Did you make it?

W Yes, Dad. It's a birthday present for Rachel.

M Good job! This bookmark ❶ _____ _____ _____ _____. It looks nice.

W Thanks. I wanted to make it in a heart shape, but Rachel really likes stars.

M I see. You drew just a smile. Why didn't you write any words on it?

W Well, I think ❷ _____ _____ _____ _____. Rachel always smiles.

M Okay. I'm sure she'll like it.

02 목적 파악

대화를 듣고, 여자가 남자에게 전화한 목적으로 가장 적절한 것을 고르시오.

① 주문을 취소하려고 ② 배송 지연을 알리려고
③ 환불 방법을 알리려고 ④ 제품 이상을 문의하려고
⑤ 배송 위치를 확인하려고

[Cellphone rings.]

M Hello.

W Hello. This is Mega Home Shopping. Is this Tom Baker?

M Yes. Speaking.

W I'm sorry, but the T-shirts you ordered ❶ _____ _____ _____ for a few days.

M Really? I need them this weekend.

W Don't worry, sir. You'll ❷ _____ _____ _____ _____.

M Okay. Could you please send them as soon as possible?

W Sure. Thank you for your understanding.

03 그림 상황에 어울리는 대화 찾기

다음 그림의 상황에 가장 적절한 대화를 고르시오.

① ② ③ ④ ⑤

① M Why didn't you come to the food festival?
　 W I couldn't because I had to ❶ _____ _____ _____ my sick cat.

② M The food here is really good.
　 W I'm glad you like it. This is my favorite place.

③ M Your cat looks so cute. What's his name?
　 W Thanks. His name is Nabi.

④ M Sorry, but dogs ❷ _____ _____ _____ here.
　 W Oh, I'm sorry. I didn't know that.

⑤ M Are you ready to order now?
　 W Not yet. Can I have some more time, please?

 Words　**01** bookmark 책갈피 **present** 선물　**02** order 주문하다 delay 미루다, 연기하다 as soon as possible 가능한 한 빨리　**03** take care of ~을 돌보다 allow 허락하다

04 특정 정보 파악 – 요일 영국식 발음 녹음

대화를 듣고, 두 사람이 만나기로 한 요일을 고르시오.

① 월요일   ② 화요일   ③ 수요일
④ 목요일   ⑤ 금요일

[Cellphone rings.]

W Hello, John. Do you remember our presentation ❶ _____ _____ _____ _____?

M Yes. Why don't we meet to talk about it?

W Are you free on Tuesday?

M I'm afraid not. I promised to ❷ _____ _____ _____ _____ with my cousin. How about Wednesday?

W Wednesday? I have a swimming lesson on Wednesday. Is Thursday good?

M Thursday is not good for me, but I'll ❸ _____ _____ _____ _____.

W Friday is okay for me, too. See you then.

05 언급되지 않은 것

다음을 듣고, Evergreen Community Center에 관해 언급되지 <u>않은</u> 것을 고르시오.

① 운영 프로그램   ② 식당 메뉴
③ 셔틀버스 운행   ④ 운영 시간
⑤ 휴관일

W Thank you for visiting Evergreen Community Center. Let me give you a ❶ _____ _____ of our center. We have a variety of programs including swimming and painting. There is a cafeteria in the basement. We offer ❷ _____ _____ _____ _____ every hour. The center is open from 9 a.m. to 7 p.m., Monday through Saturday. We ❸ _____ _____ _____ _____. We hope you'll visit us again soon. Have a nice day.

06 관계 추론

대화를 듣고, 두 사람의 관계로 가장 적절한 것을 고르시오.

① 식당 종업원 – 손님
② 경비실 직원 – 거주자
③ 음식점 배달원 – 고객
④ 택배 기사 – 물품 구매자
⑤ 주유소 직원 – 택시 기사

[Cellphone rings.]

W Hello.

M Hello. This is Michael from DK ❶ _____ _____. Is this Ms. Kim?

W Yes, speaking.

M I'm going to drop by your house in ten minutes to ❷ _____ _____ _____.

W I am sorry. There is nobody at home now.

M Then, what do you want me to do?

W Please leave it at the apartment office. I'll pick it up later today.

M Okay. I will.

📖 **Words**   **04 presentation** 발표   **promise** 약속하다   **theater** 극장   **free** 한가한   **05 brief** 간략한   **overview** 개요   **a variety of** 다양한 **basement** 지하   **06 delivery** 배달   **drop by** 잠깐 들르다   **pick up** ~을 들고 오다

Dictation Test

07 어색한 대화 찾기

다음을 듣고, 두 사람의 대화가 <u>어색한</u> 것을 고르시오.

① ② ③ ④ ⑤

① M What are you going to do during your vacation?

   W I'm going to visit my grandfather.

② M Which bag do you prefer, the red one or the black one?

   W I'll ❶ _____ _____ _____ _____.

③ M How often do you go to the movies?

   W Once or twice a month.

④ M May I ❷ _____ _____ _____?

   W Yes. I'll have a cheese sandwich, please.

⑤ M Can I borrow your pen?

   W Sure, here you are.

08 부탁한 일 파악 영국식 발음 녹음

대화를 듣고, 여자가 남자에게 부탁한 일로 가장 적절한 것을 고르시오.

① 대본 작성하기 ② 연기 평가하기
③ 소품 제작하기 ④ 연극 주제 정하기
⑤ 연극 의상 고르기

M Hi, Sunny. You look busy. What are you doing?

W Oh, Mr. Wilson. I'm preparing for ❶ _____ _____ _____ _____.

M That's right. Your class will perform a play. What is it about?

W It's about family. We want to tell ❷ _____ _____ _____ _____ in a family.

M Sounds good. Do you need any help?

W Yes, please. Could you ❸ _____ _____ _____ for the play?

M Sure. That would be fun.

09 주제 파악

다음을 듣고, 무엇에 관한 안내 방송인지 고르시오.

① 희망도서 신청 ② 학교 홈페이지 개설
③ 학교 도서관 휴관 ④ 냉방기기 사용방법
⑤ 과제 제출 장소 변경

W Attention, students. I'm Linda, the school librarian. We're sorry to announce that ❶ _____ _____ _____ _____ _____ next week from Monday to Wednesday. The air conditioner broke down and it'll ❷ _____ _____ _____ _____ _____ it. You can't use any facilities in the library, but you can put your books in the book return box in front of the library as usual. Thank you for your patience.

10 숫자 정보 파악 – 금액

대화를 듣고, 여자가 지불할 금액을 고르시오.

① $2 ② $5 ③ $7
④ $9 ⑤ $11

M Hello. Can I take your order?

W Hi. I'd like to ❶ _____ _____ _____ _____, please.

M That will be $5. If you pay $2 more, you can get a drink and fries.

W Oh, really? I'll ❷ _____ _____ _____ _____, then.

M Okay. Would you like anything else? How about dessert?

W ❸ _____ _____ _____.

M Okay. For here or to go?

W To go, please.

Words **07 prefer** ~을 좋아하다 **08 perform** 공연하다 **play** 연극 **09 librarian** 사서 **announce** 알리다, 공표하다 **break down** 고장 나다 **facilities** 설비, 시설 **as usual** 늘 그렇듯이

11 장소 추론 영국식 발음 녹음

대화를 듣고, 두 사람이 대화하는 장소로 가장 적절한 것을 고르시오.

① 체육관　　② 사진관　　③ 영화관
④ 공연장　　⑤ 미술관

W Hey, Ken. This is amazing!

M I can't believe ❶＿＿＿＿ ＿＿＿＿ ＿＿＿＿ ＿＿＿＿ of the great masters so closely!

W Me neither. Look here! These pictures seem to be so real.

M Yeah! The person ❷＿＿＿＿ ＿＿＿＿ ＿＿＿＿ seems to be looking at me.

W Right. I'd like to take some photos.

M Oh, no! We ❸＿＿＿＿ ＿＿＿＿ ＿＿＿＿ ＿＿＿＿ ＿＿＿＿ that in here.

W Okay. I didn't know that. Let's move to the next section.

12 언급되지 않은 것

다음을 듣고, Parkway School Marathon Day에 관해 언급되지 <u>않은</u> 것을 고르시오.

① 운영 책임자　　② 개최 날짜
③ 참가 대상　　④ 참가비
⑤ 접수 장소

M Hello, students. I'm Michael Lee, and ❶＿＿＿＿ ＿＿＿＿ ＿＿＿＿ ＿＿＿＿ Parkway School Marathon Day. I'm happy to tell you that we'll have the annual event on May 13th, 2017. Any of our school students can join us. Also, you can run ❷＿＿＿＿ ＿＿＿＿ ＿＿＿＿ ＿＿＿＿. This event includes ❸＿＿＿＿ ＿＿＿＿ such as a food fair and a marching band. To sign up for this event, please go to the teachers' office. Thank you.

13 도표 정보 파악

대화를 듣고, 두 사람이 사용할 회의실을 고르시오.

M Mary, which room is good for our meeting this Thursday?

W What about Room D?

M I heard that Robert will use it on that day.

W Hmm..., how about ❶＿＿＿＿ ＿＿＿＿ ＿＿＿＿ ＿＿＿＿ ＿＿＿＿ next to the lounge? They're convenient.

M But the lounge is often crowded, so those rooms may be noisy.

W You're right. Then, we have ❷＿＿＿＿ ＿＿＿＿ ＿＿＿＿, Room A and Room B.

M ❸＿＿＿＿ ＿＿＿＿ ＿＿＿＿ the room next to the restroom.

W Okay. Let's use this room.

14 주제 파악

다음을 듣고, 무엇에 관한 설명인지 고르시오.

① 자전거　　② 기차　　③ 배
④ 비행기　　⑤ 버스

W This is a vehicle. It carries ❶＿＿＿＿ ＿＿＿＿ ＿＿＿＿ ＿＿＿＿ at a time. It has restrooms that the passengers can use. Passengers ❷＿＿＿＿ ＿＿＿＿ ＿＿＿＿ ＿＿＿＿ ＿＿＿＿ and the vehicle sometimes has a snack bar. It stops at stations and people get on and get off there. It has many wheels but it can ❸＿＿＿＿ ＿＿＿＿ ＿＿＿＿ ＿＿＿＿.

Words　**11 amazing** 놀라운　**artworks** 미술품　**12 be in charge of** ~을 담당하다　**various** 다양한　**fair** 축제 마당　**marching** 행진하는　**sign up for** 등록하다　**13 lounge** 휴게실　**convenient** 편리한　**crowded** 혼잡한　**14 vehicle** 운송 수단, 차량　**carry** 나르다　**passenger** 승객

Dictation Test

15 한 일 / 할 일 파악

대화를 듣고, 남자가 할 일로 가장 적절한 것을 고르시오.

① 지하철 갈아타기 ② 극장 위치 확인하기
③ 지하철 시간 확인하기 ④ 연극 표 구매하기
⑤ 분실물 찾기

[*Cellphone rings.*]

M Hello?

W Hi, Jack. I'm on the subway but I'm going to be late.

M Why? What happened?

W I ❶_____ _____ _____. I'm sorry but I'll be there in 20 minutes.

M It's all right. We still have 30 minutes before the play starts.

W Good, I'll be there as soon as I can.

M Okay. I'm at the theater now. So, I'll ❷_____ _____ _____.

W That'll be great. Thanks.

16 특정 정보 파악 영국식 발음 녹음

대화를 듣고, 두 사람이 구입할 물건을 고르시오.

① planner ② dictionary
③ mobile phone ④ battery pack
⑤ microphone

M Ms. Park. I'm thinking about the prize ❶_____ _____ _____ _____ this year. Do you have any ideas?

W For the last two years, the winners received either a planner or a dictionary.

M I know, but many students said that they always get those.

W What about ❷_____ _____ _____? It's very practical since students use mobile devices a lot.

M That's a great idea! I'm sure our students would really like it.

W Great! Then, let's order that this time.

17 알맞은 응답 찾기

대화를 듣고, 남자의 마지막 말에 대한 여자의 응답으로 가장 적절한 것을 고르시오.

Woman: _____

① I left my wallet in the shop.
② I can't lend you my computer.
③ This coffee machine doesn't work.
④ I can't move because my back hurts.
⑤ The papers don't come out of the printer.

[*Telephone rings.*]

M ABC Office Supplies. How may I help you?

W Hi. I ❶_____ _____ _____ from your shop last week, but there's a little problem with it.

M Oh, I'm sorry for your inconvenience. What's the model number?

W The model number? Where can I find it?

M It's on the back of the printer.

W Okay. Let me see. (*pause*) It says LP-123.

M Thank you. Can you tell me ❷_____ _____ _____ _____?

📖 **Words** **15 as soon as** ~하자마자 **16 prize** 상; 상품 **battery pack** 배터리 팩 **practical** 실용적인 **device** 기기 **17 inconvenience** 불편

18 알맞은 응답 찾기

대화를 듣고, 여자의 마지막 말에 대한 남자의 응답으로 가장 적절한 것을 고르시오.

Man: _____

① Your handwriting needs more help.
② Let me tell you the website address.
③ I'm not good at solving math questions.
④ I enjoy listening to music on the Internet.
⑤ My teacher shows us how to make a blog.

M Have you _____ _____ _____ for the history presentation next Monday?
W No. I haven't even started it yet. I think I need help in making the graphs.
M I ❷ _____ _____ _____ _____ _____ about making graphs on the Internet.
W A video clip?
M Yes. It helped me a lot. The clip was about how to make graphs for beginners like us.
W It sounds helpful. ❸ _____ _____ _____ _____ it on the Internet?

19 알맞은 응답 찾기 영국식 발음 녹음

대화를 듣고, 남자의 마지막 말에 대한 여자의 응답으로 가장 적절한 것을 고르시오.

Woman: _____

① Don't worry. We can be a great team.
② Congratulations! I knew you'd win.
③ No, I'm not interested in singing at all.
④ I've never considered joining the contest.
⑤ Thanks for helping me.

W Mike, are you going to ❶ _____ _____ _____ _____?
M I'm thinking about it, but I'm scared to sing in front of people.
W Don't be. You're a good singer.
M At the last contest, I made a lot of mistakes during my song.
W Why don't we join the contest ❷ _____ _____ _____? If you are in trouble, I can help you.
M I don't know. I don't want to ❸ _____ _____ in front of everyone again.

20 상황에 맞는 말 찾기

다음 상황 설명을 듣고, 지훈이가 점원에게 할 말로 가장 적절한 것을 고르시오.

Jihoon: _____

① Then, can you make these pants shorter?
② I'm sorry, but I want to get a refund.
③ When will you get the bigger size?
④ I like this style so much.
⑤ Long pants are not my style.

M The other day, Jihoon's mother bought ❶ _____ _____ _____ _____ for him but they were too big. He wanted to exchange them for the right size, so he visited the store. However, the clerk told him that the size he wanted ❷ _____ _____ _____. He wants to ask if he could ❸ _____ _____ _____ _____. In this situation, what would Jihoon most likely say to the clerk?

Words **18** **useful** 유용한 **helpful** 도움이 되는 **19** **join** 참가하다 **scared** 겁먹은 **be in trouble** 곤경에 빠져서 **20** **the other day** 최근에
pair 한 쌍 **exchange** 교환하다 **sold out** 품절된

2017년 1회

01 대화를 듣고, 두 사람이 구입할 풍선을 고르시오.

① 　② 　③

2016년 2회

02 대화를 듣고, 남자가 여자에게 전화한 목적으로 가장 적절한 것을 고르시오.

① 숙제를 물어보기 위해

② 함께 병문안을 가기 위해

③ 친구 집에 놀러 가기 위해

④ 버스 시간을 물어보기 위해

⑤ 결석한 이유를 물어보기 위해

2017년 1회

03 다음 그림의 상황에 가장 적절한 대화를 고르시오.

①　　②　　③　　④　　⑤

2017년 2회

04 대화를 듣고, 남자가 테니스 코트를 사용할 수 없는 요일을 고르시오.

① 월요일　　② 수요일　　③ 목요일

④ 금요일　　⑤ 토요일

2017년 1회

05 다음을 듣고, Drone-X에 관해 언급되지 않은 것을 고르시오.

① 크기　　② 조종 범위　　③ 작동 시간

④ 촬영 기능　　⑤ 가격

2018년 1회

06 대화를 듣고, 두 사람이 대화하는 장소로 가장 적절한 곳을 고르시오.

① 영화관　　② 야구장　　③ 지하철역

④ 사무실　　⑤ 카페

2016년 1회

07 다음을 듣고, 두 사람의 대화가 어색한 것을 고르시오.

①　　②　　③　　④　　⑤

2016년 2회

08 대화를 듣고, 여자가 남자에게 부탁한 일로 가장 적절한 것을 고르시오.

① 아침 차려주기　　② 과제 도와주기

③ 아이들 깨우기　　④ 자명종 수리하기

⑤ 차로 자녀 등교시키기

2016년 1회

09 대화를 듣고, 여자의 마지막 말에 담긴 의도로 가장 적절한 것을 고르시오.

① 위로　　② 충고　　③ 거절

④ 요청　　⑤ 감사

2016년 1회

10 대화를 듣고, 남자가 지불할 금액을 고르시오.

① $90　　② $100　　③ $108

④ $110　　⑤ $120

11 2017년 1회

대화를 듣고, 남자가 할 일로 가장 적절한 것을 고르시오.

① 영화 시간 확인　　② 저녁 식사 준비
③ 파티 물품 구입　　④ 영화평 작성
⑤ 시험 준비

12 2017년 2회

다음을 듣고, Oakwood Flea Market에 관해 언급되지 <u>않은</u> 것을 고르시오.

① 개최 날짜　　② 취급 품목
③ 판매자 참가비　　④ 접수 장소
⑤ 신청 기한

13 2017년 2회

다음 표를 보면서 대화를 듣고, 여자가 선택할 강좌를 고르시오.

	Lesson	Date	Instructor	Price
①	A	Wednesday	Kelly	$50
②	B	Wednesday	Michelle	$70
③	C	Thursday	Kelly	$50
④	D	Thursday	Serena	$60
⑤	E	Thursday	Michelle	$70

14 2016년 2회

다음을 듣고, 무엇에 관한 설명인지 고르시오.

① 보온병　　② 정수기　　③ 병따개
④ 종이컵　　⑤ 아이스박스

15 2016년 1회

대화를 듣고, 남자가 할 일로 가장 적절한 것을 고르시오.

① 과학 숙제하기　　② 자석 가져오기
③ 실험실 청소하기　　④ 테이블 정리하기
⑤ 노트북 컴퓨터 가져오기

16 2016년 2회

대화를 듣고, 여자가 구입할 물건을 고르시오.

① milk　　② sugar　　③ honey
④ black tea　　⑤ green tea

17 2017년 1회

대화를 듣고, 남자의 마지막 말에 대한 여자의 응답으로 가장 적절한 것을 고르시오.

Woman: _____

① I failed the science test, too.
② I'll catch up with classes soon.
③ Sorry. I can't open some of your files.
④ Right. I hope this cold weather ends soon.
⑤ Sure. I'll get you my notebook this afternoon.

18 2017년 1회

대화를 듣고, 여자의 마지막 말에 대한 남자의 응답으로 가장 적절한 것을 고르시오.

Man: _____

① Sorry, I don't remember.
② That's too bad. Cheer up.
③ Why not? Let's go together.
④ Thank you. It's because of you.
⑤ Congratulations. You deserve it.

19 2017년 1회

대화를 듣고, 남자의 마지막 말에 대한 여자의 응답으로 가장 적절한 것을 고르시오.

Woman: _____

① I wish you could come to the show with me.
② I really enjoyed watching that movie.
③ I'm glad you can come with me.
④ I'm sorry you couldn't go on a family trip.
⑤ I'm disappointed that the show is canceled.

20 2016년 2회

다음 상황 설명을 듣고, 수미가 선생님에게 할 말로 가장 적절한 것을 고르시오.

Sumi: _____

① I wish my English would get better faster.
② I really enjoyed the summer camp this year.
③ Oh, it's so kind of you to plan my trip for me.
④ Where would you like to travel during the vacation?
⑤ I'm sorry, but I can't take part in the summer camp.

Dictation Test 기출문제로 마무리하는 Final Test 02 회

01 그림 정보 파악 – 사물

대화를 듣고, 두 사람이 구입할 풍선을 고르시오.

① ② ③

④ ⑤

M Hey, Amy. What are you looking at?

W Balloons. Dad, I want to get one of those.

M Which balloon are you talking about? Do you want ❶ _____ _____ _____ ?

W No. I want the elephant balloon.

M Do you mean the elephant with a hat?

W No, not that one. I'd like ❷ _____ _____ _____ _____ on its head.

M I see which one you want. Let's get it.

W Thanks, Dad.

02 목적 파악

대화를 듣고, 남자가 여자에게 전화한 목적으로 가장 적절한 것을 고르시오.

① 숙제를 물어보기 위해
② 함께 병문안을 가기 위해
③ 친구 집에 놀러 가기 위해
④ 버스 시간을 물어보기 위해
⑤ 결석한 이유를 물어보기 위해

[Cellphone rings.]

M Hello, Cathy. Are you busy now?

W Not really. I just finished my homework.

M Did you hear about Jake? ❶ _____ _____ _____ from school today. He's in the hospital.

W What happened to him?

M He broke his leg. Why don't we ❷ _____ _____ _____ this afternoon?

W Oh my! We should. Where shall we meet?

M You know the bus stop where we met yesterday? ❸ _____ _____ _____ there at 4?

W All right. See you then.

03 그림 상황에 어울리는 대화 찾기

다음 그림의 상황에 가장 적절한 대화를 고르시오.

① ② ③ ④ ⑤

① M Would you like something to drink?
   W I'd like to have a cola.

② M Can you ❶ _____ _____ _____ _____, please?
   W Sure. It's my pleasure.

③ M Do you mind if ❷ _____ _____ _____ _____ ?
   W Not at all. Go ahead.

④ M This bus is too noisy.
   W Right. I can't stand it anymore.

⑤ M You ❸ _____ _____ _____ _____, ma'am.
   W Thanks. How kind of you!

 Words   **01 balloon** 풍선   **02 finish** 끝마치다 **absent** 결석한   **03 carry** 들고 있다 **noisy** 시끄러운 **stand** 참다

04 특정 정보 파악 – 요일　영국식 발음 녹음

대화를 듣고, 남자가 테니스 코트를 사용할 수 <u>없는</u> 요일을 고르시오.

① 월요일　　② 수요일　　③ 목요일
④ 금요일　　⑤ 토요일

[Telephone rings.]
W　Hello, ABC Sports Center. How can I help you?
M　Hi, I'd like to ❶＿＿＿＿ ＿＿＿＿ ＿＿＿＿ ＿＿＿＿.
W　You can take tennis lessons once a week on Tuesdays or Thursdays.
M　How much is it per month?
W　It's 80,000 won.
M　Can I use the court on weekends?
W　No. You can only use it ❷＿＿＿＿ ＿＿＿＿ ＿＿＿＿ ＿＿＿＿.
M　Okay. Can I sign up for Thursday lessons now?
W　Sure.

05 언급되지 않은 것

다음을 듣고, Drone-X에 관해 언급되지 <u>않은</u> 것을 고르시오.

① 크기　　② 조종 범위　　③ 작동 시간
④ 촬영 기능　　⑤ 가격

W　Thank you for visiting our booth. Let me ❶＿＿＿＿ ＿＿＿＿ ＿＿＿＿ ＿＿＿＿, Drone-X. As you can see, the Drone-X is pocket-sized. ❷＿＿＿＿ ＿＿＿＿ ＿＿＿＿ ＿＿＿＿ with your smartphone. It has a control range of 100 m. Also, it can fly for about 10 minutes when ❸＿＿＿＿ ＿＿＿＿. This model is on sale for 50,000 won today only.

06 장소 추론

대화를 듣고, 두 사람이 대화하는 장소로 가장 적절한 곳을 고르시오.

① 영화관　　② 야구장　　③ 지하철역
④ 사무실　　⑤ 카페

W　John, we don't have much time. Did you ❶＿＿＿＿ ＿＿＿＿ ＿＿＿＿ for the movie, *Subway Story*?
M　No, I'm still trying. But it's difficult for me to use ❷＿＿＿＿ ＿＿＿＿ ＿＿＿＿.
W　Why don't you go and buy tickets from the clerk?
M　Look! Many people are waiting in the line over there.
W　I see. But I'm worried that we might miss the first part of the movie.
M　Just wait! I think I'm almost done.
W　Then, let me ❸＿＿＿＿ ＿＿＿＿ ＿＿＿＿ ＿＿＿＿ quickly.

07 어색한 대화 찾기

다음을 듣고, 두 사람의 대화가 <u>어색한</u> 것을 고르시오.

①　　②　　③　　④　　⑤

① W　What do you think of online shopping?
　 M　I don't think it's that convenient. I prefer visiting shops.
② W　Have you heard about a new English teacher?
　 M　I haven't heard anything.
③ W　Do you know ❶＿＿＿＿ ＿＿＿＿ ＿＿＿＿ ＿＿＿＿?
　 M　Yes. Go straight two blocks and turn right.
④ W　How often do you play soccer?
　 M　About twice a week.
⑤ W　❷＿＿＿＿ ＿＿＿＿ ＿＿＿＿ ＿＿＿＿ comedy movies?
　 M　Yes. I like horror movies a lot.

Words　**04 per** ~당　**05 introduce** 소개하다　**pocket-sized** 주머니 크기의　**range** 거리[범위]　**on sale** 할인 중인　**06 clerk** 점원　**miss** 놓치다
07 prefer ~을 선호하다

Dictation Test

08 부탁한 일 파악 영국식 발음 녹음

대화를 듣고, 여자가 남자에게 부탁한 일로 가장 적절한
것을 고르시오.

① 아침 차려주기　　　② 과제 도와주기
③ 아이들 깨우기　　　④ 자명종 수리하기
⑤ 차로 자녀 등교시키기

M　Honey, you look worried.

W　Yeah, I'm going on a business trip for the next three days.

M　Well, what's the matter, then?

W　Our kids! They usually _____ _____ _____, but midterm
exams start tomorrow.

M　Right. They're really tired these days since they're staying up so late.

W　I know. So, will you _____ _____ _____ _____ to
school for the next three days?

M　All right, I will. Should I _____ _____ _____ as well?

W　No. They can get sandwiches near the school.

09 의도 파악

대화를 듣고, 여자의 마지막 말에 담긴 의도로 가장 적절한
것을 고르시오.

① 위로　　　② 충고　　　③ 거절
④ 요청　　　⑤ 감사

M　Hey, Lisa! What brought you here to the library?

W　Hi, Brian. I came here _____ _____ _____. What are
you doing here?

M　I'm here to borrow some books for my history homework.

W　Oh, I have _____ _____ _____ as you.

M　Why don't we do our homework together after school, then?

W　I wish I could, but I've _____ _____ _____ _____.

10 숫자 정보 파악 – 금액

대화를 듣고, 남자가 지불할 금액을 고르시오.

① $90　　　② $100　　　③ $108
④ $110　　　⑤ $120

M　Excuse me. _____ _____ _____ _____ to make
copies of a calendar with photos?

W　$30 for 10 copies, and $100 for 50 copies.

M　Hmm. I actually need 40 copies, but 50 copies is a much better deal.
I guess _____ _____ 50.

W　How would you like to pay?

M　By credit card. Here it is.

W　You _____ _____ _____ _____ if you pay with this
card.

M　Great.

Words　**08 worried** 걱정하는　**give ~ a ride** ~를 태워 주다　**09 return** 반납하다　**borrow** ~을 빌리다　**10 make a copy** 복사하다　**deal**
거래

11 한 일 / 할 일 파악 영국식 발음 녹음

대화를 듣고, 남자가 할 일로 가장 적절한 것을 고르시오.

① 영화 시간 확인　② 저녁 식사 준비
③ 파티 물품 구입　④ 영화평 작성
⑤ 시험 준비

M　Finally, the exam is finished.
W　Let's _____ _____ _____ _____ and watch a movie. I really want to watch the movie, *Star Ships*.
M　Me, too. We _____ _____ _____ _____ at Farmer's Kitchen near the movie theater.
W　Sounds great.
M　Then, I'll _____ _____ _____ _____.
W　Okay. Let's meet at 5 at the restaurant.
M　See you then.

12 언급되지 않은 것

다음을 듣고, Oakwood Flea Market에 관해 언급되지 **않은** 것을 고르시오.

① 개최 날짜　② 취급 품목
③ 판매자 참가비　④ 접수 장소
⑤ 신청 기한

M　Hello, Oakwood community members. This is David Kim from City Hall. I'm happy to tell you that we'll be having the Oakwood Flea Market on October 13th, 2017. You can buy and sell ❶_____, _____, _____ _____ at this event. There is a five-dollar registration fee for sellers. ❷_____ _____ _____ the public service center if you plan to attend. Thank you.

13 도표 정보 파악 영국식 발음 녹음

다음 표를 보면서 대화를 듣고, 여자가 선택할 강좌를 고르시오.

	Lesson	Date	Instructor	Price
①	A	Wednesday	Kelly	$50
②	B	Wednesday	Michelle	$70
③	C	Thursday	Kelly	$50
④	D	Thursday	Serena	$60
⑤	E	Thursday	Michelle	$70

M　Hey, Rebecca! What are you doing here?
W　I'm checking the Sky Yoga website for a class.
M　Really? ❶_____ _____ _____ _____ there last year. Maybe I can help you.
W　Great. Hmm... I ❷_____ _____ _____ _____ every Wednesday, so I can't take it then.
M　Okay. I remember that Michelle and Serena were popular instructors.
W　Then I'm going to choose one of their classes.
M　Good. So you should choose ❸_____ _____ _____ _____ _____.
W　Well. Then, I'll take the cheaper class.

14 주제 파악

다음을 듣고, 무엇에 관한 설명인지 고르시오.

① 보온병　② 정수기　③ 병따개
④ 종이컵　⑤ 아이스박스

W　This is a special ❶_____ _____ _____ that people use in their everyday lives. Usually, it is used when people go out or travel. It is designed to keep drinks either hot or cold. It's great for people who want to ❷_____ _____ _____ on a cold day. It comes in ❸_____ _____ _____ _____. Its lid can often be used as a cup.

Words 　**11 go out** 외출하다 　**12 registration fee** 등록비 　**13 take a class** 수강하다 　**14 come in** (상품 등이) 들어오다

Dictation Test

15 한일 / 할 일 파악

대화를 듣고, 남자가 할 일로 가장 적절한 것을 고르시오.

① 과학 숙제하기   ② 자석 가져오기
③ 실험실 청소하기   ④ 테이블 정리하기
⑤ 노트북 컴퓨터 가져오기

W Kevin, we have to ❶ _____ _____ _____ _____ before our science class starts.

M Hey, Sujin. Right! What do we have to do?

W I just finished getting the tables ready. Can you bring the magnets for the experiment?

M Sure. Anything else?

W Did you ❷ _____ _____ _____ _____ that we need for class?

M Oh! I totally forgot about it.

W Then, why don't you go get the laptop computer from the teachers' office? I'll ❸ _____ _____ _____ for you.

M Thank you. I'll do that right away.

---

16 특정 정보 파악   영국식 발음 녹음

대화를 듣고, 여자가 구입할 물건을 고르시오.

① milk   ② sugar   ③ honey
④ black tea   ⑤ green tea

W Dad! What are you doing with that green tea?

M Actually, this is black tea. I was thinking of ❶ _____ _____ _____.

W Milk tea! I love that! How do you make it?

M It's very simple. Just put black tea into hot milk with ❷ _____ _____ _____ _____.

W I think it tastes better with honey. Do we have any?

M We don't, but sugar tastes almost the same as honey.

W I'd really like to ❸ _____ _____ _____ _____. I'll go buy some.

M Thanks, dear.

---

17 알맞은 응답 찾기

대화를 듣고, 남자의 마지막 말에 대한 여자의 응답으로 가장 적절한 것을 고르시오.

Woman: _____

① I failed the science test, too.
② I'll catch up with classes soon.
③ Sorry. I can't open some of your files.
④ Right. I hope this cold weather ends soon.
⑤ Sure. I'll get you my notebook this afternoon.

W Hey, Sean. Why ❶ _____ _____ _____ _____ school yesterday? I was worried.

M I had a really bad cold.

W Are you all right now?

M Yes, I ❷ _____ _____ _____.

W I'm glad to hear that.

M Thanks, but I have a lot of studying to catch up on with classes.

W Poor you. Is there anything I can help you with?

M Well, ❸ _____ _____ _____ _____ _____ from yesterday?

Words   **15 set up** 준비하다 **experiment** 실험 **teachers' office** 교무실   **16 green tea** 녹차 **black tea** 홍차   **17 bad cold** 독감 **catch up on** 만회하다

18 알맞은 응답 찾기

대화를 듣고, 여자의 마지막 말에 대한 남자의 응답으로 가장 적절한 것을 고르시오.

Man: _____

① Sorry, I don't remember.
② That's too bad. Cheer up.
③ Why not? Let's go together.
④ Thank you. It's because of you.
⑤ Congratulations. You deserve it.

M Judy, what are you going to do this weekend?
W Hmm.... Nothing special. What about you?
M I'm thinking about _____ _____ _____ _____.
W The bookstore? What are you going to buy there?
M I want to buy a new cooking magazine.
W I didn't know you're interested in cooking.
M Yes, I love to cook.
W I'd like to take a look around ❷_____ _____ _____. Can I join you?

19 알맞은 응답 찾기 영국식 발음 녹음

대화를 듣고, 남자의 마지막 말에 대한 여자의 응답으로 가장 적절한 것을 고르시오.

Woman: _____

① I wish you could come to the show with me.
② I really enjoyed watching that movie.
③ I'm glad you can come with me.
④ I'm sorry you couldn't go on a family trip.
⑤ I'm disappointed that the show is canceled.

M Hey, you look very excited today. What's up?
W Yeah, I got two tickets for the 2017 World Motor Show.
M Wow, that's great. I heard there will be ❶_____ _____ _____ _____ _____.
W I heard that, too. Would you like to go with me?
M I'd love to. When is it?
W The show is from July 4th to the 11th.
M Oh, no. ❷_____ _____ _____ _____ _____ to go on a family trip at that time.

20 상황에 맞는 말 찾기

다음 상황 설명을 듣고, 수미가 선생님에게 할 말로 가장 적절한 것을 고르시오.

Sumi: _____

① I wish my English would get better faster.
② I really enjoyed the summer camp this year.
③ Oh, it's so kind of you to plan my trip for me.
④ Where would you like to travel during the vacation?
⑤ I'm sorry, but I can't take part in the summer camp.

M Last week Sumi registered for an English camp at school during the summer vacation. Then, last night she was told that her family would ❶_____ _____ _____ for a week during the same period. Thus, she wants to tell her English teacher that she has to ❷_____ _____ _____. In this situation, what would Sumi most likely say to the teacher?

Words **18** be interested in ~에 관심이 있다 take a look around 둘러보다 **19** go on a trip 여행을 가다 **20** register for ~에 등록하다
take part in ~에 참가하다

회 미리 보는 **수능 듣기모의고사**

1번부터 17번까지는 듣고 답하는 문제입니다. 1번부터 15번까지는 한 번만 들려주고, 16번부터 17번까지는 두 번 들려줍니다. 방송을 잘 듣고 답을 하시기 바랍니다.

01 대화를 듣고, 여자의 마지막 말에 대한 남자의 응답으로 가장 적절한 것을 고르시오.

① It wasn't my fault.
② You can say that again.
③ Can you fix the report?
④ Do you mind if I borrow it?
⑤ You should tell the librarian right away.

02 대화를 듣고, 남자의 마지막 말에 대한 여자의 응답으로 가장 적절한 것을 고르시오.

① You are telling me.
② I'm sure about that.
③ Yes. It's 080-123-4567.
④ I should have changed the battery.
⑤ The repairman is not answering the phone.

03 다음을 듣고, 여자가 하는 말의 목적으로 가장 적절한 것을 고르시오.

① 지하철 운행 시간을 연장하려고
② 교통수단의 종류를 설명하려고
③ 지하철 이용 실태를 보고하려고
④ 지하철 봉사 단원들을 모집하려고
⑤ 지하철 예절의 필요성을 설명하려고

04 대화를 듣고, 성공에 대한 남자의 의견으로 가장 적절한 것을 고르시오.

① 책을 많이 읽어야 한다.
② 많은 사람들을 만나야 한다.
③ 지금 하는 일과 사랑에 빠져야 한다.
④ 다른 사람들의 충고를 잘 들어야 한다.
⑤ 어릴 때부터 자신의 재능을 잘 키워야 한다.

05 대화를 듣고, 두 사람의 관계를 가장 잘 나타낸 것을 고르시오.

① 간호사 – 환자   ② 진로 상담사 – 학생
③ 경찰관 – 자원봉사자   ④ 금융 설계사 – 고객
⑤ 면접관 – 입사 지원자

06 대화를 듣고, 그림에서 대화의 내용과 일치하지 <u>않는</u> 것을 고르시오.

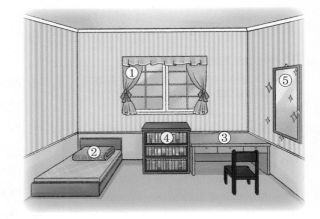

07 대화를 듣고, 남자가 할 일로 가장 적절한 것을 고르시오.

① 일정 안내하기   ② 인원 확인하기
③ 위치 안내하기   ④ 전화번호 변경하기
⑤ 숙박 요금 결제하기

08 대화를 듣고, 여자가 남자의 제안을 처음에 거절한 이유를 고르시오.

① 숙제를 해야 해서
② 남동생을 돌봐야 해서
③ 남자의 집이 너무 멀어서
④ 만화 영화를 좋아하지 않아서
⑤ 다른 친구들과 약속이 있어서

09 대화를 듣고, 남자가 추가로 지불할 금액을 고르시오.

① $5　　　② $15　　　③ $30
④ $35　　　⑤ $65

10 대화를 듣고, JK 호텔 숙박에 관해 언급되지 <u>않은</u> 것을 고르시오.

① 숙박 인원　　　② 숙박 기간
③ 숙박 시작일　　　④ 퇴실 시간
⑤ 입실 시간

11 커피에 관한 다음 내용을 듣고, 일치하지 <u>않는</u> 것을 고르시오.

① 커피는 졸릴 때 졸리지 않도록 도와준다.
② 커피를 많이 마시면 건강을 해칠 수 있다.
③ 커피 중독은 두통이나 불안감을 유발한다.
④ 중독되면 커피를 마시지 않아도 졸리지 않는다.
⑤ 커피를 과음하지 않도록 주의해야 한다.

12 다음 표를 보면서 대화를 듣고, 남자가 구입할 카레를 고르시오.

Delicious Curries

	Spiciness	Serving	Type
①	🌶	4	ready meal
②	🌶🌶	4	ready meal
③	🌶🌶	4	paste
④	🌶🌶	8	powder
⑤	🌶🌶🌶	8	powder

13 대화를 듣고, 남자의 마지막 말에 대한 여자의 응답으로 가장 적절한 것을 고르시오.

Woman: _____

① She said to say hello to you.
② My mother gave you a message.
③ No, I've got so many things to do.
④ Thanks for delivering it so quickly.
⑤ Yes. Just say, "Happy birthday, Mom."

14 대화를 듣고, 여자의 마지막 말에 대한 남자의 응답으로 가장 적절한 것을 고르시오.

Man: _____

① That is not my fault.
② Of course. I'm really into it.
③ He is not too serious about it.
④ Don't give up. You'll do better next time.
⑤ I'm looking for something interesting to watch.

15 다음 상황 설명을 듣고, George가 Kate에게 할 말로 가장 적절한 것을 고르시오.

George: _____

① Can you tell me more about it?
② I'll keep fingers crossed for you.
③ I'll call you when I find the thief.
④ Is it possible you just lost it somewhere?
⑤ Next time you go out, you should be very careful.

[16~17] 다음을 듣고, 물음에 답하시오.

16 여자가 하는 말의 목적으로 가장 적절한 것은?

① 학생들의 학업을 격려하려고
② 수업에 늦지 말 것을 당부하려고
③ 학교 행사를 손님들에게 알리려고
④ 싱가포르의 고등학교를 소개하려고
⑤ 외국에서 오는 방문객에 대해 알리려고

17 손님들에 대해 언급되지 <u>않은</u> 것은?

① 총 인원　　　② 국적
③ 도착 시간　　　④ 방문 기간 동안 하는 일
⑤ 방문 기간

Dictation Test **01**회 미리 보는 **수능 듣기모의고사**

01 | 알맞은 응답 찾기 (짧은 대화)

대화를 듣고, 여자의 마지막 말에 대한 남자의 응답으로 가장 적절한 것을 고르시오.

① It wasn't my fault.
② You can say that again.
③ Can you fix the report?
④ Do you mind if I borrow it?
⑤ You should tell the librarian right away.

😮 슬픔, 불만족, 실망의 원인에 대해 묻기 /////////
What's the matter? / What's wrong? / Why are you sad(disappointed)?

W This ❶ _____ _____ _____ _____ .
M😮 What's the matter?
W I checked out this book to write my report, but the pages I need ❷ _____ _____ .

02 | 알맞은 응답 찾기 (짧은 대화)

대화를 듣고, 남자의 마지막 말에 대한 여자의 응답으로 가장 적절한 것을 고르시오.

① You are telling me.
② I'm sure about that.
③ Yes. It's 080-123-4567.
④ I should have changed the battery.
⑤ The repairman is not answering the phone.

M I can't ❶ _____ _____ _____ .
W We can't even press any buttons. I think ❷ _____ _____ _____ _____ .
M Do you know the number of the repair center?

03 | 목적 파악

다음을 듣고, 여자가 하는 말의 목적으로 가장 적절한 것을 고르시오.

① 지하철 운행 시간을 연장하려고
② 교통수단의 종류를 설명하려고
③ 지하철 이용 실태를 보고하려고
④ 지하철 봉사 단원들을 모집하려고
⑤ 지하철 예절의 필요성을 설명하려고

W Subway is the best transportation for me, because it's very convenient and cheap. Moreover, ❶ _____ _____ _____ _____ . So, I think it would be better if we keep some etiquettes on the train. For example, it's important ❷ _____ _____ _____ _____ and leave garbage behind you. It's also important for us to give up seats to people in need. I think if we try together, we can make subway ❸ _____ _____ _____ for everyone.

Words ┃ **01 check out** 대출하다   **02 even** 심지어   **press** 누르다   **dead** 다 닳은, 수명이 다 된   **repairman** 수리 기사   **03 in need** 곤경(어려움)에 처한, 도움이 필요한

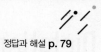

04 주제 파악

대화를 듣고, 성공에 대한 남자의 의견으로 가장 적절한 것을 고르시오.

① 책을 많이 읽어야 한다.
② 많은 사람들을 만나야 한다.
③ 지금 하는 일과 사랑에 빠져야 한다.
④ 다른 사람들의 충고를 잘 들어야 한다.
⑤ 어릴 때부터 자신의 재능을 잘 키워야 한다.

W Good evening, everyone. Tonight, we invited Mr. Smith. It's very nice to see you, Mr. Smith.

M Nice to see you.

W You are a ❶ _____ _____ _____. Did you want to be a writer from the beginning?

M Yes. Since I was an elementary school student, I have dreamed of writing stories.

W I think that made you who you are now. Can you give us some advice on how to succeed?

M If you want to succeed, you have to ❷ _____ _____ _____ _____ what you are doing. Your heart should beat when you think of it.

W Everyone should ❸ _____ _____ _____ in mind. Thank you for a great piece of advice.

M You're welcome.

05 관계 추론 영국식 발음 녹음

대화를 듣고, 두 사람의 관계를 가장 잘 나타낸 것을 고르시오.

① 간호사 – 환자   ② 진로 상담사 – 학생
③ 금융 설계사 – 고객   ④ 경찰관 – 자원봉사자
⑤ 면접관 – 입사 지원자

[Knocking Sound]

M Please come in and take a seat.

W Thank you. I'm Rachel Brown. I sent you the email yesterday.

M I've read your email carefully.

W I really appreciate it.

M You're welcome. I was very touched with ❶ _____ _____ _____ _____ _____ with the elderly.

W I have enjoyed such work. But I must choose between two roads before graduation.

M What do you mean by that?

W One is to take a job in the charity sector, and the other is to take a job at the bank.

M If financial stability is important to you, you'd better ❷ _____ _____ _____ _____ at the bank.

W Thank you for ❸ _____ _____. I will think about it carefully.

Words **04 invite** 초대하다 **beginning** 처음, 시작 **beat** (심장이) 뛰다   **05 touched** 감동 받은 **charity** 자선 단체 **sector** 부분(분야) **financial** 재정의 **stability** 안정성 **go for** ~을 택하다

Dictation Test 01회 미리 보는 수능 듣기모의고사

06 그림 정보 파악

대화를 듣고, 그림에서 대화의 내용과 일치하지 <u>않는</u> 것을 고르시오.

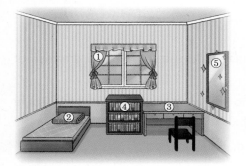

M Mom, I'm home.   **W** Did you have fun at Mike's?

M Yes, but his room was very clean.

W How was it?

M Well, the window ❶ _____ _____ _____ _____. And the blanket was folded on the bed.

W You always have many things on your desk. How about his?

M Only one book was open on the desk, and there was ❷ _____ _____ _____ _____ _____. That was it.

W Didn't he have many books?

M Yes, he had many books, but they were ❸ _____ _____ _____ _____ _____. Oh, plus, the mirror was so clean.

W Wow. I wish you were more like him.

07 한 일 / 할 일 파악

대화를 듣고, 남자가 할 일로 가장 적절한 것을 고르시오.

① 일정 안내하기   ② 인원 확인하기
③ 위치 안내하기   ④ 전화번호 변경하기
⑤ 숙박 요금 결제하기

가능성 정도 묻기 /////////////////////////
Is it possible(probable, likely, impossible) to ~?

[*Telephone rings.*]

M Hello. May I help you?

W Hi. This is Janice. I made a reservation at your hotel. ❶ _____ _____ _____ _____ _____ a little bit?

M How do you want it?

W Is it possible to book for this Friday night only?

M That's fine.

W Oh, that's good.

M Is there anything else I can do for you?

W Would you please send me ❷ _____ _____ _____ _____ _____ through email?

M Yes, ma'am. No problem.

08 이유 파악

대화를 듣고, 여자가 남자의 제안을 처음에 거절한 이유를 고르시오.

① 숙제를 해야 해서
② 남동생을 돌봐야 해서
③ 남자의 집이 너무 멀어서
④ 만화 영화를 좋아하지 않아서
⑤ 다른 친구들과 약속이 있어서

의무 표현하기 ////////////////////////
I have to(must) ~. / I should(ought to) ~. / It is required to ~.

W What are you doing tonight, Simon?

M Seohyun and Jaemin are coming over to my place to watch a movie together.

W Sounds like fun. I wish I could join you.

M You are always welcome. Please come to my house tonight.

W Thanks. But I have to babysit my brother.

M ❶ _____ _____ _____ _____ _____, too?

W No, he's too young. He will make us unable to watch the movie.

M Then, ❷ _____ _____ _____ _____ for him?

W It's very kind of you. Thank you.

---

 06 fold 개다 **mirror** 거울   **07 reservation** 예약   **08 come over (to)** ~에 들르다 **unable** 할 수 없는

09 숫자 정보 파악 – 금액 · 영국식 발음 녹음

대화를 듣고, 남자가 추가로 지불할 금액을 고르시오.

① $5 　② $15 　③ $30
④ $35 　⑤ $65

허락 요청하기

Can I ~ (, please)? / Would it be possible ~? /
Do you mind if ~? / I was wondering if I could
~?

M　Excuse me, can I exchange this for some other design?
W　Do you _____ _____ _____?
M　Yes. Here it is.
W　You bought a $30 T-shirt. You can exchange it for anything
❷ _____ _____ _____.
M　How much are these jeans?
W　They are $35.
M　Would it be possible for me to just ❸ _____ _____ _____?
W　Yes, that's possible. Do you want to do that?
M　Yes, please.

10 언급되지 않은 것

대화를 듣고, JK 호텔 숙박에 관해 언급되지 않은 것을 고르시오.

① 숙박 인원 　② 숙박 기간
③ 숙박 시작일 　④ 퇴실 시간
⑤ 입실 시간

[Telephone rings.]
M　Hello. JK Hotel. May I help you?
W　Hi. Can I ❶ _____ _____ _____ a little bit?
M　What's your name, ma'am?
W　This is Janice Brown.
M　Ms. Brown, just a moment please. You booked a deluxe room for four people. How would you like to change the schedule?
W　I booked for three days and two nights from December 23. Can I cancel ❷ _____ _____ _____ and stay from December 24?
M　It's possible, but I'm afraid that you should have called a little earlier. If you cancel today, you still have to ❸ _____ _____ _____ _____ _____.
W　Oh, then I'll just stick to the original schedule. Also, I want to check in at noon on the 23. Is that possible?
M　Yes, we will have the room ready by 12.
W　Thank you so much.
M　No problem, ma'am.

Words **09 receipt** 영수증 **price** 가격 **pay the difference** 차액을 지불하다 　**10 schedule** 일정 **stick to** ~를 고수하다 **original** 원래의 **check in** 입실하다 **possible** 가능한

11 내용 불일치

커피에 관한 다음 내용을 듣고, 일치하지 <u>않는</u> 것을 고르시오.

① 커피는 졸릴 때 졸리지 않도록 도와준다.
② 커피를 많이 마시면 건강을 해칠 수 있다.
③ 커피 중독은 두통이나 불안감을 유발한다.
④ 중독되면 커피를 마시지 않아도 졸리지 않는다.
⑤ 커피를 과음하지 않도록 주의해야 한다.

W People love drinking coffee. It tastes and smells good. When you're sleepy, it can ❶ _____ _____ _____ _____. But, drinking too much coffee can make you unhealthy. Too much coffee can cause you headaches or nervousness. Moreover, if someone who drinks too much coffee stops drinking it, he or she might ❷ _____ _____ _____ _____ _____. Coffee is a very popular drink, but you should be careful not to drink too much.

12 도표 정보 파악

다음 표를 보면서 대화를 듣고, 남자가 구입할 카레를 고르시오.

Delicious Curries

	Spiciness	Serving	Type
①	🌶	4	ready meal
②	🌶🌶	4	ready meal
③	🌶🌶	4	paste
④	🌶🌶	8	powder
⑤	🌶🌶🌶	8	powder

W Let's ❶ _____ _____ _____ _____ tonight.
M I like curry. Let's buy the spicy one.
W I can't eat spicy curry. Let's choose a two-hot-pepper curry.
M Okay. Why don't we buy ❷ _____ _____ _____ _____ and microwave it?
W No, it will be tastier if we cook it.
M Then which type do you prefer? Paste or powder?
W ❸ _____ _____ _____ is for 8 people, so we can have curry many times. Let's buy that.
M That's a good idea.

13 알맞은 응답 찾기

대화를 듣고, 남자의 마지막 말에 대한 여자의 응답으로 가장 적절한 것을 고르시오.

Woman: _____

① She said to say hello to you.
② My mother gave you a message.
③ No, I've got so many things to do.
④ Thanks for delivering it so quickly.
⑤ Yes. Just say, "Happy birthday, Mom."

😮 **모르고 있음 표현하기** ////////////////////
I don't know. / I have no idea. / I haven't got a clue.

M Can I help you?
W Yes. I want to ❶ _____ _____ _____ to my mother in Chicago.
M What kind of flowers does she like?
W Well, I don't know. What do you recommend?
M Roses and lilies are very nice at this time of year.
W Okay. A dozen red roses and five lilies, please.
M Would you like to ❷ _____ _____ _____?

📖 Words 11 **unhealthy** 건강에 해로운 **cause** 유발하다 **nervousness** 초조함 12 **ready meal** 데워 먹기만 하면 되는 **microwave** 전자레인지에 요리하다 13 **lily** 백합 **dozen** 12개짜리 한 묶음 **include** 포함하다

14 알맞은 응답 찾기 영국식 발음 녹음

대화를 듣고, 여자의 마지막 말에 대한 남자의 응답으로 가장 적절한 것을 고르시오.

Man: _____

① That is not my fault.
② Of course. I'm really into it.
③ He is not too serious about it.
④ Don't give up. You'll do better next time.
⑤ I'm looking for something interesting to watch.

😊 관심에 대해 묻기 ///////////////////////////

Do you find ~ interesting? / What are you interested in? / Are you interested in ~?

W James, where are you going?
M I'm going to the science lab.
W Again? Why do you go there so often?
M I _____ _____ _____ there. Do you want to see that?
W No, not at all. I _____ _____ _____ _____ science.
M That's too bad. I wanted to show you what I'm doing.
W Seriously, do you find it interesting?

15 상황에 맞는 말 찾기

다음 상황 설명을 듣고, George가 Kate에게 할 말로 가장 적절한 것을 고르시오.

George: _____

① Can you tell me more about it?
② I'll keep fingers crossed for you.
③ I'll call you when I find the thief.
④ Is it possible you just lost it somewhere?
⑤ Next time you go out, you should be very careful.

M George is a police officer. One day, Kate came to him and said she had been ❶ _____ _____ _____ _____. She looked very puzzled, and asked George to catch the thief. However, she ❷ _____ _____ _____ _____ _____ clearly. She only explained to him about what her wallet looked like, and where she had been robbed. But George needs more information to catch the thief, so he wants to ask her ❸ _____ _____ _____ _____ _____. In this situation, what would George most likely say to Kate?

[16~17] 다음을 듣고, 물음에 답하시오.

16 목적 파악

여자가 하는 말의 목적으로 가장 적절한 것은?

① 학생들의 학업을 격려하려고
② 수업에 늦지 말 것을 당부하려고
③ 학교 행사를 손님들에게 알리려고
④ 싱가포르의 고등학교를 소개하려고
⑤ 외국에서 오는 방문객에 대해 알리려고

W Your attention, please. This is the principal speaking. From today, we will be ❶ _____ _____ _____ at our school. The guests are students from Singapore. Their school is ❷ _____ _____ _____ _____ last year. They are very interested in what our school is like. They will arrive at about the beginning of the first class. ❸ _____ _____ _____ just as you do for two weeks from today. Please feel free to talk with them and make them feel welcome.

17 언급되지 않은 것

손님들에 대해 언급되지 않은 것은?

① 총 인원   ② 국적
③ 도착 시간   ④ 방문 기간 동안 하는 일
⑤ 방문 기간

Words **14 science lab** 과학 실험실 **so often** 그렇게 자주 **seriously** 진심으로 **15 puzzled** 당혹스러운 **thief** 도둑 **explain** 설명하다
16-17 attention 주의 (집중) **principal** 교장 **feel free to** 거리낌 없이 ~하다 **welcome** 환영받는

🎧 1번부터 17번까지는 듣고 답하는 문제입니다. 1번부터 15번까지는 한 번만 들려주고, 16번부터 17번까지는 두 번 들려줍니다. 방송을 잘 듣고 답을 하시기 바랍니다.

01 대화를 듣고, 남자의 마지막 말에 대한 여자의 응답으로 가장 적절한 것을 고르시오.

① Of course. I really like it.
② Can't you be more serious?
③ That is not one of my interests.
④ Good luck with your homework.
⑤ I have a group project to finish by next Friday.

02 대화를 듣고, 여자의 마지막 말에 대한 남자의 응답으로 가장 적절한 것을 고르시오.

① What brings you here?
② I do appreciate your help.
③ Is there anything wrong?
④ It's all my fault. I apologize.
⑤ Is this book what you had in mind?

03 다음을 듣고, 남자가 전화를 건 목적으로 가장 적절한 것을 고르시오.

① 호텔을 예약하려고
② 방문을 취소하려고
③ 만날 약속을 정하려고
④ 여행 정보를 얻으려고
⑤ 함께 여행을 떠나려고

04 대화를 듣고, 남자의 의견으로 가장 적절한 것을 고르시오.

① 다른 사람의 연구를 참고하면 안 된다.
② 자료를 찾을 때 책을 이용하는 것이 좋다.
③ 다른 사람의 도움을 받는 것은 좋지 않다.
④ 타인의 연구 자료를 사용할 때에는 출처를 밝혀야 한다.
⑤ 인터넷상의 자료를 사용하기 전에 정확한 정보인지 확인해야 한다.

05 대화를 듣고, 두 사람의 관계를 가장 잘 나타낸 것을 고르시오.

① 아빠 – 딸
② 주방장 – 사장
③ 웨이터 – 손님
④ 주방장 – 손님
⑤ 택시 운전사 – 승객

06 다음을 듣고, 들려주는 내용과 일치하는 그래프를 고르시오.

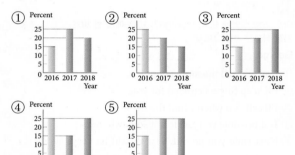

07 대화를 듣고, 남자가 할 일로 가장 적절한 것을 고르시오.

① 버스 회사에 전화해 주기
② 여자를 시청에 데려다주기
③ 시청에 가서 서류 갖다 주기
④ 시청 직원에게 문자 보내 주기
⑤ 인터넷으로 시청에 가는 버스 찾아 주기

08 대화를 듣고, 여자의 기분이 좋지 <u>않은</u> 이유를 고르시오.

① 동생이 아파서
② Kate와 다투어서
③ Kate의 몸이 좋지 않아서
④ Kate와 통화가 되지 않아서
⑤ 국제 전화 요금이 많이 나올 것 같아서

09 대화를 듣고, 남자가 지불할 금액을 고르시오.

① $20 ② $30 ③ $40

④ $50 ⑤ $60

10 대화를 듣고, 남자에 관해 언급되지 <u>않은</u> 것을 고르시오.

① 성명 ② 주소

③ 이름의 철자 ④ 생년월일

⑤ 전화번호

11 Smoothie에 관한 다음 내용을 듣고, 일치하지 <u>않는</u> 것을 고르시오.

① 새로 나온 볼펜 이름이다.

② 매우 부드럽게 써진다.

③ 여러 가지 다양한 색상이 있다.

④ 뚜껑의 색으로 볼펜의 색을 알 수 있다.

⑤ 빨리 마르지 않기 때문에 주의해야 한다.

12 다음 표를 보면서 대화를 듣고, 남자가 구입할 휴대 전화 케이블을 고르시오.

Cellphone Cables for Sale

	Brand	Length	Color	Price
①	Minibel	1 m	black	$2.50
②	Minibel	2 m	white	$3.50
③	Minibel	2 m	black	$3
④	Promac	1 m	black	$2
⑤	Promac	2 m	black	$2.50

13 대화를 듣고, 여자의 마지막 말에 대한 남자의 응답으로 가장 적절한 것을 고르시오.

Man: _____

① I'm against it.

② Oh, you shouldn't have.

③ No, thanks. I can handle it myself.

④ I'm so sorry that I'm returning it too late.

⑤ How about showing a document from the hospital?

14 대화를 듣고, 남자의 마지막 말에 대한 여자의 응답으로 가장 적절한 것을 고르시오.

Woman: _____

① No, I don't agree.

② If I were you, I'd ask a help.

③ I really appreciate your help.

④ I can't stand this work any more.

⑤ No problem. Just tell me what to do.

15 다음 상황 설명을 듣고, Tom이 Maria에게 할 말로 가장 적절한 것을 고르시오.

Tom: _____

① What happened to you?

② Don't you agree with me?

③ Do you know how to play it?

④ What do you think of this game?

⑤ What would you like to play with me?

[16~17] 다음을 듣고, 물음에 답하시오.

16 남자가 하는 말의 목적으로 가장 적절한 것은?

① 할인 품목을 알려 주려고

② 사과로 유명한 장소를 알려 주려고

③ 소지품 관리에 주의하라고 당부하려고

④ 상점의 폐점 시간을 알려 주려고

⑤ 세일 시간이 끝났음을 알려 주려고

17 Flash Sale에 대해 언급되지 <u>않은</u> 것은?

① 할인율 ② 할인 품목

③ 시작 시간 ④ 종료 시간

⑤ 진행 장소

Dictation Test 02회 미리 보는 수능 듣기모의고사

01 알맞은 응답 찾기 (짧은 대화)

대화를 듣고, 남자의 마지막 말에 대한 여자의 응답으로 가장 적절한 것을 고르시오.

① Of course. I really like it.
② Can't you be more serious?
③ That is not one of my interests.
④ Good luck with your homework.
⑤ I have a group project to finish by next Friday.

M Where are you going, Mary?
W ❶ _____ _____ _____ go to meet Michael.
M Again? ❷ _____ _____ _____ _____ him so often?

02 알맞은 응답 찾기 (짧은 대화) 영국식 발음 녹음

대화를 듣고, 여자의 마지막 말에 대한 남자의 응답으로 가장 적절한 것을 고르시오.

① What brings you here?
② I do appreciate your help.
③ Is there anything wrong?
④ It's all my fault. I apologize.
⑤ Is this book what you had in mind?

W Dad. I am home.
M ❶ _____ _____ _____ now? We're about to have a snack.
W No, thanks. ❷ _____ _____ _____ _____ _____ it.

03 목적 파악

다음을 듣고, 남자가 전화를 건 목적으로 가장 적절한 것을 고르시오.

① 호텔을 예약하려고   ② 방문을 취소하려고
③ 만날 약속을 정하려고 ④ 여행 정보를 얻으려고
⑤ 함께 여행을 떠나려고

M (beep) Hi, Isabella. I will visit San Francisco from August 14th to 22nd. I would like ❶ _____ _____ _____ _____ _____ while I stay there. Please let me know when would be convenient for you. I will inform you of my hotel in San Francisco shortly. I'm ❷ _____ _____ _____ from you soon. Bye.

Words **02 be about to** 막 ~하려 하다 **fault** 잘못 **apologize** 사과하다 **have ~ in mind** ~을 생각하다   **03 convenient** 편리한 **inform** 알리다 **shortly** 곧

04 주제 파악

대화를 듣고, 남자의 의견으로 가장 적절한 것을 고르시오.

① 다른 사람의 연구를 참고하면 안 된다.
② 자료를 찾을 때 책을 이용하는 것이 좋다.
③ 다른 사람의 도움을 받는 것은 좋지 않다.
④ 타인의 연구 자료를 사용할 때에는 출처를 밝혀야 한다.
⑤ 인터넷상의 자료를 사용하기 전에 정확한 정보인지 확인해야 한다.

M I'm sorry, but I can't ❶_____ _____ _____.

W What's the matter with it?

M Did you write this yourself?

W Of course. I wrote it without any help.

M But many parts are very similar with information on internet sites I am familiar with.

W I don't know much about insects, so I referred to some internet sites.

M But I wanted you ❷_____ _____ _____ _____, not to find the study results of others.

W I studied a lot while searching for good information. I had to check whether the information I found was right or wrong. It took a lot of time.

M But you made the work of others ❸_____ _____ _____ _____. You didn't even include your sources.

W I think you are right. I should have listed my sources.

05 관계 추론

대화를 듣고, 두 사람의 관계를 가장 잘 나타낸 것을 고르시오.

① 아빠 – 딸   ② 주방장 – 사장
③ 웨이터 – 손님   ④ 주방장 – 손님
⑤ 택시 운전사 – 승객

🗣 **기대 표현하기** //////////////////////
I can't wait for ~. / I'm looking forward to ~. / I hope ~.

M I'll cook for our dinner today. Your mom will be late.

W Well, what will you make?

M I will make fresh salad and cream sauce pasta for you.

W Wow, they sound good.

M Aren't you thirsty?

W I am, but I'll ❶_____ _____ _____ _____ _____ at least.

M It will take about 30 minutes. Wait there while watching TV.

W Okay. I'm so happy to have ❷_____ _____ _____ _____ _____. Next time, I'll make you delicious food.

M 🗣 I can't wait for it.

06 도표 정보 파악

다음을 듣고, 들려주는 내용과 일치하는 그래프를 고르시오.

M This graph shows car accident rates in recent years. The car accident rate in 2017 was ❶ _____ _____ than that of 2016. The rate in 2018 was higher than that of 2016, but was lower than that of 2017. This is because the government ❷ _____ _____ _____ the accident rate.

07 한 일 / 할 일 파악

대화를 듣고, 남자가 할 일로 가장 적절한 것을 고르시오.

① 버스 회사에 전화해 주기
② 여자를 시청에 데려다주기
③ 시청에 가서 서류 갖다 주기
④ 시청 직원에게 문자 보내 주기
⑤ 인터넷으로 시청에 가는 버스 찾아 주기

[Telephone rings.]

M Hello?

W Hi, Minho. This is me, Sarah.

M Sarah. What's up? You've just left.

W Well, I have to go to City Hall, but I forgot which bus to take. Would you ❶ _____ _____ through the Internet?

M Of course I will, but do you want me ❷ _____ _____ _____ _____ ?

W No, you don't need to. I don't want to bother you.

M I'm fine. Tell me if you want.

W No, thanks. Just ❸ _____ _____ _____ _____ I can take.

M Okay. I'll send them through text message.

08 이유 파악   영국식 발음 녹음

대화를 듣고, 여자의 기분이 좋지 않은 이유를 고르시오.

① 동생이 아파서
② Kate와 다투어서
③ Kate의 몸이 좋지 않아서
④ Kate와 통화가 되지 않아서
⑤ 국제 전화 요금이 많이 나올 것 같아서

😊 슬픔, 불만족, 실망의 원인에 대해 묻기 ////////
What's wrong? / What's the matter? / Why are you sad(disappointed)?

M You look down. What's wrong?

W Well, I'm worried.

M About what? Is somebody around you sick or something?

W Actually, I ❶ _____ _____ _____ _____ to my friend, Kate last week.

M Kate? Isn't she in America?

W Yes, that's right. I talked with her for an hour, and I'm worried about the phone bill. It ❷ _____ _____ _____ _____ .

M Don't worry. It'll be less than you expect.

Words   06 recent 최근 rate 비율 government 정부   07 search 검색하다   08 make a phone call to ~에게 전화를 걸다 phone bill 전화 요금 고지서

09 숫자 정보 파악 – 금액

대화를 듣고, 남자가 지불할 금액을 고르시오.

① $20   ② $30   ③ $40
④ $50   ⑤ $60

M Hi, I want to buy a scarf for my girlfriend. ❶ _____ _____ _____ _____?

W Sure. This one feels very soft, and it's in fashion this year.

M I think it's great. How much is it?

W It was $60 until last week, but now it's 50% off.

M Well, it sounds good, but I'm a middle school student. That's still too expensive for me.

W Okay, then you might like this one. It was ❷ _____ _____, but it's also ❸ _____ _____ _____.

M Wow, that's reasonable. I'll take it.

10 언급되지 않은 것   영국식 발음 녹음

대화를 듣고, 남자에 관해 언급되지 <u>않은</u> 것을 고르시오.

① 성명   ② 주소
③ 이름의 철자   ④ 생년월일
⑤ 전화번호

W May I help you?

M Yes, I'd like to make a membership card.

W Okay. ❶ _____ _____ _____ _____ right now. What's your name?

M My name is Kiyeol Park.

W ❷ _____ _____ _____ _____ your first name?

M It's K-I-Y-E-O-L.

W All right. Your date of birth and phone number, please.

M May 20th, 2006. My phone number is 772–9986.

W Thank you. Please wait for a moment. ❸ _____ _____ a few minutes.

11 내용 불일치

Smoothie에 관한 다음 내용을 듣고, 일치하지 <u>않는</u> 것을 고르시오.

① 새로 나온 볼펜 이름이다.
② 매우 부드럽게 써진다.
③ 여러 가지 다양한 색상이 있다.
④ 뚜껑의 색으로 볼펜의 색을 알 수 있다.
⑤ 빨리 마르지 않기 때문에 주의해야 한다.

😊 제안·권유하기
Why don't you[we] ~? / Let's ~. / What[How] about ~? / I suggest (that) we ~.

M Hi, Buddies! Now let me introduce Smoothie to you. This is a ❶ _____ _____ _____. When you write something with this, you can write smoothly. There are various colors, which will make your writing more enjoyable. You can see the color of the ball-point pen by its cover's color. Plus, it ❷ _____ _____ _____. Now you don't need to worry about your hands getting dirty. Why don't you give it a try?

Words   **09 in fashion** 유행하고 있는 **reasonable** (가격이) 적정한   **10 membership card** 회원 카드 **date** 날짜   **11 buddy** 친구 **smoothly** 부드럽게 **various** 다양한 **enjoyable** 즐거운

Dictation Test 02회 미리 보는 수능 듣기모의고사

12 도표 정보 파악

다음 표를 보면서 대화를 듣고, 남자가 구입할 휴대전화 케이블을 고르시오.

Cellphone Cables for Sale

	Brand	Length	Color	Price
①	Minibel	1 m	black	$2.50
②	Minibel	2 m	white	$3.50
③	Minibel	2 m	black	$3
④	Promac	1 m	black	$2
⑤	Promac	2 m	black	$2.50

선호 표현하기 //////////////////////////
I prefer A to B. / I('d) prefer (to) ~ (if possible). / I think A is better than B.

W Are you searching for a cellphone cable?

M Yes, I need ❶ _____ _____ _____ _____ . I am going to choose one among these.

W Are these the most popular ones?

M Yes. Which do you think looks the best?

W Minibel is usually a little more expensive than Promac, but I prefer ☺ Minibel to Promac.

M I agree. I think their products last long. I ❷ _____ _____ _____ _____ Minibel.

W How about the length?

M From my experience, the longer is the better. I think I should buy the 2-meter-long cable.

W Which color will you buy, white or black?

M Hmm, I'll buy ❸ _____ _____ _____ . It's the cheaper one of the two.

13 알맞은 응답 찾기 영국식 발음 녹음

대화를 듣고, 여자의 마지막 말에 대한 남자의 응답으로 가장 적절한 것을 고르시오.

Man: _____

① I'm against it.
② Oh, you shouldn't have.
③ No, thanks. I can handle it myself.
④ I'm so sorry that I'm returning it too late.
⑤ How about showing a document from the hospital?

이의 제기하기 //////////////////////////
I don't think so. / I don't agree (with you). / I'm against ~.

M Why are you so upset?

W I went to the library to ❶ _____ _____ _____ , and the librarian said this book is overdue and that I need to pay a big fee. So I came out without returning it.

M When was the book due?

W Three weeks ago. But I couldn't come to return it because I was ❷ _____ _____ _____ .

M Did you explain the situation? I think she can make an exception.

W ☺ I don't think so. She didn't even try to listen to me.

M Maybe many students try to ❸ _____ _____ _____ not to pay.

W Hmm. Maybe. What can I do?

(Words) **12** cable 전선 **charging** 충전 **last long** 오래 가다 **13** overdue 반납 기한이 지난 **due** 예정된 **exception** 예외 **handle** 처리하다, 다루다 **document** 문서, 서류

212 | 중학영어 듣기모의고사 **3**학년

14 알맞은 응답 찾기

대화를 듣고, 남자의 마지막 말에 대한 여자의 응답으로 가장 적절한 것을 고르시오.

Woman: _____

① No, I don't agree.
② If I were you, I'd ask a help.
③ I really appreciate your help.
④ I can't stand this work any more.
⑤ No problem. Just tell me what to do.

😊 도움 요청하기 ////////////////////

Can you give me a hand? / Could you lend me a hand? / Can I ask you for a hand ~?

W What are you doing, Dad?
M I'm ❶ _____ _____ _____ some flowers here.
W The flowers are beautiful. But, can you plant these flowers alone?
M I thought I could finish it easily, but it takes more time than I thought.
W Do you want me to help you?
M That's okay. It would be ❷ _____ _____ _____ _____.
W I have done gardening before at school. I planted flowers and grew them for several months. If I help you, ❸ _____ _____ _____ _____.
M Really? Then, can you give me a hand?

15 상황에 맞는 말 찾기

다음 상황 설명을 듣고, Tom이 Maria에게 할 말로 가장 적절한 것을 고르시오.

Tom: _____

① What happened to you?
② Don't you agree with me?
③ Do you know how to play it?
④ What do you think of this game?
⑤ What would you like to play with me?

W Maria and Tom are good friends. On Tom's birthday, Tom and his friends had a birthday party together. Maria also came to celebrate his birthday. She ❶ _____ _____ _____ _____ _____ as a birthday present. He wants to play the game with his friends but ❷ _____ _____ _____ how he should play it. So he is about to ask Maria about it. In this situation, what would Tom most likely say to Maria?

[16~17] 다음을 듣고, 물음에 답하시오.

16 목적 파악

남자가 하는 말의 목적으로 가장 적절한 것은?
① 할인 품목을 알려 주려고
② 사과로 유명한 장소를 알려 주려고
③ 소지품 관리에 주의하라고 당부하려고
④ 상점의 폐점 시간을 알려 주려고
⑤ 세일 시간이 끝났음을 알려 주려고

M Attention, shoppers. Now, the flash sale is going on. Fresh apples are ❶ _____ _____ _____. These apples are from Cheongsong, a famous place for big and sweet apples. We have 200 packages of 10 apples each for you. One person can buy only one package. This flash sale ❷ _____ _____ at 5 o'clock. It's going on ❸ _____ _____ _____ _____ right now. Come quickly and take this chance!

17 언급되지 않은 것

Flash Sale에 대해 언급되지 <u>않은</u> 것은?
① 할인율   ② 할인 품목
③ 시작 시간   ④ 종료 시간
⑤ 진행 장소

Words **14 plant** 나무를 심다 **garden** 정원을 가꾸다 **several** 몇몇의   **15 celebrate** 축하하다   **16-17 package** 포장, 꾸러미 **section** 구간, 구획

01 선호에 대해 묻고 표현하기

M Hey, Mina. Aren't these shirts nice? **Which one do you prefer?**
이봐, 미나야. 이 셔츠들 괜찮지 않니? 넌 어떤 게 더 좋아?

W The light gray one. It looks good on you.
밝은 회색인 거. 그게 너한테 잘 어울린다.

W **Which** seat **do you prefer**, an aisle or a window seat?
어떤 자리를 더 좋아하세요? 복도 쪽 아니면 창문 쪽 자리?

M A window seat, please.
창문 쪽 자리로 부탁드려요.

W We can't see the movie *Chicken Soup* then. We have two movies left.
그럼 우리는 'Chicken Soup'이라는 영화는 못 보겠다. 우린 영화 2개 남았어.

M **Which one would you prefer?**
넌 어떤 걸 더 좋아하니?

02 의도 묻고 표현하기

W Wow, we have a three-day holiday next week. **What are you going to** do?
우와, 우리 다음 주에 3일 휴가가 있어. 넌 무엇을 할 거니?

M **I'm going to** do something special.
나는 특별한 무언가를 할 거야.

W What's your plan?
네 계획은 뭐야?

M **I'm planning to** go hiking on Jiri Mountain.
나는 지리산에 등산을 할 계획이야.

M **What are you going to** write about?
넌 무엇에 대해 쓸 거야?

W I haven't decided yet. Have you?
아직 결정 못 했어. 넌 했어?

M Yes, **I'm going to** write about the people who have charged our history.
응. 난 역사를 바꾼 인물에 대해 쓸 거야.

03 바람·소원에 대해 묻고 표현하기

W Jane is really good at playing the piano.
Jane은 피아노를 매우 잘 쳐.

M You're right. **I wish I could** play like her.
맞아. 나도 그녀처럼 칠 수 있길 바라.

W Tom, today is your birthday! **What do you want to do?**
Tom, 오늘은 네 생일이야! 무엇을 하고 싶니?

M Hmm.... **I'd like to go** on a picnic with Mom and Dad.
흠…. 저는 엄마와 아빠랑 소풍을 가고 싶어요.

04 충고 구하고 표현하기

W You're right. **What should I do?**
맞아. 어떻게 해야 하지?

M **You'd better** place the computer in the living room.
너는 거실에 컴퓨터를 놓는 게 좋을 거 같아.

W No, I have a fever and a bad cough.
아니, 나는 열이 나고 심한 기침을 해.

M Oh, no. **Why don't you** take some medicine?
오, 이런. 약 좀 먹는 게 어때?

05 알고 있는지 묻고 표현하기

W **You know** that Laura is in the hospital now, **don't you?**
너 지금 Laura가 병원에 있는 것 알지, 그치?

M Yes, **I know** that.
응, 알고 있어.

M Why? **You know** you will get a penalty.
왜? 너는 불이익을 얻게 되는 걸 알잖니.

W **I know**, but I can't finish it by May 4, the due date.
알아요. 하지만 마감일인 5월 4일까지 그걸 끝마칠 수가 없어요.

06 이해 점검하고 답하기

W When you see this sign, you can't turn left.
네가 이 표지판을 보면, 너는 왼쪽으로 돌 수 없어.

M Oh, **I see.**
오, 알겠어.

W And you aren't allowed to smoke in the bedroom.
그리고 너는 침실에서 흡연을 하면 안 돼.

M Okay, **I understand.**
네, 알겠어요.

07 허락 요청하고 답하기

W Can I use your phone for a minute**?**
네 전화기 좀 잠시 써도 되니?

M Sure. Go ahead.
물론이지. 그렇게 해.

W Could you work at the restaurant for me tomorrow afternoon**?**
내일 오후에 식당에서 날 위해 일을 해 줄 수 있니?

M Of course. I'd love to.
물론이지. 좋아.

08 의견 묻고 표현하기

W What do you think of the director**?**
그 감독에 대해 어떻게 생각해?

M He's a very funny guy. **I think** he is a genius.
그는 매우 웃긴 사람이야. 내 생각에 그는 천재야.

What do you think about your math teacher**?**
네 수학 선생님에 대해 어떻게 생각해?

09 만족·불만족에 대해 묻기

How do you like your new English teacher**?**
네 새로운 영어 선생님 어때?

Are you satisfied with your babysitter**?**
너는 네 보모가 만족스럽니?

10 동의·이의 여부 답하기

M I did my science project. It was so difficult.
나 과학 숙제를 했어. 그건 너무 어려웠어.

W I agree.
나도 동의해.

M There are a lot of harmful web-sites on the Internet.
인터넷에는 많은 해로운 웹사이트가 있어.

W You're right.
맞아.

11 화남 표현하고 응대하기

W I think **I was** much too **upset** last night at the party.
어젯밤 파티에서 내가 너무 화를 냈었던 것 같아.

M No, it was my fault. I spilled coffee on your smartphone.
아니야, 그건 내 잘못이었어. 내가 네 스마트폰에 커피를 쏟았잖아.

12 걱정·두려움 표현하기

W David, where are you?
David, 어디 있니?

M I'm here in my room, Mom.
저 여기 제 방에 있어요, 엄마.

W Oh, good! **I was worried** no one would be at home.
오, 잘됐다! 집에 아무도 없을까 봐 걱정 했었어.

I'm worried about my children. They spend all their time surfing the Internet or playing computer games in their room.
나는 내 아이들이 걱정된다. 그들은 항상 방에서 인터넷 서핑을 하거나 컴퓨터 게임을 하면서 시간을 보낸다.

13 궁금증 표현하기

W I wonder if I will get a scholarship.
제가 장학금을 탈 수 있을지 궁금해요.

M Why worry? You're the best student.
왜 걱정하니? 너는 최고의 학생이야.

I was wondering, what's the best way to travel around Europe?
궁금했었는데요. 유럽 여행을 하는 최고의 방법은 무엇인가요?

14 표현 묻고 답하기

W Now, look at that sign. **What does that mean?**
이제. 저 표지판을 봐. 저건 뭘 의미하는 거야?

M It means you have to stop.
그건 네가 멈춰야 한다는 걸 의미해.

15 가능성 정도 표현하기

M Of course you're going to fish. You'll love the excitement of catching a fish.

당연히 너는 낚시하러 갈 거야. 너는 고기 잡는 것의 짜릿함을 좋아할 거야.

W **Maybe** I'll like it.

아마도 나는 좋아할 거야.

You may wonder why there's no club homepage.

너는 왜 동아리 홈페이지가 없는지 궁금할지도 모르겠다.

16 확실성 정도 표현하기

W **I am not sure**, but sometimes I want to be a singer-songwriter.

확실하지는 않지만, 가끔 나는 가수 겸 작곡가가 되고 싶어.

M Wow, great! **I'm sure** you can do it.

우와, 멋지다! 난 네가 할 수 있을 거라고 확신해.

W Do you have any idea why?

왜인지 알겠어?

M It **must have been** something I ate.

그건 내가 먹은 무언가 때문임에 틀림없어.

17 반복 요청하고 답하기

M Excuse me. Is this seat taken?

실례합니다. 여기 자리 있나요?

W I'm sorry. **I beg your pardon?**

죄송합니다. 다시 말씀해 주시겠어요?

M Oh. Will someone be using this seat?

오. 누군가 이 자리를 사용할 건가요?

18 기억·망각 묻고 답하기

W **Do you remember** what you said last week?

너 지난주에 내가 한 말을 기억해?

M Umm.... No, I don't. What was it?

음…. 아니. 뭐였지?

M Hey, Sally. Are you ready to go to Ms. Jackson's wedding?

이봐, Sally. 너 Jackson씨의 결혼식에 갈 준비됐니?

W Is it today? **I totally forgot.**

그거 오늘이니? 나 완전히 깜빡했어.

19 능력 여부 묻기

W I'm making hamburgers right now.

나는 지금 햄버거를 만들고 있어.

M **Do you know how to** make them?

너 그거 만드는 법 아니?

W Sure.

물론이지.

20 놀라움 표현하기

M You know what? Sumi failed the exam.

너 그거 알아? 수미가 시험을 망쳤대.

W **I can't believe it.**

믿을 수가 없어.

21 (도덕적) 의무 표현하기

W Let's see. I'm sorry, but all flights are booked.

어디 봅시다. 죄송합니다만, 모든 항공편의 예약이 꽉 찼습니다.

M Oh, no. **I'm supposed to** be in L.A. on Friday.

오. 이런. 저는 금요일에 L.A.에 있어야 해요.

22 주제 소개하기

Let me talk about my family. My father is a firefighter. My mother is a music teacher.

우리 가족에 대해 이야기하겠습니다. 나의 아버지는 소방관이십니다. 나의 어머니는 음악 선생님이십니다.

23 사과하기

M Don't you think it's too loud?

너무 소리가 크다고 생각하지 않니?

W **Sorry**, I'll turn the volume down.

미안, 소리 줄일게.

I'm sorry to call you so late, but the boiler isn't working.

늦은 시간에 전화해서 죄송하지만 보일러가 작동이 되지 않습니다.

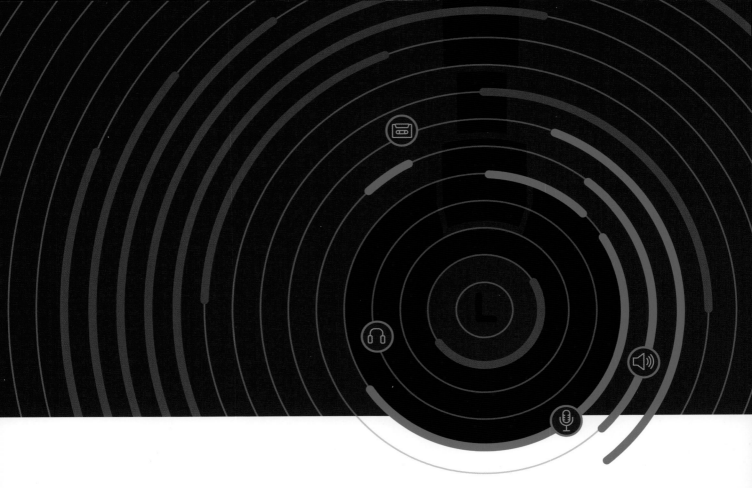

정답과 해설

중학영어
듣기모의고사 22회 3

우리는 남다른 상상과 혁신으로
교육 문화의 새로운 전형을 만들어
모든 이의 행복한 경험과 성장에 기여한다

ABOVE IMAGINATION

우리는 남다른 상상과 혁신으로
교육 문화의 새로운 전형을 만들어
모든 이의 행복한 경험과 성장에 기여한다

중학영어 **듣기모의고사** 22회
정답과 해설

3

영어 듣기모의고사

Dictation Test 01 회 　　　　　pp. 008~013

01 ❶ get an ice cream ❷ A cone ❸ a cherry on top

02 ❶ recommend a nice restaurant ❷ the new Chinese restaurant ❸ as soon as possible

03 ❶ go on a hike ❷ return it within a week ❸ What shall I buy

04 ❶ from Friday to Sunday ❷ every Tuesday and Thursday ❸ on Wednesday

05 ❶ opened in ❷ two-story building ❸ every Wednesday

06 ❶ where to ❷ don't miss the museums ❸ Keep the change

07 ❶ You'll also pass it ❷ look so tired ❸ swimming race last night

08 ❶ give a presentation ❷ how to get the materials ❸ can borrow useful books

09 ❶ just a week ❷ what you bought ❸ should spend your money wisely

10 ❶ to buy tickets ❷ twenty adults and two children

11 ❶ was writing invitation cards ❷ go to meet grandpa ❸ wash my car first

12 ❶ will be held at ❷ Only third grade students ❸ contact us

13 ❶ a cordless one ❷ the run time ❸ the cheaper the better

14 ❶ in every house ❷ round like a ball ❸ light a room

15 ❶ He got hurt badly ❷ in the hospital ❸ visit him in the hospital

16 ❶ gave them T-shirts ❷ bought new gloves ❸ buying them scarves

17 ❶ interesting classes ❷ take it together ❸ the baking class

18 ❶ work on the group project ❷ I'm afraid I can't ❸ will you come

19 ❶ stayed up all night ❷ prepare for ❸ cheer you on

20 ❶ two tickets ❷ to go with her ❸ wants to go to

01　그림 정보 파악 – 사물 | ③

해석

여 안녕하세요, 손님. 주문하시겠습니까?

남 네. 아이스크림 하나 주시겠어요?

여 물론이죠. 몇 숟갈을 떠 드릴까요?

남 두 숟갈 주세요.

여 좋아요. 콘으로 드릴까요, 컵으로 드릴까요?

남 콘으로 주세요.

여 그리고 초콜릿 시럽을 얹어 드릴까요?

남 아뇨, 괜찮아요. 위에 체리만 하나 얹어 주세요.

해설 남자는 두 스푼의 아이스크림을 콘에 담아 초콜릿 시럽 없이 체리를 얹어 주문했다.

02　목적 파악 | ①

해석

[전화벨이 울린다.]

남 여보세요?

여 여보세요? Ryan이니? 나 Susan이야.

남 안녕, Susan! 무슨 일이야?

여 가족 모임이 있는데, 괜찮은 음식점 하나 소개해 줄 수 있니?

남 너 서점 옆에 새로 생긴 중국 음식점에 대해 들어 본 적 있니?

여 아니, 들어 본 적 없어. 음식은 어떤데?

남 음식이 매우 맛이 있고 서비스가 훌륭해. 그래서 가능한 빨리 자리를 예약해야 해.

여 알겠어. 고마워.

남 천만에.

해설 여자의 두 번째 말로 보아 여자는 좋은 음식점을 추천받기 위해 전화했음을 알 수 있다.

03　그림 상황에 어울리는 대화 찾기 | ②

해석

① 남 방과 후에 하이킹 가는 게 어때?

　여 좋아. 오후 여섯 시에 도서관에서 만나자.

② 남 제가 이 책을 빌릴 수 있을까요?

　여 물론이죠. 그러나 일주일 안에 반납해야 합니다.

③ 남 당신은 어떤 종류의 책을 읽기 좋아하나요?

　여 저는 과학과 관련된 책을 읽는 것을 좋아합니다.

④ 남 너는 이 주변에 콘서트장이 어디 있는지 아니?

　여 물론이지, 저기 도서관 옆에 있어.

⑤ 남 나는 미나의 생일 선물을 고르고 있어. 뭘 사야 할까?

　여 책 한 권 선물하는 게 어때? 그녀는 독서를 즐겨 하잖아.

해설 소년이 도서관에서 책을 빌리고 있으므로 상황에 적절한 대화는 ② 이다.

04 특정 정보 파악 – 요일 | ③

해석

남 Jane, 내게 Jamie's Burger에서 햄버거 세트를 위한 무료 쿠폰이 있어. 나와 같이 갈래?

여 물론이지. 난 거기 햄버거를 좋아해.

남 잘됐네. 이번 주말에 시간이 있어?

여 아니. 난 금요일부터 일요일까지 캠핑을 갈 거야. 내일 방과 후에 만나는 건 어때?

남 내일은 화요일이지, 그렇지? 난 화요일과 목요일마다 테니스 수업이 있어.

여 그렇구나. 난 수요일에는 한가한데. 너도 수요일에 한가한지 궁금해.

남 응. 그날은 나도 좋아. 수요일 방과 후에 함께 Jamie's Burger에 가자.

여 그래. 고마워.

해설 금요일부터 일요일까지는 여자가 캠핑을 가고, 화요일과 목요일에는 남자가 테니스 수업이 있어서 안 되지만, 두 사람 모두 수요일에는 한가하다고 했다.

05 언급되지 않은 것 | ③

해석

여 Greenhill 박물관을 방문해 주셔서 감사합니다. 저희 박물관에 대해 간단히 소개해 드리도록 하겠습니다. Greenhill 박물관은 역사적이고 예술적인 작품을 보존하기 위해 1977년 문을 열었습니다. 그것은 2층짜리 건물이고 7개의 전시관을 갖추고 있습니다. 그것은 르네상스 거장이 만든 1만 점이 넘는 그림과 조각을 보유하고 있습니다. 박물관은 매일 오전 9시에서 오후 6시까지 문을 열지만, 매주 수요일마다 문을 닫습니다.

해설 Greenhill 박물관의 입장료에 관해서는 언급되지 않았다.

06 관계 추론 | ③

해석

남 안녕하세요, 어디로 가실까요?

여 Royal 호텔로 부탁합니다.

남 어디서 오셨어요? 일본인가요?

여 아니요, 저는 한국에서 왔어요.

남 아, 한국! 시간이 충분하시면, 박물관과 공연들을 놓치지 마세요.

여 감사합니다. 기억해 두겠습니다.

남 여기 런던에서 잘 머무르시길 바랍니다. 즐거운 여행되세요.

여 고맙습니다. 요금은 얼마인가요?

남 26파운드입니다.

여 여기 있습니다. 30파운드예요. 거스름돈은 가지세요.

남 대단히 감사합니다. 비의 도시 런던으로 오신 것을 환영합니다.

해설 남자가 여자에게 행선지를 묻고 요금을 받는 것으로 보아 택시 운전기사이고 여자는 택시에 탄 승객이다.

07 어색한 대화 찾기 | ⑤

해석

① 남 너 시험에 합격했구나. 축하해!

  여 고마워. 너도 합격할 거야.

② 남 너 콘서트가 언제 시작하는지 아니?

  여 응, 7시에 시작해.

③ 남 너 피곤해 보인다. 무슨 일 있니?

  여 난 지난밤 숙제가 많아서 한숨도 못 잤어.

④ 남 참 날씨가 좋구나! 소풍 가는 게 어때?

  여 좋아! 대공원에 가자.

⑤ 남 너 방과 후에 수영 강습을 받을 계획이니?

  여 나는 어젯밤에 수영 경기를 봤어.

해설 방과 후에 수영 강습을 받을 계획인지 묻는 질문에 대해 어젯밤 수영 경기를 봤다는 대답은 어색하다.

08 부탁한 일 파악 | ⑤

해석

남 안녕, Cindy! 너 오늘 바빠 보인다.

여 사실 난 다음 주 발표를 해야 하는데, 어떻게 해야 할지 모르겠어.

남 무엇에 관한 것인데?

여 미국 역사와 문화에 관한 거야. 너 지난주에 그것을 했지, 그렇지? 나에게 자료 구하는 법을 가르쳐 줄 수 있니?

남 물론이지. 난 미국 역사와 문화에 관한 책 몇 권을 읽었어. 학교 도서관에서 그것들을 빌렸지. 너도 거기에서 유용한 책들을 빌릴 수 있어.

여 오, 도와줘서 고마워.

남 천만에.

해설 여자는 남자에게 발표 자료를 구하는 방법을 물어봤다.

09 의도 파악 | ③

해석

남 엄마, 제게 용돈을 좀 더 주실 수 있나요? 책을 사야 하는데 돈이 모자라요.

여 벌써? Tommy, 네가 돈을 받은 지가 겨우 일주일밖에 안 되었는데.

남 알아요. 그렇지만 이번 주에 돈을 써야 할 데가 너무 많았어요.

여 아들아, 네가 돈으로 뭘 샀는지 말해 보렴.

남 사실 새로 나온 게임 CD를 사는 데 돈을 다 써 버렸어요.

여 저런! 너는 돈을 현명하게 써야 해. 계획된 소비는 매우 중요하단다. 알겠어?

남 네, 엄마.

해설 여자는 마지막 말로 계획된 소비의 중요성을 언급하며 남자에게 충고하고 있다.

10 숫자 정보 파악 – 금액 | ③

해석

여 안녕하세요, 여기는 Happy Adventure 공원입니다. 뭘 도와드릴까요?

남 표를 사고 싶은데요. 가격이 얼마죠?

여 어른은 20달러이고, 어린이는 10달러입니다.

남 좋아요. 어른 스무 명과 어린이 두 명을 위한 표를 주세요.

여 그런 경우, 어른 한 명은 무료입니다.

남 좋습니다, 여기 있습니다.

해설 성인 20명($20×20=$400)과 어린이 2명($10×2=$20)의 표를 구입하는데, 이 경우 어른 한 명($20)은 무료라고 했으므로 남자는 $400를 지불해야 한다.

11 한 일 / 할 일 파악 | ④

해석

남 Amanda! 너 몇 분 전에 바빠 보였어. 뭐하고 있었니?

여 친구에게 크리스마스 파티 초대장을 쓰고 있었어요.

남 그러면 그것들을 다 썼니?
여 네, 아빠. 그런데, 오늘 저녁에 할아버지를 뵈러 간다고 하지 않으셨어요?
남 그래, 근데 차가 너무 더러워. 그래서 먼저 세차부터 해야겠다. 너 세차하는 것을 도와줄 수 있니?
여 물론이죠!
해설 여자는 남자가 세차하는 것을 도와주기로 했다.

12 언급되지 않은 것 | ①
해석
여 우리는 이번 봄에 학생들을 위한 Genius 영어 말하기 대회를 엽니다. 이 대회는 4월 30일 하나 문화센터에서 실시됩니다. 대회는 3분 영어 말하기 대회를 포함하고 있습니다. 저는 그것이 여러분의 능력을 보여줄 좋은 기회가 될 것이라고 확신합니다. 오직 3학년 학생만 이 대회에 참여할 수 있습니다. 더 많은 정보를 원하시면, 800-212-6212로 저희에게 연락 주세요.
해설 Genius 영어 말하기 대회의 준비물에 관해서는 언급되지 않았다.

13 도표 정보 파악 | ②
해석
남 어떻게 도와드릴까요?
여 진공청소기를 찾고 있습니다.
남 알겠습니다. 이 5개의 모델들을 보세요. 무선 청소기를 원하시나요?
여 네. 선이 있는 것은 사용하기 약간 불편하더라고요.
남 그렇습니다. 그리고 작동 시간에 대해서는요?
여 작동 시간은 적어도 30분은 되어야 해요.
남 좋습니다. 이제 두 가지 선택권이 있어요.
여 흠… 제게는 더 저렴한 것이 더 나아요.
남 알겠습니다. 제가 가서 가져다 드리겠습니다.
해설 선이 없으면서 작동 시간이 적어도 30분이 되는 것은 ②와 ③인데, 둘 중 저렴한 것을 선택했으므로 여자가 구입할 진공청소기는 ②이다.

14 주제 파악 | ③
해석
남 매일의 일상에서 그것은 매우 중요하다. 보통 모든 집에 몇 개씩 있다. 그것은 또한 야외에서도 이용된다. 그것은 크기와 모양들이 다양하게 나오지만, 보통 작은 편이다. 그것의 몸통은 공처럼 둥글고 가느다란 목을 갖고 있다. 그것은 유리와 철로 만들어졌다. 그것은 어두울 때 방을 밝히는 데 사용된다.
해설 어두울 때 방을 밝히는 데 사용되고 몸통이 동그랗고 가느다란 목의 형태를 갖고 있으며 유리와 철로 만들어진 것은 전구이다.

15 한 일 / 할 일 파악 | ②
해석
남 Susan! 너 Michael이 어디에 있는지 아니? 나는 그를 찾을 수가 없어.
여 너 그의 사고에 대해 못 들었니? 그는 체육시간에 심하게 다쳤어.
남 정말? 안됐구나. 그러면, 그는 지금 병원에 입원해 있는 거야?
여 응. 선생님이 차로 그를 병원에 데리고 가셨어.
남 그가 빨리 회복되기를 바라.
여 나도 역시 그러기를 바라. 우리 그에게 병문안을 가는 게 어때?
남 좋은 생각이야. 언제 만날까?

여 오늘 방과 후에.
해설 남자와 여자는 방과 후에 다친 친구의 병문안을 가기로 했다.

16 특정 정보 파악 | ④
해석
여 Peter, 엄마와 아빠의 결혼기념일이 다음 주야.
남 응. 부모님께 티셔츠를 사 드리는 게 어떨까?
여 작년에 부모님께 티셔츠를 사 드렸잖아. 다른 선물을 사 드리자.
남 그럼 장갑은 어떻게 생각해?
여 내가 알기로는 엄마, 아빠는 지난주에 새 장갑을 사셨어.
남 흠… 스카프를 사 드리는 것은 어떨까?
여 그거 좋은 생각이네. 지금 사러 가자.
해설 남자와 여자는 부모님의 결혼기념일 선물로 스카프를 구입하기로 했다.

17 알맞은 응답 찾기 | ②
해석
남 Susan, 방과 후 수업 수강할 거니?
여 응, 그래. 넌 어때?
남 나도. 이번에 제빵 수업, 드럼 수업 같은 재밌는 수업이 많이 있어.
여 흥미롭네.
남 그럼 수업을 하나 선택해서 함께 그것을 수강하자.
여 좋은 생각이야.
남 난 제빵 수업을 수강할 생각이야. 함께 수강하는 것은 어때?
여 왜 안 되겠니? 그 수업을 신청하자.
① 물론이지. 좋은 것을 함께 찾아보자.
③ 내가 너무 바빠서. 다음에 너와 함께할게.
④ 날 믿어. 그것은 우리 학교에서 가장 좋은 수업이야.
⑤ 아니. 난 방과 후 수업에 관심이 없어.
해설 남자가 여자에게 제빵 수업을 함께 듣자고 제안했으므로 제안을 승낙하는 ②가 여자의 응답으로 가장 적절하다.

18 알맞은 응답 찾기 | ③
해석
여 David, 지금 외출하는 거니?
남 네. Tom과 함께 조별 과제를 하러 갈 거예요. 왜요?
여 오늘 저녁에 Kevin 삼촌의 집들이에 초대를 받았거든.
남 집들이에는 몇 시에 갈 거예요?
여 6시 정도. 그때까지는 집에 올 거야?
남 못 올 것 같아요.
여 삼촌집이 어디 있는지 알지, 그렇지?
남 네. 혼자 갈 수 있어요.
여 몇 시에 올 거야?
남 7시쯤이요. 거기에서 봐요.
① 물론이죠. 지금 4시예요.
② 아니요. 저는 그 파티에 가지 않을 거예요.
④ 문제없어요. 도와드릴 수 있어요.
⑤ 도서관에서요. 늦지 않을게요.
해설 여자가 남자에게 삼촌의 집들이에 몇 시에 올 것인지 물었으므로 7시쯤에 간다고 하는 ③이 남자의 응답으로 가장 적절하다.

19 알맞은 응답 찾기 | ①

해석

여 안녕, Mark.

남 안녕, Susan. 오늘 무척 피곤해 보여. 어젯밤에 늦게 잤니?

여 응. 밤을 새었어.

남 정말? 왜?

여 토론 대회 준비를 해야 했거든. 난 너무 초조해.

남 걱정하지 마. 넌 틀림없이 정말로 잘 할 수 있을 거야. 그런데, 대회는 언제니?

여 다음 주 월요일이야.

남 내가 가서 널 응원해도 될까?

여 **물론이지. 네가 거기 있으면 내가 더 잘 할 것 같아.**

② 내게 맡겨. 난 토론을 잘 하거든.

③ 축하해! 네가 대회에서 우승했어.

④ 정말? 어떻게 밤을 샜니?

⑤ 문제없어. 네가 그것을 준비하는 걸 도와줄게.

해설 남자가 여자의 토론 대회에 가서 응원해도 되는지 물었으므로 네가 있으면 더 잘 거라고 하는 ①이 여자의 응답으로 가장 적절하다.

20 상황에 맞는 말 찾기 | ④

해석

여 지수는 록 음악에 매료되어 있다. 록 축제가 다음 주 토요일 서울에서 열릴 것이다. 그래서 그녀는 록 축제 티켓 두 장을 구입하고, 같이 갈 사람을 찾고 있다. 그때 그녀는 Andrew가 록 축제에 가고 싶어 한다는 것을 그녀의 친구로부터 듣는다. 이런 상황에서, 지수는 Andrew에게 뭐라고 말하겠는가?

지수 **우리 함께 록 축제에 갈래?**

① 록 축제 언제 열려?

② 날 위해 티켓을 구해 줄 수 있니?

③ 이 록 축제는 정말 재미있니?

⑤ 네 친구는 록 축제에 가 본 적 있니?

해설 지수가 축제 표가 2장이 있는 상황에서 Andrew가 그 축제에 가고 싶어 하는 것을 알았으므로 ④가 답으로 적절하다.

02회 영어 듣기모의고사　pp. 014~015

01 ②	**02** ④	**03** ④	**04** ③	**05** ⑤
06 ③	**07** ②	**08** ②	**09** ③	**10** ④
11 ②	**12** ⑤	**13** ①	**14** ③	**15** ③
16 ②	**17** ④	**18** ③	**19** ②	**20** ⑤

Dictation Test 02회　pp. 016~021

01 ❶ one of these coin purses ❷ looks like a rabbit ❸ the one with glasses

02 ❶ found this wallet ❷ where you found it ❸ find its owner

03 ❶ a heavy traffic jam ❷ have to get off ❸ ten minutes to walk

04 ❶ playing badminton ❷ except for Wednesday ❸ for a group project

05 ❶ travel at speeds of ❷ light and easy to carry ❸ an hour and a half

06 ❶ saw your paintings ❷ the best exhibition ❸ ready for the interview

07 ❶ don't like ❷ something to eat ❸ a little salty

08 ❶ I'm bringing my friends ❷ Could you make a pizza ❸ won't have to wait long

09 ❶ I haven't told anybody ❷ why everybody knows ❸ I shouldn't have

10 ❶ for fifteen dollars ❷ two dollars ❸ take one

11 ❶ in thirty minutes ❷ on the table ❸ do the dishes

12 ❶ two years ago ❷ were planted and maintained ❸ to new members

13 ❶ looking for a skateboard ❷ purple and green ❸ spend more than

14 ❶ humorous name ❷ he sings and dances ❸ express your friendship

15 ❶ too hot ❷ not working ❸ have to clean it

16 ❶ I just need to bring ❷ making animals with clay ❸ have to buy some

17 ❶ my brakes were not working ❷ didn't have a car accident ❸ do for transportation

18 ❶ will move to ❷ get used to living ❸ not good at speaking English

19 ❶ looking for a toothbrush ❷ electric one ❸ What color would you like

20 ❶ very busy ❷ eat his lunch ❸ in the restaurant

01 그림 정보 파악 – 물건 | ②

해석

남 여동생 생일이 다음 주야. 그녀에게 무엇을 사 줘야 할지 모르겠어.

여 이 동전 지갑들 중 하나를 사 주는 게 어때?

남 좋은 생각이야. 동전 지갑 선택하는 것을 도와줄래?

여 물론이지. 이 개구리 동전 지갑은 어때?

남 음, 나는 그 디자인을 좋아하지 않아. 토끼처럼 보이는 이 동전 지갑이 좋아 보여. 이 지갑에 대해서 어떻게 생각해?

여 그건 귀엽게 생겼지만, 귀가 너무 길어. 내 생각에는 이 고양이처럼 생긴 동전 지갑이 더 나은 것 같아.

남 안경을 끼고 있는 동전 지갑을 말하는 거니?

여 맞아.

남 나도 그게 좋아 보인다. 그걸로 살래.

해설 남자는 안경을 끼고 있는 고양이처럼 생긴 동전 지갑을 산다고 했다.

02 목적 파악 | ④

해석

남 안녕, 꼬마 숙녀님. 무엇을 도와줄까?

여 안녕하세요, 경찰관님. 집에 가는 길에 이 지갑을 발견했어요. 저는 그것으로 무엇을 해야 할지 몰라서요.

남 그것을 어디에서 발견했는지 말해 줄래?

여 그것은 Happy 슈퍼마켓 바로 앞에 있었어요.

남 그래. 아마도 주인을 찾을 수 있을 것 같구나. 그 속에 신분증이 있네.

여 잘됐네요. 곧 주인을 찾아 주시면 좋겠네요.

해설 여자는 집에 가는 길에 지갑을 발견하여 습득물을 신고하려고 경찰서에 방문했다.

03 그림 상황에 어울리는 대화 찾기 | ④

해석

① 남 왜 또 늦었는지 이유를 말해 줄래?

　여 죄송해요. 저는 교통 체증에 갇혔어요.

② 남 버스 정류장에 있는 저 사람들을 봐.

　여 와, 버스를 기다리는 사람들이 굉장히 많이 있구나.

③ 남 우리는 다음 정류장에서 내려야 해.

　여 알았어. 내가 정지 버튼을 누를게.

④ 남 7번 버스가 국립 박물관에 가나요?

　여 아니. 길 건너에서 5번 버스를 타렴.

⑤ 남 가장 가까운 지하철역에 가려면 얼마나 오래 걸리나요?

　여 걸어서 적어도 10분은 걸립니다.

해설 남자아이가 여자에게 타야 할 버스를 물어보고, 여자가 이를 안내해 주는 그림의 상황에 적절한 대화는 ④이다.

04 특정 정보 파악 – 요일 | ③

해석

남 Jane, 체육 수업 시험 봤어?

여 아직 안 봤어. 사실은, 난 벌써 그것에 대해 걱정하고 있어. 너도 알다시피 난 배드민턴을 잘 못 치잖아.

남 내가 널 도와줄 수 있어. 난 이미 시험을 봐서 A를 받았거든.

여 네가 부러워. 우리는 다음 주 화요일에 시험을 볼 거야. 이번 주에 매일날 가르쳐 줄 수 있니?

남 어디 보자. 수요일만 제외하고 매일 널 도와줄 수 있어.

여 왜 수요일은 안 돼?

남 조별 과제 때문에 친구들을 만나야 하거든.

여 아, 알겠어. 고마워.

남 그럼 오늘 방과 후에 만나.

해설 남자는 조별 과제 때문에 수요일에 친구들을 만나야 한다고 했다.

05 언급되지 않은 것 | ⑤

해석

여 안녕하세요, 여러분. 저희를 찾아 주셔서 감사합니다. 오늘, 저는 여러분께 저희의 새로운 전동 킥보드인 'Joy'에 대해 말씀드리겠습니다. 그것은 매우 빠릅니다. 그것은 최대 시속 25킬로미터의 속도로 이동할 수 있습니다. 또한 그것은 무게가 고작 7킬로그램밖에 나가지 않기 때문에 가벼워서 가지고 다니기 쉽습니다. 완전히 충전되는데 약 1시간 30분이 걸립니다. 이것은 다른 제품에 비해서 매우 빠릅니다. 지금 'Joy'를 잠시 동안 타 보고 싶으시다면 여기 줄을 서세요.

해설 Joy의 가격에 대해서는 언급되지 않았다.

06 관계 추론 | ③

해석

남 안녕하세요, Peterson 씨. 만나 뵈어서 반갑습니다.

여 저도 만나 뵈어서 반갑습니다, Smith 씨.

남 당신의 그림을 보았어요. 그것들은 훌륭해요.

여 감사합니다.

남 이번 전시회에 만족하시나요?

여 물론, 그렇습니다. 이번이 제가 지금껏 했던 전시회 중 최고입니다.

남 잘됐어요.

여 이번 인터뷰는 이번 주 금요일 신문에 실릴 건가요?

남 네. 이제 인터뷰 준비가 되셨나요?

여 아, 네. 어서 하세요.

해설 남자는 여자를 인터뷰하고 있으므로 신문 기자임을 알 수 있고, 여자는 전시회를 열고, 자신의 그림에 만족한다고 했으므로 화가임을 알 수 있다.

07 어색한 대화 찾기 | ②

해석

① 남 이 셔츠 어때요?

　여 글쎄요. 색깔이 마음에 들지 않아요.

② 남 이 도시에서 무엇을 하고 싶으세요?

　여 이번이 두 번째 방문입니다.

③ 남 내일 먹을 것을 좀 가져와야 하나요?

　여 음, 마실 물만 좀 가져오면 됩니다.

④ 남 스테이크는 어떠셨나요?

　여 맛있었지만, 약간 짜긴 했어요.

⑤ 남 어제 당신에게 무슨 일이 있었는지 설명해 줄래요?

　여 자동차 사고를 당했어요. 그렇게 심각한 것은 아니었죠.

해설 이 도시에서 무엇을 하고 싶은지 물었는데 이번이 두 번째 방문이라고 답하는 것은 어색하다.

08 부탁한 일 파악 | ②

해석

[휴대 전화가 울린다.]

여 여보세요, Chris. 지금 집에 오는 중이니?

남 네. 함께 공부하려고 친구들을 집에 데려가는 중이에요. 괜찮죠?

여 그래. 몇 명의 친구들이 오고 있니?

남 세 명이에요. 엄마, 부탁 하나 드려도 될까요?

여 물론이지. 뭔데?

남 저희를 위해 피자를 만들어 주실 수 있나요? 친구들이 엄마가 만든 피자를 정말 좋아할 거예요.

여 좋아. 너희가 오래 기다리지 않도록 그것을 만들기 시작할게.

남 고마워요. 곧 봐요.

해설 남자는 집에 데리고 올 친구들을 위해 엄마에게 피자를 만들어 달라고 부탁했다.

09 의도 파악 | ③

해석

남 Cathy, 너 Amy를 위한 깜짝 파티에 대해 누군가에게 말한 적이 있니?

여 아니. 아무에게도 말하지 않았어.

남 내게 진실만을 말해 줘.

여	실은 Sue를 제외하고는 아무에게도 말하지 않았어.
남	오, 안 돼! 그래서 모두가 그 파티에 대해 알고 있구나.
여	뭐라고? Sue는 그것을 비밀로 하겠다고 내게 약속했어.
남	Cathy, 넌 걔가 얼마나 수다스러운지 몰랐구나.
여	오, 저런! 그녀에게 그 파티에 대해 말하지 말았어야 했는데.
해설	여자는 깜짝 파티에 대해 Sue에게 말하지 말았어야 했다며 후회하고 있다.

10 숫자 정보 파악 – 금액 | ④

해석

여	도와드릴까요?
남	저는 엄마께 드릴 선물을 사고 싶어요. 하나 추천해 주실래요?
여	이 머리핀은 어떠세요?
남	좋아요. 얼마죠?
여	10달러입니다. 15달러에 두 개를 사실 수 있어요.
남	15달러라고요? 좋아요. 두 개를 살게요. 그리고 생일 카드도 필요해요.
여	이것은 어떠신가요? 2달러입니다.
남	좋아요. 하나 사겠습니다.
해설	남자는 어머니께 드릴 머리핀 2개($15)를 사면서 생일 카드($2)도 구입했으므로 총 17달러를 지불하면 된다.

11 한 일 / 할 일 파악 | ②

해석

남	와! 맛있는 냄새가 나는구나, Kate.
여	생일 케이크가 몇 분 후면 만들어질 거야.
남	좋아. 엄마, 아빠가 30분 후에 오실 거야. 서둘러야 해.
여	꽃은 꽃병에 꽂았니?
남	물론이지. 그 꽃병을 탁자 위에 두었어.
여	잘했어. 그럼, 내가 생일 카드를 만들게.
남	그럼 내가 해야 할 것이 있을까?
여	그래. 설거지를 해 줘. 그들이 오시기 전에 부엌을 청소해야 해.
남	좋아. 내가 그 일을 할게.
해설	여자가 남자에게 설거지를 해 달라고 부탁하자 남자가 설거지를 하겠다고 했다.

12 언급되지 않은 것 | ⑤

해석

남	저희 꽃 동아리에 대한 여러분의 관심에 대해 감사드립니다. 저희 동아리는 단지 2년 전에 만들어졌지만, 흥미로운 일들을 매우 많이 해 오고 있습니다. 여러분은 정문 근처의 꽃을 본 적이 있나요? 그것들은 우리 동아리 회원들이 심어서 관리한 것입니다. 그리고 때때로 우리는 식물과 꽃 사진을 찍기 위해 야외로 가기도 합니다. 우리 동아리에 가입하고 싶으시면, 211호로 오세요. 저희는 새로운 회원들에게 아름다운 말린 꽃 책갈피를 드립니다.
해설	동아리의 가입 조건에 대해서는 언급되지 않았다.

13 도표 정보 파악 | ①

해석

남	Judy, 인터넷으로 무엇을 보고 있니?
여	난 스케이트보드를 알아보고 있는데, 어느 것을 골라야 할지 모르겠어.
남	내가 도와줄게. 먼저, 이 3킬로그램이 넘는 것은 너무 무거워.

여	맞아, 저것은 사지 않을게.
남	이것들 중에 어떤 색을 좋아하니?
여	난 파란색보다 보라색과 초록색을 더 좋아해.
남	이제 네가 선택할 수 있는 것이 두 개 남았어.
여	음, 난 스케이트보드에 100달러 넘게 쓰고 싶지 않아.
남	그렇다면 이것이 네게 완벽해 보이네.
여	맞아. 그것을 살래.
해설	3킬로그램이 넘는 것을 제외하고 보라색과 초록색인 ①과 ③ 중 100달러를 넘지 않는 것을 골랐으므로 여자가 구입할 스케이트보드는 ①이다.

14 주제 파악 | ③

해석

여	이것은 한 사람에 대한 허물없고 종종 재미있는 이름이다. 그 이름은 그의 진짜 이름, 재능, 성격 또는 외모와 관련되어 있다. 예를 들어, 나는 우리 반 친구 진수를 'Michael Jackson'이라 부른다. 왜냐하면 그가 Michael Jackson과 똑같이 노래하고 춤을 추기 때문이다. 당신은 많은 친구들에게 이것을 부여한다. 이것을 통해서 당신은 우정을 표현할 수 있고 재미를 얻을 수 있다. 그러나, 때때로 이것은 당신의 친구들의 기분을 상하게 할 수 있다.
해설	사람의 이름, 재능, 성격 또는 외모와 관련이 있고 친구와의 우정을 표현하는 것은 별명이다.

15 한 일 / 할 일 파악 | ③

해석

여	이봐, 오빠! 오늘 너무 덥지 않아?
남	응. 일기예보에서 오늘 기온이 30도까지 오른다고 했어.
여	정말? 올 여름은 너무 덥지 않으면 좋을 텐데.
남	나도 그러길 바라.
여	에어컨을 켜도 되겠어?
남	물론이지, 근데 그게 작동하지 않는 것 같아.
여	오, 저런! 그럼, 선풍기를 켜는 것은 어떨까?
남	그건 너무 더러워서, 그것을 사용하기 전에 청소해야 해.
여	알았어. 내가 당장 그렇게 할게. 난 이렇게 더운 날씨를 견딜 수가 없어.
해설	여자는 날씨가 더워서 선풍기를 쓰려고 했으나 더워서 선풍기를 사용하기 전에 선풍기를 청소하기로 했다.

16 특정 정보 파악 | ②

해석

여	Peter, 우리 내일 미술 수업 있지, 그렇지 않니?
남	그래. 넌 뭘 만들 거야?
여	종이꽃. 색종이 몇 장과 풀을 가져가기만 하면 돼.
남	멋진데! 넌 종이꽃으로 꽃다발을 만들 수도 있겠다.
여	맞아. 넌 뭘 만들 거야?
남	난 점토로 동물을 만들까 생각 중이야.
여	네 점토 동물들을 보는 것이 기다려져. 이봐, 점토와 물감을 가져오는 것을 잊지 마.
남	아, 점토가 다 떨어져서 좀 사야 하는데. 내게 상기시켜 주어서 고마워.
여	천만에.
해설	여자가 점토와 물감 가져오는 것을 잊지 말라고 하자 남자는 점토가 다 떨어졌다며 점토를 사야 한다고 했다.

17 알맞은 응답 찾기 | ④

해석
남 안녕, 수지야. 늦어서 미안해.
여 무슨 일 있었니?
남 여기 오는 길에 브레이크가 말을 듣지 않았어.
여 오, 저런. 괜찮니?
남 응, 괜찮아. 다행히 사고는 안 났어.
여 네 차는 어떻게 했어?
남 고치려고 정비소에 맡겼어.
여 그래서 앞으로 교통편은 어떻게 할 거야?
남 <u>당분간은 버스를 타야 할 거야.</u>
① 아마도 다음에.
② 나는 일하러 갈 거야.
③ 요금은 얼마니?
⑤ 당신을 알게 되어 좋았습니다. 잘 지내세요.

해설 여자가 차를 수리하는 동안 교통편은 어떻게 할 것인지 묻는 질문에 대해 당분간 버스를 탈 것이라고 말하는 ④가 남자의 응답으로 가장 적절하다.

18 알맞은 응답 찾기 | ③

해석
여 진수야, 너희 가족이 곧 미국으로 이사 갈 거라고 들었어.
남 응. 내가 거기서 잘할 수 있을지 모르겠어.
여 처음에는 좀 힘들지도 모르겠다. 하지만 거기에 사는 데 익숙해 질 거야.
남 오, 넌 2년 전에 한국으로 이사 왔지! 네게 가장 힘든 것은 무엇이었니?
여 내 경우에는, 한국어를 이해하기가 힘들었지. 너도 알다시피 나는 그때 한국어를 전혀 할 수 없었어. 그래서 매일 열심히 한국어를 공부했어.
남 음, 난 7년 동안 영어를 공부해 오긴 했어. 하지만 나는 영어로 말하는 것을 잘 못해.
여 이봐, 힘내! 나는 네가 잘할 수 있을 거라 확신해.
① 너는 나의 영어를 도와줄 수 있니?
② 네가 그곳에 제시간에 도착할 거라고 확신해.
④ 고마워. 나는 한국에서 사는 것에 만족해.
⑤ 나는 미국으로 돌아가야 해.

해설 미국으로 이민 가는 남자가 영어 때문에 걱정하고 있는 상황에서 잘할 수 있을 거라고 격려하는 ③이 여자의 응답으로 가장 적절하다.

19 알맞은 응답 찾기 | ②

해석
여 안녕하세요, 도와드릴까요?
남 안녕하세요, 저는 칫솔을 찾고 있습니다.
여 전동식을 원하세요?
남 아뇨, 그냥 일반 것으로 주세요.
여 딱딱한 것, 부드러운 것 또는 중간 것 중에는요?
남 부드러운 것이요. 치과 의사가 제 약한 치아에는 부드러운 것이 가장 좋다고 하더군요.
여 그렇군요. 어떤 색깔을 원하십니까?
남 <u>그건 별로 상관없어요.</u>
① 죄송한데, 저는 그렇게 생각하지 않아요.
③ 당신은 내 치과 의사를 좋아할 거예요.
④ 저는 지금 지불해야겠어요.
⑤ 저는 치약도 하나 원해요.

해설 어떤 색깔의 칫솔을 찾는지 물어보는 여자에게 색깔은 상관없다고 하

는 ②가 남자의 응답으로 가장 적절하다.

20 상황에 맞는 말 찾기 | ⑤

해석
남 Gary는 컴퓨터 업계에서 일한다. 오늘 그는 매우 바쁘다. 그의 상사가 그에게 추가 업무를 주었다. 그래서 그는 일을 하면서 사무실에서 점심을 먹으려고 한다. 그는 패스트푸드점에 가서 점심을 주문한다. 여종업원이 쟁반에 음식을 놓기 시작한다. 아마 그녀는 그가 식당에서 식사할 거라고 생각하는 것 같다. 이런 상황에서, Gary는 여종업원에게 뭐라고 말하겠는가?
Gary 가지고 갈 수 있게 그것을 봉투에 넣어줄 수 있나요?
① 저는 우유 대신에 콜라를 주세요.
② 치즈버거와 감자튀김을 주세요.
③ 당신은 제게 잔돈을 잘못 주셨어요.
④ 제가 늦어서 좀 서둘러 줄 수 있나요?

해설 사무실에서 점심을 먹기로 한 상황이므로 음식을 포장해 달라고 부탁하는 ⑤가 답으로 적절하다.

03회 영어 듣기모의고사				pp. 022~023
01 ①	**02** ⑤	**03** ③	**04** ④	**05** ②
06 ①	**07** ⑤	**08** ⑤	**09** ④	**10** ①
11 ⑤	**12** ③	**13** ③	**14** ③	**15** ②
16 ③	**17** ④	**18** ④	**19** ④	**20** ⑤

Dictation Test 03회 pp. 024~029

01 ❶ getting off the subway ❷ a flower pattern ❸ two small pockets

02 ❶ have a terrible headache ❷ postponed the due date ❸ see a doctor

03 ❶ the present I prepared ❷ The gift box ❸ throw out this box

04 ❶ should submit it ❷ after school tomorrow ❸ on Thursday

05 ❶ the biggest toy museum ❷ a lot of toys ❸ We are open from

06 ❶ If you try hard ❷ the final match ❸ keep your eye on

07 ❶ missed the same question ❷ your favorite dessert

08 ❶ the post office ❷ the repair shop ❸ finish my report

09 ❶ enjoyed your speech ❷ a great writer ❸ Thank you for saying that

10 ❶ at a cheaper price ❷ only paid half price

11 ❶ go on another ride ❷ eat something simple

12 ❶ services our hotel offers ❷ is cartoons ❸ the
sports channel

13 ❶ to my birthday party ❷ where Happy Pizza is ❸ It's
between

14 ❶ don't need a paper bag ❷ use less paper
❸ saving paper

15 ❶ I'm thinking of buying ❷ at the bookstore
❸ buying presents

16 ❶ in the hospital ❷ some flowers for him
❸ reading a magazine

17 ❶ a great cook ❷ wish me good luck

18 ❶ removed those rocks ❷ on the garden ❸ How
long

19 ❶ don't have enough space ❷ an extra closet
❸ put all your clothes

20 ❶ gotten some help ❷ how to say ❸ in French

---

01 그림 정보 파악 – 사물 | ①

해석

여 실례합니다. 여기가 분실물 센터인가요?

남 네. 무엇을 찾으십니까?

여 제 가방을 찾고 있어요. 지하철에서 내릴 때 자리에 그것을 두고 내렸
어요. 네모난 모양의 배낭입니다.

남 특별한 무늬가 있나요?

여 네. 꽃무늬가 있어요. 그리고 앞쪽에 조그만 주머니가 두 개 있어요.

남 좋아요. 제가 찾아볼게요. 잠시만 기다리세요.

해설 네모난 모양의 꽃무늬 배낭에 두 개의 작은 주머니가 앞쪽에 있는 가방
은 ①이다.

---

02 목적 파악 | ⑤

해석

[전화벨이 울린다.]

여 여보세요?

남 안녕, Jane. 나 Daniel이야. 너 오늘 학교 안 왔더라. 아프니?

여 안녕, Daniel. 나 심한 두통에 시달리고 있어. 그래서 다음 주 월요일
전까지 독후감을 마칠 수 있을지 모르겠어.

남 실은 좋은 소식을 알려 주려고 전화했어. 오늘 선생님께서 마감일을 다
음 주 수요일로 연기하셨어.

여 정말? 정보 고마워.

남 천만에요. 그리고 상태가 더 좋아지지 않으면, 병원에 가렴.

여 응. 그럴게.

해설 남자는 아파서 결석한 여자에게 독후감 제출일이 변경됐다는 것을 알
려 주려고 전화했다.

---

03 그림 상황에 어울리는 대화 찾기 | ③

해석

① 여 내가 이 상자를 포장해야 한다고 생각하니?

　남 내가 너라면 그렇게 할 거야.

② 여 생일 축하해! 이게 내가 너를 위해 준비한 선물이야.

　남 마음에 든다! 정말 고마워.

③ 여 선물 상자가 무척 사랑스럽네요. 고맙습니다. 여기 20,000원이요.

　남 어머니께서 이것을 좋아하시면 좋겠네요.

④ 여 너 모든 상자들을 네 방으로 옮겼니?

　남 응. 그것들은 책장 위 칸에 있어.

⑤ 여 Jim, 내 대신 이 상자를 버려 줄 수 있니?

　남 물론이죠. 더 버릴 것 있으세요?

해설 여자가 선물 상자를 계산하고 있는 상황에 적절한 대화는 ③이다.

---

04 특정 정보 파악 – 요일 | ④

해석

남 Cindy, 우리 조별 과제를 시작해야 할 것 같아.

여 그래. 다음 주 월요일까지 그것을 제출해야 하는 거지, 그렇지?

남 맞아. 우리에게는 약 1주일이 남았어.

여 내일 방과 후에 만나는 것은 어때?

남 미안하지만, 그럴 수 없어. 난 화요일마다 드럼 수업을 받거든. 수요일
에 만나는 게 어때?

여 음. 수요일에는 치과에 가야 해. 하지만 목요일과 금요일에는 한가해.

남 빠르면 빠를수록 더 좋아. 목요일에 만나자.

여 좋아. 그때 만나.

해설 화요일에 남자는 드럼 수업을 가고, 수요일은 여자가 치과에 간다. 두
사람은 남은 목요일과 금요일 중 더 이른 목요일에 만나기로 했다.

---

05 언급되지 않은 것 | ②

해석

여 안녕하세요, 여러분! 여러분께 저희 Bluebird 장난감 박물관에 대해
말씀드리고 싶습니다. Bluebird 장난감 박물관은 국내 최대의 장난감
박물관입니다. 저희는 수백 개의 인형, 자동차, 보트, 비행기, 증기기관
등을 포함하여 많은 장난감들을 보유하고 있습니다. 저희는 매일 오전
9시에서 오후 7시까지 문을 엽니다. 입장권은 어른은 25달러이고 어
린이는 15달러입니다. Bluebird 장난감 박물관을 방문하셔서 즐거운
시간을 보내세요.

해설 Bluebird 장난감 박물관의 위치에 대해서는 언급되지 않았다.

---

06 관계 추론 | ①

해석

남 Kate, 준비됐니?

여 Wilson 선생님, 저 지금 너무 긴장돼요.

남 침착하렴, Kate. 네가 열심히 하면, Lisa를 이길 거야. 틀림없어.

여 고맙습니다. Wilson 선생님.

남 Kate, 넌 정말로 열심히 연습했어. 그저 네 자신을 믿으렴.

여 선생님 덕분에, 제가 마침내 결승전에 오게 되었어요. 최선을 다할게요.

남 좋아. 항상 공에 눈을 떼지 않아야 해.

여 네, 그럴게요.

남 그래. 행운을 빌어.

해설 결승전을 앞두고 긴장하고 있는 여자를 격려하고 조언해 주는 것으로
보아 남자는 코치이고, 여자는 운동선수이다.

---

07 어색한 대화 찾기 | ⑤

해석

① 여 이 책 빌려도 될까?

　남 응, 괜찮아.

② 여 왜 그렇게 화가 났니?
　　남 같은 문제를 또 틀렸기 때문이야.
③ 여 이 병을 어떻게 여는지 아니?
　　남 한번 해 볼게.
④ 여 'app'이 무슨 뜻이니?
　　남 '응용 프로그램'이라는 뜻이야.
⑤ 여 저는 여러분이 가장 좋아하는 후식인 아이스크림에 대해 이야기하려
　　　고 합니다.
　　남 들어 주셔서 감사합니다.
해설 좋아하는 디저트인 아이스크림에 대해 이야기하고 싶다는 말에 대해
　　들어 주셔서 감사하다고 대답하는 것은 어색하다.

08　부탁한 일 파악　| ⑤
해석
여 아빠, 지금 어디에 가세요?
남 우체국에 가는데.
여 음, 그다음에 할 일이 더 있으세요?
남 아니, 그렇진 않아. 왜? 집에 오는 길에 뭐 사다 줄까?
여 아뇨. 제 휴대 전화가 고장이 났어요. 저 대신에 수리점에 좀 들려 주시
　　면 안 될까요? 저는 한 시간 안에 보고서를 마쳐야 해서 그럴 시간이
　　충분치 않아요.
남 문제없어. 내가 해 줄게.
여 고마워요, 아빠.
해설 여자는 남자에게 자기 대신 휴대 전화 수리점에 방문해 달라고 부탁
　　했다.

09　의도 파악　| ④
해석
여 Smith 선생님, 강연 잘 들었습니다.
남 고마워요.
여 저기, 저는 선생님의 책을 정말 좋아하고 그 책들로부터 값진 교훈을
　　얻었어요.
남 오, 이름이 뭐죠?
여 제 이름은 김지선이에요. 커서 선생님처럼 훌륭한 작가가 되고 싶어요.
남 김지선이라고요. 학생의 이름을 기억해 둬야겠군요. 나는 학생이 장차
　　훌륭한 작가가 될 수 있을 거라 믿어요.
여 그렇게 말씀해 주셔서 감사합니다.
해설 여자는 훌륭한 작가가 될 수 있을 거라고 격려해 주는 남자에게 감사를
　　표하고 있다.

10　숫자 정보 파악 – 금액　| ①
해석
여 와, 이 신발은 어디서 샀니? 정말 멋져 보여.
남 고마워. 남대문 시장에서 샀어.
여 거기에서 신발을 더 싼 가격에 살 수 있니?
남 응. 할인을 받으면, 싸게 살 수 있어. 나는 30,000원만 줬어.
여 나는 그 신발이 60,000원은 할 거라고 생각했어.
남 응. 이거 원래 60,000원이야. 그런데 난 겨우 반값만 치렀지.
해설 남자는 할인을 받아 60,000원짜리 신발을 반값에 구입했다고 했다.

11　장소 추론　| ⑤
해석
여 와, 이 롤러코스터 굉장하다. 그럼, 다음에는 뭐 하러 갈까?
남 뭐 좀 먹지 않을래? 나 배고파.
여 아니야. 시간이 없어. 우리는 다른 거 타러 가야 해.
남 미안한데, 나는 뭐 좀 먹고 싶어.
여 알았어. 그럼 간단한 것을 먹자.
남 좋아! 고마워.
해설 롤러코스터가 재미있다고 하고 다른 놀이기구를 타기 전에 간단히
　　무언가를 먹자고 하고 있으므로 두 사람은 놀이공원에 있음을 알 수
　　있다.

12　언급되지 않은 것　| ③
해석
남 Grand Hotel에 오신 것을 환영합니다. TV 안내를 하겠습니다. 1번
　　에서는 우리 호텔이 제공하는 서비스에 대한 정보를 얻을 수 있습니다.
　　2번은 영화 채널입니다. 하루 24시간 방영합니다. 그리고 3번은 만화
　　입니다. 4번은 CNN 뉴스, 5번은 스포츠 채널입니다. 그리고 6번은
　　패션 채널입니다.
해설 Grand Hotel에서 방영되는 방송 프로그램으로 요리 프로그램은 언
　　급되지 않았다.

13　도표 정보 파악　| ③
해석
남 Emily, 이번 토요일에 바빠?
여 아니. 왜?
남 널 내 생일 파티에 초대하고 싶어. 와서 파티를 즐길 수 있겠니?
여 물론이지. 날 네 파티에 초대해 주어서 고마워. 파티는 어디에서 할 거야?
남 ABC 쇼핑몰 안에 있는 Happy 피자에서. Happy 피자가 어디에 있
　　는지 아니?
여 음. Rainbow 슈퍼마켓 옆에 있어?
남 아니. Jason 서점과 New York 빵집 사이에 있어.
여 알겠어, 찾을 수 있겠어. 파티는 몇 시니?
남 12시야. 토요일에 만나자.
해설 남자의 생일 파티는 Happy 피자에서 열리는데, Happy 피자의 위치
　　는 Jason 서점과 New York 빵집 사이라고 했다.

14　주제 파악　| ③
해석
남 자신의 가방을 들고 시장에 가세요. 그렇게 하면 당신은 상점들이 제공
　　하는 종이 가방이 필요하지 않을 겁니다. 만약 조그만 것을 사서 종이
　　가방이 필요치 않다면 "됐습니다."라고 말하세요. 그리고 그것을 손에
　　들고 가세요. 종이를 덜 사용하는 또 다른 방법이 있습니다. 화장지 대
　　신에 자신의 손수건을 사용하면 됩니다. 이것들은 종이를 절약하는 몇
　　몇의 좋은 방법들입니다.
해설 남자는 종이를 절약하는 방법에 대해 여러 예를 들어 설명하고 있다.

15　한 일 / 할 일 파악　| ②
해석
남 어디 가니, 유나야?
여 지은이의 생일 선물을 사러 가고 있어.

남 오! 나도. 난 책을 살까 생각하고 있어. 너는 어떠니?

여 실은, 나는 좋은 생각이 나질 않아. 너를 따라가서 서점에 좋은 물건이 있는지를 봐야겠어.

남 좋아. 그런데, 벌써 다섯 시야. 그녀의 선물을 사고 같이 저녁 먹지 않을래?

여 그래, 그럼 빨리 선물 구입을 끝내자. 엄마가 저녁 여섯 시까지는 돌아오라고 하셨어.

해설 여자는 대화 직후에 친구의 생일 선물을 사러 남자와 함께 서점에 가기로 했다.

16 특정 정보 파악 | ③

해석

남 Ann, 어딜 가는 중이니?

여 입원 중인 친구를 만나러 가는 중이야. 교통사고를 당했거든.

남 아, 그 말을 들으니 유감이야. 그가 괜찮기를 바라.

여 응. 너무 심각하지는 않아. 그에게 무엇인가를 사 주고 싶은데, 무엇을 사야 할지 모르겠어.

남 꽃을 좀 사 주는 게 어때?

여 음, 많은 병원에서 꽃을 허락하지 않는다는 말을 들었어.

남 흠… 그렇다면 책은 어때?

여 불행히도, 그는 책 읽는 것을 좋아하지 않아.

남 하지만 잡지 읽는 것은 좋아할지도 몰라.

여 네 말이 맞을지도 몰라. 그는 자동차를 좋아하니까 자동차에 관한 잡지를 사야겠어. 고마워.

해설 여자는 병원에 입원 중인 친구를 위해 자동차에 관한 잡지를 사겠다고 했다.

17 알맞은 응답 찾기 | ④

해석

여 Michael, 너 뭐 하니?

남 조리사 자격증 공부를 하는 중이야.

여 와. 너 요리에 관심이 있어? 몰랐네.

남 응. 그래. 내 꿈은 위대한 한식 조리사가 되는 거야.

여 시험이 언제야?

남 이번 일요일이야. 행운을 빌어 줘.

여 너에게 행운을 빌어 줄게.

① 내가 맛을 봐도 되겠니?

② 내가 시험에 합격하면 좋겠다.

③ 일요일의 시험은 매우 짜증이 나.

⑤ 불고기 만드는 법 아니?

해설 남자가 조리 자격증 시험을 앞두고 있는 상황에서 여자에게 행운을 빌어 달라고 했으므로 행운을 빈다고 말하는 ④가 여자의 응답으로 가장 적절하다.

18 알맞은 응답 찾기 | ④

해석

여 할아버지, 정원이 훨씬 좋아졌어요! 무척 좋아요!

남 고맙구나. Amy. 지난해에 그것이 어땠는지 기억나니?

여 물론, 기억나죠. 그것은 작은 돌로 가득 찬 황무지였어요.

남 그랬지. 내가 그 돌들을 제거했단다.

여 그러고 나서 이 채소와 나무를 정원에 심으셨군요.

남 응. 그랬지.

여 와, 할아버지께서는 정원 일을 정말 열심히 하셨어요.

남 그래. 난 아직도 아주 열심히 정원 일을 하고 있단다.

여 정말요? 요즘 얼마나 오래 정원 일을 하시나요?

남 하루에 5시간 넘게 한단다.

① 일주일에 한 번이나 두 번.

② 내가 정원 가꾸기를 좋아하기 때문이지.

③ 내게는 정원이 두 개 더 있단다.

⑤ 그 정원은 여기서 멀지 않아.

해설 여자가 남자에게 요즘에 정원에서 얼마나 오래 일하고 있는지 물었으므로 하루 5시간 이상이라고 말하는 ④가 남자의 응답으로 가장 적절하다.

19 알맞은 응답 찾기 | ③

해석

남 Lisa, 네 방이 너무 지저분하구나. 네 옷들은 왜 침대와 바닥에 놓여 있니?

여 제 방이 지저분하다는 것을 알지만, 그에 대해서는 이유가 있어요.

남 그게 뭐니?

여 옷을 위한 공간이 충분하지 않아요.

남 더 큰 방을 원한다는 뜻이니?

여 음, 아니에요. 옷장이 더 필요할 뿐이에요.

남 알겠어. 네게 옷장을 사 줄게. 하지만 네 옷을 모두 옷장에 넣어 두겠다고 약속하렴.

여 물론이죠. 저도 지저분한 방은 좋아하지 않아요.

① 옷장 옮기는 것을 도와드릴게요.

② 전 그렇게 생각하지 않아요. 제 방은 깨끗해요.

④ 고맙지만 사양할게요. 저는 옷이 더 필요하지 않아요.

⑤ 고마워요. 제 새 방이 매우 마음에 들어요.

해설 남자가 옷장을 사 주는 대신 옷을 옷장에 넣어 두겠다고 약속하라고 요구했으므로 자신도 지저분한 방을 좋아하지 않는다고 말하는 ③이 여자의 응답으로 가장 적절하다.

20 상황에 맞는 말 찾기 | ⑤

해석

여 Stewart는 Judy와 프랑스를 여행하고 있다. Judy는 프랑스어를 잘 해서, 그는 그녀에게 도움을 좀 받았다. 근사한 점심을 먹고 나서, 그는 주방장에게 '고맙다'는 말을 하고 싶었다. 하지만 그는 '고맙다'는 말을 프랑스어로 어떻게 말하는지 모른다. 이런 상황에서, Stewart는 Judy에게 뭐라고 말하겠는가?

Stewart 프랑스어로 '고마워.'를 어떻게 말하니?

① 내가 살게.

② 음식은 어땠니?

③ 프랑스어를 어떻게 배웠니?

④ 'Thank you'는 무슨 뜻이야?

해설 Stewart가 프랑스인 요리사에게 감사를 표하기 위해 Judy에게 프랑스어로 감사하다고 말하는 법을 물어보는 상황이므로 ⑤가 답으로 적절하다.

01 ②	02 ⑤	03 ⑤	04 ⑤	05 ⑤
06 ①	07 ④	08 ③	09 ④	10 ④
11 ②	12 ④	13 ⑤	14 ①	15 ③
16 ③	17 ③	18 ③	19 ④	20 ④

Dictation Test 04회　　pp. 032~037

01 ❶ draw a big square ❷ two triangles ❸ color the star black

02 ❶ Did you finish packing ❷ where to get on ❸ in front of

03 ❶ cross the street ❷ any traffic light ❸ turn red

04 ❶ submit your science report ❷ submit it on Friday ❸ yellow dust problem

05 ❶ our class newspaper ❷ other high schools ❸ publish your cellphone numbers

06 ❶ eye trouble ❷ wash your hands ❸ a sick note

07 ❶ Do you mind ❷ much better than ❸ looks so heavy

08 ❶ set the table ❷ I can help you ❸ open the windows

09 ❶ won first prize ❷ practiced jumping rope

10 ❶ six dollars fifty cents ❷ fifty cents more ❸ For here

11 ❶ I miss him ❷ putting up posters ❸ put some clear photos

12 ❶ It's three-day camp ❷ The fee ❸ is limited to

13 ❶ five booths available ❷ across from the restroom ❸ take the other one

14 ❶ talk with others ❷ search for information ❸ spend too much time

15 ❶ to prepare for ❷ about my grades ❸ change my clothes

16 ❶ start giving out ❷ sit in the front ❸ half past seven

17 ❶ having an interview ❷ never thought of giving up ❸ Thank you very much

18 ❶ My favorite subject ❷ an interesting subject ❸ like solving difficult problems

19 ❶ see a movie ❷ Why don't we ❸ What time

20 ❶ take a trip ❷ heavy snow ❸ are canceled

01　그림 정보 파악 - 그림 | ②

해석

여　먼저, 큰 정사각형 하나를 그려라. 그런 다음 오른쪽 위 모서리에서 왼쪽 아래 모서리로 직선을 그려라. 이제, 당신은 하나의 커다란 정사각형 안에 두 개의 삼각형을 갖고 있다. 삼각형 중 하나에 작은 별 하나를 그려라. 하지만 그 별은 어떤 다른 선과 닿아서는 안 된다. 마지막으로, 별이 모두 검은 색이 되도록 그것을 검은색으로 칠해라.

해설　큰 정사각형을 그리고 그 안에 오른쪽 상단 모서리에서 왼쪽 하단 모서리로 이어지는 대각선을 그린 후 다른 선에 닿지 않게 삼각형 안에 검은 별을 그린 그림은 ②이다.

02　목적 파악 | ⑤

해석

[전화벨이 울린다.]

여　여보세요?

남　여보세요, Kate. 나야, Chris.

여　안녕, Chris. 무슨 일이니?

남　내일 여름 캠프를 위해서 짐은 다 꾸렸니?

여　거의 다 했어. 캠프가 기대돼.

남　나도 그래. Kate, 캠프에 가는 버스를 어디서 타야 하는지 아니? 잊어버렸어.

여　아, 그래서 전화를 한 거였어? 우리는 어린이 도서관 앞에서 버스를 탈 거야.

남　알겠어. 고마워.

여　늦지 마. 버스는 9시에 출발해.

남　걱정하지 마. 늦지 않을게. 내일 만나.

해설　남자는 여자에게 여름 캠프 버스를 타는 곳을 묻기 위해 전화했다.

03　그림 상황에 어울리는 대화 찾기 | ⑤

해석

① 여　저 버스 탈거예요, 아빠?

　남　그래, 그럴 거야. 신호등이 녹색으로 바뀌면 길을 건너자.

② 여　저기 숫자가 안 보여요. 그거 보이세요, 아빠?

　남　물론 보이지. 네 시력이 굉장히 나빠졌구나.

③ 여　멈춰요, 아빠. 여기서 길을 건너면 안 돼요.

　남　아, '건너지 마시오.' 표지판을 보지 못했구나. 고마워.

④ 여　여기에 신호등이 왜 없는지 궁금해요.

　남　많은 사람들이 여기서 길을 건너기 때문에 꼭 있어야 하는데.

⑤ 여　아빠, 제가 길을 건널게요. 거기 계세요!

　남　뒤로 물러서! 신호등이 곧 빨간색으로 바뀔 거야.

해설　아이가 뛰어서 건널목을 건너가려고 하자 길 맞은편에 있는 아빠가 손을 내저으며 걱정스러워 하는 상황에 적절한 대화는 ⑤이다.

04　특정 정보 파악 - 요일 | ⑤

해석

남　미나, 과학 보고서를 제출했니?

여　응. 월요일에 제출했어.

남　잘했네. 넌 무엇에 대해서 썼니?

여　위험에 처한 동물들에 대해 썼어. 넌 제출했어?

남　아직 아니야. 금요일에 제출할 거야.

여　넌 무엇에 대해 쓰고 있니?

남　황사에 대해서 쓰고 있어.

여　흥미롭네. 행운을 빌어.

남　고마워.

해설　남자는 아직 보고서를 쓰고 있는 중이며 금요일에 제출할 것이라고 했다.

05 언급되지 않은 것 | ⑤

해석

남 Emma, 학급 모임은 잘됐니? 우리 학급 신문을 어떻게 만들 거니?

여 우리의 급훈과 두 개의 커다란 단체 사진, 그리고 선생님과의 인터뷰를 실을 생각이에요, Brown 선생님.

남 지금까지는 좋구나. 계속해 봐.

여 그리고 몇몇 고등학교에 대한 유용한 정보와 우리 휴대 전화번호도 넣을 거예요.

남 잠깐만. 신문에 너희들의 휴대 전화번호를 실어서는 안 돼. 개인정보를 알리는 것은 안전하지 않아.

여 아, 좋은 충고예요. 감사드려요.

해설 학급 신문에 실릴 내용으로 학급 소식은 언급되지 않았다.

06 관계 추론 | ①

해석

남 당신의 눈이 모두 빨개요. 눈을 크게 뜰 수 있나요? (잠시 후) 당신은 눈병에 걸린 것 같아요.

여 오, 안 돼. 제가 어떻게 해야 하죠?

남 하루에 세 번 눈에 안약을 넣으세요. 곧 괜찮아질 겁니다.

여 다른 것은요?

남 가능한 한 자주 비누로 손을 씻는 것이 아주 중요합니다.

여 고맙습니다, 이 선생님. 제가 당신에게서 진단서를 받을 수 있을까요? 저는 담임 선생님께 그것을 드려야 하거든요.

남 그럼요. 제가 하나 써 드릴게요.

해설 여자의 눈을 진단해 주며 눈 건강을 지키기 위한 방법을 알려 주는 것으로 보아 남자는 의사이고, 여자는 환자임을 알 수 있다.

07 어색한 대화 찾기 | ④

해석

① 남 내가 네 휴대 전화를 사용해도 될까?
　여 그럼. 그렇게 해.

② 남 네 새 아파트는 좀 어때?
　여 사실, 그게 내 옛날 집보다 훨씬 더 좋아.

③ 남 너는 무엇을 주문할 거니?
　여 피자를 생각 중이야.

④ 남 그거 너무 무거워 보이는구나. 도와줄까?
　여 물론이지. 내가 도와줄게.

⑤ 남 나는 중간고사에서 형편없는 성적을 받았어.
　여 실망하지 마. 다음에 더 잘할 수 있어.

해설 무거워 보인다며 도와줘도 되는지 물어보는 남자의 말에 대해 자신이 상대방을 도와준다고 대답하는 것은 어색하다.

08 부탁한 일 파악 | ③

해석

남 엄마, 이 스파게티 맛있어 보여요.

여 고마워. 원하면 좀 맛을 보렴.

남 좋아요. (잠시 후) 와, 정말 맛있네요. 이제 상을 차려도 될까요?

여 고맙지만, 아직 아니란다, Peter. 지금 샐러드를 만드는 중이거든. 상은 내가 차릴게.

남 그래요. 제가 도와드릴 수 있는 게 있나요?

여 흠… 창문을 열어서 환기를 시켜 줄래?

남 문제없어요.

여 고마워, Peter.

해설 여자는 남자에게 창문을 열어서 환기해 줄 것을 부탁했다.

09 의도 파악 | ④

해석

여 안녕, David. 나 줄넘기 대회에서 1등을 했어.

남 아, Amy. 축하해!

여 고마워. 운이 좋았던 것 같아.

남 아니, 난 그렇게 생각하지 않아. 넌 정말 열심히 연습했어, 그렇지 않니?

여 음, 그건 사실이야. 난 매일 줄넘기 연습을 했거든.

남 그러면 넌 상을 받을 자격이 있어.

여 그렇게 말해 줘서 고마워.

남 가서 아이스크림 먹으면서 축하하자.

해설 남자는 줄넘기 대회에서 1등을 한 여자를 축하하고 있다.

10 숫자 정보 파악 – 금액 | ④

해석

여 Buger World에 오신 걸 환영합니다. 무엇을 드실 건가요?

남 안녕하세요. 불고기버거 하나랑 작은 콜라 하나 부탁합니다.

여 그 밖에 다른 것이 필요하신가요?

남 괜찮습니다.

여 음, 불고기버거가 4달러 50센트이고 콜라 작은 게 2달러예요. 그러니까, 총 6달러 50센트네요. 그런데 50센트만 더 내시면 불고기버거와 중간 크기의 콜라 그리고 감자튀김이 포함된 불고기 세트를 주문하실 수 있어요.

남 정말요? 그러면, 세트로 할게요.

여 네. 여기서 드실 건가요, 아니면 가져가실 건가요?

남 여기서 먹을 겁니다.

해설 남자는 불고기버거($4.50)와 스몰 사이즈 콜라($2)를 주문했는데, 50센트를 더 내고 불고기 세트를 주문하겠다고 했으므로 7달러를 지불해야 한다.

11 한 일 / 할 일 파악 | ②

해석

남 Jenny, 왜 슬프니?

여 고양이가 오늘 아침에 달아나 버렸어.

남 그럴리가! 안됐다.

여 지금 어디에 있을까? 너무 보고 싶어.

남 기운을 내, Jenny. 틀림없이 곧 고양이를 찾을 거야.

여 고마워. 하지만 그를 찾기 위해서 무엇을 해야 할지 모르겠어.

남 동네에 포스터를 붙이는 게 어때?

여 좋은 생각이야. 당장 포스터를 만들어야겠다.

남 포스터에 선명한 사진들을 넣는 것을 잊지 마.

여 물론이지. 고마워.

해설 고양이를 잃어버려 슬퍼하고 있는 여자에게 남자는 포스터를 붙일 것을 조언했고, 여자는 당장 포스터를 만들겠다고 했다.

12 언급되지 않은 것 | ④

해석

남 안녕하세요, 학생여러분! 여러분은 이번 여름에 여러분의 축구 실력을 다음 단계로 높이고 싶은가요? 그렇다면 저희의 여름 축구 캠프에 참가하세요. 그것은 8월 2일부터 8월 4일까지 3일 간의 캠프입니다. 10세 이상의 남학생과 여학생이면 캠프에 참가할 수 있습니다. 수업료는 점심 식사 포함 단지 100달러입니다. 캠프는 50명의 참가자로 제한되어 있습니다. 그러니 후회하지 마시고 지금 등록하세요!

해설 여름 축구 캠프 준비물에 관해서는 언급되지 않았다.

13 　도표 정보 파악 ｜ ⑤

해석

여 Peter, 다음 주 벼룩시장에서 빌릴 수 있는 부스가 5개가 있어. 어떤 것이 우리에게 가장 좋을까?

남 우리가 작년에 화장실 옆에 있는 부스를 선택했잖아. 기억해? 좋지 않았어.

여 맞아. 이번에는 화장실 옆에 있는 부스를 선택하지 말자.

남 좋아. 화장실 맞은편에 있는 이 부스들 중 하나를 선택하는 것은 어때?

여 좋은 생각이야. 안내 부스 옆의 이것이 다른 하나보다 더 나아 보이는데. 네 생각은 어때?

남 난 그렇게 생각하지 않아. 안내 부스 옆의 구역은 너무 복잡할 거야. 그것 때문에 사람들이 우리 부스를 지나칠 수도 있어.

여 네 말이 맞을지도 몰라. 그럼 나머지 다른 곳으로 하자.

해설 두 사람은 화장실 옆의 구역은 선택하지 않겠다고 하면서 화장실 맞은편으로 선택하기로 했는데, 안내 부스 바로 옆은 너무 혼잡하므로 나머지 다른 것을 선택하기로 결정했으므로 두 사람이 선택한 구역은 E 이다.

14 　주제 파악 ｜ ①

해석

남 이것은 보통 조금 비싸다. 하지만 요즘, 이것을 사용하는 사람들의 수가 늘고 있다. 사람들은 이것으로 다른 사람들과 이야기하고 사진을 찍는 것을 좋아한다. 그들은 또한 이것을 통해서 정보를 검색하고 게임을 하는 것을 좋아한다. 하지만, 사람들은 이것을 사용하는데 너무 많은 시간을 소비하지 않아야만 한다.

해설 다른 사람들과 이야기할 수 있고 사진도 찍을 수 있으며 게임과 정보 검색도 가능한 것은 스마트폰에 관한 설명이다.

15 　한 일 / 할 일 파악 ｜ ③

해석

남 Parker 선생님, 제게 시간을 내 주실 수 있나요?

여 좋아. 나는 지금 시간이 된단다.

남 지금은 아니고요. 저는 다음 체육 시간을 준비해야 해서요. 점심시간에 시간 좀 있으신가요?

여 그럼. 그런데 무슨 일이니?

남 사실, 제 성적에 대해 선생님께 말씀드릴 게 있어요. 저는 정말 좋은 고등학교에 들어가고 싶거든요. 그런데 제 성적이 오르는 것 같지가 않아요.

여 낙담하지는 마. 내가 너를 도와줄 수 있겠구나.

남 감사해요. 오, 저는 다음 체육 시간 때문에 옷을 갈아입으러 가야만 해요.

여 그래. 그럼 점심시간에 보자.

해설 선생님과 상담을 요청한 남자는 일단 다음 체육 수업을 위해 옷을 갈아입으러 가야 한다고 했다.

16 　숫자 정보 파악 – 시각 ｜ ③

해석

남 마침내, 우린 이번 주 금요일에 '개그 콘서트'를 보러 가는구나.

여 그래, 아주 신나. 우리 몇 시에 만날까?

남 흠, 그들은 오전 9시에 무료 티켓을 나눠 주기 시작해. 그러니까 8시 30분에 만나는 게 어때?

여 글쎄, 어떤 사람들은 앞쪽 자리 티켓을 받기 위해서 오전 6시부터 기다리기 시작해. 나도 앞쪽에 앉고 싶어.

남 아침 6시에 거기 가고 싶다는 말이니?

여 아니, 그게 너무 이르다는 걸 나도 알아. 7시 30분은 어떨까?

남 그래. 그게 좋겠다.

해설 여자가 7시 30분에 만나자고 하자 남자가 이를 수락하고 있다.

17 　알맞은 응답 찾기 ｜ ③

해석

남 우리는 최고의 피겨 스케이팅 선수, 김연아 씨와 함께 인터뷰를 하고 있습니다. 당신은 언제 스케이트를 타기 시작했나요?

여 제가 7살 때 스케이트를 타기 시작했어요. 14살 때는 국가대표 선수로 뽑혔죠.

남 우와, 놀랍네요! 그만둘 생각을 한 적이 있습니까?

여 가끔, 지쳐요. 하지만 포기를 생각한 적은 없습니다.

남 꽤 인상적인데요. 당신의 팬들한테 한마디 하고 싶은 게 있나요?

여 연습이 완벽을 만듭니다, 여러분. 절대 포기하지 마세요.

남 오늘 인터뷰에 응해 주셔서 대단히 감사합니다.

여 <u>별말씀을요.</u>

① 물론이죠.

② 힘내세요!

④ 정말 그렇습니다.

⑤ 다음번에는 저는 그것을 놓치지 않을 거예요.

해설 남자가 인터뷰를 마치며 여자에게 감사의 말을 전하고 있으므로 괜찮다고 말하는 ③이 여자의 응답으로 가장 적절하다.

18 　알맞은 응답 찾기 ｜ ③

해석

여 Tony, 네가 가장 좋아하는 과목이 뭐니?

남 내가 가장 좋아하는 과목은 역사야.

여 아, 몰랐어. 너는 왜 역사를 좋아하니?

남 난 과거에 무슨 일이 일어났는지 그리고 과거의 사람들이 어떻게 살았는지 배우는 것을 좋아해.

여 역사는 흥미로운 과목이지.

남 보라, 네가 가장 좋아하는 과목은 뭐니?

여 알아 맞춰 봐. 그것은 숫자, 도형, 그리고 그래프 등을 다루는 거야. 난 어려운 문제를 푸는 것을 좋아해.

남 <u>넌 수학을 좋아하는 것 같구나, 그렇지?</u>

① 내가 그 문제를 풀게.

② 음, 난 역사를 잘 못해.

④ 난 내가 무슨 과목을 좋아하는지 모르겠어.

⑤ 네 시험공부를 내가 도와줄게.

해설 여자가 자신이 좋아하는 과목이 숫자, 도형, 그래프와 관련된 것이며 어려운 문제 푸는 것을 좋아한다고 했으므로 수학을 좋아하는 것 같다고 말하는 ③이 남자의 응답으로 가장 적절하다.

19 알맞은 응답 찾기 | ④

해석

여 매일 밤 TV보는 것이 싫증나. 나가서 영화나 보자.

남 좋은 생각이야. 무엇을 보러 갈까?

여 음, 우리는 대개 드라마물을 보잖아. 기분 전환으로 만화 영화를 보러 가는 것은 어때?

남 좋아. '마다가스카'가 어떨까?

여 좋아. 그 영화는 TTC 극장에서 상영하고 있어.

남 그 극장은 가깝잖아. 몇 시에 시작하지?

여 영화 상영시간표를 확인해 보자.

① 영화를 보는 게 나을 것 같아.

② 대신 축구하자.

③ 다음 주에 시간 있니?

⑤ 상영 시간은 약 2시간이야.

해설 남자가 여자에게 영화 시작 시간을 물어보고 있으므로 영화 상영시간표를 확인해 보자고 말하는 ④가 여자의 응답으로 가장 적절하다.

20 상황에 맞는 말 찾기 | ④

해석

여 Cindy는 아버지와 함께 제주도로 여행을 갈 것이다. 그녀는 처음으로 제주도를 가게 되어 매우 신난다. 내일 아침에 그들은 서울을 떠나 제주도로 가야 하지만 오늘 뉴스에서 제주도에 눈이 많이 온다고 전한다. Cindy의 아버지는 여행사로부터 전화를 받아 제주도로 가는 모든 비행편이 많은 눈 때문에 취소된다는 말을 듣는다. 그는 Cindy에게 이것에 대해 알려 주고자 한다. 이런 상황에서, Cindy의 아버지는 Cindy에게 뭐라고 말하겠는가?

Cindy의 아버지 우리는 눈이 많이 와서 제주도에 갈 수 없단다.

① 이번은 내게도 첫 제주도 여행이야.

② 나는 제주도 여행을 하게 되어 무척 신나.

③ 내일은 날씨가 무척 추울 거야.

⑤ 눈이 많이 오고 있으니까 집에 있는 편이 나아.

해설 눈이 많이 와서 비행 편이 취소되어 여행을 갈 수 없는 상황이므로 ④가 답으로 적절하다.

05회 영어 듣기모의고사   pp. 038~039

01 ⑤	**02** ③	**03** ④	**04** ②	**05** ③
06 ④	**07** ⑤	**08** ①	**09** ②	**10** ②
11 ④	**12** ③	**13** ⑤	**14** ④	**15** ②
16 ④	**17** ⑤	**18** ③	**19** ②	**20** ②

Dictation Test 05회   pp. 040~045

01 ❶ a pretty flower vase ❷ another vase ❸ black vase with white dots

02 ❶ I've lost my dog ❷ went out ❸ if we find it

03 ❶ a new chair ❷ where my teddy bear is ❸ reach my teddy bear

04 ❶ a new smartphone ❷ after school tomorrow ❸ how abut this evening

05 ❶ We are open ❷ Admission is ❸ No outside food

06 ❶ don't have the tickets ❷ where you put them ❸ they're gone

07 ❶ borrow your notebook ❷ pass next time ❸ win the cooking contest

08 ❶ our field trip ❷ take lots of pictures ❸ send them to me

09 ❶ miss your old friends ❷ We hung out together ❸ You may invite them

10 ❶ pick them up ❷ two blouses and one skirt ❸ skirts are four dollars

11 ❶ feeling a little bad ❷ go home ❸ get some sleep

12 ❶ our new product ❷ only the size of ❸ takes only one hour

13 ❶ Could you check ❷ no experience in teaching ❸ check both subjects

14 ❶ how to protect ❷ climbing mountains ❸ take a shower

15 ❶ feel like eating ❷ clean the bathroom instead ❸ when I come back

16 ❶ water ramen ❷ some snacks ❸ he has many chopsticks

17 ❶ cut myself by mistake ❷ I've never imagined

18 ❶ exchange it ❷ Did it work ❸ your receipt

19 ❶ I don't know anybody ❷ got the wrong number

20 ❶ a dance contest ❷ feels very thirsty ❸ she has any water

01 그림 정보 파악 – 사물 | ⑤

해석

남 Diana, 네 생일 선물을 여기에서 고르는 것 어때? 내가 하나를 사 줄게.

여 오, 고마워. 예쁜 꽃병을 하나 갖고 싶어.

남 꽃병들은 저쪽에 있어. 이 꽃무늬가 있는 것이 멋져 보이네.

여 그렇구나. 하지만 나는 현대적인 것을 원해.

남 그러면 이 체크무늬가 있는 이건 어때?

여 이미 하나 가지고 있어. 와, 저기 검은색 점이 있는 하얀색 꽃병은 환상적이다.

남 응. 동일한 디자인의 또 하나의 꽃병이 있네. 하지만 그것은 다른 색이야.

여 그게 훨씬 더 예쁘구나! 저 하얀색 점이 있는 검정색 꽃병을 살게.

해설 여자는 검은색 꽃병에 흰색 점이 있는 것을 구입한다고 했다.

02 목적 파악 | ③

해석

[전화벨이 울린다.]

남 구로 경찰서입니다. 어떻게 도와드릴까요?

여 안녕하세요. 제 개를 잃어버렸어요.

남 언제, 어디에서 잃어버리셨나요?

여 한 시간 전에 저희 집에서요. 열린 문으로 개가 나가버렸어요.

남 그렇군요. 어떻게 생겼나요?

여 흰색이고 작아요. 청으로 된 옷을 입고 있어요.

남 알겠습니다. 찾으면 연락드리죠.

해설 여자는 애완견 분실 신고를 하기 위해 경찰서에 전화를 했다.

03 그림 상황에 어울리는 대화 찾기 | ④

해석

① 남 엄마, 저 새 의자가 필요해요. 제 것은 너무 낡았어요.

　 여 난 그렇게 생각하지 않아, 얘야. 그것은 그다지 낡지 않았어.

② 남 제 곰 인형이 어디에 있는지 아세요?

　 여 거실 선반 위에서 보았던 것이 기억나.

③ 남 제 로봇이 망가졌어요. 어떻게 해야 할까요?

　 여 걱정하지 마. 널 위해 내가 그것을 고쳐 줄게.

④ 남 선반에 있는 제 곰 인형에 손이 닿지 않아요. 엄마가 내려 주실래요?

　 여 물론이지. 내가 내려 줄게.

⑤ 남 엄마, 저 곰 인형이 갖고 싶어요.

　 여 그건 너무 비싸. 더 저렴한 것을 찾아보자.

해설 그림은 높은 선반 위에 있는 곰 인형에 남자아이의 손이 닿지 않는 상황이므로 가장 적절한 대화는 ④이다.

04 특정 정보 파악 – 요일 | ②

해석

[휴대 전화가 울린다.]

남 안녕, Stella. 무슨 일이니?

여 난 새 스마트폰을 살 거야. 하지만 너도 알다시피 난 전화기에 대해 잘 몰라.

남 네가 스마트폰 사는 것을 도와주길 원하니?

여 그러면 좋을 것 같아. 내일 방과 후에 한가해?

남 아니. 내일은 친구들과 야구를 할 거야. 우리는 매주 수요일마다 만나거든. 목요일에 만나는 건 어때?

여 목요일에는 바이올린 수업이 있어.

남 그렇다면 오늘 저녁에 만날래?

여 물론이지. 6시에 ABC 쇼핑몰에서 만나.

남 그래. 곧 보자.

해설 두 사람은 오늘 저녁에 만나기로 했는데 내일이 수요일이므로 오늘은 화요일이다.

05 언급되지 않은 것 | ③

해석

여 Dolphin 수족관에 오신 것을 환영합니다. 저희와 함께 물 속 생명의 경이로움을 발견하세요. 저희는 월요일부터 토요일까지 오전 9시부터 오후 8시까지 문을 열고 일요일에는 휴무입니다. 입장료는 어른은 25달러, 15세 미만의 어린이는 20달러입니다. 10명 이상의 단체는 1인당 2달러의 할인을 받을 수 있습니다. 어떠한 외부 음식이나 음료수도 허용되지 않습니다. 돌고래를 방해할 수 있으므로 돌고래가 쉬고 있을 동안 돌고래 사진을 찍는 것을 자제해 주세요. 협조해 주셔서 감사합니다.

해설 Dolphin 수족관의 편의 시설에 대해서는 언급되지 않았다.

06 심정 파악 | ④

해석

여 무슨 일이야?

남 나한테 표가 없어.

여 네 말은 표를 잃어버렸단 거니? George, 2시 30분이야. 기차는 30분 후에 떠날 거야! 내게 그것들을 받은 후에 어디에 두었는지 기억하지 못하니?

남 물론, 기억하고 있지.

여 자, 돌이켜 생각해 봐.

남 난 그것들을 내 재킷의 주머니에 넣어 두었어. 그런데 지금은 사라졌어.

해설 남자는 열차 출발 30분 전에 티켓을 잃어버린 상황이므로 당황스러울 것이다.

07 어색한 대화 찾기 | ⑤

해석

① 여 네 공책 좀 빌려도 될까?

　 남 응, 이번 주에 꼭 돌려 줘야 해.

② 여 나 영어 말하기 시험에서 떨어졌어.

　 남 포기하지 마. 다음번에는 통과할 거야.

③ 여 나 두통이 너무 심해.

　 남 병원에 가 보지 그래?

④ 여 칠판이 너무 지저분하다.

　 남 같이 청소하자.

⑤ 여 Greg이 요리 경연 대회에서 우승할 것 같아.

　 남 모든 게 내 잘못이야.

해설 Greg가 요리 경연 대회에서 우승할 것 같다는 말에 대해 모두 내 실수라고 대답하는 것은 어색하다.

08 부탁한 일 파악 | ①

해석

남 Alice, 오늘이 우리 수학여행의 마지막 날이야. 난 그것을 믿을 수가 없어.

여 나도 그래. 내일이면 우리는 학교에 돌아갈 것이고 중간고사는 다음 주야.

남 아, 여기서 더 오래 머무르면 좋겠다.

여 나도 그래. 그런데 Chris, 여기서 사진 많이 찍었니?

남 그래. 너도 내 사진들 중 일부에 있어.

여 정말? 지금 내게 보내 줄 수 있어?

남 물론이지. 버스에 탄 후에 보내 줄게.

여 고마워.

남 아, 지금 버스를 탈 시간이야. 가자.

해설 여자는 남자가 찍은 사진들 중에서 자신이 들어 있는 사진을 보내 달라고 부탁했다.

09 의도 파악 | ②

해석

여 Chris, 우리가 여기로 이사 온 지 한 달이 되었구나. 너의 새로운 학교 생활은 어떠니?

남 지금까지는 좋아요. 친구들도 많이 사귀었고요.

여 그 말을 들으니 좋구나. 네 옛 친구들은 그립지 않니?

남 물론 그립죠. 우리는 거의 매일 함께 어울려서 놀았어요.

여 기억나. 그들을 이곳에 초대하는 것이 어떠니?

남 정말이요? 그들을 다시 만나고 싶어요.

여 네가 원할 때면 언제라도 그들을 초대해도 좋아.

해설 여자의 마지막 말 You may ~.는 '~해도 좋다'라는 의미로 허락을 나타내는 표현이다.

10 숫자 정보 파악 - 금액 | ②
해석
남 안녕하세요. 도와드릴까요?
여 이 옷들을 드라이클리닝하고 싶어요.
남 그것들을 언제 찾아가고 싶으세요?
여 내일 저녁에 찾으러 와도 괜찮을까요?
남 알겠습니다. 해 보겠습니다. 자, 무엇을 가지고 오셨죠?
여 블라우스 두 장과 치마 한 장입니다. 얼마일까요?
남 블라우스는 한 벌에 2달러 50센트이고, 치마는 한 벌에 4달러입니다.
여 알겠습니다. 여기 있어요.
해설 여자는 블라우스 2개($2.50×2=$5)와 스커트 1개($4)를 드라이클리닝 맡기고 있으므로 총 9달러를 지불해야 한다.

11 한 일 / 할 일 파악 | ④
해석
남 이봐, Mary, 너 괜찮니? 조금 조용한 것 같아.
여 글쎄, 몸이 조금 안 좋은 것 같아.
남 그거 안됐구나. 내일 하루 쉬는 게 어떻겠니?
여 아침에 수업이 있어.
남 수업은 빠지렴. 내가 따라잡을 수 있도록 도울게.
여 고마워, Eric. 어쨌든 오늘은 그냥 집에 가서 잠을 좀 잘 거야.
해설 여자의 마지막 말에서 여자는 오늘 휴식을 취할 것임을 알 수 있다.

12 언급되지 않은 것 | ③
해석
남 안녕하세요, 여러분. 오늘 저는 여러분께 저희의 새로운 제품인 Genie Smart Speaker에 대해 말씀드리겠습니다. Genie Smart Speaker로 여러분은 정보를 찾을 수 있고, 음악을 들을 수 있습니다. 이것은 사과의 크기만 합니다. 그것은 2킬로그램에 불과합니다. 그것은 리모컨이나 음성으로 제어될 수 있습니다. 배터리를 충전하는 데 시간이 오래 걸리지 않습니다. 완전히 충전하는데 겨우 1시간밖에 걸리지 않습니다.
해설 Genie 스마트 스피커의 색깔에 대해서는 언급되지 않았다.

13 도표 정보 파악 | ⑤
해석
남 Rebecca, 나 학원 선생님 자리에 지원했어. 내 영문 이력서 좀 확인해 줄래? 내일 제출할 거거든.
여 알겠어. 네 이름 박도훈은 철자가 맞게 쓰였고, 너는 남자고, 네 휴대 전화 번호는 100-9123-4567이고.
남 응, 그리고 나는 가르쳐 본 경험이 없어.
여 알겠어. 그런데 너 중국어도 잘 하지 않니?
남 잘해. 하지만 나는 오직 하나의 상자에만 체크하게 되어 있는 줄 알았어.
여 그렇게 쓰여 있지 않은데. 네가 두 과목에 체크하면, 그들은 너를 더 뽑고 싶어 할 거야.
남 알았어. 도움을 줘서 고마워.
해설 남자는 영어와 중국어 모두 잘하므로 영어와 중국어 둘 다에 체크하기로 했다.

14 주제 파악 | ④
해석
여 오늘 위험한 곤충들에 의한 큰 피해가 또 있었습니다. 산행 시, 스스로를 보호하는 방법을 말씀드리겠습니다. 먼저, 긴 소매 옷과 긴 바지를 입으세요. 둘째, 돗자리 없이 풀밭에 앉지 마세요. 셋째, 곤충을 쫓을 크림이나 스프레이를 준비하세요. 마지막으로, 집에 오자마자 샤워를 하세요.
해설 여자는 산행 시 벌레를 예방하는 방법에 대해 설명하고 있다.

15 한 일 / 할 일 파악 | ②
해석
여 나는 장보러 가려고. 저녁에 무엇을 먹고 싶니?
남 음, 나는 오늘 크림 파스타를 먹고 싶은데.
여 그래. 내가 만들어 줄게.
남 원한다면 같이 갈 수 있는데.
여 대신에 화장실 청소를 좀 해 줄래?
남 문제없어. 내가 물도 끓여 놓을까?
여 아니. 내가 돌아와서 할 수 있어.
남 그래. 안전하게 운전해.
해설 남자는 여자에게 같이 쇼핑 갈 것을 제안했지만 여자는 그 대신 남자에게 화장실 청소를 부탁했다.

16 특정 정보 파악 | ④
해석
여 자, 우리 캠핑에 필요한 모든 것들을 카트에 담았니?
남 그런 것 같아. 목록을 다시 한 번 확인해 보자.
여 좋아. 물, 라면, 종이컵, 그리고 간식을 좀 샀어.
남 인스턴트 밥은 필요하지 않니?
여 아니. 내가 거기 가서 밥을 지을 수 있어.
남 하지만 일이 너무 많아질 것 같다고 생각하지 않니?
여 음, 그러네. 인스턴트 밥도 좀 사자. 젓가락은?
남 민우가 젓가락 많이 가지고 있다고 했어. 그건 그가 가져올 거야.
여 좋아.
해설 친구가 젓가락을 많이 갖고 있어서 젓가락은 구입하지 않기로 했다.

17 알맞은 응답 찾기 | ⑤
해석
여 아야!
남 무슨 일이야?
여 나 손가락을 베였어.
남 어떻게 하다가?
여 양파 자르다가 실수로 베였어.
남 아프겠다. 내가 뭐 도와줄까?
여 응. 밴드 좀 가져다줄래? 서랍 맨 위 칸에 있어.
남 그럴게. 네가 손을 벨 줄은 상상도 못 했네. 칼질에 전문가잖아.
여 **나도 마찬가지야. 더 조심했어야 했는데.**
① 그것은 맨 위 칸에 없어.
② 네일숍에 가야만 해.
③ 내 대신 다른 양파들을 잘라 줘.
④ 약국은 길 건너편에 있어.
해설 도마질 전문가인 여자가 양파를 자르다가 다친 것을 믿을 수 없다고 말하는 상황이므로 자신도 믿을 수 없다며 좀 더 주의해야 했다고 말하는 ⑤가 여자의 응답으로 적절하다.

18 | 알맞은 응답 찾기 | ③

해석

여 안녕하세요. 저는 딱 일주일 전에 여기에서 이 손목시계를 샀는데요. 벌써 작동이 되지 않아요. 새 것으로 교환하고 싶습니다.

남 정말이요? 구입하셨을 때에는 작동이 되던가요?

여 네, 몇 분 느리긴 했지만요.

남 건전지는 점검하셨나요?

여 네, 확실히 하려고 새 것으로 갈아 넣었습니다.

남 좋습니다. 영수증을 보여 주세요.

여 여기 있습니다.

남 좋습니다. 새 시계로 드릴게요.

① 그것을 착용해 보시겠습니까?

② 현금으로 하시겠어요, 아니면 신용카드로 하시겠어요?

④ 당신은 건전지를 바꿔야 할 것 같아요.

⑤ 죄송하지만, 우리는 그것에 할인을 해 드릴 수 없어요.

해설 여자가 시계를 교환하기 위해 남자에게 영수증을 건네 준 상황이므로 여자에게 새 시계를 주겠다는 ③이 남자의 응답으로 가장 적절하다.

19 | 알맞은 응답 찾기 | ②

해석

[전화벨이 울린다.]

남 여보세요?

여 여보세요, Michael? 내일 파티에 올 수 있니? 우리 집에서 열려.

남 주소가 뭐야?

여 너도 알다시피, East Street 13번지야.

남 음, 난 그 주소에 사는 사람은 하나도 몰라.

여 어, 전화 받은 분은 Michael Williams 아닌가요?

남 아니에요, 전 Michael Adams랍니다. 아무래도 전화를 잘못 거신 것 같군요.

여 귀찮게 해서 죄송합니다.

① 글쎄요, 문제되지 않습니다.

③ 저녁을 먹으러 그곳에 갈까요?

④ 전 다른 약속이 있습니다.

⑤ 당신의 시간을 뺏고 싶지 않군요.

해설 여자가 전화를 잘못 건 상황이므로 방해해서 죄송하다고 말하는 ②가 여자의 응답으로 가장 적절하다.

20 | 상황에 맞는 말 찾기 | ②

해석

여 Lisa는 댄스 대회에 출전하고 있다. 이번은 그녀가 댄스 대회에 처음 출전하는 것이다. 그녀는 다른 학생들이 춤을 매우 잘 추는 것을 본다. 그녀는 곧 무대에 올라갈 것이다. 그녀는 너무나 긴장이 된다. 그녀는 매우 목이 마르다고 느낀다. 그녀는 물을 찾지만 찾을 수 없다. 그녀는 자신의 어머니에게 물을 갖고 있는지 묻고 싶다. 이런 상황에서, Lisa는 자신의 어머니께 뭐라고 말하겠는가?

Lisa 물 있으세요?

① 제가 우승했다는 것을 믿을 수 있으세요?

③ 무대를 같이 쓸 수 있을까요?

④ 춤추는 것을 가르쳐 주실 수 있으세요?

⑤ 제가 당신을 위해 물을 갖다 드려도 될까요?

해설 댄스 대회 무대에 오르기 전에 목이 마른 Lisa가 어머니께 물을 갖고 있는지 묻는 상황이므로 Lisa가 어머니께 할 말로 적절한 것은 ②이다.

06회 영어 듣기모의고사 　　pp. 046~047

01 ④	02 ⑤	03 ②	04 ②	05 ⑤
06 ②	07 ①	08 ②	09 ⑤	10 ⑤
11 ②	12 ②	13 ③	14 ②	15 ⑤
16 ④	17 ⑤	18 ①	19 ①	20 ⑤

Dictation Test 06회 　　pp. 048~053

01 ❶ round or rectangular ❷ prefer a heart ❸ what I want

02 ❶ your membership card ❷ need to do ❸ enter your student number

03 ❶ removing those books ❷ clean the floor ❸ It's coming from

04 ❶ We have to ❷ our future jobs ❸ the nearby hospital

05 ❶ Let me tell you ❷ improve their reading ability ❸ Participation is free

06 ❶ a great painter ❷ draw everything ❸ look at my paintings

07 ❶ is larger ❷ lost your books ❸ eats insects for food

08 ❶ see a doctor ❷ exercise with me ❸ Let's play badminton

09 ❶ wanted to join ❷ Why don't you apply ❸ Just call

10 ❶ add this pen ❷ give you change

11 ❶ for tomorrow's picnic ❷ wear for tomorrow ❸ them for the picnic

12 ❶ a cat as a pet ❷ sugary treats ❸ lose a lot of hair

13 ❶ see a play ❷ cheaper ones ❸ opens early

14 ❶ a lot of resources ❷ can't leave them ❸ save them

15 ❶ beginning to snow ❷ meeting with a client ❸ call her to inform

16 ❶ dental clinic closes ❷ if it is open ❸ around six thirty

17 ❶ is dying ❷ gets enough sunshine ❸ watered it less

18 ❶ on my math test ❷ won't believe it ❸ the highest score

19 ❶ had it yesterday ❷ are very delicious ❸ to eat them

20 ❶ is still washing the dishes ❷ Unless they leave home ❸ late for the concert

01 그림 정보 파악 – 사물 | ④

해석

남 안녕하세요. 시계를 하나 사려고 하는데요. 시계 좀 보여 줄 수 있나요?

여 물론이죠. 원형과 직사각형 시계 중 어느 것을 더 좋아하시나요?

남 음, 직사각형보다는 원형을 더 좋아합니다.

여 잘 알겠어요. 그러면 꽃무늬가 있는 이 시계는 어떠세요?

남 저는 꽃은 싫어요. 저는 하트가 하나 있는 게 더 좋습니다.

여 좋아요. 그러면 이것은 어때요?

남 좋네요! 그게 바로 정확히 제가 원하던 것입니다. 그걸 할게요.

해설 남자는 하트가 중앙에 있는 둥근 시계를 원한다고 했다.

02 목적 파악 | ⑤

해석

[전화벨이 울린다.]

여 안녕하세요. 저는 Viva 도서관의 Christine Williams입니다. 어떻게 도와드릴까요?

남 안녕하세요. 회원 카드를 신청하고 싶습니다.

여 네. 학생이세요?

남 네. 저는 중학생입니다. 저는 회원 카드를 신청하고 싶습니다. 무엇을 해야 하죠?

여 저희 도서관이나 웹사이트 둘 중 하나를 방문하시기만 하면 됩니다. 학생 번호를 웹사이트에 입력해야만 합니다. 여기서 등록하려면 카드를 갖고 오세요.

남 감사합니다. 먼저 웹사이트에서 시도해 볼게요.

해설 남자는 회원 카드 신청 방법을 문의하기 위해 도서관에 전화했다.

03 그림 상황에 어울리는 대화 찾기 | ②

해석

① 남 여기 무척 덥네요. 에어컨 켰어요?

　여 아니요, 안 켰어요. 제가 켤게요.

② 남 제 방이 너무 지저분해요. 그래서 청소기로 청소할 거예요.

　여 청소기로 청소하기 전에 저 책들을 먼저 치우는 게 어때?

③ 남 엄마 대신 제가 설거지를 할게요.

　여 괜찮아. 대신에 바닥 청소를 해 줄래?

④ 남 이 책들을 반납하러 도서관에 갈 거예요.

　여 그래. 저녁 식사에 늦지 마.

⑤ 남 이 소음을 참을 수가 없어요. 어디에서 나는 거죠?

　여 밖에서 나는 거야. 아이들이 놀고 있거든.

해설 남자가 청소기로 방을 청소하려고 하고 있고 여자는 책으로 어질러진 바닥을 가리키고 있는 상황에 가장 적절한 대화는 ②이다.

04 장소 추론 | ②

해석

여 Peter, 우리 영어 숙제에 대해 이야기 하자.

남 좋아. 우리의 미래 직업에 대해 써야 하지, 그렇지?

여 그래. 우리가 미래에 갖고 싶은 직업을 갖고 있는 누군가와의 인터뷰를 포함해야 해.

남 좋아. 먼저 우리의 미래 직업에 대해 이야기해 보자. 너는 미래에 무엇이 되고 싶니?

여 난 의사가 되고 싶어. 넌 어때?

남 음, 난 어렸을 때는 경찰관이나 소방관이 되기를 원했어. 하지만 지금은 간호사가 되고 싶어.

여 잘됐네! 그럼 근처 병원에 가서 그곳의 의사와 간호사를 인터뷰하자.

남 좋은 생각이야! 내일 Peterson 종합 병원에서 만나.

해설 장래 희망이 의사와 간호사인 두 사람은 의사와 간호사를 인터뷰하기 위해 병원에서 만나기로 했다.

05 언급되지 않은 것 | ⑤

해석

여 주목해 주세요. 여러분께 저희의 여름 독서 프로그램에 관해 말씀드리겠습니다. 그것은 국립 어린이 도서관에서 개최될 것입니다. 그 프로그램은 어린이들과 10대들의 읽기 능력 향상을 위한 것입니다. 그것은 3월 10일에 시작하여 5월 10일에 끝납니다. 참가는 무료입니다. 등록은 2월 20일에 시작되며 선착순입니다. 그러니 등록하는 데 너무 늦지 마세요.

해설 여름 독서 프로그램의 참가 인원수에 대해서는 언급되지 않았다.

06 직업 및 장래 희망 | ②

해석

남 Ross 씨, 안녕하세요. 전시회가 정말 좋았어요.

여 와 주셔서 감사합니다. 그 말을 들으니 기쁘군요.

남 저는 당신처럼 훌륭한 화가가 되고 싶은 학생이에요. 그런데 저는 재능이 있는 것 같지가 않아요. 어떻게 해야 하죠?

여 그냥 당신의 꿈을 향해 열심히 연습하고, 눈에 보이는 모든 것들을 그리세요.

남 알겠습니다. 그럼. 제 그림을 나중에 한번 봐 주실 수 있으세요? 저는 제 그림이 좋은지 아닌지 모르겠어요.

여 물론이죠. 여기 제 명함이 있습니다. 이 번호로 전화 주세요.

남 그럴게요. 정말 감사합니다.

해설 남자가 여자와 같이 멋진 화가가 되고 싶다고 말하고 있으므로 여자의 직업은 화가이다.

07 어색한 대화 찾기 | ①

해석

① 여 캐나다와 중국 중에 어느 것이 더 크다고 생각하니?

　남 나는 이번에는 캐나다에 가 보고 싶어.

② 여 저쪽에 있는 여자아이 알지, 그렇지 않니?

　남 그래. 그녀는 우리 이웃이야.

③ 여 네가 책을 잃어버렸다니 안됐다.

　남 모두 내 잘못이야. 내 사물함을 잠갔어야 했는데.

④ 여 새로 오신 과학 선생님에 대해서 어떻게 생각하니?

　남 매우 똑똑하신 것 같아.

⑤ 여 이 식물은 먹이로 곤충을 먹어.

　남 우와! 아주 흥미로운데.

해설 캐나다와 중국 중에서 어떤 국가가 더 큰지 묻는 질문에 이번에 캐나다를 방문하고 싶다고 대답하는 것은 어색하다.

08 부탁한 일 파악 | ②

해석

남 보라, 안색이 안 좋아 보여.

여 요즘 굉장히 피곤한데, 왜 그런지 모르겠어.

남 병원에는 가 봤니?

여 응. 하지만 의사 선생님은 내 건강이 괜찮아 보인다고 말씀하셨어.

남 그럼 규칙적으로 운동을 해 보는 건 어때?

여　나 혼자서 규칙적인 운동을 할 수 있을지 자신이 없어. 나와 함께 운동을 해 줄 수 있어?

남　물론이지. 매일 방과 후에 배드민턴 치자.

여　고마워.

해설　규칙적으로 운동을 권하는 남자에게 여자는 혼자 운동할 자신이 없다고 하면서 함께 운동을 해 달라고 부탁했다.

09　의도 파악　| ⑤

해석

남　Mary, 뭐 보고 있어?

여　영화 동아리 포스터를 보고 있어. 이 동아리에 가입하고 싶었는데.

남　무슨 말이야?

여　나는 지원하는 것을 잊어서, 포기했어.

남　음, 마감일까지 아직 하루 남았잖아. 지금 이 동아리에 지원하지 그러니?

여　하지만 내가 너무 늦은 것 같아. 이 포스터에 의하면 선착순이잖아.

남　혹시 알아? 그냥 포스터에 있는 전화번호로 전화해 봐.

해설　남자는 선착순이라 영화 동아리에 가입하지 못할 것을 걱정하는 여자에게 동아리에 한번 전화해 보라고 제안하고 있다.

10　숫자 정보 파악 - 금액　| ⑤

해석

여　이것들은 얼마죠?

남　펜 두 개와 필통 한 개. 4,800원입니다.

여　여기 5,000원이요. 오, 잠깐만요. 이 펜을 지금 더해도 되나요? 이건 얼마예요?

남　물론 되시죠. 그건 1,200원입니다. 저한테 1,000원을 더 주시면, 거스름돈 안 드려도 되겠네요.

여　좋아요. 여기 1,000원이요.

남　감사합니다.

해설　2개의 펜과 1개의 필통을 구입하여 4,800원을 지불해야 하는데 여자는 1,200원의 펜을 하나 더 구입했으므로 6,000원을 지불해야 한다.

11　한 일 / 할 일 파악　| ②

해석

남　엉망이로구나! 민지야, 뭐 하니?

여　아빠, 내일 소풍에 입을 것이 없어요. 새 옷을 사야겠어요.

남　말도 안 돼. 너는 이렇게 옷이 많은데. 아직도 더 필요하니?

여　아빠는 이해 못 해요. 아, 내일 뭐 입어야 하지?

남　이 셔츠와 저 바지가 잘 어울리는구나. 그것들을 입도록 해. 그리고 지금 이 방을 좀 치우렴.

여　오, 전 소풍 때 그것들을 입고 싶지 않아요. 하지만 방은 치울게요.

해설　여자는 내일 소풍 갈 때 입을 옷을 고르다가 방을 어지럽혔다.

12　언급되지 않은 것　| ②

해석

남　여러분은 고양이를 좋아하세요? 만약 당신이 고양이를 애완동물로 키우기로 결심했다면, 당신이 먼저 생각해야 하는 몇몇의 것들이 있습니다. 대부분의 사람들은 고양이가 조용하다고 생각하지만, 사실 많은 고양이들은 꽤 시끄럽습니다. 또한, 고양이들에게 아이스크림과 사탕과 같은 단 음식을 주어서는 안 됩니다. 그것은 심각한 건강 문제를 야기할 수 있습니다. 여러분은 또한 대부분의 고양이가 물건을 긁는 버릇이 있다는 것을 이해할 필요가 있습니다. 마지막으로, 많은 고양이들이 일

년 내내 많은 털이 빠집니다. 이러한 점들을 고양이를 가족으로 받아들이기 전에 신중하게 생각해 주세요.

해설　고양이의 평균 수명은 언급되지 않았다.

13　도표 정보 파악　| ③

해석

여　이번 일요일에 뭐 할 계획이니?

남　나는 연극을 볼 계획이야.

여　좋은 생각이다. 같이 가도 되니?

남　좋아. 이게 내가 생각하고 있는 연극 목록이야. 어떤 게 더 좋으니?

여　음, 나는 저렴한 게 더 좋아. 8,000원이 좋아 보여.

남　좋아. 그럼 두 연극 중에서, 나는 일찍 여는 게 더 좋아. 나는 오후에는 숙제를 해야 해서.

여　문제없어. 그럼 이번 일요일 오전 8시에 만나자.

남　그래. 난 벌써 신나.

해설　두 사람은 티켓 가격이 8,000원인 연극 중에 일찍 시작하는 연극을 보기로 했다.

14　주제 파악　| ②

해석

남　지구에는 많은 사람들이 있습니다. 사람들의 수는 점점 더 많아지고 있습니다. 그들은 지구의 많은 자원들을 사용하고 있습니다. 만약 계속한다면 우리는 우리의 아들, 딸들에게 그것들을 남겨 주지 못할 수 있을 겁니다. 이제, 우리가 그것들을 절약하기 위해 무언가를 해야 할 때 입니다.

해설　인구수가 늘어나면서 자원이 부족해지는 것을 우려해서 자원 절약을 독려하고 있다.

15　한 일 / 할 일 파악　| ⑤

해석

여　눈이 내리기 시작하네요.

남　우리는 눈이 내리기 전에 출발했어야 했어요. 길이 얼어서 제시간에 맞출 수 있을 만큼 빨리 달릴 수가 없어요.

여　고객과의 중요한 회의에 늦겠어요. 어떻게 해야 하죠?

남　다행히, 제가 휴대 전화를 가져왔어요. 그녀에게 전화해서 가고 있는 중이라고 알릴게요.

여　좋은 생각이에요.

해설　눈이 많이 와 고객과의 회의에 늦을 것을 걱정하는 남자는 고객에게 전화를 걸 것이다.

16　숫자 정보 파악 - 시각　| ④

해석

여　김 선생님 치과가 언제 닫는지 아니?

남　글쎄, 확실치 않아. 왜?

여　학원 마치고 치과에 가고 싶은데, 그때 여는지 잘 모르겠어.

남　학원이 몇 시에 끝나는데?

여　오늘 수업이 하나 더 있어서, 수업이 5시 50분에 마쳐. 6시 30분쯤에 거기에 도착할 수 있을 것 같아.

남　음, 치과가 언제 닫는지는 모르지만, 6시 30분에는 열어. 전에 6시 40분에 그곳에 갔었는데, 여전히 열려 있었어.

여　잘됐다. 그럼, 시간이 충분해.

해설　여자는 치과에 6시 30분에 도착할 수 있다고 했다.

17 알맞은 응답 찾기 | ⑤

해석

여 왜 그 화분을 보고 있어?

남 내 장미가 죽어 가고 있어. 내가 뭘 잘못했는지 모르겠어.

여 그것을 어디에 두었는데?

남 바로 여기, 침실 창가 구석에. 햇볕은 충분히 쬐었을 거야.

여 얼마나 자주 물을 주었니?

남 매일 아침에.

여 음, 내 생각에는 물을 덜 줬어야 했을 것 같아.

남 그거 확실하니?

여 응. 너는 이틀마다 물을 줘야 했어.

① 그것은 모두 내 잘못인 것 같아.

② 그것은 날 슬프게 해.

③ 네가 맞다고 확신해.

④ 음, 미안하지만 나는 네 의견에 동의할 수 없어.

해설 남자가 장미에 물을 적게 주는 것이 확실한지 묻는 질문에 대해 격일로 물을 줘야 한다고 말하는 ⑤가 여자의 응답으로 가장 적절하다.

18 알맞은 응답 찾기 | ①

해석

여 아빠, 저 왔어요.

남 Emma, 너 무척 기분 좋아 보여. 오늘 학교에서 좋은 일이라도 있었던 거야?

여 네. 수학 시험을 정말 잘 봤거든요.

남 와, 그 말을 들으니 무척 기뻐.

여 믿지 못하실 거예요. 95점을 받았거든요.

남 정말 잘했구나. 축하해! 많이 향상되었어.

여 고마워요. 반에서 가장 높은 성적이에요.

남 네가 정말 자랑스럽구나.

② 난 수학을 잘 못해.

③ 낙담하지 마.

④ 넌 최선을 다하지 않았어.

⑤ 함께 수학 공부를 하자.

해설 딸이 수학 시험에서 95점을 받아 학급에서 최고 점수를 받았다는 말에 대해 정말 자랑스럽다고 말하는 ①이 남자의 응답으로 가장 적절하다.

19 알맞은 응답 찾기 | ①

해석

여 David, 저녁 먹으러 오렴.

남 엄마, 저는 안 먹어도 돼요. 지금 막 컵라면을 먹었거든요.

여 또? 너는 어제도 그거 먹었잖아. 네가 그걸 왜 그렇게 좋아하는지 모르겠다.

남 인스턴트 면은 아주 맛있잖아요. 저는 매일 그것을 먹을 수 있을 것 같아요.

여 그건 맛있지만, 건강에 안 좋아.

남 오, 일주일에 한 번은 먹어도 괜찮죠?

여 미안하지만, 그건 안 돼.

② 뉴스에서 들었어요.

③ 그거 좋은 소식인 것 같네요.

④ 저는 그걸 또 먹을 계획이에요.

⑤ 저는 즉석 식품에 매료됐어요.

해설 남자가 일주일에 한 번이라도 컵라면을 먹게 해 달라고 부탁하는 말에 대해 그럴 수 없다고 거절하는 ①이 여자의 응답으로 가장 적절하다.

20 상황에 맞는 말 찾기 | ⑤

해석

여 Judy는 어머니와 함께 자신이 가장 좋아하는 가수의 콘서트에 갈 것이다. 그 콘서트는 8시에 시작하는데 지금 이미 7시이다. 하지만 그녀의 어머니는 여전히 설거지를 하고 있고 서두르는 것처럼 보이지 않는다. 그들이 10분 이내에 집을 나서지 않는다면, 그들은 콘서트에 늦을지도 모른다. Judy는 어머니께 그것에 대해 말씀드리고 싶다. 이런 상황에서, Judy는 그녀의 어머니께 뭐라고 말하겠는가?

Judy 우리는 곧 나가야 해요, 그렇지 않으면 늦을 거예요.

① 그것은 제가 지금까지 본 콘서트 중 최고였어요.

② 8시쯤 집에 오겠다고 약속할게요.

③ 죄송하지만, 전 그 콘서트를 이미 봤어요.

④ 저는 음악을 듣는 것보다 영화를 보는 것을 더 좋아해요.

해설 어머니에게 10분 이내에 집을 나서지 않으면 콘서트에 늦을지도 모른다는 사실을 상기시켜 드려야 하므로 ⑤가 답으로 알맞다.

07회 영어 듣기모의고사 pp. 054~055

01 ①	02 ④	03 ①	04 ①	05 ④
06 ①	07 ④	08 ⑤	09 ②	10 ②
11 ②	12 ②	13 ②	14 ③	15 ⑤
16 ①	17 ①	18 ①	19 ①	20 ④

Dictation Test 07회 pp. 056~061

01 ❶ have a hot dog ❷ drink a Coke with ice ❸ get you everything

02 ❶ wondering if you know ❷ forgot to return them ❸ might have been upset

03 ❶ can sit here ❷ How often do you ❸ a free performance

04 ❶ finish another homework assignment ❷ The due date ❸ to this Thursday

05 ❶ a notebook ❷ take pictures of wildflowers ❸ to bring a hat

06 ❶ Not yet ❷ have been busy preparing ❸ I had more time

07 ❶ A piece of cake ❷ couldn't do it ❸ did a great job

08 ❶ problem with this watch ❷ is not correct ❸ can't read the manual

09 ❶ checked the weather forecast ❷ making a campfire ❸ make sure you don't leave

10 ❶ for the same price ❷ can't I get them

01 그림 정보 파악 – 사물 | ①

해석

여 여보, 나는 버터와 사과잼을 바른 토스트를 조금 먹을 거예요. 당신은 무엇을 먹을 거예요? 같은 것으로 먹기를 원하나요?

남 아니요, 나는 케첩을 바른 핫도그를 먹을 거예요.

여 마실 건요?

남 음. 얼음을 넣은 콜라를 마시고 싶어요. 당신은 어때요?

여 저는 커피를 마실 거예요. 좋아요, 여보. 그냥 여기에 있어요. 내가 당신이 원하는 모든 것을 가져다줄게요.

남 오, 정말 고마워요.

해설 남자는 얼음이 든 콜라와 핫도그를 먹는다고 했다.

02 목적 파악 | ④

해석

[전화벨이 울린다.]

남 수정아, 안녕. 무슨 일이니?

여 안녕, Michael. 네가 Sarah의 휴대 전화번호를 알고 있는지 궁금해서.

남 응. 110-2134-5678이야. 이유를 물어봐도 될까?

여 내가 오늘 허락도 없이 그녀의 교과서를 사용하고 그걸 돌려주는 걸 잊어버렸어.

남 너는 미안하다고 말하지 않니?

여 그러려고 했지만 그녀가 방과 후에 바로 떠나버렸어.

남 오, 그녀가 화가 났을 것 같아. 그녀에게 전화해서 미안하다고 말해.

여 응. 당장 전화할게.

해설 친구에게 책을 빌렸다가 돌려주지 못한 여자는 남자에게 친구의 전화번호를 묻기 위해서 전화했다.

03 그림 상황에 어울리는 대화 찾기 | ①

해석

① 여 실례합니다. 이 자리에 주인이 있나요?
　 남 아니요, 앉으셔도 되요.

② 여 어떤 운동을 가장 좋아하니?
　 남 나는 야구를 가장 좋아해.

③ 여 너 일어나서 집에 가지 그러니?
　 남 아마도 그래야 할 것 같아.

④ 여 얼마나 자주 버스를 타고 학교에 가니?
　 남 나는 절대 버스를 타고 학교에 가지 않아.

⑤ 여 티켓을 사야 하니?
　 남 아니, 그럴 필요 없어. 그건 무료 공연이야.

해설 여자가 야구장에서 자리를 가리키며 남자에게 말을 거는 상황에 적절한 대화는 ①이다.

04 특정 정보 파악 – 요일 | ①

해석

여 오늘 학교 마치고 함께 역사 보고서 쓰자.

남 미안하지만, 안 돼. 나는 이번 금요일까지 또 다른 숙제를 마쳐야 해. 나는 보고서를 이번 토요일에 쓸 거야.

여 그건 너무 늦을 거야. 보고서 마감일이 이번 목요일이잖아.

남 뭐라고? 다음 월요일 아니었어?

여 잠깐만, 너 어제 결석했었지, 맞지? Brown 선생님께서 마감일을 이번 목요일로 옮기셨어.

남 알겠어. 알려 줘서 정말 고마워.

여 천만에.

해설 여자의 두 번째 말을 통해 남자의 보고서 제출일이 다음 주 월요일에서 이번 주 목요일로 변경되었다는 것을 알 수 있다.

05 언급되지 않은 것 | ④

해석

남 여러분, 알다시피, 우리는 내일 체험학습을 갑니다. 우리는 가능한 한 많은 야생화들을 찾아볼 겁니다. 여러분들은 공책과 펜이 필요하고, 각 조마다 카메라도 필요할 겁니다. 수업시간에 우리가 함께 읽었던 야생화에 관한 책을 가져오는 것을 잊지 마십시오. 우리는 그 책을 사용해 우리가 발견하는 꽃들의 이름을 찾아볼 것입니다. 우리는 야생화 사진을 찍을 것이고, 여러분들은 체험학습 이후에 그 사진들을 가지고 보고서를 써야 합니다. 야외에 오랫동안 있을 것이기 때문에, 모자를 가져오면 좋겠습니다. 내일 뵙겠습니다.

해설 체험학습의 준비물로 야생화 사진은 언급되지 않았다.

06 심정 파악 | ①

해석

남 지우야, 내일 발표 준비 다 되었니?

여 아직이야. 게다가 상황이 그다지 좋지는 않아.

남 어째서?

여 내일이 엄마 생신이어서 내 남동생과 함께 깜짝 파티를 준비하느라 바빴거든.

남 오, 너는 분명히 바빴겠구나.

여 응. 그래서 나는 발표 준비가 안 되어 있어.

남 하지만 내일 있을 발표도 또한 네 성적에 아주 중요해.

여 알아. 시간이 더 있었으면 좋겠다. 내가 무엇을 해야만 하지?

해설 여자는 엄마의 깜짝 생일 파티를 준비하느라 바빠서 발표 준비를 소홀했다며 내일 있을 발표를 걱정하고 있다.

07　어색한 대화 찾기　| ④

해석

① 남　너의 새 소파는 어떠니?
　여　음, 정말 편안해.
② 남　식은 죽 먹기라고? 그건 무슨 의미니?
　여　그건 아주 쉬운 일이라는 의미야.
③ 남　우리 방과 후에 영화 보러 가지 않을래?
　여　미안, 나 오늘 집에 일찍 가야 돼.
④ 남　난 경주에서 이기려고 최선을 다했지만 그러지 못했어.
　여　축하해! 너 참 잘했어.
⑤ 남　너 밖에 나갈 때 불을 끄는 것을 꼭 확인해.
　여　그래, 그것을 명심할게.
해설 경주를 이기기 위해 노력했지만 이길 수 없었다고 하는 말에 대해 축하한다고 대답하는 것은 어색하다.

08　부탁한 일 파악　| ⑤

해석

남　너 지금 바쁘니? 나 조금만 도와줘. 이 시계에 문제가 있어.
여　그래. 이 시계 멋져 보인다. 그거 샀니?
남　응, 나 이거 어제 샀는데, 아직 찰 수는 없어. 시간이 맞지 않아.
여　고장 났어? 환불해 달라고 해.
남　아니, 나는 단지 이 설명서를 읽을 수가 없어. 전부 일본어로 되어 있어. 네가 일본어를 전공했다고 들었어. 이걸 내게 읽어 줄 수 있니?
여　물론 할 수 있지. 그거 내게 줘 봐. 내가 정확한 시간 맞추는 것을 도와줄게.
해설 남자는 여자에게 일본어로 된 시계 설명서를 읽어 줄 것을 부탁하고 있다.

09　의도 파악　| ②

해석

여　너 캠핑에 필요한 모든 것을 꾸리는 것을 끝냈니?
남　네, 끝냈어요. 저 갈 준비 다 됐어요. 엄마.
여　내가 금방 일기 예보를 확인했는데 너 걱정할 필요 없겠더라. 날씨가 완벽할 거야.
남　오, 정말요?
여　너희들 밤에 모닥불을 피울 거니?
남　네. 저희가 바비큐 파티를 할 거거든요.
여　불을 피울 때는 조심해야 해. 그리고 어떤 쓰레기도 남겨 둬서는 안 된다는 것을 명심하렴.
해설 여자는 마지막 말 Be careful ~.에서 캠프파이어를 하고 잔여물을 남기지 않을 것을 당부하고 있다.

10　숫자 정보 파악 – 금액　| ②

해석

남　실례합니다. 이것을 교환할 수 있을까요?
여　영수증이 있으세요?
남　네, 여기 있어요.
여　음, 30달러짜리 티셔츠를 사셨네요. 같은 가격이면 어떤 거라도 가지실 수 있어요.
남　이 청바지는 얼마인가요?
여　45달러입니다.

남　오, 그럼 안 되는 건가요?
여　아니에요, 15달러를 추가로 더 내시면 가질 수 있으세요.
남　정말요? 그럼 그걸 사겠어요.
해설 남자는 티셔츠를 청바지로 교환하면서 15달러를 추가로 지불한다고 했다.

11　장소 추론　| ②

해석

남　실례지만, 네가 Carrie니?
여　네, 당신은 Dave 삼촌이시군요.
남　와우, 너 정말 많이 컸구나. 사진이 없었다면 널 알아볼 수 없었을 거야. 다행히 네 엄마가 어제 네 사진을 내게 보내 주었지. 가족들 모두 잘 지내시지?
여　네, 모두 잘 지내세요. 엄마가 안부 전해 달라고 하셨어요.
남　네 가족 모두 다 보고 싶다. 그런데, 비행은 어땠니? 너무 오래 걸린 건 아니고?
여　오래 걸렸지요. 하지만 괜찮아요. 제 생전 처음으로 외국에 와서 매우 행복해요.
해설 남자가 여자에게 비행이 어땠냐며 오래 걸리지는 않았는지 묻고 있으므로 두 사람이 대화하는 장소는 공항이라는 것을 알 수 있다.

12　언급되지 않은 것　| ②

해석

여　주목해 주시겠어요? 저는 오늘의 상담 프로그램에 대해 다시 한 번 말씀 드리고 싶네요. 오늘 10개의 다른 고등학교에서 선생님들이 오십니다. 그분들은 여러분이 알고 싶어 하는 유용한 정보들을 주실 거예요. 그것은 점심시간 직후인 2시에 시작해서 6시에 끝날 겁니다. 프로그램은 강당에서 열릴 거예요. 가서 여러분이 입학하고 싶은 고등학교에 대한 정보를 들으세요.
해설 상담 프로그램의 참가비에 대해서는 언급되지 않았다.

13　도표 정보 파악　| ②

해석

남　너 어느 방과 후 수업을 들을 거야?
여　나는 오후 다섯 시 오십 분에 마치는 수업을 들을 거야.
남　그럼 너는 월요일과 수요일의 수업 중에서 하나를 고르겠구나.
여　맞아. 나는 A302호에서 하는 수업을 들어야 할 것 같아.
남　그거 좋다. 그거 바로 너희 교실 옆에 있잖아.
여　바로 그거야. 나는 서두를 필요가 없을 거야. 너는 뭐 들을 건데?
남　나는 코딩 수업 들을까 생각 중이야.
여　그럼 그 수업이 같은 시간에 마치네. 수업 마치고 집에 같이 가자.
남　좋은 생각이야.
해설 여자는 오후 5시 50분에 끝나고 A302호에서 하는 수업을 듣겠다고 했으므로 고급 수학 수업을 선택할 것이다.

14　주제 파악　| ③

해석

남　이것은 다양한 양념을 첨가하여 채소로 만든 전통적인 한국 반찬입니다. 이것은 대개 배추나 무로 만들어집니다. 사람들은 이것을 찌개, 부침개 혹은 볶음밥을 만드는 데 사용합니다. 오래 전에 사람들은 이것을 항아리에 담고 몇 달 동안 땅 속에 보관했습니다. 하지만 오늘날 사람들은 그 대신에 특수 냉장고를 사용합니다.

해설 주로 배추와 무로 만들어지고 예전에는 항아리에 담아 지하에 보관했던 전통적인 한국 반찬은 김치이다.

15 한 일 / 할 일 파악 | ⑤
해석
남 안 돼. 또 비가 온다. 오늘도 자전거 타러 못 가겠네.
여 네가 자전거 타러 나간 지 꽤 되었지.
남 더 이상은 못 기다리겠어. 나는 비옷을 입고 자전거를 탈 거야.
여 그건 너무 위험할 거야. 길이 매우 미끄럽고, 네가 잘 볼 수도 없잖아.
남 네가 옳아. 아마 그냥 실내 체육관에서 운동이나 해야 할 것 같아. 하지만 나는 혼자 운동하는 것을 좋아하지 않는데.
여 그럼 나랑 체육관에 배드민턴 치러 가지 않을래?
남 그거 좋다. 지금 가자.
해설 남자는 비가 와서 자전거를 못 타게 되자 여자랑 체육관에서 배드민턴을 치기로 했다.

16 특정 정보 파악 | ①
해석
여 도와드릴까요, 손님?
남 제 아들이 중학교를 졸업해서 선물을 찾고 있습니다.
여 십대들은 새 시계나 새 운동화를 좋아해요.
남 사실 그 애가 최근에 둘 다 이미 샀어요. 이 모자나 선글라스는 인기가 있나요?
여 아니요, 그것들은 십대들한테 인기가 없어요. 새 가방을 사 주시는 것은 어떤가요? 이것이 신상품이고, 저렴해요.
남 멋져 보여요. 이걸로 할게요.
해설 남자의 마지막 말을 통해 남자는 중학생 아들의 졸업 선물로 가방을 살 것을 알 수 있다.

17 알맞은 응답 찾기 | ①
해석
여 핼러윈은 어땠어, Daniel?
남 괜찮았어. 친구들과 함께 "과자를 안 주면 장난칠 거예요."라고 외치면서 마을을 돌아다녔어.
여 재밌었겠다. 옷도 차려 입었니?
남 응, 나는 드라큘라처럼 옷을 입었어.
여 그것을 봤다면 좋았을 텐데.
남 너는 어때? 핼러윈 어땠어, 미선아?
여 한국에는 핼러윈이 없지만 나는 외국 친구들 몇 명과 함께했어. 나한테는 이번이 처음이었어.
남 그랬어? 그래서 어땠는데?
여 **무척 재미있었지.**
② 그들은 그것을 좋아하지 않았어.
③ 나는 바지보다 치마가 더 좋아.
④ 여행은 중요한 교훈을 줘.
⑤ 나는 핼러윈을 경험한 적이 없어.
해설 남자가 핼러윈데이가 어땠는지 여자에게 물어본 상황이므로 즐거웠다고 답하는 ①이 여자의 응답으로 가장 적절하다.

18 알맞은 응답 찾기 | ④
해석
여 이봐, Jim! 너 오늘 안 좋아 보인다.

남 내가 태권도 시험에서 검은 띠 획득에 실패했거든.
여 그 소식을 들어 유감이다. 이번이 처음이었니?
남 아니, 사실 나 전에 세 번 실패한 적이 있어. 어떻게 하지?
여 많은 일 때문에 아마도 충분히 연습하지 못했겠지.
남 사실이야. 하지만 나는 내가 그다지 태권도에 재능이 있다고 생각하지 않아.
여 포기하지 마! 다음번에는 합격할 거야.
남 **그렇게 말해 줘서 고마워.**
① 천만에.
② 그 소식을 들어서 유감이다.
③ 나는 네 도움이 필요하지 않아.
⑤ 나는 태권도를 배우고 싶어.
해설 태권도 승급 시험에서 떨어진 남자에게 여자가 다음에는 꼭 통과할 수 있을 거라고 말한 상황이므로 그렇게 말해 줘서 고맙다고 말하는 ④가 남자의 응답으로 가장 적절하다.

19 알맞은 응답 찾기 | ①
해석
남 안녕하세요, 무언가를 찾고 계신가요?
여 네, 청바지를 좀 찾고 있어요.
남 요즘에는 사람들이 스키니진을 많이 좋아하는 것 같아요. 여기 있는 이것들 중에 하나를 한 번 입어 보시는 건 어떠세요?
여 글쎄요, 저는 스키니진을 좋아하지 않아요. 너무 꽉 조이거든요.
남 그렇다면, 제가 이 헐렁한 청바지를 추천해 드릴게요.
여 오, 마음에 들어요.
남 게다가 당신이 한 벌을 사면, 공짜로 한 벌을 더 받을 수 있어요.
여 **좋은 거래이군요.**
② 정말 슬픈 이야기네요!
③ 저는 헐렁한 청바지를 싫어해요.
④ 너무 비싸네요.
⑤ 청바지는 제가 제일 좋아하는 거예요.
해설 바지를 사러 간 여자에게 점원인 남자가 바지 하나를 사면 다른 바지 하나를 무료로 준다고 알려 준 상황이므로 좋은 거래라고 말하는 ①이 여자의 응답으로 가장 적절하다.

20 상황에 맞는 말 찾기 | ④
해석
남 Mark는 영화를 보기 위해 Jane을 만났다. 하지만, 그녀는 계속 기침을 했다. 그는 Jane에게 감기에 걸렸는지 물었고, 집에 쉬러 가도 된다고 말했다. Jane은 그녀가 감기에 걸린 것은 아니고 그녀가 단지 마실 것이 좀 필요한 것이라고 말했다. Mark는 그녀에게 음료를 사 주러 가고 싶었지만, 그녀가 정확히 무엇을 원하는지 몰랐다. 이런 상황에서, Mark는 Jane에게 뭐라고 말하겠는가?
Mark 어떤 종류의 음료를 원하니?
① 음료 잘 마셔.
② 내가 너를 집에 데려다줄게.
③ 나 오늘 몸이 좀 안 좋아.
⑤ 너는 하루에 커피를 몇 잔 마시니?
해설 Jane이 계속 기침을 하는 상황에서 마실 것이 필요하다고 했으므로 Jane에게 어떤 음료를 원하는지 묻는 ④가 답으로 적절하다.

01 ①	02 ①	03 ③	04 ⑤	05 ③
06 ⑤	07 ⑤	08 ④	09 ④	10 ①
11 ⑤	12 ⑤	13 ①	14 ②	15 ⑤
16 ②	17 ⑤	18 ④	19 ④	20 ④

Dictation Test 08회   pp. 064~069

01 ❶ designed a cup ❷ two holes on the handle ❸ for the teaspoon

02 ❶ can't make it ❷ having eye trouble ❸ go to the hospital

03 ❶ because of this stone ❷ could have fallen ❸ Watch your step

04 ❶ come with me ❷ on Wednesdays and Fridays ❸ be okay in the evening

05 ❶ as a second language ❷ as an important foreign language

06 ❶ looks like an angel ❷ rather cold-hearted ❸ have a boyfriend already

07 ❶ Turn off ❷ a bottle of milk ❸ I'm busy

08 ❶ is getting married ❷ play the violin ❸ next month

09 ❶ saw your work ❷ very impressive ❸ a talented painter

10 ❶ tip the waitress ❷ We kept waiting for ❸ I'll leave

11 ❶ with some close friends ❷ see the play ❸ with my family

12 ❶ free English camp ❷ the native English teacher ❸ read storybooks

13 ❶ this graduation party ❷ We can take Subway

14 ❶ draw a straight line ❷ with numbers ❸ in their pencil cases

15 ❶ not my bag ❷ a name tag ❸ a telephone number

16 ❶ for my skin ❷ this body cream ❸ take it

17 ❶ uses my belongings ❷ Have you told her ❸ angry at you

18 ❶ to have lunch ❷ Let's go there ❸ let me introduce her

19 ❶ write a report ❷ check out the book ❸ return it today

20 ❶ the washing machine ❷ the first time ❸ his mom's help

01   그림 정보 파악 - 사물 | ①

해석

남 나 최근에 컵을 하나 디자인했어.

여 오, 정말? 어떻게 생겼는데?

남 손잡이에 구멍이 두 개 있어. 하나는 위에 그리고 다른 하나는 아래에.

여 왜 손잡이에 구멍을 만들었니?

남 티스푼을 위해 만들었어. 이 컵을 사용하면 지저분한 탁자 위에 티스푼을 올려놓지 않아도 돼.

여 와! 넌 천재야.

해설 손잡이에 두 개의 구멍이 있어 티스푼을 꽂을 수 있는 컵은 ①이다.

02   목적 파악 | ①

해석

[전화벨이 울린다.]

여 여보세요.

남 안녕, Sarah야. 나는 Simon이야. 미안한데 나는 오늘 약속을 못 지킬 것 같아.

여 왜 못 지켜?

남 나는 눈병에 걸렸어.

여 안됐구나. 어쩌다가 눈병에 걸렸니?

남 어제 수영장에 갔었어. 거기에서 눈병에 걸린 것 같아.

여 의사의 진찰을 받으러 가 봤니?

남 아직. 점심 먹고 병원에 가 보려고.

해설 남자는 눈병에 걸려서 약속을 취소하려고 여자에게 전화를 걸었다.

03   그림 상황에 어울리는 대화 찾기 | ③

해석

① 여 제 차가 이 돌 때문에 앞으로 가지를 않아요.

　 남 제가 돌을 치워 보죠.

② 여 이 석상은 돌로 만들어졌나요? 정말 아름답군요.

　 남 틀렸어요. 그건 금속으로 만들어졌어요.

③ 여 조심해. 땅에 돌이 있어.

　 남 오! 넘어질 뻔 했네.

④ 여 해변에 아름다운 돌들이 많다.

　 남 원하면 그것들 중 하나를 가져가.

⑤ 여 발을 조심해. 페인트가 아직 마르지 않았어.

　 남 말해줘서 고마워.

해설 남자아이가 돌에 걸려 넘어질 뻔한 것을 여자가 주의를 주는 상황에 적절한 대화는 ③이다.

04   특정 정보 파악 - 요일 | ⑤

해석

여 네 손목시계 마음에 든다. 어디에서 났니?

남 남대문 시장에서 샀어.

여 나도 거기에 가고 싶다. 나랑 같이 가 줄 수 있니?

남 물론이지. 이번 주 수요일에 거기에 가는 것 괜찮니?

여 나 수요일과 금요일에는 피아노 수업이 있어. 토요일은 어때?

남 음, 나는 토요일에 약속이 있어. 하지만 저녁에는 괜찮을 거야.

여 좋아. 그럼 오후 7시에 보자.

해설 남자가 토요일엔 약속이 있지만 저녁엔 괜찮다고 했으므로 남자와 여자는 토요일 저녁에 만나기로 했다.

05 언급되지 않은 것 | ③
해석

여 세계에는 영어를 사용하는 나라들이 많이 있다. 미국, 캐나다, 영국과 호주는 사람들이 영어를 제1언어로 사용하는 국가들이다. 그리고 영어는 인도, 싱가포르, 케냐, 필리핀, 그리고 다른 많은 국가들에서 제2언어로 사용된다. 한국과 러시아와 같은 다른 나라들에서는 사람들이 중요한 외국어로서 영어를 배운다.

해설 영어가 제2언어인 나라로 러시아는 언급되지 않았다.

06 심정 파악 | ⑤
해석

남 Rebecca, 저쪽에 있는 저 소녀 예쁘다고 생각하지 않니?

여 누구? 흰 블라우스에 빨간색 바지를 입은 사람?

남 응. 천사처럼 보인다. 그녀는 성격도 좋을 거라고 확신해.

여 흠…. 나는 그녀가 천사처럼 아름답다고 생각하지 않아. 게다가, 그녀는 다소 냉담한 편이야.

남 그녀를 알고 있니?

여 응. 그녀는 우리 오빠 여자 친구야.

남 아, 안 돼. 그녀에게 이미 남자 친구가 있단 말이야?

여 안타깝게도.

해설 남자가 마음에 든 여자에게 남자 친구가 있다는 말을 듣고 실망했을 것이다.

07 어색한 대화 찾기 | ⑤
해석

① 여 에어컨을 좀 꺼 주실래요?
　남 너무 덥지 않나요?

② 여 학교에 늦지 않았니?
　남 저는 오늘 학교에 안 가요.

③ 여 집에 오는 길에 우유 한 병을 사다 줄래?
　남 좋아. 다른 것은?

④ 여 내 휴대 전화가 어디에 있어?
　남 내가 어떻게 알겠니?

⑤ 여 제 머리를 잘라야 한다고 생각하나요?
　남 전 오늘 오후에 바빠요.

해설 머리를 잘라야 할지 묻는 상대방의 말에 대해 자신이 오늘 오후에 바쁘다고 하는 대답은 어색하다.

08 부탁한 일 파악 | ④
해석

남 소진아, 부탁을 좀 해도 될까?

여 뭔데?

남 우리 담임 선생님이 곧 결혼하셔. 우리 반 애들이 결혼식을 위한 축가를 준비하고 있거든. 그래서 우리가 노래 부르는 동안 네가 바이올린을 켜줄 수 있니?

여 그러길 원하지만, 난 할 수 없어. 나는 바이올린 경연 대회까지 얼마 남지 않아서.

남 경연 대회가 언제인데?

여 다음 주야.

남 그러면, 그건 문제가 안 될 거야. 우리 선생님의 결혼식은 다음 달이야.

여 오, 잘됐다.

해설 남자는 여자에게 담임 선생님의 결혼식에서 바이올린을 연주해 줄 것을 부탁하고 있다.

09 의도 파악 | ④
해석

남 어제 나는 졸업 전시회에 가서 네 작품을 보았어.

여 정말이세요? 마음에 드셨나요?

남 매우 인상적이었단다. 정말로 네가 직접 그 그림을 그렸니?

여 네. 그 작품을 완성하는 데 정말 오랜 시간이 걸렸어요.

남 너는 재능 있는 화가가 될 것 같구나.

여 고맙습니다. 김 선생님. 그렇게 말해 주시다니 정말 친절하시군요.

해설 남자의 마지막 말 I think you will be ~.에서 여자가 재능 있는 화가가 될 것이라며 칭찬하고 있다.

10 숫자 정보 파악 – 금액 | ①
해석

남 여종업원에게 팁을 얼마나 줘야 하지?

여 10달러는 줘야지.

남 그건 너무 많아. 우리 50달러 나온 계산서의 20%잖아. 20%는 우리가 받은 서비스에 비하면 너무 많아. 우리는 그녀가 너무 느려서 음식을 계속 기다렸어.

여 음, 알아. 하지만 분명히 그녀도 친절한 서비스를 제공하기 위해 노력했을 거야.

남 나는 네 말에 동의하지 않아. 10%를 주겠어.

해설 남자는 음식 가격인 50달러의 10%를 팁으로 줄 것이라고 했다.

11 한 일 / 할 일 파악 | ⑤
해석

여 이번 주말에 뭐 할 거니?

남 토요일에는 친한 친구들과 테니스를 치고, 친구의 생일 파티에 갈 거야.

여 그럼 일요일에는?

남 공원으로 자전거를 타러 갈 거야. 너는 어때?

여 토요일 저녁에는 가족들과 연극 '햄릿'을 볼 거야. 일요일에는 숙제를 해야 해.

남 좋은 계획이구나.

해설 여자의 세 번째 말을 통해 여자는 토요일 저녁에 가족과 연극을 보러 간다는 것을 알 수 있다.

12 언급되지 않은 것 | ⑤
해석

남 방학 동안 당신의 영어를 향상시키고 싶나요? 겨울 영어 캠프에 합류하세요! 그것은 즐겁게 영어를 배울 수 있는 무료 영어캠프입니다. 선생님은 우리 학교의 영어 원어민 선생님이신 Anna Thomson 선생님입니다. 여러분은 Anna 선생님과 함께 노래 부르고, 게임을 하고, 이야기책을 읽을 겁니다. 3주간의 캠프를 통해 여러분의 영어가 상당히 향상될 거예요.

해설 겨울 영어 캠프의 수업 장소에 대해서는 언급되지 않았다.

13 도표 정보 파악 | ①
해석

여 너는 이번 졸업 파티에 참석할 거니?

남 파티가 언제인데? 나는 10월 25일에 약속이 있어.

여 26일 오후 4시야.
남 좋아. 그 파티는 어디에서 하니?
여 파티 하우스에서 있을 거야. 지하철 2호선을 타면 돼. 그리고 회비는 1만원이야.
남 알겠어. 그때 보자.
해설 졸업 파티는 10월 26일에 열린다.

14 주제 파악 | ②
해석
남 이것은 여러분이 직선을 그리기 원할 때 당신에게 필요한 무엇이다. 당신은 이것으로 사물의 길이를 측정할 수 있다. 이것은 사이즈가 다양하고, 많은 다양한 색상이 있다. 하지만, 이것은 보통 얇고 납작하며 넓은 막대로 숫자가 그 위에 쓰여 있다. 숫자가 써진 부분은 대부분 투명해서, 당신은 그것을 통해서 볼 수 있다. 많은 학생들은 이것을 그들의 필통에 넣어 다니므로, 여러분도 하나 가지고 있을지도 모른다.
해설 길이를 재고 직선을 그을 때 필요하며 숫자가 쓰여 있는 납작하고 얇은 막대는 자이다.

15 한 일 / 할 일 파악 | ⑤
해석
여 이봐, Nick! 집에 가는 길이니? 나랑 같이 가자.
남 그래. 오, 잠깐! 이거 내 가방이 아니네.
여 정말? 어떻게 그런 일이 일어났지?
남 아마 내가 실수로 다른 누군가의 가방을 가져왔나봐.
여 누구 가방인데? 이름표나 어떤 거라도 있니?
남 오, 그래. 전화번호가 적힌 이름표가 있어. 네 전화기를 써도 될까?
여 어서 써.
해설 남자는 가방의 이름표를 발견하고 주인에게 전화하기 위해 여자에게 휴대폰을 빌렸다.

16 특정 정보 파악 | ②
해석
남 도와드릴까요?
여 저는 샤워 후 피부에 바를 것이 필요합니다.
남 이 바디 로션은 어떠세요? 이것은 요즘 매우 인기가 있습니다.
여 제 피부는 매우 건조해서, 저는 크림을 선호합니다.
남 그러면 저는 이 바디 크림을 추천합니다.
여 이거 써 봐도 되나요?
남 물론이죠. 써 보세요. 그것은 향이 매우 좋아요.
여 네, 그러네요. 이걸로 할게요.
남 같은 향의 립밤이나 샴푸가 있습니다. 그것들도 한 번 써 보시겠어요?
여 아니오, 괜찮아요. 그것들은 다음에 써 볼게요.
해설 여자는 샤워 후에 바르기 위한 용도로 바디 크림을 사겠다고 했다.

17 알맞은 응답 찾기 | ⑤
해석
남 왜 그렇게 화가 났니?
여 우리 언니하고 문제가 있어서. 언니는 나한테 묻지 않고 내 물건을 사용해서 난 그것이 짜증이 나.

남 네가 그것에 대해 어떻게 느끼는지 언니에게 얘기해 봤니?
여 실은, 언니가 아닌 아빠께 말씀 드려왔어.
남 그러면 언니는 네가 아빠께 말한 것에 대해 네게 화가 났겠구나.
여 맞아. 내가 어떻게 해야 할까?
남 너의 아빠가 아닌 언니에게 얘기하려고 노력해 봐.
① 경찰을 부르는 게 좋겠어.
② 너는 잘못된 어떤 것도 하지 않았어.
③ 어쨌든 그녀는 내 말에 귀 기울이지 않을 거야.
④ 너는 그가 화가 난 이유를 그에게 물어야 해.
해설 언니가 잘못한 일을 아빠에게 말해 언니가 화낼 것을 걱정하는 여자에게 아빠가 아닌 언니와 대화하라고 조언하는 ⑤가 남자의 응답으로 가장 적절하다.

18 알맞은 응답 찾기 | ④
해석
여 안녕, Tom. 점심 먹으러 가니?
남 응, 그래. 너 이 주변에 좋은 식당 아니?
여 저 모퉁이 근처에 괜찮은 데가 있어.
남 점심 먹었니? 거기 같이 가자.
여 좋아. 나는 오랫동안 거기에 가지 않았어. 이 사람은 너의 친구니?
남 아, 그녀를 소개해 줄게. 내 여동생 Jane이야.
여 만나서 반가워, Jane.
① 나는 그렇게 생각하지 않아.
② 너 어떻게 지냈니?
③ 오래간만이야, Jane.
⑤ 내가 충분한 시간이 있는지 모르겠어.
해설 남자가 여자에게 여동생을 소개하고 있으므로 만나서 반갑다고 하는 ④가 여자의 응답으로 가장 적절하다.

19 알맞은 응답 찾기 | ④
해석
여 너 과학에 관한 책을 읽고 보고서를 썼니?
남 아니, 아직 못 했어. '인간의 몸'이라는 책을 빌리려고 도서관에 갔는데, 그게 벌써 대출되었더라. 오늘 하나 사야 할 것 같아.
여 너 이 책 말하는 거니?
남 응, 그거 맞아. 너 이 책에 관해 보고서를 썼니?
여 응. 내가 지난주에 이 책을 대출했고, 이미 숙제를 다 해서 오늘 반납하러 가려고 했어.
남 내가 이 책을 너 대신 내일 반납하면 안 될까?
① 그 책은 다 팔렸어.
② 유감스럽지만 환불받을 수 없을 거야.
③ 지난주에 그 책을 반납했어야지.
④ 도서관에 가는 길을 내게 알려 줄 수 있니?
해설 남자는 숙제를 하기 위해 책이 필요하고 여자는 숙제를 끝마쳤으므로 책을 사용한 후 대신 책을 반납할 것을 제안하는 ④가 남자의 응답으로 가장 적절하다.

20 상황에 맞는 말 찾기 | ④
해석
여 Coby는 오늘 자신의 교복을 빨기로 결심했다. 그래서 그는 세탁기에 그것을 넣었다. 세탁 후에, 그는 그 교복을 다림질해야 한다는 것을 알았다. 그러나 그는 다림질을 하는 것이 처음이다. 그래서 그는 엄마의 도움이 필요하다고 생각한다. 이런 상황에서, Coby는 엄마에게 뭐라고 말하겠는가?

Coby <u>다리미를 사용하는 방법을 말해 줄 수 있나요?</u>

① 다리미가 고장 났어요.
② 다리미를 어디에 놓으셨어요?
③ 왜 제가 교복을 빨아야 하나요?
⑤ 세탁기를 이용하는 것은 쉽지 않아요.

해설 Coby가 다리미를 사용해 본 적이 없어서 어머니의 도움이 필요한 상황이므로 ④가 답으로 적절하다.

09회 영어 듣기모의고사　　pp. 070~071

01 ⑤	02 ⑤	03 ③	04 ⑤	05 ⑤
06 ⑤	07 ①	08 ②	09 ④	10 ②
11 ①	12 ④	13 ④	14 ③	15 ①
16 ①	17 ③	18 ①	19 ⑤	20 ②

Dictation Test 09회　　pp. 072~077

01 ❶ very long hair ❷ sunglasses over his hair ❸ his necklace

02 ❶ moved in next door ❷ some pumpkin pie I made ❸ be good neighbors to

03 ❶ keep that in mind ❷ the most popular dishes ❸ feel much like eating

04 ❶ the movie theater ❷ at a shoe repair shop ❸ have it fixed

05 ❶ sends school notices ❷ get a membership ❸ will expire

06 ❶ rounded shoulders ❷ correct your posture ❸ an exercise program

07 ❶ doesn't look good on ❷ to brush your teeth ❸ do better next time

08 ❶ feed my cat ❷ is dead ❸ borrow mine

09 ❶ What brought you here ❷ is not high either ❸ should rest for a while

10 ❶ one adult ❷ one kid ❸ have to pay for yourself

11 ❶ might play this song ❷ Let's finish this hamburger

12 ❶ hear about her new album ❷ who the surprise guest is

13 ❶ his car is ready ❷ the cost of the repairs

14 ❶ buy things at a store ❷ get a refund ❸ prove that you bought it

15 ❶ already broken ❷ for a new one ❸ want us to exchange

16 ❶ just decided to interview ❷ going one day earlier

17 ❶ make a reservation ❷ What time ❸ at six o'clock

18 ❶ Let me help you ❷ When will she arrive at

19 ❶ I want to buy ❷ the most popular model ❸ can control this

20 ❶ a math teacher ❷ didn't seem to understand it ❸ to solve it

---

01 그림 정보 파악 - 인물 | ⑤

해석
남 넌 뭘 보고 있니?
여 이건 내가 가장 좋아하는 가수의 사진이야.
남 와, 그는 머리가 매우 길구나.
여 응. 그가 패션 리더라고 생각하지 않니?
남 솔직히 나는 그의 스타일이 마음에 안 들어. 선글라스를 머리에 쓰고 있잖아. 그에게 잘 어울리는 것 같지 않아.
여 왜 그래. 그의 목걸이를 봐. 너무 멋지잖아.
남 너무 여자 같아. 왜 여자아이들은 그와 같은 가수들에 열광하지? 이해가 안 돼.

해설 머리가 길고, 선글라스를 머리 위에 두고 있으며 목걸이를 한 사람은 ⑤이다.

02 목적 파악 | ⑤

해석
여 실례합니다. 누구 계세요?
남 네. 누구세요?
여 안녕하세요, 제 이름은 Jessica예요. 어제 옆집으로 이사 왔어요.
남 아, 안녕하세요. 만나서 반갑습니다. 저는 민수예요.
여 저도 만나서 반가워요. 여기 제가 만든 호박 파이를 좀 가져왔어요. 좀 드셔 보세요.
남 와, 감사합니다. 매우 맛있어 보이네요.
여 서로에게 좋은 이웃이 되면 좋겠어요.
남 저도 그래요.

해설 어제 이사 온 여자가 자신을 소개하러 옆집 이웃을 방문하여 인사하고 있다.

03 그림 상황에 어울리는 대화 찾기 | ③

해석
① 여 좋은 생각이 나면, 메모해 두는 것이 중요해.
　 남 알겠어. 명심할게.
② 여 저녁에 뭐 먹고 싶은 거 있니?
　 남 아니, 넌 어때?
③ 여 이 식당에서 가장 유명한 요리가 무엇인가요?
　 남 불고기가 가장 인기 있습니다.
④ 여 나는 이 식당에 너무나 많은 사람들이 있어서 정말로 놀랐어.
　 남 그래. 나는 요리들의 맛이 너무 궁금해.
⑤ 여 Tommy, 저녁이 준비되었다.
　 남 전 별로 먹고 싶지 않아요, 엄마.

해설 여자가 식당에서 음식을 주문하는 상황에 적절한 대화는 ③이다.

04 장소 추론 | ⑤
해석
[휴대 전화가 울린다.]
남 여보세요?
여 Dave. 너 벌써 극장이니?
남 아직 아니야. 나는 지하철역이야. 왜?
여 가는 길에, 내 신발 굽이 부러졌어. 나는 지금 구두 수리점에 있어.
남 오래 걸리니?
여 아니야, 약 20분 안에 고칠 수 있을 거야. 너 수리점이 어디인지 아니?
남 응, 알아. 지금 거기로 갈게.
해설 여자의 신발 굽이 부러져 수리를 해야 해서 두 사람은 구두 수리점에서 만나기로 했다.

05 언급되지 않은 것 | ⑤
해석
여 JW 중학교는 모든 학부모님들께 '학교 공지' 앱을 휴대 전화에 설치하시기를 강력히 추천합니다. 이 무료 앱은 학교 공지들을 휴대 전화로 보내 주어서, 중요한 공지를 또 놓칠까 봐 걱정하실 필요가 없습니다. 이 앱을 사용하시려면, 회원 가입을 하셔야 합니다. 학교는 아이의 학년과 반을 확인한 후 회원을 승인할 것입니다. 여러분의 회원권은 이 해 말에 만료됩니다. 서비스는 다음 달부터 시작되므로, 이 달 말 전에 가입을 해 두세요.
해설 School Notice 앱의 서비스 종료일에 대해서는 언급되지 않았다.

06 관계 추론 | ⑤
해석
여 허리가 아파요. 제 자세가 좋지 않은 것 같아요.
남 죄송하지만 맞으세요. 어깨가 굽으셨네요.
여 제가 이것에 관해 할 수 있는 것이 있나요?
남 꾸준히 운동하시면 도움이 됩니다. 자세를 바르게 하도록 제가 도와드리겠습니다.
여 제가 운동하러 얼마나 자주 와야 할까요?
남 제 의견으로는, 적어도 일주일에 세 번은 오셔야 합니다.
여 그러면 그렇게 할게요. 정말 열심히 운동할 거예요.
남 좋아요. 그러면 제가 회원님께 적절한 운동 프로그램을 만들어 볼게요. 이제, 스트레칭부터 시작하죠.
해설 남자가 여자의 운동을 도와주며 여자를 위해 개인 운동 프로그램을 만들어 본다고 했으므로 남자는 여자의 개인 운동 지도사이고 여자는 회원임을 알 수 있다.

07 어색한 대화 찾기 | ①
해석
① 여 내일 파티에 무엇을 입으시겠어요?
　 남 그건 네게 어울리지 않는 것 같아.
② 여 액션 장면이 매우 현실적이어서 놀랐어.
　 남 응, 요즘은 영화들이 정말로 현실적이야.
③ 여 치아를 건강하게 유지하려면 어떻게 해야 하나요?
　 남 하루에 세 번 이를 닦는 것이 매우 중요합니다.
④ 여 너무 실수를 많이 해서 대회에서 상을 못 받았어.
　 남 실망하지 마. 다음에는 더 잘할 거야.

⑤ 여 길을 잃으신 것 같네요. 도움이 필요하세요?
　 남 네. 서울역에 가는 법을 알려 주시겠어요
해설 내일 있을 파티에서 무엇을 입을 거냐고 묻는 질문에 대해 그것은 너에게 어울리지 않는다고 대답하는 것은 어색하다.

08 부탁한 일 파악 | ②
해석
남 걱정스러워 보인다. 왜 그러니?
여 음, 나는 내 고양이가 걱정돼. 내가 오늘 아침에 고양이 밥 주는 것을 잊었어. 굶주리고 있을 지도 몰라. 점심시간에 집에 가야 할까 봐.
남 엄마가 주셨을 수도 있잖아. 엄마께 전화 드려서 확인해 보지 않을래?
여 좋은 생각이야. 하지만 내 휴대 전화 배터리가 다 닳았어.
남 그럼 내 것을 빌려줄까?
여 그래도 되니? 오래 얘기하지는 않을 거야.
남 괜찮아. 그렇게 해.
해설 여자는 엄마가 고양이에게 밥을 주었는지 확인하기 위해 남자에게 휴대 전화를 빌려 달라고 부탁했다.

09 의도 파악 | ④
해석
남 안녕하세요, 김 선생님.
여 안녕하세요. 어떻게 오셨나요?
남 음, 두통이 심해서요.
여 기침을 하거나 콧물이 나나요?
남 아니요. 열도 높지 않아요. 감기는 아닌 것 같아요.
여 하루에 몇 시간 주무세요?
남 네 시간 정도지만, 피곤하거나 졸리지는 않아요.
여 그건 좋은 신호가 아니에요. 제 생각에, 당분간은 쉬셔야 해요.
해설 여자는 두통이 있는 남자에게 한동안 쉬어야 한다고 충고하고 있다.

10 숫자 정보 파악 - 금액 | ②
해석
여 도와드릴까요?
남 안녕하세요. 돌고래 쇼 표 두 장을 사고 싶은데요.
여 어른 둘이세요?
남 아니요, 어른 하나와 아이 하나요.
여 어른 표는 10달러입니다. 일곱 살 이하의 어린이 표는 무료이고, 일곱 살이 넘는 어린이는 7달러예요.
남 제 아들은 여섯 살이에요.
여 그럼 아들 몫은 지불하실 필요 없으세요. 그냥 선생님 것만 내시면 돼요.
남 좋아요, 돈 여기 있습니다.
해설 일곱 살 이하 어린이는 무료라고 했는데 남자의 아들은 여섯 살이므로 남자는 성인용 티켓 값인 10달러만 지불하면 된다.

11 장소 추론 | ①
해석
여 진수야, 이 음악에 대해 어떻게 생각해?
남 음, 굉장히 경쾌하다. 난 맘에 들어. 왜?
여 우리가 이 노래를 학교 축제에서 연주하면 어떨까 생각 중이야.
남 좋은 생각이다. 이 노래는 완벽할 거야.
여 우리 이 음악 CD를 사서, 함께 연주 연습을 하지 않을래?

남　좋아. 이 햄버거만 다 먹고 나가자. 이 식당 근처에 음반 가게가 있어.
여　좋아.
해설　남자가 햄버거를 다 먹고 식당 주변에 있는 음반 가게에 가자고 했으므로 두 사람이 대화하고 있는 장소는 식당이다.

12　언급되지 않은 것 | ④
해석
남　여러분, 안녕하세요. 저는 '음악캠프'의 진행자인 Michael입니다. 오늘, 우리는 Kimberley Clark를 만나서 그녀의 새 앨범에 대해 들어 보겠습니다. 그녀는 그녀의 히트곡들 중 한 곡인 '바람의 노래'를 부를 것입니다. 또한 그녀는 스튜디오에서 깜짝 손님에게 전화 통화를 할 건데요. 그 손님은 그녀의 가장 친한 친구이며 또한 가수라고 합니다. 깜짝 손님이 누구일지 정말 궁금하군요. 채널 고정해 주세요.
해설　라디오 방송에서 깜짝 손님의 이름은 언급되지 않았다.

13　도표 정보 파악 | ④
해석
[전화벨이 울린다.]
여　여보세요?
남　여보세요. Adams 씨와 통화할 수 있나요?
여　지금은 안 계신데요. 메시지를 전해 드릴까요?
남　네, 저는 Max 자동차 정비소의 Max예요. 그의 차가 다 수리되어 전화드립니다.
여　알겠습니다. 다른 것은요?
남　Adams 씨께 수리비가 50달러라고 전해 주시겠어요? 그리고 저에게 다시 전화해 달라고 전해 주세요.
여　알겠습니다. 그렇게 전해 드리죠.
남　고맙습니다.
해설　수리비는 15달러가 아니라 50달러이다.

14　주제 파악 | ③
해석
여　가게에서 물건을 살 때, 여러분은 이것을 받습니다. 많은 사람들은 그냥 이것을 버리지만, 사실 이것을 갖고 있는 것은 매우 중요합니다. 여러분이 환불을 받아야 할 때나 어떤 것을 교환해야 할 때, 이것은 당신이 그 가게에서 그것을 샀다는 것을 증명해 줄 것입니다.
해설　물건을 산 후에 받으며 물건을 환불하거나 교환할 때 필요한 것은 영수증이다.

15　한 일 / 할 일 파악 | ①
해석
남　안녕하세요. 어떻게 도와드릴까요, 손님?
여　안녕하세요. 이 선풍기를 지난달에 샀어요. 한 달밖에 안 썼는데, 벌써 고장 났네요.
남　저희가 한번 볼까요? 고쳐 드릴 수 있는데요.
여　아뇨, 저는 환불을 받고 싶어요.
남　죄송합니다만, 손님께서는 벌써 한 달 동안 사용하셨어요. 환불받기 어려우세요.
여　그럼 새 것으로 바꿀 수 있나요?
남　네, 그것은 가능하지만 같은 모델로만 입니다. 그것을 교환해 드릴까요?
여　네, 그러면 돼요.
해설　여자는 고장 난 선풍기를 새 물건으로 교환해 달라고 했다.

16　숫자 정보 파악 – 날짜 | ①
해석
여　Brian, 인터뷰 숙제 마쳤니?
남　아니, 이제 막 이모를 인터뷰하기로 결정했어. 디자이너시거든.
여　정말? 나도 같이 가도 되니? 디자이너를 인터뷰하고 싶었거든.
남　물론이지. 언제 보러 갈까? 6월 10일에서 21일까지는 바쁘다고 하셨어.
여　그럼 6월 9일은 어때?
남　음, 미안하지만 그날은 내가 약속이 있어. (6월 9일보다) 하루 일찍 가는 건 어때?
여　좋아. 나는 괜찮아.
해설　두 사람은 남자의 이모가 바쁜 기간을 피해 6월 8일에 인터뷰를 하러 가기로 했다.

17　알맞은 응답 찾기 | ③
해석
[전화벨이 울린다.]
남　Sky 라운지입니다. 무엇을 도와드릴까요?
여　이번 주 토요일에 네 명을 예약하고 싶습니다.
남　언제 방문하시겠습니까, 손님?
여　여섯 시 정각에 갈 겁니다.
남　전화번호와 성함을 남겨 주세요.
여　제 이름은 김지수입니다. 저의 휴대 전화번호는 010-1101-5678이에요.
남　성함의 철자를 불러 주실 수 있으세요?
① 제가 그것을 뭐라고 말해야 하나요?
② 미리 주문을 하려고 합니다.
④ 죄송하지만 그날은 모두 예약되었습니다.
⑤ 저를 따라오시면 테이블로 안내해 드리겠습니다.
해설　여자는 식당 예약을 하기 위해 이름을 남기고 있으므로 이름의 철자를 다시 묻는 ③이 남자의 응답으로 가장 적절하다.

18　알맞은 응답 찾기 | ①
해석
[전화벨이 울린다.]
남　여보세요?
여　여보세요. Kenny, 나 Julie야. 오늘 오후에 바쁘니?
남　아니, 별로. 왜?
여　그럼 내 부탁 좀 들어 줄래?
남　물론이지. 내가 도와줄게. 뭔데?
여　내 여동생이 오늘 오후에 캐나다에서 집에 와. 그런데 내가 오늘밤 늦게까지 일을 해야 해. 내 대신 그녀를 좀 태우러 가 줄 수 있니?
남　물론이야. 동생이 공항에 언제 도착하는데?
여　그녀는 오후 5시쯤에 올 거야.
② 그녀를 만나는 게 정말 기대돼.
③ 미안한데, 내가 너무 바빠서 그녀를 데리러 갈 수 없어.
④ 그녀는 공항에서 오후 10시에 떠날 거야.
⑤ 그녀는 짧은 머리에 안경을 쓰고 있어.
해설　남자가 여자의 언니를 공항으로 마중하는 상황에서 언니가 언제 도착하는지 물어봤으므로 5시쯤 도착할 것이라고 말하는 ①이 여자의 응답으로 가장 적절하다.

19 알맞은 응답 찾기 | ⑤

해석

여 도와드릴까요, 손님?

남 네, 부탁드려요. 저는 오븐을 사고 싶은데요.

여 집에서 사용하실 겁니까?

남 네. 너무 크지 않았으면 좋겠어요.

여 이것이 가장 인기 있는 모델입니다.

남 이 디자인이 좋아요. 조작하기는 쉬운가요?

여 네, 그렇습니다. 간단히 다이얼을 돌려서 오븐을 조작하실 수 있으세요.

남 좀 더 자세히 설명해 주실 수 있으세요?

① 잘하셨어요.

② 이해가 되세요?

③ 저도 당신의 말에 동의합니다.

④ 제 말이 무슨 뜻인지 아시겠어요?

해설 여자가 남자에게 오븐 조작 방법을 알려 준 상황에서 좀 더 자세히 설명해 달라고 요청하는 ⑤가 남자의 응답으로 가장 적절하다.

20 상황에 맞는 말 찾기 | ②

해석

남 한 선생님은 수학 교사이다. 어느 날, 그녀의 학생 중 하나인 정수가 그녀에게 수학 문제 푸는 법을 물었다. 그녀는 그에게 푸는 법을 보여 주었지만 그는 이해한 것 같지 않았다. 그녀는 그를 이해시키기 위해 그에게 그것을 푸는 방법을 다시 말해 줘야겠다고 생각한다. 이런 상황에서, 한 선생님은 정수에게 뭐라고 말하겠는가?

한 선생님 다시 설명해 줄게.

① 천만에.

③ 네 도움에 정말로 감사해.

④ 날 다시 도와주겠니?

⑤ 수학 점수가 또 형편없을까 봐 걱정돼.

해설 정수가 수학 문제 풀이를 이해하지 못하는 것 같아 다시 설명해 주려고 하는 상황이므로 ②가 답으로 적절하다.

10회 영어 듣기모의고사 — pp. 078~079

01 ④	02 ③	03 ⑤	04 ⑤	05 ②
06 ①	07 ③	08 ④	09 ③	10 ④
11 ④	12 ④	13 ④	14 ⑤	15 ⑤
16 ④	17 ④	18 ②	19 ⑤	20 ⑤

Dictation Test 10회 — pp. 080~085

01 ❶ an exercise you can do ❷ raise your arms

02 ❶ a nice pizza place ❷ where it is ❸ I can find it

03 ❶ a fashion model ❷ a five minute walk away ❸ Try this one

04 ❶ can't use it ❷ it will be open ❸ on Friday

05 ❶ Her name ❷ fourteen years old ❸ speaks French

06 ❶ Dad called you ❷ should have done ❸ I am really sorry

07 ❶ It was great ❷ Don't give up ❸ Never mind

08 ❶ I'm here in ❷ in the laundry box ❸ socks in the basket

09 ❶ studied the whole night ❷ too tired to take ❸ can't agree with you more

10 ❶ four dollars for five ❷ nine dollars for five ❸ five pears and five oranges

11 ❶ repair my cellphone ❷ dropped it ❸ has to check it

12 ❶ send a package ❷ based on ❸ you have to

13 ❶ an invitation text message ❷ Julie's birthday party this evening ❸ at Pizza Factory

14 ❶ not good for your health ❷ cause various adult diseases

15 ❶ some more chicken ❷ do the dishes ❸ throw away the food waste

16 ❶ change the date ❷ I'd like to come back

17 ❶ give it a try ❷ You're doing great ❸ that's enough for today

18 ❶ a lot of fun ❷ nearby a seashore ❸ should come with me

19 ❶ Where did you ❷ go there together ❸ next Saturday

20 ❶ travel to Japan ❷ see his concert ❸ can't book a ticket

01 그림 정보 파악 – 인물 | ④

해석

여 많은 사람들이 비행기로 여행을 할 때 피로를 느낀다. 여기에 장시간 비행 시 시차증을 줄일 수 있도록 좌석에서 할 수 있는 운동 방법이 있다. 먼저, 똑바로 앉아라. 손가락을 모으고, 팔꿈치를 일직선으로 유지하고, 손바닥을 바깥으로 한 채 팔을 가슴 높이까지 올려라. 앞쪽으로 허리를 굽힌 다음 편안한 자세를 취해라.

해설 바로 앉아서 손가락을 모은 채 팔꿈치를 일직선으로 쭉 편 다음 손바닥을 바깥으로 한 채 팔을 가슴 높이까지 올린 후 앞쪽으로 허리를 굽힌 자세는 ④이다.

02 목적 파악 | ③

해석

[휴대 전화가 울린다.]

여 안녕, Alex. 무슨 일이야?

남 안녕, Patti. 네가 나한테 네 아파트 근처에 괜찮은 피자 가게가 있다고 말한 적 있지. 아주 유명한 요리사가 그 가게를 경영한다고.

여 응, Jamie's Kitchen이야.

남 맞아. 그게 정확하게 어디에 있는지 말해 줄 수 있니?

여 너 우리 아파트가 어디에 있는지는 알지, 그렇지?

남 응.

여 그건 우리 아파트의 정문 건너편에 있어.

남 오, 찾을 수 있을 것 같아. 고마워.

해설 남자는 식당의 위치를 물어보기 위해 여자에게 전화했다.

03 그림 상황에 어울리는 대화 찾기 | ⑤

해석

① 남 너는 미래에 뭐가 되고 싶니?

　여 나는 패션모델이 되고 싶어.

② 남 사용 가능한 방이 있나요?

　여 죄송하지만, 지금은 없네요.

③ 남 제가 백화점에 어떻게 갈 수 있을까요?

　여 이쪽으로 직진하세요. 걸어서 5분 거리입니다.

④ 남 이 근처에 새로 생긴 옷가게에 대해 들어 봤니?

　여 아니, 몰라.

⑤ 남 이게 저한테 너무 작아요. 좀 더 큰 것이 있나요?

　여 물론이죠. 이것을 입어 보세요.

해설 남자의 티셔츠가 작아 보여 다른 옷을 권하는 대화로 적절한 것은 ⑤
이다.

04 특정 정보 파악 – 요일 | ⑤

해석

여 실례합니다. 테니스 코트가 여전히 수리 중인가요?

남 네. 오늘은 사용하실 수 없습니다.

여 왜 이렇게 오래 걸리나요? 지난 수요일에 시작했는데, 오늘이 벌써 화
요일이잖아요.

남 거의 다 되었어요. 금요일부터 사용하실 수 있을 겁니다.

여 수리가 거의 다 되었다면, 내일 코트에서 테니스 치는 것은 안 되나요?

남 안전 조사관이 목요일에 올 거예요. 금요일에 다시 오세요.

해설 남자가 여자에게 금요일에 테니스 코트를 다시 이용할 수 있다고 했다.

05 언급되지 않은 것 | ②

해석

남 오늘 우리 학교로 전학 온 여러분의 새 친구를 소개합니다. 그녀의 이
름은 Celine이고, 열네 살이에요. 보이는 것처럼, 그녀는 한국인이 아
닙니다. 그녀는 프랑스에서 와서 프랑스어로 말합니다. 그녀는 막 한국
으로 이사해서 한국어를 잘하지는 못합니다. 한국의 모든 것이 그녀에
게 새롭습니다. 부디 그 상황을 이해해 주고, 그녀를 잘 대해 주길 바랍
니다. 모두 좋은 친구가 될 수 있기를 바랍니다.

해설 새로 전학 온 친구의 취미에 관해서는 언급되지 않았다.

06 심정 파악 | ①

해석

여 Tom, 너는 지금 몇 시인 줄 아니?

남 죄송해요, 엄마. 다시는 늦지 않을게요.

여 아빠가 너한테 10번도 더 전화하셨어. 어디에 있었니?

남 학급 친구들 중 몇 명이랑 농구를 하고 있었어요. 제 휴대 전화 배터리
가 나가서 전화할 수 없었어요.

여 친구들의 휴대 전화 중에 하나를 사용할 수도 있었을 텐데.

남 맞아요. 제가 그랬어야만 했는데. 정말 죄송해요.

여 이번이 처음이 아니잖아. 뭐가 문제니?

남 정말 죄송해요, 엄마. 약속할게요. 다시는 늦지 않을 거예요.

해설 남자가 계속 집에 늦게 오는 상황이므로 여자는 화가 났을 것이다.

07 어색한 대화 찾기 | ③

해석

① 남 영화는 어땠니?

　여 좋았어. 나는 배우들에게 마음을 빼앗겼어.

② 남 나는 오늘 아침에 우산을 잃어버렸어.

　여 너무 안됐구나.

③ 남 포기하지 마! 너는 다음번에는 성공할 거야.

　여 그 소식을 들어 유감이다.

④ 남 너는 내 말에 동의하니?

　여 사실은, 그렇지 않아.

⑤ 남 다 내 잘못이야. 제발 나를 용서해 줘.

　여 오, 괜찮아. 신경 쓰지 마.

해설 다음번에는 잘될 거라며 포기하지 말라고 독려하는 말에 유감이라고
대답하는 것은 어색하다.

08 부탁한 일 파악 | ④

해석

여 Ronald, 너는 어디 있니?

남 여기 제 방에 있어요, 엄마.

여 당장 이리 나와.

남 네. 무슨 일이에요?

여 바닥에 있는 네 양말을 좀 봐! 내가 여러 번 말했지. 양말을 벗어서 빨
래 통에 넣어야 한다고.

남 정말 죄송해요. 다음에는 양말을 그 통에 넣을게요.

여 알겠다.

해설 여자는 남자에게 벗은 양말을 빨래 통에 넣어 줄 것을 부탁하고 있다.

09 의도 파악 | ③

해석

여 좋은 아침.

남 안녕, 너는 시험 준비는 다 됐니?

여 난 밤새 공부했어.

남 너는 전혀 안 잤다고 말하는 거니?

여 응, 시험을 치르는 동안 깨어 있을 수 없을 것 같아.

남 잠을 안 자고 공부하는 것은 너를 너무 피곤하게 만들어서 너는 시험을
잘 치를 수가 없어. 내가 전에 말했었잖아.

여 맞아, 나는 예전에 그것을 깨닫지 못했는데, 이제는 네 말에 완전 동의해.

해설 여자의 마지막 말 I can't agree with you more.은 동의를 하는
표현이다.

10 숫자 정보 파악 – 금액 | ④

해석

남 안녕하세요.

여 안녕하세요, 제가 할머니께 드릴 과일이 좀 필요한데요.

남 이 배들을 사가세요. 달고 과즙이 많아요.

여 얼마예요?

남 하나에 1달러지만, 다섯 개에 4달러예요.

여 이 오렌지들은 어때요?

남 하나에 2달러인데, 다섯 개에 9달러예요.

여 알겠어요. 배 다섯 개랑 오렌지 다섯 개를 살게요.

남 감사합니다. 할머니께서 그것들을 좋아하실 거라고 확신해요.

해설 여자는 배 5개와 오렌지 5개를 구입했으므로 총 13달러를 지불해야
한다.

11 장소 추론 | ④
해석
여 어떻게 도와드릴까요?
남 안녕하세요, 제가 휴대 전화를 수리 받아야 하는데요.
여 문제가 뭐죠?
남 화면이 깨졌어요. 문자 메시지를 읽을 수가 없어요.
여 왜 그런 거예요?
남 제가 실수로 계단에서 그것을 떨어뜨렸거든요.
여 알겠습니다. 이 양식을 기입해 주실 수 있나요?
남 네. 요금은 얼마가 들까요?
여 글쎄요. 우선 수리하시는 분이 그것을 확인해 보셔야 합니다.
해설 남자는 휴대 전화 화면이 고장 나서 이를 수리하기 위해 서비스 센터에
방문했다.

12 언급되지 않은 것 | ④
해석
여 여러분이 우체국에서 소포를 보내기 원할 때, 여러분은 그것을 주중
오전 9시부터 오후 6시 사이에 가져가야 합니다. 우편 요금은 여러분
의 소포의 무게에 근거하여 결정됩니다. 소포가 더 무거울수록, 요금이
더 높아집니다. 여러분은 그것을 보낼 때 요금을 지불하거나, 받는 사
람이 요금을 지불하도록 할 수 있습니다. 모든 소포에 관해서, 여러분
은 여러분과 받는 사람 둘 다의 이름, 주소와 전화번호를 상자에 써야
합니다.
해설 소포를 발송할 때 소포의 무게 한도는 언급되지 않았다.

13 도표 정보 파악 | ④
해석
여 와, 금요일이다. 오늘 기분은 어떠니, David?
남 좋아. 너는 Julie에게서 초대 문자 하나 받았지, 그렇지?
여 뭐라고? (잠시 후) 오, 지금 막 확인했어.
남 음, 그냥 네가 오늘 저녁에 있는 Julie의 생일 파티에 갈 건지를 나에게
알려 주면 돼.
여 응, 가고 싶어. 6시에 Pizza Factory에서 하는 거 맞지?
남 맞아.
해설 생일 파티가 이루어지는 시간은 금요일인 오늘 저녁이다.

14 주제 파악 | ⑤
해석
남 정크푸드에 대해 들어본 적이 있습니까? 많은 사람들이 그것을 좋아합
니다. 그것은 아마도 그것이 간단하고 맛이 아주 좋기 때문일 겁니다.
하지만 당신은 그것이 당신의 건강에 좋지 않다는 것을 알 필요가 있습
니다. 그것들은 매우 고열량이고 당분이 많은 음식입니다. 너무 많은 정
크푸드를 먹는 것은 다양한 성인병을 일으킬 수 있습니다. 그런 음식들
을 먹지 않으려고 노력하고 더 많은 야채를 먹도록 해 보세요.
해설 정크푸드의 안 좋은 점에 대해 설명하며 정크푸드가 고칼로리이고 설
탕 함유량이 높으며 여러 성인병을 유발할 수 있다는 점을 언급했다.

15 한 일 / 할 일 파악 | ⑤
해석
남 훌륭한 저녁이었어요, 엄마. 나는 엄마가 세계 최고의 요리사라고 확신
해요.
여 고마워. 치킨을 좀 더 먹겠니, Eric?
남 아니에요. 많이 먹었어요.
여 그래, 그러면 이제 나는 설거지를 할게.
남 제가 도와드릴 수 있는 일이 있을까요, 엄마?
여 아니야. 괜찮아. 너는 그냥 방에 가서 숙제를 하렴.
남 엄마, 그럼 제가 음식물 쓰레기를 버릴게요.
여 오, 정말? 그래, 그거 좋겠구나.
해설 남자는 엄마에게 자신이 음식물 쓰레기를 버린다고 했다.

16 숫자 정보 파악 – 날짜 | ④
해석
남 Star 여행사입니다.
여 안녕하세요, 제가 비행 날짜를 바꿀 수 있을 지 궁금합니다.
남 그럼요. 성함이 어떻게 되시죠?
여 Judy Park입니다.
남 네. 8월 6일에 시드니로 떠나셔서 8월 10일에 돌아오시는군요.
여 네, 그러려고 했는데, 8월 9일에 돌아오고 싶어요.
남 잠시만 기다리세요. (잠시 후) 네, 비행을 바꾸실 수 있어요.
여 감사합니다.
해설 여자는 8월 10일에서 9일로 돌아오는 비행 편을 바꿨다.

17 알맞은 응답 찾기 | ④
해석
여 아빠, 저는 자전거를 더 이상 탈 수 없을 것 같아요.
남 그냥 시도해 봐, Dorothy. 너는 할 수 있어.
여 오, 안 돼요, 아빠. 너무 무서워요.
남 잘하고 있단다, 얘야.
여 지금은 멈춰야 할 거 같아요.
남 좋아. 아마도 오늘은 충분한 것 같아.
여 자전거를 타는 게 아주 어렵네요. 쉬울 줄 알았어요.
남 포기하지 마, 얘야. 다음에는 더 잘할 거야.
여 <u>알겠어요. 내일 해 볼게요, 아빠.</u>
① 그걸 해낼 수 있으세요, 아빠.
② 자전거를 좀 사 주세요, 아빠.
③ 저는 지난주에 자전거를 탔어요, 아빠.
⑤ 방금 전에 어디 계셨었어요, 아빠?
해설 남자가 여자에게 자전거 타는 것을 포기하지 말라고 독려하고 있는 상
황이므로 내일도 시도해 보겠다고 말하는 ④가 여자의 응답으로 가장
적절하다.

18 알맞은 응답 찾기 | ②
해석
남 너 방학이 어땠니?
여 정말 재미있었어. 나는 조부모님 댁에서 방학 내내 지냈어.
남 어디 사시는데?
여 부산에. 해안가에 사셔. 나는 바닷가에서 매일 놀았어.
남 정말 재미있었던 것 같다. 부러워. 내 방학은 지루했어.

여　아마 너는 다음 여름에 나랑 같이 가야 할 것 같아.

남　<u>그러면 정말 좋을 것 같아.</u>

① 나도 정말 재미있었어.

③ 내 조부모님들은 도시에 사셔.

④ 나는 다른 나라에 한 번도 가 본 적이 없어.

⑤ 나는 바다보다는 산이 더 좋아.

해설　여자가 남자에게 다음에 함께 조부모님 댁을 방문할 것을 제안한 상황이므로 좋을 거라며 기대하는 ②가 남자의 응답으로 가장 적절하다.

19 알맞은 응답 찾기 | ⑤

해석

여　내 새 가방 어떠니?

남　잘 어울린다. 어디서 샀니?

여　N 서울 타워 기념품 가게에서 샀어.

남　거기가 가방도 파는 줄 몰랐네.

여　언제 거기 같이 가 볼래? 둘러보기도 좋은 곳이고 괜찮은 식당들도 있어.

남　좋아. 다음 주 토요일은 어떠니?

여　<u>가고 싶지만, 이미 계획이 있어.</u>

① 행운을 빌게.

② 나는 새 가방은 필요 없어.

③ 그 가게가 어디라고 생각하니?

④ 나는 N 서울 타워가 어디 있는지 몰라.

해설　남자가 N 서울 타워를 방문할 것을 제안하고 있으므로 가고 싶지만 계획이 있다고 말하는 ⑤가 여자의 응답으로 가장 적절하다.

20 상황에 맞는 말 찾기 | ⑤

해석

여　유진이는 일본으로 여행 갈 계획이다. 그녀가 여행하는 동안, Yuhki Kuramoto의 피아노 공연이 도쿄에서 열릴 것이다. 그녀는 정말 그의 공연을 보고 싶어 한다. 하지만 웹사이트는 일본어로만 정보를 제공한다. 그래서 그녀는 표를 예매할 수가 없다. 그녀는 일본어를 잘하는 친구에게 전화한다. 이런 상황에서, 유진이는 친구에게 뭐라고 말하겠는가?

유진　<u>일본어로 된 웹사이트에서 예약하는 것을 도와줄 수 있니?</u>

① 일본으로 돌아오지 그래?

② 네 피아노 콘서트는 언제 시작하니?

③ 너는 일본으로 혼자 여행한 적 있니?

④ 지난번에 네가 사 줬던 티켓이 얼마였지?

해설　유진이가 일본 여행 중에 콘서트를 예약하고 싶은데 일본어 사이트만 존재하는 상황에서 일본어를 잘하는 친구에게 할 말로 ⑤가 알맞다.

11^회 영어 듣기모의고사				pp. 086~087
01 ③	02 ④	03 ②	04 ③	05 ②
06 ①	07 ③	08 ⑤	09 ③	10 ④
11 ④	12 ③	13 ⑤	14 ③	15 ②
16 ②	17 ⑤	18 ③	19 ②	20 ④

Dictation Test 11^회 pp. 088~093

01 ❶ last jumper ❷ is going to jump ❸ The bar has fallen

02 ❶ out of toilet paper ❷ Do you want ❸ a lot of work

03 ❶ Go straight one block ❷ turn left ❸ be on your left

04 ❶ Nothing special ❷ supposed to finish ❸ at the park until three o'clock

05 ❶ your new book ❷ wrote the book ❸ wrote a fairy tale

06 ❶ change these coins into bills ❷ how much they are worth ❸ than I expected

07 ❶ possible that I enter ❷ make a reservation ❸ bank account number

08 ❶ should take ❷ look it up ❸ with the bus information

09 ❶ Why are you going ❷ as early as possible ❸ you have a point

10 ❶ The blocks look nice ❷ you cannot use ❸ any more

11 ❶ book about bananas ❷ like to buy it ❸ paying for it

12 ❶ Every day this week ❷ The guests are students from ❸ take classes with you

13 ❶ which concert to go ❷ would be fine ❸ who are aged under seven

14 ❶ with time and weather ❷ becomes gray ❸ have rain soon

15 ❶ probably stay home ❷ Going fishing ❸ pick you up

16 ❶ the game start ❷ take about ten minutes

17 ❶ at midnight ❷ no public transportation ❸ can take her

18 ❶ Bluetooth earphones ❷ then try mine

19 ❶ on the subway ❷ I kept you waiting

20 ❶ pretty satisfied ❷ a membership card ❸ get a discount

01 그림 정보 파악 – 운동 경기 | ③

해석

남　여기는 올림픽 경기장입니다. 마지막 도약 선수인 영국의 Ted Johnson이 곧 뛰겠습니다. 바의 높이는 2미터 30센티미터입니다. 이제 그는 마지막 시도를 시작합니다. 그리고 점프합니다! 아! 바에 부딪힙니다. 바가 떨어졌습니다. 다쳤을까요? 아닙니다. 그는 괜찮습니다. 그는 일어나서 걸어 나가지만 매우 실망한 것 같습니다.

해설 한 선수가 2.3m 높이의 바를 뛰어넘으려고 시도했지만 부딪혀서 바가 떨어진 상황이므로 높이뛰기에 대한 중계방송이라는 것을 알 수 있다.

02 목적 파악 | ④
해석
[전화벨이 울린다.]
남 여보세요.
여 여보세요. Brian, 너 아직 마트에 있니?
남 응, 막 음료를 골랐어. 왜? 뭔가 필요하니?
여 응. 지금 막 우리가 화장실 휴지가 떨어졌다는 걸 알았어. 좀 사다 줄래?
남 문제없어. 너 지금 뭐 하고 있니? 집에 바로 갔으면 좋겠어?
여 아니, 괜찮아. 나는 책을 선반에 정리하고 있어. 일이 많다.
남 집에 가기 전에, 운동복 코너를 잠시 둘러볼게. 너무 힘들게 일하지 마.
여 알겠어. 집에 오면 보자.
해설 여자는 아직 마트에 있는 남자에게 휴지를 사다 줄 것을 부탁하기 위해서 전화했다.

03 그림 정보 파악 – 길 찾기 | ②
해석
여 실례합니다. 르네상스 호텔에 어떻게 가는지 아시나요?
남 오, 저는 그 호텔에서 묵고 있어요. 제가 길을 가르쳐 드리죠. 한 블록 직진하시다가 좌회전하세요. 오, 아니, 우회전하세요.
여 한 블록 직진하다가 우회전이요. 그다음에는요?
남 한 블록 더 직진해서 좌회전하세요. 왼편에 있을 거예요.
여 알겠습니다. 도와주셔서 무척 감사합니다.
남 천만에요.
해설 출발하는 지점에서 한 블록 직진하여 오른쪽으로 꺾어 한 블록 더 간 후에 왼쪽으로 꺾은 후 왼쪽에 있는 곳은 ②이다.

04 장소 추론 | ③
해석
여 내일 학교 사생 대회 끝나고 뭐 할 거니?
남 특별한 일 없는데.
여 영화 보러 가자.
남 좋아. 지금 영화표 예매할까?
여 그러자. 2시에 'Star Trek Into Darkness'는 어떠니?
남 농담하니? 우리 그때까지 공원에 있을 거야.
여 정말? 정오 무렵에 그림 그리는 것 끝마치는 것 아니야?
남 아니야. 정오 무렵에 그림 그리고, 정오에 점심 먹어. 그런 후에 3시까지 공원에 있을 거야.
여 알겠어. 그러면 4시 영화를 보자.
해설 두 사람은 학교 사생 대회 때문에 내일 오전부터 오후 3시까지 공원에 있을 것이라고 했다.

05 직업 및 장래 희망 | ②
해석
남 최 작가님. 만나게 되어 반갑습니다.
여 안녕하세요, 초대해 주셔서 감사합니다.
남 이 쇼에 모시게 되어 우리가 기쁩니다. 작가님의 신간을 읽었습니다. 줄거리가 감동적이고, 창의적이었어요.

여 마음에 드셨다니 기쁘네요.
남 어떻게 그 책을 쓰셨는지 말씀해 주시겠어요?
여 사람들은 보통 동화는 아이들만을 위한 것이라고 생각해요. 하지만 그렇지가 않거든요. 우리는 모두 진심으로 동화를 갈망하지요.
남 그것이 당신이 어른들을 위한 동화를 쓰신 이유군요.
여 맞습니다.
해설 남자는 여자가 쓴 새 책을 읽었고, 여자에게 새 책을 쓴 계기에 대해 물어보는 것으로 보아 여자의 직업은 작가이다.

06 관계 추론 | ①
해석
남 도와드릴까요?
여 이 동전들을 지폐로 바꾸고 싶어요.
남 와, 동전을 많이 모았군요. 동전들을 기계에 넣어서 얼마인지 보죠.
여 얼마나 걸릴까요?
남 2분 이내로 걸릴 거예요. (삐 소리) 다 됐습니다. 45달러네요.
여 와, 예상했던 것보다 더 많군요. 감사합니다.
남 천만에요.
해설 여자가 모아 둔 동전을 지폐로 바꾸려고 은행에 온 상황이므로 남자는 은행 직원이고, 여자는 고객이다.

07 어색한 대화 찾기 | ③
해석
① 여 좀 조용히 해 주시겠어요? 소리가 너무 크네요.
   남 제가 그랬나요? 죄송합니다.
② 여 배고프지 않니?
   남 배고파 죽겠어. 뭔가를 먹고 싶어.
③ 여 극장에 지금 들어가도 되나요?
   남 극장은 소방서 옆에 있습니다.
④ 여 그 음식점을 예약했니?
   남 아니. 너무 바빴어. 나 대신 해 줄 수 있니?
⑤ 여 은행 계좌번호 좀 알려 주세요.
   남 잠깐만요. 확인해 봐야 해요. 전 그것을 외우고 있지 않거든요.
해설 극장에 들어가는 것이 가능한지 묻는 말에 대해 극장이 소방서 옆에 있다고 대답하는 것은 어색하다.

08 부탁한 일 파악 | ⑤
해석
[전화벨이 울린다.]
남 여보세요?
여 아빠, 저예요.
남 Sarah? 너 금방 나갔잖아. 무슨 일이니?
여 음, 국립 박물관에 가는 길이었는데 어떤 버스를 타야 하는지 잊어버렸어요. 알려 주실 수 있으세요?
남 잠깐 기다려. 내가 스마트폰으로 찾아볼게.
여 제가 그걸 어디다가 적어 놨는데, 어디다 적어 두었는지 모르겠어요.
남 그럴 수도 있지. 급하면 내가 거기에 차로 태워다 줄까?
여 아니오, 괜찮아요. 시간이 많아요.
남 알겠어. 내가 네게 버스 정보를 문자로 보내 줄게.
여 좋아요. 고마워요.
해설 여자는 남자에게 박물관으로 가는 버스 정보를 알려 달라고 부탁했다.

09 의도 파악 | ③
해석
남 피시방에 가자.
여 다음에. 나는 집에 가려고.
남 왜 집에 이렇게 일찍 가? 뭐 할 일 있어?
여 오늘 역사 보고서를 끝내야 해.
남 하지만 제출일 일주일 전이잖아.
여 나는 과제를 가능한 한 빨리 끝내려고 노력하는 편이야. 중요한 일을 끝마치고 쉴 때 더 마음이 편안해.
남 네 말이 맞는 것 같아. 나도 똑같이 해야겠어.
해설 남자는 중요한 일을 빨리 끝내고 쉬는 게 더 여유롭다는 여자의 말에 동의하며 여자의 말대로 해 보겠다고 했다.

10 숫자 정보 파악 – 금액 | ④
해석
남 안녕하세요, 저는 3살짜리 제 사촌을 위한 장난감을 하나 사고 싶은 데요.
여 그 나이의 아이들은 블록이나 인형을 좋아하죠. 어떤 것이 더 나으세요?
남 블록이 멋져 보이네요. 얼마예요?
여 50달러이지만, 쿠폰이 있으면 10% 할인을 받을 수 있어요.
남 이거 사용 가능한 쿠폰인가요?
여 어디 볼게요. 오, 이 쿠폰을 더 이상 사용하실 수 없습니다. 보이세요? 지난달까지였어요.
남 알겠습니다. 어쨌든 블록을 사도록 할게요.
해설 남자는 할인 쿠폰의 유효 기간이 지난달에 끝나 블록을 정가인 50달러에 구입했다.

11 장소 추론 | ④
해석
남 넌 뭘 읽고 있니?
여 바나나에 관한 책이야.
남 그것들에 관한 흥미 있는 내용이 있니?
여 응. 너 어떤 바나나는 안에 딱딱한 씨가 있다는 것을 알았니?
남 정말? 재미있네.
여 응, 나는 이 책이 마음에 들어. 나는 이것을 사고 싶다.
남 내가 너라면, 도서관에 가서 그 책을 빌릴 텐데.
여 음, 난 책 사는 걸 좋아해. 계산하고 나서 바로 올게.
해설 여자가 책을 보다가 책을 구입하겠다고 했으므로 두 사람이 대화하는 장소는 서점이다.

12 언급되지 않은 것 | ③
해석
여 좋은 아침입니다. 교장입니다. 여러분들은 작년에 홍콩의 한 학교를 방문했던 것을 기억하십니까? 이번 주 내내, 우리는 특별한 손님들의 학교 방문이 있을 예정입니다. 손님들은 홍콩의 Saint Mark's 학교의 학생들입니다. 우리는 그들이 오늘 아침 아홉 시에 도착할 것으로 예상합니다. 그들은 여러분과 함께 수업을 듣고 점심 식사를 함께할 것입니다. 그들이 환영 받는 느낌이 들도록 해 주시고, 그들이 우리 학교에서 즐거운 한 주를 보낼 수 있도록 도와주세요.
해설 학교를 방문하는 손님들에 관해 언급되지 않은 것은 총 방문 인원이다.

13 도표 정보 파악 | ⑤
해석
남 음악 숙제를 마쳤니?
여 아직. 어떤 콘서트를 가야 할지 결정을 못 했거든.
남 서울 오케스트라 콘서트에 함께 가는 건 어떠니?
여 좋아. 언제 어디에서 콘서트를 하는데?
남 7월 28일과 29일에 화이트 아트센터에서 열려.
여 난 29일이 좋아. 관람료는 얼마야?
남 R석은 20달러, S석은 15달러, 그리고 A석은 12달러야.
여 A석이 내게 좋겠다. 그나저나 나 여동생을 데려가고 싶은데. 나이 제한이 있니?
남 있어. 7세 미만의 어린이는 공연장에 입장할 수 없어.
해설 7세 미만의 아이들은 음악회 입장이 불가능하다.

14 주제 파악 | ③
해석
남 당신은 이것을 하늘에서 볼 수 있습니다. 이것은 공기 중의 작은 물방울들이 모인 것입니다. 이것의 색깔은 시간과 날씨에 따라 바뀝니다. 예를 들어, 이것의 색깔은 해질녘에는 붉은색이 되고, 밤에는 남색이 됩니다. 또한, 이것이 회색이 되면, 당신은 곧 비가 올 거라고 추측할 수 있습니다.
해설 공기 중의 작은 물방울이 모여 시간에 따라 붉은색이 되기도 하고, 남색이 되기도 하며 회색이 되면 비가 올 것을 추측할 수 있는 것은 구름에 관한 설명이다.

15 한 일 / 할 일 파악 | ②
해석
남 안녕, Monica. 오늘 오후에 뭘 할 것인지 말해 줘.
여 확실하지 않아. 아마도 집에서 책을 볼 거야. 너는?
남 음, 난 낚시를 하러 갈 계획이야. 나랑 같이 갈래?
여 물론이지. 가고 싶어. 낚시 가는 것이 집에서 책을 읽는 것보다 훨씬 더 재미있을 것 같아.
남 좋아! 1시쯤에 데리러 갈게.
여 그때 보자.
해설 여자는 남자가 오후에 낚시를 가는데 함께 가기로 했다.

16 숫자 정보 파악 – 시각 | ②
해석
남 내일 농구 경기를 보기 위해 몇 시에 만날까?
여 경기는 몇 시에 시작하는데?
남 오후 7시에 시작해. 버스 정류장에서 6시 30분에 만나는 거 어때?
여 그때는 교통체증이 있을 거야. 5시 30분에 만나면 어떻겠니?
남 음, 나 피아노 수업이 5시 30분에 끝나. 버스 정류장까지 가는데 약 10분이 걸릴 거야.
여 좋아. 5시 40분에 만나. 햄버거를 사서 버스 정류장으로 갈게.
남 좋아.
해설 두 사람은 5시 40분에 버스 정류장 앞에서 만나기로 했다.

17 상황에 맞는 말 찾기 | ⑤
해석
여 Judy의 친구들 중 한 명이 자정에 여는 꽃 시장에 대해 Judy에게 말해 주었다. Judy는 그 시장을 보러 가고 싶지만, 그녀는 밤에 혼자 그곳에 가는 것이 걱정된다. 게다가, 자정에는 대중교통이 없고 Judy는 어떻게 그곳에 갔다가 집에 오는지도 알지 못한다. Judy는 그녀의 아버지가 그녀를 그곳에 데려다주기를 바란다. 이런 상황에서, Judy는 아버지께 뭐라고 말하겠는가?

Judy 저와 함께 꽃 시장에 가 주실 수 있으세요?

① 그거 정말 좋겠네요.
② 저는 그렇게 많이 꽃을 좋아하지는 않아요.
③ 죄송하지만 저는 갈 필요가 없어요.
④ 제가 그 시장에 가도 괜찮을까요?

해설 여자는 꽃 시장이 한밤중에 열려서 아버지와 함께 꽃 시장에 가면 좋겠다고 생각하므로 ⑤가 답으로 적절하다.

18 한 일 / 할 일 파악 │③
해석
여 너 무엇을 검색하고 있니?
남 나는 블루투스 이어폰을 검색 중이야. 그게 아주 멋지고 편리해 보여서.
여 그것들은 자주 충전해야 해. 그것들은 또한 잃어버리기도 쉬워.
남 하지만 내가 찾은 것을 봐. 이것은 최신 모델인데, 너무 멋져 보여.
여 그래, 그럼 내 것을 며칠 동안 먼저 써 봐. 그런 다음에 그것들을 살지 말지를 결정해.
남 좋은 생각이다. 너는 그것을 자주 안 쓰니?
여 안 써. 나는 쓰던 것이 더 좋더라. 내가 내일 그것들을 가져다줄게.
남 정말 고마워.
해설 남자는 블루투스 이어폰을 구입하기 전에 여자의 이어폰을 빌려서 사용해 보려고 하고 있다.

19 알맞은 응답 찾기 │③
해석
남 안녕, Helen. 늦어서 미안해.
여 무슨 일이 있었니?
남 가방을 잃어버렸어. 지하철에 두고 내렸어.
여 안됐구나. 그래서 어떻게 했니?
남 지하철역에 있는 분실물 센터에 가서 신고를 했어.
여 좋은 생각이야! 찾았으면 좋겠다.
남 나도 그래. 어쨌든 너무 오래 기다리게 해서 정말 미안해.
여 괜찮아. 이런 일들은 있게 마련이야.
① 네가 새 것을 사길 바라.
② 오, 굉장하다! 더 좋을 수가 없어.
④ 날 위해 그걸 해 주다니 친절하구나.
⑤ 문제없어. 다음에 더 잘할 수 있어.
해설 남자가 가방을 잃어버려 분실물 센터에 다녀오느라 약속 시간에 늦어서 여자에게 사과하고 있는 상황이므로 괜찮다고 말하는 ③이 여자의 응답으로 가장 적절하다.

20 알맞은 응답 찾기 │④
해석
남 우리 가게의 차들이 어떠세요?
여 음, 꽤 만족스럽네요.
남 감사합니다. 다시 방문해 주시겠어요?
여 물론이지요. 회원 카드를 받을 수 있나요?
남 네. 여기에 이름을 쓰고 그 옆에 서명해 주세요.
여 그래요. 이걸로 할인을 받을 수 있나요?
남 네. 저희 직원에게 카드를 꼭 보여 주세요.

① 그거 아주 좋은 생각이네요.
② 할인을 받을 수 있으면 좋겠어요.
③ 물론이죠. 얼마나 많이 할인해 주세요?
⑤ 아니요, 자신의 장바구니를 가지고 다니셔야 합니다.
해설 여자가 회원 카드로 할인을 받을 수 있는지 물어봤으므로 가능하다며 카드를 직원에게 보여 줘야 한다고 말하는 ④가 남자의 응답으로 가장 적절하다.

12회 영어 듣기모의고사 pp. 094~095

01 ⑤	**02** ⑤	**03** ④	**04** ③	**05** ④
06 ①	**07** ③	**08** ⑤	**09** ③	**10** ④
11 ③	**12** ③	**13** ⑤	**14** ⑤	**15** ①
16 ④	**17** ①	**18** ⑤	**19** ③	**20** ⑤

Dictation Test 12회 pp. 096~101

01 ❶ online shopping ❷ this cap on it ❸ your shirt and pants online
02 ❶ to visit my sister ❷ she looks very thin ❸ have a good time
03 ❶ return this book ❷ you lost my book ❸ Take a look at
04 ❶ Do you want me ❷ at the furniture section ❸ let's go to
05 ❶ will be displayed ❷ Whenever I take a picture ❸ where you took these pictures
06 ❶ I'm going to have ❷ I can't wait ❸ right after school
07 ❶ shouldn't be late ❷ on your right ❸ hope to visit
08 ❶ I didn't bring one ❷ the closest store instead ❸ I need to buy
09 ❶ helping me with it ❷ Let's go to ❸ let me treat you
10 ❶ I'd like to buy ❷ make a bouquet ❸ for a nice bouquet
11 ❶ choose a movie ❷ to get tickets ❸ move to a restaurant
12 ❶ my pet dog ❷ He loves apples ❸ do a special trick
13 ❶ on Mondays and Wednesdays ❷ The class is in ❸ there's no textbook
14 ❶ to save water ❷ not all of it ❸ costs a lot
15 ❶ do this vacation ❷ do volunteer work ❸ make bread for the kids

16 ❶ make an appointment ❷ can't make it on
   Monday ❸ half an hour later
17 ❶ carrying her baby ❷ heavy bags ❸ to help her
18 ❶ There's something wrong ❷ gas station
   ❸ walk to get some gas
19 ❶ about an old woman ❷ she helped poorer
   people ❸ gave food and clothes
20 ❶ major in French ❷ dreams can change ❸ my
   favorite song

01 그림 정보 파악 – 사물 | ⑤

해석

여 Sam, 너 오늘 멋지다.

남 고마워. 온라인 쇼핑을 좀 했어.

여 네 신발이 마음에 든다. 어느 사이트에서 그것들을 샀니?

남 나는 그것들을 GD 쇼핑몰에서 샀어. 그곳에서 이 모자도 샀어.

여 나머지 것들은? 네 셔츠랑 바지도 온라인으로 주문했니?

남 응. 하지만 이 손목시계는 아버지가 주신 생일 선물이야.

여 그건 네 셔츠랑 매우 잘 어울린다.

해설 손목시계는 온라인으로 주문한 물건이 아니라 남자가 아버지께 받은
생일 선물이다.

02 목적 파악 | ⑤

해석

[전화벨이 울린다.]

남 여보세요?

여 안녕, Kevin. 나 Linda야. 나는 뉴욕에서 전화하고 있어.

남 정말? 언제 거기 갔었니?

여 나는 내 여동생을 방문하려고 어제 여기에 왔어. 그녀는 공부하러 이곳
에 혼자 와 있거든.

남 오, 몰랐어. 거기에서 그녀는 어떻게 지내니?

여 그녀는 괜찮아. 그런데 많이 야위어 보여.

남 그곳에서 여동생과 즐거운 시간을 보내길 바랄게.

여 그럴게. 안녕!

해설 여자의 두 번째 말에서 여자는 여동생을 보러 뉴욕에 간 것임을 알 수
있다.

03 그림 상황에 어울리는 대화 찾기 | ④

해석

① 남 너 도서관에 가는 중이니?

   여 응. 나는 이 책을 반납하려고 해.

② 남 너는 이 책이 어땠니?

   여 나는 아직 그것을 다 끝내지 못했어.

③ 남 지난주에 네가 빌려간 내 책을 잃어버렸다고 말했니?

   여 미안해. 모두 내 잘못이야.

④ 남 이것은 누구의 책이니?

   여 아, 그거 내 거야. 그것을 찾아 여기저기를 살피고 있었어.

⑤ 남 좋은 전자책 있니?

   여 응, 있어. 이거 봐봐.

해설 여자가 남자가 들고 있는 책이 자신의 것이라고 대답하는 상황에 적절
한 대화는 ④이다.

04 장소 추론 | ③

해석

여 Brian, 너 우리가 너의 새 침대를 사러 오늘 쇼핑하러 갈 것을 기억하지,
그렇지?

남 물론이죠. 학교 앞에서 만날까요?

여 아니. 네 학교는 백화점에서 가깝잖아. 거기서 4시에 보자.

남 제가 지하철역에서 기다릴까요?

여 그럴 필요 없어. 백화점 정문에서 만나자.

남 엄마가 먼저 가구를 둘러보시는 게 더 좋을 것 같아요. 8층 가구 코너
에서 만나요.

여 그거 좋은 생각이다. 침대를 찾는데 시간이 오래 걸리지 않으면, 그 후
에 네가 제일 좋아하는 초밥 집에 가자.

남 완벽한데요.

해설 남자의 침대를 사러 가기로 한 두 사람은 백화점 8층의 가구 코너에서
만나기로 했다.

05 직업 및 장래 희망 | ④

해석

여 우와! 이 사진들 전부 네가 찍었니?

남 물론이지. 그것들은 이번에 전시될 사진들이야.

여 정말 멋진 사진들이구나.

남 고마워. 나는 사진을 찍을 때마다, 최고의 장면을 얻으려고 온갖 노력을
다하지.

여 대단해. 이 사진들 어디서 찍었는지 궁금해.

남 파리의 여러 장소에서 찍었어.

여 그곳들은 아주 훌륭해! 나도 언젠가 파리에 가고 싶어.

해설 남자는 파리에서 찍은 사진을 전시할 것이라고 했으므로 남자의 직업
은 사진작가이다.

06 심정 파악 | ①

해석

여 방과 후에 뭐 할 거야?

남 나는 민수랑 아이스크림을 먹으러 갈 거야. 그의 집 근처에 유명한 아
이스크림 가게가 있어.

여 와, 나는 정말 아이스크림 좋아해. 너희와 같이 가도 되니?

남 물론이지. 그 가게는 매우 인기가 있어서, 우리가 늦으면 못 먹을 수도
있어.

여 너무 기대된다. 언제 만날까?

남 학교 끝나면 바로 만나자.

여 그럼 방과 후 바로 너의 교실로 갈게.

남 좋아. 그때 보자.

해설 여자는 방과 후에 유명한 아이스크림 가게를 방문하는 것을 몹시 기대
하고 있다.

07 어색한 대화 찾기 | ③

해석

① 여 그의 새 앨범을 어떻게 생각해?

   남 아주 마음에 들어.

② 여 너 다시는 늦어서는 안 될 것 같구나.

   남 네. 일찍 올게요.

③ 여 버스가 언제 오기로 되어 있니?

   남 버스 정류장은 네 오른편에 있어.

④ 여 무엇을 드시겠어요?

남 커피를 먹겠습니다.
⑤ 여 이번 방학에 무엇을 하고 싶니?
남 일본에 있는 이메일 친구를 방문하고 싶어.
해설 언제 버스가 오는지 묻는 말에 대해 버스 정류소가 오른쪽에 있다고 대답하는 것은 어색하다.

08 부탁한 일 파악 | ⑤
해석

여 아, 밖에 비가 오네. 우산 있니?
남 응, 있어. 너는 없니?
여 아니, 안 가져왔어.
남 그럼 내가 오늘 너를 집에 데려다줄게. 같이 쓰자.
여 음, 대신 가장 가까운 상점으로 데려다줄래?
남 물론이지. 새 것 사려고?
여 응, 나는 하나를 살 필요가 있거든. 고마워.
해설 여자는 집까지 같이 우산을 쓰자는 남자에게 대신 우산을 사기 위해 가까운 상점에 데려다줄 것을 부탁했다.

09 의도 파악 | ③
해석

남 너의 발표는 대단했어. 정말 감동적이었어.
여 내 발표를 도와줘서 고마워. 너 없이는 해낼 수 없었을 거야.
남 아니야, 할 수 있었을 거야. 나는 네가 얼마나 열심히 일했는지 알거든.
여 고마워. 그런데, 배고프지 않니?
남 응, 배고프다. 저녁시간이야.
여 건물 앞에 있는 새 식당에 가자.
남 좋은 생각이야. 그곳의 음식을 먹어 보고 싶었어.
여 오늘은 내가 너를 대접하게 해 줘. 네게 고맙거든.
해설 여자는 마지막 말 Please let me ~.에서 남자에게 식사를 대접하겠다고 제안하고 있다.

10 숫자 정보 파악 – 금액 | ④
해석

여 안녕하세요. 도와드릴까요, 손님?
남 음, 딸에게 줄 꽃을 좀 사고 싶습니다.
여 이 빨간 장미는 어떠세요?
남 좋아요. 얼마인가요?
여 한 다발에 15달러입니다. 빨간 장미와 어울리는 보라색 팬지는 좀 어떠세요? 10달러밖에 안 해요.
남 오, 좋은 생각이에요. 꽃으로 꽃다발을 만드나요?
여 네, 그래요. 꽃다발을 만드는데 7달러만 더 내시면 됩니다.
남 좋습니다. 예쁜 꽃다발을 만들어 주세요.
여 문제없어요.
해설 남자는 15달러짜리 빨간 장미 한 다발과 10달러짜리 보라색 팬지 한 다발을 구입한 후 꽃다발을 만들어 달라고 요청했으므로 꽃다발을 만드는 비용 7달러를 추가해 32달러를 지불해야 한다.

11 장소 추론 | ③
해석

남 민지야, 늦어서 매우 미안해.
여 오, James. 괜찮아. 책을 읽고 있었어. 이제 영화를 고를까?
남 글쎄, 여기에 사람들이 너무 많다고 생각하지 않니? 사람들이 표를 사

려고 줄을 길게 서서 기다리고 있네.
여 응. 인기 있는 영화의 표는 이미 매진이야.
남 우선 식당으로 옮기지 않을래? 저녁 식사 후에 영화를 보는 게 나을 것 같아.
여 그거 좋은 생각이다. 같이 맛있는 저녁을 먹자.
남 좋아.
해설 두 사람은 영화를 고르고 있는데 인기 있는 영화의 표가 품절되었다고 이야기하고 있는 것으로 보아 두 사람이 대화하는 장소는 영화관이다.

12 언급되지 않은 것 | ③
해석

남 저의 애완견 Bingo를 소개합니다. Bingo는 갈색 털이 있는 두 살짜리 푸들입니다. 그는 산책을 아주 좋아해서, 저는 비가 오지 않는다면 매일 밤 Bingo와 산책을 하러 갑니다. 그가 사과를 좋아하지만 너무 많이 주지 않으려고 신경 쓰고 있습니다. 그는 또한 특별한 재주가 있습니다. 제가 손을 내밀 때 Bingo가 그의 발을 제 손에 올립니다. 그는 정말로 귀엽고 똑똑합니다. 저희 집에 오시면 Bingo와 함께 놀 수 있습니다.
해설 남자의 애완동물인 Bingo의 크기에 대해서는 언급되지 않았다.

13 도표 정보 파악 | ⑤
해석

남 Mary, 난 방과 후 중국어 수업이 듣고 싶어. 무슨 요일에 수업이 있는지 아니?
여 수업은 월요일과 수요일에 있어.
남 알겠어. 오, 어디로 그리고 몇 시에 가야 하는지 모르는데.
여 수업은 205호 실에서 오후 3시 40분에 시작한대.
남 교재를 사야 하니?
여 아니, 이 수업에는 교재가 없어. 그러니까 너는 어떤 것도 살 필요가 없어.
남 좋은데. 정보 고마워.
해설 방과 후 수업에 교재가 없다고 했으므로 ⑤가 대화의 내용과 일치하지 않는다.

14 주제 파악 | ⑤
해석

여 모든 사람들은 우리가 물을 절약해야 한다는 것을 압니다. 하지만, 정말 실천은 하시나요? 많은 사람들은 우리가 물을 절약해야 한다고 생각하지 않습니다. 그들은 우리가 사용할 수 있는 물이 많다고 말합니다. 맞습니다, 우리 주변에는 많은 물이 있어요, 하지만 그것 전부가 식수는 아닙니다. 우리가 마실 수 있는 물을 만드는 데는 많은 돈이 듭니다. 물을 절약하는 것은 에너지를 절약하는 것입니다.
해설 식수를 만드는 데 많은 돈이 든다는 것을 언급하면서 수자원을 절약해야 한다고 강조하고 있다.

15 한 일 / 할 일 파악 | ①
해석

남 이번 방학에 뭐 할 거야?
여 이번 여름에 캄보디아에 갈 거야.
남 와! 앙코르와트와 같은 볼 곳이 많이 있다고 들었어.
여 응, 나도 거기 갈 수 있으면 좋겠다.
남 그게 무슨 말이니?

여　사실, 나는 거기 봉사 활동을 하러 갈 예정이야. 관광할 시간이 있을 것 같지 않아.

남　너 정말 대단하다. 거기서 무엇을 할 건데?

여　나는 아이들을 위해 빵을 만들 거야.

해설　여자의 마지막 말로 여자는 캄보디아에서 아이들을 위해 빵을 만들 것 임을 알 수 있다.

16　숫자 정보 파악 - 시각 | ④

해석

여　한 박사님 병원입니다. 도와드릴까요?

남　제가 건강 검진을 받을 필요가 있어서 진료 약속을 잡고 싶습니다.

여　검진을 마지막으로 언제 받으셨나요?

남　약 일 년 전에 한 번 검진을 받았어요.

여　그렇군요. 월요일 2시 30분에 오실 수 있으세요?

남　죄송하지만, 월요일에는 갈 수 없어요.

여　화요일 2시 30분은 어떠세요?

남　음, 30분 늦게 가도 괜찮을까요?

여　괜찮아요. 그때 뵙죠.

해설　남자는 건강 검진을 받기 위해 3시에 병원을 예약했다.

17　상황에 맞는 말 찾기 | ①

해석

여　진수는 부산에 계신 그의 할머니를 뵈러 가는 중이었다. 그는 기차에 올라타서 기차가 출발하기를 기다렸다. 진수는 그의 곁에 앉으려고 하는 한 젊은 여성을 보았다. 그녀는 아기를 안고 있었고, 무거운 가방 들을 들고 있었다. 그 순간, 아기가 울기 시작했고, 그녀는 매우 당황 스러워 보였다. 이런 상황에서, 진수는 그녀를 돕기 위해 뭐라고 말하겠 는가?

진수　① 제가 도와드릴까요?

② 가방 드는 것을 도와주실 수 있나요?

③ 저는 이 가방을 환불받고 싶어요.

④ 나는 당신의 아기가 너무 많이 울지 않았으면 좋겠네요.

⑤ 그걸 제게 주세요. 제가 지불할 차례예요.

해설　아이와 무거운 가방을 들고 있는 여성이 아이가 울어 당황하자 진수가 여성을 돕고 싶어 하는 상황이므로 ①이 답으로 적절하다.

18　한 일 / 할 일 파악 | ⑤

해석

여　왜 우리는 멈춰 섰지? 우리는 길 한복판에 있어.

남　뭔가 잘못됐나 봐. 차가 갑자기 멈췄어.

여　그걸 고치는 방법을 모르니?

남　무슨 문제가 있는지 모르겠네. 오, 우리는 기름이 떨어졌구나.

여　오, 세상에! 이 근처에 주유소가 하나 있어. 내가 걸어가서 기름을 사 올게.

남　좋아. 그럼, 나는 여기에 있을게.

해설　기름이 없어 갑자기 차가 멈춘 상황에서 여자가 가까운 주유소까지 걸 어간다고 했다.

19　알맞은 응답 찾기 | ③

해석

남　무엇을 읽고 있니?

여　한 할머니에 관한 기사를 읽고 있어.

남　좀 더 이야기해 주겠니?

여　그녀는 사용한 캔이나 병을 모아 돈을 벌었어. 그녀는 가난했지만, 그 돈으로 그녀보다 더 가난한 사람들을 도왔어.

남　더 자세히 말해 줘.

여　그녀는 매년 가난한 사람들에게 음식과 옷을 드렸대. 대단하지 않아? 그녀에 대해 어떻게 생각해?

남　③ 나 역시 그녀가 매우 존경스럽구나.

① 음, 나는 그렇게 생각하지 않아.

② 다음에는 더 잘할 거야.

④ 나는 이미 지난주에 그 기사를 읽었어.

⑤ 그녀는 곧 돌아와야 할 것 같아.

해설　가난하지만 다른 가난한 사람을 돕는 여성에 대해 어떻게 생각하는지 물었으므로 자신 또한 그녀를 존경한다고 말하는 ③이 남자의 응답으 로 가장 적절하다.

20　알맞은 응답 찾기 | ⑤

해석

남　나는 대학에서 프랑스어를 전공할 거야.

여　정말이야? 믿을 수가 없네.

남　뭐가 그렇게 놀랍니?

여　넌 항상 음악가가 되고 싶다고 말했잖아.

남　너도 알다시피, 꿈은 바뀔 수 있는 거야. 어쨌든 나는 프랑스어 수업도 미리 들을 거야.

여　무엇 때문에 프랑스어 애호가가 되었니?

남　프랑스 노래들 듣다가 프랑스어에 매료되었거든. 내가 가장 좋아하는 노래 들어 볼래?

여　⑤ 물론이지. 그 노래를 들려 줘.

① 나는 프랑스에 가본 적이 없어.

② 충고해 줘서 고마워.

③ 음악가가 되는 건 어때?

④ 나는 프랑스어 수업에 흥미가 없어.

해설　남자가 자신이 좋아하는 프랑스 노래를 들어 보라고 권유하고 있으므 로 노래를 들어 보겠다고 말하는 ⑤가 여자의 응답으로 가장 적절하다.

13회　영어 듣기모의고사　pp. 102~103

01 ①	02 ①	03 ④	04 ⑤	05 ②
06 ③	07 ③	08 ②	09 ⑤	10 ②
11 ②	12 ②	13 ④	14 ⑤	15 ①
16 ②	17 ⑤	18 ⑤	19 ⑤	20 ④

Dictation Test 13회　pp. 104~109

01 ❶ do the stretching we learned　❷ stand straight
　❸ touch our toes

02 ❶ make a reservation　❷ There are ten of us
　❸ What's your name

03 ❶ go straight two blocks　❷ turn right　❸ a flower shop

04 ❶ preparing our group presentation ❷ this Friday ❸ decide the topic

05 ❶ transferred to this school ❷ why you moved to ❸ your new school life

06 ❶ do you mind if ❷ I've lost it ❸ maybe someone found it

07 ❶ Would you mind ❷ appreciate your help

08 ❶ I can't have lunch ❷ to get it ❸ buy milk and bread

09 ❶ keep in touch with ❷ won't be easy but

10 ❶ fifty percent off ❷ That'll be sixty dollars

11 ❶ Are there any good seats ❷ I have no seats ❸ on the second floor

12 ❶ basic information ❷ how they made you feel ❸ what you want to do

13 ❶ may I speak to ❷ has been canceled ❸ this afternoon

14 ❶ try not to run ❷ don't like waiting for

15 ❶ my new cellphone back ❷ I used it in class ❸ in the teachers' office

16 ❶ tomorrow is their wedding anniversary ❷ Two years later

17 ❶ to buy some fruit ❷ also very expensive ❸ buy some apples instead

18 ❶ clean the classroom ❷ borrow some books ❸ doing my homework

19 ❶ make a lot of noise ❷ run around all day long ❸ What should I do

20 ❶ the same question ❷ I'm getting old ❸ It can happen

01 　그림 정보 파악 – 인물　| ①

해석

여 우리 5시간 동안 공부하고 있었어.

남 오, 정말?

여 나는 우리가 약간의 휴식을 취하고 잠시 쉬어야 한다고 생각해.

남 혹은 예전에 체육시간에 배웠던 스트레칭을 해보는 건 어떨까?

여 그거 좋은 생각이다. 어떻게 하는지 기억나니?

남 당연하지. 아주 간단해. 우선 우리는 똑바로 서야 해. 그리고 무릎을 구부리지 않은 상태에서 양손을 발가락에 닿게 노력해야 해.

해설 똑바로 선 후에 무릎을 구부리지 않고 양손을 발가락에 대는 자세는 ①이다.

02 　목적 파악　| ①

해석

[전화벨이 울린다.]

남 안녕하세요. Judy Palace 식당입니다.

여 오늘 밤으로 예약하고 싶습니다.

남 알겠습니다. 몇 시죠?

여 8시요.

남 8시요. 일행이 몇 분이시죠?

여 우리는 10명입니다. 그리고 채식주의자를 위한 요리가 있나요? 우리 중 세 명이 채식주의자여서요.

남 물론이죠. 저희는 몇 가지 채식주의자용 요리가 있어요. 성함과 전화번호가 어떻게 되시죠?

여 Olivia Ross이고, 081-2254-3312입니다.

해설 여자는 식당을 예약하려고 남자에게 전화를 걸었다.

03 　그림 정보 파악 – 길 찾기　| ④

해석

여 실례합니다. 가장 가까운 버스 정류장이 어디에 있는지 아시나요?

남 네. 두 블록만 곧장 가신 다음에 모퉁이에서 오른쪽으로 도세요.

여 두 블록 가서 오른쪽으로 돌아요?

남 네. 그리고 나서, 몇 걸음만 걸어가시면 꽃집과 동물병원을 볼 수 있을 거예요. 버스 정류장은 그것들 사이에 있어요. 분명 찾기 쉬울 거예요.

여 알겠습니다. 매우 감사합니다.

남 천만에요.

해설 출발하는 곳에서 두 블록을 직진한 후 모퉁이에서 오른쪽으로 돈 후 꽃집과 동물병원 사이에 있는 곳은 ④이다.

04 　특정 정보 파악 – 요일　| ⑤

해석

남 우리 조별 발표를 준비하기 시작해야 할 것 같아.

여 좋은 생각이야. 이번 주에 학교 마치고 만나서 이야기해 보자.

남 나는 이번 금요일에 치과에 가야 해. 다른 날은 괜찮아.

여 나는 화요일과 목요일에 오후 학교 수업이 있어. 월요일은 어때?

남 좋아. 그럼 월요일에 주제를 정하고, 수요일에 자료를 준비하자.

여 완벽해.

해설 남자는 금요일에 치과에 가야 해서 조별 모임을 할 수 없다고 했다.

05 　직업 및 장래 희망　| ②

해석

여 실례합니다, 선생님. 제가 학교 식당에 들어가려면 여기에서 줄을 서야 하나요?

남 응, 그렇단다. 너는 낯이 익어 보이지 않는구나.

여 저는 3학년 지나라고 합니다. 저는 오늘 이 학교로 전학을 왔어요.

남 어디 출신이니?

여 대구에서 왔어요.

남 왜 서울로 이사 왔는지 물어봐도 될까?

여 아빠가 서울에서 일하기 시작하셨거든요.

남 그렇구나. 여기 새로운 학교생활이 마음에 들었으면 좋겠구나.

여 감사합니다.

해설 여자의 두 번째 말로 여자는 오늘 학교에 전학 온 학생이라는 것을 알 수 있다.

06 　심정 파악　| ③

해석

여 David, 나와 잠시 얘기를 나눌 수 있니?

남 그럼, 지민아. 무슨 일이니?

여　한 달 전에 내가 너에게서 영어 소설책을 한 권 빌렸던 거 기억하니?

남　응, 그래.

여　내가 그것을 잃어버린 것 같아. 정말 미안해.

남　하지만 지민아, 내가 어제 내 책상 위에서 그 책을 발견했어. 나는 네가 그것을 거기에 놓아두었다고 생각했었는데.

여　아니야. 오, 아마도 누군가 그것을 발견하고 책에 있는 너의 이름을 본 거 같아.

해설　여자는 남자의 소설책을 잃어버려 걱정했는데 누군가 이름을 보고 남자에게 찾아 준 상황이므로 여자는 안심했을 것이다.

07　어색한 대화 찾기　| ③

해석

① 남　내가 그 제안을 받아들여야 한다고 생각하니?

　여　당연하지.

② 남　너 왜 그렇게 화가 났어?

　여　나는 누군가 내 샌드위치를 훔쳐가서 화가 났어.

③ 남　제 사진을 한 장 찍어 주실 수 있나요?

　여　당연하지요. 제가 좀 바빠서요.

④ 남　나는 서점이 언제 닫는지 궁금해.

　여　오후 10시에 닫아.

⑤ 남　감사합니다. 당신의 도움에 정말 감사드려요.

　여　천만에요.

해설　사진을 찍어 줄 수 있는지 부탁하는 말에 대해 당연하다고 말하며 지금 바쁘다고 대답하는 것은 어색하다.

08　부탁한 일 파악　| ②

해석

남　선미야, 점심 먹으러 가자.

여　나 오늘 너희들이랑 점심 못 먹어. Steve랑 Jane이랑 가.

남　왜? 다이어트하니?

여　아니야. 내 과학 보고서를 가져오는 것을 잊었는데 그것을 오늘 내야 해.

남　그래서 점심시간 동안 그걸 다시 쓰게?

여　아니, 그걸 가지러 집에 갈 거야.

남　그럼 서둘러야겠네. 점심 먹을 시간이 없겠다.

여　그래서, 우유랑 빵 좀 사다 줄래? 나중에 돈 줄게.

남　그럴게. 돌아오면 보자.

해설　여자는 숙제를 가지러 집에 갔다 와야 한다며 남자에게 빵과 우유를 사 올 것을 부탁했다.

09　의도 파악　| ⑤

해석

남　서영아, 너 일주일만 있으면 캐나다로 떠나지, 그렇지?

여　응. 나 정말 슬퍼.

남　기운 내! 네가 우리를 영원히 떠나는 게 아니야. 우리와 연락할 수 있어.

여　네 말이 맞아.

남　그런데 너는 캐나다에서 얼마나 공부할 거니?

여　나는 캐나다에서 3년 동안 공부할 계획이야.

남　그건 쉽지 않겠지만, 내가 너의 행운을 빌어 줄게!

해설　남자는 캐나다에 공부하러 가는 여자에게 행운을 빌어 주고 있는 상황이다.

10　숫자 정보 파악 - 금액　| ②

해석

남　도움이 필요하신가요?

여　네. 이 티셔츠가 얼마인가요?

남　40달러입니다. 당신이 이것을 하나 사면 다른 하나는 50% 할인해 드립니다.

여　아주 좋네요. 그렇다면, 제가 이것과 저것을 사고 싶어요.

남　훌륭한 선택이세요. 60달러가 되겠네요.

여　알겠습니다. 여기 100달러짜리 지폐가 있어요.

남　감사합니다. 여기에 거스름돈이 있습니다.

해설　40달러인 티셔츠 하나를 구입하면 동일한 다른 티셔츠는 50% 할인해 주므로 여자는 60달러를 지불하면 되는데, 100달러를 지불했으므로 거스름돈으로 40달러를 받을 것이다.

11　장소 추론　| ②

해석

남　다음 공연을 위한 좋은 좌석이 1층에 있습니까?

여　네, 왼쪽 편에 좋은 좌석이 몇 자리 있습니다.

남　좋습니다. 좌석 배치도를 볼 수 있을까요?

여　네, 바로 여기 있습니다. 몇 좌석이나 필요하십니까?

남　두 자리만요.

여　죄송합니다만, 연달아 있는 좌석은 없습니다.

남　오, 저희는 함께 앉고 싶어요.

여　알겠습니다. 그렇다면 2층의 좌석들은 어떠신가요?

남　네, 좋습니다.

해설　남자가 다음 공연의 자리를 문의하고 있고 여자가 이를 안내하는 것으로 보아 대화가 이루어지는 장소는 공연장이다.

12　언급되지 않은 것　| ②

해석

여　만약 좋은 독후감을 쓰고 싶다면, 다음에 말하는 것을 시도해 보세요. 좋은 독후감은 제목이나 작가와 같은 책에 관한 기본 정보를 포함해야 합니다. 또한 여러분은 감명 깊은 부분의 요약과, 그 부분에 관한 여러분의 느낌도 써야 합니다. 가장 중요한 것은 여러분이 독서 후에 하고 싶은 것을 쓰는 것입니다. 짧아도 괜찮습니다. 여러분의 독서 경험을 여러분 자신의 인생에 결부시키기 위해 그저 최선을 다해야 합니다.

해설　좋은 독서 감상문의 조건으로 언급되지 않은 것은 독후감의 길이이다.

13　도표 정보 파악　| ④

해석

[전화벨이 울린다.]

남　여보세요?

여　안녕하세요, Lisa와 통화할 수 있을까요?

남　미안합니다. 그녀가 지금 없네요. 메시지 남겨드릴까요?

여　네, 그렇게 해 주세요.

남　알겠습니다. 잠시 기다리세요. (잠시 후) 준비됐어요.

여　저는 Michelle이라고 합니다. Lisa에게 우리 티타임이 취소되었다고 전해 주세요. 그것은 오늘 오후에 태풍이 상륙할 것이기 때문입니다.

남　알겠습니다. 또 다른 게 있나요?

여　아니요. 그게 다예요. 고맙습니다.

해설 티타임은 오늘 오후 태풍의 상륙 때문에 변경된 것이 아니라 취소되었다.

14 주제 파악 | ⑤
해석
여 사람들은 위층으로 혹은 아래층으로 이동하기 위해 이것을 사용한다. 당신은 커다란 건물에서 이것을 발견할 수 있다. 당신은 이것을 사용할 때 조심해야만 한다. 난간을 잡고, 뛰지 않는 것이 좋다. 사실, 당신은 엘리베이터를 사용한다면 층과 층 사이를 훨씬 더 빠르게 이동할 수 있다. 하지만 나는 이것을 사용하는 것을 선호한다. 왜냐하면 버튼을 누른 후 엘리베이터를 기다리는 것을 좋아하지 않기 때문이다.
해설 커다란 건물에서 위층과 아래층으로 이동하기 위해 사용되며 엘리베이터보다 선호한다고 했으므로 에스컬레이터라는 것을 알 수 있다.

15 한 일 / 할 일 파악 | ①
해석
남 안녕, Judy! 나는 오늘 내 새 휴대 전화를 돌려받을 거야.
여 그게 무슨 말이야?
남 나는 일주일 전에 새 휴대 전화를 샀어. 그런데 그날 수업시간에 그걸 사용해서 영어 선생님이 가져가셨거든.
여 수업시간에 휴대 전화를 사용했다고?
남 응, 그러지 말았어야 했다는 걸 알아.
여 그래서 그게 교무실에 일주일간 보관됐었구나.
남 맞아. 오, 나 휴대 전화 찾으러 가야겠다. 또 보자.
해설 남자는 휴대 전화를 돌려받기 위해 교무실에 방문할 것이다.

16 숫자 정보 파악 – 연도 | ②
해석
남 안녕, Laura.
여 민호야, 안녕. 너 여기에서 뭐하니?
남 내일이 부모님 결혼기념일이라서 부모님을 위한 선물을 좀 찾아보고 있어.
여 그분들은 언제 결혼하셨는데?
남 그들은 1997년에 결혼하셨다고 들었어. 2년 뒤에 내가 태어났지.
여 너의 쌍둥이 여동생들은? 그들은 언제 태어났니?
남 그들은 서울에서 월드컵이 개최되었던 2002년에 태어났어.
해설 남자의 부모님이 1997년에 결혼하시고, 2년 뒤에 남자가 태어났다고 했으므로 남자는 1999년도에 태어났음을 알 수 있다.

17 상황에 맞는 말 찾기 | ⑤
해석
남 민수는 과일을 좀 사러 시장에 갔다. 그는 딸기를 아주 좋아하기 때문에, 과일 가게 아저씨에게 딸기를 좀 싸 달라고 부탁했다. 하지만, 그가 자세히 보았을 때, 그는 딸기가 신선하지 않다는 것을 발견했다. 게다가 그것들은 또한 너무 비쌌다. 이제 그는 딸기 사는 것을 원하지 않고 대신에 사과를 좀 사고 싶다. 이런 상황에서, 민수는 점원에게 뭐라고 말하겠는가?
민수 딸기 대신에 사과를 살 수 있을까요?
① 다시 한 번 말씀해 주시겠어요?
② 이 딸기에 대해 어떻게 생각하세요?
③ 딸기에 대해 할인을 받을 수 있을까요?

④ 딸기와 사과 중에 어떤 것이 더 나은가요?
해설 민수는 딸기가 신선하지 않아 사과를 사고 싶은 상황이므로 ⑤가 답으로 적절하다.

18 한 일 / 할 일 파악 | ⑤
해석
여 너 오늘 방과 후에 뭘 할 거니?
남 나는 오늘 교실을 청소해야 해. 그리고 도서관에서 책을 좀 빌릴 계획이야.
여 그리고 그 후에는 집에 가니?
남 응, 나는 숙제를 하고 나서 피자를 만들 거야.
여 피자를 만든다고?
남 응, 내 사촌 동생이 오늘 오거든. 그녀를 위해 피자를 만들 거야.
여 우와! 나는 네가 요리를 잘하는지 몰랐어!
해설 남자가 방과 후에 할 일 중에 사촌 동생을 데리러 가는 것은 없다.

19 알맞은 응답 찾기 | ⑤
해석
남 너 화가 나 보인다. 무슨 일이니?
여 나는 위층에 있는 사람들을 더 이상 참을 수가 없어. 그들이 많은 소음을 만들거든.
남 어떤 종류의 소음을 말하는 거니?
여 그들은 아이들이 있는 거 같은데 그 아이들이 온종일 뛰어다녀. 그것뿐만 아니라, 누군가 심지어 밤에 피아노를 연주해.
남 정말 안됐구나.
여 어떻게 해야 할까?
남 나는 네가 위층에 가서 그들에게 그것들에 대해 얘기해야 한다고 생각해.
① 너는 그들에게 사과해야 해.
② 너는 소음을 내서는 안 돼.
③ 너는 밤에 피아노를 쳐서는 안 돼.
④ 나는 우리 아이들과 더 많은 시간을 보내야 해.
해설 여자의 위층 집 이웃이 소음을 만드는 상황이므로 위층에 올라가서 이 문제에 대해 말하라고 권유하는 ⑤가 남자의 응답으로 가장 적절하다.

20 알맞은 응답 찾기 | ④
해석
여 수빈아, 저녁으로 뭐 먹고 싶니?
남 엄마, 5분 전에 제게 같은 질문을 하셨잖아요.
여 오, 내가 그랬니? 그것에 대한 기억이 전혀 안 나는구나.
남 정말요? 전 상관없다고 대답했어요.
여 휴, 내가 늙어가나 보다. 요새 종종 잊어버려.
남 그런 말씀 마세요. 누구에게나 그런 일은 때때로 일어날 수 있어요. 엄마, 힘내세요!
여 그렇게 말해줘서 고맙구나, 아들아.
① 나는 벌써 저녁을 먹었어.
② 흥미롭구나.
③ 비빔밥을 먹는 게 어떠니?
⑤ 네가 무엇을 의미하는지 내게 분명하지 않구나.
해설 자꾸 깜빡하는 것 같다며 자책하는 엄마에게 아들이 위로의 말을 건넨 상황이므로 고맙다고 말하는 ④가 여자의 응답으로 가장 적절하다.

01 ③	02 ④	03 ③	04 ①	05 ①
06 ①	07 ②	08 ⑤	09 ③	10 ④
11 ②	12 ⑤	13 ②	14 ④	15 ②
16 ⑤	17 ②	18 ⑤	19 ③	20 ⑤

Dictation Test 14회　　　pp. 112~117

01 ❶ changed my mind ❷ want to have sushi
02 ❶ for over two years ❷ gotten a raise ❸ what I can do
03 ❶ bring my umbrella ❷ Let's share ❸ is broken
04 ❶ bought them yesterday ❷ in the park last Sunday ❸ visited the repair shop
05 ❶ We'll be landing at ❷ fasten your seat belts ❸ the plane stops
06 ❶ type this letter ❷ make three copies ❸ Send one to the president
07 ❶ the final exam start ❷ What are your plans
08 ❶ missing classes ❷ can you let me know ❸ tell him about it
09 ❶ have a problem ❷ your English will get better
10 ❶ have an iced tea ❷ in total ❸ Give me a cup
11 ❶ it's a long line ❷ get five in one cab
12 ❶ starting in June ❷ a former national player ❸ every Monday
13 ❶ in the first row ❷ sit at the back ❸ behind me
14 ❶ to protect your feet ❷ have your shoes on ❸ they have any holes
15 ❶ can't work on my report ❷ should leave for the library
16 ❶ make an appointment ❷ In the afternoon ❸ you're scheduled to
17 ❶ a presentation project ❷ give her the materials ❸ one more day
18 ❶ I'd really like to go ❷ prefer to study by myself ❸ a home tutor for me
19 ❶ where the nearest bus stop ❷ come with you ❸ appreciate it
20 ❶ cure sick people ❷ Why did you

01　그림 정보 파악 – 사물 | ③
해석
남 우리 빨리 주문하자. 나는 일본식 라면을 먹을 거야.
여 좋아. 어디 보자. 와, 많은 종류의 음식을 제공하는 구나.
남 너도 라면을 먹고 싶다고 했지, 그렇지?
여 아니, 나 마음이 바뀌었어. 초밥을 먹고 싶어.

남 너는 라면을 먹을 게 아니었으면, 여기에 올 이유가 없어. 이곳은 라면으로 유명하거든.
여 그건 다음번에 먹어 볼래. 지금은 초밥이 먹고 싶어.
남 흠… 좋아. 너 좋을 대로 해.
해설 여자는 마음을 바꾸어 라면 대신 초밥을 주문하기로 했다.

02　목적 파악 | ④
해석
여 Johnson 씨, 잠깐 말씀 좀 나눌 수 있을까요?
남 물론이죠. 들어와요. 뭘 도와줄까요?
여 음, 아시다시피, 저는 여기서 2년 이상 일해 왔어요.
남 네. 계속하세요.
여 그런데 아직 월급 인상이 안 되었어요.
남 알겠어요. 나는 당신이 항상 열심히 일하는 것 알아요. 내가 그 문제에 대해 무엇을 할 수 있을지 알아볼게요.
여 대단히 고맙습니다.
해설 여자는 남자에게 급여를 인상해 줄 것을 요구하기 위해 면담했다.

03　그림 상황에 어울리는 대화 찾기 | ③
해석
① 남 나 우산 안 가져왔는데.
　여 나도 안 가져왔어.
② 남 계단에 이 액체가 뭐지?
　여 내가 실수로 물을 엎질렀어.
③ 남 비가 오기 시작하네. 어쩌지?
　여 내 우산 같이 쓰자.
④ 남 너 눈 오는 날 좋아하니?
　여 아니, 나는 비 오는 날이 더 좋아.
⑤ 남 앗, 내 우산이 부러졌네.
　여 걱정 마. 더 이상 비가 안 와.
해설 비가 오는 상황에서 우산이 없어 걱정하는 남자에게 여자가 우산을 씌워 주고 있는 상황에 적절한 대화는 ③이다.

04　장소 추론 | ①
해석
남 이봐, 너는 새 선글라스를 샀구나. 그거 너한테 잘 어울려.
여 고마워. 어제 백화점에서 샀어.
남 예전 선글라스는 어쩌고?
여 지난 일요일에 공원에서 우리 개와 놀고 있었는데 우리 개가 내 선글라스를 물어뜯었어.
남 그거 안됐다.
여 나는 다음날에 수리점에도 가봤는데 소용없더라고.
남 잊어. 어쨌든 넌 더 멋진 선글라스를 샀잖니.
여 맞아.
해설 여자는 지난 일요일에 개와 함께 공원에서 놀았다고 했다.

05　직업 및 장래 희망 | ①
해석
여 신사 숙녀 여러분, 주목해 주시겠습니까? 우리는 10분 후에 Kennedy 공항에 착륙할 예정입니다. 안전벨트를 착용하시고 휴대 전화는 전원을 꺼 주세요. 비행기가 완전히 멈출 때까지 자리를 지켜 주십시오. 고맙습니다.

해설 비행기 착륙 전 안내 방송을 하고 있으므로 여자의 직업은 비행 승무원이다.

06 관계 추론 | ①
해석
남 이 편지를 타자 쳐 줄 수 있어요?
여 물론이죠. 언제까지 필요하신 건가요?
남 2시까지 필요해요.
여 그게 다인가요?
남 그리고 나서 세 부를 복사해 줄래요?
여 물론이죠. 세 부요.
남 네. 한 부는 사장님께 드리고, 한 부는 마케팅부에. 그리고 한 부는 파일에 보관해 두세요. 고마워요.
여 천만에요. 그것은 제가 해야 할 제 일인걸요.
해설 남자는 여자에게 타이핑과 복사 등의 일을 시키고 있으므로 두 사람의 관계는 상사와 비서임을 알 수 있다.

07 어색한 대화 찾기 | ②
해석
① 여 학교에서 휴대 전화를 사용하는 것에 대해 어떻게 생각하니?
   남 내 생각에 그건 필요해.
② 여 기말고사가 언제 시작하니?
   남 그건 월요일까지야.
③ 여 케이크 좀 먹어 보지 그러니?
   남 배불러. 여기 오는 길에 샌드위치를 먹었거든.
④ 여 이번 주말에 네 계획이 뭐니?
   남 광주에 계신 조부모님을 뵈러 갈 거야.
⑤ 여 넌 보통 몇 시에 자니?
   남 10시에. 그런데 어제는 12시까지 깨어 있었어.
해설 기말고사가 언제 시작하는지 묻는 질문에 대해 월요일까지라고 대답하는 것은 어색하다.

08 부탁한 일 파악 | ⑤
해석
[전화벨이 울린다.]
남 여보세요?
여 Mathew. 나 지민이야. 좀 나아졌니?
남 응, 어제보다는 낫지만, 오늘 학교를 갈 수 있을 것 같지는 않아. 수업을 빠지는 것이 걱정이 된다.
여 걱정 마. 내가 너를 위해 수업 자료를 모으고 있어.
남 정말 고마워. 그런데, 너 Jake의 전화번호를 알려 줄 수 있니?
여 문자로 보낼게. 왜?
남 오늘 그 애랑 내가 도서부 당번인데, 그 애가 혼자 일해야 해. 그것에 대해 이야기해야 할 것 같아.
여 나랑 일정을 바꾸자. 내가 그 애랑 오늘 일하고 너는 금요일에 일해.
해설 남자는 여자에게 Jake의 전화번호를 알려 달라고 부탁했다.

09 의도 파악 | ③
해석
여 이봐, 진호야. 너 우울해 보인다. 무슨 일이니?
남 음, 나는 나의 미래가 걱정이 돼.
여 너의 미래? 뭐가 되고 싶은데?

남 나는 국제 변호사가 되고 싶은데, 한 가지 문제가 있어.
여 그게 뭔데?
남 내 영어 실력이 그렇게 좋지 않아.
여 힘 내! 나는 네가 더 연습하면 영어 실력이 좋아질 거라고 확신해.
해설 국제 변호사가 되고 싶은데 영어 실력이 좋지 않다며 걱정하는 남자를 여자가 연습을 하면 잘할 수 있다며 격려하고 있다.

10 숫자 정보 파악 – 금액 | ④
해석
남 주문하시겠어요?
여 네. 아이스티 한 잔과 크림치즈 토스트 하나를 먹고 싶어요.
남 다른 것도 필요하세요?
여 아뇨. 그게 다예요.
남 네. 총 21달러입니다.
여 알겠습니다. 여기 제 신용카드입니다.
남 음, 저희가 행사를 하고 있는데요. 손님이 20달러 이상 사셔서 손님은 단돈 2달러에 컵을 사실 수 있어요.
여 좋습니다. 컵도 하나 주세요.
해설 여자는 아이스티와 크림치즈 토스트를 21달러에 구입한 후 행사 중인 컵을 구입했으므로 총 23달러를 지불해야 한다.

11 장소 추론 | ②
해석
여 오, 줄이 기네요.
남 네. 우리는 기다려야 할 것 같아요.
여 우리 일행이 다섯 명이에요. 택시 한 대에 다섯 명이 못 탈 거예요.
남 네, 맞아요. 택시가 두 대 필요하겠어요.
여 Ken, 당신이 아이들을 데리고 첫 번째 택시를 타세요.
남 좋아요. 잠깐만요! 식당 이름이 Pizza Hat인가요?
여 네, 그래요.
해설 줄이 길다고 말하며 다섯 명이 타야 할 택시 개수를 정하고 있으므로 두 사람이 대화하는 장소는 택시 승차장이다.

12 언급되지 않은 것 | ⑤
해석
남 안녕하세요. 우리는 6월에 시작하는 벨리 댄스 수업을 제공합니다. 여름을 위해 체중을 감량할 계획을 하신다면, 오셔서 수업을 들으세요. 선생님은 전 국가대표 선수인 Grace Kim입니다. 수업은 매주 월요일 오후 5시 30분에 있습니다. 특별한 이벤트도 있는데요. 이번 주까지 등록하는 분들께는 10% 할인을 해 드립니다.
해설 벨리 댄스의 수업 장소에 대해서는 언급되지 않았다.

13 도표 정보 파악 | ②
해석
여 안녕, Tom.
남 안녕, 수영아. 여기 와서 앉아.
여 첫 줄에는 안 앉을래. 그건 칠판이랑 너무 가까워.
남 뒤에 앉으려고?
여 아니, 그래도 발표를 위해 좋은 자리에 앉고 싶어. 둘째 줄이나 셋째 줄에 앉을 거야.

남 그럼 내 뒤에 앉아.
여 좋아. 그럴게.
해설 남자는 첫째 줄에 앉아 있고, 여자는 남자의 뒤에 앉겠다고 했으므로 여자는 두 번째 줄에 앉을 것이다.

14 주제 파악 | ④
해석
남 이것은 당신이 일 년 내내 매우 자주 착용하는 것이다. 당신은 대부분 그것을 당신의 발을 보호하기 위해 착용한다. 이것은 다양한 디자인과 사이즈로 출시된다. 요즘에 다수의 이것 위에는 귀여운 캐릭터들이 있다. 여러분이 신발을 신고 있다면 사람들은 여러분이 그것을 신고 있는지 아닌지 볼 수 없을 수도 있다. 비록 사람들이 이것을 볼 수 없을지라도, 신기 전에 그것에 구멍이 있는지를 확인해야 한다.
해설 발을 보호하기 위해 신는 것이고, 신발 안에 착용하는 것은 양말이다.

15 한 일 / 할 일 파악 | ②
해석
남 여보, 저게 무슨 소리죠? 온종일 시끄럽네요.
여 길 건너 초등학교가 운동회를 한다고 들었어요.
남 나는 이런 소음 속에서 보고서 작업을 할 수가 없어요.
여 그러면 도서관에 가지 그래요?
남 하지만 나는 컴퓨터를 써야 한단 말이에요.
여 노트북 컴퓨터를 사용할 수 있는 열람실이 있잖아요.
남 오, 듣던 중 반가운 소리네요. 지금 당장 도서관으로 출발해야겠어요.
해설 남자는 초등학교 운동회 날 들리는 소음 때문에 집중이 안 돼 도서관에 간다고 했다.

16 숫자 정보 파악 – 날짜와 시각 | ⑤
해석
여 Smith 병원입니다. 무엇을 도와드릴까요?
남 저는 Mickey Arnold입니다. 17일 금요일에 예약을 할 수 있을까요?
여 가능합니다. Arnold 씨. 오전과 오후 중 언제 하시겠어요?
남 오후예요.
여 오후 4시에 오실 수 있나요?
남 좋아요.
여 그러면 17일 금요일 오후 4시에 오시도록 일정이 잡혀 있습니다.
남 감사합니다.
해설 남자는 17일 오후 4시로 병원 진료를 예약했다.

17 상황에 맞는 말 찾기 | ②
해석
여 민우와 Jane은 같은 조이다. 그들은 발표 과제가 있어서 민우가 발표 자료를 만들고 Jane이 발표를 하기로 결정했다. 그는 그녀에게 월요일까지 자료를 주겠다고 약속했다. 그는 주말 동안 열심히 작업했지만, 자료 만드는 것을 끝마치지 못했다. 그는 하루만 더 있으면 그것을 마칠 수 있을 것이라고 생각한다. 이런 상황에서, 민우는 Jane에게 뭐라고 말하겠는가?
민우 나는 하루가 더 필요할 것 같아.
① 네가 좋아해서 좋아.
③ 이해해 줘서 고마워.

④ 내가 왜 너에게 전화하기를 원하니?
⑤ 우리 프레젠테이션이 언제니?
해설 민우가 약속한 날까지 자료를 만들지 못한 상황이므로 하루가 더 필요하다고 말하는 ②가 답으로 알맞다.

18 한 일 / 할 일 파악 | ⑤
해석
남 겨울 방학 동안 너의 계획은 무엇이니, Becky?
여 난 정말 미국에 가서 공부하고 싶어.
남 재미있겠다!
여 내가 "그러고 싶다"고 했잖아. 그건 너무 비싸서 불가능해.
남 안됐구나. 나는 세 개의 학원 수업을 들을 거야. 너도 나와 함께 그것들을 듣는 게 어때?
여 글쎄, 너 내가 도서관에서 혼자 공부하는 것을 더 좋아하는 거 알잖아.
남 하지만 넌 항상 잠들어 버리잖아.
여 맞아. 그게 우리 엄마가 겨울 방학 동안 내게 가정교사를 구해 두신 이유야.
남 오, 그렇구나.
해설 여자의 어머니가 겨울 방학 동안 입주 가정교사를 구했다고 했으므로 여자는 겨울 방학 동안 선생님과 집에서 공부할 것이다.

19 알맞은 응답 찾기 | ③
해석
남 실례합니다. 가장 가까운 버스 정류장이 어디 있는지 아시나요?
여 네. 저기 높은 빨간색 건물이 보이나요?
남 네, 보입니다.
여 좋아요, 그냥 그쪽으로 직진하세요. 당신은 그 건물에 도착하기 전에 아주 좁은 거리를 발견할 수 있을 겁니다. 거기에서 우회전하시고 약 1분 동안 걸어가면 커다란 우체통이 보일 거고 그리고….
남 죄송합니다만, 못 알아듣겠어요. 다시 말씀해 주시겠어요?
여 음, 그냥 제가 같이 갈게요. 가시죠.
남 오, 정말이요? 정말 감사해요.
여 천만에요.
① 몸 건강하세요!
② 맞습니다.
④ 당신은 정말 좋으시군요!
⑤ 당신은 그곳에 또 갈 수 있어요.
해설 여자가 버스 정류장에 함께 가 주겠다고 하자 남자가 감사하다고 한 상황이므로 천만에요라고 말하는 ③이 여자의 응답으로 가장 적절하다.

20 알맞은 응답 찾기 | ⑤
해석
남 넌 왜 의사가 되었니?
여 우리 할머니가 살아계실 때 중병을 앓으셨어. 그래서, 의사가 되기로 결심했어.
남 아. 너는 너의 할머니처럼 아픈 사람들을 고쳐 주려고 의사가 되었구나.
여 맞아.
남 잘됐다. 넌 의사로서 정말 행복해 보여.
여 응, 그건 그렇고, 나는 네 꿈이 가수가 되는 것이라고 들었어. 넌 왜 의사가 되었니?

남 <u>우리 부모님은 항상 내가 의사가 되기를 원하셨거든.</u>
① 나는 가수로서도 행복해.
② 나는 가수가 아니라 의사야.
③ 난 네 꿈을 절대 못 잊을 거야.
④ 너는 노래를 잘 부르고, 춤도 잘 추곤 했었지.
해설 여자가 남자에게 의사가 된 이유를 물은 상황이므로 그 이유를 답하는
⑤가 남자의 응답으로 가장 적절하다.

15회 영어 듣기모의고사   pp. 118~119

01 ③	02 ③	03 ①	04 ⑤	05 ⑤
06 ③	07 ⑤	08 ②	09 ①	10 ④
11 ①	12 ④	13 ④	14 ②	15 ②
16 ⑤	17 ③	18 ⑤	19 ①	20 ③

Dictation Test 15회   pp. 120~125

01 ❶ bought a doll ❷ raising its right hand ❸ its smiling face

02 ❶ got two tickets ❷ come with me ❸ miss this chance

03 ❶ do look nice ❷ give me a ride ❸ they are too expensive

04 ❶ Are we going to ❷ it's better to buy ❸ at Martin's house

05 ❶ my order ❷ drop by with it immediately ❸ I'll get it

06 ❶ I'm late ❷ hadn't brought my wallet ❸ there was a traffic jam

07 ❶ I was fascinated by ❷ It's all my fault ❸ save a lot of energy

08 ❶ have dinner at home ❷ a few onions

09 ❶ what day it was yesterday ❷ You don't need to wait ❸ You are right

10 ❶ use a special delivery service ❷ I'll use that

11 ❶ have to wait ❷ see the doctor ❸ for the patients

12 ❶ came from ❷ bright yellow ❸ two or three times

13 ❶ five people ❷ a four-star difficulty room ❸ This room's time limit

14 ❶ listen to music alone ❷ into your ears ❸ can bring them anywhere

15 ❶ You look dirty ❷ right after your shower

16 ❶ I'd like to order ❷ when can I get ❸ Our school sports day

17 ❶ good at singing ❷ wants to know his opinion

18 ❶ planted a seed ❷ a bit cold ❸ in a sunny place

19 ❶ had a traffic accident ❷ was not a serious ❸ didn't get hurt at all

20 ❶ wrote her diary ❷ I'm very curious ❸ Are you sure

01 그림 정보 파악 – 사물 | ③

해석
남 Jean, 너의 일본 여행은 어땠어?
여 아주 좋았어. 여기, 너를 주려고 인형을 사 왔어.
남 와, 이 고양이 무척 귀엽게 생겼다.
여 봐, 이것은 머리 옆에 오른손을 들고 있어. 이 인형은 우리에게 행운을 가져다준대.
남 그거 좋네. 나는 목에 있는 붉은 리본이 마음에 들어.
여 나는 그것의 웃는 얼굴도 마음에 들었어. 네가 좋아하니 기쁘다.
남 정말 고마워.
해설 머리 옆에 오른손을 들고 웃는 얼굴을 하고 있으며 목에 빨간 리본을 한 고양이는 ③이다.

02 목적 파악 | ③

해석
[전화벨이 울린다.]
남 여보세요?
여 안녕, Jim. 나 미나야. 너 팝 음악에 관심 있니?
남 응, 있어. 그건 왜 물어?
여 나는 오늘 밤에 있는 팝 콘서트 표 두 장을 방금 얻었거든. 나랑 같이 갈 수 있니?
남 음, 난 도서관에 가려고 했지만, 이 기회를 놓치고 싶지 않아. 그게 몇 시에 어디에서 하니?
여 예당 홀에서 7시에 해.
남 좋아. 거기서 6시 30분에 만나.
여 좋아. 그때 봐.
해설 여자는 남자와 함께 콘서트에 가려고 전화했다.

03 그림 상황에 어울리는 대화 찾기 | ①

해석
① 여 저 이것을 입으니 괜찮아 보여요?
   남 당신은 멋져 보여요.
② 여 나를 위해 이것을 들고 계실 수 있나요?
   남 물론이죠. 어서 주세요.
③ 여 이 편지들을 우편으로 보낼 수 있을까요?
   남 네. 우표가 좀 필요하신가요?
④ 여 호텔까지 좀 태워 주시겠어요?
   남 물론이죠. 타세요.
⑤ 여 이 신발에 대해 어떻게 생각하세요?
   남 너무 비싼 것 같아요.
해설 옷 가게에서 새로운 옷을 입어보는 상황에 적절한 대화는 ①이다.

04 장소 추론 | ⑤

해석

남 우리 오늘 민지 생일 선물을 사러 갈 거니?

여 그럴 필요 없어. 내가 어제 음반 가게에 가서 그녀가 원하는 CD를 샀어.

남 그럼 케이크는? 내가 제과점에 가서 케이크를 살까?

여 내일 사는 게 나을 것 같아. 오늘 방과 후에 Martin의 집으로 와. 그가 어디에 사는지 아니?

남 응, 알아. 거기서 뭐 하게?

여 민지 생일 파티를 위한 파티용 소품을 준비할 거야. 학교 정문에서 만나서 같이 가는 게 어때?

남 아니야. 오늘은 네가 나보다 먼저 끝나잖아.

여 알았어. 그럼 Martin의 집에서 보자.

해설 두 사람은 Martin의 집에서 만나서 민지의 생일 파티를 위한 소품을 준비하기로 했다.

05 직업 및 장래 희망 | ⑤

해석

[전화벨이 울린다.]

남 여보세요?

여 여보세요. 제 주문에 대해 여쭤보려고 전화드렸습니다.

남 죄송하지만, 그것에 대해 더 이야기해 주시겠어요?

여 네. 여기는 Elm가 141번지예요. 저는 한 시간 전에 전화로 프라이드 치킨을 주문했어요. 그런데 아직 그것이 도착하지 않았어요.

남 확인해 보겠습니다. 음, 여기 있네요. 즉시 이것을 가지고 들를게요.

여 좋아요. 저희는 너무 배가 고파요.

남 네. 되도록 빨리 가져다 드릴게요.

해설 여자가 치킨을 1시간 전에 주문했는데 아직 배달이 안 되었다고 남자에게 문의하고 있고 남자가 바로 들르겠다고 했으므로 남자의 직업은 배달원이라는 것을 알 수 있다.

06 심정 파악 | ③

해석

남 선생님, 늦어서 죄송해요.

여 괜찮다. 하지만 왜 늦었니? 너는 보통 제시간에 오잖아.

남 제가 버스를 기다리고 있었는데, 지갑을 가지고 오지 않았다는 걸 알았어요.

여 너는 집에 돌아갔니?

남 네, 그래야 했어요. 제가 버스 정류장으로 돌아왔을 때, 버스가 막 떠났어요.

여 운이 없었구나.

남 네, 그래서 택시를 탔는데, 차가 막히는 거예요.

여 그래서 늦었구나.

남 네. 오늘 아침은 엉망이었어요.

해설 버스를 기다리다가 지갑을 갖고 오지 않은 것이 생각 나 집에 다시 갔다 왔는데 버스는 이미 떠나서 택시를 타느라 늦은 남자는 짜증났을 것이다.

07 어색한 대화 찾기 | ⑤

해석

① 남 나는 Mike Ashley가 득점할 것 같아.

여 확실해? 나는 그럴 것 같지 않은데.

② 남 인도로의 여행은 어땠니?

여 나는 아름다운 경치에 마음을 빼앗겼지.

③ 남 오, 너 내 책을 잃어버렸다고 했니?

여 미안해. 다 내 잘못이야.

④ 남 나는 노래를 잘 못 부르는 것 같아. 나는 가수가 될 수 없을지도 몰라.

여 포기하지 마. 계속 연습하면, 할 수 있어.

⑤ 남 재활용을 하면 많은 에너지를 절약할 수 있어. 내게 동의하지 않니?

여 응, 나는 2년 동안 저축하고 있어.

해설 재활용이 많은 에너지를 절약할 수 있다는 의견에 동의하는지 물어보는 말에 대해 2년 동안 돈을 저금하고 있다는 대답은 어색하다.

08 부탁한 일 파악 | ②

해석

남 엄마, 아직도 그 드라마를 보고 계세요?

여 응, 이거 굉장히 재미있어. 같이 보자.

남 아니에요, 저는 책을 좀 빌리러 나가려던 참이었어요. 5시까지 올게요.

여 그래. 그럼 집에서 저녁 먹을 거지, 그치?

남 네, 그래요.

여 그럼 집에 오는 길에 양파를 조금 사 올 수 있겠니? 양파가 떨어졌네.

남 네. 제게 맛있는 요리를 해 주세요.

여 그래.

해설 여자는 남자에게 집에 오는 길에 양파를 사 오라고 부탁했다.

09 의도 파악 | ①

해석

여 너 어젯밤 8시에 전등을 껐니?

남 무슨 말이야?

여 너 어제가 무슨 날인지 몰랐니?

남 어제는 4월 22일이었고, 월요일이었지. 그게 왜?

여 4월 22일은 '지구의 날'이야. 이 날에 사람들은 에너지를 절약하기 위해 8시부터 10분간 전등을 꺼.

남 그거 멋진 생각이다. 내년에 나도 참여해야겠다.

여 내년까지 기다릴 필요 없어. 네가 전등을 쓰지 않을 때 전등을 끌 수도 있는 걸.

남 네 말이 맞아.

해설 남자는 쓰지 않는 전등을 끄는 것으로 에너지 절약에 동참할 수 있다는 여자의 말에 동의하고 있다. You are right.는 상대방의 말에 동의하는 표현이다.

10 숫자 정보 파악 - 금액 | ④

해석

남 실례합니다. 이 소포를 부산으로 보내고 싶은데요.

여 그래요. 그것의 무게를 잴게요. (잠시 후) 1kg이네요. 그럼 6천원입니다. 안에 무엇인가요?

남 접시예요.

여 그것들은 쉽게 깨져서 당신은 특별 배달 서비스를 이용해야 합니다.

남 오, 그건 얼마인데요?

여 3천원 더 비쌉니다.

남 좋아요, 그럼 그걸 이용할게요.

해설 1kg의 소포를 보내는 비용은 6,000원이나 특별 배달 서비스 이용비 3,000원을 추가로 지불해야 하므로 남자는 총 9,000원을 지불해야 한다.

11 장소 추론 | ①
해석

남 실례합니다. 제가 30분 동안 기다렸는데요. 얼마나 더 오래 기다려야 하나요?
여 죄송하지만, 오늘은 바쁜 날이에요. 하지만, 분명 10분 안에 진료를 받으실 수 있을 거예요.
남 알겠습니다. 이제 막 여기 있는 책을 전부 다 봤어요.
여 그럼, 저기 있는 간식 좀 드시겠어요?
남 저 간식들은 환자들 거예요?
여 그럼요.
해설 여자가 남자에게 10분 후에 의사를 만날 수 있을 거라고 했으므로 두 사람이 대화하고 있는 장소는 병원이다.

12 언급되지 않은 것 | ④
해석

여 해바라기는 일 년밖에 살지 못합니다. 이 꽃은 원래 북아메리카에서 왔습니다. 그것은 보통 2~3m 높이이고, 밝은 노란색입니다. 만약 당신이 이것을 기르고 싶다면, 일주일에 두 번이나 세 번 물을 주어야 합니다. 그리고 그것을 아시나요? 사실, 이 꽃은 항상 태양을 향하지는 않습니다.
해설 해바라기를 심는 시기는 언급되지 않았다.

13 도표 정보 파악 | ④
해석

남 지수랑 Sam이랑 탈출 게임하러 가는 거 어때?
여 좋아. 나 항상 탈출 게임 해 보고 싶었어. Mary도 함께 가지 않을래?
남 좋지. 제일 쉬운 것으로 시작해야 할까?
여 아니, 좀 더 어려운 것들 중에 하나를 해 보자.
남 그러면, 우리는 다섯 명이야. 별 네 개 난이도 방을 해 보자. 그러면 우리는 선택권이 하나밖에 없어.
여 네 말이 맞아. 시간은 무슨 뜻이야?
남 그것은 우리가 모든 문제를 풀어야 하는 시간이야. 이 방의 시간제한은 70분이네.
여 아, 나 벌써 신난다. 예약하자.
남 그래.
해설 별 4개짜리 난이도 게임을 5명의 인원이 70분 동안 한다고 했으므로 ④번을 선택할 것이다.

14 주제 파악 | ②
해석

남 당신이 혼자 음악을 듣고 싶을 때, 이것들은 아주 유용합니다. 음악을 들으려면, 당신은 이것들을 음악 재생기에 연결하고 당신의 귀에도 꽂아야 합니다. 이것들은 무겁거나 크지 않아서, 어디에나 가지고 다닐 수 있습니다. 하지만 당신이 이것들을 가지고 다닐 때, 선들이 심각하게 꼬일지도 모릅니다. 그러니 주의하세요.
해설 음악을 들을 때 사용하고 어디에나 들고 다닐 수 있지만 선이 꼬일 수도 있어 조심해야 하는 것은 이어폰이다.

15 한 일 / 할 일 파악 | ②
해석

남 엄마, 저 왔어요.
여 Bob, 너 바깥에서 놀았니? 너는 지저분해 보이는구나.

남 네, 저는 친구들이랑 축구를 했어요. 옷 갈아입으러 갈게요.
여 근데 샤워도 해야 할 것 같구나.
남 네. 그런데, 뭐 만드세요? 매우 좋은 냄새가 나요.
여 이건 미트볼 스파게티야. 거의 다 되었어. 샤워 마치고 바로 돌아와. 같이 저녁 먹자.
남 좋아요.
해설 축구를 하고 집에 돌아온 남자는 대화 직후에 샤워를 할 것이다.

16 숫자 정보 파악 – 날짜 | ⑤
해석

[전화벨이 울린다.]
남 여보세요. 여기는 T-zone입니다. 무엇을 도와드릴까요?
여 안녕하세요. 저는 체육대회에 사용할 30장의 L 사이즈 분홍색 티셔츠를 주문하고 싶은데요, 오늘 그것들을 주문하면 10월 10일까지 받을 수 있나요?
남 정말 죄송하지만 어려울 것 같습니다. 오늘이 벌써 10월 8일이에요.
여 그러면 언제 저희가 그것을 받을 수 있나요?
남 당신은 11일에 그것을 받으실 수 있습니다.
여 저희의 체육대회는 10월 12일이라서 괜찮을 거예요.
남 감사합니다. 가능한 한 빨리 보내 드릴게요.
해설 여자의 세 번째 말에서 체육대회 날짜가 10월 12일이라는 것을 알 수 있다.

17 상황에 맞는 말 찾기 | ③
해석

남 Maggie는 그녀의 남동생과 함께 음악 프로그램을 보고 있었는데 그녀가 가장 좋아하는 가수가 나왔다. 그녀는 남동생에게 그 가수가 노래를 매우 잘하고, 춤을 매우 잘 춘다고 말했다. 그러나 남동생은 아무 말도 하지 않았다. 그녀는 그의 의견을 알고 싶다. 이런 상황에서, Maggie는 남동생에게 뭐라고 말하겠는가?
Maggie 나에게 동의하지 않니?
① 무슨 일이니?
② 그건 내 잘못이야. 사과할게.
④ 무엇이 너를 그렇게 생각하게 만들었니?
⑤ 그 이야기가 흥미롭다고 생각하니?
해설 자신이 좋아하는 가수가 노래와 춤을 잘 춘다고 남동생에게 말했는데 남동생이 반응이 없는 상황이므로 내 말에 동의하지 않냐고 묻는 ③이 답으로 적절하다.

18 한 일 / 할 일 파악 | ⑤
해석

여 너 무엇을 보고 있니?
남 내 식물을 보고 있어.
여 네 식물? 그 화분에는 아무것도 없는데.
남 알아. 내가 씨앗을 심은 지 일주일이 되었어. 그런데 아무 일도 일어나지 않고 있어. 문제가 뭐지?
여 음. 물은 충분히 줬니?
남 물론 그랬지.
여 이 방이 좀 추운 것 같다. 햇볕이 잘 드는 곳에 두어야 할지도 몰라.
남 오, 그렇게 해 봐야 되겠다.
해설 여자는 화분을 햇볕이 드는 곳으로 옮겨야 한다는 남자의 조언대로 해 보겠다고 했다.

19 알맞은 응답 찾기 | ①

해석

[전화벨이 울린다.]

남 Alice, 안녕. 무슨 일이니?

여 저기, 나 3시까지 못 가겠어.

남 무슨 일인데?

여 나는 방금 교통사고가 났어.

남 뭐? 넌 괜찮아?

여 응. 심각한 건 아니었어. 내가 타고 있던 버스가 승용차랑 부딪쳤어.

남 너 확실히 괜찮은 거야?

여 난 전혀 안 다쳤어.

남 <u>그것 정말 다행이다.</u>

② 그 말을 들으니 유감이다.

③ 실망하지 마.

④ 다시는 차를 운전하지 마.

⑤ 나는 네가 곧 낫길 바라.

해설 여자가 교통사고가 났지만 다치지 않았다고 했으므로 다행이라고 말하는 ①이 남자의 응답으로 가장 적절하다.

20 알맞은 응답 찾기 | ③

해석

여 Tom, 뭐 하고 있니?

남 오, 엄마. 저는 책을 읽고 있어요. 이 책은 정말 재미있어요.

여 너는 그 책에 패나 빠져 있구나. 무슨 이야기인데?

남 이건 Anne Frank라는 소녀에 관한 이야기예요. 그녀는 제2차 세계 대전 동안 일기를 썼어요.

여 오, 나는 그 책을 알아.

남 그녀가 전쟁에서 살아남았나요? 정말 궁금해요.

여 내가 알기로는, 그녀는 전쟁이 끝나기 전에 죽었어.

남 너무 슬프네요. 그거 확실해요?

여 <u>응, 그거 확실해.</u>

① 그거 내 관심을 매우 끄는걸.

② 아니야. 그건 네 잘못이 아니었어.

④ 나는 더 연습해야만 했어.

⑤ 포기하지 마. 너는 그 책을 끝낼 거야.

해설 남자가 책의 주인공이 전쟁이 끝나기 전에 죽었다는 것이 확실하냐고 물어본 상황이므로 확실하다고 말하는 ③이 여자의 응답으로 가장 적절하다.

16회 영어 듣기모의고사   pp. 126~127

01 ④	02 ⑤	03 ③	04 ④	05 ③
06 ③	07 ⑤	08 ④	09 ②	10 ①
11 ②	12 ③	13 ④	14 ③	15 ③
16 ⑤	17 ③	18 ①	19 ②	20 ③

Dictation Test 16회   pp. 128~133

01 ❶ a cellphone case ❷ Is there anything special ❸ put the letters

02 ❶ have a phone installed ❷ The earliest day

03 ❶ a plastic bag ❷ going grocery shopping

04 ❶ How about ❷ would like a scarf ❸ take it

05 ❶ What were you doing ❷ can prove ❸ check your room

06 ❶ look worried ❷ I'm supposed to answer ❸ not be able to understand

07 ❶ Have you heard about ❷ have left home earlier ❸ enough space to do that

08 ❶ do the household chores ❷ buy a cake ❸ something for dinner

09 ❶ didn't feel well ❷ I didn't know that ❸ should have gone

10 ❶ the most popular ones ❷ Three small Cokes ❸ I'd like to have two

11 ❶ check in ❷ for one night ❸ Please sign here

12 ❶ a lot of underwater animals ❷ can take a bus

13 ❶ played against ❷ three to one

14 ❶ very hard and thin ❷ They keep growing ❸ the tips of your fingers

15 ❶ feel like eating ❷ Can we make it ❸ go to the market

16 ❶ provide tour guide services ❷ it's ten thirty ❸ begin in half an hour

17 ❶ worried about her ❷ instead of skipping meals

18 ❶ did you finish ❷ get a package ❸ come over there

19 ❶ background music ❷ found any suitable songs ❸ What does it mean

20 ❶ the best way to ❷ How long will it take ❸ going by bus

01 그림 정보 파악 - 사물 | ④

해석

여 안녕하세요, 제가 여동생을 위한 휴대 전화 케이스를 살 생각인데요. 하나 추천해 주실래요?

남 물론입니다. 이 곰을 좀 보세요. 그리고 이 토끼도 마찬가지로 귀엽지요.

여 음, 이것들은 너무 흔해요. 그녀를 위해 제가 살 수 있는 특별한 것이 있을까요?

남 이 손으로 뜨개질 한 케이스도 좋아요.

여 하지만 제 생각에 그건 쉽게 더러워질 것 같아요.

남 그렇다면 이건 어떠세요? 우리는 이것 위에 당신의 여동생 이름의 글자들을 넣을 수 있어요.

여 근사하네요. 그것으로 할게요.

해설 동생의 이름을 새길 수 있는 휴대 전화 케이스는 ④이다.

02 목적 파악 | ⑤

해석

[전화벨이 울린다.]

남 여보세요. 무엇을 도와드릴까요?

여 네, 저는 전화를 설치하고 싶습니다.

남 당신의 성함과 주소를 말씀해 주시겠어요?

여 네. 제 이름은 Janet Miller입니다. 주소는 Train가 20번지입니다.

남 감사합니다. 전화를 설치할 수 있는 가장 빠른 날짜는 이번 주 금요일입니다. 괜찮으세요?

여 좋습니다. 고맙습니다.

해설 여자는 전화 설치를 신청하려고 전화를 걸었다.

03 그림 상황에 어울리는 대화 찾기 | ③

해석

① 여 여기에서 드실 건가요, 아니면 가져가실 건가요?
　남 가져가겠습니다.

② 여 제가 슈퍼마켓에 어떻게 갈 수 있을까요?
　남 오, 그건 바로 저기에 있어요.

③ 여 비닐봉지가 필요하신가요?
　남 네. 하나만 주세요.

④ 여 당신은 어디로 가시나요?
　남 저는 식료품을 사러 갑니다.

⑤ 여 제가 오후 3시 기차표를 살 수 있을까요?
　남 죄송합니다. 그 좌석들은 모두 매진입니다.

해설 마트에서 점원이 비닐봉지를 건네는 상황에 적절한 대화는 ③이다.

04 그림 정보 파악 – 사물 | ④

해석

여 도와드릴까요, 손님?

남 네, 아내에게 줄 선물을 찾고 있어요.

여 알겠습니다. 핸드백은 어떠세요?

남 아니요. 그녀는 이미 핸드백을 많이 갖고 있어요.

여 그렇다면 아마도 스카프를 좋아하실지도 몰라요. 이것 어떠세요?

남 오, 아름답네요! 얼마죠?

여 55달러 75센트입니다.

남 그것으로 하죠.

해설 남자는 아내에게 줄 선물로 스카프를 산다고 했다.

05 직업 및 장래 희망 | ③

해석

여 실례합니다. Turner 씨. 어제 오후 7시경에 당신은 무엇을 하고 있었나요?

남 저는 저녁으로 스파게티를 요리하고 있었습니다.

여 그게 확실한가요?

남 네, 가족들에게 물어보세요. 그리고 심지어 제 이웃들인 Kevin과 Linda도 제가 그들과 함께 있었다는 것을 증명할 수 있어요.

여 흠… 당신이 누군가 소리 지르는 것을 들었을 때가 몇 시였나요?

남 아마도 대략 8시쯤이었을 겁니다. 우리는 그때 막 저녁을 끝내려고 했었어요.

여 제가 당신의 방을 확인해 봐도 될까요?

남 그럼요, 그러세요.

해설 여자는 남자의 알리바이를 조사하며 남자의 방을 조사하고 있으므로 형사라는 것을 알 수 있다.

06 심정 파악 | ③

해석

여 너 걱정스러워 보인다.

남 오늘 있을 말하기 시험 때문에 그래.

여 그건 무슨 종류의 시험이니?

남 우리 영어 선생님이 질문 몇 개를 하실 거고, 나는 그것들에 대해 대답을 해야만 해.

여 너무 걱정하지 마. 나는 네 영어 실력이 그 시험에 합격할 만큼 충분히 좋다고 확신해.

남 하지만 그가 내게 어떤 종류의 질문들을 물어보실지 궁금해. 나는 그 질문들을 이해할 수 없을 지도 몰라. 내가 어떻게 해야 하지?

여 긴장 풀어. 괜찮을 거야.

해설 남자는 영어 말하기 시험을 앞두고 긴장하고 있다.

07 어색한 대화 찾기 | ⑤

해석

① 남 고기와 생선 중 어떤 것이 더 좋으신가요?
　여 생선이 더 좋습니다.

② 남 'read-a-thon(독서 마라톤)'에 대해 들어 봤니?
　여 아니, 들어 본 적 없어. 그게 뭔데?

③ 남 너 그녀를 위한 선물로 무엇을 살 거니?
　여 나는 인형을 살까 생각하고 있어.

④ 남 우리 학교에 늦었어.
　여 응. 조금 더 일찍 집을 나서야만 했어.

⑤ 남 우주에서 물을 마시는 것이 가능한가요?
　여 아니. 우리는 그것을 하기에 충분한 공간을 가지고 있지 않아.

해설 우주에서 물을 마시는 것이 가능하냐고 질문했는데 그것을 할 충분할 공간이 없다고 말하는 것은 어색하다.

08 부탁한 일 파악 | ④

해석

여 오늘이 엄마의 생일이야. 그녀를 위해 특별한 무언가를 하자.

남 우리 그녀를 위해 집안일들을 하지 않을래? 내가 청소를 하고, 네가 빨래를 하는 거야.

여 엄마는 기뻐하실 거야. 설거지는?

남 네가 설거지를 하면, 내가 쓰레기통을 비울게.

여 그래. 쓰레기통을 비운 다음에 엄마를 위해 케이크를 사러 갈 수 있니? 나는 저녁에 먹을 것을 준비할게.

남 문제없어. 엄마가 우리의 깜짝 선물을 좋아하시면 좋겠어.

해설 여자는 남자에게 쓰레기를 버린 후 엄마의 생일 케이크를 살 것을 부탁했다.

09 의도 파악 | ②

해석

남 너 어젯밤에 어디에 있었니?

여 그게 무슨 말이야?

남 우리는 Amy의 생일 파티에 초대되었는데 네가 거기에 없었어.

여 아, 나는 온종일 몸이 안 좋았어. 그런데 지금은 괜찮아.

남 그게 이유였구나. 너는 Amy의 삼촌이 Justin Bieber의 매니저라는 것을 알고 있었니?

여 정말? 나는 몰랐어.

남 그가 그녀를 놀래 주려고 Justin Bieber를 파티에 데리고 왔어.

여 농담하는 거지. Justin은 내가 가장 좋아하는 가수란 말이야.

남 나도 알아. 그는 심지어 우리를 위해 노래도 불러 줬어.

여 오, 안 돼! 내가 거기에 갔어야야 했는데.

해설 여자는 자신이 좋아하는 가수가 친구의 생일 파티에 온 것을 알고 생일 파티에 가지 않은 것을 후회하고 있다.

10 숫자 정보 파악 - 금액 | ①

해석

여 King Burgers에 오신 것을 환영합니다.

남 안녕하세요. 어떤 종류의 버거가 있나요?

여 우리는 다양한 버거를 가지고 있습니다만, 치즈버거와 치킨버거가 가장 인기 있는 메뉴입니다.

남 좋네요. 치즈버거 하나랑 치킨버거 두 개 주시겠어요?

여 알겠어요. 마실 것도 드릴까요?

남 얼음을 넣은 콜라 작은 것 세 잔 주세요.

여 다른 것은요?

남 오, 감자튀김 두 개를 주문하고 싶어요.

여 네. 여기서 드실 건가요 아니면 가져가실 건가요?

남 가져가겠습니다.

해설 남자는 치즈버거 1개와 치킨버거 2개를 주문하고 콜라 작은 것 3개와 프렌치프라이 2개를 주문했으므로 총 20달러를 지불해야 한다.

11 장소 추론 | ②

해석

남 안녕하세요. 투숙 수속을 밟고 싶은데요.

여 성함을 말씀해 주시겠어요?

남 네, 제 이름은 Larry Kim입니다.

여 잠시만 기다려 주세요. 딱 하룻밤만 묵으시나요?

남 맞습니다.

여 어떻게 지불하시겠습니까?

남 신용카드로요.

여 신용카드를 주시겠습니까?

남 여기 있습니다.

여 여기 서명을 해 주시죠.

해설 여자가 남자에게 하루 숙박하는 게 맞는지 묻고, 남자가 숙박 요금을 결제하며 체크인을 하고 있는 상황이므로 두 사람이 대화하고 있는 장소는 호텔이다.

12 언급되지 않은 것 | ③

해석

여 Blue Planet 수족관에 대해 들어 본 적이 있나요? 만약 당신이 런던에 방문할 계획이라면 이 환상적인 곳을 놓치지 마세요. 당신은 많은 수중 동물을 관람할 수 있고 심지어 먹이를 줄 수도 있습니다. 식당과 선물 가게도 있으니, 오셔서 이 모든 것들을 즐기세요. 우리는 매일 오전 10시부터 오후 6시까지 문을 엽니다. 당신은 이곳에 오기 위해서 Big Ben에서 버스를 탈 수 있습니다. 감사합니다.

해설 Blue Planet 수족관의 입장료에 관해서는 언급되지 않았다.

13 도표 정보 파악 | ④

해석

남 5월 29일에 나는 야구 경기를 보기 위하여 Dodger 경기장에 갔다. Dodgers는 Angels와 경기했다. 솔직히 말해서 나는 한국인 선수인

류현진이 Dodgers에서 뛰기 때문에 Dodgers를 더 좋아한다. 그날, 최종 점수는 3:1이었다. 더 좋은 소식은 그 경기의 MVP가 류현진이었다는 것이다.

해설 경기의 최종 점수는 3:1이므로 ④가 일치하지 않는다.

14 주제 파악 | ③

해석

여 이것은 여러분의 몸의 일부입니다. 여러분 몸의 대부분의 부분들과는 달리, 이것은 매우 단단하고 얇습니다. 이것이 매우 단단하기 때문에, 누군가는 이것이 뼈의 일부라고 생각할 지도 모릅니다. 하지만, 그것은 사실 피부의 일부입니다. 그것은 조금씩 계속 자라기 때문에 사람들은 그것을 가끔씩 자릅니다. 그것은 기본적으로는 여러분의 손가락 끝을 보호합니다. 많은 사람들은 그들의 손을 멋져 보이게 하려고 광택제로 꾸미기도 합니다.

해설 손끝을 보호하기 위한 몸의 단단한 부분이라고 했으므로 손톱에 관한 설명임을 알 수 있다.

15 한 일 / 할 일 파악 | ③

해석

남 나 너무 배고파.

여 나도 그래. 김밥이 먹고 싶어.

남 김밥? 그게 뭔데?

여 그건 유명한 한국 음식이야.

남 어떻게 생겼는데?

여 초밥처럼 생겼지만 김밥 안에는 날 생선이 없어.

남 우리가 그것을 집에서 만들 수 있을까?

여 당연하지. 하지만 그것을 만들기 위해서는 몇 가지가 필요해.

남 그렇다면 장부터 보러 가자.

여 그래, 가자.

해설 두 사람은 집에서 김밥을 만들기 위해 장을 보러 간다고 했다.

16 숫자 정보 파악 - 시각 | ⑤

해석

남 와! 이 국립 박물관은 세계에서 가장 큰 박물관들 중에 하나야.

여 놀랍다!

남 그들은 하루에 두 번 투어 가이드 서비스를 제공하네. 너 관심 있니?

여 당연하지. 시간을 확인해 보자.

남 어디 보자. 지금이 10시 30분이니까. 첫 번째 투어는 이미 시작했어.

여 맞아. 두 번째 것이 30분 후에 시작하네. 우리 기다릴까?

남 그래, 기다리자. 기다리는 동안 이 지도를 읽는 게 어떨까?

여 그거 좋은 생각이다.

해설 지금이 10시 30분인데 다음 박물관 투어는 30분 뒤에 시작한다고 했으므로 투어는 11시에 시작될 것이다.

17 상황에 맞는 말 찾기 | ③

해석

여 지호와 Lisa는 가장 친한 친구이다. Lisa는 요즘 살이 찌고 있다고 생각해서 매일 점심을 거르기 시작한다. 그녀와 가장 친한 친구들 중에 한 명으로서 지호는 그녀가 건강해 보이지 않아서 정말 걱정스럽다. 지호는 그녀에게 식사를 거르는 것 대신에 무언가를 하라고 말하고 싶다. 이런 상황에서, 지호는 Lisa에게 뭐라고 말하겠는가?

지호 너는 체육관에서 운동하는 게 어떠니?
① 너는 저녁도 걸러야 해.
② 너는 먼저 미안하다고 말해야 할 것 같아.
④ 나는 내가 너무 살이 찌고 있는 것 같아 걱정이야.
⑤ 네가 한가할 때 함께 점심을 먹는 것은 어때?
해설 Lisa에게 체중을 조절하기 위해 밥을 거르는 것 대신 다른 것을 추천
     하고 싶은 상황이므로 ③이 답으로 적절하다.

18 한 일 / 할 일 파악 | ①
해석
[휴대 전화가 울린다.]
남 안녕, Jenny. 무슨 일이니?
여 준아, 너 숙제 다 끝냈니?
남 응.
여 그러면 우리 집에 올래? Jack과 규리도 여기 있어.
남 그럴 수 없을 거 같아. 나 지금 소포도 받아야 하고 방 청소도 지금 해
    야 하거든. 그런 다음에는 컴퓨터를 수리하러 수리점에도 가야 해.
여 우리는 오후 8시까지 여기에 있을 거야.
남 정말? 그러면 아마 오후 5시에 거기에 갈 수 있을 거야.
여 그래, 그때 보자.
해설 남자는 이미 숙제를 끝마쳤다.

19 알맞은 응답 찾기 | ②
해석
남 너 뭐 하고 있니?
여 음악을 듣고 있어요. 저는 연극의 배경 음악을 고르고 있어요.
남 네가 학교 축제를 위한 연극의 음악 감독이니?
여 네. 이거 생각보다 더 어렵네요.
남 적절한 노래를 좀 찾았니?
여 네, 하지만 어떤 것을 쓸 지는 결정하지 않았어요. 이거 들어 보실래요?
남 이것 좋은데. 제목이 뭐야?
여 'Gracias Mi Amigo'예요.
남 'Gracias Mi Amigo?' 그게 무슨 뜻이니?
여 '고마워 내 친구야'라는 뜻이에요.
① 나도 그것을 듣고 놀랐어.
③ 너는 그 노래를 부르는 방법을 아니?
④ 의미를 이해하는 것은 매우 중요해.
⑤ 나는 이 노래가 연극에 매우 잘 어울릴 것이라고 생각해.
해설 남자가 여자에게 노래 제목의 의미를 물었으므로 노래 제목의 의미를
     알려 주는 ②가 여자의 응답으로 가장 적절하다.

20 알맞은 응답 찾기 | ③
해석
여 실례합니다. 뭐 좀 물어 봐도 될까요?
남 물론이죠. 무엇인가요?
여 Toronto 동물원으로 가는 가장 좋은 길을 말씀해 주시겠어요?
남 오, 그것은 여기에서 멀지 않아요. 걸어서도 갈 수 있고 버스를 타서 갈
    수도 있어요.
여 제가 걸으면 얼마나 걸릴까요?
남 30분 정도 걸릴 거예요.
여 그럼, 버스를 타면요?
남 약 15분이요.

① 일주일에 두 번이요.
② 택시를 탑시다.
④ 태워 드릴까요?
⑤ 당신의 말에 전적으로 동의해요.
해설 Toronto 박물관에 가는데 버스로 얼마나 걸리는지 물었으므로 15분
     정도 걸린다는 ③이 남자의 응답으로 가장 적절하다.

17회 영어 듣기모의고사 pp. 134~135

01 ④	02 ⑤	03 ③	04 ④	05 ④
06 ④	07 ①	08 ②	09 ④	10 ②
11 ①	12 ⑤	13 ⑤	14 ④	15 ④
16 ④	17 ④	18 ①	19 ③	20 ④

Dictation Test 17회 pp. 136~141

01 ❶ choose some nice curtains ❷ look too childish
   ❸ prefer the checked ones
02 ❶ missed the flight ❷ have an important meeting
   ❸ a train ticket to
03 ❶ that novel ❷ computer games for five hours
   ❸ is out of order
04 ❶ what else they have ❷ have plans until Friday
   ❸ on Saturday
05 ❶ by accident ❷ just sell cellphones here ❸ buy
   a new one
06 ❶ Will you come to ❷ invited many friends ❸ I
   can't wait to see
07 ❶ go out for tea ❷ go for vacation ❸ park your car
08 ❶ Let me check ❷ am supposed to go to ❸ call
   for a taxi
09 ❶ I've heard that ❷ ask you a favor ❸ I'd rather
   not
10 ❶ These three sweaters ❷ seventy dollars total
11 ❶ put our bags ❷ climbing was so hard ❸ to get
   to the top
12 ❶ free this Saturday ❷ get off at
13 ❶ good spots for that flowerpot ❷ on the
   bookshelf ❸ the desk
14 ❶ food cold and frozen ❷ a big piece of ice ❸ by
   electricity
15 ❶ giving her seat to ❷ she might be having ❸ my
   seat
16 ❶ the report due on ❷ hand it in by tomorrow
17 ❶ passed two stations ❷ was going to be late

18 ❶ sent her a text message ❷ call her
19 ❶ practice for the show ❷ see your performance
   ❸ I go to see
20 ❶ a free drink coupon ❷ rather complicated
   ❸ when is the coupon available

01 그림 정보 파악 – 사물 | ④
해석
남 새 집이 마음에 드니?
여 나는 그 집이 좋은데, 좀 더 안락한 장소로 꾸미고 싶어. 좋은 커튼을 고르는 것 좀 도와줘.
남 좋아. 이 곰 인형 무늬가 있는 이것들은 어떠니?
여 내 스타일은 아냐. 너무 유치하잖아.
남 너 꽃무늬도 안 좋아하지, 그렇지?
여 꽃무늬 질색이야. 이 체크무늬 커튼이 괜찮지 않니?
남 모르겠어, 내 타입은 아닌데. 이 줄무늬가 더 낫지 않니?
여 음, 나는 체크무늬가 더 좋아.
해설 여자의 마지막 말에서 체크무늬 커튼을 선호한다고 했다.

02 목적 파악 | ⑤
해석
[전화벨이 울린다.]
남 여보세요?
여 안녕, Laurence. 나야.
남 수지야, 너 지금쯤 비행기 안에 있기로 되어있지 않니? 어떻게 전화한 거야?
여 나는 항공편을 놓쳐서, 지금 공항에 있어.
남 어째서?
여 내가 비행 스케줄을 착각했어.
남 오, 저런. 너는 목포에서 중요한 회의가 있다면서. 내가 도울 일이 있으면 좋겠다.
여 실은, 나는 네 도움이 필요해. 목포행 기차표가 있는지 좀 확인해 줄래?
남 그럴게. 인터넷으로 확인하고 전화 줄게.
해설 비행기 탑승을 놓친 여자는 남자에게 목포행 기차표를 구매 가능한지 확인을 부탁하기 위해서 전화했다.

03 그림 상황에 어울리는 대화 찾기 | ③
해석
① 여 우리 같이 축구하자.
   남 아니, 난 농구하고 싶어.
② 여 너는 그 소설에 푹 빠진 것 같아.
   남 응. 이것을 읽는 것을 멈출 수가 없어.
③ 여 이봐, 너는 다섯 시간 동안 컴퓨터 게임을 하고 있구나.
   남 딱 5분만 더 할게. 이게 마지막 단계란 말이야.
④ 여 얼마나 오랫동안 공부하고 있니?
   남 막 시작했어.
⑤ 여 오, 내 컴퓨터가 고장 난 것 같아.
   남 어디 보자. 내가 고쳐 볼게.
해설 엄마가 컴퓨터 게임을 하는 아들에게 주의를 주는 상황에 적절한 대화는 ③이다.

04 특정 정보 파악 – 요일 | ④
해석
여 이 샌드위치 정말 맛있다. 너 이거 어디서 샀니?
남 그거 우리 집 근처 제과점에서 샀는데.
여 언제 나를 그곳에 데려가 줘. 다른 빵은 무엇이 있는지 보고 싶어.
남 그래. 그럼 같이 샌드위치 사러 가자. 이번 금요일은 어때?
여 미안하지만 안 돼. 이번 목요일에 갈 수 있을까?
남 아니, 금요일까지는 못 가. 그럼 이번 주말은 어때?
여 나는 좋아. 어느 요일이 더 낫니?
남 토요일에 올래? 일요일은 확실하지 않아.
여 토요일 좋아.
해설 두 사람은 토요일에 샌드위치를 사러 가기로 했다.

05 직업 및 장래 희망 | ④
해석
남 무엇을 도와드릴까요?
여 안녕하세요, 제가 실수로 변기에 제 휴대 전화를 떨어뜨렸는데 그것이 작동하지 않아요.
남 여기에서는 휴대 전화 판매만 한답니다. 그러니, 휴대 전화를 고치시려면 수리점에 방문하셔야 해요.
여 그렇군요. 가장 가까운 서비스센터가 어디에 있는지 말씀해 주시겠어요?
남 용산역에 있어요.
여 도와주셔서 감사해요.
남 뭘요. 하지만 고치려면 돈이 많이 드실 거예요. 그럴 경우, 새로운 것을 사시는 것이 더 나으니, 이곳에 또 들러 주세요.
여 그럴게요, 감사해요.
해설 남자의 두 번째 말에서 남자는 휴대 전화 판매만 하고 있을 뿐이라고 했으므로 남자의 직업은 휴대 전화 판매자이다.

06 심정 파악 | ④
해석
여 안녕, Ted. 내일 우리 집에 올래? 파자마 파티를 할 거야.
남 너희 부모님은 어쩌고?
여 여행 가셔서, 일주일 후에 돌아오셔.
남 좋다. 너는 친구들을 많이 초대했니?
여 물론이지. Julie, Monica, Luke 그리고 Tony가 올 거야.
남 Luke라고 말했니? 나는 초등학교 이후로 그를 못 봤어. 나는 그를 너무 보고 싶어. 좋아. 나는 내일 너의 집에 갈게.
해설 남자는 오랜만에 친구들을 만날 생각으로 잔뜩 기대하고 있다.

07 어색한 대화 찾기 | ①
해석
① 여 물 좀 끓여 줄래요?
   남 알겠어요. 차 마시러 나갑시다.
② 여 이 인형들은 판매용인가요?
   남 아뇨. 그것들은 전시품의 일부입니다.
③ 여 너는 휴가 때 어디 갔니?
   남 나는 그냥 텔레비전을 보면서 집에 있었어.
④ 여 너 아직 방 청소를 안 했니?
   남 네. 저는 숙제하느라 바빴어요.
⑤ 여 당신은 여기에 차를 대시면 안 됩니다.
   남 저는 여기가 개인 주차 공간인 줄 몰랐네요.

해설 물 좀 끓여 달라는 말에 대해 차 한 잔하러 나가자고 대답하는 것은 어색하다.

08 부탁한 일 파악 | ②
해석
남 아직도 3시야?
여 이상하네. 아까 전에 시계를 봤을 때 3시였는데.
남 내 휴대 전화 시계를 확인해 볼게. 세상에. 4시 30분이야.
여 시계 배터리가 다 된 것이 분명해.
남 어떻게 하지? 난 사촌 동생 만나러 5시까지 서울역에 가야 하는데.
여 지하철로 30분 만에 서울역에 가는 건 불가능해. 택시를 타는 게 어때?
남 그래야겠어. 내가 가방을 챙길 동안 택시를 좀 불러 줄래?
여 물론이야.
해설 남자는 약속 시간에 늦지 않기 위해 자신이 짐을 싸는 동안 여자에게 전화로 택시를 불러 달라고 부탁했다.

09 의도 파악 | ④
해석
여 실례합니다만, 당신은 Josh Austin 씨가 아니세요? 사인 한 장만 해 주실래요?
남 음, 저 아닌데요.
여 앗, 죄송해요.
남 아뇨, 아닙니다. 그런데 저는 그 가수를 많이 닮았다는 이야기를 들어봤습니다.
여 부탁 하나만 드려도 될까요?
남 뭔데요?
여 저랑 사진 한 번만 찍어 주실래요? 친구들은 제가 Josh를 만났다고 믿을 거예요.
남 안 그러는 게 좋겠어요. 제가 Josh인 척한다는 사실을 Josh Austin 이 알면 좋아하지 않을 겁니다.
여 오, 그렇겠네요.
해설 가수 Josh Austin인 척하며 사진 찍어 달라는 여자의 제안을 남자가 거절했다.

10 숫자 정보 파악 – 금액 | ②
해석
남 안녕하세요, 저는 제 옷을 가지러 왔어요. 그것들은 전부 드라이클리닝 되었나요?
여 네. 여기 스웨터 세 장과 코트 하나가 손님 것 맞죠?
남 맞습니다. 얼마죠?
여 모두 70달러입니다.
남 와, 그렇게 비싸요?
여 드라이클리닝을 하는 데에 스웨터 한 장에 15달러고요, 코트는 25달러거든요.
남 알겠습니다. 여기에 100달러짜리 지폐가 있습니다.
해설 남자는 드라이클리닝 비용으로 70달러를 지불해야 하는데 100달러를 건넸으므로 30달러의 거스름돈을 받을 것이다.

11 장소 추론 | ①
해석
여 우리는 아직도 도착 못했니? 나는 잠시 쉬고 싶어.
남 좋아. 여기에 우리 가방들을 놓자.

여 나는 등산이 이렇게 힘든 줄 알았더라면, 대신 해변에 갔을 텐데.
남 네가 해변에 갔다면, 너는 그것을 후회했을 거야. 거긴 너무 붐벼.
여 그럴 수도, 아닐 수도 있지. 어쨌든, 다리가 너무 아프다.
남 가방 이리 줘. 정상까지 가려면 15분밖에 안 걸릴 거야.
해설 여자는 등산이 이렇게 힘든지 알았다면 대신 해변에 갔을 것이라고 말했고, 남자가 정상까지 15분 남았다고 했으므로 두 사람은 산에 있음을 알 수 있다.

12 언급되지 않은 것 | ⑤
해석
여 메시지를 남겨주세요. (삐 소리)
남 안녕, Natalie. 나는 최근에 새 집으로 이사해서 파티를 계획하고 있어. 이번 주 토요일에 시간 되면 12시까지 우리 집에 와. 너는 3번 버스를 타고 지산역에서 내리면 돼. Jenny가 우리 집에 와봤으니까 연락해서 같이 와도 돼. 토요일에 볼 수 있기를 바라.
해설 파티의 참석 인원에 관해서는 언급되지 않았다.

13 그림 정보 파악 | ⑤
해석
여 이 작은 화분을 어디다 놓을지 모르겠어.
남 화분 놓을 좋은 자리가 많이 있잖아. 문이랑 책장 사이도 비어 있고.
여 그냥 바닥에 놓기는 싫어.
남 침대 머리 위는 어때?
여 내가 침대에 있을 때 그것을 실수로 건드릴까봐 걱정돼.
남 그럼, 책장 위는? 네가 실수로 그것을 거기에서 건드릴 것 같지 않은데.
여 맞아. 하지만 공간이 충분한 것 같지 않아.
남 아, 책상이 가장 좋겠다. 책상 앞에 큰 창문이 있잖아.
여 좋은 생각이다. 꽃은 해가 많이 필요하지. 여기 놓을래.
해설 여자는 앞에 큰 창문이 있는 책상 위에 화분을 두기로 했다.

14 주제 파악 | ④
해석
남 그것은 음식을 차갑게 하거나 냉동된 상태로 유지시킵니다. 예전에 그 것은 보통 안에 큰 얼음 조각을 넣은 나무로 된 상자였습니다. 요즘 그 것은 금속으로 만듭니다. 그리고 그것은 꽤 큰 직사각형의 상자입니다. 그리고 그것은 하나 혹은 두 개의 문을 가지고 있습니다. 그것은 전기 로 작동될 수 있습니다.
해설 음식을 냉장이나 냉동 상태로 유지하고 크고 직사각형이며 하나 또는 두 개의 문이 있는 것은 냉장고이다.

15 한 일 / 할 일 파악 | ④
해석
여 경로석에 앉은 저 젊은 여자를 봐. 앞에 계신 노인분께 자리를 양보하지 않고 있네.
남 그녀는 그녀 나름의 이유가 있을지도 모르지.
여 예를 들면?
남 아마도 그녀가 다리 부상으로 고통 받고 있거나, 아니면 아기를 가졌는 지도 모르잖아. 그렇게 생각하지 않니?
여 네 말이 맞을지도 모르겠다. 내가 내 자리를 노인분께 양보해 드리는 게 낫겠다.

남 정말 친절하구나!
해설 여자는 노인에게 자신의 자리를 양보하겠다고 말했다.

16 숫자 정보 파악 – 날짜 | ④
해석
남 미란아, 잠시 이야기 좀 할 수 있니?
여 물론이죠, 김 선생님.
남 너 아직 리포트 제출을 안 했더구나.
여 네? 보고서 제출은 5월 20일까지 아닌가요?
남 아니, 12일까지였고, 오늘은 벌써 16일이구나.
여 내일까지 제출할게요.
남 알겠다.
해설 오늘이 5월 16일인데 내일까지 과제를 제출하겠다고 했으므로 여자가 과제를 제출할 날짜는 17일이다.

17 상황에 맞는 말 찾기 | ④
해석
여 Peter는 Judy를 만나기 위해 지하철을 탔다. 그는 너무 피곤해서 잠시 낮잠을 잤다. 그러나 Peter가 눈을 떴을 때, 그는 두 정거장을 지나쳤다는 사실을 알았다. 그가 늦을 것은 분명했다. Judy는 만날 장소에 있을 것이다. 이런 상황에서, Peter는 Judy에게 뭐라고 말하겠는가?
Peter 미안한데, 나 조금 늦을 것 같아.
① 다시 늦지 말아줘.
② 너는 집에 가는 길이니?
③ 나는 지하철을 탈 거야.
⑤ 우리는 모임 장소를 바꿀 필요가 있어.
해설 깜빡 잠이 들어 두 정거장을 지나 약속 장소에 늦게 도착하는 상황이므로 ④가 답으로 적절하다.

18 한 일 / 할 일 파악 | ①
해석
남 모두 다 왔니? 우리 놀이공원으로 출발하자.
여 잠깐, 민주가 아직 안 왔어.
남 오, 그녀가 어제 배가 아프다고 말하지 않았니?
여 그랬지. 그녀는 아직 아픈가 봐. 그래서 내가 5분 전에 그녀에게 문자 메시지를 보냈어.
남 그녀가 휴대 전화를 확인 못 할 수도 있어. 그녀에게 전화해 줄래?
여 좋아.
해설 민주가 문자 메시지를 보지 못할 수도 있으므로 전화를 걸기로 했다.

19 알맞은 응답 찾기 | ③
해석
여 너 이제 동아리에 가니?
남 응, 우리 다음 주 공연을 위해 연습해야 해.
여 공연에 못 가서 미안해.
남 이해해. 중요한 가족 행사가 있잖아.
여 하지만 나는 정말 너의 공연을 보고 싶어.
남 음, 사실은, 우리 내일 리허설이 있는데.
여 정말? 내가 가서 보면 안 될까?
남 물론 괜찮지. 네가 원하면 와.
① 아마 가능할 거야.
② 네가 실수를 했어.

④ 누가 시간과 장소를 내게 말해 줄 수 있을까?
⑤ 미안하지만 너의 공연을 보러 갈 수 없을 것 같아.
해설 여자가 리허설에 가도 되는지 물었으므로 원하면 오라고 말하는 ③이 남자의 응답으로 가장 적절하다.

20 알맞은 응답 찾기 | ④
해석
여 축하드립니다! 오늘 저희 가게의 100번째 손님이십니다.
남 제가요? 놀랍군요.
여 선물로 저희가 당신께 무료 음료 쿠폰을 드립니다.
남 좋네요. 감사합니다.
여 여기 쿠폰 있습니다. 저희 홈페이지에 방문하셔서, 이 번호들을 써 넣으시고 간단한 설문 조사를 작성해 주세요.
남 휴, 다소 복잡한걸요.
여 5분 이내로 걸릴 거예요.
남 좋아요, 해 볼게요. 이 쿠폰은 언제까지 유효한가요?
여 당신은 9월 말까지 그것을 사용하실 수 있으세요.
① 내일 다시 와 주세요.
② 이것이 저희 웹사이트 주소입니다.
③ 그 설문 조사를 수행해 주셔서 감사합니다.
⑤ 당신은 이 쿠폰으로 어떤 종류의 음료든 다 드실 수 있어요.
해설 무료 음료 쿠폰이 언제까지 사용 가능한지 물었으므로 9월 말까지 사용 가능하다고 말하는 ④가 여자의 응답으로 가장 적절하다.

18회 영어 듣기모의고사 pp. 142~143

01 ④	02 ①	03 ④	04 ①	05 ⑤
06 ②	07 ④	08 ④	09 ⑤	10 ③
11 ⑤	12 ④	13 ④	14 ③	15 ②
16 ②	17 ②	18 ④	19 ⑤	20 ⑤

Dictation Test 18회 pp. 144~149

01 ❶ a crosswalk sign ❷ can ride a bicycle ❸ can't turn left ❹ have to stop

02 ❶ drop by your place ❷ give it back ❸ passing by your place

03 ❶ We are going to ❷ paint my room ❸ near the statue

04 ❶ change the plan ❷ bring my purse ❸ at the front gate

05 ❶ The lights went out ❷ may have lost everything ❸ am I going to do

06 ❶ I wish ❷ tell me how you improved ❸ I should try it

07 ❶ Can you hear me ❷ Have you been to ❸ both of them

08 ❶ a hard time waking up ❷ couldn't hear it ❸ I'll ask her

09 ❶ in the recycling bin ❷ a lot of energy ❸ you'll be bothered

10 ❶ a chicken sandwich ❷ fifteen dollars each ❸ half and half

11 ❶ the schedule for today ❷ taking a group picture ❸ in case it rains

12 ❶ show the librarian ❷ three books in total ❸ within two weeks

13 ❶ What time is the show ❷ bring your camera ❸ I'm afraid not

14 ❶ you wear on your head ❷ for your safety ❸ protect their head

15 ❶ not home now ❷ leave a message ❸ he just came

16 ❶ the right time to buy ❷ I have an appointment ❸ How about meeting

17 ❶ is looking at ❷ forgot to bring ❸ to lend him one

18 ❶ go out for dinner ❷ going dancing ❸ not good at bowling

19 ❶ She's been crying ❷ she failed ❸ should go and comfort her

20 ❶ I've watched this movie ❷ an action movie star ❸ who is your hero

---

01 그림 정보 파악 – 사물 | ④

해석

여 저 표지판은 무엇이지? 엄마와 아이의 그림이 있네.

남 그건 횡단보도 표지판이야.

여 그렇구나. 그리고 자전거가 있는 저 표지판을 무엇을 의미하니?

남 그것은 네가 거기에서 자전거를 탈 수 있다는 것을 의미해.

여 응. 그리고 저 표지판은? 그것은 무엇을 의미해?

남 네가 저 표지판을 보면, 너는 좌회전을 할 수 없어.

여 오, 그렇구나. 저 표지판은 어때?

남 그건 네가 정지해야 한다는 걸 의미해.

해설 대화에 주차 금지 표지판은 언급되지 않았다.

02 목적 파악 | ①

해석

[전화벨이 울린다.]

여 여보세요?

남 Mary, 나 Mike야. 너 지금 어디니?

여 나 집이야. 남동생이랑 영화 보고 있어. 무슨 일이야?

남 내가 지금 너희 집에 들러서 빌린 게임을 돌려줘도 되니?

여 우리 집까지 올 필요는 없는데. 내일 학교에서 돌려줘도 돼.

남 마침 너희 집을 지나게 되었어. 이것만 돌려주고 금방 갈게. 5분 안에

거기 갈 거야.

여 그럼 알겠어. 곧 만나.

해설 남자는 여자에게 빌렸던 게임을 돌려주기 위해 여자에게 전화했다.

03 그림 상황에 어울리는 대화 찾기 | ④

해석

① 남 선생님, 우리는 오늘 무엇을 하나요?

　여 우리는 이 단편소설을 읽고 그것 중 가장 인상 깊은 장면을 그릴 거야.

② 남 나는 내 방을 칠할 거야. 파란색과 노란색 중에 무슨 색이 나을 거라고 생각해?

　여 파란색이 어때? 파란색이 이 방에 더 잘 어울릴 것 같아.

③ 남 너 그거 아니? 이 그림의 작가가 눈이 안 보인대.

　여 정말? 그럼 이 그림은 어떻게 그렸대?

④ 남 내가 네 사진을 찍어 줄게. 저기 동상 옆에 가서 서.

　여 그래. 나 괜찮아 보이니?

⑤ 남 이 책은 그림에 관한 충분한 정보가 없어. 그렇게 생각하지 않니?

　여 맞아. 작가가 그것들에 대해 더 썼어야 해.

해설 남자가 사진기를 들고 여자에게 동상 옆으로 가라고 손짓하고 있는 상황에 적절한 대화는 ④이다.

04 장소 추론 | ①

해석

남 우리 방과 후에 학교 정문 앞에서 만날 거지, 그치?

여 음, 미안하지만, 우리 계획을 변경해야 할 것 같아. 우리 극장에서 만날 수 있니?

남 물론이지, 근데 무슨 일이야?

여 내 지갑을 가져오는 것을 깜빡했어. 집에 가서 가지고 오려고.

남 네가 원하면 내가 네게 돈을 빌려줄게.

여 정말? 내일 네게 꼭 갚을게. 오, 종이 친다. 나는 우리 반으로 돌아가야겠어.

남 그럼 원래 약속대로 정문에서 보는 거지?

여 그래. 이따 보자.

해설 두 사람은 계획을 바꿔 극장 앞에서 보기로 했다가 다시 원래의 계획대로 학교 정문에서 만나기로 했다.

05 심정 파악 | ⑤

해석

여 맙소사!

남 무슨 일이야?

여 갑자기 전기가 나갔어. 난 컴퓨터로 작업을 하고 있었는데.

남 저장했니?

여 아니, 완전히 깜박 잊었어. 자료를 모두 잃어버렸을지도 몰라.

남 이봐, 내게 생각이 있어. 내가 널 돕도록 Peter를 데려올게. 그 애가 그 파일을 복구할 수 있을 거야. 그 애는 컴퓨터 전문가야.

여 그런데 그가 이걸 복구하지 못하면, 나는 어떻게 하지?

해설 여자는 컴퓨터 작업 중에 갑자기 전기가 나가 컴퓨터로 작업하고 있던 파일을 날려 버린 상황이므로 당황스러울 것이다.

06 관계 추론 | ②

해석

남 미나야. 나는 네가 영어 듣기 시험에서 만점을 받았다고 들었어.

여 응, 내가 만점을 받은 것은 이번이 처음이야.

남 나도 영어를 잘했으면 좋겠다. 네가 점수를 어떻게 올렸는지 말해 줘.

여 음, 특별한 건 없어. 문제집 하나 사서 MP3 파일을 반복해서 들었거든.

남 그게 다야?

여 응, 진짜야.

남 맞아. 나도 그것을 시도해 봐야겠다.

해설 남자가 여자에게 영어 듣기 시험에서 만점을 받은 비결을 물어보며, 그 방법을 시도해 보겠다고 했으므로 두 사람 모두 학생이라는 것을 알 수 있다.

---

07 <u>어색한 대화 찾기</u> | ④

해석

① 여 제 말 들리세요?

　남 네, 하지만 명확하게는 안 들려요.

② 여 뭐라고 불러 드리면 될까요?

　남 Jake라고 불러 주세요.

③ 여 이 커피숍은 너무 붐비는군요.

　남 다른 곳에 갈까요?

④ 여 현대 미술관에 가 봤나요?

　남 저는 그림 그리는 데 소질이 없어요.

⑤ 여 빨간 것과 흰 것 중에 어느 것이 더 나아요?

　남 저는 둘 다 좋아요.

해설 현대 미술 박물관에 가 본 적이 있는지 묻는 질문에 대해 그림 그리는 것을 잘한다고 답하는 것은 어색하다.

---

08 <u>부탁한 일 파악</u> | ④

해석

남 선생님, 늦어서 죄송해요.

여 왜 늦었니? 너는 보통 정시에 오잖아.

남 음, 저희 엄마께서 일을 시작하셔서, 이제 아침에 집에서 혼자 있어요. 저를 깨워 주는 사람이 없어서 때때로 아침에 일어나는 것이 힘들어요.

여 알람을 설정해 놓았니?

남 했는데, 오늘은 그것을 못 들었어요.

여 Ann이 네 집 근처에 살더라. 그 애와 같이 올 수 있겠다.

남 그럼 좋은데, 제가 그 애랑 그렇게 친하지 않아요. 괜찮은지 그 애에게 물어봐 주실 수 있으세요? 그럼 제가 그 애가 학교에 올 때 초인종을 눌러 달라고 부탁할게요.

여 그래. 내가 너를 위해서 그것은 할 수 있을 것 같다.

해설 남자는 여자에게 Ann이 학교 가는 길에 자신의 집 초인종을 눌러 주는 게 괜찮은지 물어봐 줄 것을 부탁했다.

---

09 <u>의도 파악</u> | ⑤

해석

남 Sarah. 네가 이 종이를 쓰레기통에 버렸니?

여 네, 제가 그랬어요. 뭐가 문제죠?

남 종이는 재활용 쓰레기통에 버려야 해. 네가 그것을 쓰레기통에 버리면, 그것은 땅에 묻혀 버릴 거야.

여 하지만 종이는 묻혀도 괜찮을 것 같은데요.

남 우리가 종이를 만드는 데 많은 에너지를 사용해야 하고 우리는 이 종이를 다시 사용할 수 있다는 거지.

여 제가 쓰레기까지도 신경 써야 한다는 것이 정말 귀찮아요.

남 네 기분을 이해하지만 만약 네가 지금 그것에 관해 신경 쓰지 않으면, 너는 미래에는 그것에 의해 더 많이 귀찮게 될 거야.

해설 남자는 여자에게 종이를 재활용 쓰레기통에 버려야 한다고 충고하고 있다.

---

10 <u>숫자 정보 파악 - 금액</u> | ③

해석

여 이 제과점에는 많은 다양한 종류의 빵이 있구나.

남 멋지다. 나는 블루베리 쿠키랑 초콜릿 머핀을 먹고 싶어.

여 탁월한 선택이야. 나는 치킨 샌드위치를 먹을래.

남 얼마지?

여 쿠키랑 머핀은 각각 15달러이고 샌드위치는 20달러야.

남 반반씩 내자. 음식을 같이 먹을 수 있잖아.

여 좋아.

해설 남자와 여자는 블루베리 쿠키와 초콜릿 머핀 그리고 치킨 샌드위치를 구입하기로 했고 절반씩 지불하기로 했으므로 남자는 50달러의 반인 25달러를 지불하면 된다.

---

11 <u>장소 추론</u> | ⑤

해석

여 오늘의 일정을 말씀드리겠습니다. 9시에 버스를 타고 자유의 여신상으로 이동할 겁니다. 그곳에서 단체 사진을 찍은 후에 우리는 브루클린 다리에 가서 점심시간까지 그곳에 있을 거예요. 2시에는 센트럴 파크에 갈 예정이지만, 비가 오는 경우에는 대신 현대 미술관에 갈 겁니다. 그 이후에는 5시에 라디오시티 뮤직홀에 갈 거예요.

해설 오후 2시에 비가 올 경우 현대 미술관에 갈 것이라고 했다.

---

12 <u>언급되지 않은 것</u> | ④

해석

남 이제, 책을 대출하는 법을 알려 드리겠습니다. 여러분이 빌리고 싶은 책을 선택해서 사서에게 가져다주세요. 사서에게 학생 신분증도 보여 줘야 합니다. 사서는 여러분의 학번과 이름을 확인하고 책을 대출하게 해 줄 겁니다. 여러분은 총 세 권을 빌릴 수 있고, 2주 안에 그 책들을 반납해야 합니다. 만약 2주 안에 책을 반납하지 않으면, 여러분은 책을 더 대출할 수 없을 것입니다.

해설 원하는 책을 찾는 법은 언급되지 않았다.

---

13 <u>도표 정보 파악</u> | ④

해석

남 6월 21일에 김연아의 아이스 쇼 'Winter Dream'을 보러 가지 않을래? 그것이 그녀의 마지막 아이스 쇼래.

여 우와, 놓치고 싶지 않아. 쇼가 몇 시인데?

남 저녁 7시부터 9시까지야.

여 그리고 입장료는 얼마야?

남 30달러부터 100달러까지 있어. 하지만 우리 삼촌이 내게 무료 티켓 두 장을 주셨어.

여 멋지다! 내가 저녁을 살게.

남 고마워. 그리고 카메라 가져오는 것 잊지 말고.

여 쇼 중간에 사진을 찍어도 괜찮아?

남 아니, 그렇진 않은데, 쇼가 끝나고 그녀의 사진을 찍을 수 있을지도 모르잖아.

해설 아이스 쇼의 가격은 30달러부터 100달러까지라고 했다.

14 주제 파악 | ③

해석

남　이것은 머리에 쓰는 것이며 둥근 모양입니다. 이것은 쉽게 깨지지 않는 특별한 물질로 만들어지고 패션을 위한 것이 아닙니다. 그것은 안전을 위한 것이죠. 다시 말해, 사람들은 머리를 보호하기 위해 이것을 착용합니다. 예를 들어, 사람들은 자전거나 인라인 스케이트를 탈 때 이것을 착용합니다.

해설　머리를 보호하고 안전을 위해 쓰며 쉽게 부서지지 않는 재질로 만들어진 둥근 것으로 자전거나 인라인스케이트를 탈 때 쓰기도 하는 것은 헬멧이다.

15 한 일 / 할 일 파악 | ②

해석

[전화벨이 울린다.]

남　여보세요?

여　이봐, David. 우리 집에서 같이 숙제하자.

남　음, 누구세요? David는 지금 집에 없는데요.

여　저는 Bella예요. 당신은 David의 형인 Jack인가요?

남　응. David는 식료품점에 가서 5분 안에 돌아올 거야. 메시지를 남기겠니?

여　제가 그냥 잠시 후에 전화 할게요.

남　오, 그가 방금 왔다. 잠깐만 기다려.

해설　여자가 남동생에게 전화를 건 상황으로 식료품점에 다녀온 남동생이 방금 집에 왔다며 잠시만 기다리라고 했으므로 남자는 남동생에게 전화를 바꿔 줄 것이다.

16 숫자 정보 파악 – 시각 | ②

해석

남　JJ 신발 가게가 오늘만 70퍼센트 할인 판매한다는 소식 들었니?

여　정말? 장화를 살 적당한 때가 왔구나.

남　나는 슬리퍼 한 켤레 사야겠다.

여　그럼, 우리 같이 가자.

남　좋아. 나는 3시부터 5시까지 약속이 있어. 그것 말고는 오후 내내 시간이 있어.

여　5시 이후에는 틀림없이 붐빌 거야. 점심 식사 직후에 가자.

남　좋아. 1시에 만날까?

여　좋아. 그곳에 가는 게 너무나 기다려진다.

해설　두 사람은 점심 식사 후 1시에 만날 것이다.

17 상황에 맞는 말 찾기 | ②

해석

여　Andy는 오늘 미술 수업이 있다. 그는 채색 도구를 가져오기로 되어 있었고 그는 중요한 것을 빠뜨렸다는 것을 알았다. 그는 그림붓을 빠뜨린 것이다! 그는 오늘의 미술 수업 동안 그림붓 없이는 아무것도 할 수 없다. 그러나 그때 그는 그의 친한 친구인 영미가 그림붓이 많이 있는 것을 보고 그녀가 그에게 하나를 빌려주었으면 한다. 이런 상황에서 Andy는 영미에게 뭐라고 말하겠는가?

Andy　나한테 그림붓 하나만 빌려줄 수 있니?

① 물론, 그렇게 해.

③ 너는 오늘 무엇을 그릴 거야?

④ 우리 지금 미술실로 가야 하니?

⑤ 다음번에 내게 더 많은 그림붓을 가져오라고 상기시켜 줘.

해설　그림붓을 빠뜨리고 온 Andy는 그림붓이 필요하므로 영미에게 그림붓을 빌려 달라고 부탁하는 ②가 답으로 적절하다.

18 한 일 / 할 일 파악 | ④

해석

남　Sally, 너 이번 주말에 뭘 할 계획이니?

여　우리 저녁 먹으러 나가자. 그 후에는 새로 나온 Brad Pitt 영화를 볼까 생각 중이었어.

남　저녁 식사는 좋은데. 나 그 영화는 이미 봤어.

여　음, 그럼 춤추러 가는 것은 어때?

남　미안하지만, 내가 춤추는 것은 안 좋아하는 거 알잖아.

여　볼링 치는 것은 어떨까?

남　볼링을 잘하지는 못하지만 재미있을 것 같아.

여　그래, 그러면 토요일 5시에 만나자.

해설　두 사람은 토요일에 저녁을 먹고 볼링을 치기로 했다.

19 알맞은 응답 찾기 | ⑤

해석

남　Claire는 어디에 있니? 나는 그녀를 어디에서도 못 찾겠네.

여　그녀는 화장실에 있어.

남　지금 한 시간이나 흘렀어. 그녀는 화장실에서 뭐하고 있니?

여　그녀는 울고 있어.

남　왜?

여　그녀는 반장으로 당선될 거라고 확신했었는데 떨어졌거든.

남　오, 우리가 가서 위로해 줘야 하지 않을까?

여　시간이 최고의 약이야. 여기서 그냥 기다리자.

① 내가 가서 약을 좀 사 올게.

② 나는 그녀가 반장이 되길 바라.

③ 그녀는 네가 오기를 기다렸어.

④ 내가 너라면, 나는 그녀를 선택했을 거야.

해설　남자가 울고 있는 Claire를 위로해 줘야 할지 여자에게 물었으므로 시간이 약이라며 여기서 그냥 기다리자고 하는 ⑤가 여자의 응답으로 가장 적절하다.

20 알맞은 응답 찾기 | ⑤

해석

남　너 뭐 보고 있니?

여　'Rush Hour'를 보고 있어.

남　너 Jackie Chan의 영화를 또 보는 거야?

여　응. 나는 이 영화를 10번 이상 봤어.

남　너는 왜 같은 영화를 계속해서 다시 보니?

여　그건 Jackie Chan이 내 영웅이기 때문이야. 언젠가 나는 그 사람 같은 액션 영화 스타가 될 거야.

남　오, 그게 바로 네가 태권도와 쿵푸를 배우는 이유니?

여　응. 그런데, 너의 영웅은 누구니?

남　팝의 황제인 Michael Jackson이야.

① 그는 내 취향이 아니야.

② Jackie Chan의 영화.

③ 나는 대신에 유도를 배워.

④ 나는 그 영화에 대해 몰라.

해설　여자가 남자에게 남자의 영웅은 누구냐고 물은 상황이므로 Michael Jackson이라고 답한 ⑤가 남자의 응답으로 가장 적절하다.

01 ⑤	02 ④	03 ②	04 ③	05 ③
06 ①	07 ①	08 ②	09 ④	10 ⑤
11 ⑤	12 ③	13 ②	14 ①	15 ②
16 ⑤	17 ③	18 ⑤	19 ⑤	20 ⑤

Dictation Test 19회　　pp. 152~157

01 ❶ a big heart in the middle　❷ birthday message inside the heart　❸ make stripes outside

02 ❶ take a look at it　❷ come over here　❸ to fix your computer

03 ❶ put your watch　❷ half past nine　❸ do my homework

04 ❶ Why don't we meet　❷ buy some snacks　❸ Then let's meet at

05 ❶ is not working　❷ on a hot afternoon　❸ buy some ice cream

06 ❶ by any chance　❷ the same elementary school　❸ call me a little kid

07 ❶ How did you like　❷ wear a seat belt　❸ I feel like

08 ❶ huge fan of yours　❷ Could I have your autograph　❸ appreciate it

09 ❶ a threat to them　❷ it might bite you　❸ go close to dogs

10 ❶ how much the fare　❷ Here we are　❸ keep the change

11 ❶ good at basketball　❷ can't play any more　❸ finish the class early

12 ❶ fresh bananas　❷ will finish at　❸ the grocery section

13 ❶ still a lawyer　❷ She's working at　❸ have the same number

14 ❶ wet your hands　❷ It's important to rub　❸ dry them

15 ❶ do something fun　❷ difficult to get tickets　❸ in the park

16 ❶ buy pencils and erasers　❷ must have bought one

17 ❶ the classroom key　❷ she's almost at　❸ open the classroom

18 ❶ cough medicine　❷ you're not feeling well　❸ a hot lemon drink

19 ❶ I've had enough　❷ My doctor suggested　❸ Why did your doctor

20 ❶ you look down　❷ I got nothing　❸ no talent in drawing

01　그림 정보 파악 – 사물　| ⑤

해석

남　초콜릿 크림으로 생일 케이크를 장식하는 방법을 알려 드리겠습니다. 먼저, 케이크의 가운데에 큰 하트를 하나 그리세요. 그런 후, 하트 안에 생일 메시지를 쓰세요. 이제, 하트 바깥쪽에 줄무늬를 만들기 위해 선들을 그리세요. 하트 안쪽에는 선을 긋지 않도록 하시고요.

해설　케이크 중앙에 큰 하트를 그리고 하트 안에 생일 메시지를 쓴 다음 하트 밖에 줄무늬로 선을 그린 케이크는 ⑤이다.

02　목적 파악　| ④

해석

[휴대 전화가 울린다.]

남　안녕, Michelle. 무슨 일이야?

여　안녕, Scott. 내 컴퓨터가 또 고장 났어. 지금 와서 봐 줄 수 있니?

남　나는 지금 집을 떠날 수가 없어. 엄마가 소포를 받아달라고 부탁하셨거든. 배달하시는 분이 한 시간 후에 도착하신다고 했어.

여　그럼, 너는 오후에는 여기에 들를 수 있겠네, 그렇지?

남　응. 소포 받은 후에 컴퓨터 고치러 거기에 갈게.

여　좋아. 고마워.

해설　여자는 자신의 컴퓨터가 고장 나서 컴퓨터 수리를 부탁하기 위해 남자에게 전화했다.

03　그림 상황에 어울리는 대화 찾기　| ②

해석

① 남　너는 하루에 시간을 몇 번이나 확인하니?

　　여　모르겠어. 그건 나의 버릇인 것 같아.

② 남　시계를 마지막으로 어디에 두었니?

　　여　전혀 기억이 안 나.

③ 남　조심해! 차가 오고 있어.

　　여　큰일 날 뻔했다. 고마워.

④ 남　봐. 벌써 아홉 시 삼십 분이야.

　　여　그건 불가능해.

⑤ 남　너는 두 시간 동안이나 텔레비전을 보고 있어.

　　여　그래요. 이제 숙제하러 갈게요.

해설　여자의 잃어버린 시계를 찾는 상황에 적절한 대화는 ②이다.

04　장소 추론　| ③

해석

남　우리 이번 토요일에 같이 놀기로 한 거 기억하니?

여　응, 그래. 우리 소풍 갈 거잖아. 우리 어디서 만날까?

남　식당에서 만나서 점심으로 김밥을 좀 사는 게 어때?

여　내가 집에서 과일이랑 김밥을 좀 쌀 거야. 너는 그냥 간식을 좀 사면 돼.

남　그럼 코리아 마트에서 만나서 같이 간식을 사자.

여　그래. 우리 거기서부터 같이 공원으로 가자.

남　좋아. 자전거 대여소로 가서 자전거를 빌리는 건 어때?

여　좋은 생각이야. 나는 벌써 신난다.

남　나도 그래.

해설　소풍을 가기로 한 남자와 여자는 마트에서 만나서 같이 간식을 사기로 했다.

05 심정 파악 | ③

해석

남 Jenny, 날씨가 너무 더웠지, 그렇지?

여 네, 김 선생님. 우리 모두가 땀을 많이 흘리고 있는데 에어컨이 작동하지 않아요. 선풍기를 켜는 것으로는 충분하지 않아요.

남 이해한다. 하지만 그건 우리가 전기를 절약해야 하기 때문이야.

여 알아요. 하지만 저는 오늘 같이 더운 오후에는 에어컨을 사용하고 싶어요.

남 대신에 내가 너희들 모두에게 아이스크림을 사 주마. 그러니까 반장에게 지금 당장 교무실로 오라고 전하렴.

여 와! 정말 감사합니다. 김 선생님.

해설 땀이 많이 나지만 에어컨이 고장 나 에어컨을 틀지 못하는 상황에서 여자는 짜증이 났지만 선생님이 아이스크림을 사 준다고 하여 기뻤을 것이다.

06 관계 추론 | ①

해석

남 실례합니다. 당신은 혹시 Susan 아닌가요?

여 네, 맞아요. 제가 당신을 아나요?

남 알지. 우리는 같은 초등학교에 다녔잖아. Lincoln 초등학교 말이야. 나 기억 안나?

여 아뇨. 저는 아직 누구신지 모르겠어요.

남 나는 Jason이야. 내가 키가 아주 작아서 너는 나를 작은 꼬맹이라고 부르곤 했잖아.

여 아! Jason. 그 작은 꼬맹이! 너는 키가 훨씬 더 컸구나.

남 그런 소리 많이 들어. 어쨌든 우리 어디 가서 이야기 좀 나누자.

해설 두 사람은 같은 초등학교를 다닌 동창 사이이다.

07 어색한 대화 찾기 | ①

해석

① 남 일본으로 여행 갔던 건 어땠니?

　여 나는 그 여행을 즐길 수 있으면 좋겠어.

② 남 그는 피아노 경연 대회에서 1등을 했어.

　여 뭐? 농담하는 거겠지.

③ 남 안전벨트를 매는 것은 아주 중요해.

　여 네 말에 동의해.

④ 남 내가 창문을 열어도 될까?

　여 응, 그렇게 해.

⑤ 남 너 저녁 뭐 먹고 싶니?

　여 나는 피자를 먹고 싶어.

해설 여행이 어땠냐는 질문에 대해 즐거운 여행이 됐으면 좋겠다고 대답하는 것은 어색하다.

08 부탁한 일 파악 | ②

해석

여 실례합니다. 당신은 박지성 씨인가요?

남 네, 그렇습니다.

여 어머나! 저 진짜 당신의 팬이에요.

남 매우 감사합니다.

여 항상 TV에서 보던 사람을 내가 보고 있다니 믿기지가 않네요. 이 공원 근처에 사시나요?

남 아니요. 여기에는 친구를 만나러 왔어요.

여 그렇군요. 이 축구공에 당신의 사인을 받을 수 있을까요?

남 물론이지요. 이름이 어떻게 되시죠?

여 Lisa예요. 오, 멋지네요. 정말 감사합니다.

해설 여자는 남자에게 축구공에 사인해 줄 것을 부탁했다.

09 의도 파악 | ④

해석

여 저 개를 봐! 정말 귀엽다. 가서 쓰다듬어 주고 싶어.

남 그건 좋은 생각이 아닌 것 같아. 너 저 개 아니?

여 아니, 하지만 대부분의 개들은 우호적이잖아.

남 그렇지만, 너는 네가 그들에게 위협이 될 수 있다는 것을 알아야 해.

여 무슨 말이야?

남 만약 그 개가 너를 알지 못하면, 네가 그 개를 해치려고 한다고 생각할 수도 있잖아. 개들이 겁을 먹으면 너를 물지도 몰라.

여 내가 우호적이라는 것을 개들도 알 수 있지 않을까 생각해.

남 그럼 너는 거대한 우호적인 낯선 사람이 되겠지. 그건 너에게도 위험해.

여 그래. 이제 이해가 된다. 모르는 개들에게 가까이 가지 말아야겠다.

남 그래. 개의 주인에게 먼저 물어봐야 해.

해설 남자는 여자에게 개를 만지지 않도록 경고하고 있다.

10 숫자 정보 파악 – 금액 | ⑤

해석

여 저는 Twin Tower 호텔에 가려고 해요.

남 알겠습니다.

여 요금이 얼마나 될까요?

남 아마 22달러와 23달러 사이 정도가 될 것입니다.

여 좋습니다.

남 (잠시 후) 다 왔습니다. Twin Tower 호텔입니다. 21달러 65센트입니다.

여 여기 25달러가 있습니다. 거스름돈은 가지세요.

남 감사합니다.

해설 실제 택시 요금은 21.65달러이나 여자는 25달러를 택시 기사에게 지불하면서 거스름돈은 택시 기사에게 가지라고 했으므로 여자가 지불한 금액은 25달러이다.

11 장소 추론 | ⑤

해석

여 상혁아, 너 정말 농구를 잘하는구나.

남 고마워. 그런데 나 더 이상 못 하겠다. 오늘 너무 더워.

여 맞아, 그리고 나는 배가 고파. 몇 시니?

남 12시 30분이야. 점심시간까지 10분 남았네.

여 체육 선생님께 수업을 일찍 끝내 달라고 부탁드려 보자. 그러면 우리는 학교 식당에서 긴 줄을 설 필요가 없잖아.

남 좋은 생각이긴 한데 선생님이 승낙하실까?

여 모르겠어. 하지만 시도해 볼 수는 있잖아.

남 맞아. 해 보자. 오, 선생님이 이쪽 코트로 오고 계셔.

해설 두 사람은 체육 수업 시간에 농구 연습을 하면서 대화를 나누고 있으므로 학교 체육관에 있음을 알 수 있다.

12 언급되지 않은 것 | ③

해석

남 고객 여러분께 알려 드립니다. 수입 과일에 대한 타임 세일이 곧 시작할 예정입니다. 신선한 바나나가 40% 할인 중이고, 파인애플과 자몽은 20% 할인하고 있습니다. 또한, 10달러 이상 사시면 다음 방문에 사용하실 수 있는 10% 할인 쿠폰을 드립니다. 이 타임 세일은 오후 두 시부터이며 오후 4시 혹은 재고가 소진되면 그 전에 종료됩니다. 이 좋은 기회들을 잡기 위해 빨리 식료품 구역으로 오세요.

해설 쿠폰을 지급하는 기준 금액은 안내가 되었으나, 품목별 가격은 언급되지 않았다.

13 도표 정보 파악 | ②
해석

남 이봐요, Cindy. Elly Brown은 여전히 변호사인가요?
여 네, 그래요.
남 그녀는 아직도 KM Law에서 일하나요?
여 더 이상 일하지 않습니다. 지금 그녀는 Kim & Johnson에서 일하고 있어요. 사무실은 뉴욕에 5번가에 있습니다.
남 그녀는 아직도 East 23번가에서 살고 있나요?
여 네, 그래요.
남 그녀는 여전히 같은 전화번호를 사용하나요? 001-0908인가요?
여 네, 맞아요.

해설 Kim & Johnson 사무실은 5번가에 있다.

14 주제 파악 | ①
해석

여 당신이 집으로 돌아오면, 여러분은 이것을 해야 합니다. 먼저, 따뜻한 물에 손을 적시세요. 비누를 가지고 여러분 손의 양쪽 면과 손가락들을 비비는 것이 중요합니다. 여러분은 이것을 약 15초에서 20초 동안 할 필요가 있습니다. 마지막으로 손을 헹구고 깨끗한 수건으로 말리세요.

해설 손을 씻는 방법을 자세히 설명하고 있다.

15 한 일 / 할 일 파악 | ②
해석

여 Jason, 이번 주말에 뭔가 재미있는 것을 하지 않을래?
남 박물관에서 공룡 전시회가 있어.
여 난 공룡을 좋아하지 않아.
남 콘서트는 어때?
여 음, 표를 구하기 힘들어.
남 그러면, 영화 보러 가자.
여 아니, 차라리 야외로 나가고 싶어.
남 리버 공원?
여 그래. 공원에서 쉬면서 신선한 공기를 마시고 싶어.
남 좋아. 토요일에 전화할게.

해설 두 사람은 이번 주말에 상쾌한 공기를 즐기고 휴식을 취하기 위해 공원에 가기로 했다.

16 특정 정보 파악 | ⑤
해석

여 안녕, Jack. 너는 여기에서 무엇을 살 거니?
남 안녕 효린아, 내 사촌 동생이 곧 초등학교에 입학해서 나는 그녀에게 작은 선물을 주고 싶어. 하지만 나는 무엇을 사야 할지 결정을 못하겠어.
여 연필과 지우개를 사는 게 어때?
남 난 그것들을 사려고 했어. 하지만 또 어떤 게 있을까?
여 글쎄, 여자아이들은 그리기를 좋아하거든. 이 크레용과 스케치북도 사.
남 그거 좋은 생각이다. 내가 그녀를 위해 책가방도 사야 할까?

여 아마도 아닐 거야. 나는 그녀의 부모님들께서 이미 하나 사셨을 거라고 확신해.
남 아마 네 말이 맞겠다. 고마워.

해설 남자는 사촌 동생의 부모님이 이미 가방을 사 주었을 것 같다며 가방은 구입하지 않았다.

17 상황에 맞는 말 찾기 | ③
해석

남 George는 보통 그의 반에서 가장 먼저 학교에 도착한다. 매일 아침, 그는 교무실에서 교실 열쇠를 가지고 교실을 연다. 하지만, 그는 오늘 매우 늦게 일어났고 그가 보통 가던 시간까지 학교에 갈 수가 없을 것이다. 그래서, George는 그의 반 친구인 민지에게 전화를 걸었다. 다행스럽게도 그녀는 거의 학교이다. 그는 그녀에게 오늘 교실을 열어 달라고 부탁하고 싶다. 이런 상황에서, George는 민지에게 뭐라고 말하겠는가?

George 오늘 네가 교실을 여는 것이 가능하니?
① 그거 안심이다.
② 김 선생님께 내가 늦을 거라고 말해 줄 수 있니?
④ 너 교무실 가는 법을 아니?
⑤ 네가 나 대신에 교실 문을 열도록 되어 있어.

해설 George는 민지에게 오늘 자기 대신에 교실 문을 열어 줄 것을 부탁하고 싶으므로 ③이 답으로 적절하다.

18 한 일 / 할 일 파악 | ⑤
해석

여 Max, 의사가 뭐래?
남 내게 기침약을 처방해 주고 쉬라고 했어.
여 쉬라고? 하지만 나는 우리가 진행하고 있는 이 프로젝트에 네 도움이 꼭 필요해.
남 알아. 걱정 마. 이 일이 끝날 때까지는 집에 가지 않을 거야.
여 몸도 안 좋은데 도와줘서 고마워. 우리 점심 먼저 먹자.
남 고맙지만 됐어. 그런데 난 아픈 목을 위해 뜨거운 것을 마시고 싶어.
여 내가 너의 목을 위해 뜨거운 레몬차를 만들어 줄게.
남 고마워.

해설 여자는 목이 아픈 남자에게 뜨거운 레몬차를 만들어 주겠다고 했다.

19 알맞은 응답 찾기 | ⑤
해석

남 이 아이스크림 정말 맛있다.
여 좀 더 먹을래?
남 아니, 많이 먹었어.
여 정말이야? 아이스크림 애호가가 무슨 일이래?
남 더 이상 아니야. 의사 선생님이 살 빼라고 권하셨거든.
여 의사 선생님이 왜 그렇게 권하셨대?
남 그녀는 내가 체지방이 많아서 다이어트가 필요하다고 말했어.
① 맞아. 아이스크림을 더 먹자.
② 응. 나는 최근에 살을 너무 많이 뺐어.
③ 꼭 그렇지는 않아. 나는 살을 찌울 필요가 있어.
④ 그녀는 내가 아이스크림을 피해야 한다고 말하지 않았어.

해설 여자가 남자에게 의사 선생님이 체중 감량을 제안한 이유를 물었으므로 그 이유를 답하는 ⑤가 남자의 응답으로 가장 적절하다.

20 알맞은 응답 찾기 | ⑤

해석

남 엄마, 저 집에 왔어요.

여 안녕, 얘야. 오늘 어땠니?

남 괜찮았어요.

여 그런데 너 우울해 보이는구나. 안 좋은 일이라도 있니?

남 오늘 지난주에 참가했던 그림 그리기 대회의 결과가 나왔어요.

여 오, 정말? 내게 말해 주렴.

남 아무것도 못 탔어요, 엄마. 죄송해요.

여 괜찮아. 네가 최선을 다했잖아. 그게 가장 중요한 거란다.

남 하지만 저 정말 열심히 연습했어요. 아마 제가 그림 그리기에 재능이 없나 봐요.

여 <u>낙담하지 마. 너는 다음에 더 잘할 거야.</u>

① 너는 더 열심히 할 필요 없어.

② 너 그 대회에 참여하는 게 어때?

③ 내가 네게 말했잖아. 너는 좀 자는 게 나을 거라고.

④ 괜찮아. 나는 네가 나를 이해해 주기를 바라.

해설 남자가 그림 그리기 대회에서 수상하지 못해 좌절하는 상황이므로 좌절하지 말라며 격려하는 ⑤가 여자의 응답으로 가장 적절하다.

20회 영어 듣기모의고사   pp. 158~159

01 ①	**02** ④	**03** ③	**04** ①	**05** ②
06 ⑤	**07** ③	**08** ⑤	**09** ②	**10** ③
11 ④	**12** ②	**13** ①	**14** ⑤	**15** ④
16 ②	**17** ①	**18** ②	**19** ③	**20** ②

Dictation Test 20회   pp. 160~165

01 ❶ has three sides ❷ four sides and four points ❸ aren't touching each other

02 ❶ You asked me to ❷ which book to buy ❸ the red one

03 ❶ I don't know where ❷ go straight for a while ❸ on your right

04 ❶ why don't we visit ❷ every Friday ❸ Monday's fine

05 ❶ Can you move it ❷ work at a hospital ❸ your left leg

06 ❶ wearing it inside out ❷ laughing at me ❸ too worried

07 ❶ Did you do well ❷ try these shoes on ❸ you left it

08 ❶ like a summer vacation ❷ visited the museums ❸ swam almost every day

09 ❶ a math textbook ❷ can I borrow it ❸ won't forget your kindness

10 ❶ just for today ❷ the red one ❸ take this cap with

11 ❶ you can use this court ❷ passed by ❸ Can I play

12 ❶ had an umbrella ❷ a globe of the world ❸ new mystery books

13 ❶ you're watching another drama ❷ I'm sure you won't like ❸ you've been watching

14 ❶ important to have breakfast ❷ a cereal bar ❸ Instead of skipping breakfast

15 ❶ get a refund ❷ only exchange them ❸ not more expensive than

16 ❶ got one hour before ❷ the tickets for

17 ❶ she visited a phone shop ❷ who came before her ❸ have her cellphone repaired

18 ❶ tiny pieces of plastic ❷ they can't grow properly ❸ other things that have

19 ❶ about a used car ❷ looking for a small car ❸ perfect condition

20 ❶ going to a concert ❷ to pay more money ❸ Why don't you get

01 그림 정보 파악 – 도형 | ①

해석

여 제가 여러분이 그려야 하는 도형을 설명해 드리겠습니다. 우선, 큰 원이 하나 있습니다. 그 안에는 두 개의 작은 도형이 있습니다. 왼쪽에 있는 것은 세 변과 세 점이 있습니다. 오른쪽의 다른 것은 네 변과 네 점이 있습니다. 각각의 도형에서, 모든 변의 길이는 같습니다. 이 두 도형은 서로 닿아 있지 않습니다.

해설 큰 원 안에 2개의 도형을 그려야 하는데 왼쪽에는 정삼각형을 그리고 오른쪽에는 정사각형을 그린 것은 ①이다.

02 목적 파악 | ④

해석

[전화벨이 울린다.]

여 여보세요?

남 Maria, 나 Ken이야. 나 K 서점에 와 있어. 네가 나한테 'Gentle Math'를 사다 달라고 부탁했잖아.

여 응, 부탁해. 나는 문제 풀이를 더 연습해야 하거든.

남 그런데 여기 세 종류 책이 있어. 어떤 것을 사야 하는지 모르겠어. 녹색, 노란색 그리고 빨간 것이 있네.

여 알려 주는 것을 잊었네. 내가 필요한 것은 빨간 색이야. 그거 얼마니?

남 만 삼천 원이야.

여 내가 나중에 만 삼천 원을 줄게. 내일 학교로 그것을 가져다줘. 정말 고마워.

남 천만에. 내일 봐.

해설 서점에 있는 남자는 세 종류의 수학 교재 중에 어떤 책을 사야 하는지 묻기 위해 여자에게 전화했다.

03 그림 정보 파악 – 길 찾기 | ③

해석

남 실례합니다. 저 좀 도와주시겠어요?

여 물론이죠.

남 저는 이 주변을 관광하고 있는데, JK 호텔이 어디에 있는지 모르겠어요.

여 음, 어디 봅시다. 세 번째 신호등에서 좌회전해서 조금만 직진하세요. 당신의 오른편에 그 호텔이 있을 거예요.

남 여기서 얼마나 걸리죠?

여 아마도 10분 정도요.

남 고맙습니다.

해설 남자가 찾는 호텔은 세 번째 신호등에서 좌회전해서 조금 직진한 후 오른편에 있다고 했으므로 ③이다.

04 특정 정보 파악 – 요일 | ①

해석

남 너 그림 보는 거 좋아하니?

여 응. 나는 그림에 아주 관심이 많아.

남 그럼 우리 최근에 문을 연 미술관에 같이 방문해 보는 게 어때?

여 그러고 싶어. 우리 언제 갈까?

남 그 미술관은 수요일에는 닫아. 이번 목요일은 어때?

여 나는 목요일에는 못 가. 나는 매주 화요일과 목요일에 요가 수업이 있어.

남 음, 나는 금요일마다 바이올린 수업이 있어. 그럼 우리 월요일에 갈까? 너무 갑작스럽니?

여 전혀 아니야. 월요일 괜찮아. 그때 가자.

해설 남자와 여자는 월요일에 미술관에 가기로 했다.

05 직업 및 장래 희망 | ②

해석

남 실례합니다. 제가 비명소리를 들었는데요. 도와드릴까요?

여 네. 제가 계단에서 미끄러졌어요.

남 다리를 움직일 수 있나요?

여 못 움직이겠어요. 정말 아파요.

남 제가 한 번 볼게요. 저는 병원에서 일하고 있거든요.

여 정말 잘됐네요! 당신이 여기 계셔서 정말 다행이에요! 제 다리에 문제가 생겼나요?

남 오, 왼쪽 다리가 부러졌어요. 먼저 구급차를 부를게요.

여 정말 고맙습니다.

해설 남자는 병원에서 근무하고 있다며 계단에서 넘어진 여자의 상태를 검진하고 있으므로 의사임을 알 수 있다.

06 심정 파악 | ⑤

해석

여 내 연설 어땠니? 솔직히 말해 줘.

남 난 네 연설에 매료되었어. 그런데 네 티셔츠가 조금….

여 뭐? 오, 저런! 나 티셔츠를 뒤집어 입고 있었잖아! 왜 내게 말해 주지 않았니?

남 나는 네가 연설을 시작하고 나서야 알아챘어.

여 오, 모두가 내 티셔츠를 쳐다보고 비웃었던 이유가 바로 그거구나.

남 너무 걱정하지 마.

해설 여자는 발표를 하고 난 후 티셔츠를 거꾸로 입은 것을 발견했으므로 당황스러울 것이다.

07 어색한 대화 찾기 | ③

해석

① 여 너 시험 잘 쳤니?

　 남 그것에 대해 내게 묻지도 마.

② 여 제가 문 열어 드릴게요.

　 남 정말 친절하시군요.

③ 여 제가 이 신발들 신어 봐도 될까요?

　 남 많이 드세요. 그것들은 맛있어요.

④ 여 손님, 여기에 커피와 샌드위치 나왔습니다.

　 남 음, 그것들은 제가 주문한 것이 아닌데요.

⑤ 여 기다려요! 이거 그쪽 휴대 전화인가요? 교실에 두고 간 것 같은데요.

　 남 오, 제 것입니다. 감사해요.

해설 신발을 신어 봐도 되는지 물어봤는데 마음껏 먹으라고 대답하는 것은 어색하다.

08 한 일 / 할 일 파악 | ⑤

해석

남 안녕, Sandra. 겨울 방학 어땠니?

여 내게는 여름 방학 같았어.

남 무슨 의미야?

여 호주에서 겨울을 보냈거든. 거기는 여름이잖니.

남 겨울에 더운 날씨가 상상이 안 된다. 너는 거기에서 뭐 했니?

여 나는 박물관, 동물원을 방문했고 거의 매일 수영했어. 넌 어땠어?

남 나는 가족들과 함께 스키 리조트에 갔어. 그것 역시 재미있었어.

해설 여자는 겨울 방학에 호주에서 여름을 즐겼다고 했고, 스키를 탄 것은 여자가 아니라 남자이다.

09 의도 파악 | ②

해석

여 늦어서 미안해. 앗, 나 집에 필통이랑 수학 교과서를 두고 왔어!

남 뭐? 확실해?

여 응, 나 30분 후에 수학 수업에 들어가야 해. 내가 쓸 수 있는 연필 한 자루와 종이 몇 장이 있니?

남 물론이지.

여 그리고 만약 수학 교과서가 있으면 내게 그걸 빌려도 될까?

남 응, 여기 있어. 나는 첫 수업이 영어라서 괜찮아.

여 너의 친절을 잊지 않을게!

해설 여자는 마지막 말로 남자의 친절을 잊지 않겠다고 말하며 교과서를 빌려준 것에 대해 감사를 나타내고 있다.

10 숫자 정보 파악 – 금액 | ③

해석

여 안녕하세요, 저는 어깨에 메는 가방을 하나 사고 싶은데요.

남 이 빨간 가방 어떠세요? 오늘만 25달러에 판매되고 있습니다.

여 좋네요. 이것 말고 다른 색상도 있나요?

남 푸른색과 흰색도 있는데 그것들은 40달러예요.

여 오, 정말요? 저는 빨간색으로 할게요.

남 알겠습니다. 그러면 가방과 함께 이 모자도 사시는 게 어떠세요? 그것들은 아주 잘 어울리는데요.

여 귀엽네요. 얼마인가요?

남 그건 10달러입니다.

여　그것도 살게요. 여기 50달러 있습니다.

남　거스름돈 여기에 있습니다.

해설　여자는 25달러인 빨간색 숄더백과 10달러인 모자를 구입했으므로 총 35달러를 지불하면 되는데, 50달러를 지불했으므로 거스름돈으로 15 달러를 받을 것이다.

11　장소 추론　| ④

해석

남　오늘은 이것으로 마치겠고, 연습하고 싶으시면, 11시까지 이 코트를 사용하실 수 있습니다.

여　김 선생님, 고맙습니다. 당신의 테니스 수업은 항상 매우 재미있어요.

남　정말 기쁘네요. 더 연습하실 거예요?

여　물론이죠. 제 아파트 단지에는 테니스 코트가 없어요. 그런데, 지난 토요일에 당신이 브런치 먹는 것을 보았어요.

남　당신도 그 식당에 있었어요?

여　아니요. 저는 그냥 식당을 지나쳐 갔어요. 저는 제 개를 산책시키러 공원에 가는 길이었어요.

남　그렇군요. 저는 그 식당 근처에서 테니스 수업을 가르쳐요.

여　저는 그 식당 주변에 있는 테니스 코트가 매우 좋다고 들었어요. 언제 그 코트에서 테니스를 쳐 봐도 될까요?

남　그럼요. 제가 언제 그 테니스 코트에 초대할게요.

해설　두 사람은 테니스 강습이 끝난 후 테니스 코트에서 대화하고 있다.

12　언급되지 않은 것　| ②

해석

남　어제는 Sam의 생일이었다. 그는 많은 선물을 받았다. 한 네모난 상자는 파란색이었는데 그 안에는 우산이 들어 있었다. Sam의 누나는 그에게 크고 둥근 꾸러미를 주었다. 그는 그것이 공이라고 생각했지만 지구본이었다. 그의 형은 그에게 그가 원했던 것인 스마트폰을 주었다. 그리고 그의 아버지는 그에게 새로 나온 추리소설 책들을 선물했다.

해설　Sam은 생일 선물로 우산, 지구본, 스마트폰, 추리소설 책은 받았지만, 공은 받지 않았다

13　도표 정보 파악　| ①

해석

남　Sandy, 너 또 다른 드라마를 보고 있구나, 그건 제목이 뭐니?

여　이것의 제목은 '러빙유'야.

남　그것은 재미있니?

여　그다지. 네가 원하면 채널을 돌려도 돼.

남　고마워. 오, 야구 경기가 막 끝났네. TV에 뭐 재미있는 거 없을까?

여　우리 TV 편성표를 확인해 보자. 나는 네가 '내셔널 지오그래픽'이나 뉴스 채널을 좋아하지 않을 거라고 확신해.

남　그런 것들은 지겨워. 5번 채널에서 하는 '코미디 하우스'는 어때니?

여　그건 요새 재미없어.

남　그러면 그냥 네가 보던 '러빙유'나 보자.

해설　남자는 여러 채널을 보다가 여자가 보던 드라마 '러빙유'를 다시 보자고 했으므로 1번 채널을 볼 것이다.

14　주제 파악　| ⑤

해석

남　여러분은 학교에 늦지 않기 위해 보통 아침 식사를 거르나요? 아침 식사를 하는 것은 중요합니다. 그러나 아침에 충분한 시간이 없다고요?

여기에 여러분을 위한 곡물 바가 있습니다. 이것은 건강에 좋을 뿐만 아니라 맛있답니다. 게다가 열량이 낮기 때문에 살찔 걱정을 하지 않아도 되죠. 아침 식사를 거르는 대신에 이 곡물 바와 함께 여러분의 하루를 시작하세요.

해설　아침을 거르지 않고 간단하게 먹을 수 있는 식사 대용품인 곡물 바를 광고하고 있다.

15　한 일 / 할 일 파악　| ④

해석

여　도와드릴까요?

남　제가 이 바지를 지난달에 구입했는데요, 저한테 잘 맞지 않습니다.

여　사이즈를 변경하고 싶으세요?

남　아니오, 환불을 받고 싶습니다.

여　정확하게 언제 그것들을 구입하셨어요? 영수증이 있으세요?

남　여기 있어요. 5월 25일에 샀네요.

여　그 품목을 세일 중에 구입하셨으므로, 그 품목은 교환만 가능합니다. 더 큰 사이즈를 입어 보시겠어요?

남　별로 그러고 싶지 않네요. 그것을 티셔츠로 교환할 수 있을까요?

여　네, 손님. 티셔츠가 바지보다 비싸지 않다면요.

해설　남자는 바지를 환불 받을 수 없자 바지를 티셔츠로 교환했다.

16　숫자 정보 파악 - 시각　| ②

해석

여　서둘러! 우리 늦었어.

남　무슨 말이야? 영화가 시작하려면 한 시간이 남았는데.

여　하지만 거기까지 가는 데 30분이나 걸려. 그게 문제야.

남　이해가 안 돼. 왜 그게 문제야?

여　음, 나는 인터넷으로 8시 영화표를 예매했어. 그리고 우리는 영화가 시작되기 30분 전에 표를 찾아야 해.

남　오, 몰랐어. 어서 움직이자.

해설　영화를 8시로 예매했고 영화가 시작하기까지 1시간이 남았으므로 현재 시각은 7시이다.

17　상황에 맞는 말 찾기　| ①

해석

남　Kate의 휴대 전화 화면이 깨져서 그녀는 수리를 받기 위해 휴대 전화 가게를 방문했다. 수리 기사는 화면을 교체해 줄 수는 있지만 최소 2시간은 걸릴 것 같다고 말했다. 그녀 앞에 이미 많은 사람들이 있었다. Kate는 시간이 많이 없어서 다음번에 다시 오겠다고 말했다. 그러자 그는 수리된 휴대 전화를 배달 서비스로 보내 줄 수 있다고 말했다. Kate는 자신의 휴대 전화가 고쳐진 채로 집에 배달되기를 원했다. 이런 상황에서, Kate는 수리 기사에게 뭐라고 말하겠는가?

Kate　그러면 휴대 전화를 배달해 주시겠어요?

② 수리비는 얼마인지 말씀해 주세요.

③ 집에 도착하는데 얼마나 걸리나요?

④ 그러면 당신의 집 주소를 여기 남겨 주세요.

⑤ 새로운 화면으로 교체해 주세요.

해설　Kate는 휴대 전화가 고쳐진 채로 배달되기를 원하는 상황이므로, 휴대 전화를 집으로 배달해 달라고 하는 ①이 답으로 적절하다.

18 [한 일 / 할 일 파악] | ②

해석

남 너 미세 플라스틱에 관한 뉴스 들은 적 있니?

여 아니. 미세 플라스틱이 뭔데?

남 그것들은 아주 작은 플라스틱 조각들이야. 치약과 같은 사람들이 매일 쓰는 물건에 많이 있어. 유감스럽게도 미세 플라스틱은 결국 바다로 흘러들어 간대.

여 그게 문제를 일으키는 거야?

남 응. 만약 동물들이 그것을 먹으면, 제대로 자라지 못한대. 그리고 사람들이 해양 동물들을 먹기 때문에, 우리도 미세 플라스틱을 먹을 수 있는 거지.

여 와. 당분간 해산물은 못 먹겠다. 당장 집에 가서 내 치약에 미세 플라스틱이 있는지 봐야겠다.

남 미세 플라스틱이 있는 다른 것들도 찾아봐.

해설 여자는 집에 가서 치약에 미세 플라스틱이 들어 있는지 확인해 보겠다고 했다.

19 [알맞은 응답 찾기] | ③

해석

남 도와드릴까요?

여 안녕하세요, 중고차에 대한 정보를 좀 얻고 싶습니다.

남 마음속에 특별히 생각해 둔 것이 있나요?

여 경차를 찾고 있어요.

남 이것은 어때요? 겨우 9,000달러로 정말 저렴한 가격이에요.

여 몇 년도에 만들어졌죠?

남 2016년이요. 거의 새 것이에요.

여 좋네요. 사고가 난 적이 있나요?

남 전혀요. 거의 완벽한 상태입니다.

여 <u>그러면 시운전을 해 볼 수 있나요?</u>

① 저는 운전을 전혀 못 합니다.

② 다음 주가 좋겠네요.

④ 운전면허증이 있나요?

⑤ 그것을 고치는 데에 얼마나 걸릴까요?

해설 남자가 추천하는 중고차가 완벽한 상태라고 했으므로 시운전을 해 볼 수 있는지 묻는 ③이 여자의 응답으로 가장 적절하다.

20 [알맞은 응답 찾기] | ②

해석

여 John, 오늘 밤에 어떤 계획이 있니?

남 특별한 계획은 없어.

여 나랑 오늘 밤에 음악회에 가는 거 어때?

남 미안하지만 안 되겠어. 음, 난 별로 기분이 안 좋아.

여 이봐, 무슨 일인데 그래?

남 아마 나는 내 아파트에 더 이상 살지 못할지도 몰라. 집주인이 내가 이곳에 더 있으려면 더 많은 돈을 지불해야 한다고 말했어.

여 동거인을 구해서 생활비를 나누는 게 어때?

남 <u>그거 좋은 생각이야.</u>

① 천만에.

③ 여기서 널 보니 기쁘다.

④ 내가 언제 떠나야 해?

⑤ 아니, 나는 이곳에 산 적이 없어.

해설 여자가 남자에게 동거인을 구해서 생활비를 나누라고 조언해 준 것에 대해 좋은 생각이라고 말하는 ②가 남자의 응답으로 가장 적절하다.

21회 영어 듣기모의고사 pp. 166~167

01 ③	02 ④	03 ②	04 ②	05 ⑤
06 ④	07 ②	08 ②	09 ③	10 ③
11 ④	12 ④	13 ②	14 ①	15 ④
16 ⑤	17 ⑤	18 ①	19 ④	20 ④

Dictation Test 21회 pp. 168~173

01 ❶ I'd like to buy ❷ Could you recommend ❸ with white stars

02 ❶ Could you send a file ❷ I need to work ❸ after emailing you

03 ❶ We don't use ❷ any special reason

04 ❶ I need to get them ❷ can get them on Tuesday ❸ have them ready

05 ❶ Let's take a picture ❷ pose was perfect ❸ after taking this photo

06 ❶ Wait where is it ❷ can't find my wallet ❸ waiting in line behind you

07 ❶ bought a handkerchief ❷ No I haven't ❸ don't need to

08 ❶ doesn't work ❷ checking out the plug ❸ power is not on

09 ❶ making slippers ❷ make a video ❸ I bet you'll be surprised

10 ❶ need to pay fifty dollars ❷ cannot use both of them ❸ use the coupon

11 ❶ ride it ❷ it's really exciting ❸ after you ride it

12 ❶ written a new book ❷ There is a bonus event

13 ❶ the world in fifty years ❷ the end of August ❸ send the work by email

14 ❶ made from milk ❷ turns to oily liquid ❸ high in fat

15 ❶ not the green one ❷ go and exchange it ❸ buy the red one

16 ❶ will she be back ❷ Any time after ❸ the rest of the afternoon

17 ❶ some volunteer work ❷ which book ❸ pick the best book

18 ❶ shouldn't have ordered ❷ have it wrapped ❸ eat it later

19 ❶ stay up all night ❷ a cold drink

20 ❶ doing a survey ❷ any of our programs ❸ What did you think

01 그림 정보 파악 – 사물 | ③

해석

여 Clark, 가운데에 선이 두 개 있는 이 배낭은 어때? 나 이거 사고 싶은데.

남 너 똑같은 스타일로 하나 가지고 있지 않니? 새로운 스타일을 시도해 봐.

여 흠… 시도해 볼게. 날 위해 하나를 추천해 줄래?

남 리본이 달린 이것 어떠니?

여 나는 그건 마음에 들지 않아.

남 그러면, 하얀색 별들이 그려져 있는 이 검정색은 어때?

여 좋다. 그걸로 살래.

해설 여자는 흰 별들이 있는 검정색 가방을 사겠다고 했다.

02 목적 파악 | ④

해석

여 아들, 이 시간에 무슨 일이니?

남 엄마, 지금 집에 계세요?

여 응. 왜 그러니?

남 파일 하나를 제 이메일로 보내 주시겠어요? 파일 제목은 '과학 과제'예요.

여 알겠어. 너 그걸 가져가지 않았구나, 그렇지?

남 네. USB에 파일을 저장해서 가지고 오는 걸 깜빡했거든요. 지금 모둠원들과 프로젝트 작업을 해야 해요.

여 알겠다. 이메일을 보내고 나서 전화할게.

해설 남자는 파일을 이메일로 보내 줄 것을 요청하려고 여자에게 전화했다.

03 그림 상황에 어울리는 대화 찾기 | ②

해석

① 남 도움 좀 주실래요?

여 물론이죠. 무엇을 도와드릴까요?

② 남 우리는 악수할 때 왼손을 쓰지 않습니다.

여 오, 몰랐네요. 죄송합니다.

③ 남 왼손으로 어쩜 그렇게 잘 쓰세요?

여 음, 전 왼손잡이거든요.

④ 남 우리는 먹을 때 오른쪽 손만 사용합니다.

여 특별한 이유라도 있나요?

⑤ 남 포크를 사용하지 그러니?

여 나는 젓가락을 사용하는 게 더 편해.

해설 여자가 왼손을 내밀고 있고 이에 대해 남자가 화를 내는 상황에 적절한 대화는 ②이다.

04 특정 정보 파악 – 요일 | ②

해석

[전화벨이 울린다.]

남 여보세요. T마켓입니다. 도와드릴까요?

여 여보세요. 저는 테디베어 티셔츠 25개를 주문하고 싶습니다. 이번 주 목요일까지 받아야 해요.

남 정말 죄송하지만 수요일이 휴일이라서 그것은 불가능합니다. 오늘 주문하시면 이번 금요일까지 보내드릴 수 있습니다.

여 하지만 저희 체육대회가 금요일이에요. 이번 목요일까지는 받아야 해요.

남 가지러 오실 수 있으시면, 화요일에 받으실 수 있어요. 하지만 오늘 지불을 완료해 주실 때에만 가능합니다. 저희 가게 주소는 웹사이트에 있습니다.

여 갈 수 있어요. 정말 감사합니다. 언제 가면 돼요?

남 여섯 시쯤 오세요. 준비해 놓겠습니다.

해설 여자는 화요일에 가게에 직접 가서 티셔츠를 받아 오기로 했다.

05 직업 및 장래 희망 | ⑤

해석

남 컷. 한 번 더 찍어요.

여 음, 제가 또 뭘 잘못 했나요?

남 이번에는 당신이 아니었어요. 사실, 당신의 자세는 완벽했어요.

여 그러면 뭐가 잘못되었나요?

남 파리 한 마리가 당신 주변을 날아다니고 있었거든요.

여 그렇군요. 이번이 마지막이면 좋겠네요.

남 나도 그러길 바랍니다. 이 사진을 찍고 쉬도록 하죠.

해설 남자는 여자의 사진을 반복해서 찍고 있는 것으로 보아 남자의 직업은 사진작가이다.

06 심정 파악 | ⑤

해석

여 얼마인가요?

남 모두 15달러입니다. 현금으로 내시겠어요, 카드로 내시겠어요?

여 카드로 낼게요. 잠깐, 어디에 있지?

남 음, 무슨 문제라도 있으신가요?

여 제 지갑을 어디에서도 찾을 수가 없네요. 잠깐만 저를 기다려 주시겠어요?

남 알겠습니다. 하지만, 다음 분께 차례를 양보해 주시겠어요? 손님 뒤에 많은 분들이 기다리고 계셔서요.

여 오, 그걸 몰랐네요. 죄송해요.

남 괜찮습니다.

해설 여자는 계산을 하려고 하는데 지갑이 어디 있는지 모르는 상황이므로 당황스러울 것이다.

07 어색한 대화 찾기 | ②

해석

① 여 가방 들어 드릴까요? 무거워 보이는데요.

남 감사하지만 전 괜찮아요.

② 여 Tim의 생일 선물로 뭘 살 거니?

남 그는 손수건을 샀어.

③ 여 새로운 식당에 가 봤니?

남 안 가 봤어. 거긴 뭐로 유명하니?

④ 여 한 시간 내에 그 보고서를 끝낼 수 있겠어요?

남 물론이죠, 저는 정말 빠르게 타이핑할 수 있어요.

⑤ 여 제 조리도구를 가져와야 하나요?

남 그럴 필요 없어요. 우리는 모든 도구를 다 가지고 있거든요.

해설 Tim의 생일 선물로 무엇을 살 것인지 묻는 질문에 대해 그가 손수건을 구입했다고 대답하는 것은 어색하다.

08 이유 파악 | ②

해석

남 안녕, Jenny. 너는 복사기에 무슨 문제가 있니?

여 응. 작동이 안 돼. 무엇이 문제인지 알아내지 못하겠어.

남 용지함은 확인했니?

여 물론이지. 그건 괜찮아. 휴, 난 기계에 대해서는 잘 모르겠어.

남 뭐가 문제인지 한번 보자. 우리 플러그 점검부터 시작하는 게 어때?

여 그건 꽂혀 있어.

남 오! 그런데 전원이 아직 켜져 있지 않구나.

여 이런 바보 같은 실수라니!

해설 남자의 마지막 말에서 복사기의 전원이 꺼져 있었음을 알 수 있다.

해석

남 너 뭐 만드니?

여 저는 슬리퍼를 만들고 있어요. 한번 보실래요?

남 이것들은 매우 편안해 보이는구나. 이것들을 어떻게 만들었니?

여 만드는 법을 보여 드릴게요.

남 너는 정말 창의적이구나. 우리 비디오를 만들어서 그것을 인터넷에 올리는 것은 어때?

여 재미있을 것 같지만, 누가 관심을 가질 것 같지 않아요.

남 날 믿어. 나는 네가 이것에 대한 사람들의 생각으로 놀랄 것이라고 확신해.

해설 남자는 자신의 작품을 인터넷에 올리는 것을 주저하는 여자에게 사람들의 좋은 반응을 확신하며 격려하고 있다.

10 숫자 정보 파악 – 금액 | ③

해석

여 제 새로운 헤어스타일이 마음에 드네요. 얼마를 지불해야 하죠?

남 마음에 드신다니 다행이에요. 50달러를 지불하셔야 합니다.

여 네? 50달러라고 하셨어요?

남 네. 머리 자르는 데 20달러, 염색하는 데 30달러예요.

여 그렇군요. 저 회원 카드도 있고 할인 쿠폰도 있어요.

남 죄송하지만, 둘 다를 사용하실 수는 없어요. 회원 카드로 10% 할인을 받으시거나 쿠폰으로 30% 할인을 받으실 수 있어요.

여 알겠어요. 쿠폰을 사용할게요.

해설 여자는 총 50달러를 지불해야 하는데 30% 할인 쿠폰을 사용하겠다고 했으므로 35달러만 지불하면 된다.

11 장소 추론 | ④

해석

여 Jack, 나 저 롤러코스터 탔는데, 너무 재밌었어. 한 번 더 타도 될까?

남 또? 너 무섭지 않니?

여 아니, 정말 재미있어. 너도 나와 함께 탈래?

남 절대 안 타. 레일만 봐도 울렁거려.

여 좋아, 나 혼자 탈게.

남 재미있게 타렴. Amy, 나 오렌지 주스를 마시고 싶어. 타고 나서 스낵 바로 와.

여 그럴게.

해설 여자는 롤러코스터를 한 번 더 타고 싶다고 남자에게 말하고 있는 것으로 보아 두 사람이 대화하고 있는 장소는 놀이공원이라는 것을 알 수 있다.

12 언급되지 않은 것 | ④

해석

여 베스트셀러 작가인 Babara Jones가 'Jenny의 비밀'이라는 신간을 집필하였습니다. 그녀는 5월 31일 정글 서점에서 사인회를 할 것입니다. 사인회는 오후 3시에 시작하여 두 시간 동안 이어질 것입니다. 보너스 행사도 있답니다. 책을 두 권 사시면, 세 번째 권은 무료로 드립니다.

해설 저자 사인회에 관해 저자의 책 내용은 언급되지 않았다.

13 도표 정보 파악 | ②

해석

남 Amy, 이번 디자인 대회에 관심 있니?

여 오, 그래. 그 대회에 정말 참가하고 싶어.

남 그럼, 50년 후의 세계에 대한 네 자신의 작품을 만들어야 해.

여 주제가 흥미롭구나. 제출 기한을 아니?

남 8월 말까지야. 너 그거 알아? 1등 상이 iPad래.

여 정말? 이메일로 작품을 보내는 것이 가능하니?

남 응. 더 많은 정보를 원하면 그들의 웹사이트 www.designcompetition.com을 방문하면 돼.

해설 디자인 경연 대회 작품의 제출 기한은 8월 31일이다.

14 주제 파악 | ①

해석

여 이것은 우유로 만들어집니다. 이것은 냉장고에서는 딱딱하지만 열이 가해지면 기름기가 있는 액체로 변하죠. 당신은 이것을 빵에 펴 발라 먹거나, 아니면 야채나 고기를 볶을 때 사용합니다. 쿠키나 케이크를 구울 때도 이것이 필요하죠. 이것은 지방이 많이 함유되어 있어서 너무 많이 먹는 것은 좋지 않습니다.

해설 우유를 재료로 만들어졌으며 빵에 발라 먹고 야채와 고기를 튀기기 위해 사용하며 쿠키와 케이크를 구울 때 필요한 것은 버터이다.

15 한 일 / 할 일 파악 | ③

해석

남 엄마, 사 오라고 말씀하신 양념 여기에 있어요.

여 고맙다. 잠깐, 이거 녹색 병이잖아.

남 네. 녹색 병이라고 하셨잖아요, 아닌가요?

여 아니, 녹색 병 말고 빨간 병을 사오라고 했지.

남 앗. 그냥 사용하면 안 되나요?

여 안 돼. 완전히 다른 양념이야.

남 음, 제가 가서 그것을 교환해 오기를 원하시나요?

여 흠, 어쨌든 이것도 필요할 수도 몰라. 그것을 여기에 두고 빨간 걸 사오렴. 그래 줄래?

남 알겠어요.

해설 남자는 양념을 잘못 사 와서 양념을 새로 사러 갈 것이다.

16 숫자 정보 파악 – 시각 | ⑤

해석

[전화벨이 울린다.]

남 여보세요. 제가 Nicole과 통화할 수 있을까요?

여 죄송하지만 그녀는 지금 외출 중입니다.

남 알겠어요. 그녀는 몇 시에 사무실에 돌아올까요?

여 확실하지 않습니다.

남 알겠습니다. 점심시간에는요?

여 잠시만요. 확인해 보죠. (잠시 후) 아니요, 그녀는 디자이너와 점심을 먹을 것입니다.

남 아! 그럼 언제 전화를 드리면 될까요?

여 3시 이후로 언제든지요. 그녀는 오후의 나머지는 사무실에 있을 예정입니다.

남 좋아요. 그때 다시 전화하죠. 감사합니다.

해설 Nicole은 3시 이후에는 언제든지 통화가 가능하다고 했다.

17 상황에 맞는 말 찾기 | ⑤

해석

여 Tom은 초등학교 학생들을 위한 봉사 활동을 준비하고 있다. 그는 그들에게 책을 읽어 주기로 되어 있어서, 지난주에 책을 몇 권 골랐다. 하히도 그의 여동생 Ann은 초등학교 학생이다. 그는 Ann에게 그가 갖고 있는 책들 중에서 가장 좋은 책을 골라 달라고 부탁하고 싶다. 이런 상황에서, Tom은 Ann에게 뭐라고 말하겠는가?

Tom 너는 어떤 책이 가장 재미있니?

① 그거 정말 실망스럽다.
② 내게 동의하지 않니?
③ 왜 그렇게 생각하니?
④ 이 책보다 저 책보다 더 나은 것 같아.

해설 Tom이 가진 책 중에서 어떤 책이 가장 좋은지 묻는 표현을 골라야 하므로 ⑤가 답으로 적절하다.

18　한 일 / 할 일 파악 | ①

해석
여 저녁 다 먹었니?
남 응, 나 충분히 먹었어, 배불러.
여 그러면 왜 이렇게 많이 시켰니? 마지막에 순대는 주문하지 않아야 했어.
남 그것도 좀 맛보고 싶었단 말이야. 하지만, 나는 더 못 먹겠어.
여 좋아. 그러면 그것들을 싸 가서 나중에 먹자.
남 좋은 생각이야.

해설 저녁 식사를 많이 해 배부른 두 사람은 남은 음식을 싸가기로 했다.

19　알맞은 응답 찾기 | ④

해석
여 John, 뭐 하고 있니?
남 오, 엄마. 저는 기말시험 때문에 공부하고 있어요.
여 졸리지 않니? 시간이 너무 늦었다.
남 어쩔 수 없어요. 저는 아직 이 책도 다 못 끝냈는데 읽을 책이 더 있어요. 밤을 새야 할 것 같아요.
여 힘든 밤이 되겠구나. 내가 도와줄 수 있는 게 있니?
남 네. 저 벌써 졸려요. 저를 깨워 줄 차가운 음료를 가져다 주시겠어요?
여 물론이지. 콜라와 오렌지 주스 중에 어떤 게 더 좋겠니?
남 콜라가 오렌지 주스보다 더 나은 것 같아요.

① 고마워요. 그걸 정말 좋아해요.
② 아니요. 그게 뭔데요?
③ 아마 그는 오렌지 주스를 더 좋아할 거예요.
⑤ 저는 시험이 끝나면 영화를 보러 갈 거예요.

해설 여자가 남자에게 콜라와 오렌지 주스 중 어떤 것을 선호하는지 물었으므로 콜라가 더 낫다고 말하는 ④가 남자의 응답으로 가장 적절하다.

20　알맞은 응답 찾기 | ④

해석
남 실례합니다. 저는 채널 7 TV에서 나왔는데요. 설문 조사를 하고 있습니다. 몇 가지 질문을 드려도 될까요?
여 좋아요.
남 우선 어젯밤에 TV를 시청하셨나요?
여 예, 저녁 먹고 나서요. 8시경부터요.
남 저희 프로그램 중 어떤 거라도 보셨나요?
여 네, 거의 저녁 내내 봤죠. 11시까지요.
남 그럼, '야생 동물들의 하루'를 보셨겠네요. 그 프로그램에 대해 어떻게 생각하세요?
여 아주 재미있어요. 전 그런 야생 동물에 대한 프로그램을 좋아해요.

① 동물들을 조심하세요.
② 저는 집에서 강아지 한 마리와 고양이 한 마리를 키웁니다.
③ 저는 절대 저녁에 내 아이가 TV를 보도록 하지 않아요.
⑤ 좋은 생각이군요! 나는 당신이 그 프로그램들을 봐야 한다고 생각해요.

해설 TV 프로그램에 대한 의견을 묻고 있는 상황이므로 매우 흥미로우며 야생 동물을 다룬 프로그램을 좋아한다고 말하는 ④가 여자의 응답으로 가장 적절하다.

22회 영어 듣기모의고사　pp. 174~175

01 ③	02 ①	03 ②	04 ④	05 ⑤
06 ⑤	07 ②	08 ③	09 ①	10 ③
11 ④	12 ③	13 ③	14 ⑤	15 ④
16 ⑤	17 ⑤	18 ①	19 ④	20 ⑤

Dictation Test 22회　pp. 176~181

01 ❶ as a side dish　❷ allergic to seafood　❸ bring you a pork cutlet

02 ❶ at the moment　❷ send him a package　❸ receive the package

03 ❶ turn the music down　❷ No problem　❸ I'd love to dance

04 ❶ Closed Thursdays　❷ a bus tour on Friday　❸ the day after tomorrow

05 ❶ job at a hotel　❷ be a hotel manager

06 ❶ never expected that　❷ Are you kidding　❸ wouldn't think of camping

07 ❶ how to fix the radio　❷ am worried about

08 ❶ Cash or card　❷ left them in　❸ can't accept your check

09 ❶ I really wanted to　❷ How did you　❸ are the best

10 ❶ than I had expected　❷ too far away　❸ for the first floor

11 ❶ has caught a cold　❷ prepare some medicine　❸ before she goes to bed

12 ❶ The departure gate　❷ snow outside　❸ are about to board at

13 ❶ May I speak to　❷ has been changed　❸ call me this afternoon

14 ❶ a piece of cloth　❷ wipe sweat off　❸ use it again

15 ❶ clean the house on Saturday　❷ if you could help me

16 ❶ buy some strawberries　❷ Try some blueberries　❸ blueberries are really delicious

17 ❶ likes window shopping ❷ clerk often comes and asks

18 ❶ going shopping this evening ❷ Can't you delay it ❸ a lot more fun

19 ❶ Didn't you like ❷ an upset stomach ❸ a glass of soda

20 ❶ a graduation present ❷ Can I see ❸ Could you wrap this up

01 　그림 정보 파악 – 사물 ｜③
해석

남　주문하시겠어요?

여　저는 무엇을 먹을 것인지 아직 결정하는 중이에요. 여기 버거는 맛있나요?

남　네, 맛있어요. 하지만 곁들임 요리로만 미니 버거를 제공합니다.

여　알겠습니다.

남　메인 요리로는 특별한 해산물 스파게티가 있습니다.

여　고맙지만 괜찮습니다. 제가 해산물에 알레르기가 있어서요. 저는 해산물보다 육류가 더 좋아요.

남　그러면 돈가스를 가져다 드릴까요?

여　네, 그것으로 해야겠네요.

남　알겠습니다, 손님.

해설　여자는 해산물 알레르기가 있어 돈가스를 주문했다.

02 　목적 파악 ｜①
해석

[전화벨이 울린다.]

여　안녕하세요. ABC 회사의 Anna Johns입니다. 뭘 도와드릴까요?

남　안녕하세요. 저는 Fred입니다. White 씨와 통화할 수 있나요?

여　죄송합니다. 그는 지금 출장 중이세요. 메시지를 남겨 드릴까요?

남　글쎄요. 저는 그에게 소포를 보내고 싶습니다. 회사 주소 좀 알려 주시겠습니까?

여　물론입니다. 주소는 Greehill에 있는 Shine Road의 65번지입니다. 다른 것은요?

남　소포를 받으시면, 제게 전화를 다시 부탁드려요.

여　알겠습니다.

남　도움 주셔서 고맙습니다.

해설　남자는 소포를 보내려고 하는데 주소를 몰라서 이를 물어보기 위해 전화했다.

03 　그림 상황에 어울리는 대화 찾기 ｜②
해석

① 여　네가 가장 좋아하는 노래는 뭐니?

　 남　난 이 노래가 제일 좋아. 너는?

② 여　이봐, 음악 소리 좀 낮춰 줄래?

　 남　뭐라고? 더 크게 말해. 안 들려.

③ 여　난 342번 곡을 부르고 싶어.

　 남　그래. 내가 그 번호를 눌러 줄게.

④ 여　콘서트 표 두 장을 주시겠어요?

　 남　어디에 앉으시겠어요?

⑤ 여　난 너랑 춤추고 싶어.

　 남　좋아. 난 오랫동안 너에게 춤을 신청하고 싶었어.

해설　음악 소리가 너무 커서 이를 줄여 달라고 하는 상황에 적절한 대화는 ②이다.

04 　특정 정보 파악 – 요일 ｜④
해석

남　와! 이 국립 미술관은 정말 크다. 안 그래?

여　응, 엄청나네. (잠시 후) 오, 이런! 오늘은 개관하지 않는 것 같아.

남　무슨 소리야?

여　봐. "목요일은 휴관"이라고 쓰여 있잖아.

남　그럼, 우리 내일 와야 하겠구나.

여　그런데 잠깐만. 금요일에는 버스 관광을 가기로 되어 있잖아.

남　맞아. 그럼, 모레는 어때?

여　나는 좋아.

남　좋아.

해설　두 사람은 버스 투어가 있는 금요일 다음날인 토요일에 박물관을 관람하기로 했다.

05 　직업 및 장래 희망 ｜⑤
해석

여　이제 우리가 대학을 졸업하려면 몇 달밖에 안 남았어.

남　넌 졸업하면 뭐 할 거니?

여　음, 난 호텔에 취직하고 싶어.

남　흥미롭게 들리는구나. 그 일에 대한 다음 계획은 어떻게 돼?

여　난 호텔 지배인이 되고 싶고 언젠가는 호텔을 경영하고 싶어.

남　열심히 일하면 넌 호텔을 살 만큼 충분히 부유해질 거야.

해설　여자의 마지막 말을 통해 여자의 장래 희망이 호텔 지배인이라는 것을 알 수 있다.

06 　심정 파악 ｜⑤
해석

남　할머니와 할아버지께서 어디로 휴가를 가실 건지 맞춰 봐.

여　마이애미? 하와이?

남　아니! 다른 곳들을 생각해 봐!

여　난 포기했어. 어디로 가시는데?

남　콜로라도로 캠핑을 가실 거래! 결코 상상도 못했지, 그렇지?

여　뭐? 캠핑? 농담하니?

남　아니야. 그분들은 진지하셔. 호텔은 질리셨대.

여　멋지다. 난 60대에 캠핑은 생각도 못할 거야.

해설　여자는 할아버지와 할머니가 캠핑을 간다는 소식을 듣고 자신이 60대라면 캠핑을 갈 생각을 못했을 것이라고 말하며 놀라고 있다.

07 　어색한 대화 찾기 ｜②
해석

① 남　이 셔츠를 입어 봐도 되나요?

　 여　물론이죠. 탈의실은 저쪽에 있습니다.

② 남　라디오를 고치는 방법을 아니?

　 여　아니, 동의하지 않아.

③ 남　스테이크를 어떻게 요리해 드릴까요?

　 여　완전히 익혀 주세요.

④ 남　우울해 보여. 무슨 일이니?

　 여　내 수학 시험이 걱정되네.

⑤ 남 이 소포를 부치고 싶어요.
　　여 네. 어디로 보내고 싶으신 거죠?
해설 라디오 고치는 방법을 묻는 질문에 대해 반대한다고 대답하는 것은 어색하다.

08 이유 파악 | ③
해석
남 이 서류 가방으로 살게요.
여 어떻게 지불하시겠어요? 현금으로요, 카드로요?
남 여행자 수표를 받으시나요?
여 네, 손님. 여권이나 다른 신분증 있으세요?
남 아니오, 저는 그것들을 호텔방에 두고 왔습니다.
여 죄송합니다, 손님. 그런 경우에, 저희는 수표를 받을 수 없습니다. 현금으로 지불하셔야 할 것 같습니다.
남 음, 그러면, 여기 100달러짜리 지폐가 있어요.
해설 남자는 신분증을 호텔 방에 두고 와서 수표로 지불할 수 없다고 했다.

09 의도 파악 | ①
해석
여 June의 포스터가 음반 가게에서 다 팔렸어.
남 너 음반 가게에서 돌아오는 길이니?
여 응. 정말 슬프다. June의 포스터들 중에 하나를 정말 갖고 싶었는데. 그는 내가 가장 좋아하는 가수야.
남 내가 갖고 있는 걸 맞춰 봐.
여 그게 뭐니? June의 포스터? 어떻게 얻었니?
남 방과 후 바로 음반 가게에 가서 두 개를 샀어. 이게 네 거야.
여 오, 네가 최고야! 내가 내일 점심을 살게.
해설 여자는 자신을 위해 포스터를 구매한 남자의 친절한 행동에 대해 기뻐하며 감사를 표현하고 있다.

10 숫자 정보 파악 – 금액 | ③
해석
여 콘서트홀에서 가장 좋은 좌석표가 얼마죠?
남 60달러입니다. 무대 바로 앞에 있죠.
여 오, 제가 지불하려고 예상했던 것보다 훨씬 더 비싸네요.
남 가장 저렴한 것은 15달러입니다.
여 위치가 어디죠?
남 3층입니다.
여 너무 멀리 떨어져 있네요. 아무 것도 볼 수 없을 거예요.
남 2층석은 25달러이고 1층은 45달러입니다.
여 음, 제가 음악회를 즐기려면, 1층 표를 사는 것이 좋겠네요.
해설 여자는 콘서트를 즐기기 위해 1층에 있는 좌석을 구입하겠다고 했으므로 45달러를 지불할 것이다.

11 장소 추론 | ④
해석
남 도와드릴까요?
여 네. 제 딸이 감기에 걸렸어요.
남 네. 그것에 대해 더 자세히 말씀해 주시겠어요?
여 그녀는 어젯밤부터 기침을 꽤 많이 했어요. 약 좀 처방해 주시겠어요?
남 따님이 몇 살이죠?
여 4살입니다.

남 이 알약은 어린이의 기침에 잘 듣습니다. 자기 전에 두 알을 먹으세요.
여 고맙습니다, 그럴게요.
해설 여자가 딸의 증상을 남자에게 설명하며 약을 준비해 달라고 한 것으로 보아 두 사람이 대화하는 장소는 약국이다.

12 언급되지 않은 것 | ③
해석
여 토론토로 가는 CX417편의 승객 여러분, 안녕하십니까. 탑승구가 37A로 변경되었습니다. 또한 바깥에 눈이 내리고 있어서 약간의 지연이 있겠습니다. 우리는 4시 정각에 탑승할 예정입니다. 대단히 죄송하며 이해해 주셔서 감사합니다.
해설 안내 방송 중 기장을 소개하는 내용은 없었다.

13 도표 정보 파악 | ③
해석
[전화벨이 울린다.]
여 여보세요, Belle Company입니다.
남 Lopez 씨와 통화할 수 있을까요?
여 죄송합니다. 자리에 안 계세요. 메시지를 남겨 드릴까요?
남 네. 저는 Smith라고 합니다. 부디 그녀에게 모임 시간이 금요일 11시에서 1시 30분으로 변경되었다고 전해 주세요.
여 알겠습니다.
남 그리고 오늘 오후에 저에게 전화해 달라고 전해 주시겠어요? 제 전화번호는 0356-4031번입니다.
여 알겠습니다. 그럴게요.
해설 만나는 시간은 금요일 11시에서 1시 30분으로 변경되었다.

14 주제 파악 | ⑤
해석
남 이것은 사람들이 가지고 다니는 천 조각으로, 보통 멋진 무늬가 있습니다. 사람들이 이것을 가지고 다닐 때에는 이것들 사각형 모양으로 접어서 주머니나 가방에 넣습니다. 여러분은 이것으로 여러분의 얼굴 땀을 닦거나, 이것으로 손을 말릴 수 있습니다. 그것이 지저분해지면 그것을 씻어서 말린 후에 다시 쓸 수 있습니다. 어떤 사람들이 그것을 목 주변에 묶기도 하고, 어떤 사람들은 멋지게 보이기 위해 그것을 그들의 재킷 앞주머니에 넣기도 합니다.
해설 정사각형 모양으로 접어 가지고 다니는 천 조각으로 얼굴의 땀을 닦아내거나 손을 말릴 때 쓰는 것은 손수건이다.

15 한 일 / 할 일 파악 | ④
해석
남 난 '위대한 게츠비'를 보고 싶어. 너 이번 주 토요일에 시간 있어?
여 그 영화 일요일에 봐도 될까? 토요일에는 집안 청소를 해야 할 것 같아.
남 난 좋아. 그리고 네가 집을 청소하는 것을 내가 도와줄 수 있을 것 같아.
여 네가 도와준다면 나야 고맙지. 우리 집에 아침 10시에 올래?
남 그럴게.
여 그런데 그 영화 지루하게 들리네.
남 아니야. 환상적이라고 들었어. 내 말 믿어.
해설 남자는 토요일에 여자의 집 청소를 도와주기로 했다.

16 특정 정보 파악 | ⑤

해석

여 도와드릴까요, 손님?

남 딸기를 좀 사고 싶어요. 오늘 딸기 괜찮아요?

여 딸기는 이제 철이 지났어요. 제철 과일을 시도해 보시는 게 어떠세요?

남 무엇을 추천하세요?

여 수박도 좋고, 포도랑 토마토가 아주 신선해요.

남 수박은 어제 샀어요. 포도랑 토마토를 먹어 봐도 될까요?

여 물론이죠. 블루베리도 좀 드셔 보세요. 그것도 오늘 아주 싸게 나왔어요.

남 아, 이 블루베리 정말 맛있네요. 이걸 살게요.

해설 남자는 포도와 토마토, 블루베리를 먹어 보고 블루베리를 사겠다고 했다.

17 상황에 맞는 말 찾기 | ⑤

해석

남 Susan은 시간 여유가 있을 때마다 아이쇼핑을 즐긴다. 그녀에게 그것은 그냥 재미있는 놀이이다. 그것은 어떤 새로운 상품이 시장에 나와 있는지 볼 기회를 제공한다. 그녀가 아이쇼핑을 즐길 때, 점원이 종종 와서 도움이 필요한지 묻는다. 이런 상황에서, 그녀는 점원에게 뭐라고 말하겠는가?

Susan 괜찮아요. 저는 그냥 둘러보고 있어요.

① 그것을 살게요.

② 저는 현금으로 지불할게요.

③ 제가 할인을 받을 수 있나요?

④ 그것들은 얼마죠?

해설 Susan이 아이쇼핑을 즐기고 있는데 점원이 Susan에게 다가와 도움이 필요한지 물었으므로 자신은 단지 구경하고 있을 뿐이라고 말하는 ⑤가 답으로 적절하다.

18 한 일 / 할 일 파악 | ①

해석

여 Brian, 뭐 하고 있니?

남 오, Cindy, 지금 막 학기말 리포트를 끝냈어. 무슨 일이니?

여 음, 오늘 저녁에 난 쇼핑하러 갈 거야. 함께 갈래?

남 그러고 싶지만 오늘 저녁에 약속이 있어.

여 오, 뭔데? 미룰 수 없니?

남 학교 축제 계획을 짜기 위해 Susan을 만날 거야.

여 이봐! 쇼핑이 훨씬 더 재미있을 거야. 그리고 내가 저녁 살게.

남 흠… 좋아. Susan에게 전화할게.

해설 두 사람은 오늘 저녁에 쇼핑을 하기로 했다.

19 알맞은 응답 찾기 | ④

해석

남 손님, 제가 해 드릴 게 있을까요?

여 아니오, 괜찮습니다.

남 이곳 음식이 마음에 안 드시나요?

여 아니오, 좋아요. 왜 물으시죠?

남 음식을 많이 남기셔서, 음식에 만족하지 않으시나 궁금하네요.

여 아, 이거요. 매우 마음에 들었는데요, 제가 체한 것 같아요. 그냥 먹지를 못하겠어요.

남 알겠습니다. 탄산음료 한 잔 가져다 드릴까요? 그게 배를 편안하게 해 줄 수도 있어요.

여 네. 그럼 정말 좋을 것 같아요.

① 바싹 익혀 주세요.

② 물론 아니지요. 이걸 다 먹어버릴 거예요.

③ 후식을 좀 주문하고 싶은데요.

⑤ 요리들이 너무 맛있어서 놀랐어요.

해설 남자가 여자에게 탄산음료를 권하고 있으므로 탄산음료를 마시면 좋을 것 같다고 말하는 ④가 여자의 응답으로 가장 적절하다.

20 알맞은 응답 찾기 | ⑤

해석

남 무엇을 보여 드릴까요, 부인?

여 저는 제 조카의 졸업 선물을 사려고 합니다.

남 하나 추천해 드릴까요?

여 물론이죠. 무엇인가요?

남 전자 사전은 어떠세요?

여 오, 좋아요. 신상품을 볼 수 있을까요?

남 물론이죠. 진열되어 있는 빨간 것이 가장 인기 있는 상품이에요.

여 멋져 보이네요. 얼마인가요?

남 가격을 살펴보겠습니다. 120달러입니다. 그 상품은 세일 중이에요.

여 좋아요. 그걸로 할게요. 이거 포장 좀 해 주시겠어요?

남 물론입니다. 잠시만 기다려 주세요.

① 아니요, 그렇지 않습니다. 손님.

② 죄송합니다만, 저는 지금 가야 합니다.

③ 죄송합니다만, 저희는 현금만 받습니다.

④ 멋진 선물을 제게 주셔서 감사합니다.

해설 여자가 물건을 포장해 달라고 부탁한 상황이므로 몇 분만 기다려 달라고 말하는 ⑤가 남자의 응답으로 가장 적절하다.

기출문제로 마무리하는 Final Test 01 회   pp. 182~183

01 ④	02 ②	03 ④	04 ⑤	05 ②
06 ④	07 ②	08 ⑤	09 ③	10 ③
11 ⑤	12 ④	13 ②	14 ②	15 ④
16 ④	17 ⑤	18 ②	19 ①	20 ②

Dictation Test 01 회   pp. 184~189

01 ❶ looks like a star ❷ a smile is enough

02 ❶ will be delayed ❷ get them by this Friday

03 ❶ take care of ❷ are not allowed

04 ❶ will be next week ❷ go to the theater ❸ be free on Friday

05 ❶ brief overview ❷ a free shuttle bus ❸ are closed every Sunday

06 ❶ delivery company ❷ deliver your order

07 ❶ pay by credit card ❷ take your order

08 ❶ the school festival play ❷ a story about love ❸ choose the clothes

09 ❶ the library will be closed ❷ take three days to fix

10 ❶ have a cheese burger ❷ pay two dollars more ❸ Not for today

11 ❶ I'm seeing the artworks ❷ in this picture ❸ are not allowed to do

12 ❶ I'm in charge of ❷ with your family members ❸ various programs

13 ❶ using one of the rooms ❷ two rooms left ❸ Let's not use

14 ❶ a lot of passengers ❷ can buy snacks on board ❸ only run on rails

15 ❶ missed my stop ❷ buy the tickets

16 ❶ for the speaking contest ❷ a battery pack

17 ❶ bought a printer ❷ what the problem is

18 ❶ finished making graphs ❷ watched a useful video clip ❸ Where can I find

19 ❶ join the singing contest ❷ as a team ❸ look bad

20 ❶ a pair of pants ❷ was sold out ❸ get his money back

---

01 그림 정보 파악 – 사물 | ④

해석

남 Emily, 네 책상에 책갈피가 있네. 네가 만들었니?

여 네, 아빠. Rachel을 위한 생일 선물이에요.

남 잘 만들었구나! 이 책갈피는 별처럼 보이네. 좋아 보이는 구나.

여 감사해요. 저는 이것을 하트 모양으로 만들고 싶었는데. Rachel은 별을 정말로 좋아해요.

남 그렇구나. 너는 단지 웃는 모양을 그렸네. 왜 그 위에 아무 말도 쓰지 않았니?

여 음, 저는 웃는 모양이 충분하다고 생각해요. Rachel은 항상 웃거든요.

남 그렇구나. 나는 그 애가 이것을 좋아할 것이라고 확신한단다.

해설 여자는 Rachel의 생일 선물로 아무 말도 쓰지 않고 웃는 모양만 있는 별 모양의 책갈피를 만들었다.

---

02 목적 파악 | ②

해석

[휴대 전화가 울린다.]

남 여보세요.

여 여보세요. 여기는 Mega 홈쇼핑입니다. Tom Baker 씨 되시나요?

남 네. 맞습니다.

여 죄송합니다만, 주문하신 티셔츠가 며칠 동안 (배송이) 지연될 것입니다.

남 정말요? 저는 그 티셔츠가 이번 주말에 필요해요.

여 걱정하지 마세요, 고객님. 그 티셔츠를 이번 주 금요일까지는 받으실 겁니다.

남 알겠어요. 가급적 빨리 보내 주실 수 있으세요?

여 물론이죠. 이해해 주셔서 감사합니다.

해설 여자는 남자가 주문한 티셔츠의 배송 지연을 알리려고 남자에게 전화를 했다.

---

03 그림 상황에 어울리는 대화 찾기 | ④

해석

① 남 왜 음식 축제에 오지 않았니?

  여 나는 아픈 고양이를 돌봐야 했기 때문에 갈 수 없었어.

② 남 여기 음식 정말 맛있어.

  여 네가 좋아해서 기뻐. 여기는 내가 정말 좋아하는 곳이야.

③ 남 고양이가 정말 귀엽네요. 고양이 이름이 뭐예요?

  여 감사합니다. 고양이 이름은 Nabi예요.

④ 남 죄송합니다만, 강아지는 여기 들어올 수 없습니다.

  여 오, 죄송해요. 저는 그것을 몰랐어요.

⑤ 남 지금 주문할 준비되셨습니까?

  여 아직이요. 시간을 좀 더 가져도 될까요?

해설 남자가 애완동물 입장 금지 표시를 가리키며 강아지를 들고 있는 여자를 제지하고 있는 상황에 어울리는 대화는 ④이다.

---

04 특정 정보 파악 – 요일 | ⑤

해석

[휴대 전화가 울린다.]

여 여보세요, John. 우리 발표가 다음 주인 거 기억하니?

남 응. 만나서 발표에 대해 얘기하는 게 어때?

여 화요일에 시간되니?

남 안타깝지만 안 돼. 사촌이랑 극장에 가기로 약속했어. 수요일은 어때?

여 수요일? 나 수요일에 수영 수업이 있어. 목요일 괜찮니?

남 목요일은 내가 안 될 것 같은데, 금요일엔 시간이 될 것 같아.

여 금요일은 나도 좋아. 그때 보자.

해설 남자는 화요일이 안 되고, 여자는 수요일과 목요일이 안 된다고 했다. 마지막 부분에서 두 사람 모두 금요일은 좋다고 하며 만나기로 했다.

---

05 언급되지 않은 것 | ②

해석

여 Evergreen 시민 문화 센터에 방문해 주셔서 감사합니다. 우리 센터에 대해 간략한 설명을 해 드리겠습니다. 우리 센터에는 수영과 그림을 포함한 다양한 프로그램들이 있습니다. 지하에는 구내식당도 있습니다. 우리는 매시간 무료 셔틀버스를 제공합니다. 센터는 월요일부터 토요일, 오전 9시부터 오후 7시까지 열려 있습니다. 우리는 매주 일요일에 닫습니다. 우리는 여러분이 우리 센터를 곧 다시 방문하기를 희망합니다. 좋은 하루 보내세요.

해설 Evergreen 시민 문화 센터의 식당 메뉴는 언급되지 않았다.

---

06 관계 추론 | ④

해석

[휴대 전화가 울린다.]

여 여보세요.

남 여보세요. 저는 DK 택배 회사의 Michael입니다. 김 선생님이신가요?

여 네. 접니다.

남 제가 당신이 주문하신 것을 배달하기 위해 10분 후에 당신 집에 들를 예정입니다.

여 죄송해요. 지금 집에 아무도 없어서요.

남 그러면, 제가 어떻게 해 드리길 원하시나요?

여 그걸 아파트 사무실에 맡겨 주세요. 제가 나중에 찾아갈게요.

남 네. 그렇게 하겠습니다.

해설 여자가 주문한 물품을 남자가 배달한다고 했으므로 남자는 택배 기사이고 여자는 물품 구매자이다.

07 어색한 대화 찾기 | ②

해석

① 남 너는 방학 동안에 무엇을 할 거야?
　 여 할아버지 댁을 방문할 거야.

② 남 빨간 가방과 검은 가방 중 어느 것이 더 마음에 드시나요?
　 여 신용카드로 계산할게요.

③ 남 너는 얼마나 자주 영화를 보러 가니?
　 여 한 달에 한 번 혹은 두 번.

④ 남 주문을 받아도 될까요?
　 여 네. 치즈 샌드위치로 주세요.

⑤ 남 당신의 펜을 빌릴 수 있을까요?
　 여 그럼요. 여기 있습니다.

해설 빨간 가방과 검은 가방 중 어느 것이 더 마음에 드는지 묻는 질문에 신용카드로 계산한다고 답하는 것은 어색하다.

08 부탁한 일 파악 | ⑤

해석

남 안녕, Sunny. 바빠 보이는구나. 뭐 하고 있니?

여 아, Wilson 선생님. 저 학교 축제 연극을 위한 준비를 하고 있어요.

남 맞아. 너희 반은 연극 공연을 할 거지. 무엇에 관한 연극이니?

여 가족에 관한 내용이에요. 저희는 가족의 사랑에 관한 이야기를 하고 싶어요.

남 좋구나. 혹시 도움이 필요하니?

여 네. 연극을 위한 의상을 골라 주실 수 있으신가요?

남 그럼. 재밌겠는걸.

해설 여자는 남자에게 연극 의상을 골라 줄 것을 부탁했다.

09 주제 파악 | ③

해석

여 주목해 주세요, 학생 여러분. 저는 학교 도서관 사서 Linda입니다. 다음 주 월요일부터 수요일까지 도서관이 휴관한다는 소식을 알리게 되어 유감입니다. 에어컨이 고장 나서 수리하는데 3일이 걸릴 예정입니다. 도서관 내에 어떤 시설도 이용하실 수 없습니다만, 평소대로 도서관 앞에 있는 도서 반납함에 여러분의 책을 넣으실 수는 있습니다. 기다려 주셔서 감사합니다.

해설 에어컨을 수리하는 동안 도서관이 휴관한다는 것을 알리기 위한 안내 방송이다.

10 숫자 정보 파악 – 금액 | ③

해석

남 안녕하세요. 주문하시겠습니까?

여 안녕하세요. 치즈버거 하나 주세요.

남 5달러입니다. 2달러를 더 지불하시면, 음료와 감자튀김을 받으실 수 있습니다.

여 오, 정말요? 그러면, 2달러를 더 지불할게요.

남 알겠습니다. 다른 거 필요하신 거 있으세요? 디저트는 어떠신가요?

여 오늘은 괜찮아요.

남 좋습니다. 여기에서 드실 건가요? 아니면 가져가실 건가요?

여 가져갈게요.

해설 여자는 5달러인 치즈버거에 음료와 감자튀김을 받기 위해 2달러를 더 지불하기로 했으므로 총 7달러를 지불하면 된다.

11 장소 추론 | ⑤

해석

여 야, Ken. 이거 멋지다!

남 나는 위대한 화가들의 예술 작품을 이렇게 가까이에서 보고 있다는 사실이 믿기지 않아.

여 나도 그래. 여기 좀 봐! 이 그림들은 정말 사실적으로 보여.

남 그래! 이 그림 속에 있는 사람은 나를 쳐다보고 있는 듯 해.

여 그러네. 나 사진을 좀 찍고 싶어.

남 오, 안 돼! 여기에서 그렇게 하는 게 허락되지 않아.

여 그래. 그런 것을 몰랐어. 다음 구역으로 이동하자.

해설 두 사람은 예술 작품을 보고 있고, 사진 찍는 것이 금지되어 있는 곳에서 대화를 나누고 있으므로 두 사람이 대화하는 장소가 미술관임을 알 수 있다.

12 언급되지 않은 것 | ④

해석

남 안녕하세요. 학생 여러분, 저는 Michael Lee입니다. 저는 Parkway 학교 마라톤의 날을 담당하고 있습니다. 우리가 2017년 5월 13일에 이러한 연례행사를 갖게 될 거라는 것을 전할 수 있어서 기쁩니다. 우리 학교 학생이라면 누구든 함께하실 수 있습니다. 또한, 여러분의 가족들과 함께 달리실 수도 있어요. 이 행사는 음식 축제 마당과 밴드 행진과 같은 다양한 프로그램을 포함하고 있습니다. 이 행사에 등록하기 위해서 교무실로 가 주세요. 고맙습니다.

해설 Parkway 학교 마라톤의 날의 참가비에 관해서는 언급되지 않았다.

13 도표 정보 파악 | ②

해석

남 Mary, 어떤 방이 이번 주 목요일 회의에 좋을까?

여 방 D는 어때?

남 Robert가 그날에 그 방을 사용한다고 들었어.

여 흠…. 휴게실 옆에 있는 방들 중에서 하나를 사용하는 것은 어떨까? 그 방들은 편리해.

남 그런데 휴게실은 종종 혼잡해서 휴게실 옆에 있는 방은 시끄러울 거야.

여 네가 맞아. 그러면, 우리에게는 방 A와 방 B, 두 개의 방이 남았어.

남 화장실 옆에 있는 방은 사용하지 말자.

여 알겠어. 이 방을 사용하자.

해설 방 D는 다른 사람이 사용하기로 하였고, 휴게실 옆에 있는 방은 시끄러울 것 같아 사용하지 않기로 했다. 방 A와 방 B 중 화장실 옆에 있는 방은 남자가 사용하지 말자고 했으므로 결국 방 B를 사용할 것임을 알 수 있다.

14 주제 파악 | ②

해석

여 이것은 운송 수단입니다. 한 번에 많은 승객을 태울 수 있습니다. 승객들이 이용할 수 있는 화장실이 있습니다. 승객들은 탑승한 후에 스낵을 구입할 수 있고, 이 운송 수단은 때로로 스낵바를 구비하고 있기도 합니다. 이것은 역에서 멈추며 사람들은 그곳에서 타고 내립니다. 이것은 많은 바퀴가 있지만 철길에서만 달릴 수 있습니다.

해설 화장실과 스낵바가 있고, 철길에서만 달릴 수 있으며 역에서 멈추는 운송 수단은 기차이다.

15 한 일 / 할 일 파악 | ④

해석

[휴대 전화가 울린다.]

남 여보세요?

여 안녕, Jack. 나 지하철에 있는데, 늦을 것 같아.

남 왜? 무슨 일 있었어?

여 내릴 역을 놓쳤어. 미안하지만, 20분 안에는 도착할 거야.

남 괜찮아. 연극 시작하기 전에 아직 30분이 있어.

여 다행이야. 가능한 한 빨리 갈게.

남 알겠어. 내가 지금 극장에 있어서 표를 살게.

여 그러면 정말 좋을 것 같아. 고마워.

해설 남자가 극장에 먼저 도착해서 연극 표를 구입하기로 했다.

16 특정 정보 파악 | ④

해석

남 박 선생님. 저는 올해 말하기 경연 대회를 위한 상품에 대해 생각하고 있어요. 아이디어 있으세요?

여 지난 2년 동안, 우승자들은 일정 계획표나 사전을 받았어요.

남 알지만, 많은 학생들이 항상 그것들을 받는다고 말하거든요.

여 배터리 팩은 어때요? 학생들이 모바일 기기를 많이 사용하기 때문에 매우 실용적일 거예요.

남 정말 좋은 생각이에요! 학생들이 매우 좋아할 것이라고 확신해요.

여 좋아요! 그러면, 이번에는 그것을 주문할게요.

해설 남자와 여자는 올해 말하기 경연 대회 우승자에게 줄 상품으로 배터리 팩을 주문하기로 했다.

17 알맞은 응답 찾기 | ⑤

해석

[전화벨이 울린다.]

남 ABC 사무용품점입니다. 어떻게 도와드릴까요?

여 안녕하세요. 저는 지난주에 당신의 가게에서 프린터를 구입했는데, 프린터에 약간의 문제가 있습니다.

남 오, 불편을 드려 죄송합니다. 모델 번호가 무엇인가요?

여 모델 번호요? 어디서 찾을 수 있나요?

남 프린터 뒤에 있습니다.

여 알겠습니다. 잠시만요. (잠시 후) LP-123입니다.

남 감사합니다. 문제가 무엇인지 말해 주실 수 있으세요?

여 종이가 프린터에 걸렸어요.

① 저는 가게에 제 지갑을 놓고 왔어요.

② 저는 당신께 제 컴퓨터를 빌려줄 수 없어요.

③ 이 커피 기계는 작동하지 않아요.

④ 저는 등을 다쳐서 움직일 수 없어요.

해설 남자가 프린터에 어떤 문제가 있는지 물었으므로 종이가 프린터에 걸려 있다고 말하는 ⑤가 여자의 응답으로 가장 적절하다.

18 알맞은 응답 찾기 | ②

해석

남 다음 주 월요일에 있을 역사 발표를 위한 그래프 만드는 것을 끝냈니?

여 아니. 아직 시작도 못했어. 그래프 만드는데 도움이 필요한 것 같아.

남 나는 인터넷에서 그래프 만들기에 대한 유용한 비디오 클립을 봤어.

여 비디오 클립?

남 응. 그것은 나를 많이 도와주었어. 그 클립은 나와 같은 초보자들을 위한 그래프 만드는 방법에 관한 것이었어.

여 유용하게 들린다. 내가 인터넷에서 그것을 어디서 찾을 수 있을까?

남 내가 웹사이트 주소를 알려 줄게.

① 네 손글씨는 좀 더 도움이 필요해.

③ 나는 수학 문제 푸는 것을 잘하지 못해.

④ 나는 인터넷에서 음악을 듣는 것을 즐겨.

⑤ 내 선생님이 블로그 만드는 방법을 보여 주셨어.

해설 여자가 그래프 만들기에 대한 비디오 클립을 어디서 찾을 수 있는지 물었으므로 웹사이트 주소를 알려 준다는 ②가 남자의 응답으로 가장 적절하다.

19 알맞은 응답 찾기 | ①

해석

여 Mike, 노래 경연 대회에 참가할 거야?

남 그것에 대해 생각 중인데, 나는 사람들 앞에서 노래 부르는 것이 두려워.

여 그러지마. 너는 훌륭한 가수야.

남 지난 경연 대회에서, 나는 노래를 부르는 동안 실수를 많이 했어.

여 팀으로 경연 대회에 참가하는 것이 어떨까? 네게 난처한 상황이 생기면, 내가 너를 도와줄게.

남 모르겠어. 나는 모두 앞에서 좋지 않은 모습을 다시는 보이고 싶지 않아.

여 걱정하지 마. 우리는 좋은 팀이 될 수 있을 거야.

② 축하해! 네가 우승할 줄 알았어.

③ 아니, 나는 노래 부르는 것에 전혀 관심이 없어.

④ 나는 경연 대회에 참가하는 것을 고려한 적이 없어.

⑤ 나를 도와줘서 고마워.

해설 남자가 노래 경연 대회 참가를 앞두고 걱정하고 있으므로 걱정하지 말라고 격려하는 ①이 여자의 응답으로 가장 적절하다.

20 상황에 맞는 말 찾기 | ②

해석

남 최근에, 지훈이의 엄마는 지훈이를 위해 바지 한 벌을 샀지만, 바지가 너무 컸다. 지훈이는 바지를 맞는 사이즈로 교환하고 싶어서 그 가게를 방문했다. 그러나, 점원은 그에게 그가 원하는 사이즈가 품절되었다고 말했다. 그는 돈으로 되돌려 받을 수 있는지 묻고 싶었다. 이런 상황에서, 지훈이는 점원에게 뭐라고 말하겠는가?

지훈 죄송하지만, 환불받고 싶습니다.

① 그러면, 이 바지를 짧게 만들어 줄 수 있나요?

③ 언제 더 큰 사이즈를 받을 수 있으세요?

④ 저는 이 스타일이 정말 좋아요.

⑤ 긴 바지는 제 스타일이 아니에요.

해설 지훈이는 원하는 바지 사이즈가 품절되었다는 점원의 말에 그 바지를 돈으로 되돌려 받고 싶은 상황이므로 ②가 답으로 적절하다.

01 ④	**02** ②	**03** ⑤	**04** ⑤	**05** ④
06 ①	**07** ⑤	**08** ⑤	**09** ③	**10** ①
11 ①	**12** ⑤	**13** ⑤	**14** ①	**15** ⑤
16 ③	**17** ⑤	**18** ②	**19** ①	**20** ⑤

Dictation Test 02회   pp. 192~197

01 ❶ the rabbit balloon ❷ the one with a ribbon

02 ❶ He was absent ❷ go visit him ❸ How about meeting

03 ❶ help me carry these bags ❷ I open the window ❸ can have my seat

04 ❶ register for tennis lessons ❷ from Monday to Friday

05 ❶ introduce our new product ❷ You can control it ❸ the battery is fully charged

06 ❶ finish buying tickets ❷ this ticketing machine ❸ get some popcorn and drinks

07 ❶ where the bank is ❷ Why do you like

08 ❶ get up early ❷ give them a ride ❸ make them breakfast

09 ❶ to return books ❷ the same homework ❸ already finished my homework

10 ❶ How much is it ❷ I'll order ❸ get ten percent off

11 ❶ go out to eat ❷ can also eat dinner ❸ check the movie schedule

12 ❶ toys books and clothing ❷ Please register at

13 ❶ I took a class ❷ have a dance class ❸ one of these two classes

14 ❶ type of bottle ❷ drink hot water ❸ many sizes and shapes

15 ❶ set up for the experiment ❷ bring the laptop computer ❸ get the magnets

16 ❶ making milk tea ❷ some sugar or honey ❸ try it with honey

17 ❶ were you absent from ❷ feel much better ❸ can I borrow your notes

18 ❶ going to the bookstore ❷ at the comic books

19 ❶ a lot of nice cars ❷ I already have a plan

20 ❶ take a trip ❷ cancel her registration

---

01 그림 정보 파악 – 사물 | ④

해석

남 이봐, Amy. 뭘 보고 있니?

여 풍선들이요. 아빠, 저것들 중에 하나 갖고 싶어요.

남 어떤 풍선 말하는 거니? 토끼 풍선을 원하니?

여 아니요. 저는 코끼리 풍선을 원해요.

남 모자를 쓴 코끼리 말하는 거니?

여 아니요, 그거 아니에요. 저는 머리에 리본이 달린 것을 갖고 싶어요.

남 네가 어떤 것을 원하는지 알겠다. 그것을 사자.

여 고마워요, 아빠.

해설 여자는 리본이 달린 코끼리 풍선을 갖고 싶다고 했다.

02 목적 파악 | ②

해석

[휴대 전화가 울린다.]

남 안녕, Cathy. 너 지금 바쁘니?

여 그렇게 바쁘지 않아. 방금 숙제를 끝냈거든.

남 너 Jake 소식 들었어? 오늘 학교에 결석했대. 병원에 있대.

여 그에게 무슨 일이 생긴 거니?

남 다리가 부러졌대. 우리 오늘 오후에 그를 방문하는 게 어떠니?

여 오 이런! 당연히 그래야지. 어디서 만날래?

남 어제 우리가 만났던 버스 정류장 알지? 거기에서 4시에 만나는 게 어때?

여 그래. 그때 보자.

해설 남자는 여자와 함께 친구의 병문안을 가기 위해 전화했다.

03 그림 상황에 어울리는 대화 찾기 | ⑤

해석

① 남 음료수 좀 드시겠어요?
   여 저는 콜라를 마시고 싶어요.

② 남 이 가방을 좀 옮기는 것을 도와주시겠어요?
   여 물론이죠. 제 기쁨입니다.

③ 남 제가 창문을 열어도 괜찮을까요?
   여 전혀요. 어서 하세요.

④ 남 이 버스는 너무 시끄러워요.
   여 그래요. 저는 더 이상 참을 수 없어요.

⑤ 남 아주머니, 제 자리에 앉으세요.
   여 고맙습니다. 정말 친절하시네요!

해설 남자가 임신한 여자에게 자리를 양보하고 있는 상황에 적절한 대화는 ⑤이다.

04 특정 정보 파악 – 요일 | ⑤

해석

[전화벨이 울린다.]

여 안녕하세요, ABC 스포츠 센터입니다. 어떻게 도와드릴까요?

남 안녕하세요, 저는 테니스 수업을 등록하고 싶습니다.

여 당신은 화요일 또는 목요일에 일주일에 한 번 테니스 수업을 들을 수 있습니다.

남 한 달에 얼마인가요?

여 80,000원입니다.

남 주말에 코트를 사용할 수 있나요?

여 아니요. 월요일부터 금요일에만 사용하실 수 있습니다.

남 알겠습니다. 지금 목요일 수업에 등록해도 될까요?

여 물론이죠.

해설 주말에는 테니스 코트를 이용할 수 없다고 했다.

05 언급되지 않은 것 | ④

해석

여 저희 부스를 방문해 주셔서 감사합니다. 저희의 새로운 상품인 Drone-X에 대해 소개해 드리겠습니다. 여러분이 보시다시피, Drone-X는 주머니에 들어갈 수 있는 크기입니다. 여러분은 그것을 스마트폰으로 통제할 수 있습니다. 100미터 범위 안에서 통제할 수 있지요. 또한, 배터리가 완전히 충전됐을 때 그것은 10분 정도 비행할 수 있습니다. 이 모델은 오늘만 5만원에 할인해 드리고 있습니다.

해설 Drone-X의 촬영 기능에 관해서는 언급되지 않았다.

06 장소 추론 | ①

해석

여 John, 우리 시간이 많이 없어. 영화 '지하철 이야기'에 대한 영화 티켓 사는 거 끝났니?

남 아니, 나는 아직 노력 중이야. 하지만 이 티켓 기계를 이용하는 것은 내게 어려운 일이야.

여 가서 직원에게 티켓을 사는 것은 어떠니?

남 봐! 많은 사람들이 저기 줄 서서 기다리고 있어.

여 알아. 하지만 나는 우리가 영화 첫 부분을 놓칠까 봐 걱정돼.

남 잠깐만 기다려! 나 거의 끝난 것 같아.

여 그러면, 내가 팝콘하고 음료 좀 빨리 사 올게.

해설 남자는 영화 티켓을 구입하고 있고, 여자는 영화의 첫 부분을 놓칠까 봐 걱정하면서 팝콘하고 음료를 빨리 사 온다고 했으므로 두 사람이 대화하는 장소는 영화관임을 알 수 있다.

07 어색한 대화 찾기 | ⑤

해석

① 여 온라인 쇼핑에 대해 어떻게 생각해?
　남 그렇게 편리하다고 생각하지 않아. 나는 가게에 방문하는 걸 더 좋아해.
② 여 새로 오신 영어 선생님에 대해 들어 본 적 있니?
　남 어떤 것도 듣지 못했어.
③ 여 은행이 어디에 있는지 아세요?
　남 네. 두 블록 직진하셔서 우회전 하시면 돼요.
④ 여 너는 축구를 얼마나 자주 하니?
　남 1주일에 두 번쯤 해.
⑤ 여 너는 코미디 영화를 왜 좋아하니?
　남 맞아. 나는 공포 영화를 많이 좋아해.

해설 코미디 영화를 좋아하는 이유를 물었는데 공포 영화를 많이 좋아한다고 답하는 것은 어색하다.

08 부탁한 일 파악 | ⑤

해석

남 여보, 당신 걱정스러워 보여요.

여 네, 저 3일간 출장 가잖아요.

남 음, 그런데 뭐가 문제예요?

여 우리 애들이요! 애들이 보통 일찍 일어나지만 내일 중간고사가 시작하거든요.

남 맞아요. 그들이 요즘 매우 늦게까지 깨어 있느라 정말 피곤해 하지요.

여 알아요. 그래서 당신이 앞으로 3일 동안 아이들을 학교에 좀 태워다 줄래요?

남 좋아요. 그럴게요. 아침도 만들어 줘야 할까요?

여 아니요. 학교 근처에서 샌드위치를 살 수 있어요.

해설 여자는 남자에게 차로 아이들을 등교시켜 줄 것을 부탁했다.

09 의도 파악 | ③

해석

남 이봐, Lisa! 네가 도서관에는 무슨 일이야?

여 안녕, Brian. 책을 반납하러 왔어. 너는 여기서 뭐하고 있어?

남 나는 역사 숙제를 위한 책을 몇 권 빌리러 왔어.

여 오, 나도 너랑 똑같은 숙제가 있는데.

남 그럼 우리 방과 후에 함께 숙제하면 어떨까?

여 그렇게 하면 좋긴 하겠지만, 나는 이미 숙제를 끝냈어.

해설 여자는 이미 숙제를 끝냈기 때문에 남자가 함께 숙제를 하자는 제안을 거절했다.

10 숫자 정보 파악 - 금액 | ①

해석

남 실례합니다. 사진이 있는 달력을 복사하는 게 얼마인가요?

여 10장에 30달러이고, 50장에 100달러입니다.

남 흠. 저는 사실 40장이 필요한데요. 50장을 복사하는 게 훨씬 좋겠네요. 50장을 주문해야 할 거 같아요.

여 요금은 어떻게 지불하실 건가요?

남 신용카드로요. 여기 있습니다.

여 이 카드로 결제하면 10% 할인을 받습니다.

남 좋네요.

해설 남자는 달력을 50장 복사하였고, 카드로 결제하면서 10% 할인을 받으므로 90달러를 지불하면 된다.

11 한 일 / 할 일 파악 | ①

해석

남 마침내, 시험이 끝났어.

여 우리 밖에 나가서 밥도 먹고 영화도 보자. 나는 영화 'Star Ships'를 정말로 보고 싶어.

남 나도 그래. 우리는 영화관 근처에 있는 Farmer's Kitchen에서 저녁 식사도 할 수 있어.

여 좋은데.

남 그럼, 내가 영화 스케줄을 확인할게.

여 그래. 식당에서 5시에 만나자.

남 그때 봐.

해설 남자는 영화를 보러 가기 전에 영화 스케줄을 확인하기로 했다.

12 언급되지 않은 것 | ⑤

해석

남 안녕하세요, Oakwood 주민 여러분. 시청에서 일하고 있는 David Kim입니다. 우리가 2017년 10월 13일에 Oakwood 벼룩시장을 개최하게 될 거라는 사실을 전할 수 있어서 기쁩니다. 여러분은 장난감과 책 그리고 옷을 이 행사에서 사고 팔 수 있습니다. 판매자 여러분께는 5달러의 등록비용이 있습니다. 참석을 계획하고 있으시다면, 민원실에 등록해 주세요. 감사합니다.

해설 Oakwood 벼룩시장의 신청 기한에 관해서는 언급되지 않았다.

13 도표 정보 파악 | ⑤

해석

남 이봐, Rebecca! 여기서 뭐 하고 있어?

여 나는 수업을 위해 Sky 요가 웹사이트를 확인하고 있어.

남 정말로? 나는 작년에 거기에서 수업을 들었어. 아마도 내가 너를 도와줄 수 있을 거야.

여 좋아. 흠… 나는 매주 수요일마다 춤 수업이 있어서 그때는 못 가.

남 알겠어. 나는 Michelle과 Serena가 인기 있는 강사들이었다는 걸 기억해.

여 그러면 그 선생님들의 수업 중 하나를 선택할래.

남 좋아. 그래서 너는 이 두 개의 수업 중에 하나를 선택해야 할 거야.

여 음. 그러면, 나는 더 저렴한 수업을 선택할래.

해설 춤 수업이 있는 수요일을 제외하고, Michelle과 Serena의 수업 중 더 저렴한 수업은 D이다.

14 주제 파악 | ①
해석

여 이것은 사람들이 그들의 일상생활에서 사용하는 특별한 형태의 병입니다. 보통, 사람들이 외출하거나 여행할 때 사용됩니다. 이것은 음료를 뜨겁게 혹은 차갑게 유지하기 위해 고안되었습니다. 추운 날 뜨거운 물을 마시고 싶어 하는 사람들에게 좋습니다. 다양한 사이즈와 모양으로 나옵니다. 뚜껑은 종종 컵으로 사용될 수 있습니다.

해설 음료를 뜨겁게 혹은 차갑게 유지하고, 추운 날 뜨거운 물을 마실 때 사용하는 병은 보온병이다.

15 한 일 / 할 일 파악 | ⑤
해석

여 Kevin, 우리는 과학 수업이 시작하기 전에 실험 준비를 해야 해.

남 이봐, 수진. 맞다! 우리가 뭘 해야 하지?

여 내가 테이블 준비를 방금 끝냈어. 네가 실험을 위한 자석을 가져다줄 수 있니?

남 물론이지. 또 다른 것은?

여 너 우리가 수업에서 필요한 노트북 컴퓨터를 가져왔니?

남 오! 그것에 대해 완전히 잊고 있었어.

여 그럼 네가 교무실에 가서 노트북 컴퓨터를 가져올래? 자석은 내가 가져올게.

남 고마워. 지금 당장 할게.

해설 남자는 과학 수업 준비를 위해 여자의 부탁을 받고 교무실에서 노트북 컴퓨터를 가져오기로 했다.

16 특정 정보 파악 | ③
해석

여 아빠! 녹차로 뭐 하시는 거예요?

남 사실, 이건 홍차란다. 밀크티를 만들까 생각하고 있었어.

여 밀크티! 저 그거 정말 좋아해요! 그건 어떻게 만드는 거예요?

남 아주 간단해. 그냥 홍차를 설탕이나 꿀 조금과 함께 뜨거운 우유에 넣으면 돼.

여 제 생각에는 꿀을 넣는 게 맛이 더 좋을 것 같아요. 저희 꿀 있나요?

남 없는데. 설탕도 꿀이랑 거의 똑같은 맛을 낸단다.

여 저는 정말로 꿀을 넣고 만들어 보고 싶어요. 제가 가서 조금 사 올게요.

남 고맙구나. 얘야.

해설 여자는 밀크티를 만들 때 사용할 꿀을 구입할 것이다.

17 알맞은 응답 찾기 | ⑤
해석

여 이봐, Sean. 너 어제 왜 학교에 결석했니? 걱정했잖아.

남 감기가 좀 심했어.

여 지금은 괜찮니?

남 응. 훨씬 좋아졌어.

여 그 말을 들으니 기쁘다.

남 고마워. 하지만 수업에서 따라잡아야 할 것들이 아주 많아.

여 안됐네. 내가 도와줄 수 있는 게 있을까?

남 음, 어제 노트 필기한 것 좀 빌릴 수 있니?

여 당연하지. 오늘 오후에 내 노트를 갖다 줄게.

① 나도 과학 시험을 통과하지 못했어.

② 나는 곧 수업 내용을 따라잡을 거야.

③ 미안해. 내가 네 파일 중 몇 개를 열 수 없어.

④ 맞아. 이 추운 날씨가 곧 끝나길 바라.

해설 남자가 학교에 결석해서 노트 필기를 빌려줄 것을 부탁했으므로 오후에 노트를 갖다 준다고 말하는 ⑤가 여자의 응답으로 가장 적절하다.

18 알맞은 응답 찾기 | ③
해석

남 Judy, 이번 주말에 뭐 할 거야?

여 흠… 특별한 건 없어. 너는?

남 나는 서점에 갈까 생각 중이야.

여 서점? 거기에서 뭐 사게?

남 새로 나온 요리 잡지를 사고 싶어.

여 네가 요리에 관심이 있는지는 몰랐네.

남 응, 나 요리하는 걸 좋아해.

여 나는 만화책 코너를 둘러보고 싶은데. 너와 함께 가도 될까?

남 왜 안 되겠어? 함께 가자.

① 미안하지만, 기억나지 않아.

② 너무 안됐다. 힘내.

④ 고마워. 네 덕분이야.

⑤ 축하해. 너는 그럴 만한 자격이 있어.

해설 여자가 서점에 함께 가자고 제안했으므로 함께 가자고 답하는 ③이 남자의 응답으로 가장 적절하다.

19 알맞은 응답 찾기 | ①
해석

남 이봐, 너 오늘 아주 신나 보이네. 무슨 일이야?

여 응, 나 2017 세계 모터쇼 표가 2장이 생겼거든.

남 와, 멋진데. 거기에 멋진 자동차들이 아주 많을 거라고 하던데.

여 나도 들었어. 너 나랑 함께 갈래?

남 그러고 싶어. 그게 언제인데?

여 쇼는 7월 4일부터 11일까지야.

남 오, 안 돼. 그때 가족 여행을 갈 계획을 이미 세웠거든.

여 네가 나와 함께 그 쇼에 갈 수 있으면 좋을 텐데.

② 나 그 영화를 정말 재미있게 봤어.

③ 네가 나와 함께 갈 수 있어서 기뻐.

④ 네가 가족 여행을 갈 수 없었다니 유감이다.

⑤ 그 쇼가 취소되었다니 정말 실망이야.

해설 여자가 모터쇼에 같이 가자고 제안했는데 남자가 이미 계획이 있다고 말한 상황이므로 아쉬움을 표현하는 ①이 여자의 응답으로 가장 적절하다.

20 상황에 맞는 말 찾기 | ⑤
해석

남 지난주에 수미는 여름 방학 동안 학교에서 진행되는 영어 캠프에 등록했다. 그리고 나서, 지난밤 그녀는 그녀의 가족이 같은 기간에 1주일간 여행을 갈 거라는 말을 듣게 되었다. 그래서 그녀는 등록을 취소해야 한다고 영어 선생님께 말하고 싶다. 이런 상황에서, 수미는 선생님께 뭐라고 말하겠는가?

수미 죄송하지만, 여름 캠프에 참가할 수 없을 것 같아요.

① 제 영어 실력이 더 빨리 향상됐으면 좋겠어요.
② 올해 여름 캠프는 정말 즐거웠어요.
③ 오, 저를 위해 여행 계획을 짜 주시다니 정말 친절하시군요.
④ 방학 동안에 어디를 여행하고 싶으신가요?

해설 영어 캠프를 참가하기로 한 기간 동안에 가족 여행을 가기로 했으므로 여름 캠프에 참가할 수 없을 것 같다고 말하는 ⑤가 답으로 적절하다.

01회 미리 보는 수능 듣기모의고사 | pp. 198~199

01 ⑤	02 ③	03 ⑤	04 ③	05 ②
06 ③	07 ③	08 ②	09 ①	10 ④
11 ④	12 ④	13 ⑤	14 ②	15 ①
16 ⑤	17 ①			

Dictation Test 01회 | pp. 200~205

01 ❶ makes me really angry ❷ are missing
02 ❶ open the door ❷ the battery is dead
03 ❶ it's always on time ❷ not to make noise ❸ a useful transportation
04 ❶ very successful writer ❷ fall in love with ❸ keep your words
05 ❶ your work as a volunteer ❷ go for the job ❸ your advice
06 ❶ curtain was neatly tied ❷ a cup next to it ❸ all put on the bookshelf
07 ❶ Can I change the schedule ❷ the location of the hotel
08 ❶ Why don't you bring him ❷ how about animation movies
09 ❶ have the receipt ❷ the same price ❸ pay the difference
10 ❶ change my schedule ❷ the first day ❸ pay for the other night
11 ❶ help you stay awake ❷ feel tired all day long
12 ❶ have curry for dinner ❷ a ready meal curry ❸ The powder type
13 ❶ send some flowers ❷ include a message
14 ❶ do some experiments ❷ have a fear of
15 ❶ robbed of her wallet ❷ couldn't explain about the accident ❸ what happened in more detail

16~17 ❶ having special guests ❷ the school we visited ❸ They'll take classes

01 알맞은 응답 찾기 (짧은 대화) | ⑤

해석
여 이거 나를 정말 화나게 한다.
남 왜 그래?
여 내가 이 책을 보고서를 쓰려고 대출했는데, 내가 필요한 페이지들이 다 없어졌어.
남 문제를 해결하기 위해 사서한테 당장 말해야 해.
① 그건 내 잘못이 아니었어.
② 전적으로 동의해.
③ 너 보고서를 고칠 수 있니?
④ 내가 그거 빌려도 되니?

해설 빌린 책에서 필요한 페이지가 찢겨져 있어 화가 난 여자에게 사서에게 당장 말하라고 하는 ⑤가 남자의 응답으로 가장 적절하다.

02 알맞은 응답 찾기 (짧은 대화) | ③

해석
남 문을 열 수가 없어.
여 심지어 어떤 버튼도 누를 수가 없어. 건전지가 다 되었나봐.
남 수리 센터 전화번호를 아니?
여 응. 080-123-4567이야.
① 그렇고말고.
② 나는 그것에 관해 확신해.
④ 내가 건전지를 갈았어야 하는데.
⑤ 수리 기사가 전화를 받지 않고 있어.

해설 남자가 수리 센터의 전화번호를 아는지 물어봤으므로 전화번호를 알려주는 ③이 여자의 응답으로 가장 적절하다.

03 목적 파악 | ⑤

해석
여 지하철은 내게 최고의 교통수단인데, 그 이유는 매우 편리하고 저렴하기 때문이다. 게다가 그것은 항상 정시에 온다. 그래서 나는 우리가 지하철에서 예절을 지킨다면 더 좋을 거라고 생각한다. 예를 들어, 시끄럽게 떠들지 않고 쓰레기를 남기지 않는 것이 중요하다. 도움이 필요한 사람들에게 자리를 양보하는 것도 우리에게 역시 중요하다. 나는 우리가 함께 노력한다면, 우리는 지하철을 모든 사람들에게 유용한 교통수단으로 만들 수 있다고 생각한다.

해설 지하철에서 우리 모두가 예절을 지키면 더 나아질 것이라며 지하철 예절을 지킬 것을 강조하고 있다.

04 주제 파악 | ③

해석
여 안녕하세요, 여러분. 오늘 밤은 Smith 씨를 초대했습니다. 만나서 매우 반갑습니다, Smith 씨.
남 만나서 반갑습니다.
여 당신은 매우 성공한 작가이신데요. 처음부터 작가가 되고 싶었나요?
남 네. 제가 초등학생이었을 때부터, 이야기를 쓰는 것을 꿈꿔 왔습니다.
여 그게 지금의 당신을 만든 것 같습니다. 성공하는 법에 대해 조언을 주신다면요?
남 성공하고 싶으면 자신이 하는 일과 사랑에 빠져야 합니다. 그것을 생각하면 가슴이 뛰어야 하지요.

여 모든 분들이 당신의 말을 모두 기억했으면 좋겠군요. 훌륭한 조언 감사합니다.

남 천만에요.

해설 남자는 성공하기 위한 방법으로 지금 하는 일과 사랑에 빠져야 한다고 조언했다.

05 관계 추론 | ②

해석

[문 두드리는 소리]

남 들어와서 앉으세요.

여 감사합니다. 저는 Rachel Brown입니다. 제가 선생님께 어제 이메일을 보냈습니다.

남 학생이 보낸 이메일을 정성 들여서 읽었어요.

여 정말 감사합니다.

남 천만에요. 저는 학생이 어르신들과 함께한 봉사 활동에 매우 감동을 받았어요.

여 저는 그러한 활동을 즐겨 했습니다. 하지만 저는 졸업하기 전에 두 갈래의 길 사이에서 반드시 선택해야 합니다.

남 그게 무슨 의미인가요?

여 하나의 길은 자선 단체 분야에서 직업을 갖는 것이고, 다른 하나는 은행에서 직업을 갖는 것입니다.

남 만약 경제적 안정성이 학생에게 중요하다면, 은행에서 직업을 얻는 것이 더 나을 거예요.

여 조언해 주셔서 감사합니다. 선생님의 조언을 신중히 생각해 보겠습니다.

해설 졸업을 하기 전에 진로 선택에 있어서 고민을 하고 있는 여자에게 남자가 조언해 주고 있는 상황이므로 진로 상담사와 학생 사이에 이루어진 대화임을 알 수 있다.

06 그림 정보 파악 | ③

해석

남 엄마, 저 왔어요.

여 Mike의 집에서 잘 놀았니?

남 네. 그런데 그 애 방이 매우 깨끗했어요.

여 어땠기에?

남 음, 창문 커튼이 단정히 묶여 있었어요. 그리고 이불이 침대 위에 개어져 있었고요.

여 네 책상에는 늘 물건이 많이 있잖니. 그 애의 책상은 어땠니?

남 책 한 권만 책상 위에 펴져 있었고요, 그 옆에 컵이 하나 있었어요. 그게 다예요.

여 그 애는 책이 많지 않니?

남 네, 책이 많았는데요, 모두 책장에 꽂혀 있었어요. 오, 게다가 거울이 정말 깨끗하더라고요.

여 와. 네가 그 애 같다면 좋으련만.

해설 책상 위에 책 한 권과 그 옆에 컵이 있다고 했는데 책상 위에 아무것도 없다.

07 한 일 / 할 일 파악 | ③

해석

[전화벨이 울린다.]

남 여보세요. 도와드릴까요?

여 여보세요, 저는 Janice입니다. 당신의 호텔에 예약을 했는데요. 일정을 좀 변경할 수 있을까요?

남 어떻게 하고 싶으세요?

여 이번 주 금요일 하룻밤만 예약하는 게 가능할까요?

남 괜찮습니다.

여 오, 잘됐네요.

남 제가 해 드릴 다른 일이 있을까요?

여 호텔 위치를 이메일로 보내 주시겠어요?

남 네, 손님. 물론입니다.

해설 여자가 남자에게 호텔의 위치를 이메일로 보내 달라고 부탁했다.

08 이유 파악 | ②

해석

여 Simon, 오늘 밤에 뭐 하니?

남 서현이랑 재민이가 함께 영화를 보러 우리 집에 올 거야.

여 재미있겠다. 나도 갈 수 있으면 좋을 텐데.

남 넌 언제나 환영이지. 오늘 밤에 우리 집에 와 줘.

여 고마워. 하지만 나는 남동생을 돌봐야 해.

남 그 애도 데려오지 그래?

여 아니야, 그 애는 너무 어려. 걔는 우리가 영화를 볼 수가 없게 만들 거야.

남 그럼 걔를 위한 만화 영화는 어때?

여 넌 정말 친절하구나. 고마워.

해설 여자는 남동생을 돌봐야 해서 남자의 제안을 처음에 거절했다.

09 숫자 정보 파악 - 금액 | ①

해석

남 실례합니다. 이것을 다른 디자인으로 교환할 수 있을까요?

여 영수증 있으세요?

남 네, 여기 있어요.

여 30달러짜리 티셔츠를 사셨네요. 그것을 같은 가격의 어떤 것과도 교환하실 수 있으세요.

남 이 청바지는 얼마인가요?

여 35달러입니다.

남 제가 차액을 지불하고 이것과 바꿀 수 있나요?

여 그것도 가능합니다. 그렇게 하시겠어요?

남 네. 그렇게 해 주세요.

해설 남자는 티셔츠와 청바지의 차액인 5달러만 지불하면 된다.

10 언급되지 않은 것 | ④

해석

[전화벨이 울린다.]

남 여보세요. JK 호텔입니다. 도와드릴까요?

여 여보세요. 제가 일정을 조금 변경할 수 있나요?

남 성함이 어떻게 되세요, 손님?

여 Janice Brown입니다.

남 Brown 씨, 잠깐만 기다려 주세요. 디럭스 룸에 네 명을 예약하셨네요. 일정을 어떻게 변경하실 겁니까?

여 제가 12월 23일부터 2박 3일을 예약했어요. 첫 날을 취소하고 12월 24일부터 머무를 수 있나요?

남 그것은 가능한데요, 죄송하지만 조금 더 일찍 전화 주셨으면 좋았을 것 같습니다. 오늘 취소하시면 여전히 다른 날도 지불하셔야 합니다.

여 아, 그럼 원래 일정대로 할게요. 또, 제가 23일 정오에 입실하고 싶은데요. 그것은 가능한가요?

남 네, 저희가 열두 시까지 방을 준비시켜 두겠습니다.

여　정말 감사합니다.
남　천만에요, 손님.
해설　여자는 자신의 객실 퇴실 시간에 관해서는 언급하고 있지 않다.

11　내용 불일치　| ④
해석
여　사람들은 커피 마시는 것을 매우 좋아합니다. 그것은 맛도 향도 좋습니다. 그것은 당신이 졸릴 때 깨어 있도록 도와줄 수도 있습니다. 하지만 커피를 너무 많이 마시는 것은 당신의 건강에 해로울 수 있습니다. 너무 많은 커피는 여러분에게 두통이나 초조함을 유발할 수 있습니다. 게다가 커피를 많이 마시는 사람이 그것을 마시는 것을 멈추면 그들은 하루 종일 피곤함을 느끼게 될지 모릅니다. 커피는 매우 인기 있는 음료이지만, 과음하지 않도록 조심해야 합니다.
해설　커피를 많이 마시는 사람은 커피를 그만 마셨을 때 하루 종일 피곤하다고 했다.

12　도표 정보 파악　| ④
해석
여　오늘 저녁으로 카레를 먹자.
남　나 카레 좋아해. 매운 거 사자.
여　나는 너무 매운 카레는 못 먹어. 고추 두 개짜리 카레를 선택하자.
남　그래. 우리 데워 먹기만 하면 되는 카레를 사서 전자레인지에 요리하지 않을래?
여　아니야. 우리가 요리하는 것이 더 맛있어.
남　그럼 어떤 형태가 더 좋아? 반죽 아니면 가루?
여　가루 타입은 8명을 위한 거니까, 우리는 카레를 여러 번 먹을 수 있어. 저걸 사자.
남　그거 좋은 생각이다.
해설　여자는 고추 두 개가 그려진 가루 타입의 카레를 8인분을 사겠다고 했다.

13　알맞은 응답 찾기　| ⑤
해석
남　도와드릴까요?
여　네. 시카고에 계신 어머니께 꽃을 보내고 싶어요.
남　어머니는 어떤 종류의 꽃을 좋아하시나요?
여　글쎄요, 잘 모르겠어요. 어떤 것을 추천하시겠어요?
남　이맘때에는 장미와 백합이 아주 좋습니다.
여　좋습니다. 붉은 장미 12송이와 백합 5송이 주세요.
남　메시지도 넣으시겠어요?
여　네. 그냥 "생신 축하드려요, 엄마."라고 해 주세요.
① 그녀가 당신에게 안부를 전해 달라고 했어요.
② 저희 엄마가 당신에게 메시지를 주셨어요.
③ 아니요, 저는 할 것들이 너무 많았어요.
④ 그것을 이렇게 빨리 배달해 주셔서 감사해요.
해설　남자가 엄마에게 메시지를 보낼 거냐고 물어봤으므로 생일을 축하한다고 전해 달라는 ⑤가 여자의 응답으로 가장 적절하다.

14　알맞은 응답 찾기　| ②
해석
여　James, 어디 가니?
남　난 과학 실험실에 가고 있어.

여　또? 왜 거기에 그렇게 자주 가니?
남　거기서 실험을 좀 하고 있어. 그거 보고 싶니?
여　아니, 전혀. 난 과학에 공포증이 있어.
남　유감이다. 네게 내가 하고 있는 것을 보여 주고 싶었는데.
여　진심으로 넌 그게 재미있니?
남　물론이지. 나는 정말 푹 빠져 있어.
① 그건 내 잘못이 아니야.
③ 그는 그것에 대해 많이 심각하진 않아.
④ 포기하지 마. 다음에는 더 잘할 거야.
⑤ 나는 흥미로운 볼거리를 찾고 있어.
해설　여자가 남자에게 과학에 흥미를 느끼는지 물어봤으므로 과학에 푹 빠져있다고 말하는 ②가 남자의 응답으로 가장 적절하다.

15　상황에 맞는 말 찾기　| ①
해석
남　George는 경찰이다. 어느 날, Kate가 그에게 와서 그녀가 지갑을 도둑맞았다고 말했다. 그녀는 매우 당황해 보였고, George에게 도둑을 잡아 달라고 부탁했다. 하지만, 그녀는 그 사건에 대해 명확히 설명하지 못했다. 그녀는 단지 그에게 그녀의 지갑이 어떻게 생겼는지, 그리고 그녀가 어디서 도난을 당했는지만 설명했다. 하지만, George는 그 도둑을 잡기 위해서 더 많은 정보가 필요해서, 그는 그녀에게 무슨 일이 일어났는지 더 상세히 물으려고 한다. 이런 상황에서, George는 Kate에게 뭐라고 말하겠는가?
George　그것에 대해 더 말해 줄 수 있나요?
② 행운을 빌게요.
③ 도둑을 찾으면 전화할게요.
④ 단지 어디선가 잃어버렸을 가능성이 있나요?
⑤ 다음에 나갈 때는 매우 조심해야 해요.
해설　George가 도둑을 잡기 위해 도둑에 대한 정보가 더 필요한 상황이므로 도둑에 대해 좀 더 말해 달라고 요구하는 ①이 답으로 적절하다.

16~17　목적 파악 / 언급되지 않은 것　| ⑤, ①
해석
여　집중해 주세요. 교장입니다. 오늘부터 우리는 학교에 특별한 손님을 모실 것입니다. 그 손님들은 싱가포르의 학생들입니다. 그들의 학교는 작년에 우리가 방문했던 학교입니다. 그들은 우리 학교가 어떤지에 대해 매우 관심이 있습니다. 그들은 1교시 시작할 무렵에 도착할 겁니다. 그들은 오늘부터 2주일 동안 여러분들처럼 수업을 들을 것입니다. 그들과 마음껏 대화하고 그들을 환영해 주세요.
해설
16 여자는 외국에서 방문객이 온다는 사실을 알리기 위해 방송을 했다.
17 손님들의 총 인원에 대해서는 언급되지 않았다.

02회 미리 보는 수능 듣기모의고사　pp. 206~207

01 ⑤	02 ③	03 ③	04 ④	05 ①
06 ①	07 ⑤	08 ⑤	09 ①	10 ②
11 ⑤	12 ③	13 ⑤	14 ⑤	15 ③
16 ①	17 ③			

01 ❶ I'm going to ❷ Why do you meet

02 ❶ Are you hungry ❷ I don't really feel like

03 ❶ to drop by your office ❷ looking forward to hearing

04 ❶ accept this report ❷ to study about insects ❸ look like your own

05 ❶ get my drink by myself ❷ my daddy as a cook

06 ❶ much higher ❷ tried to lower

07 ❶ search it ❷ to drive you there ❸ tell me the buses

08 ❶ made a phone call ❷ will cost so much

09 ❶ Can you recommend one ❷ forty dollars ❸ fifty percent off

10 ❶ I'll get you one ❷ How do you spell ❸ It'll take

11 ❶ brand-new ball-point pen ❷ dries very quickly

12 ❶ a long charging cable ❷ should buy one from ❸ the black one

13 ❶ return my book ❷ in the hospital ❸ make an excuse

14 ❶ trying to plant ❷ too hard for you ❸ you could finish this soon

15 ❶ gave him a board game ❷ he doesn't know

16~17 ❶ discounted fifty percent ❷ will finish ❸ in the fruit section

---

01   알맞은 응답 찾기 (짧은 대화) | ⑤

해석

남   Mary야. 어디 가니?

여   Michael을 만나러 가고 있어.

남   또? 왜 그를 그렇게 자주 만나니?

여   다음 주 금요일까지 끝내야 할 조별 과제가 있어.

① 당연하지. 나는 그것을 정말 좋아해.

② 너는 더 심각할 수 없니?

③ 그건 내 관심사가 아니야.

④ 너의 과제에 행운을 빌어.

해설   남자가 여자에게 Michael을 자주 만나는 이유를 물었으므로 그 이유를 답하는 ⑤가 여자의 응답으로 가장 적절하다.

---

02   알맞은 응답 찾기 (짧은 대화) | ③

해석

여   아빠. 저 집에 왔어요.

남   지금 집에 오니? 우리는 막 간식을 먹으려던 참이었어.

여   고맙지만 괜찮아요. 정말 그럴 기분이 아니에요.

남   무슨 일이 있었니?

① 여기에 왜 왔니?

② 도와줘서 정말 고마워.

④ 모두 내 잘못이야. 사과할게.

⑤ 이 책이 네가 생각하고 있던 거니?

해설   남자가 학교에서 돌아온 여자에게 간식을 권했는데 간식을 먹을 기분이 아니라고 말한 상황이므로 무슨 일이 있는지 묻는 ③이 남자의 응답으로 가장 적절하다.

---

03   목적 파악 | ③

해석

남   (삐 소리) 안녕, Isabella. 나는 8월 14일부터 22일까지 샌프란시스코를 방문할 거야. 나는 거기에 머무르는 동안 네 사무실에 들르고 싶어. 언제가 네게 편할지 나에게 좀 알려 줘. 네게 곧 샌프란시스코에서 내가 묵을 호텔을 알려 줄게. 빨리 소식 듣기를 고대하고 있을게. 안녕.

해설   남자는 샌프란시스코에 방문하는 동안 만날 약속을 정하기 위해 전화를 걸었다.

---

04   주제 파악 | ④

해석

남   미안하지만, 이 보고서는 받을 수가 없구나.

여   무슨 문제가 있나요?

남   이거 너 혼자 힘으로 썼니?

여   물론이죠. 아무 도움을 받지 않고 썼어요.

남   하지만 많은 부분들이 내가 아는 인터넷 사이트의 정보와 비슷해.

여   저는 곤충에 대해 많이 알지 못해서 몇몇 인터넷 사이트들을 참고했어요.

남   하지만 나는 네가 곤충에 대해 공부하는 것을 원했지, 다른 사람들의 연구 결과를 찾는 것을 원한 것은 아니었어.

여   저는 적절한 정보를 검색하는 동안 많이 공부했어요. 저는 제가 찾은 정보가 맞는지 틀렸는지를 확인해야 했어요. 그것은 시간이 많이 걸렸어요.

남   하지만 너는 다른 사람들의 작업물을 너의 것인 것처럼 보이게 만들었구나. 너는 심지어 출처도 첨부하지 않았어.

여   선생님 말씀이 맞는 것 같아요. 제가 자료 출처를 적었어야 했어요.

해설   남자는 여자에게 보고서를 쓸 때 참고 자료의 출처를 명시해야 한다고 강조하고 있다.

---

05   관계 추론 | ①

해석

남   오늘은 내가 저녁을 준비할 거야. 너의 엄마는 늦으실 거야.

여   음, 무엇을 만드실 거예요?

남   널 위해 신선한 샐러드와 크림소스 파스타를 만들 거란다.

여   와, 좋아요.

남   목 안 마르니?

여   말라요, 하지만 적어도 제 음료는 제가 스스로 가져올 거예요.

남   30분 정도 걸릴 거야. TV 보면서 저기서 기다리렴.

여   좋아요. 아빠를 요리사로 두다니 매우 행복해요. 다음에는 제가 맛있는 음식 만들어 드릴 게요.

남   정말 기대되는구나.

해설   남자가 저녁을 만드는 상황에서 여자가 아빠를 요리사로 두어서 행복하다고 말했으므로 두 사람의 관계는 아빠와 딸이라는 것을 알 수 있다.

---

06   도표 정보 파악 | ①

해석

남   이 그래프는 최근 몇 년간의 교통사고율을 나타내고 있다. 2017년도의 교통사고율은 2016년보다 훨씬 높았다. 2018년도의 비율은 2016

년도의 비율보다는 높지만 2017년에 비해서는 낮아졌다. 이것은 교통
사고율을 낮추기 위해 정부가 노력했기 때문이다.

해설 2017년의 교통사고율이 2016년보다 훨씬 높다고 하였고, 2018년
교통사고율은 2017년보다는 낮으나 2016년보다 높다고 했으므로
①이 알맞다.

07 한 일 / 할 일 파악 | ⑤

해석

[전화벨이 울린다.]

남 여보세요?

여 안녕, 민호야. 나야, Sarah.

남 Sarah. 무슨 일이니? 너 금방 나갔잖아.

여 저기, 나 시청에 가야 하는데 어떤 버스를 타야하는지 잊어버렸어. 인터
넷으로 검색해 줄래?

남 물론 할 수 있는데, 내가 너를 거기에 태워 줄까?

여 아니야, 그럴 필요 없어. 나는 너를 괴롭히고 싶지 않아.

남 나는 괜찮아. 원하면 말해.

여 고맙지만 괜찮아. 그냥 내가 탈 수 있는 버스를 말해 줘.

남 그래. 문자 메시지로 보내 줄게.

해설 여자가 남자에게 자신이 탈 수 있는 버스를 말해 달라고 부탁했으므로
남자는 여자를 위해 시청에 가는 버스를 찾아 줄 것이다.

08 이유 파악 | ⑤

해석

남 너 우울해 보인다. 뭐가 잘못되었니?

여 음, 걱정이 되어서 그래.

남 뭐에 관해서? 주변에 누가 아프기라도 한 거니, 뭐니?

여 사실은, 지난주에 내 친구 Kate와 전화를 했어.

남 Kate? 그녀는 미국에 있지 않니?

여 그래, 맞아. 나는 한 시간이나 통화를 했어. 전화 요금이 너무 걱정 돼.
그것은 너무 많이 나올 거야.

남 걱정 마. 네 예상보다 적을 거야.

해설 여자는 미국에 있는 친구와 전화를 해서 전화 요금이 너무 많이 나올
것 같다며 걱정하고 있다.

09 숫자 정보 파악 – 금액 | ①

해석

남 안녕하세요, 제가 여자 친구 주려고 스카프를 사고 싶은데요. 하나 추천
해 주실 수 있나요?

여 그럼요. 이게 아주 부드럽고 올해 유행이에요.

남 좋다고 생각해요. 얼마예요?

여 그게 지난주까지는 60달러였지만 지금은 50% 할인입니다.

남 음, 아주 좋네요. 하지만 저는 중학생이에요. 그 가격도 여전히 저에게
는 너무 비싸네요.

여 알았어요, 그러면 당신은 이게 마음에 들 거예요. 이건 40달러였지만
역시 50% 할인입니다.

남 와우, 적절하네요. 그것을 살게요.

해설 남자는 40달러짜리 스카프를 50% 할인 받아 20달러에 구입했다.

10 언급되지 않은 것 | ②

해석

여 도와드릴까요?

남 네, 회원 카드를 만들고 싶습니다.

여 알겠습니다. 바로 하나 드리겠습니다. 성함이 어떻게 되세요?

남 제 이름은 박기열입니다.

여 이름의 철자를 어떻게 쓰나요?

남 K-I-Y-E-O-L입니다.

여 좋아요. 생년월일과 전화번호를 알려 주세요.

남 2006년 5월 20일입니다. 제 전화번호는 772-9986입니다.

여 감사합니다. 잠깐만 기다려 주세요. 몇 분 걸릴 겁니다.

해설 남자는 회원 카드를 만드는 데 주소는 언급하지 않았다.

11 내용 불일치 | ⑤

해석

남 안녕, 친구들! 이제 제가 여러분에게 Smoothie를 소개할게요. 이것은
새로운 볼펜이에요. 이것으로 뭔가를 쓸 때, 여러분은 부드럽게 쓸 수
있어요. 다양한 색깔이 있어서 글쓰기가 더 즐거울 거예요. 볼펜의 색을
뚜껑의 색으로 알 수 있어요. 게다가, 그것은 매우 빨리 말라요. 이제 손
이 더러워지는 것을 걱정할 필요가 없어요. 한번 써 보지 않을래요?

해설 Smoothie 펜의 장점은 빨리 마르는 것이라고 했다.

12 도표 정보 파악 | ③

해석

여 너 휴대 전화 케이블을 검색하고 있니?

남 응. 나는 긴 충전 케이블이 필요해. 나는 이것들 중에서 하나를 선택할
거야.

여 이것들이 가장 인기 있는 것들이야?

남 응. 어떤 것이 제일 나아 보인다고 생각하니?

여 Minibel이 보통 Promac보다는 조금 더 비싸지만, 나는 Promac보
다는 Minibel을 선호해.

남 동의해. 그것의 상품들이 오래 가는 것 같아. Minibel에서 하나를 사야
겠다.

여 길이는?

남 내 경험으로는, 더 길수록 더 좋아. 2미터 케이블을 사야 할 것 같아.

여 어떤 색을 살 거야, 흰 색 아니면 검정색?

남 흠, 나는 검정색을 살 거야. 이게 둘 중에서 더 싸.

해설 남자는 Minibel의 2미터짜리 케이블 중 더 저렴한 검정색을 사겠다고
했다.

13 알맞은 응답 찾기 | ⑤

해석

남 왜 그렇게 화가 났니?

여 내 책을 반납하러 도서관에 갔는데, 사서 선생님이 이 책이 반납 기한이
지났고 내가 많은 연체료를 내야 한다고 말씀하셨어. 그래서 반납하지
않고 그냥 나왔어.

남 반납일이 언제였는데?

여 3주 전. 하지만 나는 병원에 입원해서 그것을 반납하러 올 수가 없었
잖아.

남 너의 상황을 말씀드렸어? 좀 봐주실 것 같은데.

여 나는 그렇게 생각하지 않아. 심지어 내 말을 듣지 않으려고 하시더라고.

남 아마 많은 학생들이 연체료를 내지 않으려고 변명을 하려고 할 거야.

여 흠. 그럴지도 모르지. 내가 무엇을 할 수 있을까?

남 병원에서 서류를 받아서 보여 드리면 어때?

① 나는 반대야.

② 오, 너는 그렇게 하면 안 됐어.

③ 고맙지만 괜찮아. 혼자 해결할 수 있어.

④ 그것을 너무 늦게 돌려줘서 정말 미안해.

해설 남자에게 문제를 해결할 방법을 물었으므로, 해결 방법을 제안하는 ⑤ 가 남자의 응답으로 가장 적절하다.

14 알맞은 응답 찾기 | ⑤

해석

여 뭐 하세요, 아빠?

남 여기에 꽃을 좀 심으려고 하고 있어.

여 꽃들이 아름다워요. 하지만, 혼자서 이 꽃들을 심으실 수 있으세요?

남 난 그것을 쉽게 끝마칠 수 있을 거라고 생각했지만, 내가 생각한 것보다 시간이 더 걸리는 것 같아.

여 제가 도와드릴까요?

남 괜찮아. 너에게는 너무 어려운 일이야.

여 전에 학교에서 정원 꾸미기를 해 본 적이 있어요. 꽃을 심고 몇 달이나 키웠는걸요. 제가 도와드리면, 이걸 금방 끝내실 거예요.

남 정말? 그럼 좀 도와주겠니?

여 **물론이죠. 뭘 해야 할지만 말씀해 주세요.**

① 아니요, 동의하지 않아요.

② 내가 당신이라면, 난 도움을 청할 거예요.

③ 도와주셔서 정말 고맙습니다.

④ 이 일을 더 이상 참을 수가 없어요.

해설 남자가 여자가 자신을 도와줄 수 있는지 확인하고 있으므로 문제없다며 할 일이 무엇인지 말해 달라고 하는 ⑤가 여자의 응답으로 가장 적절하다.

15 상황에 맞는 말 찾기 | ③

해석

여 Maria와 Tom은 좋은 친구이다. Tom의 생일에 Tom과 그의 친구들은 함께 생일 파티를 했다. Maria도 그의 생일을 축하하러 왔다. 그녀는 그에게 생일 선물로 보드 게임을 주었다. 그는 그 게임을 친구들과 하고 싶지만 그것을 어떻게 해야 할지를 모른다. 그래서 그는 그것에 관해 Maria에게 물어보려고 한다. 이런 상황에서, Tom은 Maria에게 뭐라고 말하겠는가?

Tom 그것을 어떻게 하는지 아니?

① 네게 무슨 일이 생겼니?

② 나에게 동의하지 않니?

④ 이 게임을 어떻게 생각하니?

⑤ 나와 무슨 놀이를 하고 싶니?

해설 Tom이 선물 받은 보드 게임을 하는 방법을 모르는 상황이므로 게임을 하는 방법을 아는지 물어보는 ③이 할 말로 적절하다.

16~17 목적 파악 / 언급되지 않은 것 | ①, ③

해석

남 고객님들께 알려 드립니다. 지금 반짝 세일이 진행 중입니다. 신선한 사과가 50퍼센트 할인합니다. 이 사과들은 크고 달콤한 사과로 유명한 곳인 청송에서 왔습니다. 우리는 여러분들을 위한 사과를 10개씩 200묶음을 가지고 있습니다. 한 사람에 한 묶음만 살 수 있습니다. 이 반짝 세일은 5시 정각에 끝납니다. 바로 지금 과일 코너에서 진행 중입니다. 빨리 오셔서 이 기회를 잡으세요!

해설

16 남자는 사과를 할인하고 있다는 것을 알리기 위해 방송하고 있다.

17 Flash Sale 시작 시간에 대해서는 언급되지 않았다.

기본서	▶	All that	중학 영어 학습에 필요한 모든 것 **올댓 중학 영어**	중등 1~3학년
영역별	▶	**TAPA**	영어 고민을 한 방에 타파! 영역별·수준별 학습 시리즈, **TAPA!**	중등 1~3학년
독해	▶	**READER'S BANK**	초등부터 고등까지 새롭게 개정된 10단계 맞춤 영어 전문 독해서, **리더스뱅크**	(예비) 중등~고등 2학년
독해	▶	중등 수능독해	기출문제를 통해 독해 원리를 익히며 단계별로 단련하는 수능 학습서, **중등 수능독해**	중등 1~3학년
문법·구문	▶	마법같은 블록구문	마법같이 영어 독해력을 강화하는 구문 학습서, **마법같은 블록구문**	중등 3~고등 2학년
문법	▶	Grammar in	3단계 반복 학습으로 완성하는 중학 영문법, **그래머 인**	중등 1~3학년
문법	▶	악마의 문법책을 찢어라	알맹이 4법칙을 통해 문장을 쉽게 이해하는 **악마의 문법책을 찢어라**	중등 1~고등 2학년
듣기	▶	중학영어 듣기모의고사 22회	영어듣기능력평가 완벽 대비 듣기 실전서, **중학영어 듣기모의고사**	중등 1~3학년
어휘	▶	VOCA PICK	주제별로 한 번, 빈출도순으로 또 한 번, 중등 내신 및 수능 대비, **완자 VOCA PICK**	중등 1~3학년

VISANG

발행일 2018년 7월 1일
펴낸날 2018년 7월 1일
펴낸곳 (주)비상교육
펴낸이 양태회
신고번호 제2002-000048호
출판사업총괄 최대찬
개발총괄 채진희
개발책임 구세나
디자인책임 김재훈
영업책임 이지웅
마케팅책임 이은진
품질책임 석진안
대표전화 1544-0554
주소 서울특별시 구로구 디지털로33길 48
　　　대륭포스트타워 7차 20층

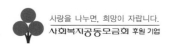

사랑을 나누면, 희망이 자랍니다.
사회복지공동모금회 후원 기업